Research Anthology on Applying Social Networking Strategies to Classrooms and Libraries

Information Resources Management Association
USA

Volume IV

IGI Global
PUBLISHER of TIMELY KNOWLEDGE

Published in the United States of America by
IGI Global
Information Science Reference (an imprint of IGI Global)
701 E. Chocolate Avenue
Hershey PA, USA 17033
Tel: 717-533-8845
Fax: 717-533-8661
E-mail: cust@igi-global.com
Web site: http://www.igi-global.com

Library of Congress Cataloging-in-Publication Data

Names: Information Resources Management Association, editor.
Title: Research anthology on applying social networking strategies to
  classrooms and libraries / Information Resources Management Association,
  editor.
Description: Hershey PA : Information Science Reference, 2022. | Includes
  bibliographical references. | Summary: "This reference book presents
  contributed chapters that describe the applications, tools, and
  opportunities provided by the intersection of education and social
  media, considering the ways in which social media encourages learner
  engagement and community participation"-- Provided by publisher.
Identifiers: LCCN 2022030171 (print) | LCCN 2022030172 (ebook) | ISBN
  9781668471234 (hardcover) | ISBN 9781668471241 (ebook)
Subjects: LCSH: Social media in education. | Libraries and social media. |
  Online social networks--Educational applications | Online social
  networks--Library applications.
Classification: LCC LB1044.87 .R46 2022 (print) | LCC LB1044.87 (ebook) |
  DDC 371.33/44678--dc23/eng/20220920
LC record available at https://lccn.loc.gov/2022030171
LC ebook record available at https://lccn.loc.gov/2022030172

British Cataloguing in Publication Data
A Cataloguing in Publication record for this book is available from the British Library.

All work contributed to this book is new, previously-unpublished material. The views expressed in this book are those of the authors, but not necessarily of the publisher.

For electronic access to this publication, please contact: eresources@igi-global.com.

List of Contributors

Table of Contents

Section 2
Development and Design Methodologies

Volume II

Section 3
Tools and Technologies

Volume III

Section 4
Utilization and Applications

Section 5
Organizational and Social Implications

Section 6
Managerial Impact

Section 7
Critical Issues and Challenges

Preface

The introduction of social media has given many communities the opportunity to connect and communicate with each other at a higher level than ever before. Many organizations, from businesses to governments, have taken advantage of this important tool to conduct research and enhance efficiency. Libraries and educational institutions have also made use of social media to enhance educational marketing, engage with learning communities, adapt educational tools, and more.

Staying informed of the most up-to-date research trends and findings is of the utmost importance. That is why IGI Global is pleased to offer this four-volume reference collection of reprinted IGI Global book chapters and journal articles that have been handpicked by senior editorial staff. This collection will shed light on critical issues related to the trends, techniques, and uses of various applications by providing both broad and detailed perspectives on cutting-edge theories and developments. This collection is designed to act as a single reference source on conceptual, methodological, technical, and managerial issues, as well as to provide insight into emerging trends and future opportunities within the field.

The *Research Anthology on Applying Social Networking Strategies to Classrooms and Libraries* is organized into seven distinct sections that provide comprehensive coverage of important topics. The sections are:

1. Fundamental Concepts and Theories;
2. Development and Design Methodologies;
3. Tools and Technologies;
4. Utilization and Applications;
5. Organizational and Social Implications;
6. Managerial Impact; and
7. Critical Issues and Challenges.

The following paragraphs provide a summary of what to expect from this invaluable reference tool.

Section 1, "Fundamental Concepts and Theories," serves as a foundation for this extensive reference tool by addressing crucial theories essential to implementing social networking into classrooms and libraries. The first chapter, "Social Media and the Future of the Instructional Model," by Prof. Soha Abdeljaber of Rising Leaders Academy, USA and Prof. Kathryn Nieves Licwinko of New Jersey City University, USA, provides the latest information on social media and its application in the instructional model. The chapter contains information on how social media enhances learning, especially at times where remote learning is necessary, such as COVID-19. The last chapter, "Facebook in the International Classroom," by Prof. Inna P. Piven of Unitec Institute of Technology, New Zealand, explores international students' learning experiences with Facebook-based activities within the eight-week study term known as the intensive mode of course delivery. By implementing participant observation and two asynchronous Facebook focus groups, the study investigates the potential values of Facebook for learning from international students' perspective.

Section 2, "Development and Design Methodologies," presents in-depth coverage of the design and development of social networking implementation. The first chapter, "Bridging Activities: Social Media for Connecting Language Learners' in-School and Out-of-School Literacy Practices," by Prof. Ellen Yeh of Columbia College Chicago, USA and Prof. Svetlana Mitric of University of Illinois at Chicago, USA, applies pedagogically-focused project design by using Instagram as a platform to investigate how the use of social media such as Instagram in a multimodal digital storytelling model could bridge the skills English language learners (ELLs) learn in the classroom to out-of-school literacy practices. The last chapter, "Social Media, Cyberculture, Blockchains, and Education: A New Strategy for Brazilian Higher Education," by Prof. Matheus Batalha Moreira Nery of Uninassau, Brazil; Prof. Magno Oliveira Macambira of Universidade Estadual de Feira de Santana, Brazil; Prof. Marlton Fontes Mota of Universidade Tiradentes, Brazil; and Prof. Izabella Cristine Oliveira Rezende of Uninassau, Brazil, contributes to the debate of the uses of social media, cyberculture, and blockchain technology for the development of educational strategies. It reviews the existing scientific literature on social networking, social media, cyberculture, and blockchains related to Brazil.

Section 3, "Tools and Technologies," explores the various tools and technologies used in classrooms and libraries for social networking. The first chapter, "Using Social Media in Creating and Implementing Educational Practices," by Profs. Inna P. Piven and Robyn Gandell of Unitec Institute of Technology, New Zealand, examines the use of social media as a couse management tool, the use of social media to enhance student-centered learning and the need for institutional support for using social media in educational contexts. The last chapter, "Is Twitter an Unexploited Potential in Indian Academic Libraries? Case Study Based on Select Academic Library Tweets," by Prof. Swapan Kumar Patra of Tshwane University of Technology, South Africa, maps the Indian libraries' Twitter activities, taking academic libraries as case study.

Section 4, "Utilization and Applications," describes the opportunities and challenges of social networking implementation. The first chapter, "Navigating the Shortcomings of Virtual Learning Environments via Social Media," by Profs. Puvaneswary Murugaiah and Siew Hwa Yen of School of Distance Education, Universiti Sains Malaysia, Penang, Malaysia, uncovers the shortcomings of the use of virtual learning environments (VLEs) for language learning in several Malaysian institutions of higher learning. It also highlights the use of social media in addressing the barriers. The last chapter, "Nexus Between Social Network, Social Media Use, and Loneliness: A Case Study of University Students, Bangladesh," by Prof. Md. Aminul Islam of University of Liberal Arts Bangladesh, Bangladesh and Prof. Bezon Kumar of Rabindra University, Bangladesh, explores how real-life social network and social media use are related to loneliness among university students in Bangladesh.

Section 5, "Organizational and Social Implications," includes chapters discussing the impact of social networking on education and library organizations and beyond. The first chapter, "Identifiable Problems in Social Media: Concerning Legal Awareness Within Academic Libraries," by Prof. Amy D. Dye-Reeves of Murray State University, USA, serves as a primer for academic librarians on helping patrons with disabilities receive, protect, and understand disseminated content on a multitude of popular social media networking platforms. The content of the chapter provides introductory material on the Americans with Disabilities Act (ADA) and the Family Educational Rights and Privacy Act. The last chapter, "Using Twitter to Form Professional Learning Communities: An Analysis of Georgia K-12 School Personnel Discussing Educational Technology on Twitter," by Profs. Charles B. Hodges, Lucas John Jensen, and Mete Akcaoglu of Georgia Southern University, USA, diescusses teacher professional development taking place on Twitter in Georgia, USA.

Section 6, "Managerial Impact," covers the internal and external impacts of social networking within education and library administration. The first chapter, "Social Media in Tertiary Education: Considerations and Potential Issues," by Prof. Ann M. Simpson of Unitec Institute of Technology, New Zealand, addresses some of the considerations and potential issues that impact our use of social media in the higher education classroom. It examines social media as an educational tool in higher education, possible pedagogies for social media use, potential educational contexts, and privacy concerns raised by social media use in educational environments. The last chapter, "Social Media Integration in Educational Administration as Information and Smart Systems: Digital Literacy for Economic, Social, and Political Engagement in Namibia," by Profs. Sadrag Panduleni Shihomeka and Helena N. Amadhila of University of Namibia, Namibia, explains that there are various groups on Facebook where youthful education administrators can use to post educational information and discuss pertinent issues concerning their institutions.

Section 7, "Critical Issues and Challenges," presents coverage of academic and research perspectives on challenges to social networking in education and libraries. The first chapter, "Making Social Media More Social: A Literature Review of Academic Libraries' Engagement and Connections Through Social Media Platforms," by Prof. Elia Trucks of University of Denver, USA, explores how academic libraries have used social media for broadcasting information, responsive communication, and engagement. The last chapter, "Social Media Usage for Informal Learning in Malaysia: Academic Researcher Perspective," by Prof. Mohmed Y. Mohmed Al-Sabaawi of Department of Management Information Systems, College of Administration and Economics, University of Mosul, Iraq; Prof. Halina Mohamed Dahlan of Information Systems Department, Azman Hashim International Business School, Universiti Teknologi Malaysia, Malaysia; and Prof. Hafiz Muhammad Faisal Shehzad of Department of Computer Science and IT, University of Sargodha, Pakistan, explores the use of social media for informal learning, barriers, benefits, and effect of individual factors.

Although the primary organization of the contents in this multi-volume work is based on its seven sections, offering a progression of coverage of the important concepts, methodologies, technologies, applications, social issues, and emerging trends, the reader can also identify specific contents by utilizing the extensive indexing system listed at the end of each volume. As a comprehensive collection of research on the latest findings related to social networking in education and library practices, the *Research Anthology on Applying Social Networking Strategies to Classrooms and Libraries* provides pre-service teachers, teacher educators, faculty and administrators of both K-12 and higher education, librarians, archivists, government officials, researchers, and academicians with a complete understanding of the applications and impacts of social networking. Given the vast number of issues concerning usage, failure, success, strategies, and applications of social networking applied to classrooms and libraries, the *Research Anthology on Applying Social Networking Strategies to Classrooms and Libraries* encompasses the most pertinent research on the applications, impacts, uses, and strategies of social networking.

Chapter 78

The Usage of Social Networking Sites for Informal Learning:
A Comparative Study Between Malaysia Students of Different Gender and Age Group

Lay Shi Ng
Universiti Kebangsaan Malaysia, Bangi Selangor, Malaysia

Siew Ming Thang
Universiti Kebangsaan Malaysia, Bangi Selangor, Malaysia

Noorizah Mohd. Noor
Universiti Kebangsaan Malaysia, Bangi Selangor, Malaysia

ABSTRACT

Nowadays, social networking sites (SNSs) on the Internet are increasingly being utilised as a learning tool for study and school-related issues. In Malaysia, most public schools do not allow students to bring their cell phones to school. Hence, learning activities involving SNSs can only be carried out after school hours. This article will refer to learning that takes place outside the school environment as "informal learning" as these activities are unstructured and are not undertaken in a formal educational setting. Through a questionnaire, the present study investigated the perceptions of 799 secondary-school Malaysian secondary school students towards the using of the SNSs for informal learning purposes. Data was analysed quantitatively and comparisons across gender and age were made. The findings revealed that Malaysian students have generally accepted the SNSs as an alternative learning environment with evidence showing that the difference in usage between gender is significant to a certain extent and less so for age.

DOI: 10.4018/978-1-6684-7123-4.ch078

INTRODUCTION

The popularity of social networking sites (SNSs) has rapidly increased over the past few years in Malaysia. The Global Web Index (2015) revealed that Malaysia has the second highest penetration of social networking usage among Internet users in Asia. It was further reported that on average a Malaysian with a social networking account spends 2.8 hours per day on SNSs. Now with the widespread use of smartphones, it is believed that the time spent on SNSs will continue to rise. SNSs such as Facebook, Instagram, WhatsApp and WeChat are the most commonly used Internet-based social spaces in Malaysia, particularly among young individuals.

Boyd and Ellison (2007) defined a social networking system as a web-based service that allows individuals to do the following: i) build public or semi-public profile in a system, (ii) share a connection, and (iii) view and cross-list their relationship with others in the system. Such systems enable easy and rapid connection with friends, families, classmates, customers and clients. In addition, SNSs are also seen as media that allows people to come together around an idea or topic of interest. In fact, SNSs are increasingly being leveraged as a learning tool, especially for today's tech-savvy students. According to Lai et al. (2013), many students are immersed in out-of-school online activities. When using digital media, students engage in a new learning culture which is very different from what they have been enculturated in traditional schools. Many studies have revealed the potential of using social networking for learning purposes (Selwyn, 2009; Griffith & Liyanage, 2008). However, it is not possible to use it as a tool for learning in Malaysian secondary schools due to the constraint of not allowing students to bring their cell phones to schools. Thus, it would be interesting to find out to what extent students use SNSs for learning purposes outside the classroom which has been defined as "informal learning" in this study. This definition is in line with that of Livingstone (1999) and Marsick and Watkins (2001). Livingstone (1999) described informal learning as any activity involving the pursuit of understanding, knowledge or skill which occurs outside the curricula of educational institutions, or the courses or workshops offered by educational or social agencies. Marsick and Watkins (2001) further described it as intentional but unstructured, contextualized learning.

It has long been documented that gender differences exist and influence how individuals engage in everyday activities. Some research findings also show that there are significant gender differences between how men and women adopt and use technology (Chun, 2013). Some studies undertaken in the Malaysian context which explored users' purposes in using SNSs found gender difference to be an influencing factor. According to Misra et al. (2015), attraction towards SNSs varied between male and female students. Mazman and Usluel (2011) earlier reported that significant gender differences were also found when young adults used SNSs to maintain existing relationships, make new relationships, pursue academic purposes and follow specific agendas. This study extends on these studies in its attempt to investigate how differences in gender and age affect students' usage of SNSs for informal learning purposes. Findings of this study will add to the current body of research, conducted on the effects of social networking on Malaysian secondary school students.

The following research questions specifically seek to investigate whether there are differences in usage for the following categories of students: (a) between male and female students, (b) between students of two different age-groups:

1.   What types of SNSs usage patterns are displayed among the different categories of Malaysian secondary school students?

2. How much time do these different categories of students spend on SNSs?
3. To what extent do these different categories of students use SNSs for learning and what types of learning do they focus on?
4. What are the differences in usage of SNSs for informal learning purposes of the different categories of students?

RELATED LITERATURE

Social Networking Sites

Social networking was introduced 15 to 20 years ago. Since then it has grown from a niche to a mass online activity, in which millions of Internet users (from different ages, cultures and education levels) are engaged in during their leisure time and at their workplace (Misra et al., 2015; Mazman & Usluel, 2011). Its impact cannot be overstated. Social networking is the most popular online activity worldwide accounting for nearly 1 in every 5 minutes spent online in October 2011, and reaches 82 percent of the world's Internet population, representing 1.2 billion users around the globe (ComScore, 2011). According to Lenhart et al. (2010), young people are much more likely than older adults to use social networks. Several studies conducted in the U.S. found that 80% of online teens use social network sites, Facebook being the most popular, with 93% of those teens reporting its use (Manago et al., 2008). Likewise, it was reported that Malaysians were spending more than three hours on their smartphones each day, where 40% of users' time was spent on social networking and chatting (Vserv, 2015).

Gender and Age Differences in Using SNSs

It is generally believed that male and female tend to use SNSs differently. Joiner et al. (2012) reported that females use social networking more than males. Women have been found to use SNSs more for connecting with people, while men have been found to use SNSs more for seeking information. Studies also showed that when men open social media accounts to network, they are more often looking to form new relationships, while women are more focused on sustaining existing ones (Social Media Today, 2016). When using SNSs, women were reported to disclose more about relationships with others (i.e. family, friends, significant others) and scenarios where relationships tend to be the central focus (e.g. holidays), whereas men were reported to disclose more information related to entertainment (e.g. sports) (Bond, 2009).

A Pew Research Center survey in 2015 found that Pinterest, Facebook and Instagram have a larger female user base, while online discussion forums like Reddit, Digg or Slashdot attract a greater share of male users. Another survey undertaken by Pew Research Center in the same year also found a strong gender gap in the way that teenagers make friends online. It was reported that 78% of girls who made friends online did so through SNSs, like Facebook or Instagram, while only 52% of boys made their online friends through SNSs. While these explain how men and women use SNSs differently, a report of ComScore (2011) showed females to be more active on SNSs. A look at gender differences in social networking engagement found that, across global regions, females age 15 and older spend more time social networking than their male counterparts.

Although many studies have found that male and female differ in their interaction with technology, not much is known about the gender differences in e-learning. According to Cuadrado-García et al. (2010), there has been little empirical evidence regarding the effects of gender differences and e-learning and the few studies that existed had revealed contradictory results. For instance, Liu and Yu (2013) stated that teenage boys in the United Kingdom used computers more often than girls and were more comfortable when doing so. On the other hand, Bruestle et al. (2009) believed that e-learning, through its flexible and interactive learning approach favoured women. Many research studies supported this finding by suggesting that female's poorer performance was a result of poorer access to technology (Kirkup & Von Pru¨mmer, 1997).

In addition, surveys have found substantial differences in social media use according to age. According to a report published by Pew Research Center, in 2018, 88% of the Americans between the ages of 18-29 used SNSs. However, the social media adoption rate of Americans between 30-49 was 78%, while older age group (50-64) was 64%. Women were more likely than men to use social media. The report also revealed that a majority of Americans used Facebook and YouTube, but young adults (especially those age 18-24) were especially heavy users of Snapchat and Instagram.

In USA, the age group between 35-44 displayed dominant use of SNSs across the social web (Briansolis.com, 2010). According to a survey by Sproutsocial (2017), more than 60% of Americans age above 34 preferred to use Facebook, while only 33% of Millennials preferred Facebook and 25% of younger Millennials (ages 18-24) identified Instagram as their favourite social media network. In Malaysia, over 90% of Internet users used SNSs. Older age group reported a lower rate of Internet use compared to younger group. Only 7.5% of Malaysians age 50-64 used Internet (MCMC, 2017). Hence, it is obvious that the usage of social media is higher among young Malaysians than the older age group.

SNSs and Informal Learning

Many studies have dealt with the uses of SNSs in learning and learners' opinions toward the use of SNSs for learning. According to Pempek, Yermolayeva, and Calvert (2009), SNSs expose students to an extensive range of discourse functions and online writing that enhances critical literacy and language skills, and launches creative deployment of language play. Lai et al., (2013) stated that using technologies in informal settings can be more motivating and engaging than using technologies in school settings as informal learning often engages students in real life problems and uses community resources. Students with a collaborative learning preference have been found to use SNSs more frequently for informal learning (Vivian & Barnes, 2010). Some suggested that high school students use SNSs to connect with other students for homework and group projects (Boyd, 2008). SNSs can actively encourage online community building, extending learning beyond the boundaries of the classroom (Smith, 2009; Brady, Holcomb, & Smith, 2010). According to Tiene (2000), written communication on cyberspace enables students to take part in discussions at a time convenient to them and articulate their ideas in more carefully thought-out and structured ways. Deng and Tavares (2013) stated that web-based discussions can contribute to the development of students' reflective ability and critical thinking skills. The ability to explore unasked questions inside a less formal atmosphere, getting a strong voice through web technology, and getting a location to go over issues within an open, public format are other provisions of social media (Kirkup, 2010).

Learning online as well through SNSs can be considered as an informal way of learning. According to Laskaris (2015) informal learning gives the highest level of learning with the deepest cognitive impact.

Different age and gender groups may participate in informal learning activities for different personal interest. According to Farah and Melati (2013), Malaysian teenagers tend to use SNSs to gather specific information for the purpose of completing assignments given by their teachers in school. On the other hand, older age group use SNSs to access information and issues related to challenges associated with later life such as retirement, aging, and health, family and finances (Nimrod, 2013). Although people of different age groups learn different types of knowledge through SNSs, they all generally gather knowledge from multiple sources to establish a pattern and then decide what to believe and practise. There is still a lack of studies in the Malaysian context exploring the use of SNSs as an informal learning tool. Hence this study will add new knowledge to this field.

METHOD

Participants

A convenience sampling approach was used to recruit 799 students from three types of schools located in the Klang Valley and Selangor in Malaysia, i.e. an urban school, a sub-urban school and a rural school. The reason for choosing the three types of schools was to give a convincing representation of the different types of schools found in Malaysia. However, the choice of actual schools depended on the willingness of the principals to allow their students to participate in the study. A brief description of each type of school is given below:

The urban school is situated about 17 km from Kuala Lumpur. It is a secondary co-education school where the medium of instruction for all subjects except English and Bahasa Malaysia is in Mandarin. All of the students come from National Type Chinese School (with Mandarin as the medium of instruction). The performance of students in this school for the PT3/ UPSR (Primary Three/Primary Six) examinations is generally mixed with high and average performing students.

The suburban school is about 30 km from Kuala Lumpur. The students are Malay male and female students who come from national primary schools. The medium of instruction for all subjects except English is in Malay. The performance of students for the PT3/UPSR examinations in this school is mixed ranging from good to below average. Their proficiency in English is generally average. Students in this school generally speak Malay at home, come from middle income families where most of their parents are civil servants, and they live around Putrajaya.

The rural co-education school is about 30 km from Kuala Lumpur. It is a normal type of Malaysian school where students are drawn from the surrounding areas. The medium of instruction for all subjects except English is in Malay. However, the students in this school come from mixed primary school background. Some would have studied their primary education in a National Type Chinese school (with Mandarin as the medium of instruction, some in National Type Tamil schools (with Tamil as the medium of instruction) and some in National school (with Malay as the medium of instruction). The performance of students in this school for the PT3/UPSR examinations is mixed with more low performing students than high performing students.

In addition to that, only Form Two (14 years old) and Form Four (16 years old) students from the three different types of schools were utilised for this study. This was due to the fact that it was not possible to obtain permission from the Ministry of Education to conduct the research on examination classes (i.e. Form Three and Form Five students). Form Two students represented lower secondary school students who were generally assumed to be less exposed to technology than the Form 4 students who represented upper secondary school students. The truth of this assumption would also be investigated in this study.

The sample of this study consists of 50.9% female and 49.1% male, and they were secondary school students of age 14 and age 16 from the three different types of school mentioned above. The following table gives a breakdown of students according to the age, gender and school type.

Table 1. Breakdown of students from the three different types of school

School	Students Age 14						Students Age 16						Overall Total	Overall %
	F	%	M	%	Total	(%)	F	%	M	%	Total	(%)		
Urban	42	21.8	48	24.7	90	23.3	53	24.8	60	30.3	113	27.4	203	25.4
Suburban	67	34.7	82	42.3	149	38.5	69	32.2	80	40.4	149	36.2	298	37.3
Rural	84	43.5	64	33.0	148	38.2	92	43.0	58	29.3	150	36.4	298	37.3
Total	193	100	194	100	387	100	214	100	198	100	412	100	799	100

Key: F=Female; M=Male

Instrument

In this study, the role of SNSs in teenagers' informal language learning experiences was measured through a questionnaire survey that consists of two sections:

1. Section A elicits demographic information of the students;
2. Section B elicits information from the students regarding their use of SNSs for informal language learning purposes This section consists of 8 items with a four-point Likert scale comprising responses that varied from 1 (Never) to 4 (all the time).

Research Procedure

An e-mail was sent to the person-in-charge of each school to ask for permission to conduct the questionnaire survey during school hours. The participants were given approximately 15 minutes to complete the questionnaire survey. Participants were assured of their anonymity and were informed that participation was voluntary and that they would receive a small gift as a token of appreciation for participating in this study. The questionnaire was only distributed to Form Two (14 years old) and Form Four (16 years old) students from the three different types of schools.

Data Analysis

The questionnaire data were analysed using SPSS (Statistical Package for the Social Sciences)- what version 17. Descriptive and inferential statistical tools were used. The descriptive data analysis involved comparing of mean scores and ranking of items. Inferential statistics analysis involved the use of T-test to measure the significance of the difference in mean scores between male and female students.

RESULTS

Analysis of Baseline Data

The overall breakdown of students according to age-groups and genders are shown in Table 2. The number of boy and girl respondents is roughly equivalent.

Table 2. Breakdown of respondents

	Female	Male
Age 14	193	194
Age 16	214	198
Total	407	392

Spending time on SNSs appears to be part of most Malaysian teenagers' daily activities. As shown in Table 3, the four most popular SNSs among the students in this study are Facebook, WhatsApp, Instagram and WeChat with rankings that vary with age groups and genders. The only variation is age 16 female students who ranked Twitter as number 4.

Table 3. SNSs that students are members to according to genders and age

SNSs Frequented by Students	Age 14								Age 16							
	F	%	R	M	%	R	T	%	F	%	R	M	%	R	T*	%
Facebook	303	85.8	1	167	86.1	1	470	86.0	285	78.3	2	173	87.4	1	458	81.5
WhatsApp	263	74.5	2	152	78.3	2	415	75.9	305	83.8	1	172	86.9	2	477	84.9
Twitter	174	49.3	5	56	28.9	5	230	42.0	220	60.4	4	94	47.5	5	314	56.0
Instagram	263	74.5	2	113	58.2	4	376	68.7	261	71.7	3	128	64.6	4	389	69.2
WeChat	215	60.9	4	137	70.6	3	352	64.4	210	57.7	5	137	69.2	3	347	61.7
Line	84	23.8	7	48	24.7	7	132	24.1	70	19.2	8	42	21.2	7	112	19.9
Tumblr	71	20.1	8	11	5.7	8	82	15.0	73	20.1	7	25	12.6	8	98	17.4
Pinterest	52	14.7	9	9	4.6	9	61	11.2	35	9.6	9	10	5.1	9	45	8.0
Skype	115	32.6	6	55	28.4	6	170	31.1	133	36.5	6	70	35.4	6	203	36.1
Total no. of respondents to Qs*	353	100		194	100		547	100	364	100		198	100		562	100

Key: R = Rank; T=Total; Qs=Questionnaires

For this study, spending less than 5 hours on SNSs per day is considered as spending a reasonable amount of time on social networking and spending more than 5 hours on SNSs is considered as "excessive use". This is calculated based on the assumption that students need 8 hours of sleep per night and 7 hours to attend school leaving them with 9 hours for other activities. If more than 5 hours (i.e.55%) of this remaining time is used for SN, then they are left with only 4 hours (i.e. 45%) for important activities such as taking their meals, doing their homework, other recreational activities and relaxation.

It can be seen in Table 4 that between 61.8% and 67.7% students from both age groups and genders spend less than 5 hours on SNSs. However, the rest (which is between 32.3% to 38.2% students of both age groups and genders) spend over 5 hours on SNSs which is considered excessive. Thus, although the findings indicate that the pattern of usage is higher for less than 5 hours, the percentage of usage of above 5 hours is above 30% which is a pattern that we should be concerned with as it may lead to even higher usage in the near future. In addition to that, it appears that generally age 16 students spend less time on SNSs than age 14 students. Out of the four groups, the male students age 16 is the group that spent the least amount of time on SNSs (67.7% spent less than 5 hours on SN) whereas female students age 14 spent the most amount of time on SNSs (38.2% spend more than 5 hours on SNSs).

Table 4. Time spent on SNSs per day according to genders and age

Time Spent Social Networking Sites	Age 14					Age 16				Total
	Female	%	Male	%	Total	Female	%	Male	%	
Less than 2 hours	80	22.8	55	28.6	135	74	20.4	46	23.6	120
2 to 5 hours	137	39.0	66	34.4	203	165	45.5	86	44.1	251
5+ to 8 hours	78	22.2	30	15.6	108	80	22.0	36	18.5	116
More than 8 hours	56	16.0	41	21.4	97	44	12.1	27	13.8	71
Total (Valid)	351	100	192	100	543	363	100	195	100	558

Comparing the Differences in the Usage of SNSs for Informal Learning for Different Categories of Students

For analysis of use of SNSs for the informal learning, both descriptive and inferential tools were used. For descriptive analysis, a mean score of 2.5 and above is taken as inclining to "often". The learning items showed in Table 5 reveal the different ways age 14 students use SNSs for informal learning. The Age 14 female students have 9 out of 14 items (64.3%) that are inclined to "often". Out of these 9 items, 4 of them (44.6%) are on learning of English. As for the Age 14 male students, 6 out of 14 items (42.9%) are inclined to "often". Out of these 6 items, 3 items (50%) are on the learning of English. These findings suggest that the age 14 female students use SNSs for learning (including in the learning of English) more often than the age 14 male students.

Inferential statistics were used to support or refute the findings from the descriptive analysis. Inferential statistical data analysis was undertaken using T-tests to identify the statistically significant results. Most research studies use a cut-off of 5% (that is the p-value is less than 0.05). This is the p-value that is used for this research study. In view of that only significant findings were displayed and items with significantly higher mean scores were highlighted.

Table 6 revealed that out of 14 items, only 5 items displayed significant differences. The mean scores of age 14 female students are significantly higher than age 14 male students for these 5 items. This suggests that age 14 female students undertake these learning activities significantly more than age 14 male students. There are no significant differences between the female and male students in the use of the other items. The findings from the inferential analysis confirm that of the descriptive analysis in showing that age 14 female students use SNSs for informal learning more that age 14 male students.

Table 5. The usage of SNSs for informal language learning purposes according to genders (age 14)

Item	Students Age 14	Male			Female		
		N	Mean	Rank	N	Mean	Rank
1	Gain new knowledge	194	2.90	1	192	2.90	1
2	Give you a chance to communicate in English	194	2.78	2	192	2.62	4
3	Discuss lessons with friends	194	2.59	3	193	2.86	2
4	Learn from communicating with friends	194	2.56	4	192	2.74	3
5	Learn new words in English	194	2.53	5	193	2.55	7
6	Provide information related to your studies	194	2.51	6	193	2.59	5
7	Improve English through chatting with others	194	2.43	7	191	2.58	6
8	Improve English by reading articles or other people's writing	192	2.41	8	190	2.54	8
9	Form a study group to discuss homework	194	2.25	9	192	2.53	9
10	Use an online dictionary to find new words in English	194	2.14	10	192	2.40	10
11	Learn from communicating with teachers	194	1.98	11	191	2.02	12
12	Learn how to pronounce words from an online dictionary	193	1.93	12	193	2.02	12
13	Learn words in foreign language	194	1.93	12	193	2.13	11
14	Form a group to chat in English	193	1.80	14	191	1.90	14

Key: 4 = "all the time", 3 = "often", 2 = "sometimes" and 1 = "never".

Table 6. Comparison of mean scores across gender for age 14 students

Item	Students Age 14	Male			Female			t	df	SD
		N	Mean	SD	N	Mean	SD			
3	Discuss lessons with friends	194	2.59	0.89	193	2.86	0.80	3.15	384	0.002
4	Learn from communicating with friends	194	2.56	0.95	192	2.74	0.92	1.92	384	0.05
9	Form a study group to discuss homework	194	2.25	0.97	192	2.53	0.95	2.84	384	0.05
10	Use an online dictionary to find new words in English	194	2.14	0.93	192	2.40	0.90	2.82	384	0.005
13	Learn words in foreign language	194	1.93	0.99	193	2.13	0.93	2.02	385	0.04

Descriptive analysis was also undertaken on age 16 male and female students. As shown in Table 7 for age 16 female students there are 10 learning items (71.4%) incline to "often". Out of these 10 items, 4 items (40%) are on the learning of English. The age 16 male students have 9 items (64.4%) inclined to "often" and out of these 5 items (55.5%) are on the learning of English. Thus, the difference between age

16 male and female students is less distinct. A comparison across age groups reveal that age 16 students appear to use SNSs for learning to a larger extent than age 14 students including in the learning of English.

The inferential analysis in Table 8 revealed that only 3 items out of the 14 items displayed significant differences. The mean scores of age 16 female students are significantly higher than male students for 2 items and significantly lower for one item. These findings confirm that of the descriptive analysis. The difference between the age 16 male and female students is less clearly defined.

Table 7. The usage of SNSs for informal language learning purposes according to genders (age 16)

Item	Students Age 16	Male			Female		
		N	Mean	Rank	N	Mean	Rank
1	Gain new knowledge	196	3.11	1	214	3.07	1
2	Give you a chance to communicate in English	195	2.90	2	214	2.96	3
3	Discuss lessons with friends	196	2.81	4	213	3.01	2
4	Learn from communicating with friends	195	2.82	3	213	2.92	4
5	Learn new words in English	195	2.63	8	213	2.77	6
6	Provide information related to your studies	195	2.75	5	212	2.82	5
7	Improve English through chatting with others	195	2.68	7	213	2.73	7
8	Form a study group to discuss homework	195	2.70	6	214	2.67	8
9	Improve English by reading articles or other people's writing	192	2.59	9	210	2.63	9
10	Use an online dictionary to find new words in English	195	2.43	10	213	2.61	10
11	Learn from communicating with teachers	195	2.38	11	212	2.20	13
12	Learn how to pronounce words from an online dictionary	193	2.23	12	213	2.28	11
13	Learn words in foreign language	195	2.06	13	213	2.21	12
14	Form a group to chat in English	193	2.03	14	211	1.97	14

Key: 4 = "all the time", 3 = "often", 2 = "sometimes" and 1 = "never".

Table 8. Comparison of mean scores across gender for age 16 students

Item	Students Age 16	Male			Female			t	df	p-Value
		N	Mean	SD	N	Mean	SD			
3	Discuss lessons with friends	196	2.81	0.92	213	3.01	0.82	2.35	407	0.02
10	Use an online dictionary to find new words in English	195	2.43	0.89	213	2.61	0.87	2.13	406	0.03
11	Learn from communicating with teachers	195	2.38	0.91	212	2.20	0.83	2.34	391	0.04

Ranking of the Types of Learning Undertaken for the Different Categories of Students

With regard to the top five rankings, as shown in Tables 4 and 5, the "gain new knowledge" item has the highest ranking for all groups suggesting that students see this as the most important thing they can gain from the SNSs. The next three items are on learning through interaction with others suggesting that social interaction online has its benefits. The fifth item, "Learn new words in English", has some variations in rankings. This item is preferred more by the age 14 students than the age 16 students.

With regard to the bottom five items, they are all the same with some slight variation in ranking. Three of these items are on learning alone and one on learning through the help of a teacher and the final on learning through a group chat.

OVERALL DISCUSSION

This study investigated the use of SNSs for learning purposes by Malaysian male and female secondary of two different age groups. Four research questions were addressed in the study. First question looked into the SNSs patterns that Malaysian secondary school students preferred. The findings revealed that SNSs that are popular among students age 14 and students age 16 are not different in types but in ranking only. In addition, this finding was similar for both male and female students. Generally, all students chose Facebook, WhatsApp, Instagram and WeChat as the first four choices except age 16 students who indicate a preference of Twitter as the fourth choice. This is in line with the findings of Global Web Index (2015) which suggests that there is no apparent difference in patterns of use between male and female students as well as between students of different age groups.

The second research question explored the amount of time the different categories of students spent on SNSs to get an idea of the extent of use. The study revealed that on the whole over 60% of students spent less than 5 hours on SNSs. However, it is disturbing to note that over 30% students spent over five hours on SNSs which would indicate 'excessiveness of use' and may lead to abuse in the future. Thus, it is important at this juncture to investigate to what extent they are using the SNSs for informal learning. A deeper analysis indicated that generally age 16 students spent less time on SNSs than age14 students. For across genders, the findings revealed that male students spent less time on social networking than female students. The findings across gender are in line with that of Joiner et al. (2012) and ComScore (2011).

The third research question investigated to what extent the different categories of students use SNSs for informal learning and the types of learning they focus on. The findings revealed that the students did use SNSs for learning with the highest usage among age 16 female students (71.4%) and the lowest usage among age 14 male students (42.9%). The figures are encouraging and they suggest that students' involvement in SNSs have indeed brought about reasonable amount of informal learning. This finding supports that of Lai et al., (2013) that showed that students do use technologies for informal learning to improve themselves.

With regard to types of use, generally students from both age groups often used it for learning of English on an average level with a range of 44% to 55.5%. With regard to other types of learning, SNSs were often used for gaining of knowledge and information, various types of interactions and for vocabulary improvement.

With reference to types of learning preferred, generally for all groups it appeared that gaining new knowledge was seen as the most important followed by learning through interactions and learning new words in English. The least preferred types of learning by all the groups were almost the same which included learning alone, learning through the help of a teacher and learning through a group chat. These findings corroborated previous findings (Boyd, 2008; Smith, 2009; Brady, Holcomb and Smith, 2010) that show SNSs can be used for informal learning for a variety of purposes. However, there seem to be less preference for activities that have to be performed alone or with the support of the teachers.

The last research question investigated whether there were any differences in usage of SNSs for informal learning between male and female students and between students age 14 and age 16. The overall findings revealed that generally age 16 students used SNSs for learning more than age 14 students. In addition to that the difference in usage between age 16 male and female students was less apparent than in the case of age 14 male and female students. In the case of age 14 students, the female students used SNSs for learning more than the male students. T-tests confirmed these findings. This finding supported that of Misra et al. (2015) which revealed a variation in attraction towards SNSs between male and female students. It also supported findings of Mazman and Usluel (2011) in reporting that difference in gender also influenced types and preference of use.

IMPLICATIONS AND CONCLUSION

In conclusion, it is possible to say that Malaysian students age 14 and 16 have used SNSs for informal learning to a reasonable extent and that their involvement in SNSs has beneficial effects. This study has identified the types of learning these students are involved in and they encompass a variety of learning activities: ranging from the search for knowledge and information, learning through interactions and gaining new knowledge. However, the students show lower preference for activities that involve self-learning and teacher involvement. The differences between male and female do exist in terms of learning types and preferences, but the differences are limited.

Social networking has become an essential part of life for most Malaysian secondary school students and that it serves not only as a primary tool for communication and socialization but also a tool in assisting students' education development outside the classroom. The findings of this research can help teachers and parents understand how lower secondary and upper secondary male and female students learn after school. It is also believed that this research can help school teachers design meaningful activities involving the use of SNSs for learning purposes. Apart from that, this research may also help to expand methods for teaching languages in classroom contexts since the findings show that informal online engagement leads to successful language learning. According to the Global Information Technology Report 2015 by Dutta et al. (2015), Malaysia was ranked 32nd out of 143 countries listed in the Networked Readiness Index 2015, and it is the only country in Asia that was featured in the top 60. The report also revealed that the internet access in schools was ranked 34th out of 143. This clearly indicates that it will not be difficult for Malaysian schools to harness social networking as an educational tool.

Although this research has successfully achieved its objectives, there are unavoidable limitations that need to be mentioned here. It has to be admitted that there is a possibility of sample selection bias in this study. The study has targeted a fairly narrow demographic segment, namely, secondary school students (age 14 and 16) from three schools located in the Klang Valley and Selangor. In addition to that the findings would have been richer if other variables such as different types of schools, different ethnic origins and different social economic status were investigated. However, it is not possible to explore all of them within the scope of this study. It is possible that this narrow focus may have limited the generalisability of the results to Malaysian school population as a whole. Hence, for future research, it is recommended that a more extensive study covering more variables and wider demographic segments be undertaken.

ACKNOWLEDGMENT

This paper was part of a research project (Code SK-2015-003) funded by the Malaysian Communications and Multimedia Commission (MCMC).

REFERENCES

Bond, B. J. (2009). He posted, she posted: Gender differences in self-disclosure on social networking sites. *Rocky Mountain Communication Review*, *6*(2), 29–37.

Boyd, D. M., & Ellison, N. B. (2007). Social network sites: Definition, history, and scholarship. *Journal of Computer-Mediated Communication*, *13*(1), 210–230. doi:10.1111/j.1083-6101.2007.00393.x

Boyd, D. M. (2008). *Taken Out of Context: American teen sociality in networked publics. (Ph.D. Dissertation)*. Berkeley, CA: School of Information, University of California-Berkeley. Retrieved from https://www.danah.org/papers/TakenOutOfContext.pdf

Brady, K., Holcomb, L., & Smith, B. (2010). The use of alternative social networking sites in higher educational settings: A case study of the e-learning benefits of Ning in education. *Journal of Interactive Online Learning*, *9*(2), 151–170.

Briansolis. (2010). The age of social networks. Retrieved from https://www.briansolis.com/2010/03/the-age-of-social-networks/

Bruestle, P., Haubner, D., Schinzel, B., Holthaus, M., Remmele, B., Schirmer, D., & Reips, U. D. (2009). Doing E-learning/doing gender? Examining the relationship between students' gender concepts and E-learning technology. In *Proceedings of the 5th European Symposium on Gender & ICT Digital Cultures: Participation - Empowerment – Diversity, University of Bremen*.

Chun, W. S. M. (2013). An exploration of gender differences in the use of social networking and knowledge management tools. *Journal of Information Technology Management*, *24*(2), 20–31.

ComScore. (2011). It's a social world: Social networking leads as top online activity globally, accounting for 1 in every 5 online minutes. Retrieved from https://www.comscore.com/Insights/Press-Releases/2011/12/Social-Networking-Leads-as-Top-Online-Activity-Globally

Cuadrado-García, M., Ruiz-Molina, M. E., & Montoro-Pons, J. D. (2010). Are there gender differences in e-learning use and assessment? Evidence from an interuniversity online project in Europe. *Procedia: Social and Behavioral Sciences*, *2*(2), 367–371. doi:10.1016/j.sbspro.2010.03.027

Deng, L., & Tavares, N. (2013). From Moodle to Facebook: Exploring students' motivation and experiences in online communities. *Computer Educ*, *68*, 167–176. doi:10.1016/j.compedu.2013.04.028

Dutta, S., Geiger, T., & Lanvin, B. (2015). The global information technology report 2015. Retrieved October 2016 from http://www3.weforum.org/docs/WEF_Global_IT_Report_2015.pdf

Yusop, F. D., & Sumari, M. (2013). The use of social media technologies among Malaysian youth. *Procedia: Social and Behavioral Sciences, 103*, 1204–1209. doi:10.1016/j.sbspro.2013.10.448

Global Web Index. (2015). Quarterly report on the latest trends in social networking. Retrieved from https://www.globalwebindex.net/hs-fs/hub/304927/file-2812772150pdf/Reports/GWI_Social_Summary_Report_Q1_2015.pdf

Griffith, S., & Liyanage, L. (2008). An introduction to the potential of social networking sitesin education. In *Proceedings of the Second Emerging Technologies Conference 2008*, Wollongong, Australia.

Joiner, R., Gavin, J., Brosnan, M., Cromby, J., Gregory, H., Guiller, J., ... Moon, A. (2012). Gender, Internet experience, Internet identification and Internet anxiety: A ten year follow-up. *Cyberpsychology, Behavior, and Social Networking, 15*(7), 370–372. doi:10.1089/cyber.2012.0033 PMID:22690795

Kirkup, G., & von Prümmer, C. (1997). Distance education for European women: The treats and opportunities of new educational forms and media. *European Journal of Women's Studies, 4*(1), 39–62. doi:10.1177/135050689700400104

Kirkup, G. (2010). Academic blogging: Academic practice and academic identity. *London Review of Education, 8*(1), 75–84. doi:10.1080/14748460903557803

Lai, K. W., Khaddage, F., & Knezek, G. (2013, January). Student technology experiences in formal and informal learning. In *WCCE 2013: Learning while we are connected: Proceedings of the IFIP Computers in Education 2013 World Conference* (pp. 290-290). Nicolaus Copernicus University Press.

Laskaris, J. (2015). 6 Benefits of informal learning. *Talentslms.com*. Retrieved from https://www.talentlms.com/blog/6-benefits-of-informal-learning/

Lenhart, A., Madden, M., & Hitlin, P. (2010). Social media and mobile internet use among teens and young adults. *Pew Internet & American Life Project*. Retrieved from https://files.eric.ed.gov/fulltext/ED525056.pdf

Liu, C. Y., & Yu, C. P. (2013). Can Facebook use induce well-being? *Cyberpsychology, Behavior, and Social Networking, 16*(9), 674–678. doi:10.1089/cyber.2012.0301 PMID:24028138

Livingstone, D. W. (1999). Exploring the icebergs of adult learning: Findings of the first Canadian survey of informal learning practices. Centre for the Study of Education and Work, OISE/UT, Toronto. Retrieved from https://tspace.library.utoronto.ca/bitstream/1807/2724/2/10

Malaysian Communications and Multimedia Commission. (2017). Internet users survey 2017. Retrieved from https://www.mcmc.gov.my/skmmgovmy/media/General/pdf/MCMC-Internet-Users-Survey-2017.pdf

Marsick, V. J., & Watkins, K. E. (2001). Informal and incidental learning. *New Directions for Adult and Continuing Education, 89*(89), 25–34. doi:10.1002/ace.5

Manago, A. M., Taylor, T., & Greenfield, P. M. (2012). Me and My 400 Friends: The anatomy of college students' Facebook networks, Their Communication Patterns, and Well-Being. *Developmental Psychology*, *48*(2), 369–380. doi:10.1037/a0026338 PMID:22288367

Mazman, S. G., & Usluel, Y. K. (2011). Gender differences in using social networks. *The Turkish Online Journal of Educational Technology*, *10*(2), 133–139.

Misra, N., Dangi, S., & Patel, S. (2015). Gender differences in usage of social networking sites and perceived online social support on psychological well being of youth. *The International Journal of Indian Psychology*, *3*(1), 63–74.

Nimrod, G. (2013). Applying gerontographics in the study of older Internet users. *Journal of Audience & Perception Study*, *10*(2), 46–64.

Pempek, T. A., Yermolayeva, Y. A., & Calvert, S. L. (2009). College students' social networking experiences on Facebook. *Journal of Applied Developmental Psychology*, *30*(3), 227–238. doi:10.1016/j.appdev.2008.12.010

Pew Research Center. (2018). Social media use in 2018. Retrieved from http://www.pewinternet.org/2018/03/01/social-media-use-in-2018/

Selwyn, N. (2009). Faceworking: Exploring students' education-related use of "Facebook". *Learning, Media and Technology*, *34*(2), 157–174. doi:10.1080/17439880902923622

Smith, B. V. (2009). *Use of online educational social networking in a school environment.* Unpublished master's thesis, North Carolina State University, Raleigh, NC. Retrieved from http://www.ncolr.org/jiol/issues/pdf/9.2.4.pdf

Social Media Today. (2016). Gender-specific behaviors on social media and what they mean for online communications. Retrieved from https://www.socialmediatoday.com/social-networks/gender-specific-behaviors-social-media-and-what-they-mean-online-communications

Sproutsocial. (2017). The Q1 2017 Sprout social index-The social generations: Millennials ask, Gen X buys & Baby Boomers observe. Retrieved January 2018 from https://sproutsocial.com/insights/data/q1-2017/

Tiene, C. D. (2000). Online discussions: A survey of advantages and disadvantages compared to face-to-face discussions. *Journal of Educational Multimedia and Hypermedia*, *9*(4), 371–384.

Vivian, R., & Barnes, A. (2010). Social networking: From living technology to learning technology? In C.H. Steel, M.J. Keppell, P. Gerbic et al. (Eds.), Curriculum, Technology & Transformation for an unknown Future. Proceedings of Ascilite Sydney 2010 (pp. 1007–1019).

Vserv. (2015). Smartphone user Persona report (SUPR) 2015. Retrieved from https://www.vserv.com/vserv-unveils-first-smartphone-user-persona-report-supr-malaysia/

This research was previously published in the International Journal of Computer-Assisted Language Learning and Teaching (IJCALLT), 8(4); pages 76-88, copyright year 2018 by IGI Publishing (an imprint of IGI Global).

Chapter 79

Nexus Between Social Network, Social Media Use, and Loneliness:
A Case Study of University Students, Bangladesh

Bezon Kumar

https://orcid.org/0000-0003-4489-431X

Rabindra University, Bangladesh

Md. Aminul Islam

https://orcid.org/0000-0001-5636-3140

University of Liberal Arts Bangladesh, Bangladesh

ABSTRACT

This paper mainly explores how real-life social network and social media use are related to loneliness among university students in Bangladesh. To carry out this paper, primary data and several methods are used. This paper uses Lubben Social Network Scale and UCLA loneliness scale to measure the level of real life social network and loneliness, respectively. Besides Pearson's partial correlation matrix is used to find out the correlation between social network, social media use, and loneliness. The study finds that students are averagely engaged in real-life social network and moderately lonely. The study also finds a significantly positive relationship between social media (Facebook) use and loneliness, and a significantly negative relationship between real life social network and loneliness. This paper calls for the students to be careful in using social media and be engaged more in real life social network to avoid loneliness.

DOI: 10.4018/978-1-6684-7123-4.ch079

INTRODUCTION

One of the most defining characteristics of the human being is their need for meaningful social connection and they feel pain without it. The need for interaction with others is deeply embedded in human being genetic code. Cacioppo and Patrick (2009) metaphorically termed loneliness as social pain but is very much similar to physical pain or hunger. By using functional magnetic resonance imaging (FMRI), they found that loneliness and social isolation or rejection activates the same parts of the brain as physical pain. Researchers often use the terms loneliness and social isolation interchangeably. Contrarily, Valtorta and Hanratty (2012) argued that these two terms are completely distinct concepts. For them, individuals can be lonely despite having numerous persons to interact with. On the other hand, an individual may not feel lonely despite being isolated from the social world or not having a huge number of active social connections. So, loneliness is a two dimensional phenomenon– both social and emotional. Social loneliness can be measured by a number of connections of a person has. On the other hand, emotional loneliness can be understood in terms of quality of the relationship and desired companionship. Lack of social contacts and interactions and lack of meaningful quality and quantity relationship lead to social isolation (Victor and Bond, 2009).

Latest modern communication technologies and social media platforms have connected to each other today than ever before. Internet, mobile phone and social Medias are the key factors to this connections. According to the statistics of International Telecommunication Union (ITU), about 51.2 per cent of the global populations (3.9 billion) used the internet actively by the end of 2018 (ITU, 2019). This figure has been changed to more than 56 percent (4.33 billion) by July 2019 (Statista, 2019). According to The Global State of Digital in 2019 Report, worldwide the number of social media users was 3.484 billion and mobile phone users was 5.112 billion in 2019 while on an average people had 7.6 social media accounts around the world and daily time spent on social was 142 minutes a day (Smith, 2019).

Bangladesh is a country of the third world with 16.8 million population. The access to and use of communication technologies are increasing rapidly in the country. The number of internet users in the country reached at 96.199 million and the number of mobile phone subscribers reached at 161.772 million at the end of June, 2019 in Bangladesh (BTRC, 2019). Several reports reveals that Bangladesh is in the third position in terms of 'growing number of Facebook users'. About 92 million people in the country use internet in multiple devices. Among them, 34 million are active in using various social media platforms which is about 20 percent of the total population in 2019. The table below shows picture of total population, internet and Facebook users in Bangladesh in comparison to South Asia and Global perspective.

Table 1. Internet users and 2019 population statistics for Asia

Asia Region	Population (2019 Est.)	Population. % World	Internet Users 30-June-2019	Penetration (% Population)	Internet % Users	Facebook 31-Dec-2018
Asia Only	4,241,972,790	55.0	2,200,658,148	51.9	49.8	867,984,000
Rest of World	3,474,250,419	45.0	2,221,836,474	64.0	50.2	1,331,444,570
All the World	7,716,223,209	100.0	4,422,494,622	57.3	100.0	2,199,428,57
Bangladesh	168,065,920		94,445,000	56.2		28,000,000

Source: https://www.internetworldstats.com/stats3.htm

Figure 1. Individuals using the internet per 100 inhabitants around the world, 2018

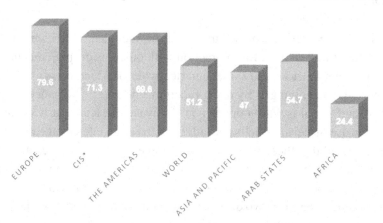

Bangladesh is now passing through the massive transformations and constant changes in terms of its economic development, penetration of technology, mobility of people and the structure and function of the society. Such development has increased urbanization which demanded new living spaces which resulted in increasing number of high rise building. In the past, Bangladesh mainly had individually owned houses but the economic development brought high rise buildings which has introduced new spheres of social relationships. The rise of mobile communication technologies and social media around the world has led changes in the forms of social interaction. In combination with urbanization, modernization and social media's popularity, the social interactions have been going through changes. Similar is the case in a developing country like Bangladesh. Over last few decades, Bangladeshi population migrated from rural areas to urban areas searching for better education and job purposes, which has increased the number of urban populations. Globalization and modernization also played a significant role in contributing to the transformation of urban life, especially to the forms of social interaction. As social institutions, the universities and the university students are not distant island of the society. Rather, they are the significant part of the society, who lead the transformation and changes.

People are now spending too much time communicating and interacting with others. Yet several studies show that people feel increasingly alone and the sense and feeling of loneliness are becoming an epidemic in modern society (Alberti, 2018; Killeen, 1998; Wood, 2013; Brown and Wood, 1953 and Kar-Purkayastha, 2010). However, a critical look into how technology-mediated communication affects users to offer mixed and conflicting results. Some studies show that use of social media such as Facebook is linked to depressive symptoms (Steers et al. 2014 and Alshammari et al. 2017), feelings of isolation (Song et al. 2014), self-esteem and sense of belonging (Tobin et al. 2014), sleep disturbance (Wolniczak et al. 2013 and Levenson et al. 2016) and frequency of social media use initially predicted decreased loneliness and increased happiness (Pittman, 2018). Another study found that there is a relationship between loneliness, depression and internet addiction, and loneliness and internet addiction are risk factors for depression (Demir, 2016). While some other studies indicate that Facebook didn't make people lonely, rather lonely people were more likely to use the social media site (Song et al. 2014). In an online social networking experiment, Deters and Mehl (2012) found that status updating activities on Facebook decrease loneliness. In a study, Lin et al. (2016) found that there association between the amount of time spent on social media and level of depression. Their results indicate that individuals who spend more time using social media are more likely to be depressed. Blanchnio et al. (2018) indicated that among young Polish people, friendship decreases loneliness and loneliness decreases Facebook intrusion. Scott, et al. (2018) found that there is a positive relationship between posting photo and narcissism. However, their results reveal that in the case of loneliness and shyness the relationship is negative. Meanwhile, narcissists are more frequently update about their achievements, diet, and exercise, and individuals with outgoing characteristics post more frequently update about their social activities. Another study found that Facebook 'Likes' less likely to affect the self-esteem of people with the purpose (Burrow and Rainone, 2017). However, Facebook profiles raise users' self-esteem and affect behavior (Toma, 2013).

Some contrasting views about the impact of social media on face-to-face connections are also found. Researchers note that more interactions on social media are replacing face-to-face connections. Meanwhile, other researchers argue that social media does not decrease face-to-face interactions (Hall et al. 2018). No statistically significant association was found between loneliness and Facebook use (Yavich et al., 2019). However, studies suggest that more reliance on social technology instead of face to face interaction create a feeling of social isolation. In a meta-analysis, Huang ((2010) investigated forty studies to find out the relationship between depression, loneliness, self-esteem, and life satisfaction. Its results show that there is a small detrimental effect of Internet use on psychological well-being. Another study finds that social interaction on Facebook may decline subjective well-being in young adults, while it is increased as a result of frequent interactions with supportive "offline" social networks (Kross et al. 2013).

A growing body of researches indicates that loneliness has multiple causes and effects on the human body and mind (Cohen, 2004 and Umberson and Montez, 2010). Results of several studies suggest that suffering from loneliness for a long time can lead to changes in the cardiovascular (Xia and Li, 2018 and Valtora et al. 2016), nervous systems (Cacioppo and Patrick, 2009 and Zelikowsky et al, 2018), health behavior (Winkel et al. 2017), immune and mortality risk (Cole et al. 2015; Holt-Lunstad, et al. 2015 and Steptoe et al. 2013) and loneliness deteriorates the productivity of human being which ultimately decelerates the economic growth of a country (Ahmed, 2018). In the cases, the determining factors are the structural characteristics and types of social networks (Medevene, et al. 2015), quality and quantity of the relationship (Wiseman et al. 2006; Schmidt and Sermat, 1983 and Valtorta and Hanratty, 2012). For example, Cohen (2004) explored three aspects of social relations and their associated health outcomes. The researcher found that social relationships-social support, social integration, and negative interaction-strongly affect both physical and mental health. Another study revealed the mechanism in which age, socioeconomic status, and other factors contribute to social isolation and poorer mental health (Alberti, 2018). Contrarily, Weeks, et al. (1980) argued the relationship between loneliness and depression is not causal, meaning that neither causes directly the other, though the origins of the both are same.

For a comprehensive understanding, the role of social media in mental health can be outlined as the interpersonal-connection-behaviors framework. For them, social media sites can benefit people when they use it for meaningful social connections. On the contrary, the use of the sites can cause harm through multiple ways such as isolation and social comparison. Hunt et al. (2018) found that the limited use group showed significant reductions in loneliness and depression over three weeks compared to the control group. Balchi and Olkun (2015) revealed a positive relationship between the loneliness of foreigners and Facebook usage that implies social network usage is increasing with rising loneliness level. Similarly, Karakose et al. (2016) revealed that students most commonly share photographs and videos on Facebook for spending leisure time. In addition, they have found that there is a statistically significant relationship between the time participants spend on Facebook and their Facebook addiction scores. Primack et al. (2017) found that young adults with high social media use seem to feel more socially isolated than their counterparts with lower social media use. In addition, Masthi et al. (2017) revealed that private school students were more prone to social media addiction and a multitude of physical, psychological and behavioral problems was observed among social media users. Shettar et al. (2017) found that more than one-fourth (26%) of the study participants had Facebook addiction and 33% had a possibility of Facebook addiction. Besides, they have also found that there was a significant positive correlation between the severity of Facebook addiction and extent of experience of loneliness.

In another theoretical model, Nowland et al. (2017) the researchers note that the relationship between loneliness and social internet use is bidirectional and dynamic. According to the model, social technologies can be a strong tool for reducing loneliness when it is used to enhance existing relationships and forge new social connections. On the contrary, the technologies can increase the 'social pain' of interaction and feelings of loneliness when people use it as a scope for escaping from the reality of life and social world. So, it can be argued that the impact of Facebook use is two dimensional- it can deteriorate and improve mental health conditions.

A causal association between social network and health is well established by the wealth of empirical shreds of evidence in various recent cross-sectional, longitudinal, experimental and quasi-experimental studies, most from western perspectives. But the mechanisms through which social relationships affect mental health remain to be explored from the context of developing countries like Bangladesh. Many factors are found in the earlier studies which affects loneliness among the people of Bangladesh. For instance, Pervin and Ferdowshi (2016) examined the relationship between suicidal ideation and depression, loneliness, hopelessness among University students in Bangladesh. They found that suicidal ideation was positively correlated with depression, loneliness and hopelessness. In the context of Bangladesh, mostly young people are found depressed and lonely after the significant visible inclusion of internet particularly after using of various social Medias like Facebook. In addition, Kabir et al. (2018) found that students feel lonely for anxiety, stress and so on. Although very few study has been carried out on loneliness in Bangladesh, to the best of knowledge of the researchers, this is the first study which explores the relationship between mental health (loneliness) and real-life social network and virtual social media use (Facebook) in the context of private university students in Bangladesh. This study is an effort to fill up the gap and this study investigates the structure of real and social media and their relationship with loneliness.

METHODOLOGY

Study Area and Sample Selection

This paper is mainly based on primary data. For carrying out this paper, Rajshahi district among 64 districts of Bangladesh is selected randomly as the study area. There are four universities in Rajshahi district of which two are public university and the rest two are private. As this study focuses only on the private university, public universities are ignored here. Among two private universities, one university is selected randomly and the selected university is Varendra University. The university has about 5000 students in 3 faculties such as Arts and Social Sciences, Business, and Science and Engineering faculties. From the university registrar office, the list of faculty wise students is collected and these faculties are assigned as a stratum. Using the stratified sampling method, sample is determined. The number of sample size is determined using the following formula stated by Taro Yamane.

$$n = \frac{N}{1 + Ne^2},$$

where, n = sample size, N= population size and e = rate of precision (0.05).

$$n = \frac{5000}{1 + 5000\left(0.05^2\right)} = 370$$

Data are collected from 370 students of different faculties randomly with a well-structured questionnaire from January to June 2019 through face to face interview.

Empirical Methods

This study uses three distinct empirical methods. To measure the level of real life social network and loneliness among university students, 6 items Lubben Social Network Scale (LSNS-6) is used following Jobe and White (2007) and Cecen (2008). The LSNS-6 total score is an equally weighted sum of these six items. The scale consisted of 6 items, and scores for each question ranged from zero to five. The score zero indicated minimal social integration and five indicated substantial social integrations. The total score was an equally weighted sum of the 6 items. Scores ranged from 0 to 30 with higher scores indicated a greater level of social support and low risk for isolation. A score less than 12 indicated a person with an extremely limited social network and high risk for isolation. Authors of this study also tried to understand the level of social network of the respondents by dividing total score in three categories. A score of 0-10.00 indicated extremely lower or limited social network, 10.01-20.00 indicated average or moderate social network and 20.01- 30.00 indicated higher or strong social network.

Besides measuring the level of real life social network, the study measures the level of loneliness. To measure the level of loneliness, this study uses twenty items the University of California and Los Angeles (UCLA-20) loneliness scale consisting with 10 negatively stated (lonely) and 10 positively stated (non-lonely) items following Jobe and White (2007) and Cecen (2008). The estimated score of this index ranges from 0 to 60 (Russell et al. 1980). The score zero means student is not lonely while the score 60 means student is highly lonely. More specifically, the score ranges from 0 to 20.00 reveals the lower level of loneliness, the score ranges from 20.01 to 40.00 and 40.01 to 60.00 reveal the moderate level and severe level of loneliness, respectively.

After being informed with the level of real life social network and the level of loneliness, the study uses Pearson's partial correlation matrix to find out the correlation between real life social network, social media use (Facebook use) and loneliness among the university students. Variables considered in the Pearson's partial correlation matrix are described in Table 2.

Table 2. Description of the variables included in the Pearson's correlation test

Variables	Types	Measurement
Age (AG)	Continuous	Age of the students (years)
Gender (GN)	Dummy	1 if the student is male, 0 otherwise
Romantic relationship (RR)	Dummy	1 if the student has romantic relationship, 0 otherwise
Study year (SY)	Continuous	Student's studying year
Time spent on Facebook (TSF)	Continuous	Total hours spent in Facebook by the student in a day
Real life social network (RLSN)	Continuous	Measured by Lubben Social Network Scale
Loneliness (LN)	Continuous	Measured by UCLA Loneliness Scale

RESULTS AND DISCUSSION

Descriptive Analysis

This section presents the students' demographic and Facebook use related features like age, gender, study year, hours spent on Facebook per day, years of Facebook use and so on. The result is analyzed with SPSS 23.00 and presented in Table 3.

Table 3 shows that about 43 percent of students are aged between 20 to 22 years while 62 percent of students are male. It is also found that most of the students read in the fourth year and use Facebook from 1 to 2 years. Majority of the students (58 percent) use Facebook for keeping contact with others and mostly they spent time on Facebook for viewing friends' update. From this analysis, it is found that most of the students (32 percent) spent time on Facebook from 2 to 3 hours a day. At the same time, the study also finds that most of the students (68 percent) share various links on their Facebook timeline. Interestingly, the study finds that the majority of the students (32 percent) never changed their profile picture in last three months.

Reasons behind Updating Facebook Status

Reasons behind updating the Facebook status of the students are analyzed through SPSS 23.00 and presented in Table 4. This analysis has been done for checking whether students update status when they feel lonely.

The above table shows the causes of updating Facebook status. The study finds eleven causes behind updating Facebook status and they are ranked according to the order of their mean value. It is found that to share memorable moments is the topmost reason behind updating Facebook status. The study finds that about 50 of percent students update their Facebook status just for this reason. On the other hand, to express feelings, to make people aware of any important issue are the second and third reasons behind updating Facebook status. Similarly, to earn name and fame is the lowest reason behind updating Facebook status. About 3 percent of students update their Facebook status for this reason. From this analysis, it is found that students mainly update Facebook status not only to express loneliness but also to share memorable moments.

Table 3. Demographic and Facebook use related features of students

Variables	Categories	Percentage
Age (years)	18.00-20.00	18.50
	20.01-22.00	43.00
	22.01-24.00	32.50
	24.01 and above	6.00
Gender	Male	62.00
	Female	38.00
Year of Study	First	23.50
	Second	17.90
	Third	24.80
	Fourth	33.80
Years of Facebook use	1.00 and below	32.10
	1.01 2.00	33.30
	2.01-3.00	23.50
	3.01 and above	11.10
Purpose of using Facebook	Passing time	11.5
	A kind of addiction	9.4
	Keeping contact with others	58.1
	Entertainment	20.9
Major Facebook activities	Making new friendship	15.4
	Viewing friends' updates	79.5
	Uploading photo/selfie	5.1
Time spent on Facebook per day (hours)	1.00 and below	15.40
	1.01 -2.00	24.80
	2.01-3.00	32.50
	3.01 and above	27.40
Sharing of link	Yes	67.9
	No	32.1
Frequency of changing profile picture in last three months	Never	32.1
	Once	5.1
	Twice	22.2
	Thrice	15.4
	Fourth and above	25.2

Lubben Social Network Scale

Lubben Social Network Scale (LSNS) is measured through the MS Excel 2013 and the result is presented in tabular form in the following table.

Table 4. Reasons behind updating a Facebook status

Reasons	Percentage of total	Mean	Rank
To share memorable moments	50.00	0.50	1
To express feelings	48.70	0.49	2
To make people aware about various issues	40.20	0.40	3
To express joys	38.00	0.38	4
To express rudeness, anger and egotism indirectly	19.70	0.20	5
To express depression	15.80	0.16	6
To get rid of loneliness	13.70	0.14	7
To express personality	11.10	0.11	8
To bring to light the skill, knowledge and appearance	10.30	0.10	9
To get like and comments	6.80	0.07	10
To earn name and fame	3.40	0.03	11

Source: Field survey, 2019

Table 5. Level of real life social network of students

Levels of social network	Frequency	Percentage
Lower level (0.00 to 10.00)	71	19.23
Average level (10.01 to 20.00)	213	57.69
Higher level (20.01 to 30.00)	86	23.08
Total	370	100

Note: Average level of real life social network of all students is average i.e. 15.02.
Source: Field survey, 2019

Table 5 shows that about 19 percent of students in the study area are lower engaged in real life social network. On the other hand, the majority of the students (58 percent) in the study area are averagely engaged in real life social network while 23 of percent students are highly engaged in real life social network. From the analysis, it is also found that the level of real life social network among the university students in the study area is 15. This interprets that students are averagely engaged in real life social network in the study area.

UCLA Loneliness Scale

UCLA Loneliness Scale is measured through the MS Excel 2013 and the result is presented in tabular form in the following table.

Table 6 shows only 35 percent of students in the study area suffered from lower level loneliness. On the other hand, it is found that most of the students (51 percent) in the study area suffered from the moderate level of loneliness while 13 percent of students severely suffered from loneliness. From this analysis, it is also found that the level of loneliness among the university students in the study area is 27. This interprets that students suffered from loneliness moderately in the study area.

Table 6. Level of loneliness of university students in Bangladesh

Levels of loneliness	Frequency	Percentage
Lower level (0 to 20.00)	131	35.47
Moderate level (20.01 to 40.00)	190	51.28
Severe level (40.01 to 60.00)	49	13.25
Total	370	100

Note: Average level of loneliness of all students is moderate i.e. 26.86.
Source: Field survey, 2019

Correlations among Different Characteristics and Loneliness

Correlations among various characteristics and loneliness are analyzed by Pearson's partial correlation matrix though SPSS 23.00 and presented in Table 7.

Table 7. Correlations among different characteristics and loneliness

	AG	GN	RR	SY	HF	RLSN	LN
AG	1						
GN	-.157**	1					
RR	-.036	-.057	1				
SY	.126*	-.372**	.183**	1			
TSF	.187**	-.038	-.114*	-.339**	1		
RLSN	-.095	-.219**	-.094	.111*	.051	1	
LN	-.040	.466**	-.186**	-.689**	.443**	-.234**	1

Note: ** and * means 1 percent and 5 percent levels of significance (two-tailed test)
Source: Survey data, 2019

Pearson's partial correlation test reveals the correlation among variables. The above table shows the correlation of some variables with loneliness. All tests were two-tailed and conducted at 5% level of significance. From the above table, it is found that there is a significant correlation between all variables and loneliness except age. The above table reveals that there is a perfect correlation of a particular variable with that variable and the correlation coefficient is one. The estimated correlation coefficient 0.466** reveals that there is a positive correlation between gender and loneliness which is significant at 1 percent level of significance. The estimated correlation coefficient of the romantic relationship and study year with loneliness are -0.186** and -0.689**, respectively. Similarly, 0.443** and -0.234** shows the correlation of Facebook use and real life social network with loneliness. These values interpret that there is a positive and significant relationship between Facebook use and loneliness while a negative relationship exists between real life social network and loneliness.

Although there is a negative relationship between the age of students and the level of loneliness, the relationship is not statistically significant. This finding is consistent with the results of many studies related to the loneliness of students (Cassidy and Asher, 1992). The findings of the study also shows that there is a positive and significant relationship between gender and level of loneliness which reveals that female students are lonelier than male students. This finding may be interpreted by the fact that female students in the study area cannot move freely everywhere anytime with anyone and cannot share their feeling with others, consequently, they have to stay at home in most cases. For this reason, they got depressed and feel lonelier than male students. This study also finds that there is a negative and significant relationship between the romantic relationship and the level of loneliness. This can be interpreted by the fact that students who are in a romantic relationship are less lonely than students who are not in any romantic relation as students enjoying romantic relationship can share their both positive and negative feelings with their partners but others cannot do that. Thus, romantic relationship holder students do not suffer from loneliness but the others. Weiss (1973) and Ozdemir and Tuncay (2008) have found the similar findings. On the other hand, a negative and significant relationship has been found between study year and loneliness. This finding explains that if a student reads in the higher class, the level of loneliness of those students will be relatively lower than students who read in the lower class. Because students read in higher class has many friends and acquainted persons in the university and they can adapt themselves in their university life. As a result, they do not get depressed and do not suffer from loneliness. The study also finds that the level of loneliness among university students differentiates over the time spent on Facebook. This result is positively and significantly correlated which implies that the more the students spent time on Facebook, the more they are lonelier. This finding may be explained by the fact that students' views of others improvements or updates on social media for a long times and staying without family and friends result mental dissatisfaction which makes students lonely. This result is in line with Deters and Mehl (2012). Contrarily, it is found that the students who engaged mostly in real life social network are less lonely than others. The finding is consistent with the result found by Holt-Lunstad et al. (2015).

CONCLUSION

This paper investigates two separate research questions. First, what is the level of real life social network and the level of loneliness among the university students in Bangladesh? Second, what is the correlation between real life social network, social media, and loneliness? To find out the solution to these questions, this paper uses primary data and several methods, and finds some interesting results. Results are interesting in two different aspects. First, the study finds that university students of Bangladesh have an average level of real life social network and a moderate level of loneliness. Second, the study finds that gender and hours on Facebook are positively and significantly while romantic relationship, study year and real life social network are negatively and significantly related to the level of loneliness of university students. Therefore, the study recommends that students should be more engaged in real life social network and romantic relationship, and be careful in using social media to get rid of the effects of loneliness. As researchers of this paper were constraint by time and money, small sample was taken. Authors here suggest taking a big sample in doing further study on it.

ACKNOWLEDGMENT

This research has not received grant from any funding agency in the public, commercial or non-profit sectors.

REFERENCES

Ahmed, O. (2018). Relationship between loneliness and mental health among first-year undergraduate students: Mediating role of timeline browsing and chatting on Facebook. *International Journal of Contemporary Education*, *1*(2), 86–94. doi:10.11114/ijce.v1i2.3625

Alberti, B. F. (2018). This "modern epidemic": Loneliness as an emotion cluster and a neglected subject in the history of emotions. *Emotion Review*, *10*(3), 242–254. doi:10.1177/1754073918768876

Alshammari, A., Al-Harbi, M., Alhamidah, A., Alreshidi, Y., & Abdulrahim, O. (2017). Association between social media use and depression among Saudi population. *Annals of International Medical and Dental Research*, *4*(1). doi:10.21276/aimdr.2018.4.1.ME7

Balchi, S., & Olkun, E. O. (2015). The relation between loneliness in social life and Facebook usage. *Proceedings of the 16th International Academic Conference*. Academic Press. doi:10.20472/IAC.2015.016.015

Blachnio, A., Przepiorka, A., Wolonciej, M., Mahmoud, A. B., Holdos, J., & Yafi, E. (2018). Loneliness, friendship, and Facebook intrusion. a study in Poland, Slovakia, Syria, Malaysia, and Ecuador. *Studia Psychologica*, *60*(3), 183–194. doi:10.21909p.2018.03.761

Brown, L., & Wood, M. (1953). Paths of Loneliness: The individual isolated in modern society. *American Sociological Review*, *18*(6), 712. doi:10.2307/2088145

BTRC. (2019). Internet Subscribers in Bangladesh June, 2019. Retrieved from http://www.btrc.gov.bd/telco/internet

Burrow, A., & Rainone, N. (2017). How many likes did I get?: Purpose moderates links between positive social media feedback and self-esteem. *Journal of Experimental Social Psychology*, *69*, 232–236. doi:10.1016/j.jesp.2016.09.005

Cacioppo, J., & Patrick, W. (2009). *Loneliness: Human Nature and the Need for Social Connection.* New York: Norton. Retrieved from https://psycnet.apa.org/record/2008-07755-000

Cassidy, J., & Asher, S. R. (1992). Loneliness and peer relations in young children. *Child Development*, *63*(2), 350–365. doi:10.2307/1131484 PMID:1611939

Cecen, A. R. (2008). The effects of gender and loneliness levels on ways of coping among university students. *College Student Journal*, *42*, 510–516. Retrieved from https://eric.ed.gov/?id=EJ816934

Cohen, S. (2004). Social relationships and health. *The American Psychologist*, *59*(8), 676–684. doi:10.1037/0003-066X.59.8.676 PMID:15554821

Cole, S., Capitanio, J., Chun, K., Arevalo, J., Ma, J., & Cacioppo, J. (2015). Myeloid differentiation architecture of leukocyte transcriptase dynamics in perceived social isolation. *Proceedings of the National Academy of Sciences of the United States of America, 112*(49), 15142–15147. doi:10.1073/pnas.1514249112 PMID:26598672

Demir, Y. (2016). The relationship between loneliness and depression: Mediation role of internet addiction. *Educational Process International Journal, 5*(2), 97–105. doi:10.12973/edupij.2016.52.1

Deters, F., & Mehl, M. (2012). Does posting Facebook status update increase or decrease loneliness? An online social networking experiment. *Social Psychological & Personality Science, 4*(5), 579–586. doi:10.1177/1948550612469233

Hall, J., Kearney, M., & Xing, C. (2018). Two tests of social displacement through social media use. *Information Communication and Society, 10*, 1–18. doi:10.1080/1369118x.2018.1430162

Holt-Lunstad, J., Smith, T., Baker, M., Harris, T., & Stephenson, D. (2015). Loneliness and social isolation as risk factors for mortality. *Perspectives on Psychological Science, 10*(2), 227–237. doi:10.1177/1745691614568352 PMID:25910392

Huang, C. (2010). Internet use and psychological well-being: A meta-analysis. *Cyberpsychology, Behavior, and Social Networking, 13*(3), 241–249. doi:10.1089/cyber.2009.0217 PMID:20557242

Hunt, M. G., Marx, R., Lipson, C., & Young, J. (2018). No more FOMO: Limiting social media decreases loneliness and depression. *Journal of Social and Clinical Psychology, 37*(10), 751–768. doi:10.1521/jscp.2018.37.10.751

ITU. (2019). ITU World Telecommunication /ICT Indicators database. Retrieved from https://www.itu.int/en/ITU-D/Statistics/Pages/stat/default.aspx

Jobe, L. E., & White, S. W. (2007). Loneliness, social relationships, and a broader autism phenotype in college students. *Personality and Individual Differences, 42*(8), 1479–1489. doi:10.1016/j.paid.2006.10.021

Kabir, M. A., Sultana, F., Ibrahim, M., Islam, M. M., Rahman, M. M., Islam, M. J., & Bayen, S. (2018). Evaluation of stress, loneliness and depression among residential and non-residential students of Dhaka University: Case-control study. *Pharmaceutical Science and Technology, 2*(1), 1–6. doi:10.11648/j.pst.20180201.11

Kar-Purkayastha, I. (2010). An epidemic of loneliness. *Lancet, 376*(9758), 2114–2115. doi:10.1016/S0140-6736(10)62190-3 PMID:21167590

Karakose, T., Yirci, R., Uygun, H., & Ozdemir, T. Y. (2016). Relationship between high school students' Facebook addiction and loneliness status. *Eurasia Journal of Mathematics. Science and Technology Education, 12*, 2419–2429. doi:10.12973/eurasia.2016.1557a

Killeen, C. (1998). Loneliness: An epidemic in modern society. *Journal of Advanced Nursing, 28*(4), 762–770. doi:10.1046/j.1365-2648.1998.00703.x PMID:9829664

Kross, E., Verduyn, P., Demiralp, E., Park, J., Lee, D., Lin, N., ... Ybarra, O. (2013). Facebook use predicts declines in subjective well-being in young adults. *PLoS One, 8*(8), e69841. doi:10.1371/journal.pone.0069841 PMID:23967061

Levenson, J., Shensa, A., Sidani, J., Colditz, J., & Primack, B. (2016). The Association between social media use and sleep disturbance among young adults. *Preventive Medicine, 85*, 36–41. doi:10.1016/j.ypmed.2016.01.001 PMID:26791323

Lin, L., Sidani, J., Shensa, A., Radovic, A., Miller, E., Colditz, J., ... Primack, B. A. (2016). Association between social media use and depression among US young adults. *Depression and Anxiety, 33*(4), 323–331. doi:10.1002/da.22466 PMID:26783723

Masthi, N. R. R. M., Pruthvi, S., & Mallekavn, P. (2017). A comparative study on social media addiction between public and private high school students of urban Bengaluru, India. *ASEAN Journal of Psychiatry, 18*, 206–215.

Medvene, L., Nilsen, K., Smith, R., Ofei-Dodoo, S., DiLollo, A., Webster, N., ... Nance, A. (2015). Social networks and links to isolation and loneliness among elderly HCBS clients. *Aging & Mental Health, 20*(5), 485–493. doi:10.1080/13607863.2015.1021751 PMID:25808879

Nowland, R., Necka, E., & Cacioppo, J. (2017). Loneliness and social internet use: Pathways to reconnection in a digital world? *Perspectives on Psychological Science, 13*(1), 70–87. doi:10.1177/1745691617713052 PMID:28937910

Ozdemir, U., & Tuncay, T. (2008). Correlates of loneliness among university students. *Child and Adolescent Psychiatry, 2*, 1–6. doi:10.11866/1753-2000-2-29 PMID:18851744

Pervin, M. M., & Ferdowshi, N. (2016). Suicidal ideation in relation to depression, loneliness and hopelessness among university students. *Dhaka University Journal of Biological Sciences, 25*(1), 57–64. doi:10.3329/dujbs.v25i1.28495

Pittman, M. (2018). Happiness, loneliness, and social media: perceived intimacy mediates the emotional benefits of platform use. *The Journal of Social media in Society, 7*, 164-176.

Primack, B. A., Shensa, A., Sidani, J. E., Whaite, E. O., Lin, L. Y., Rosen, D., ... Miller, E. (2017). Social media use and perceived social isolation among young adults in the U.S. *American Journal of Preventive Medicine, 53*(1), 1–8. doi:10.1016/j.amepre.2017.01.010 PMID:28279545

Russell, D., Peplau, L. A., & Cutrona, C. E. (1980). The revised UCLA loneliness scale– concurrent and discriminate validity evidence. *Journal of Personality and Social Psychology, 39*(3), 472–480. doi:10.1037/0022-3514.39.3.472 PMID:7431205

Schmidt, N., & Sermat, V. (1983). Measuring loneliness in different relationships. *Journal of Personality and Social Psychology, 44*(5), 1038–1047. doi:10.1037/0022-3514.44.5.1038

Scott, G., Boyle, E., Czerniawska, K., & Courtney, A. (2018). Posting photos on Facebook: The impact of narcissism, social anxiety, loneliness, and shyness. *Personality and Individual Differences, 133*, 67–72. doi:10.1016/j.paid.2016.12.039

Shettar, M., Karkal, R., Kakunje, A., Mendonsa, R. D., & Chandran, V. V. M. (2017). Facebook addiction and loneliness in the post-graduate students of a university in southern India. *The International Journal of Social Psychiatry, 63*(4), 325–329. doi:10.1177/0020764017705895 PMID:28504040

Smith, K. (2019). *126 Amazing Social Media Statistics and Facts*. Retrieved from https://www.brandwatch.com/blog/amazing-social-media-statistics-and-facts/#section-10

Song, H., Zmyslinski-Seelig, A., Kim, J., Drent, A., Victor, A., Omori, K., & Allen, M. (2014). Does Facebook make you lonely?: A meta analysis. *Computers in Human Behavior*, *36*, 446–452. doi:10.1016/j.chb.2014.04.011

Statista, (2019). Global digital population as of July 2019 (in millions). Retrieved from https://www.statista.com/statistics/617136/digital-population-worldwide/

Steers, M., Wickham, R., & Acitelli, L. (2014). Seeing everyone else's highlight reels: How Facebook usage is linked to depressive symptoms. *Journal of Social and Clinical Psychology*, *33*(8), 701–731. doi:10.1521/jscp.2014.33.8.701

Steptoe, A., Shankar, A., Demakakos, P., & Wardle, J. (2013). Social isolation, loneliness, and all-cause mortality in older men and women. *Proceedings of the National Academy of Sciences of the United States of America*, *110*(15), 5797–5801. doi:10.1073/pnas.1219686110 PMID:23530191

Tobin, S., Vanman, E., Verreynne, M., & Saeri, A. (2014). Threats to belonging on Facebook: Lurking and ostracism. *Social Influence*, *10*(1), 31–42. doi:10.1080/15534510.2014.893924

Toma, C. (2013). Feeling better but doing worse: Effects of Facebook self-presentation on implicit self-esteem and cognitive task performance. *Media Psychology*, *16*(2), 199–220. doi:10.1080/15213269.2012.762189

Umberson, D. K., & Montez, J. (2010). Social relationships and health: A flashpoint for health policy. *Journal of Health and Social Behavior*, *51*(1 suppl), S54–S66. doi:10.1177/0022146510383501 PMID:20943583

Valtorta, N., & Hanratty, B. (2012). Loneliness, isolation and the health of older adults: Do we need a new research agenda? *Journal of the Royal Society of Medicine*, *105*(12), 518–522. doi:10.1258/jrsm.2012.120128 PMID:23288086

Valtorta, N., Kanaan, M., Gilbody, S., & Hanratty, B. (2016). Loneliness, social isolation and social relationships: What are we measuring? A novel framework for classifying and comparing tools. *BMJ Open*, *6*(4), e010799. doi:10.1136/bmjopen-2015-010799 PMID:27091822

Victor, C., Scambler, S., & Bond, J. (2009). *The social world of older people: Understanding Loneliness and Social Isolation in Later Life*. Maidenhead: Open University Press.

Weeks, D., Michela, J., Peplau, L., & Bragg, M. (1980). Relation between loneliness and depression: A structural equation analysis. *Journal of Personality and Social Psychology*, *39*(6), 1238–1244. doi:10.1037/h0077709 PMID:7205551

Weiss, R. S. (1973). *Loneliness: The experience of emotional and social isolation London*. MIT Press. Retrieved from https://mitpress.mit.edu/ books/loneliness

Winkel, V. M., Wichers, M., Collip, D., Jacobs, N., Derom, C., & Thiery, E. (2017). Unraveling the role of loneliness in depression: The relationship between daily life experience and behavior. *Psychiatry*, *80*, 104–117. doi:10.1080/00332747.2016.1256143

Wiseman, H., Mayseless, O., & Sharabany, R. (2006). Why are they lonely? Perceived quality of early relationships with parents, attachment, personality predispositions and loneliness in first-year university students. *Personality and Individual Differences*, *40*(2), 237–248. doi:10.1016/j.paid.2005.05.015

Wolniczak, I., Cáceres-DelAguila, J., Palma-Ardiles, G., Arroyo, K., Solís-Visscher, R., Paredes-Yauri, S., ... Bernabe-Ortiz, A. (2013). Association between Facebook dependence and poor sleep quality: A study in a sample of undergraduate students in Peru. *PLoS One*, *8*(3), e59087. doi:10.1371/journal.pone.0059087 PMID:23554978

Wood, C. (2013). Loneliness: A silent epidemic. *Independent Nurse*, *6*. doi:10.12968/indn.2013.17.6.99114

Xia, N., & Li, H. (2018). Loneliness, social isolation, and cardiovascular health. *Antioxidants & Redox Signalling*, *28*(9), 837–851. doi:10.1089/ars.2017.7312 PMID:28903579

Yavich, R., Davidivutch, N., & Frenkel, Z. (2019). Social media and loneliness - forever connected? *Higher Education Studies*, *9*(2), 10–21. doi:10.5539/hes.v9n2p10

Zelikowsky, M., Hui, M., Karigo, T., Choe, A., Yang, B., Blanco, M., ... Anderson, D. J. (2018). The neuropeptide controls a distributed brain state induced by chronic social isolation stress. *Cell*, *173*(5), 1265–1279. doi:10.1016/j.cell.2018.03.037 PMID:29775595

This research was previously published in Innovative Management and Business Practices in Asia; pages 228-243, copyright year 2020 by Business Science Reference (an imprint of IGI Global).

Section 5
Organizational and Social Implications

Chapter 80

Identifiable Problems in Social Media:
Concerning Legal Awareness Within Academic Libraries

Amy D Dye-Reeves
https://orcid.org/0000-0002-1268-4265
Murray State University, USA

ABSTRACT

The chapter serves as a primer for academic librarians on helping patrons with disabilities receive, protect, and understand disseminated content on a multitude of popular social media networking platforms. The content of the chapter provides introductory material on the Americans with Disabilities Act (ADA) and the Family Educational Rights and Privacy Act. The first part of the chapter discusses the inclusion of best practices and web accessibility applications for structuring written incorporation to help all patrons understand the expressed material within social media networking pages. The second part of the chapter discusses the importance of respecting patron privacy within FERPA guidelines. This section discusses social networking pages and best practices for helping safeguard the patron's identity concerning inadvertent HIPAA violations.

INTRODUCTION

This chapter serves as an introductory primer that provides academic librarians with detailed context on how to better assist and inform disabled patrons through social media platforms. The following paragraphs educate informational professionals concerning issues within Americans with Disability Act (ADA) and the Family Educational Rights and Privacy Act of 1974 (FERPA). As a short disclaimer, this chapter serves only as a primer that simply provides information literacy to help aid patrons with disabilities. This chapter does not serve as a directive in terms of legality issues, in which specific issues, should always be directed to the assigned university personnel within that specific institution.

DOI: 10.4018/978-1-6684-7123-4.ch080

The first part of the chapter discusses the careful consideration of social media platforms for patrons with disabilities (ADA compliance) and provides a list of applications that enhances and enriches content comprehension. The second part of the chapter discusses FERPA (Family Educational Right and Privacy Act) and provides a list of associated practices on helping patrons understand the importance non-disclosure information, such as HIPPA (Health Insurance Portability and Accountability Act) based information. The chapter ends with a recommendation section that provides a short list of professional development opportunities.

According to Merriam-Webster (2018), social media is defined as the "form of electronic communication (such as websites for social networking and microblogging) through which users create online communications to share information, ideas, personal messages, and other content (such as videos)" (Webster, 2018). In today's fast pace environment, social media is being used outside of personal correspondence. The social networking pages provide opportunities that are often being explored by corporations, pre and post-secondary education, and beyond.

Nancy Flynn (2012), *The Social Media Handbook* explains that employers must "manage social media use effectively in order to protect (their) organization's assets, reputation, and future" (Flynn, 2). However, the definition of social media should be treated as a living organism whose definition can change rapidly due to the nature of technological advancements.

The 2018 current landscape of popular social media networking sites include *Facebook, Twitter, Instagram, Snapchat and YouTube*. Each page provides a unique venue for both formal and informal conversations. According to a recent survey from the Pew Research Center (2018) revealed that a majority of adults (age 24 and older) within the United States chose *Facebook* and *YouTube* as the preferred social media platform. Whereas the younger Americans preferred a wide variety of social networking pages and used them on a frequent basis. The collected data from the Pew Research Center indicated that "some 78% of 18-24-year-olds use Snapchat, and a sizable majority of these users (71%) visit the platform multiple times a day. Similarly, 71% of Americans in this age group now use Instagram and close to half (45%) are Twitter users." (Pew Research Center, 2018). Interesting enough, *Facebook* is the most widely used social media platform where over 68 percent of adults within the United States prefer this networking page. (Pew Research Center, 2018). Another top performing networking site included *YouTube* (a popluar video sharing platform system) that uses social elements such as vlogs. Vlogs range in the promotion of consumer-based products to personal viewpoints on a multiple of subject matters. The Pew Research Center showed that over three-quarters of adults in America used this platform. Additionally, over, ninety-four percent of 18 to 24 years old utilized this particular product. (Pew Research Center,2018). This informational data allows academic librarians to consider what social networking pages might work best for both promotional and instructional service purposes.

MAIN FOCUS OF THE CHAPTER

Understanding the Americans With Disabilities Act (ADA)

The Americans with Disabilities Act (ADA) is a "civil rights law that prohibits discrimination against individuals with disabilities in all areas of public life, including jobs, schools, transportation, and all public and private places that are open to the general public. (ADA National Network, 2018). ADA prohibits any type of discrimination based on the "basis of disability in employment, state, and local government, public accommodations, commercial facilities, transportation, and telecommunications" (ADA Guide 2018—www.ada.gov/cguide.htm). Additionally, the rights of students with disabilities are protected under the Vocational Rights Act of 1973 (United States Department of Education, 2004).

This legislative act was signed into effect during the year 1990. President George H.W. Bush stated the legislation was "powerful in its simplicity" (Nolan, 2006, p. 367). The Former Attorney General Dick Thornburgh stated the ADA legislation a "great leap forward in the civil rights movement". (Thornburgh 1991, 375). The main purpose of the law allows for those with disabilities to gain the same rights and privileges as the general population. The law guarantees equal opportunities to those needing extra attention with general accommodations (such as public transportation, employment, and communication mechanisms). "University faculty members are most familiar with the reasonable accommodations requirements or appropriate academic adjustment as stated in section 504 subpart E of the Disabilities Act "(Rodriguez, 2011, p. 544). It's important to note that ADA is broken down into five different service categories: Employment, State and Local Government, Public Accommodation, Telecommunications, and Miscellaneous Provisions.

The audience's familiarity with the Americans with Disability Act often begins with Public Accommodation. This initial knowledge often begins with public signage (including public restrooms and parking regulations). A great example within academic libraries would be helping patrons remove books that are physically out of reach on higher placed shelving. The closest section on ADA compliance concerning social media would be the *Telecommunications (Title IV)*. The Title IV of Americans with Disabilities Act "sets forth two major requirements to expand telecommunications services for individuals with hearing impairments: telecommunications relay services and closed captioning of all federally-funded TV public service announcements". (Explanation of the Contents of the Americans with Disabilities Act: Disability Rights Education and Defense Fund, pp. 199). The Federal Communications Center (FCC) implemented the Title V Act on August 1, 1991. Upon research, the emphasis was placed upon two issues: hearing and voice carry over recognition systems. The hearing carries over (HCO) allows the "a person with a speech disability is able to listen to the voice of the other party and, in reply, the operator speaks the text as typed by the person with the speech disability. The operator does not type the conversation." (Explanation of the Contents of the Americans with Disabilities Act: Disability Rights Education and Defense Fund, pp.200). The voice carries over (VCO) provides a person(s) with a hearing disability to "speak directly to the other party, and the operator types the response back to the person with hearing disability. The operator does not voice any conversation." (Explanation of the Contents of the Americans with Disabilities Act: Disability Rights Education and Defense Fund, pp.200). The main objective was to provide equal participation to all user groups. The congressional committees indicated the longevity of ADA stating that it must "keep pace with the rapidly advancing technology of the times". (HR Rep 101-485). The discussion on the advancement of technology eventually gave way to the ADA Amendment Act of 2008.

"In response to several Supreme Court decisions and U.S. Equal Employment Opportunity Commission (EEOC) regulations concerning the Americans with Disabilities Act (ADA), the President of the United States signed into law the ADA Amendments Act of 2008 (ADAAA). Congress signed ADAAA, which will take effect January 1, 2009, in order to correct a trend by the EEOC and Courts of decreasing the breadth of the ADA". (Race and Dornier 2009, p. 357). The original amendment of ADA was appealed due to the lack of expansive disability coverage expanding past the Courts and the Equal Employment Opportunity Commission. The term "disability" was loosely labeled and lacked extensive coverage. The current ADA and ADDAA coverage for chapter content purposes expands to the collegiate setting providing reasonable accommodations for both students and faculty members. In today's electronic environment, colleges and universities are constantly changing content management systems and library resources to accommodate all students regardless of disability status. The next section highlights how academic libraries can use auxiliary aids and assistive technologies (plain language and alternative texts) to help patrons understand posts made within social media.

Using Auxiliary Aids and Assistive Technologies (Plain Language and Alternative Text) for Americans With Disability Compliance

The personal participation for those with disabilities on social media network sites can be difficult to maneuver digitally. Therefore, technology has greatly enhanced a person with disabilities comprehension of social media postings.

The types of disabilities associated with social media technology limitations include: blindness, low vision, limited physical mobility and auditory learning. The patron experiencing a disability related to blindness will encounter the need for usage software that enables auditory readability. This software specifically reads what's on the screen (clicking links or texts) and produces the text into a Braille component for patrons with visual impairments.

The first type of technological limitations is assisting patrons with low vision disabilities. The W3C-Web Accessibility Initiative (https://www.w3.org/WAI/people-use-web/tools-techniques) provides information on utilizing software produced to help read the size of the text. This software helps reformat to a small or a larger monitor to help to enhance learning for all users.

Patrons with limited physical mobility (i.e.: arm and hand impairments) use a variety of virtual keyboards. These type of virtual keyboard includes alternative mice that help produce needed computer-based work.

The final type of incorporation system for disabled users includes a voice dictation system. The voice dictation system allows users to speak and command the conveyed text into a word processing system. The benefits include grammar checks and word prediction software to allow users to produce the best information possible. An example would be website entitled: Voice Dictation (https://dictation.io) . The website provides online speech recognition without typing.

Identifiable Problems: Using Auxiliary Aids and Assistive Technologies

The following issues play a large role in the encompassing of the development and implementation of social media pages within academic libraries.

Beginning with the United States Public Law (100-407) that denotes that any item, piece of equipment or product system whether acquired commercially, off the shelf, modified or customized, that is used to increase or improve functional capabilities of individuals with disabilities" (Public Law 100-407). Section III discusses the necessity of making reasonable modifications for users. The usage of auxiliary aids provides persons with disabilities access to screen- reader software and voice recognition over the phone or website formats.

The statue and regulations of aids are broken down into four major categories. "(1) aids and services for making aural materials accessible to individuals with hearing impairments, (2) aids and services for making the visual material accessible to individuals with visual impairments, (3) acquisition or modification of equipment or devices. (4) other similar services and actions such as furnished closed captioning and screen readers" (Legal Information Institute, 42 U.S.C 12103)

The Sub Section two of the state and regulations of aids within the major categories aligns perfectly with two major components for ADA compliance within websites. This specific sub section discusses the concepts of alternative text and plain language used within the holistic markup of the website.

Plain language provides users with the following: short logical sentences and conversational tone. This language is designed with the content in mind to help break the content down logically. The Center for Plain Language provides a five-step checklist for website organization. The five steps included "identify and describe the target audience, structure the content to guide the reader through it, write the content in plain language, use information design to help readers see and understand and work with the target user groups to test the design and content". (Center for Plain Language website, 2018). This allows users to find what is needed quickly without having to struggle with a problematic interface.

The second key component would be alternative text ("alt text). The alternative text provides a level of the descriptions associated with the image allowing the user to understand the context to their fullest possible extent. The nature of the alternative text will not alter or change the websites purpose. The text only adds a single line of coding describing the image holistically. The website designer utilizing alternative text does not need extensive training on coding. An example of alternative text can be found within the image properties of the content management system of Spring Share's product of LibGuides. The designer can add any type of alternative text associated with the image below the URL link. The alternative text features can also be found within Facebook, Twitter, and Instagram for digital incorporation. The following paragraph discusses how to help enhance the provided context for persons with limited visual and auditory disabilities.

Tackling Social Media Postings for Both the Visual and Auditory Disabled Patron

Social media does provide users with the unique opportunity to communicate in a variety of expressed manners. This includes both a verbal (example: Snap Chat) and a written form of expression (example Twitter). It's important to note that social media content can the ebb and flow of the rhythmical pattern of change can happen systematically in order to avoid unforeseen perils of possible emerging opportunities. For academic librarians, an identifiable problem would be providing accessibility for all patrons. The process begins by investigating some of the top social media websites (Facebook, Instagram, Snapchat, Twitter, and YouTube). A majority of social networking pages provides accessibility information for patrons experiencing disabilities. Table 1 provides helpful links to specific information regarding accessibility requirements for both Twitter and YouTube

Table 1. Links to accessibility requirements

Facebook	https://www.facebook.com/help/accessibility
Twitter	https://help.twitter.com/en/using-twitter/picture-descriptions
YouTube(Google Related Products)	https://www.google.com/accessibility/products-features.html

At present, Instagram and Snapchat does not provide official statements concerning accessibility. However, Instagram users can hear the words of what text looks like with the help of using alternative text. Alternative text with Instagram does not contain a word limitation like the networking site of Twitter. Therefore, disabled users can understand the image regarding the written language on their screen. The best technique would be to add the words ALT text below the hashtag information.

In terms of Snapchat, The Perkins School for the Blind does provide a 2018 guide to using Snap Chat with patrons that have low vision restrictions. This website http://www.perkinselearning.org/technology/blog/snapchat-and-low-vision) discusses the importance of both voiceover and large picture text. The voiceover application improves the quality of understanding concerning the narration of videos. The next section explores a multitude of ways to make social media understandable for those experiencing both visual and auditory disabilities.

Careful Considerations for Social Media Posts

This section provides a short chart, Table 2, discussing the problems identified within social media postings that effect both visual and auditory disabled patrons. The academic librarian might want to consider the following information before creating a social media post.

Table 2. Types of posts and accessibility considerations

Types of Posts	What content should be avoided for those with visual impairments? (think about imagery and adding alternative text (alt text)
Length of Posts (example: Word Count)	Using short and precise language for clarity of understanding. For example, in 2018, Twitter is limited to 280 characters per posts. Keep in mind that Voiceover for the visually impaired can be lengthy to hear. Therefore, the post needs to directly correspond to what is happening within that particular image.
Format (example: Content)	Think about Text vs Visual Images (Instagram vs Twitter). What format works best for your chosen content? Think about those experiencing problems with visual limitations? How might they view your content (if an image was unattached?) Would the content viewer still understand the overall message?
Visual Hashtags	The Voiceover feature (available as a downloadable attachment for the visually impaired on Google Play) will dictate the words on the screen. It's important to limit how many hashtags are being used. This can be confusing for those that cannot seem the image in front of them.
Captioning and GIFS (Images)	Within social media platforms, it's important to make note of who is being represented within a particular photo. This should include the location and other important details. A person with visual limitations needs descriptions concerning who., what, where, and how things are being represented within a particular photograph. Remember to be mindful of what is being represented and how it's being replicated with someone with visual limitations. Additionally, the moving "GIFS" can pose a problem for those with visual limitations.
Emoticons (Emoji)	Cannot be Translated using a Voiceover Audio Program. Therefore, those with visual impairments cannot understand the full context of the post with the use of emoji throughout a social media posting.

The proceeding section provides a starter set of accessibility tools concerning social media platforms to help academic librarians best serve their entire user population.

Incorporating Web Accessibility Into Social Media Platforms (ADA Compliance)

The average academic university libraries serves patrons ranging in population from hundreds to thousands on a daily basis. The services offered include: consultations, programming and instructional sessions. These are just a few services offered within most academic university units. The social media strategic personnel or administer with the university libraries will need to provide alternative methods of disseminating information. Table 3 provides a list of ADA Compliant Accessibility Tools for thoughtful implementation of future services.

Table 3. ADA compliant accessibility tools

Implementation Accessibility Tool Name	URL Address	Primary Functionality Features
DANYA This Social Media Accessibility Google Handout-DLH Holdings Corporation	https://www.youtube.com/watch?v=DKXXXKtFRNlQ&t=64s	This Google Handout Video Session discusses improvements within existing and emerging social media technological tools for social media accessibility.
Easy Chirp	www.easychirp.com	Created by Dennis Lembree. This is a Third-party web-based interface aimed at Twitter users. Features shorter URLs, direct messaging, navigational and search saving tools
Tota11y- provides from the Khan Academy.	http://khan.github.io/tota11y/	Provides the website designer with possible accessibility violations through a browser-enabled plugin system.
Site Improve Accessibility Checker	https://chrome.google.com/webstore/detail/siteimprove-accessibility	Evaluates web pages for accessibility problems using Google Chrome.
Usability.Gov (provided by the Department of US Health and Human Services).	https://www.usability.gov	Provides content strategies, visual design basics, and user experience basics for providing digital content.
Wave Web Accessibility Tools	http://wave.webaim.org http://wave.webaim.org/extension/	Wave Web provides Informational Instruction on how to evaluate current accessibility within thousands of web pages. The second link provides information on web accessibility using a Browser Extension.
W3 Accessibility Testing	https://www.w3.org/wiki/Accessibility_testing	The W3 Accessibility Testing page provides a reference point for understanding usability (including Testing requirements)
Web AIM: Web Accessibly in Mind. (provided by the Center for Persons with Disabilities-Utah State University).	https://webaim.org/	The Center for Person with Disabilities (Utah State University) provides accessibility training content and up to date practices within the field of website compliance

Respecting Patron Privacy on Social Media Networking Pages

The following sections discuss the importance of understanding patron privacy and how to avoid the accidental posting of provided personal information to a large scale audience. The preceding paragraphs will discussion FERPA (Family Educational Rights and Privacy Act) and provide the best strategies for incorporation within an academic library setting.

FERPA: What Does It Mean? The Direct Effects of Social Media Compliance

"The Family Educational Rights and Privacy Act (FERPA) 20 U.S.C. § 1232g; 34 CFR Part 99) is a federal law that protects the privacy of student educational records" (US Department of Education 2018). FERPA was signed into law by President Gerald Ford on August 21, 1974, with an effective date of November 19, 1974. This law was enacted ninety days after the official presidential signage. (Department of Education 2004)

"FERPA was enacted as a new § 438 of the General Education Provisions Act (GEPA) called "Protection of the Rights and Privacy of Parents and Students," coded 20 U.S.C. § 1232g. It was also commonly referred to as the "Buckley Amendment" after its principal sponsor, Senator James Buckley of New York. FERPA was offered as an amendment on the Senate floor and was not the subject of committee consideration. Accordingly, traditional legislative history for FERPA was first enacted is unavailable." (Department of Education, 2004). It's important to note that "Congress has amended FERPA a total of nine times in the nearly 28 years since its enactment". (U.S Department of Education, 2004). The major legislative changes include the Campus Security Act (1900), Higher Education Amendments of 1992 and 1998, and the USA Patriot Act of 2001.

This federal law applies to all schools that receive any type of federal funding within the United States Department of Education Programs. The law explicitly states that "schools may disclose, without consent, "directory information" such as a student's name, address, telephone number, date and place of birth, honors and awards, and dates of attendance." (U.S Department of Education, 2018). However, the school must communicate with eligible students within a reasonable amount of time. This includes making the request for the school to disclose any type of specified directory of information.

In the digital environment, the faculty member cannot post any type of identifiable information about a student's educational progress on any social media networking platform such as Facebook, Twitter, Instagram, etc. This extends to social media within libraries concerning the sharing, posting, and publishing of any type of digital content as part of a student's educational record. FEPRA does not specifically prohibit any type of social media usage in the classroom or other related settings (Diaz et al., 2010, Lavagnino 2010). Marek and Skrabut (2017) suggest that "higher education institutions in the United States most often limit themselves to reiterating federal government statements about the requirements of FERPA and/or the specific items the school has defined as releasable, and the procedure by which the students can have some or all of these items withheld." (p.17) The standard language is well defined and broadly used and there is little incentive for institutions to "reinvent the wheel". The continued growth of technology leads to the high attention of privacy within education concerning social media as a type of record collecting. In Biegl (2012) article questioned educational privacy within legal case law and the need for revisionary changes regarding privacy regulation.

Ultimately, the academic librarian needs to consider revisiting the laws attached to FERPA ensuring complete compliance. A great starting point would be looking at the Student Privacy 101 website (https://studentprivacy.ed.gov/?src=fpco) provided by the United States Department of Education. The website includes a section for parents, students and post-secondary officials. Another important step would be discussing these types of related laws with a university lawyer and any attached university personnel concerning guidance per a university-specific social media account.

Understanding FERPA and Social Media Privacy for Disabled Patrons

This section provides an insight into helping both adjunct and faculty members at the university level concerning social media postings. The academic librarian often works with faculty members concerning specific instructional sessions and other related needs. A greater example being the digital scavenger hunt. First, this would be limited to those with visual impairments. Secondly, the academic librarian would choose to use a form of social media (i.e.: Twitter, Facebook or Instagram). Many participants may not feel comfortable with personally identifiable information being disseminated on the web to achieve a specific academic goal. Therefore, it's important for everyone to be aware of the privacy of student progress and the dissemination of information. In the past five years, faculty members have been incorporating social media tools to enhance the student learning experience. The networking pages used by faculty members include Facebook, Instagram, and Twitter. However, in 2018 most are using Snapchat and Instagram exclusively. The Pew Research Center for Internet & Technology (2018) reports that "Some 78% of 18- to 24-year-olds use Snapchat, and a sizeable majority of these users (71%) visit the platform multiple times per day. Similarly, 71% of Americans in this age group now use Instagram and close to half (45%) are Twitter users." (Pew Research Center, 2018) This technology shift allows students to collaborative groups within a flexible environment. In terms of faculty member's usage, a survey conducted by Moran, Seaman & Tinti- Kane (2011) showed that over 80 percent of all faculty members were having students complete an assignment using some form of social media. The results of this survey are not surprising concerning social media usage continues to be on the rise. Therefore, all academic professional needs to be made aware of the Family Educational Rights Privacy Act (FERPA).

The legislative law concerning FERPA protects all identifiable information concerning a student's personal academic record. The law does not specifically discuss a protocol for the digital dissemination of student records. Lavagino (2010) article entitled: "Policy as an enabler of student engagement" argued that creative course content on social platforms should not fall under FERPA law unless it's physically achieved by the course instructor, which would be considered a type of educational record. Upon implementing a social media platform, faculty members should always consult existing social media policies within the university. If none exist, the faculty member will need to consult the universities communication procedure manual. Lavagino suggests the guidelines for creation would include three inclusion categories: legal procedures, technical assistance, and educational rights. These c guidelines provide participants with additional policies, alternative assignments, constant forms, and providing faculty members with FERPA checklist for later investigation.

The audience needs to make note that FERPA does not specifically discuss or prohibit the use of social tools within digital classroom or the university library digital settings. It's important to remember that social media did not exist when FERPA was first enacted. Therefore, there is no current agreement on student postings in social media correlating to "educational records". In Lavagnino (2010) article discussed how content created on a social media platform should not fall under FERPA law unless it's archived physically by the instructor. Therefore, this case would be considered an "educational record". Faculty members using social media websites for classroom construction may not be aware of the multiple privacy issue concerns.

One major concern includes data breaches within the issued software. "These particular issues can develop into different legal and the security concerns that are related to identity management, infrastructure, risk management, legislative and regulatory compliance, integrity control, access control and other risks that are dependent on the cloud computing provider". (Almudawi, N.,2016, p.31). The invasion of data privacy can intellectually hurt both corresponding parties. The social ramifications of using a public social media platform include that of cyberbullying, profile hacking and digital identity theft. These important issues are needed for faculty members to reflect upon implantation.

According to Schwartz and Solove (2011) discusses that "congress neither revisited FERPA'S reliance on the concept of "educational records", nor created a more basic right to the block the release of student records for commercial purposes. As for universities, they remain able to sell essential student contact information to credit card companies, such as data is considered "directory information", hence not an education (al) record." (p. 1823)

Ultimately, if public information can be pieced together using "directory information", then the Family Educational Right Privacy Act would be applicable. Gross and Acquisit (2015) analyzed 4,000 Carnegie Melon University Facebook profiles and outlined the potential threats to privacy containing in the personal information included on this networking site utilized by students. These potential threats include the ability to reconstruct users' social security numbers and using information found in profiles, such a date of birth. These types of "public records" make it easy to identify any given individual. The discussed risks make it easy for third party vendors to create a digital portfolio on personal behavior.

The aforementioned statements provided context into understanding FERPA and the risks associated when students provide personal forms of information within a very public social media platform. The preceding paragraph provides best practices that will help alleviate privacy issues within social media postings.

Best Practices for Social Media Postings (Concerning FERPA and HIPAA)

The nature of this section denotes helpful tips on helping patrons not to disclose identifiable information. This can be especially important for patrons with disabilities concerning HIPAA (Health Insurance Portability and Accountability Act) First, it's important to stress and reiterate to patrons and associated staff members that social media is not concerned a private space. Therefore, an academic library should attempt to post all information from a neutral and bipartisan approach. The social media manager for the academic library should "screen" postings for any type of FERPA or HIPAA potential violations.

A suggestion for future development for academic libraries would be the creation and implementation of a social media policy. The social media policy will formalize a library's strategic guidance and will strengthen its position on social media usage. The American Libraries Association, Intellectual Freedom Committee in June of 2019 approved the Social Media Guidelines for Public and Academic Libraries. "This document provides a policy and implementation framework for public and academic libraries engaging in the use of social media" (American Libraries Association, Social Media Guidelines for Public and Academic Libraries, 2018). A section of the document entitled "Staff Responsibilities" discusses how "library staff should protect patron privacy and confidentiality whenever possible. Social media platforms should not be used to collect information about the library's users. Information shared by patrons on the library's social media should not be kept by the library or used for other purposes." (American Libraries Association, Social Media Guidelines for Public and Academic Libraries, 2018). Delaney (2011) article entitled "Apps &Web 2.0: Legal risks from using the internet in class" provides three strategies for success: legal, technical, and educational. Each section provided alternative assignments, FERPA checklists and consent forms for future incorporation.

A final recommendation would be looking at the American Libraries Association Code of Ethics. The Code of Ethics provides a helpful reference for intellectual property and privacy concerning the ethical codes within the library profession.

SOLUTIONS AND RECOMMENDATIONS

The first solution and recommendations for social media usage and persons with expressed disabilities begins with awareness. The awareness process begins by looking at the language found within the Americans with Disabilities Act (ADA) and the Family Educational Rights Privacy Act (FERPA). The background requirements should start as a basis when considering a social media platform that would be friendly for all patrons. The complete documents can be found on the United States Department of Justice Website for ADA and the United States of Education Website for FERPA.

The second step would be looking at your specific universities handbook and communication offices concerning the proper route concerning the dissemination of information. A meeting with the university lawyer can provide additional context and a working framework for understanding the expectations and standards for specific social media networking accounts.

The third step concern is the future of technology and the rapid succession of change. Therefore, the academic librarian must continuously look for new and updated technology to help all patrons understand all given context within a social media account. A great website for ADA Compliance and social media advancement would be the Digital Gov website (https://digital.gov/index.html). The website is run by the US General Administration (an associate page with the US Government) with a section dedicated to social media and accessibility. For FERPA, the academic librarian is encouraged to look at the Protecting Student Privacy website (https://studentprivacy.ed.gov/Apps). The website is run by the US Department of Education. Each is maintained by the government and can provide insight into new laws and technology advancements to help their patrons be successful within their given environment.

CONCLUSION

The purpose of the chapter was aimed towards a primer approach to helping patrons with disabilities. The chapter discussed how the Americans with Disabilities Act and the Family Educational Act effects usability in terms of disseminating information through the means of social media. This chapter only provided best practices and suggestions for possible incorporation within an academic library setting. Therefore, this chapter is not a directive in terms of handling social media lawsuits concerning the affirmation laws. Therefore, the reader should always consider having lengthy conversations concerning legality with the assigned personnel attached to a specific university.

REFERENCES

W3C. (2018). *Accessibility Testing*. Retrieved July 18, 2018 from, https://www.w3.org/wiki/Accessibility_testing

ADA National Network: Information, Guidance, and Training on the Americans with Disabilities Act (2018). *What is the Americans with Disabilities Act (ADA)?* Retrieved July 13, 2018 from, https://adata.org/learn-about-ada

Almudawi, N. A. (2016). Cloud computing privacy concerns in social networks. *International Journal of Computer*, *22*(1), 29–36.

American Library Association. (2018). *Social Media Guidelines for Public and Academic Libraries.* Retrieved August 14, 2018 from, http://www.ala.org/advocacy/intfreedom/socialmediaguidelines

Boyd, D. M., & Ellison, N. B. (2007). Social network sites: Definition, history, and scholarship. *Journal of Computer-Mediated Communication*, *13*(1), 210–230. doi:10.1111/j.1083-6101.2007.00393.x

Center for Persons with Disabilities, Utah State University. (2018). *Web AIM: Web Accessibility in Mind.* Retrieved June 17, 2018 from, https://webaim.org

Center for Plain Language. (n.d.). *5 Steps to Plain Language.* Retrieved June 16, 2018 from, https://centerforplainlanguage.org/learning-training/five-steps-plain-language/

Charnigo, L., & Barnett-Ellis, P. (2007). Checking out Facebook. com: The impact of a digital trend on academic libraries. *Information Technology and Libraries*, *26*(1), 23. doi:10.6017/ital.v26i1.3286

Chrome Web Store. (2018). *Site Improve Accessibility Checker.* Retrieved September 10, 2018 from, https://chrome.google.com/webstore/detail/siteimprove-accessibility/efcfolpjihicnikpmhnmphjhhpicll jc?hl=en-US

Delaney, S. (2011). Apps & Web 2.0: Legal risks from using the internet in class. *Distance Education Report*, *15*(9), 5–7.

DLH Holdings Corp. (2014, May 5). *T.H.I.S Social Media Accessibility Google Hangout.* Retrieved June 13, 2018 from, https://www.youtube.com/watch?v=DKXXKtFRNlQ

Facebook Help Center. (2018). *Accessibility.* Retrieved July 8, 2018 from, https://www.facebook.com/help/accessibility

Flynn, N. (2012). *The Social Media Handbook: Rules, Policies, and Best Practices to Successfully Manage Your Organization's Social Media Presence, Posts, and Potential.* San Francisco, CA: Pfeiffer.

Google Accessibility Center. (2018). *Products and Features.* Retrieved June 5, 2018 from, https://www.google.com/accessibility/products-features.html

Gross, R., Acquisti, A., & Heinz, J. III., H. (2005). Information revelation and privacy in online social networks (The Facebook Case). *WPES'05: Proceedings of the 2005 ACM Workshop on Privacy in the Electronic Society*, 71-80. 10.1145/1102199.1102214

Jarrow, J. E. (1997). What is a reasonable accommodation? [Web log article]. *DAIS (Disability Access Information and Support).* Retrieved May 5, 2018 from, http://www.daisweb.com/

Johnson, C., & Burclaff, N. (2013, April). Making social media meaningful: connecting missions and policies. *Imagine, innovate, inspire: Proceedings of the ACRL 2013 Conference.* Retrieved June 16, 2018 from, http://www.ala.org/acrl/sites/ala.org.acrl/files/content/conferences/confsandpreconfs/2013/papers/JohnsonBurclaff_Making.pdf

Khan Academy. (2018). *Tota11y: An Accessibility Visualization Toolkit.* Retrieved September 19, 2018, from http://khan.github.io/tota11y/

Lavagnino, M. B. (2010). *Policy as an enabler of student engagement.* Retrieved May 30, 2018, from https://er.educause.edu/articles/2010/10/policy-as-an-enabler-of-student-engagement

Legal Information Institution. (n.d.). *42 U.S. Code § 12103 - Additional definitions.* Retrieved July 31, 2018 from, https://www.law.cornell.edu/uscode/text/42/12103

Lembree, D. (2018). *Easy Chirp.* Retrieved June 4, 2018 from, https://www.easychirp.com

Marek, M. W., & Skrabut, S. (2017). Privacy in Educational use of Social Media in the US. *International Journal on E-Learning, 16*(3), 265–286.

Moran, M., Seaman, J., & Tinti-Kane, H. (2011). *Teaching, Learning, and Sharing: How Today's Higher Education Faculty Use Social Media.* Retrieved from: http://www.pearsonlearningsolutions.com/educators/pearson-social-media-survey-2011-bw.pdf

Nolan, M. (2005). A Difference of Opinion: Reconciling the Court's Decision in Tennessee v. Lane. *S. Ill. ULJ, 30,* 357

Pew Research Center. (2018). *Social Media Use in 2018.* Retrieved June 10, 2018, from, http://www.pewinternet.org/2018/03/01/social-media-use-in-2018/

PUBLIC. L. (1988). LAW 100-407 and 103-218. *Technology-related assistance for individuals with disabilities.* Public, Law 100-1047, 102 STAT. 1044. Retrieved May 18, 2018 from, https://www.gpo.gov/fdsys/pkg/STATUTE-102/pdf/STATUTE-102-Pg1044.pdf

Race, P. A., & Dornier, S. M. (2009). ADA Amendments Act of 2008: The effect on employers and educators. *Willamette Law Review, 46,* 357.

REP. H. (1990). NO. 101-485 (III), 101st Cong., 2d Sess. (1990), reprinted in 1990 USCCAN 478-79. In The conference committee report also states that the phrase" clarifies that this prohibition [against discrimination] applies to any person who owns, leases (or leases to), or operates a place of public accommodation." Joint Explanatory Statement of the Committee of Conference, 101st Cong. 2d Sess.

Rodriguez, J. E. (2011). *Social Media Use in Higher Education: Key Areas to Consider for Educators.* Retrieved May 4, 2018 from, https://our.oakland.edu/handle/10323/2153

Schwartz, P. M., & Solove, D. J. (2011). The PII problem: Privacy and a new concept of personally identifiable information. *NYUL Rev., 86,* 1814.

Social Media. (n.d.). In *Merriam-Webster's collegiate dictionary.* Retrieved May 10, 2018 from, https://www.merriam-webster.com/dictionary/social%20media

Thornburgh, D. (1991). The Americans with Disabilities Act: What It Means to All Americans. *Temp. LR, 64*, 375.

Twitter Help Center. (2018). *How to Make Images Accessible for People?* Retrieved July 17, 2018 from, https://help.twitter.com/en/using-twitter/picture-descriptions

United States Department of Education. (2004). *Legislative History of Major FERPA Provisions.* Retrieved August 4, 2018 from, https://www2.ed.gov/policy/gen/guid/fpco/ferpa/leg-history.html

United States Department of Education. (2018). *Family Educational Rights and Privacy Act (FERPA).* Retrieved August 4, 2018 from, https://www2.ed.gov/policy/gen/guid/fpco/ferpa/index.html

United States Department of Education. (2018). *Student Privacy 101: Student Privacy at the U.S. Department of Education.* Retrieved August 4, 2018 from, https://studentprivacy.ed.gov/?src=fpco

United States Department of Health & Human Services. (2018). *Usability.Gov: Improving the User Experience.* Retrieved August 4, 2018 from, https://www.usability.gov

United States Department of Justice. (2009). *A Guide to Disabilities Rights Laws.* Retrieved August 4, 2018 from, https://www.ada.gov/cguide.htm

United States General Services Administration. (2018). *DigitialGov.* Retrieved August 4, 2018 from, https://digital.gov/

WAVE. (2018). *Homepage.* Retrieved July 18, 2018 from, http://wave.webaim.org

ADDITIONAL READING

Al-Daihani, S. M., & Abrahams, A. (2016). A text mining analysis of academic libraries' tweets. *Journal of Academic Librarianship, 42*(2), 135–143. doi:10.1016/j.acalib.2015.12.014

American Libraries Association. (2017). *Professional Ethics.* Retrieved July 13, 2018, from, http://www.ala.org/tools/ethics

American Libraries Association. (2018). *Social Media Guidelines for Public and Academic Libraries.* Retrieved July 13, 2018, from, http://www.ala.org/advocacy/intfreedom/socialmediaguidelines

Harrison, A., Burress, R., Velasquez, S., & Schreiner, L. (2017). Social media use in academic libraries: A phenomenological study. *Journal of Academic Librarianship, 43*(3), 248–256. doi:10.1016/j.acalib.2017.02.014

Marek, M. W., & Skrabut, S. (2017). Privacy in Educational use of Social Media in the US. *International Journal on E-Learning, 16*(3), 265–286.

Rodriguez, J. E. (2011). Social media use in higher education: Key areas to consider for educators. Retrieved October 14, 2018, from, https://our.oakland.edu/handle/10323/2153

Stvilia, B., & Gibradze, L. (2014). What do academic libraries tweet about, and what makes a library tweet useful? *Library & Information Science Research, 36*(3-4), 136–141. doi:10.1016/j.lisr.2014.07.001

Stvilia, B., & Gibradze, L. (2017). Examining undergraduate students' priorities for academic library services and social media communication. *Journal of Academic Librarianship*, *43*(3), 257–262. doi:10.1016/j.acalib.2017.02.013

United States Department of Education. *Family and Educational Rights and Privacy Act (FERPA)*. Retrieved May 16, 2018 from, https://www2.ed.gov/policy/gen/guid/fpco/ferpa/index.html

United States Department of Justice. *Information and Technical Assistant on the Americans with Disability Act*. Retrieved May 16, 2018 from, https://www.ada.gov/

This research was previously published in Social Media for Communication and Instruction in Academic Libraries; pages 119-133, copyright year 2019 by Information Science Reference (an imprint of IGI Global).

Chapter 81
Library and Information Science Female Undergraduate Preference for Facebook as Information Sharing Tool

Adeyinka Tella

https://orcid.org/0000-0002-5382-4471

University of South Africa, South Africa

Oluwole Olumide Durodolu

https://orcid.org/0000-0003-2734-8165

University of South Africa, South Africa

Stephen Osahon Uwaifo

Delta State University, Abraka, Nigeria

ABSTRACT

This study has examined the library and information science female undergraduates' preference for Facebook as an information-sharing tool. A survey approach was adopted using a questionnaire to collect data from 457 LIS female undergraduate students drawn from five library schools in Nigeria. The findings of the study have demonstrated that most significant factors that lead to the use of Facebook for information sharing among LIS female undergraduate students are user-friendly nature of the tool, personal gain, enjoyment, and self-efficacy while the least factors are social engagement and empathy. User-friendliness nature of Facebook has the highest correlation with the preference for Facebook as an information-sharing tool by female students followed by enjoyment while learning and empathy are the least correlated factors.

DOI: 10.4018/978-1-6684-7123-4.ch081

INTRODUCTION

Social networking site is increasingly the most popular forms of communication on the Internet. Generally, social networking websites (SNS) facilitate communication and information sharing between people. It has been argued repeatedly that people turn to those in their social network for information rather than going to formal sources (Savolainen, 2017). As social network sites (SNSs) have been shown to connect individuals to people with whom they have a previously established offline connection (Lampe., Ellison,& Steinfield, 2006), as well as connecting different degrees of relational closeness (Gilbert & Karahalios, 2009), it is likely that people turn to SNSs as an efficient way to tap these connections for sharing information.

Among the accessible social networking sites, Facebook has become an increasingly important tool for people engaging in a range of communication behaviours, including requesting help from their social network to address information needs. Social networking websites, such as Facebook, are member-based Internet communities which allow participants to post profile information, such as usernames and photographs, and to interact with others in innovative ways, such as sending public or private online messages or sharing photos online (Pempek, Yermolayeva & Calvert, 2009).

Currently, it is projected that 2.41 billion are monthly active users of Facebook during the second quarter of 2019 (Clement, 2019). With these statistics, Facebook has become the most significant social network worldwide. It was reported in the third quarter of 2012 that the number of active Facebook users surpass one billion, making it the first social network ever to achieve this (Clement, 2019). Active users in this context are those who have logged in to Facebook during the last 30 days. In the previous reported quarter, Facebook stated that 2.7 billion people were using at least one of Facebook's core products (Clement, 2019). It can be seen from here that the growing percentage increase in the number of users of Facebook reveals its potential as favourite tool for sharing information, particularly among the female gender.

As an appropriate tool for Internet communication, Facebook has become an essential part of Internet users' lives. Facebook become part of people's day-to-day existence. According to the research results, 65% of the users log on to Facebook each day, and 85% of the users log on to Facebook at least once a week, which shows that Facebook-is getting more and more popular, and is becoming one of the crucial tools for interpersonal interaction (Tella, et al. 2014; Tella & Babatunde, 2017). Bhattacherjee (2001) commented that system acceptance is an essential factor for users' adoption of the system. Nevertheless, to observe from a long-term viewpoint, whether the system is accepted has something to do with whether users "continue to use" that system. Hence, for Facebook, it is an issue worthy of investigating currently how the users mainly the female undergraduate keep on preferring Facebook as a platform to share information.

Information sharing is an essential motivation for people to join virtual communities (Ridings and Gefen 2004). Social networking websites (e.g. Facebook) empower their users to share different kinds of information such as ideas, pictures, and videos with just a few clicks. From only using the usual way of sharing information like discussion, distribution of documents via postage, sharing information via electronic media, social network or media is now trending as an information-sharing tool (Dahri & Yunus, 2017).

As Dahri and Yunus (2017) indicated, there are many social media platforms that are famously used globally including Facebook, Youtube, Whatsapp, FB messenger, Instagram, WeChat, Google+, Line, Twitter, Sino Weibo, Linkedin and Skype. However, based on the available statistic from the literature (e.g. Clement, 2019), of most active social media platforms, Facebook tops the list as the most preferred social network. The factors identified for Facebook preference are (Dahri & Yunus, 2017): opportunity of accessing it on different digital devices such as desktop, laptops, tablet, computers, smartphones and smart television; opening Facebook account is free, but users are only required to register and create profile which their names, geographical location, educational background among others; opportunity of embarking on activities like adding friends, exchange messages, post status and updates, upload digital photos, share video, receive and post notices when friends and relations update their status, play games, etc. Moreover, users have the opportunity to create or join groups that have the same or common interest that can be in different categories like work-related, school, hobbies, sports, music, entertainment, show-business, etc.

Available data have also confirmed that men and women use social network services (SNSs) such as Facebook differently and with different frequencies (Acquisti & Gross, 2006; Joinson, 2008). Generally, several researchers have found that women tend to use SNSs more than men and for different and more social purposes especially to explicitly foster social connections. A study conducted by Pew Research Renters found that women were more avid users of social media (Pew Research Center, 2015). Similarly, a Pew Research Center report in 2015 revealed that 73% of online men and 80% of online women used social networking sites (Facebook). Complementing these data, a study conducted in United States as of May 2019, reported that 55.4 per cent of U.S Facebook audience were female and 44.6 per cent of users were male (Clement, 2019). All of these data generally affirmed that the preference for the use of Facebook is high among female compared to their male counterpart.

From the literature, it is observed that studies have focused on the use of social networking sites in general, limited studies have considered the preference for Facebook as tool for information sharing especially by the female undergraduate students. Available current studies on Facebook have primarily focused on connecting friends and relatives and self-disclosure concerns. Little or no consideration has been paid to explain or illuminate the rationale behind the preference for Facebook as a tool for information sharing. It is also observed that investigation of the reasons behind the preference especially among the female undergraduate in Nigerian Universities has been so neglected. Thus far, literature seems to affirm there are more female users of Facebook than male (Clement, 2019). Related studies available (e.g. Oh & Syn, 2014), looked at motivations for Sharing Information and Social Support in Social Media: A Comparative Analysis of Facebook, Twitter, Delicious, YouTube, and Flickr; while (Dahri & Yunus, 2017) examined the effectiveness of social media as knowledge management sharing tool in government agency: a case study. None of these two studies considers female preference for using Facebook for information sharing.

Furthermore, limited number of studies have considered the Library and Information Science (LIS) female undergraduate students even though they use Facebook to a great extent particularly as a discussion forum for most of their courses and others. Therefore, it is considered imperative to examine LIS undergraduate preference for Facebook as tool for sharing information in view of the fact that the study will reveal the rationale behind the preference by female undergraduates, and that the outcomes will add more to the available data and literature on Facebook usage. In addition, part of the expectations of this study is that it will be an essential source of reference in the field of Librarianship and Information Science as it will serve as the baseline for further research in this area.

Objectives of the Study

The main objective of this study was to examine library and information science female undergraduates' preference for Facebook as an information-sharing tool. Specifically, the study:

1. The rationale behind the preference for Facebook as an Information sharing tool.
2. Identify the types of activities preference on Facebook by LIS female undergraduate students.
3. Determine the devices preference for accessing Facebook by LIS female undergraduate students.
4. Find out which type of Facebook activity puts LIS female undergraduate more at risk for developing problematic usage.

Literature Review

Facebook is a social networking website where users can post comments, share photographs and post links to news or other interesting content on the web, chat live, and watch short-form video. It is a social networking site that makes it easy for users to connect and share with family and friends online. It is an American online social media and social networking service based in Menlo Park, California. It is designed for college students and was created in 2004 by Mark Zuckerberg while he was enrolled at Harvard University. In other words, it is a famous free social networking website that allows registered users to create a profile, upload photos and video, send messages and keep in touch with friends, family and colleagues.

As succinctly put by (Oh & Syn, 2014), Facebook contains multiple channels for information seeking, including dyadic and group messaging, as well as network-wide interaction via status updates. Facebook also enables users to passively view the information-sharing and seeking activities of their network via the News Feed and can respond to network members' information requests, either by commenting directly on an update or through another channel.

The distinguishing characteristics that make Facebook the most popular social networking site for sharing information include event, timeline, social plug-in, embedded in post, turn off push notifications, relationship status, Facebook messenger, the like button, news feed, and photos (VCPost, 2019).

- **Event:** this enables users to know who among friend is, for instance celebrating birthday, updating social life. Event is the users' feature that enables them to understand what is going on with friends.
- **Timeline:** The timeline feature enables pictures, new friends and other contents to flow smoothly and ceaselessly in a wider, double-barrel river. Though was criticized but still preferred than old wall which was highly cramped.
- **Social plug-in**: This feature enables users to comment on article read. With social plug-ins, users can make comments on various sites. Just by logging-in to the Facebook account and post comments directly on the site where the comment is made.
- **Embedded in post:** This seems to be the most advantageous feature of Facebook over other social media platforms. By posting articles, videos and pictures on Facebook, the linked content is delivered right in the post. Due to this, the users do not have to make another click.
- **Turn off push notifications**: Through the tab of Facebook application, the user can easily switch off push notifications. User need not to always be informed about what is happening to friends.

- **Relationship status**: Through this feature, it is easier for Facebook users to determine whether the user met recently is single, engaged, married or in an open relationship. By invitation to become Facebook friend, it can be confirmed quickly by looking at the profile of the users and check their relationship status.
- **Facebook messenger**: Through this Facebook application, messages popping up intermittently. Some users may show a likeness to the chat while others become annoyed.
- **The like button:** The feature enables users to indicate their likeness for a post by typing the word 'like' Yes' and so on as a sign of approving the comment. Users need to click on the button to indicate this.
- **Newsfeed:** Users can receive push updates for new content on a site by subscribing to the site's news feed.
- **Photos**: this feature is the most popular on Facebook. It was launched in October 2005. Photo is a feature that enables users to post their pictures online.

Facebook and Information Sharing

In a related dimension, literature has revealed factors that determine and or motivate Facebook users to prefer it as a tool for sharing information. For instance, Mittal (2018) indicated that Facebook is popularly preferred because it is user-friendly in nature, being a source of information and creation of emotional bonding. Similarly, Oh and Syn (2014) identified ten motivation framework for sharing information and social support in social media had been developed based on the literature review. They are:

- *Reputation:* This is known as external rewards that geared people to contribute and share information in communities, share information because they would like to be known, regarded and respected among other users, increase the number of friends, and followers or as active contributors within the platform they are actively been a part.
- *Reciprocity*: This is an exercise of exchanging things with others for mutual benefits especially privileges granted by one person to another. As indicated in social exchange theory by Blau (1964), reciprocity does not mean give and take in one on one relationship; however, it is generalised reciprocity that explains one to many relationships among peer users. In other words, Facebook users may share information as paying back the favour received from others.
- *Enjoyment*: Similar to pleasure and amusement. It is the state or process of taking pleasure in something. It is one of the self-motivated and intrinsic or personal factors that enable users of Facebook to have a preference for it and feel and enthusiastic about using it for the sharing of information. People may share information because they are interested in exchange information for entertainment, have fun, or while away time (Quan-Haase & Young, 2010). It is also possible that they consider being a part of social media as a hobby or find information and share with those who need it (Lin & Lu, 2011)
- *Self-efficacy:* As put forward by Bandura (1997), it is one's belief in one's ability to succeed in a specific situation or accomplish a task. This is popularly adopted to understand information sharing in communities (Constant et al., 1994). Facebook users who have a preference by self-efficacy may perceive themselves as worthy of creating, finding and distributing information to others. They may also feel a sense of remarkable deed when they make useful information available to others.

- *Community of Interest*: Social media users may have a feeling of bond and loyalty to some types of social media like Facebook which they use often. They may as a result of this creates a group of interest or community to promote such on particular topics of interest, promote it to develop the community and encourage different activities within the community.
- *Social engagement:* social involvement and participation are one of the main reasons that people actively take part in social media (Quan-Haase & Young, 2010). User may decide to share information with the sole aim to communicate their peer users or collaborate with them in proffering solution to identified problems or enjoy a sense of belonging to others.
- Altruism: This is kind of self-sacrifice or self-denial where an individual displays disinterested and selfless concern for the wellbeing of others. It factors in the motivation that results in a preference for information sharing in social media (Hsu & Lin, 2008). It is considered in the literature as the most influential motivation that makes people voluntarily gather information and provide it to answer questions from others (Oh, 2012). Social media users, such as Facebook would show interest to help others without expecting external rewards.
- Personal gain: This is a significant advantage, commercially driven, in which social media users may expect to obtain by sharing information. It is an external reward, mainly if there are monetary incentives (Deci & Ryan, 1985). Facebook users may willingly release information related to their business and use social media as a channel to sell or advertise their products or services.
- Learning: People may want to participate in the activity of social media to enable them to learn. They may want to lean by exchanging information with one another and to be informed with updated information about the topics they are interested.
- Empathy: this remains the ability to understand and share in the feelings of others. It is a concern with caring for others' feeling or circumstances. According to Oh (2012); in the case of empathy, social media is a venue for people to gather to provide social and emotional support for one another. Social media users may with those who have trouble finding information or those who have similar information needs or concerns as theirs.

Social networking sites and Facebook in particular, can be used in various ways and can enable various motives (Ellison., Steinfield & Lampe, 2007), including but not limited to entertainment, social sharing, information seeking, relationship maintenance (such as interacting with an existing offline social network), and emotional coping (e.g. facing boredom, loneliness or negative effect (Ryan, Chester, Reece, & Xenos, 2014). Particularly, Facebook usage preferences have been related to its positive and negative use (Andreassen, 2015; Rae & Lonborg, 2015; Yang & Brown, 2013). Communication that is directed (for instance one on one exchanges), was found to have more impact on social capital that does broadcasting or passive consumption of social news (Burke, Kraut & Marlow, 2011). In furtherance to this, Baek, Bae and Jang (2013) pointed out that the alternative effects of social (that is unidirectional, such as chatting other's status or profile) online activates: social activities were negatively correlated with a perceived correlated with a perceived feeling of loneliness, whereas para-social activates were positively related with it. Similarly, wellbeing was to increase when time spent on Facebook was used to maintain relationships but to decrease when it was used to create new relationships (Rae & Lonborg, 2015).

Related Studies

Researchers in several disciplines have addressed how people use Facebook, as well as outcomes associated with use. Previous studies have established that individuals used the site more to connect with pre-existing offline connections than to meet new people (Lampe, Ellison, & Steinfield, 2006) and that specific types of profile information (e.g., those hard to fake, like contact information and organizational membership) predicted network size (number of Friends) (.Lampe, Ellison, & Steinfield, 2007). More recent studies have established a typology of Facebook uses, including relationship maintenance, social surveillance, and social interaction (Joinson, 2008; Papacharissi & Mendelson, 2011).

Rothen, Briefer, Deleuze, Karila, Andreassen, and Achab (2018) explored the heterogeneity of Facebook usage and determine which kind of Facebook activity predicts problematic usage; and tested whether specific impulsivity facets predict problematic use of Facebook. To this end, a sample of Facebook users ($N = 676$) completed an online survey assessing usage preferences (e.g., types of activities performed), symptoms of problematic Facebook use and impulsivity traits. Results indicated that explicit usage preferences (updating one's status, gaming via Facebook, and using notifications) and impulsive characteristics (positive and negative urgency, lack of perseverance) are associated to problematic Facebook use. This study underscores that labels such as Facebook "addiction" are deceptive and that focusing on the actual activities accomplished on SNSs is fundamental when considering dysfunctional usage. Additionally, this study clarified the role of impulsivity in problematic Facebook use by building on a theoretically driven model of impulsivity that assumes its multidimensional nature. The current study differs significantly from this study as it's only focused on Facebook a resource or tool for sharing information by the LIS undergraduate students.

Tella and Babatunde (2017), examined the determinant of continuance intention of Facebook usage among female library and information science (LIS) undergraduates selected from Four Library Schools in the Nigerian universities. The survey design approach was adopted and questionnaire was used for data collection. Collected data were analysed using percentages and frequency count; multiple correlation and regression. The results revealed that the inter-correlation exists between the dependent variable (continuance intention of Facebook usage) and the independent variables (i.e. Peer Influence, User Friendliness, sense of belonging, perceived enjoyment, Satisfaction, security, Facebook interface quality and attractiveness and perceived benefits) and jointly as indicated by the R-square value explained or predicted 49.4% of the variations in the LIS female undergraduates continuance intention of Facebook usage. The result generally suggests that the entire continuance intention dimensions/ factors significantly correlates with Facebook continuance intention. This study is different from the current study in view of the fact that the current study focuses of preference for Facebook as a tool for sharing information while the former focused continuance intention of Facebook usage by the female LIS undergraduate students.

Dahri and Yunus (2017) reviewed the effectiveness of social media as a knowledge management sharing tool in a government agency, which is Department of Chemistry Malaysia. As technology evolved, the tools to share knowledge have diversified. From just using the usual way of sharing information like discussion, distribution of documents via postage, sharing information via electronic media, social network or media is now trending as an information-sharing tool. The research reviewed the situation regarding the effectiveness of using social media as a knowledge-sharing tool in a government organization which is filled with red tapes, rules and regulations. The study included a brief conclusion and variety sources of references cited for better understanding and clear thought.

Oh and Syn (2014) examined the influential factors that inspire active and eager participation, and what motivate social media users to share their personal experiences, information and social support with anonymous others. A variety of information-sharing activities in social media, including creating postings, photos, and videos in 5 different types of social media: Facebook, Twitter, Delicious, You-Tube, and Flickr, were observed. Ten factors: enjoyment, self-efficacy, learning, personal gain, altruism, empathy, social engagement, community interest, reciprocity, and reputation, were tested to identify the motivations of social media users based on reviews of major motivation theories and models. Findings from this study indicated that all of the 10 motivations are influential in encouraging users' information sharing to some degree and strongly correlate with one another. At the same time, motivations differ across the 5 types of social media, given that they deliver different information content and serve different purposes. Understanding such differences in motivations could benefit social media developers and those organisations or institutes that would like to use social media to facilitate communication among their community members. The study suggested that appropriate types of social media could be chosen that would fit their own purposes and they could develop strategies that would encourage their members to contribute to their communities through social media.

Lampe, Vitak, Gray, and Elliso, (2012) in a study of 614 staff members at a large university, examined how social capital, network characteristics, and use of Facebook were related to how useful individuals find Facebook to be for informational purposes and their propensity to seek different types of information on the site. The study demonstrated that bridging social capital and engagement with one's network through directed communication behaviours are important predictors of these dimensions of information seeking; furthermore, a number of demographic and usage behaviour differences exist between those who choose to engage in information-seeking behaviours on Facebook and those who do not. When predicting information-seeking behaviours, a significant interaction between users' perceptions of Facebook as appropriate for purposes beyond the purely social and their engagement with their network was discovered.

In line with the review of previous related studies, it is evident that most of the studies on the use of Facebook for information and knowledge sharing were conducted outside the sore of Nigeria. In addition there seems to no study as known to the authors that examine female students of Facebook for knowledge sharing. Similarly, limited studies have focused on female LIS student use of Facebook for information sharing. These are the gaps in literature that this study identified and made efforts to fill.

METHODOLOGY

Research Design

The design adopted for this research is a survey. The survey is a data collection tool used to gather information about individuals. Surveys are commonly used in LIS research to collect self-report data from study participants. A survey may focus on factual information about individuals, or it might aim to collect the opinions of the survey takers. This design gives room for the researcher to cover a substantial percentage of respondents (students) in the schools that are covered in the study. The survey design method was adopted because it has been prominently used in previous related studies.

Area of the Study

The study covers the department of library and information science in four selected universities in the South West and North Central Nigeria. The universities include Kwara State University, Malete, Ilorin; University of Ilorin, Ilorin, University of Ibadan, Ibadan, Federal University, Oye-Ekiti, and Tai-Solarin University of Education, Ijebu-Ode.

The Population of the Study

The population for the study includes all the female undergraduates' students in the department of library and information science in the afore-mentioned selected universities. They include all the female undergraduates in the departments from two hundred level (year 2) to the final year students in four hundred level (year 4). The year students were excluded from the study because they are considered new to the system and may not much about the importance of taking part in research. See Table 1 for details.

Sampling Technique

The total enumerative sample method was adopted. This is due to the small size of the populations of female students in the department of library and information science in the participating universities. A total enumerative sampling otherwise known as census is a study of every unit, everyone, or everything, in a population. It is known as a total enumeration, which means a complete count. According to Babbie (2013), if a study population is small and less in number; it may be preferable to do a census of everyone in the population, rather than a sample. A census is attractive for small population necessary for given combinations of precision, confidence levels, and variability (Kothari, 2013 & Creswell, 2014). This approach has a high level of accuracy and provides complete statistical coverage over space and time. In other words; the researcher sampled all the female undergraduates' students in the department of library and information science in year 2 to 4 in the five selected universities. The sample size obtained amounted to 540. This represents the sample for this study (see Table 1).

Research Instrument

The research instrument used for data collection in this study was a questionnaire. This was used to gather the in-depth factual information desired. The questionnaire is both open and closed-ended. The questionnaire was divided into two parts, part one consists of demographic characteristics of the respondents. Parts two consists of section A, B, C, D, E, with each section targeted at capturing data on each of the variables in the study. Some items in the instrument were adapted from previous related studies (e.g. Oh & Syn, 2014; Rothen et al., 2018) and modified to suit the purpose in this study, while others were derived from the literature.

Validation and Reliability of the Instrument

In other to validity the instrument used for data collection in this study, it was given to two experts in Library and Information Science whose research area includes the use of social networks. The comments and suggestion of these experts lead to the modification of the instrument thereby authenticating the face and content validity of the instrument. The reliability of the instrument used in the study were found to be section A, r = 0.95, B, r = 0.81, C, r = 0.87, D, r = 0.88 and E r =0.78, while the overall reliability of the entire scale return an r =0.86.

Results

Table 1 reveals the demographic information of the respondents. The result shows that most respondents were student of university of Ilorin library and information science department (34.4%), while University of Ibadan respondents were (21.2%), Federal University Oye-Ekiti were (8.3%), Kwara state university Library and Information Science female undergraduate respondents were (26.3%) and Tai-Solarin University of Education (TASUED) respondents were (9.8%). The result on the age of the respondents shows that those between ages 16 -19 years constituted the majority with (50.5%), while those between the age range of 20-24years were (42.5%) and those ages 25-29 years were (5.5%) while those in the age range of 30 years and above were (1.5%).

Table 1. Demographic Distribution of Respondents (N=154)

Demographics	Frequency	Percent (%)
Gender		
Female	457	100
Age		
16-19 years	231	50.5
20-24 years	194	42.5
25-29 years	25	5.5
30 years +	7	1.5
Total	457	100.0
Institution		
Uni. Of Ilorin	157	34.4
Uni. Of Ibadan	97	21.2
Fed. Uni. Oye-Ekiti	38	8.3
Kwara State Uni.	120	26.3
Tai-Solarin Uni. Of Education	45	9.8
Total	**457**	**100.0**

Objective 1: Determine the rationale behind the preference for Facebook as an Information sharing tool.

The findings in table 2 reveal that the user-friendly nature of Facebook is the major reason why female undergraduate LIS students use it for sharing information. This is demonstrated by the ($\bar{x}$ value = 3.98, SD =0.81). Next to this is for personal gain with ($\bar{x}$ = 3.71, SD =1.80). Others followed in this order: source of information with ($\bar{x}$ = 3.68; SD =0.82); self-efficacy with ($\bar{x}$ = 3.66; SD =0.81); reputation ($\bar{x}$ = 3.58; SD = 0.82) and enjoyment ($\bar{x}$ = 3.51; SD =0.80). However, other factors identified but their values are below the average mean of 3.50 are creation of emotional bond with ($\bar{x}$ =3.44, SD = 0.84); community of interest ($\bar{x}$ = 3.44; SD. 0.76); social engagement ($\bar{x}$ = 3.38, SD. 0.70); and empathy ($\bar{x}$ = 3.01; and SD = 0.73). This implies that the most significant factors that lead to the use of Facebook for information sharing among LIS female undergraduate students are user-friendly nature of the tool and personal gain while the least factors are social engagement and empathy.

Table 2. Rationale behind the preference for Facebook as Information sharing

The Rationale for Facebook Preference	Number	Mean	SD	Correlational r- Values
User Friendly in nature	457	3.98	0.81	0.87
Source of information	457	3.68	0.82	0.78
Creation of emotional bonding	457	3.44	0.84	0.62
Reputation	457	3.58	0.82	0.70
Reciprocity	457	3.25	0.84	0.69
Enjoyment	457	3.51	0.80	0.83
Self-efficacy	457	3.66	0.81	0.81
Community of Interest	457	3.41	0.76	0.61
Social engagement	457	3.38	0.77	0.71
Altruism	457	3.33	0.70	0.53
Personal gain	457	3.71	1.80	0.82
Learning	457	3.11	0.71	0.55
Empathy	457	3.01	0.73	0.45
Facebook Preference	457	4.00	0.96	1.00

Correlation is sign* at 0.1
Average Mean = 3.50

Going a little further, the correlational analysis of the factors that determine which of them significantly correlates with using Facebook as a tool for information sharing was conducted. The results reveal that user-friendliness nature of Facebook has the highest correlation with (r = 0.87), followed by enjoyment (r =0.83), personal gain followed with (r = 0.82), then, self-efficacy (r = 0.81), and source of information (r= 0.78), while factors with less significant correlational values are learning (r = 0.55) and empathy (r = 0.45). This implies that user-friendliness nature of Facebook has the highest correlation, followed by enjoyment while learning and empathy were the least correlated factors with the use of Facebook for knowledge sharing. This means that these factors can as well predict the sharing of information on Facebook by the LIS female undergraduate students.

Objective 2: Identify the types of activities preference on Facebook by LIS female undergraduate students.

Looking at the types of activities preference on Facebook by LIS female undergraduate for sharing information, the results reveal that reading news is the best ($\bar{x}$ = 4.6 and SD =1.98). This is immediately preceded by reading friends timelines ($\bar{x}$ = 4.6 and SD = 1.95) and to update status ($\bar{x}$ = 4.6, SD 1.93).

However the least type of activities preferred are viewing friends' pictures with ($\bar{x}$ = 4.6, SD 1.7), gaming, ($\bar{x}$ = 1.6 and SD =1.8); uploading music ($\bar{x}$ = 4.6, SD= 1.1) and uploading audio and video ($\bar{x}$. 4.6; SD = 0.9). The result implies that activities preference on Facebook by LIF female undergraduate students are reading news, reading friends' timelines and updating status while the least activities preference is uploading music, audio and video.

Table 3. Types of activities preference on Facebook by LIS female undergraduate

Rationale for Facebook Preference	Number	Percentage	Mean	SD	Rank
Reading the news	457	100	4.57	1.98	1
Reading Friends timelines	451	98.7	4.57	1.95	2
Updating Status	445	97.4	4.56	1.93	3
Commenting	400	87.5	4.57	1.73	6
Contributing to Group	403	88.2	4.56	1.75	5
Sharing stuff from the Internet	383	83.8	4.57	1.65	8
Viewing friends pictures	389	85.1	4.57	1.68	7
Gaming	407	89.1	4.56	1.76	4
Uploading Music	260	56.9	4.56	1.11	9
Uploading audio/video	201	44.0	4.56	0.86	10

Objective 3: Determine the devices preference for accessing Facebook by LIS female undergraduate students.

On the devices preferred by Female LIS undergraduate students for sharing information on Facebook, the findings reveal use of smartphones as the prominent device preferred by LIS female students to share information (56%), followed by library desktop (22.3%) and tablets (15.8%) while personal computer is the least preferred device for sharing information on Facebook (5.9%). This implies that smartphones are device preferably used by LIS female undergraduate students to share information on Facebook.

Table 4. Devices Preference for Accessing Facebook to Sharing Information

Devices	No	Percentage	Rank
Personal computers	27	5.9	4
Library Desktops	102	22.3	2
Smartphones	256	56.0	1
Tablets	72	15.8	**3**
Total	**457**	**100.0**	

Objective 4: Find out which type of Facebook activity puts LIS female undergraduate more at risk for developing problematic usage.

Facebook, as practically known is one of the social networking sites. The common belief is that social networking sites usually have negative impact on the users based on the erroneous belief that some of the activities users engaged on the platform put them at risk for developing problematic usage. The findings in this study reveal that out ten activities female undergraduates engages in sharing information on Facebook, four were identified as having the capability of putting users at risk. These are uploading audio and video which was strongly agreed to by (99.1%). This is followed by sharing stuff from the internet which was strongly agreed to by (97.1%), viewing friends pictures which were strongly agreed to (94.3%). These factors have significant percentage values that confirm that the significant activities that can put female students at risk of problematic usage of Facebook. This implies that uploading audio/video, sharing stuff from the Internet, viewing friend's pictures and reading friends' timelines are activities that put female students on the risk of usage of Facebook.

Table 5. Type of Facebook activity That Puts LIS female undergraduate more at risk for developing problematic usage

Rationale for Facebook Preference	Strongly Agree	Strongly Disagree	Don't Know
Reading the news	3(0.6%)	450(98.5%)	4(0.9%)
Reading Friends timelines	431(94.3%)	11(2.4%)	15(3.2%)
Updating Status	5(1.1%)	449(98.2%)	3(0.6%)
Commenting	2(0.4%)	450(98.5%)	5(1.1%)
Contributing to Group	5(1.1%)	447(97.8%)	5(1.1%)
Sharing stuff from the Internet	444(97.1%)	8(1.8%)	5(1.1%)
Viewing friends pictures	439(96.1%)	11(2.4%)	7(1.5%)
Gaming	0(0%)	450(98.5%)	7(1.5%)
Uploading Music	201(44.0%)	220(48.1%)	36(7.9%)
Uploading audio/video	453(99.1%)	4(0.9%)	0 (0%)

Discussion of Findings

The most significant factors that lead to the use of Facebook for information sharing among LIS female undergraduate students are user-friendly nature of the tool and personal gain, enjoyment and self-efficacy while the least factors are social engagement and empathy. It worthy of note that users will always use any social media that is user-friendly to all short of activities. Not this alone, users will never cease using any tool that results in personal gain just like the use of Facebook in this study has demonstrated. In the same vein, users will always be happy to use any tool that gives them joy. There is doubt that Female students derive joy in using Facebook because they able to meet with old friends, colleagues and relatives, share information with them, see their pictures and even have opportunity of chatting with them. Therefore, these results are not a coincidence. The finding agrees with the report of the study conducted by Oh and Syn (2014) which tested factors that identified the motivations of social media users based on reviews of major motivation theories and models. Findings from the study indicated that all of the 10(enjoyment, self-efficacy, learning, personal gain, altruism, empathy, social engagement, community interest, reciprocity, and reputation) are influential in encouraging users' information sharing to some degree and strongly correlate with one another. Similarly, the finding by Tella and Babatunde (2017) which reported that peer influence, user-friendliness, sense of belonging, perceived enjoyment, Satisfaction, security, Facebook interface quality and attractiveness and perceived benefits) jointly explained or predicted the variations in the LIS female undergraduates continuance intention of Facebook usage lend credence to the present finding in this study. This is because two significant factors from their study relate to the factors identified in the current study which are user-friendliness and enjoyment.

User-friendliness nature of Facebook has the highest correlation, followed by enjoyment while learning and empathy were the least correlated factors with the use of Facebook for knowledge sharing. This finding again correlates with Tella and Babatunde (2017) report which demonstrated that user-friendliness had the highest correlational value with the Facebook usage continuance intention. However, the current study does not focus on continuance intention but since both address use, confirm that the fact that the two studies are related.

Activities preference on Facebook by LIF female undergraduate students are reading news, reading friends' timelines and updating status while the least activities preference is uploading music, audio and video. Just like applicable to another social network usage. These activities are relevant to the activities carrying out in other related social networking sites such as Twitter, linkdln and others.

The finding showcase that uploading audio/video, sharing stuff from the Internet, viewing friend's pictures and reading friends' timelines are activities that put female students on the risk of usage of Facebook. There is no doubt that these activities identified usually cause troubles for the users irrespective of gender. Viewing a friend's picture, for instance, can change one's behaviour through the practising of one sees or trying to emulate it. One an individual read as well can put him or her risk. All of these confirm the common saying that what we see, hear and think can make us misbehave. The report by (Rothen, Briefer, Deleuze, Karila, Andreassen, & Achab, 2018) which explored the heterogeneity of Facebook usage and determine which kind of Facebook activity predicts problematic usage; and tested whether specific impulsivity facets predict problematic use of Facebook and reported that specific usage preferences (updating one's status, gaming via Facebook, and using notifications) and impulsive traits (positive and negative urgency, lack of perseverance) are associated to problematic Facebook use confirm the current finding in this study.

Smartphones are device preferably used by LIS female undergraduate students to share information on Facebook. This finding is also not a coincidence in view of the fact that smartphones use is now commonplace among undergraduates generally. They prefer using this device to do anything because of its convenience, mobility, ease of use and user-friendliness, and it saves time. There is no need for the students to go the library to use the library desktop or whatever.

CONCLUSION

This study has examined the library and information science female undergraduates' preference for Facebook as an information-sharing tool. So far, the findings of the study have demonstrated that most significant factors that lead to the use of Facebook for information sharing among LIS female undergraduate students are user-friendly nature of the tool, personal gain, enjoyment and self-efficacy while the least factors are social engagement and empathy. User-friendliness nature of Facebook has the highest correlation with the preference for Facebook as information sharing tool by female students followed by enjoyment while learning and empathy were the least correlated factors. Activities preference on Facebook by LIS female undergraduate students are reading news, reading friends' timelines and updating status while the least activities preference are uploading music, audio and video. Just like applicable to another social network usage. Uploading audio/video, sharing stuff from the Internet, viewing friend's pictures and reading friends' timelines are activities that put female students on the risk of usage of Facebook. Smartphones is the device preferably used by LIS female undergraduate students to share information on Facebook.

Recommendations

Based on the findings in this study, it is recommended that female students should desist from activities that will put them at risk of problematic usage when sharing information on Facebook. Enjoyment has been identified as one of the factors that make female LIS undergraduate students make use of Facebook. This enjoyment should not be taking for granted because they are students. They should allow Facebook activities to consume the time they supposed to use for study so they can perform to expectation.

Implication of the Study

The findings of the study have demonstrated that most significant factors as user-friendly nature of Facebook, personal gain, enjoyment and self-efficacy and the least factors as social engagement and empathy. The implication of these is that as much as Facebook continue to be user friendly, it will continue to attract more female users. Since female users prefer technology that is flexible and devoid of complexity to use.

Another implication is that female undergraduate will not engage in any technology in which they derive no enjoyment. This is the more reasons why currently the number of female users of Facebook is currently more than their male counterpart. This is as a result of the enjoyment female users derived from using the Facebook.

Future Research Opportunities

The study has been able to cover only the female Library and Information Science undergraduates. This is rather limited. In light of this, future reseacrcher can consider increasing the scope of the study to cover more ground such involing female undergraduate from other disciplines. In fact, a comparative analysis of undergraduate use and preference for Facebook would be an interesting piece too. In addition, examination of female undergraduates use of other related social media may as well be considered.

REFERENCES

Acquisti, A., & Gross, R. (2006). Imagined communities: Awareness, information sharing, and privacy on Facebook. Privacy Enhancing Technologies. Lecture Notes in Computer Science, 4258, 36–58. doi:10.1007/11957454_3

Andreassen, C. S. (2015). Online Social Network Site Addiction: A Comprehensive Review. *Current Addiction Reports, 2*(2), 175–184. doi:10.100740429-015-0056-9

Bhattacherjee, A. (2001). An empirical analysis of the antecedents of electronic commerce service continuance. *Decision Support Systems, 32*(2), 201–214. doi:10.1016/S0167-9236(01)00111-7

Burke, M., Kraut, R., & Marlow, C. (2011). Social Capital on Facebook: Differentiating uses and users. *Proc. SIGCHI Conf. Human. Factors Computer System*, 571–580. 10.1145/1978942.1979023

Clement, J. (2019). *Number of Facebook users worldwide 2008-2019.* https://www.statista.com/statistics/264810/number-of-monthly-active-facebook-users-worldwide/

Clement, J. (2019). *Facebook user share in the United States 2019, by gender.* https://www.statista.com/statistics/266879/facebook-users-in-the-us-by-gender/

Creswell, W. J. (2014). *Research Design, Qualitative, Quantitative and Mixed Methods Approaches.* Sage.

Dahri, A. F. & Yunus, A.M. (2017). The Effectiveness of Social Media as Knowledge Management Sharing Tool in Government Agency: A Case Study. *International Journal of Academic Research in Business and Social Sciences, 7*(120), 1189-1199.

Ellison, N. B., Steinfield, C., & Lampe, C. (2007). The Benefits of Facebook "Friends:" Social Capital and College Students' Use of Online Social Network Sites. *Journal of Computer-Mediated Communication, 12*(4), 1143–1168. doi:10.1111/j.1083-6101.2007.00367.x

Gilbert, E., & Karahalios, K. (2009). Predicting tie strength with social media. In *Proceedings of the 27th international conference on Human factors in computing systems.* ACM.

Joinson, A. N. (2008). Looking at, looking up or keeping up with people?: motives and use of Facebook. In *Conference on Human Factors in Computing Systems (CHI).* Florence, Italy: ACM Press.

Kothari, C. R. (2013). *Research methodology: Theory and Techniques* (2nd rev. ed.). New Age Publishers; doi:10.1145/1357054.1357213

Lampe, C., Ellison, N., & Steinfield, C. (2006). A Face(book) in the Crowd: Social Searching vs. Social Browsing. In *ACM Special Interest Group on Computer-Supported Cooperative Work.* ACM Press. doi:10.1145/1180875.1180901

Lampe, C., Ellison, N., & Steinfield, C. (2007). Profile Elements as Signals in an Online Social Network. In *ACM Conference on Human Factors in Computing Systems.* ACM Press.

Lampe, C., Vitak, J., Gray, R., & Elliso, N. B. (2012). *Perceptions of Facebook's Value as an Information Source.* CHI 2012, Austin, TX.

Mittal, P. (2018). *What are some unique characteristics makes "Facebook" as Successful?* Retrieved from https://www.quora.com/What-are-some-unique-characteristics-makes-Facebook-as-Successful

Papacharissi, Z., & Mendelson, A. (2011). Toward a new(er) sociability: Uses, gratifications and social capital on Facebook. In *Media perspectives for the 21st century.* Routledge.

Pew Research Center. (2015). *Men catch up with women on overall social media use.* Retrieved https://www.pewresearch.org/fact-tank/2015/08/28/men-catch-up-with-women-on-overall-social-media-use/

Rae, J. R., & Lonborg, S. D. (2015). Do motivations for using Facebook moderate the association between Facebook use and psychological well-being? *Frontiers in Psychology*, *6*, 771. doi:10.3389/fpsyg.2015.00771 PMID:26124733

Rothen, S., Briefer, J.-F., Deleuze, J., Karila, L., Andreassen, C. S., Achab, S., Thorens, G., Khazaal, Y., Zullino, D., & Billieux, J. (2018). Disentangling the role of users' preferences and impulsivity traits in problematic Facebook use. *PLoS One*, *13*(9), e0201971. doi:10.1371/journal.pone.0201971 PMID:30183698

Ryan, T., Chester, A., Reece, J., & Xenos, S. (2014). The uses and abuses of Facebook: A review of Facebook addiction. *Journal of Behavioral Addictions*, *3*(3), 133–148. doi:10.1556/JBA.3.2014.016 PMID:25317337

Savolainen, R. (2017). Everyday life information seeking: Approaching information seeking in the context of "way of life". *Library & Information Science Research*, *17*(3), 259–294. doi:10.1016/0740-8188(95)90048-9

VCPost. (2019). *Ten features that made Facebook the most used social Media site.* Retrieved https://www.vcpost.com/articles/27824/20140925/10-features-made-facebook-used-social-media-site.htm

Yang, C., & Brown, B. B. (2013). Motives for using Facebook, patterns of Facebook activities, and late adolescents' social adjustment to college. *Journal of Youth and Adolescence*, *42*(3), 403–416. doi:10.100710964-012-9836-x PMID:23076768

This research was previously published in Recent Developments in Individual and Organizational Adoption of ICTs; pages 245-261, copyright year 2021 by Information Science Reference (an imprint of IGI Global).

Chapter 82
Exploring the Use of Social Media Platforms by Public Universities

Mohanad Halaweh
https://orcid.org/0000-0001-8045-8457
Al Falah University, Dubai, UAE

Ahmed Kamel
Al Falah University, Dubai, UAE

Robin Kabha
Al Falah University, Dubai, UAE

Moataz Elbahi
Al Falah University, Dubai, UAE

Reem Yousef
Al Falah University, Dubai, UAE

ABSTRACT

The use of social media platforms by university students and teachers has been found to facilitate the learning and teaching processes. This includes providing opportunities for students to share and discuss relevant ideas and issues, thus making the task more enjoyable and raising the level of achievement. This study explored the use of social media platforms by public universities in Egypt. It investigated how these universities utilized social media platforms, and whether they are used for educational purposes or not. The data was collected from 21 universities using a questionnaire survey of 2100 undergraduate and postgraduate students. The official social media pages of each university were surveyed and analyzed using content analysis method. The results revealed that the use of social media platforms by public universities was for the purpose of communicating with the general public more than the students. This study also found that the majority of students consider social media platforms of their universities to be useless and not supporting their academic studies. This paper offers practical implications and recommendations for universities' decision makers and social media developers.

DOI: 10.4018/978-1-6684-7123-4.ch082

1. INTRODUCTION

The number of social media users around the world has arisen over the last years. It is expected to reach 3 billion by 2021 (Benedek, 2018). Facebook, for example, was the first social network platform that reached one billion monthly active users by the first quarter of 2017. Social media networks have been used for many different purposes including education (Greenhow & Lewin, 2016), commerce (Chen, Lu, & Wang, 2017), healthcare (Hubbell, 2018), politics (Sabatovych, 2019), and many more. The literature review on the role of social media in education has covered a different range of topics such as the relationship between social media and educational outcomes, learning patterns and best practices, and students' online participation. In addition, some previous studies (e.g., Chugh & Ruhi, 2018; Price et al., 2018) have examined the role of social media networks in shaping students' attitudes to collaboratively share and manage learning materials. Although there is much research that has shown positive relations between the use of social media platforms and students' learning process, there is still limited research that has investigated the use of social media platforms by public universities. Some developing countries, such as Egypt, started to consider the role of social media platforms in developing students' learning (Sobaih & Moustafa, 2016). In Egypt, there are currently 48 million active users on the Internet (52%) with 30% uses social media platforms. Facebook users reached about 27 million users in which 23 million of them uses mobile phones to access their Facebook pages.

The majority of social media users in Egypt consists of young people who are eager to use the social network for education purpose (Easa, 2019). Egypt has a total of 63 universities and academic institutions, of which 27 are state-sponsored universities. The number of students enrolled in these universities until 2018 is about 3.3 million students (www.youm7.com). Despite the large number of university students and the widespread use of technology, our preliminary study showed a notable lack of using learning management system (LMS) among students in most Egyptian government universities. This can be reasoned to the difficulties in obtaining the required financial and technological resources for these universities to effectively use LMS. As a result, some universities have been adopting other communication tools to help students and instructors share and manage the relevant learning resources. Therefore, exploring the use of social media platforms among students of public universities in Egypt is essential for understanding students' behavioral intentions to adopt technology for learning purposes. Despite the extensive literature on social media and learning and mainly "informal learning", there has been little evidence of using them for "formal learning" which is directed and mandated by universities. In addition, there seems to be little empirical basis for this assumption (Greenhow & Lewin, 2016). Thus, this study explored whether social media platforms can be used for promoting students' learning development, and if so, to what extends, and how they are used by students and universities. Outcomes from this study can highlight the needs of the Egyptian public universities to utilize social media platforms as an educational tool, and maximize the benefits offered by them to enhance their students' learning experience.

This paper has been divided into five sections. Section two reviews the literature. Section three presents the research methodology. Section four presents the research findings, followed by the implications and discussions of the results, and the conclusion.

2. LITERATURE REVIEW

Social media platforms (Twitter, Facebook, YouTube, Wikis, and Blogs) allow students to create, navigate, communicate, share and collaborate. Experiences from such practices may enable students to enable the students to develop competence (Bugawa & Mirzal, 2018). Many previous studies (e.g., Al-Samarraie & Saeed, 2018; Balakrishnan & Gan, 2016; Gleason & Von Gillern, 2018) have reported the potential of using social media platforms in helping students to communicate easily, exchange knowledge, and find new resources of information related to their subjects. Aspects of this include making the learning process more interactive, attractive and efficient. In addition, integrating social media into classroom approaches has made a paradigm shift from teacher and teaching to 'learner-centered' and learning, also called 'personalized' education system (Chawinga, 2017). Much of previous studies have focused on the benefits of social media platforms, particularly in facilitating interaction between the instructor and students, sharing of relevant material, engaging students in collaborative projects that require the creation, editing and management of content, and enabling more independent, lifelong learning (Dabbagh & Kitsantas, 2012; Ha, Joa, Gabay, & Kim, 2018; Jordan & Weller, 2018; Price et al., 2018).

A recent study by Niu (2019) reviewed 57 empirical studies on the use of social networking websites for different academic purposes. The review revealed that the majority of the surveyed studies reported positive effects of using Facebook for academic purposes. The author also reported that Facebook is an effective tool for academic communication, especially in promoting student-centered learning. However, the use of Facebook as Learning Management System (LMS) is still under-studied. In addition, Facebook may not be suitable for teaching all academic subjects.

Over the past decade, many studies have investigated the relationship between the use of social media networks and the learning opportunities they present. For example, Al-Rahmi and Othman (2013) reported that students' collaboration through social media may positively influence students' academic performance. Eid and Al-Jabri (2016) found a significant positive relationship between both chatting and online discussion, and knowledge sharing. Another study by Evans (2014) found that using social media may not necessarily influence students' attendance of main academic classes .

Prior research also pointed out that the use of certain social network websites (e.g., Facebook) can help in developing student-teacher relationships outside of the classroom (Sheldon, 2015; Schwartz, 2009). Some previous studies have also considered the use of 'Facebook friendships' to be useful for mentoring and advising students (DiVerniero and Hosek, 2011; Sheldon, 2015). This is especially needed when some students feel shy to discuss personal and confidential issues with their tutors in a face-to-face manner (Puzio, 2013). However, the extensive use of Facebook friendships among students might also lead them to invade their tutors' privacy. Therefore, instructors need to set boundaries for their relationships with students (Schwartz, 2009).

Despite the positive results of using social media in education, the current knowledge about the use of social media by university students is still limited and this is due to the inclined nature of these mediums, such as cultural resistance, pedagogical issues, as well as the differences among academics. According to Madge, Meek, Wellens, and Hooley (2009), certain social media platforms might be more useful for informal rather than formal learning. Meanwhile, previous research highlighted the negative impacts of using social media for learning purposes. For example, it was found that time spent on Facebook may negatively affect students' grades (Kirschner & Karpinski, 2010). Moreover, our review of the literature showed that social networking websites may negatively influence students' social interactions, emotional health problems, and work completion (Kitsantas et al., 2016; Tandoc, Ferrucci, & Duffy, 2015).

Also, multitasking in Facebook, in the form of doing school work and other irrelevant activities, is distractive to the learning process, which may negatively influence students' academic performance (Andersson, Hatakka, Grönlund, & Wiklund, 2014). Based on these, it is anticipated that understanding the use of social media platforms in the Egyptian universities can help optimize resources utilization with maximal impact on students. Therefore, this study attempted to answer the following questions: "Which social media platforms are currently in use by public universities and their students in Egypt?", "What is the purpose of using these platforms in these universities?", and "What are the reasons for the students' low use of the university social media platforms". Answering these questions may offer practical implications and recommendations for universities' decision makers and social media developers in Egypt.

3. RESEARCH METHODOLOGY

The purpose of this study was to explore the extent of using social media platforms in the public universities of Egypt for educational/learning purposes. In Egypt, there are 63 universities in which 27 are government-sponsored universities, 4 are non-profit universities, 20 are private universities owned by the private sector, and 12 are higher academic institutions. In this study, only governmental (public) universities were considered.

The current study employed two quantitative methods: contents analysis and questionnaire. Figures 1 shows the overall methodology for conducting this research work, including the steps, tools and techniques for data collection and analysis.

The use of quantitative content analysis conforms to the scientific method and produce reliable findings (Macnamara, 2005). It helps summarizing and quantifying messages (Neuendorf, 2002), as well as helping the researcher determine the frequency of specific ideas, phrases, concepts, terms in texts and make comparisons in order to describe or explain communicative behavior (Allen, 2017). Content analysis can be applied manually or using computerized system which automates the word count, based on in-built dictionary or researcher developed dictionary. The use of computerized algorithms is mainly to resolve words with more than one meaning and identify different words that have the same meaning (Short & Palmer, 2008).

In this study, the collection and analysis of social media data were accomplished by using Facepager and Matlab software (see Figure 2). The Facepager software (Jünger & Keyling, 2019) was used to retrieve the data from the main social media platforms of each public university. The period of data collection was from February 2018 to the end of April 2018. The collected data from the social media platforms were exported into a CSV format and then imported into Matlab program. The content analysis was done using the Text Analytics tool in Matlab. This toolbox provides algorithms and visualizations for preprocessing, analyzing, and modeling text data. Using this tool, the keywords identifying the categories of the posts (for example, Education, Learning, learn identifies the education category) were detected and counted. The results of this process, including the categories (e.g., Education, Entertainment, and University News) are shown in Figures 9 and Figure 10.

In addition to that, and in order to simplify the process of gathering data from students of the selected universities, a total of 15 research assistants were recruited to distribute randomly the questionnaire to 2100 participants from 21 universities, seeking at least 100 participants from each university. 53% of the sample were male and 47% were female. The majority of the respondents (94%) were between 18 and 23 years old, 6% were between 23 and 29 years (post graduate students).

Figure 1. Research methodology

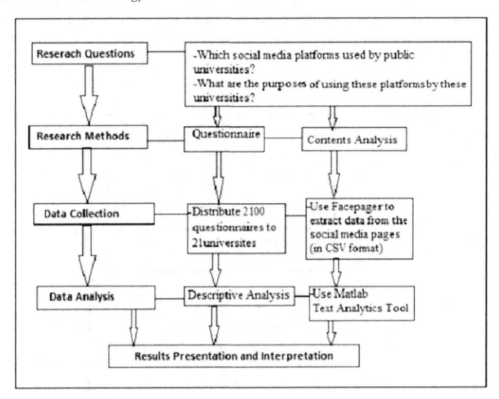

4. RESULTS

4.1. The Utilized Social Media Platforms by Public Universities and Their Students in Egypt

This section reports the main research findings of this study. Our results showed that Facebook was reported to be the most used social media platform by students in Egypt with an average usage percent of 91.6%, followed by YouTube (29%) and Twitter (27.3%) (see Figure 3). The use of social network platforms among universities was consistent between students and the rest of Egyptian society. The general statistics shows that more than 37% of the population uses Facebook, noting that the use of the remaining social media platforms at the community level was much less than Facebook.

The results show that the use of students to the Facebook platform can be associated with its popularity among the Egyptian society, especially with many governmental and non-governmental organizations adopts it as a means of communication between them and the public.

The participants were also asked to determine the number of social media platforms used. Figure 4 shows that the majority of students used two or more social media platforms. Interestingly, 97.5% of the surveyed participants were found to use social media platforms with only 52 participants (representing around 2.5%) who do not use any social media platforms. It was noticed that most of the students who are not using social media platforms were female students. Those students were mostly undertaking courses at universities located in upper Egypt, where the society limit access to social media sites for females. Overall, these results indicate a high rate of social media platforms usage and that should motivate the universities to invest in developing communications via social media platforms and utilizing it for various learning purposes.

Figure 2. Steps for data collection and analysis

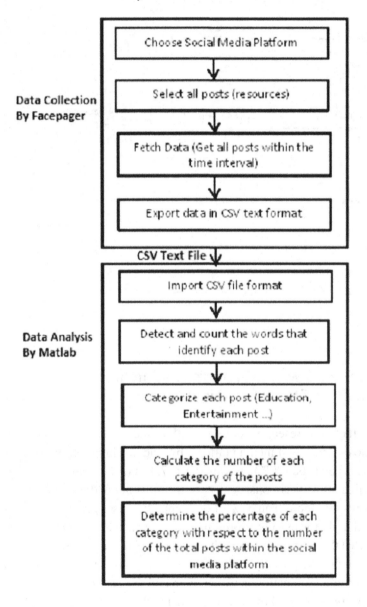

Figure 5 shows the results of surveying the selected universities with regard to their use of social media platforms. The results revealed that 21 universities had an official page on Facebook, 19 universities had an official page on Twitter, 12 universities had official page on YouTube, and 9 universities had an official page on Google+. The results also showed the use of many social networking platforms. For example, 13 public universities were found to use several platforms to help them represent their sub-entities within a single entity, such as the use of multiple accounts to represent different sub-departments under one administration or college. However, these universities may consider associating multiple sites/pages to one single social media network.

Figure 3. Frequency of using social media platforms by students in Egypt

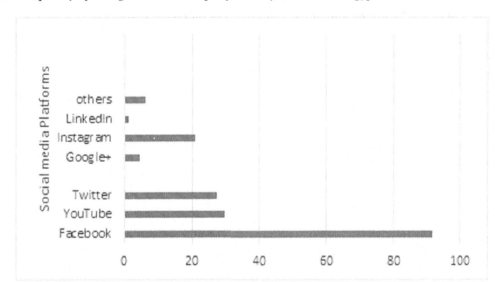

Figure 4. The number of social media platforms used by students

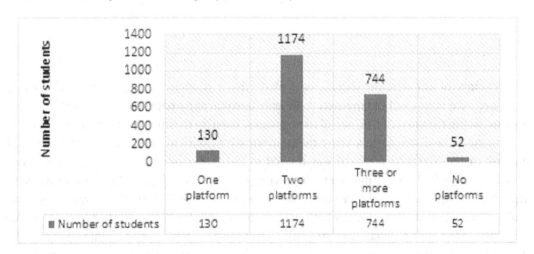

Table 1 shows the social media platforms used by each university and the number of audiences in each platform. Most of the universities were found to use four social media platforms, such as Facebook, Twitter, YouTube, and Google+. However, there were few universities used Instagram (Damanhour) and LinkedIn (Alexandria), which indicates their limited relevance to the public universities' initiatives in Egypt. A shown in Table 1, four universities (Cairo, Ain Shams, Banha, and Mansoura) were reported to have five social media accounts each, four universities (Damanhour, Assiut, Suez, and Zakazeek) were found to use four social media platforms, six universities (Beni_suef, Portsaid, South of Valley, Tanta, Fayoum, and Monfia) were found to use three platforms only, six universities (Kafer elshiekh, Helwan, Al Azhar, Menia, Aswan, and Suhag) were found to use two social media platforms each, and only one university used six social media platforms (Alexandria).

Figure 5. The number of governmental universities used social media platforms

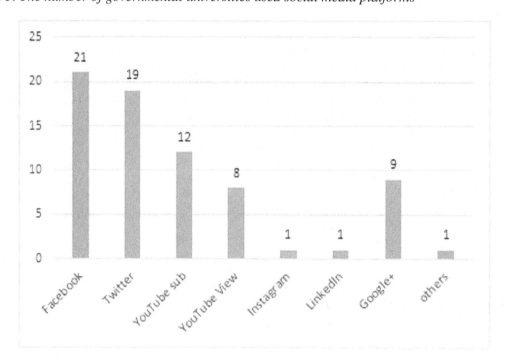

The percentage of using certain social media platforms (e.g., Facebook, YouTube, and Twitter) was found to exceed the number of the registered students in some universities, which implies that not only students were using the universities' social media pages, but also the employees of the same university, previous graduates, and other users using the platforms for political reasons. Our study showed that students' use of the YouTube platform was limited to the subscription and the view of instructional videos. All the identified universities had a high view rate on YouTube (73.88%). However, students' subscription to the official page of each university was as low as 0.49%. Overall, these results imply that Facebook is a dominant platform used by both universities and students. Facebook, Twitter and YouTube are recognized as the most popular platforms among Egyptian students. The present social communication platforms used in the community does not cost the universities any additional costs to operate and maintain. With the exception of Cairo University, most of the activities performed by public universities on these platforms were mainly to increase the effectiveness and the interaction of the online learning community in which individual and group 'reflection' play a crucial role.

Table 1. Social media uses by governmental universities in Egypt

University	Facebook	Twitter	YouTube		Instagram	LinkedIn	Google+	Others
			sub	views				
Cairo	952,979	6,483	877	24,297			1,109	
Ain Shams	487630	407	10	49				27,160
Helwan	170851	2628						
Al Azhar	51704	6.031						
Alexandria	24158	2,523	907	54,004		76,892	806	
Menia	22996	652						
Assiut	59596	371	189				172	
Banha	39293	2,131	320	65,129			225	
beni_suef	54604	1,324					56	
Damanhour	5179	65	58		52			
Fayoum	45194		184	6,062				
Kafer elshiekh	132109		484					
Aswan	1053	102						
Portsaid	16534	2,097					82	
Mansoura	181312	739	35,355	5,853,253			93	
Monfia	13898	203		1,144				
Suhag	49694	1211						
South of Valley	7858	547					76	
Suez	12 071	69	13	99				
Tanta	8715	65	23	1 339				
Zakazeek	7249	49	112	9 712			168	

4.2 The Purpose of Using Social Media Platforms

To assess the extent to which students in public universities are using social media platforms, a questionnaire was administrated to them to ask about their use of these platforms. Surprisingly, 95% of the students said they were not using social media platforms for academic purposes (see Figure 6). Only few students (3.75%) reported the use of social media platforms for different learning purposes. The results of the study indicate that there was a lack of opportunities for electronic academic communication between students and their universities. If there is continuity, it was very limited, informal, and depends on individual initiatives of the faculty members and students. This indicates that the opportunity to use an easy, available, cheap and widespread technological alternative is wasted by the public universities in Egypt.

The results also revealed that, as shown in Figure 7, the main purposes of using these platforms were to follow university news and events, entertainment, and to stay in touch with friends. The results revealed that universities' use of social media networks to connect academics with their students was low.

Figure 6. The utilization of social media platforms by university students

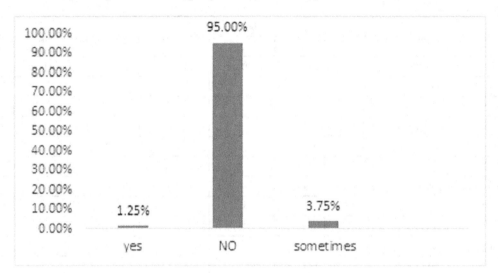

Figure 7. The utilization of social media platforms by public universities

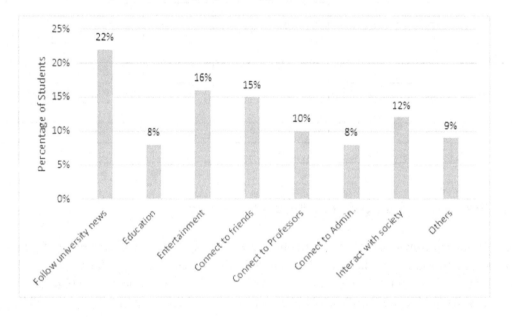

The Reasons for the Students' Low Use of the University Social Media Platforms in Egypt

As shown in Figure 8, the majority of students (1265 (60%) of the surveyed participants) expressed that 'useless' information was the main reason for not interacting or using the official pages of their universities' social media platforms. In addition, 260 students (12%) declared that they were not actively interacting with the official social page of their universities because the contents were not related to their learning needs. Other students (265, 12.62%) said that the contents provided were boring.

Figure 8. Main reasons for not using social media platforms

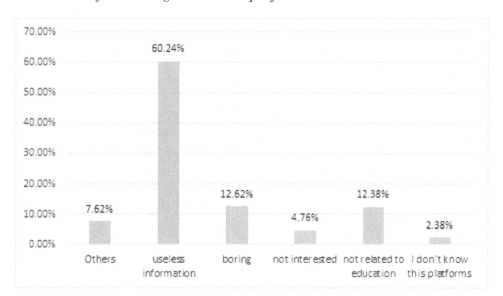

As mentioned earlier, Facebook and YouTube were the commonly used social media platforms by most public universities in Egypt. To better understand the reasons behind this use, we used a content analysis method to study the publications on the official pages of each public university on Facebook and YouTube. Figures 9 and 10 present the results of the content analysis. As shown in Figure 9, the use of Facebook for publishing educational contents on the official pages of the selected universities was lower than university news and academics news. As shown in Figure 10, the content analysis of the YouTube platform revealed the same results with 2% of total use for educational purposes, while the highest usage was reported for publishing academic news (21%), followed by students' news (18%), and community engagement (17%). Such news stories may not necessarily attract the students, especially when the topic is not relevant to the interests and lives of the students. 29% of the official news posted by the public universities in Egypt were mostly related to the university administration. News coverage topics such as opening new facilities, receiving guests, following-up of daily work practices were also commonly posted on the Facebook platform. The use of YouTube in these universities was also associated with publishing community reports (13.50%), which shows the potential of this platform in distributing information about the relevant community issues.

Based on these, it can be anticipated that the content of social networking platforms in the Egyptian universities is not relevant to the students' needs and interests which, as a result, stop them from using it again. In addition, the lack of focus on students' activities, educational process, achievements and their sports and cultural activities was apparent in universities' posting on social media platforms. Therefore, the posting process of online contents of these universities may need to be supervised by specialized academics to increase the effectiveness of their pages.

Figure 9. Content analysis of Facebook usage

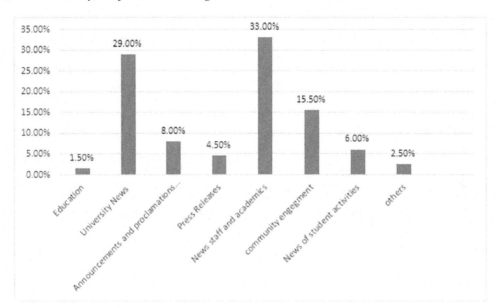

Figure 10. Content analysis of YouTube usage

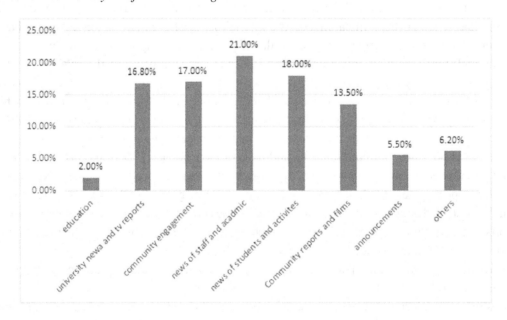

5. DISCUSSION AND IMPLICATIONS

Despite the high rate of using social media platforms in Egypt, it was found that the use of these platforms for educational purposes was very limited by students in public universities. The results showed that majority of public universities in Egypt were not efficiently using social media platforms for promoting certain learning and teaching activities. Facebook and YouTube were the main social media channels used by public universities in Egypt. However, their uses were limited to news posting and events-related promotion. Our results are also in line with the work of Tur, Marín-Juarros and Carpenter (2017), who reported that students' use of social network websites is mainly to access information and this because students are unfamiliar with using them as educational tools. This was also supported by Talaue, Alsaad, AlRushaidan and AlHagail (2018) who reported that using social networks by university students was mainly to search for friends and classmates, but not for learning purposes. In addition, our result can be also linked to the finding of Akintola, Taiwo, and Adesegun (2018), which found that not all lecturers were skilled in the use of social networking websites for teaching.

The findings showed some evidence of using social media sites by public universities in Egypt, which is recognized as a form of informal learning. A recent study has confirmed that the application of social media in educational context is largely initiated by the students themselves and not by their teachers (Chugh & Ruhi, 2018). Therefore, it is suggested that Egyptian universities may, in the future, focus on introducing social learning strategies in order to enhance the general perceptions of their students. This may also involve motivating teachers to organize various collaborative learning activities with their students in social media sites. By doing so, students may find the contents and activities more interesting and related to their learning needs. In addition, engaging students a collaborative problem-solving task using video resources from the YouTube platform can increase students' access to the learning materials and improve their communication with their instructors.

Educational decision makers are also encouraged to find realistic ways for integrating social media platforms into the current curriculum, which requires engaging students in weekly online discussions. In addition, future research is still needed to explore different usage patterns of social media can influence students' intentions to accept this technology in learning. This requires decision makers to adopt policies and develop the necessary guidance that would help or encourage teachers and students to use them in the future. The findings of this study also showed that since the majority of students reported experience in using social media networks, then the acceptance ratio from student and teachers to use these platforms for educational purposes would be higher and more feasible than the traditional learning systems (LMS).

The interesting thing about using social media as an educational tool is that it can connect central universities with students from rural areas. This supports the initiative "education for all" and the shifting toward what we call "open education".

The results showed that news posting was the main reason for using social media platforms by public universities in Egypt. This is due to the potential of these platforms to communicate universities with a larger audience, particularly to promote their programs, attract and recruit students from different countries. The results also showed low usage of LinkedIn, which brings up the question of its efficiency in the educational setting of Egyptian public universities. Therefore, Egyptian universities may increase their usage of LinkedIn by hiring higher quality educators. academic staff may also consider creating an account on LinkedIn to connect with professional people around the world, thus opening new opportunities for collaboration and knowledge exchange.

For social media developers (e.g. Facebook), there is an urgent need to add the relevant teaching and learning functionalities for students and teachers to use. Facebook, for example, might develop new version called Facebook Academia that is more tailored to serve the needs of students. Similarly, developers might integrate the common features of social network websites (e.g., Facebook and twitter) into LMS, thus students' acceptance will be high as they have already used them.

Further work on comparison of different social network websites and strategies for using them in education and learning is required. Moreover, future research might identify the activities and needs of instructors and students in the learning environment and evaluate the appropriateness of the social network websites to meet most of these needs.

6. CONCLUSION

This study explored the current utilization of social media platforms by students and public universities in Egypt. The results showed that the Facebook was the most commonly used social media tool in Egypt, followed by YouTube and Twitter. For students, the main purpose of visiting the social media platforms was to follow the news of their university. We found that the use of these platforms for educational purposes was very limited in Egyptian universities. Some of the reasons were mostly devoted to the appropriateness of information provided and low interest in the provided services.

This research provides some practical contributions to university decision makers. It suggests that public universities may need to implement policies, and provide trainings that would help or encourage instructors and students to effectively use social network websites in learning and teaching. Also, universities may consider providing all students and instructors with a compulsory course on the role of social network websites in teaching and learning. This study also provides suggestions for software developers to develop new learning tools in social media platforms to use in education context, or duplicate the features and functionalities of these platforms in LMS in order to increase students' acceptance and use.

Finally, the results of this study were based on data collected from public universities and so, they cannot be generalized to private universities. As such, future research may conduct comparative study to explore the use of the social media networks by private universities.

REFERENCES

Akintola, M. A., Taiwo, Y. H., & Adesegun, O. O. (2018). Lecturers'readiness towards the integration of social media for teaching in a Nigerian university. *International Journal for Innovative Technology Integration in Education, 1*(1), 57–64.

Al-Rahmi, W., & Othman, M. (2013). The impact of social media use on academic performance among university students: A pilot study. *Journal of Information Systems Research and Innovation, 4*(12), 1-10.

Al-Samarraie, H., & Saeed, N. (2018). A systematic review of cloud computing tools for collaborative learning: Opportunities and challenges to the blended-learning environment. *Computers & Education, 124,* 77–91.

Alhakim, H. A., Emam, O., & El-Mageed, A. A. (2018). Architecting decision support system for allocating budget at egyptian universities. *Journal of Computer Sciences and Applications, 6*(2), 56–63.

Allen, M. (2017). *The Sage encyclopedia of communication research methods.* SAGE Publications.

Andersson, A., Hatakka, M., Grönlund, Å., & Wiklund, M. (2014). Reclaiming the students–coping with social media in 1: 1 schools. *Learning, Media and Technology, 39*(1), 37–52.

Balakrishnan, V., & Gan, C. L. (2016). Students' learning styles and their effects on the use of social media technology for learning. *Telematics and Informatics, 33*(3), 808–821.

Benedek, I. (2018). Instagram as a tool for destination branding–case study on the major cities of romania. *Journal of Media Research-Revista de Studii Media, 11*(2), 43–53.

Bugawa, A. M., & Mirzal, A. (2018). The impact of web 2.0 technologies on the learning experience of students in higher education: A review. *International Journal of Web-Based Learning and Teaching Technologies, 13*(3), 1–17.

Chawinga, W. D. (2017). Taking social media to a university classroom: Teaching and learning using twitter and blogs. *International Journal of Educational Technology in Higher Education, 14*(1), 3.

Chen, A., Lu, Y., & Wang, B. (2017). Customers' purchase decision-making process in social commerce: A social learning perspective. *International Journal of Information Management, 37*(6), 627–638.

Chugh, R., & Ruhi, U. (2018). Social media in higher education: A literature review of facebook. *Education and Information Technologies, 23*(2), 605–616.

Dabbagh, N., & Kitsantas, A. (2012). Personal learning environments, social media, and self-regulated learning: A natural formula for connecting formal and informal learning. *The Internet and higher education, 15*(1), 3–8.

DiVerniero, R. A., & Hosek, A. M. (2011). Students' perceptions and communicative management of instructors' online self-disclosure. *Communication Quarterly, 59*, 428–449.

Easa, N. F. (2019). Social media strategies and students' satisfaction at egyptian universities. *International Journal of Customer Relationship Marketing and Management, 10*(1), 1–16.

Eid, M. I., & Al-Jabri, I. M. (2016). Social networking, knowledge sharing, and student learning: The case of university students. *Computers & Education, 99*, 14–27.

Evans, C. (2014). T witter for teaching: Can social media be used to enhance the process of learning? *British Journal of Educational Technology, 45*(5), 902–915.

Gleason, B., & Von Gillern, S. (2018). Digital citizenship with social media: Participatory practices of teaching and learning in secondary education. *Journal of Educational Technology & Society, 21*(1), 200–212.

Greenhow, C., & Lewin, C. (2016). Social media and education: Reconceptualizing the boundaries of formal and informal learning. *Learning, Media and Technology, 41*(1), 6–30.

Ha, L., Joa, C. Y., Gabay, I., & Kim, K. (2018). Does college students' social media use affect school e-mail avoidance and campus involvement? *Internet Research, 28*(1), 213–231.

Hubbell, E. R. (2018). Leading through evidence and experience: How social media provides a real-time platform for disseminating what works in education. *Australian Educational Leader, 40*(3), 16.

Jordan, K., & Weller, M. (2018). Academics and social networking sites: Benefits, problems and tensions in professional engagement with online networking. *Journal of Interactive Media in Education*, 1.

Jünger, J., & Keyling, T. (2018). *Facepager. An application for generic data retrieval through APIs.* Retrieved September 2018, https://github.com/strohne/Facepager/

Kirschner, P. A., & Karpinski, A. C. (2010). Facebook® and academic performance. *Computers in Human Behavior*, *26*(6), 1237–1245.

Macnamara, J. (2005). Media content analysis: Its uses; benefits and best practice methodology. *Asia Pacific Public Relations Journal*, *6*(1), 1–34.

Madge, C., Meek, J., Wellens, J., & Hooley, T. (2009). Facebook, social integration and informal learning at university:It is more for socialising and talking to friends about work than for actually doing work. *Learning, Media and Technology*, *34*(2), 141–155.

Neuendorf, K. (2002). *The Content Analysis Guidebook*. Sage Publications.

Niu, L. (2019). Using Facebook for Academic Purposes: Current Literature and Directions for Future Research. *Journal of Educational Computing Research*, *56*(8), 1384–1406.

Price, A. M., Devis, K., LeMoine, G., Crouch, S., South, N., & Hossain, R. (2018). First year nursing students use of social media within education: Results of a survey. *Nurse Education Today*, *61*, 70–76. PMID:29179050

Puzio, E. (2013). Why can't we be friends? How far can the state go in restricting social networking communications between secondary school teachers and their students? *Cardozo Law Review*, *34*(3), 1099–1127.

Sabatovych, I. (2019). Use of sentiment analysis for predicting public opinion on referendum: A feasibility study. *The Reference Librarian*, 1–10.

Schwartz, H. L. (2009). Facebook: The new classroom commons? *The Chronicle of Higher Education*, *56*(6), B12–B13.

Sheldon, P. (2015). Understanding students' reasons and gender differences in adding faculty as Facebook friends. *Computers in Human Behavior*, *53*, 58–62.

Short, J. C., & Palmer, T. B. (2008). The Application of DICTION to Content Analysis Research in Strategic Management. *Organizational Research Methods*, *11*(4), 727–752.

Sobaih, A. E. E., & Moustafa, M. A. (2016). Speaking the same language: The value of social networking sites for hospitality and tourism higher education in egypt. *Journal of Hospitality & Tourism Education*, *28*(1), 21–31.

Talaue, G. M., Alsaad, A., AlRushaidan, N., & AlHagail, A. (2018). The impact of social media on academic performance of selected college students. *International Journal of Advanced Information Technology*, *4*, 27–35.

Tandoc, E. C., Ferrucci, P., & Duffy, M. (2015). Facebook use, envy, and depression among college students: Is facebooking depressing? *Computers in Human Behavior, 43*, 139–146.

Tur, G., Marín-Juarros, V., & Carpenter, J. (2017). Using twitter in higher education in Spain and the USA. *Comunicar, 25*(51), 19–28.

Youm7. (2018). الإحصاء: 3.03 مليون طالب مقيدين بالتعليم العالى للعام الجامعى 2016-2017. Retrieved September 2018, https://www.youm7.com/story/2018/5/6/الإحصاء-مليون-03-3-طالب-مقيدين-بالتعليم-العالى-للعام-الجامعى/3780304

This research was previously published in the International Journal of Web Portals (IJWP), 12(2); pages 41-56, copyright year 2020 by IGI Publishing (an imprint of IGI Global).

Chapter 83
Importance of Social Media to Create Environmental Awareness in Sustainable Higher Education System

T. Phani Madhavi
Sathyabama University, India

ABSTRACT

This chapter mainly addresses on the importance of social media to achieve the environmental sustainability in higher education system comprised of universities, colleges, and training institutions, which is responsible for skills development, personal development, and knowledge generation. Higher education systems play a critical role to develop the values and attitudes of the individuals and to create environmental awareness about the several issues There are many environmental issues such as global warming, waste management, environmental pollution in a global community. It is a mandatory requirement to create environmental awareness about the effects of environmental hazards. Due to rapid increase in living standards and industrialization, all the individuals as well as organizations should act in environmentally responsible ways and also promote sustainable practices for the protection of the environment.

INTRODUCTION

Over a past decade, the communication methods has been changed drastically by usage of social media networking sites like Facebook, Twitter, LinkedIn, You tube .There are several advantages of social media in higher education system particularly students can create a bond with institution, it encourages the interaction between students community, increases the student participation in team projects, enhances the video conferencing abilities, develops the better collaborative activities, it provides the rich e-learning media facilities etc. Social media become an effective marketing and communication tool in higher education system across the world for disseminating information such as daily events, press releases, publications, latest updates, upcoming events, achievements of the students, staff as well as organization,

DOI: 10.4018/978-1-6684-7123-4.ch083

admission advertisements, recruitment details, information distribution and communication to support teaching activity and for many other benefits. The information included in social media platforms have the power to spread to other social media fora within few seconds. Social media have been used by environmentalists to conduct environmental awareness campaigns and to promote environmental education.

The term social media is defined as "a group of Internet-based applications that build on the ideological and technological foundations of Web 2.0, and that allow the creation and exchange of user-generated content" (Kaplan & Haenlein, 2010). There are a plethora of Internet services that can be classified as social media, with Facebook and Twitter being two of the most common platforms (Staff, 2011). Twitter encourages word-of-mouth and discussion through short messages which are tied to events and/or people. Facebook encourages social networking and accessing of aggregated social network information through a personalised dashboard. Facebook provides the facilities for users to share content to their network of contacts of various types of content, such as text, links, images and videos. Conversely, Twitter provides limited facilities for sending short messages and embedding images (Tobey & Manore, 2014). Social media platforms have been shown to be effective tools to communicate and support interaction (Tobey & Manore, 2014). Environmental awareness is seen as a component to the education process and helps with creating change (Staff, 2011). The greater the number of aware and informed individuals; the more likely societies will take some form of action to affect environmental change. In higher educational institutions it has been proven that students have a basic awareness of environmental issues but are ignorant on strategies to address these issues (Thomas, 2004).

THE USAGE OF SOCIAL NETWORK IN HIGHER EDUCATION

Social media has become more popular among older and younger generations primary means of interacting and connecting with the world. Social network sites are primarily defined as web-based services that allow individuals to (1) construct a public or semi-public profile within a bounded system, (2) articulate a list of other users with whom they share a connection, and (3) view of traverse their list of connections and those made by others within the system, their participants are not necessarily "networking" or looking to meet new people (Boyd & Ellison, 2008).

Numerous studies about use of Social Networking Sites as a new space for improving communication among students including learning outcomes show that this is new educational tools (Tiryakioglu& Erzurum, 2011), and that online social networking activities are becoming more relevant in the education context (Hamid, Chung & Kurnia, 2009), or as a space with new facilities that significantly influences the behavior of students around the world (Pay, Hosseini & Shakouri, 2013). Also, SNSs have potential to become a valuable resource for supporting students' educational communication and collaboration with faculty (Roblyer et al. 2010; Griffith & Liyanage, 2008). These were the reasons for numerous SNS studies published in influential international journals from 2004 to 2013 (Tsai et al.,2013) and for increasing number of higher education instructors that began to combine distance education delivered through SNSs (Brady, Holcomb & Smith, 2010; Tiryakioglu& Erzurum, 2011). So, in the context of educational environment and tools there is estimation that social networks support students' using and improving their academic performance, inquiry, and alternative thinking skills. The literature has shown evidence of some efforts made to appropriate and repurpose technologies to support educational activities (Hamid, Chang & Kurnia, 2009) as well as use of the Internet for individuals' development (Ceyhan, 2013).

The implementation of Social Network in higher education can alter from communication media, information media, marketing media, sharing, announcement, feedback, task assignment, complain and examination. Effectiveness of Social Network media utilization depends on some important components such as, the attitude of user, the background and behavior of user, University policy on internet access the behavior of university communication, the role and rule of Social Network in daily communication. The impact of social media has a great potential to enhance the learning experience through active interaction and participation. Even though there are debates on the use of social media for learning, educators and scholars are seeking to find ways on how to utilize the social media in higher education environment.

UTILISING THE SOCIAL MEDIA FOR ENVIRONMENTAL SUSTAINABILITY AWARENESS

Higher education plays a crucial role for shaping students and staff to create environmental awareness and changing the attitude of future generations in order to promote and preserve the natural environment. Universities should take the responsibility through their education system for educating the younger generations towards importance of environmental sustainability, so as to impede the climate change, global warming and environmental degradation. The exponential growth of population andrapid indus-trialization have adverse impact on the environment which leads to the extreme and unusual changes on global climate. Hence the necessity of providing environmental awareness was raised among the student fraternity. Practices conducted at the university-level, such as recycling, reduction of electricity and water consumption, riding abicycle on and to the campus and paper reduction comprised environmental sustainability practices that can be shared (Higgitt, 2006; Sobreiro & Jabbour, 2007; Barata*et al.*, 2011; Zhang *et al.*, 2011; Efthymiou*et al.*, 2013; Pappas *et al.*, 2013).

Social networks can provide different kinds and levels of information that are important to us (Krätzig & Warren-Kretzschmar, 2014). Some researchers found that social media provides enormous opportuni-ties to encourage environmental activism (Arbatani & Labafi, 2016). The study (Mooney &Winstanley, 2013) found that harnessing the pro-social aspects of Twitter could prove a useful tool in informing the public better about environmental problems. The social media can be used as a part of course curricu-lum to explain, record and to carry out hands-on activities to promote the environmental sustainability initiatives to the community. For Example social media, such as YouTube, can be used as a means of communication. Social media could be utilized as a potent platform to establish dynamic participation and involvement by being an environmental volunteers. Apart from creating environmental awareness, social media can be engaged to serve environmental communication. Many national and international organizations have already raised the importance of social media for awareness raising campaigns. For example, Greenpeace is one of the popular environmental projects using social media intensely and actively to advertise its campaigns. In addition, Biodiversity loss is one of the major serious problems facing the world, and it is a problem that will not just vanish. The European Commission's 2010 campaign in the category of Environment and Ecology has won a prestigious "European Excellence Award" in the field of communication. This campaign has a strong social media component to highlight awareness of biodiversity loss. Social media tools facilitate two-way communication by providing direct channels of communication between organizations and the publics such as coordinating events and group meetings (Williams, Page, & Petrosky, 2014; Wright & Hinson, 2009). Social media also allows communicators to reach the audiences in their own space, which is important because many environmental behaviors involve personal behaviors such as recycling and turning off lights (Williams, Page, & Petrosky, 2014). LinkedIn is also one of the most popular social media among the professionals. In this social media platform the green message can be conveyed to the society.

CONCLUSION

The importance of creating environmental awareness using social media as a tool in higher education environment would enhance the good behavioral conduct of students towards environmental sustainability. Higher Education institutions should play a vital role in creating awareness on global environmental issues through social media for the benefit of the natural environment by developing appropriate curriculum, syllabus and training. Universities can play a leadership role as agents of sustainable development (James & Card, 2012). Campus sustainability leaders can communicate procedural knowledge, prompts or reminders, issue awareness, and social motives to forge a culture of environmental sustainability (Aronson & O'Leary, 1982; De Young, 1989; 2000; Katzev & Mishima,

1992). Researchers have argued that policies, such as vision, implementation of environmental management system and Green University ambitions are all done in the attempt to create more environmental sustainability awareness (Gao et al., 2006; Sammalisto & Brorson, 2008; Jinliang et al., 2010; Barata et al., 2011; Aklin et al., 2013). The participation of green champions using social media as a tool has a greater impact towards greener outcomes and greening the community. The environmental sustainability components should be combined in all academic disciplines using social media in order to change the attitude and behaviors of learning community through communicating the information towards achieving the sustainable development.

This chapter suggest a proposal towards the application of digital technology in higher education system by considering the unique policies of individual University or Institute on usage of social networking sites as a significant tool inside the campus, for the development of environmental awareness to promote sustainability in higher academic environment through learning process and to achieve the sustainable green transformation and also transforming Universities into green and sustainable campuses for the protection of natural environment.

REFERENCES

Aklin, M., Bayer, P., Harish, S. P., & Urpelainen, J. (2013). Understanding environmental policypreferences: New evidence from Brazil. *Ecological Economics*, *94*, 28–36. doi:10.1016/j.ecolecon.2013.05.012

Arbatani, R., & Labafi, S. (2016). Effects of Social Media on the Environmental Protection Behaviour of the Public. *International Journal of Environmental of Research*, *10*, 237–244.

Aronson, E., & O'Leary, M. (1982). The relative effectiveness of models and prompts on energy conservation: A field experiment in a shower room. *Journal of Environmental Systems*, *12*(3), 219–224. doi:10.2190/UBD5-4Y9B-61EF-WUM6

Barata, E., Cruz, L., & Ferreira, J.-P. (2011). Parking at the UC campus: Problems and solutions. *Cities (London, England)*, *28*(5), 406–413. doi:10.1016/j.cities.2011.04.001

Boyd, D. M., & Ellison, N. B. (2008). Social network sites.Definition, history and scholarship. *Journal of Computer-Mediated Communication*, *13*(1), 210–230. doi:10.1111/j.1083-6101.2007.00393.x

Brady, K. P., Holcomb, L. B., & Smith, B. V. (2010). The Use of Alternative Social Networking Sites in Higher Educational Settings: A Case Study of the E-Learning Benefits of Ning in Education. *Journal of Interactive Online Learning*, *9*(2), 151–170.

Ceyhan, A. A. (2013). Investigation of Adolescents' Internet Use Motives. *The Online Journal of Counseling and Education*, *2*(3), 1–15.

De Young, R. (2000). New ways to promote proenvironmental behavior: Expanding and evaluating motives for environmentally responsible behavior. *The Journal of Social Issues*, *56*(3), 509–526. doi:10.1111/0022-4537.00181

Efthymiou, D., Antoniou, C., & Waddell, P. (2013). Factors affecting the adoption of vehicle sharing systems by young drivers. *Transport Policy*, *29*, 64–73. doi:10.1016/j.tranpol.2013.04.009

Gao, C., Hou, H., Zhang, J., Zhang, H., & Gong, W. (2006). Education for regional sustainable development: Experiences from the education framework of HHCEPZ project. *Journal of Cleaner Production*, *14*(9-11), 994–1002. doi:10.1016/j.jclepro.2005.11.043

Griffith, S., & Liyanage, L. (2008). An introduction to the potential of social networking sites in education. In I. Olney, G. Lefoe, J. Mantei, & J. Herrington (Eds.), *Proceedings of the Second Emerging Technologies Conference 2008* (pp. 76-81). Wollongong: University of Wollongong. Retrieved November 2, 2009, from http://ro.uow.edu.au/etc08/9

Hamid, S., Chung, S., & Kurnia, S. (2009). Identifying the use of online social networking in higher education. *Proceedings ascilite Auckland: Poster presentation*, 419-422. Retrieved from http://www.ascilite.org.au/conferences/auckland09/procs/hamid-poster.pdf

Higgitt, D. (2006). Finding space for education for sustainable development in the enterprise economy. *Journal of Geography in Higher Education*, *30*(2), 251–262. doi:10.1080/03098260600717331

James, M., & Card, K. (2012). Factors contributing to institutions achieving environmental sustainability. *International Journal of Sustainability in Higher Education*, *13*(2), 166–176. doi:10.1108/14676371211211845

Jinliang, W., Miaoyuan, Z., Xuejuan, T., Maoheng, H., Shen, X., Yinxia, G., & Jing, G. (2010). Opportunities and challenges for environmental education at Yunnan's institutions of higher learning. *Chinese Education & Society*, *43*(2), 82–93. doi:10.2753/CED1061-1932430208

Kaplan, A. M., & Haenlein, M. (2010, January). Users of the world, unite! The challenges and opportunities of Social Media. *Business Horizons*, *53*(1), 59–68. doi:10.1016/j.bushor.2009.09.003

Katzev, R., & Mishima, H. R. (1992). The use of posted feedback to promote recycling. *Psychological Reports*, *71*(1), 259–264. doi:10.2466/pr0.1992.71.1.259

Krätzig, S., & Warren-Kretzschmar, B. (2014). Using Interactive Web Tools in Environmental Planning to Improve Communication about Sustainable Development. *Sustainability*, *6*(12), 236–250. doi:10.3390u6010236

Mooney, P., & Winstanley, A. (2013). Evaluating Twitter for Use in Environmental Awareness Campaigns. *Geotechnology Research Group*, *1*, 1–4.

Pappas, E., Pierrakos, O., & Nagel, R. (2013). Using Bloom's Taxonomy to teach sustainability in multiple contexts. *Journal of Cleaner Production*, *48*, 54–64. doi:10.1016/j.jclepro.2012.09.039

Roblyer, M. D., McDaniel, M., Webb, M., Herman, J., & Witty, V. J. (2010). Findings on Facebook in higher education: Comparison of collegefaculty and students uses and perceptions of social networking sistes. *Internet and Higher Education*, *13*(3), 134–140. doi:10.1016/j.iheduc.2010.03.002

Salek Pay, B., Hosseini, S. H., & Shakouri, H. G. (2013). Why do students use virtual social networks in Iran: A system approach. *Interdisciplinary Description of Computer System*, *11*(1), 108-122. http://www.indecs.eu/2013/indecs2013-pp108-122.pd

Sammalisto, K., & Brorson, T. (2008). Training and communication in the implementation ofenvironmental management systems (ISO 14001): A case study at the University of Gavle, Sweden. *Journal of Cleaner Production*, *16*(3), 299–309. doi:10.1016/j.jclepro.2006.07.029

Sobreiro, V. A., & Jabbour, C. J. C. (2007). Toward a greener university: Some lessons fromthe Brazilian experience. *Environmental Quality Management*, *16*(4), 69–73. doi:10.1002/tqem.20142

Staff, C. (2011). *Environmental Awareness, Education and Training Strategy Table of contents*. White Paper.

Thomas, I. (2004). Sustainability in tertiary curricula: What is stopping it happening? *International Journal of Sustainability in Higher Education*, *5*(1), 33–47. doi:10.1108/14676370410517387

Tiryakioglu, F., & Erzurum, F. (2011). Use of Social Networks as an Education Tool. *Contemporary Educational Technology*, *2*(2), 135–150.

Tobey, L. N., & Manore, M. M. (2014). Social media and nutrition education: The food hero experience. *Journal of Nutrition Education and Behavior*, *46*(2), 128–133. doi:10.1016/j.jneb.2013.09.013 PMID:24220043

Tsai, C. W., Shen, P. D., & Chiang, Y. C. (2013). The Application of Social Networking Sites (SNSs) in e-Learning and Online Education Environments: A Review of Publications in SSCI-Indexed Journals from 2004 to 2013. *International Journal of Web-Based Learning and Teaching Technologies, 8*(3). Retrieved from http://www.igi-global.com/article/the-application-of-social-networking-sites-snss-in-e-learning-and-onlineeducation-environments/102695

Williams, K. C., Page, R. A., & Petrosky, A. R. (2014). Green Sustainability and New Social Media. *Journal of Strategic Innovation and Sustainability*, *9*(1/2), 11–33.

Wright, D. K., & Hinson, M. D. (2009, March). *An analysis of the increasing impact of social and other new media on public relations practice.* Paper presented to the 12th Annual International Public Relations Research Conference, Miami, FL.

Zhang, N., Williams, I. D., Kemp, S., & Smith, N. F. (2011). Greening academia: Developing sustainable waste management at higher education institutions. *Waste Management (New York, N.Y.), 31*(7), 1606–1616. doi:10.1016/j.wasman.2011.03.006 PMID:21450452

Chapter 84
Social Media and Social Bonding in Students' Decision-Making Regarding Their Study Path

Amir Dirin

(iD) https://orcid.org/0000-0002-4851-5711

Haaga-Helia University of Technology, Finland

Marko Nieminen

Aalto University, Finland

Ari Alamäki

Haaga-Helia University of Applied Science, Finland

ABSTRACT

Students are often unsure of how to select the right study path at a higher educational institution. They either lack knowledge of a proposed study path or they do not manage to learn more before making their selection. Universities often apply various approaches, such as printed or online course curricula, to facilitate the selection process. Yet these approaches are often inefficient because they do not attract students' attention, or they provide ambiguous descriptions. Moreover, these descriptions are not provided to students through the right channels. The study reveals that students use different digital channels in various contexts to perform their educational activities. The study reveals that the use of social media applications in an educational context results in social bonding among students. The results of the study can help educators select appropriate channels that match students' expectations of a reliable and trustworthy interaction medium.

DOI: 10.4018/978-1-6684-7123-4.ch084

INTRODUCTION

Smart device usage at educational institutions has evolved at a rapid pace. The use of technology in mobile learning (M-learning) application design has also evolved quickly. Dirin and Nieminen (2018) divided the evolution of M-learning user experience into three distinct eras. A technology-focused approach (Era 1) is no longer sufficient for persuading learners to use an M-learning application. Neither does ease-of-use nor usability offer sufficient distinctive characteristics for successful M-learning services (Era 2). In the third and current era of M-learning user experience, the emphasis has moved toward engaging and emotional factors. In addition to M-learning applications, students widely apply various digital channels in their educational activities.

Students' study path selection after their first semester is often dependent on concerns, for example, about how they can improve their knowledge, their judgement of their own competence, and the extent to which they feel the university offers them the skills they need for their chosen career. Salmela and Read (2017) demonstrated that students often start university with high motivation, but over time, their motivation levels drop and feelings of stress and pressure develop. The students' mental models are constructed according to their learning experiences (Piaget & Brown, 1985), in which digital channels play a crucial role.

A Finnish Ministry of Education and Culture (2010) report indicated that 75% of high school graduates apply to attend higher educational institutions immediately after graduation, of which only 40% get through on the first attempt and the rest gain admission on the second and third attempts. In addition, many factors influence whether students successfully and smoothly graduate from higher education on time (Määttä & Uusiautti, 2011).

The aim of this study was to reveal students preferred digital channels and social media when selecting their course and study paths . Skaniakos, Penttinen, and Lairio (2014) demonstrated that peer monitoring is an important part of pastoral care for first-year students in higher education. Määttä and Uusiautti (2011) presented four factors that impact one's study path: first, the experience, habit, and ability that students develop during their studies; second, the instructors' mentoning skills; third, the curriculum; and fourth, the university community in general, such as the studying atmosphere and study culture.

Digital channels and social media have become important means of interacting in contemporary life. We use these channels for communication, socializing, decision-making, and taking effective actions. Digital touchpoints, such as websites, email, search engines, social media, video content communities, discussion forums, and blogs (Hallikainen, Alamäki, & Laukkanen, 2018), enable individuals to interact with each other, access consumer content, and perform numerous other actions. Students at higher educational institutions often utilize these channels at various stages of their studies. For example, they may use them for learning, communication, or research purposes; for getting acquainted with new students; for learning about forthcoming courses; and for skill development (e.g., Dirin, Alamäki, & Suomala, 2019; Nguyen, Muilu, Dirin, & Alamäki, 2018).

Digital touchpoints and channels are used often in marketing and advertising to evoke emotions. Straker and Wrigley (2016) demonstrated that engaging with customers through digital channels has a significant impact on growth and revenue. In an educational context, we lack a proper systematic approach for using digital channels to assist students in their educational experiences, including study path selection. In this study, "digital channels" were defined as all those online and mobile applications and services that students use to engage with peers and educational institutions to communicate, perform education-related tasks, or socialize. Furthermore, "study path" encompassed the study models that students required to complete their B.Sc. degree program. The aim of this study was to reveal the digital touchpoints and channels that students in the Business Information Technology (BITe) department of the University of Applied Sciences (UAS) often apply to engage with peers about different study path options. Figure 1 presents the typical process of study path selection at a Nordic institution of higher education.

Figure 1. Study path selection process at a Nordic higher educational institution

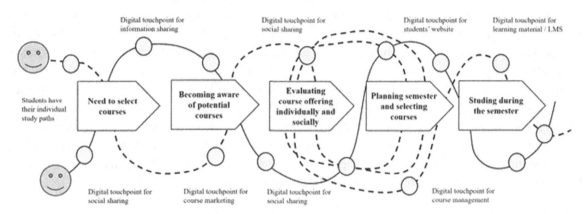

RELATED RESEARCH

Educational institutions have always used technology to support their educational offerings (Selwyn, 2011). Yet the remarkable development of information technology has transformed educational systems and processes (Fu, 2013). This development enables us to explore entirely new frameworks for teaching and learning. Traditional lecture-based teaching is often considered insufficient for deep learning and acquisition of the contextual understanding of a subject. With the increased popularity of new social media and work-related digital services, our lives have become overwhelmed with new digital channels and touchpoints. Various researchers have investigated these digital channels and touchpoints and their potential in the marketing sector (Hallikainen et al., 2018; Straker, Wrigley, & Rosemann, 2015). Kannan and Li (2017) developed a framework for digital channels and touchpoints in the marketing process, while Straker et al. (2015) focused on the opportunities that digital touchpoints provide for practitioners to open up a channel of communication with their customers. Straker et al. classified digital touchpoints into four categories: functional, social, community, and corporate. They showed that each of these four categories has a unique role in the context of digital channels. Aligned with this, Baxendale, Macdonald, and Wilson (2015) examined potential digital touchpoints in marketing, for example, in brand advertising, relative advertising, in-store communications, word of mouth (WOM), peer observation, and traditional media, such as editorials. Moreover, Straker and Wrigley (2016) demonstrated that emotional engagement is the essence of the study of digital touchpoints. In an educational context, Khanna, Jacob, and Yadav (2014) identified touchpoints for higher education marketing and branding, framing higher education as the service provider and students as the customer.

Technologies have brought about huge changes to the ways in which educational institutions offer education. M/E-learning offers great freedom and flexibility in terms of accessing knowledge anywhere, anytime (Philp, 2004). The freedom afforded by new technologies, however, has not changed students' behavioral engagement (Li, Qi, Wang, & Wang, 2014). In digital education, user engagement and user experience with learning applications play a crucial role. Huang, Jang, Machtmes, and Deggs (2012) investigated the roles of perceived playfulness and resistance to change in learning with mobile English learning outcomes (MELOs). Their results demonstrated that playfulness and self-management of learning had positive influences on MELOs. In the same year, Terras and Ramsay (2012) identified five important psychological challenges posed by mobile devices for M-learning. Cleveland-Innes, Ally, Wark, and Fung (2013) published similar research on emotional presence in M-learning. Their study focused on the use of mobile devices among graduate students pursuing their studies online and examined what effect (if any) their use had on emotional presence. In addition, Seraj and Wong (2014) investigated students' perceptions of learning through mobile devices. Their findings showed that lecturers and students raised many interactivity and flexibility issues regarding the effectiveness of learning applications especially when learning a technical subject. Moreover, Capuano, Mangione, Pierri, and Salerno (2014) addressed issues of personalization and contextualization of learning experiences in information and services management. Bachl, Tomitsch, Wimmer, and Grechenig (2010) investigated the design challenges of user experience in the context of multi-touch interfaces. The challenges that they identified (such as individual differences, input-based challenges, and accessibility) can be tackled either technologically, through a proper user interface design, or by a hardware solution.

Social Bonding

The social bond theory was proposed by Hirschi (1969). According to this theory, acceptance of social norms may prevent individuals from committing crimes or delinquency. Therefore, social bond theory suggests that an individual who has solid relationships with peers and family members may accept the surrounding social conditions and be unlikely to commit illegal acts. Hirschi identified the following fours factors of social bond theory. First, *attachment* refers to individual emotional connections to others, such as parents, teachers, and friends. It also includes the value that individuals place on others' opinions. Second, *commitment* refers to the goals that individuals set for themselves, such as educational or occupational goals. The reasoning is that an individual who is committed to a goal is less likely to risk losing the chance to achieve that goal. Third, *involvement* refers to an individual's daily activities, such as schoolwork, sports, hobbies, or work-related tasks. Lastly, *belief* refers to an individual's beliefs regarding the social and moral norms.

Hirschi (1969) employed the social bond theory to explore whether strong attachments to society prevent deflection from social norms. Similarly, Bryan et al. (2012) demonstrated that social bonds impact educational outcomes. Bishop, Bishop, Gelbwasser, Green, and Zuckerman (2003) showed that parental support has a stronger influence on children's educational success than friends' support does.

Peguero, Ovink, and Ling (2016) identified a correlation between social bonding at school and dropout for racial and ethnic minorities. They used national survey data to show that social bonding factors, such as attachment, academic and sports involvement, commitment, and belief, influence the dropout rates of racial and ethnic minorities.

In contemporary life, social media has become a strong instrument for establishing social bonds and social well-being (Burke, Marlow, & Lento, 2010). Cao, Lu, Dong, Tang, and Li (2013) investigated the role of social media as the main communication platform for supporting real-time information sharing in social bonding and bridging. Aligned with this, Phua, Jin, and Kim (2017) investigated the influence of social networking on social bridging and social bonding by receiving gratification through the media, which satisfies social and leisure needs.

Social Media in the Educational Context

Social networking services, such as Facebook, Twitter, Google+, and LinkedIn, have become popular globally. According to Jin, Chen, Wang, Hui, and Vasilakos (2013), social networking services play a significant role in peoples' lives. Lu and Churchill (2013) revealed that social patterns in a social networking environment appear to enhance social engagement, and the utilization of social networking platforms supports productive and meaningful learning. According to Watermeyer (2010), social networking services are new, innovative pedagogical tools that support creative interaction and new ways of learning science. Furthermore, Rehm and Notten (2016) discussed the contribution of Twitter to teachers' continuous competence development by analyzing hashtag conversations among German-speaking teachers.

In addition to social networking, communication applications, such as WhatsApp, Telegram, Instagram, Viber, IMO, and Discord, have become popular and are competitors of social networking services. Sutikno, Handayani, Stiawan, Riyadi, and Subroto (2016) compared WhatsApp, Telegram, and Viber and identified WhatsApp as the best instant messaging platform. Similarly, Montag et al. (2015) demonstrated that WhatsApp is the driving force in communication applications. Khodarahimi and Fathi (2017) showed that the level of anxiety of WhatsApp users was less than that of users of other social networking applications. According to data published online, in 2018, the average time that people spent on social networking sites was 144 minutes per day, which is an increase of 1 hour or 62.5% since 2012 (BroadbandSearch, 2020). Social media has also begun to play a significant role in higher education (Al-Qaysi & Al-Emran, 2017) for information sharing, as a learning management system, and to assist students in making decisions by enabling direct access to teachers and peers. Kumar and Nanda (2019) identified that educational institutions use social media as potential media to reach a large youth audience. Therefore, they concluded that social media is a good marketing instrument for higher education students. Furthermore, Dumpit and Fernandez (2017) investigated higher education students' adoption of social media. They applied the technology accepted model (TAM), perceived norm, and perceived playfulness in their study, and their results demonstrated that perceived ease of use, perceived usefulness, subjective norm, and playfulness are important predictors of students' social media usage behavior.

We are moving toward life-long learning wherein learning happens such that it corresponds with the learner's needs. Hence, we expect to see social media play an increasingly strong role as learning happens through sets of connected smart gadgets with the associated applications. Therefore, the learner's attention and focus are extending from mobile devices to other "cool" technologies and services, such as smart watches and associated social media. Chen, Grossman, Wigdor, and Fitzmaurice (2014) presented an interactive system exploring a design space of interactions between a smart phone and smart watch. This design indicates that interaction and input media for gadgets are emerging on the basis of devices and service capabilities. The emergence of a symphony of applications for smart phones and digital channels has facilitated and enhanced the use of smart devices and social media in the education system.

Structure of UAS Degree Programs and Major Selections

The overall structure of degree programs at UAS is as follows ("Studyinfo.fi," n.d.). UAS provides students with solid knowledge of, and research opportunities in, their chosen fields and professional specializations. The professional studies provide competencies and expertise in a specific field that the student chooses from the course curriculum depending on their interest, motivation, and recommendations of others, such as teachers, current students, and peers. In addition, there are elective studies that students often select from other degree programs or even other UAS campuses. Furthermore, during the practical training period, students gain experience in their professional field via hands-on job experience. The final stage of bachelor's degree studies is a thesis, depending on the student's selected study path and specialization. Various factors affect students' selection of a study path and major. For example, Malgwi, Howe, and Burnaby (2005) stated that for female students, the driving factor is their aptitude for the subject, whereas male students are motivated by the potential for career advancement and job opportunities. Arcidiacono, Hotz, and Kang (2012) suggested that future earnings primarily influence a student's major selection. However, in addition to future earnings, Wiswall and Zafar (2013) identified the student's ability as the main factor for major selection. Furthermore, Workman (2015) demonstrated that parents influence students in making this decision.

RESEARCH METHODOLOGY AND PROCESS

This section provides a general description of the research approach and process. The study was a qualitative study and its main objective was to learn students' opinions on digital touchpoints and social media's support with their study path selection. Furthermore, the study was intended to explore the social bonding that facilitates students' search for further help and information based on the digital channels. Therefore, an interview and a survey were selected as appropriate methods for obtaining students' opinions.

Research Questions

To investigate the role of digital channels in students' study path choices and course selection, this study aimed to answer the following research questions:

1. What are the digital channels used by students prior to study path selection?
2. What are the roles of digital channels in study path selection?
3. What are the major opportunities and challenges associated with the digital channels?

Research Methods

In this study, we applied qualitative research methods to learn about user attitudes and behavior regarding study path selection and managing coursework. As part of our approach, we conducted a semi-structured interview (Cohen & Crabtree, 2006). Livesey (2010) recommended semi-structured interviews because they allow respondents to express their opinions on specific subjects. Furthermore, Livesey stated that the objective of semi-structured interviews is to learn respondents' viewpoints on an specific issue rather than identifying general behavior. The semi-structured interview was conducted with a focus group. According to Longhurst (2010), a focus group should contain between 6 and 12 participants who represent the target users. Additionally, we administered a survey to collect opinions. Story and Tait (2019) identified surveys as a method of gathering evidence, attitudes, and knowledge. In this vein, Fink (2010) stated that surveys also enable people to describe and compare behavior. Therefore, in this study, the survey and semi-structured interview complemented each other for learning students' attitudes concerning how social media and social bonding impact their decision-making.

Participants

To learn about students' digital channel usage, we conducted our semi-structured interview and a survey with a group of students in their second semester of higher education. We selected students randomly at a Finnish university (UAS) during the fall 2018 semester. We conducted an interview with a student advisor, the head of the BITe department, and four students between 18 and 30 years old (of whom two were male and two were female). Table 1 presents the overall user profile. The participants in this study represent both the faculty (i.e., the head of the department and a study advisor) and the students.

Table 1. User profiles

Users	Title	Gender	Most used App in education	Learning App
U1	Department head	Male	Teams/WhatsApp	-
U2	Student advisor	Female	WhatsApp, Email	-
U3	Student	Male	WhatsApp, Skype, Telegram, Email	YouTube/Search engine
U4	Student	Male	WhatsApp, Discord, GitHub, YouTube, Email	YouTube/Search engine, Moodle
U5	Student	Female	WhatsApp, Telegram, Facebook, YouTube, Search engine, Discord	MOOCs, YouTube/Search engine, Moodle
U6	Student	Male	WhatsApp, Telegram, Facebook, YouTube, Search engine	YouTube, Search engine, Moodle

In addition to the interviews, we conducted a short survey (n = 40) with students in their second semester to learn about their use of various channels for decision-making prior to their course and study path selections.

RESULTS

Interview Results

What are the digital channels that students use prior to selecting their study path? The interview data indicate that none of the participants use a dedicated M-learning app at school. However, they regularly use publically available digital channels, such as WhatsApp, YouTube, and search engines ("We have created a WhatsApp group for our classroom activity" – U3, U4, U5, U6). This is also shown in Figure 3, which indicates that WhatsApp is the most commonly used tool (used by 79.2% of participants) after

Moodle, which is a university default online learning platform. This aligns with the findings of Kaur (2017) on the use of WhatsApp in a collaborative learning environment.

What are the roles of digital channels in study path selection? The interview analysis shows that students' course and study path selections go through several stages. We identified that the course selection starts with awareness of a potential course from individual course planning or the course curriculum ("Online course curriculum is the first step to introducing the course" – U1; "We help students plan in advance for the course, but I am not an expert on all courses, so students often change what we plan" – U2). Therefore, the existing online information was good for promoting awareness, but it did not sufficiently help the students make their selection. Thus, awareness in this context is associated with previous experience, personal interest, or just simply an appealing course name ("Sometime I attend the course just because I like the course name" – U4). The survey and interview demonstrate that students may be familiar with the name of a course, but not its content and objectives ("Check the course curriculum, but it is not clear... lots of new terms" – U4 and U6). At the start of the course, students often establish a WhatsApp group for organizing social interactions ("We engage with each other through WhatsApp, since we established a specific classmate channel during our orientation week" – U5). This channel is strictly for students, with no staff involvement. They use this channel to get to know each other, to socialize, and to exchange ideas. Learning about the courses and teachers actually started from this channel ("We also share our findings about the courses and teachers in this channel" – U5 and U6). This channel greatly impacts course selection ("I often discuss with the previous semester's students about their experience with courses and teachers, then accordingly, I select the course" – U3, U4, U5, U6).

Survey Results

The participants who took part in the survey were in their second semester and had recently selected their study path. They were between 19 and 42 years old and of various nationalities, including Finnish, Chinese, South Korean, Vietnamese, Somalian, Ukraine, Philippines, Mexican, Japan, Austria, and German. The majority of students stated that a laptop is the main device on which they perform their educational activities. Figure 2 presents an overview of the devices used for educational purposes.

Figure 2. Overview of devices used in an educational context

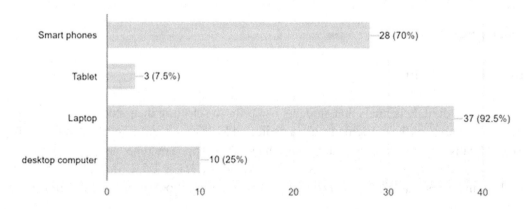

1562

Students use various social media for educational purposes. The main tool that they employ in university is the learning platform Moodle (used by 87.5%), while WhatsApp is their primary social media tool (used by 80%). Figure 3 presents the usage of social media by students for educational purposes.

Figure 3. Students' use of social media for educational purposes

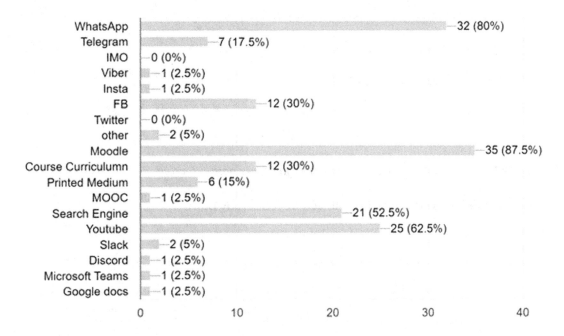

Which of the following SM do you use in educational context

40 responses

In addition to the above, during the interview, participants mentioned that channels such as GitHub, MS Teams, and Discord are used widely, for example, to share programming codes with peers. The digital channels that students use for personal reasons differ slightly from those that they use for educational purposes. In their personal lives, 90% of students use WhatsApp and 57.5% use Instagram and 55% Facebook. Figure 4 demonstrates the common social media tools that students use in their personal lives.

Students were also asked where they had learned about their course and study path options. The survey results underline online course curricula as the most common source of information. Figure 5 presents the most commonly used channels for study path selection.

Students stated that digital channels make their school life easier by offering more freedom and flexibility. Figure 6 demonstrates that the majority of students felt that using digital channels offers them greater freedom in their education.

Figure 4. Students' social media usage in their personal lives

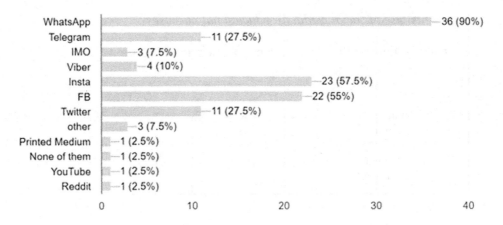

Figure 5. Most commonly used digital channels for study path selection

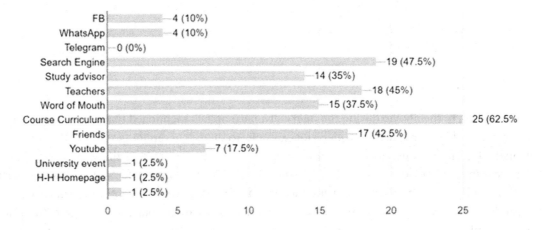

DISCUSSION

In the contemporary educational setup, students have the option to use various digital channels in different contexts. Identifying the channels that students employ for educational and social purposes can enable us to devise new solutions for facilitating their educational journey. The learner-centric touchpoints solution (Wong, 2012) can facilitate engaging students more closely with course implementation, selecting the best channels for engagement, and constructing a friendlier educational environment.

Figure 6. Students' experience of freedom through digital channels

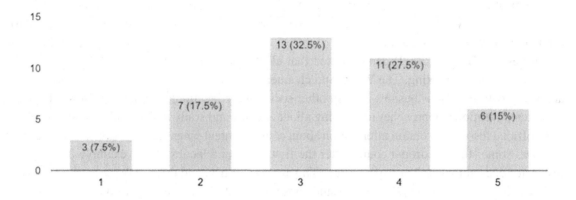

I have more freedom at the school because of SM

40 responses

Smart phones have become popular among students as potential educational tools, and they often use them to perform their educational tasks via a proper digital channel. As shown in Figure 2, smart phones (at 70%) are the most commonly used devices after laptops (at 92.5%). Mobile penetration is the result of the existence of services and applications that students can access on these devices to perform their daily and educational tasks. Furthermore, according to the interview analysis, none of the participants use any dedicated mobile learning applications. Instead, all participants utilize available digital channels, such as Moodle and search engines, and social media, such as WhatsApp, YouTube, GitHub, and Telegram, to perform their educational duties. This corresponds with our survey results, which surprisingly indicate that 15% of students still use the printed medium despite the fact that 2.5% of students use the printed medium in their personal lives. This finding echoes Casselden and Pears' (2019) investigation of students' preferences for using ebooks from academic libraries. It also aligns with Kay and Lauricella's (2011) findings regarding the benefits of soft copy note-taking, as opposed to hard copy note-taking, for students.

We identified that students' course and study path selections often go through several stages. The course selection starts with the awareness of a potential course, which happens either through individual course planning or through course curricula recommended by educational institutions. The findings reveal that the existing online information was good for generating awareness about courses, but it was insufficient for making decisions about courses and study paths. Awareness is associated with previous experience regarding a topic, personal interest in a study path, or the fact that course names in the selected study path appeal to students. In all cases, the results indicate that printed or online course curricula do not provide sufficient information to students. Moore and Shulock (2011) showed that supporting students in selecting their study program promotes program completion.

Furthermore, Hoad et al. (2017) revealed that media affects students' major selection. Their findings indicated that mediated referents and news following resulted in students choosing to study journalism, while others selected, for example, communications-related majors. In the present study, we also identified the impact of social media on study path selection. The survey and interview results indicate that social and community channels have become important tools for course and study path selections.

Furthermore, students often establish a WhatsApp group for organizing social activities and sharing course information when they start university, and they do not invite lecturers or other staff into these groups. Our findings also validate previous research on the use of WhatsApp among students, such as that of Bouhnik and Deshen (2014), who identified four main reasons why students use WhatsApp: communicating with peers, socializing, initiating dialogue, and encouragement. Similarly, we identified that students use WhatsApp to get acquainted, socialize, and exchange ideas about a course, and to help each other with course assignments.

Steffes and Burgee (2009) demonstrated that electronic word of mouth (eWOM) communication influences decision-making. The WhatsApp channel also functions as eWOM in the context of course and study path selections besides playing other social and educational supporting roles. In addition to these unconventional approaches to learning about courses and study paths, students often use Moodle as an official resource to obtain information about course content when participation is approved by their lecturer. Some students drop a course after the first or second lecture if, for example, the topic or the instructor does not meet their expectations. This process of trial and error, moving back and forth from different courses, can often result in the student missing out on the whole period or semester. Dropout from a course or from school is an important issue that has been widely investigated by researchers such as Dekker, Pechenizkiy, and Vleeshouwers (2009) and Bayer, Bydžovská, Géryk, Obšívač, and Popelínský (2012). Our findings indicate that social media through sharing information reduces trial and error dropout from courses.

The interview and survey show that students often use various digital channels and means, such as WhatsApp, WOM, Moodle, search engines, Facebook, and YouTube, to get help, develop skills, perform educational activities, and carry out group work (see Figure 3). As U3 noted, "For group work, we use Facebook in some project-based courses," which Hew (2011) also identified. In addition, U4 stated, "Often, I use YouTube to learn further, specifically in [my] programming course," which aligns with the findings of Moghavvemi, Sulaiman, Jaafar, and Kasem (2018) regarding students' use of this digital channel in the educational context. However, the aforementioned digital channel usage depends on the stage of the course, the context, and the content of the course.

Research on social media usage in the educational context is on the rise. For example, researchers are investigating how social media helps students adjust to college (e.g., Deandrea, Ellison, Larose, Steinfield, and Fiore, 2012), the role of social media in students' academic performance (Media, 2015), and the impact of social media on students' grades and engagement (Junco Heiberger, and Loken, 2011). In our study, we focused on the role of social media in students' study path and major selections. The analysis indicates that students use various digital channels in selecting their study paths (see Figure 5). Aligning with the categories of digital touchpoints identified by Straker et al. (2015), we found that the course curriculum (used by 62.5%) represents the corporate touchpoint (which we can rename as the organizational touchpoint in an educational context). It delivers university-generated content and this content and use are controlled by the educational organization. Search engines (used by 47.5%) and WOM (used by 37.5%) are the second and third most-used channels. Search engines represent "functional digital" channels, which offer means for finding and consuming digital content. Friends, teachers, study advisors, and university events represent social or community channels, which enable students to communicate. Students use digital social channels, such as YouTube (17.5%), WhatsApp (10%), and Facebook (10%), most frequently to communicate or develop their competencies. Our third research question focused on the major opportunities and challenges associated with the range of channels. We found that digital channels must connect to the study path because their role varies depending on the phase of the study path.

Before they make their course selection, students tend to have different needs and demands for finding information and communicating about the study path for which they have a passion.

The survey and semi-structured interview analyses revealed that course and study path selections are carried out on the basis of what is depicted in Figure 5. That is, the first phase is awareness of the course through online materials, WOM, and social networking channels. This phase attracts the initial attention of most students before they begin their course and study path selections. During the next stage, which we call the "consideration phase," students use channels such as WhatsApp, search engines, and YouTube to collect further information in order to choose or drop a course. During the next phase, students select a course and start to develop competence on the topic by attending lectures. Moreover, students often use WhatsApp, email, Facebook, and YouTube for projects and group work and to understand the learning materials more efficiently. Figure 7 presents the course and study path selection process.

Figure 7. The process of study path selection and common digital channel use

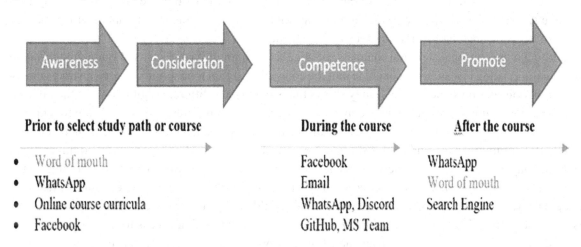

After taking a course, those students who have gained sufficient knowledge will promote the course to their peers. Therefore, social media as an enhanced tool in the educational context constructs Hirschi's (1969) social bonding among students.

Finally, this study revealed that students rarely use printed materials prior to or during their studies (even those materials that instructors hand out during lectures).

A major challenge associated with social media usage in the educational context is the number of social media applications that students have at their disposal. This variation confused students as to which one would be the best application for their purposes. The second major challenge is the fragmentation of social media applications, such as using WhatsApp for communication, Google Docs for sharing files, and GitHub for sharing codes. Therefore, a dedicated social networking application is needed to cover the essential needs of students.

This study focused on students' opinions of the role of social media at BITe. We applied a qualitative research methodology including a semi-structured interview and survey to answer the research questions. These two methods complemented each other for gathering and analyzing data from the target group. Therefore, we consider the findings to be valid and reliable.

CONCLUSION

Technological advancements have always impacted educational institutions' strategic planning and educational offerings. Today, students perform their educational duties through different digital channels and by applying various digital tools. During course and study path selection, students go through various phases, such as awareness, consideration, competence, and promotion. In each of these phases, students often use relevant digital channels depending on the nature of the task at hand. These digital channels, such as WhatsApp, Facebook, and Discord, are not primarily intended for educational purposes. However, these tools have become part of the educational performance toolkit. Thus, students learn and study in a multi-channel learning environment where they use functional, social, community, and organizational touchpoints for finding information, communicating, making decisions, and completing course assignments. Some educational institutions provide their own digital channels, but many of the channels that students use are their own selections and are outside the control of educational institutions and faculty. The latest developments in digital channel usage indicate that we are moving away from a single smart device service or application and heading toward multiple touchpoints that interact in a chain of decision-making toward a collective digital channel.

Although the concepts of digital channels and digital touchpoints have been used synonymously quite often in the existing research, we conclude that the concept of digital touchpoints better illustrates the use of digital tools among students. This study shows that students use different digital tools in the different phases of their studies, and they have many options to choose from. Thus, digital tools are touchpoints for the formal education process, courses, and administrative tasks rather than official channels. Physical and digital communication and administration are now blended as students seamlessly combine digital tools and physical encounters to facilitate retrieving and sharing information. Therefore, we suggest that more research be done on digital touchpoints as part of the physical activities and encounters that raise students' awareness of their educational context. This could clarify the role of channels and touchpoints, as the concept of "channels" refers more to an official way of obtaining access to the service provider and "touchpoint" connotes integrated and non-formal ways of carrying out everyday tasks in the blended digital and physical world.

As a future study, we plan to expand this research with other degree programs. Collecting more data will enable us to generalize our findings.

REFERENCES

Al-Qaysi, N., & Al-Emran, M. (2017). Code-switching usage in social media: A case study from Oman. *International Journal of Information Technology and Language Studies*.

Arcidiacono, P., Hotz, V. J., & Kang, S. (2012). Modeling college major choices using elicited measures of expectations and counterfactuals. *Journal of Econometrics*, *166*(1), 3–16. Advance online publication. doi:10.1016/j.jeconom.2011.06.002

Bachl, S., Tomitsch, M., Wimmer, C., & Grechenig, T. (2010). Challenges for designing the user experience of multi-touch interfaces. *Workshop on Engineering Patterns for Multi-Touch Interfaces*.

Baxendale, S., Macdonald, E. K., & Wilson, H. N. (2015). The impact of different touchpoints on brand consideration. *Journal of Retailing*, *91*(2), 235–253. Advance online publication. doi:10.1016/j. jretai.2014.12.008

Bayer, J., Bydžovská, H., Géryk, J., Obšívač, T., & Popelínský, L. (2012). Predicting drop-out from social behaviour of students. *Proceedings of the 5th International Conference on Educational Data Mining, EDM 2012.*

Bishop, J. H., Bishop, M., Gelbwasser, L., Green, S., & Zuckerman, A. (2003). *Nerds and freaks: A theory of student culture and norms.* Brookings Papers on Education Policy., doi:10.1353/pep.2003.0002

Bouhnik, D., & Deshen, M. (2014). WhatsApp goes to school: Mobile instant messaging between teachers and students. *Journal of Information Technology Education*, *13*, 217–231. Advance online publication. doi:10.28945/2051

BroadbandSearch. (2020). *Average time spent daily on social media (latest 2020 data).* Retrieved from https://www.broadbandsearch.net/blog/average-daily-time-on-social-media

Bryan, J., Moore-Thomas, C., Gaenzle, S., Kim, J., Lin, C. H., & Na, G. (2012). The effects of school bonding on high school Seniors' academic achievement. *Journal of Counseling and Development*, *90*(4), 467–480. Advance online publication. doi:10.1002/j.1556-6676.2012.00058.x

Burke, M., Marlow, C., & Lento, T. (2010). Social network activity and social well-being. *Conference on Human Factors in Computing Systems - Proceedings.* 10.1145/1753326.1753613

Cao, Q., Lu, Y., Dong, D., Tang, Z., & Li, Y. (2013). The roles of bridging and bonding in social media communities. *Journal of the American Society for Information Science and Technology*, *64*(8), 1671–1681. Advance online publication. doi:10.1002/asi.22866

Capuano, N., Mangione, G. R., Pierri, A., & Salerno, S. (2014). Personalization and contextualization of learning experiences based on semantics. *International Journal of Emerging Technologies in Learning*, *9*(7), 5–14. doi:10.3991/ijet.v9i7.3666

Casselden, B., & Pears, R. (2019). Higher education student pathways to ebook usage and engagement, and understanding: Highways and cul de sacs. *Journal of Librarianship and Information Science.* Advance online publication. doi:10.1177/0961000619841429

Chen, X. A., Grossman, T., Wigdor, D. J., & Fitzmaurice, G. (2014). Duet: Exploring joint interactions on a smart phone and a smart watch. *Proceedings of the 32nd Annual ACM Conference on Human Factors in Computing Systems - CHI '14*, 159–168. 10.1145/2556288.2556955

Cleveland-Innes, M., Ally, M., Wark, N., & Fung, T. (2013). Emotional presence and mobile learning: Learner-driven responses in a wireless world. *European Journal of Open, Distance and E-Learning*, *16*(2).

Cohen, D., & Crabtree, B. (2006). *Semi-structured interviews recording semi-structured interviews.* Qualitative Research Guidelines Project.

Deandrea, D. C., Ellison, N. B., Larose, R., Steinfield, C., & Fiore, A. (2012). Serious social media: On the use of social media for improving students' adjustment to college. *Internet and Higher Education*, *15*(1), 15–23. Advance online publication. doi:10.1016/j.iheduc.2011.05.009

Dekker, G. W., Pechenizkiy, M., & Vleeshouwers, J. M. (2009). Predicting students drop out: A case study. *EDM'09 - Educational Data Mining 2009: 2nd International Conference on Educational Data Mining.*

Dirin, A., Alamäki, A., & Suomala, J. (2019). Gender differences in perceptions of conventional video, virtual reality and augmented reality. *International Journal of Interactive Mobile Technologies.* doi:10.3991/ijim.v13i06.10487

Dirin, A., & Nieminen, M. (2018). The three eras of mobile learning user experience. In *Communications in Computer and Information Science* (vol. 865, pp. 207–220). Retrieved from

Dumpit, D. Z., & Fernandez, C. J. (2017). Analysis of the use of social media in higher education institutions (HEIs) using the technology acceptance model. *International Journal of Educational Technology in Higher Education.* doi:10.1186/s41239-017-0045-2

Fink, A. (2010). Survey research methods. In International Encyclopedia of Education. doi:10.1016/B978-0-08-044894-7.00296-7

Fu, J. S. (2013). ICT in education: A critical literature review and its implications. *International Journal of Education and Development Using Information and Communication Technology, 9*(1), 112–125.

Hallikainen, H., Alamäki, A., & Laukkanen, T. (2018). Individual preferences of digital touchpoints: A latent class analysis. *Journal of Retailing and Consumer Services.* doi:10.1016/j.jretconser.2018.07.014

Hew, K. F. (2011). Students' and teachers' use of Facebook. *Computers in Human Behavior, 27*(2), 662–676. Advance online publication. doi:10.1016/j.chb.2010.11.020

Hirschi, T. (1969). *Causes of Delinquency.* Academic Press.

Hoag, A., Grant, A. E., & Carpenter, S. (2017). Impact of media on major choice: Survey of communication undergraduates. *NACADA Journal, 37*(1), 5–14. Advance online publication. doi:10.12930/NACADA-15-040

Huang, R. T., Jang, S. J., Machtmes, K., & Deggs, D. (2012). Investigating the roles of perceived playfulness, resistance to change and self-management of learning in mobile English learning outcome. *British Journal of Educational Technology, 43*(6), 1004–1015. doi:10.1111/j.1467-8535.2011.01239.x

Jin, L., Chen, Y., Wang, T., Hui, P., & Vasilakos, A. V. (2013). Understanding user behavior in online social networks: A survey. *Communications Magazine, IEEE, 51*(9), 144–150. doi:10.1109/MCOM.2013.6588663

Junco, R., Heiberger, G., & Loken, E. (2011). The effect of Twitter on college student engagement and grades. *Journal of Computer Assisted Learning, 27*(2), 119–132. Advance online publication. doi:10.1111/j.1365-2729.2010.00387.x

Kannan, P. K., & Li, H. A. (2017). Digital marketing: A framework, review and research agenda. *International Journal of Research in Marketing, 34*(1), 22–45. Advance online publication. doi:10.1016/j.ijresmar.2016.11.006

Kaur, S. (2017). Use of WhatsApp instant messenger among undergraduate degree students of D.A.V. College Pundri (Kaithal) Haryana: A study. *International Journal of Information Movement.*

Kay, R. H., & Lauricella, S. (2011). *Exploring the benefits and challenges of using laptop computers in higher education classrooms: A formative analysis.* Canadian Journal of Learning and Technology/La Revue Canadienne de l'Apprentissage et de la Technologie., doi:10.21432/t2s598

Khanna, M., Jacob, I., & Yadav, N. (2014). Identifying and analyzing touchpoints for building a higher education brand. *Journal of Marketing for Higher Education, 24*(1), 122–143. Advance online publication. doi:10.1080/08841241.2014.920460

Khodarahimi, S., & Fathi, R. (2017). The role of online social networking on emotional functioning in a sample of Iranian adolescents and young adults. *Journal of Technology in Human Services, 35*(2), 120–134. Advance online publication. doi:10.1080/15228835.2017.1293587

Kumar, V., & Nanda, P. (2018). Social media in higher education. *International Journal of Information and Communication Technology Education.* Advance online publication. doi:10.4018/ijicte.2019010107

Kumar, V., & Nanda, P. (2019). Social media in higher education: A framework for continuous engagement. *International Journal of Information and Communication Technology Education, 15*(1), 97–108. Advance online publication. doi:10.4018/IJICTE.2019010107

Li, F., Qi, J., Wang, G., & Wang, X. (2014). Traditional classroom vs e-learning in higher education: Difference between students' behavioral engagement. *International Journal of Emerging Technologies in Learning, 9*(2), 48–51. doi:10.3991/ijet.v9i2.3268

Livesey, C. (2010). *Focused (semi-structured) interviews.* Sociology Central.

Longhurst, R. (2010). Semi-structured interviews and focus groups. *Journal of Chemical Information and Modeling.* Advance online publication. doi:10.1017/CBO9781107415324.004

Lu, J., & Churchill, D. (2013). The effect of social interaction on learning engagement in a social networking environment. doi:10.1080/10494820.2012.680966

Määttä, K., & Uusiautti, S. (2011). How to enhance the smoothness of university students' study paths? *International Journal of Research Studies in Education.* doi:10.5861/ijrse.2012.v1i1.16

Malgwi, C. A., Howe, M. A., & Burnaby, P. A. (2005). Influences on students' choice of college major. *Journal of Education for Business, 80*(5), 275–282. Advance online publication. doi:10.3200/JOEB.80.5.275-282

Media, S. (2015). Social media and academic performance: Does the intensity of Facebook activity relate to good grades? *Schmalenbach Business Review.*

Ministry of Education and Culture. (2010). *Student survey 2010—University students' subsistence and studying.* Retrieved from http://www.minedu.fi/OPM/Julkaisut/2010/Opiskelijatutkimus_2010.html

Moghavvemi, S., Sulaiman, A., Jaafar, N. I., & Kasem, N. (2018). Social media as a complementary learning tool for teaching and learning: The case of YouTube. *International Journal of Management Education, 16*(1), 37–42. Advance online publication. doi:10.1016/j.ijme.2017.12.001

Montag, C., Błaszkiewicz, K., Sariyska, R., Lachmann, B., Andone, I., Trendafilov, B., Eibes, M., & Markowetz, A. (2015). Smartphone usage in the 21st century: Who is active on WhatsApp? *BMC Research Notes*, *8*(1), 331. Advance online publication. doi:10.118613104-015-1280-z PMID:26238512

Moore, C., & Shulock, N. (2011). *Sense of direction: The importance of helping community college students select and enter a program of study.* Institute for Higher Education Leadership & Policy, CSU Sacramento.

Nguyen, N., Muilu, T., Dirin, A., & Alamäki, A. (2018). An interactive and augmented learning concept for orientation week in higher education. *International Journal of Educational Technology in Higher Education*, *15*(1), 35. Advance online publication. doi:10.118641239-018-0118-x

Peguero, A. A., Ovink, S. M., & Li, L. Y. (2016). Social bonding to school and educational inequality: Race/ethnicity, dropping out, and the significance of place. *Sociological Perspectives*. Advance online publication. doi:10.1177/0731121415586479

Phua, J., Jin, S. V., & Kim, J. (2017). Uses and gratifications of social networking sites for bridging and bonding social capital: A comparison of Facebook, Twitter, Instagram, and Snapchat. *Computers in Human Behavior*, *72*, 115–122. Advance online publication. doi:10.1016/j.chb.2017.02.041

Piaget, J., & Brown, T. (1985). The equilibration of cognitive structures: The central problem of intellectual development. *American Journal of Education.* Advance online publication. doi:10.1002ce.3730610403

Rehm, M., & Notten, A. (2016). Twitter as an informal learning space for teachers!? The role of social capital in Twitter conversations among teachers. *Teaching and Teacher Education*, *60*, 215–223. doi:10.1016/j.tate.2016.08.015

Salmela-Aro, K., & Read, S. (2017). Study engagement and burnout profiles among Finnish higher education students. *Burnout Research*, *7*, 21–28. Advance online publication. doi:10.1016/j.burn.2017.11.001

Selwyn, N. (2011). Education & technology. Key issues & debates. *Neurological Sciences: Official Journal of the Italian Neurological Society and of the Italian Society of Clinical Neurophysiology.*

Seraj, M., & Wong, C. Y. (2014). Lecturers and students' perception on learning Dijkstra's shortest path algorithm through mobile devices. *International Journal of Interactive Mobile Technologies*, *8*(3), 19–24. doi:10.3991/ijim.v8i3.3745

Skaniakos, T., Penttinen, L., & Lairio, M. (2014). Peer group mentoring programmes in Finnish higher education—Mentors' perspectives. *Mentoring & Tutoring*, *22*(1), 74–86. Advance online publication. doi:10.1080/13611267.2014.882609

Steffes, E. M., & Burgee, L. E. (2009). Social ties and online word of mouth. *Internet Research*, *19*(1), 42–59. Advance online publication. doi:10.1108/10662240910927812

Story, D. A., & Tait, A. R. (2019). Survey research. *Anesthesiology*, *130*(2), 192–202. Advance online publication. doi:10.1097/ALN.0000000000002436 PMID:30688782

Straker, K., & Wrigley, C. (2016). Emotionally engaging customers in the digital age: The case study of "Burberry love.". *Journal of Fashion Marketing and Management*, *20*(3), 276–299. Advance online publication. doi:10.1108/JFMM-10-2015-0077

Straker, K., Wrigley, C., & Rosemann, M. (2015). Typologies and touchpoints: Designing multi-channel digital strategies. *Journal of Research in Interactive Marketing, 9*(2), 110–128. Advance online publication. doi:10.1108/JRIM-06-2014-0039

Studyinfo.fi. (n.d.). *Finnish universities of applied sciences (UAS)*. Retrieved from https://studyinfo.fi/wp2/en/higher-education/polytechnics-universities-of-applied-sciences/

Sutikno, T., Handayani, L., Stiawan, D., Riyadi, M. A., & Subroto, I. M. I. (2016). WhatsApp, Viber and Telegram: Which is the best for instant messaging? *International Journal of Electrical and Computer Engineering*. doi:10.11591/ijece.v6i3.10271

Terras, M. M., & Ramsay, J. (2012). The five central psychological challenges facing effective mobile learning. *British Journal of Educational Technology, 43*(5), 820–832. doi:10.1111/j.1467-8535.2012.01362.x

Watermeyer, R. (2010). Social network science: Pedagogy, dialogue, deliberation. *Journal of Science Communication, 9*(1), 1–9. doi:10.22323/2.09010204

Wiswall, M., & Zafar, B. (2013). Determinants of college major choice: Identification using an information experiment. *The Review of Economic Studies*. Advance online publication. doi:10.1093/restud/rdu044

Wong, L. H. (2012). A learner-centric view of mobile seamless learning. *British Journal of Educational Technology, 43*(1), E19–E23. Advance online publication. doi:10.1111/j.1467-8535.2011.01245.x

Workman, J. L. (2015). Parental influence on exploratory students' college choice, major, and career decision making. *College Student Journal*.

This research was previously published in the International Journal of Information and Communication Technology Education (IJICTE), 17(1); pages 88-104, copyright year 2021 by IGI Publishing (an imprint of IGI Global).

Chapter 85
Effects of Social Network Information on Online Language Learning Performance: A Cross-Continental Experiment

Abrar Al-Hasan
https://orcid.org/0000-0002-1662-6417
Kuwait University, Kuwait

ABSTRACT

This study examines the value and impact of social network information on a user's language learning performance by conducting an online experiment in a peer-to-peer collaborative language learning marketplace. Social information or information about others in one's network can present a socially networked learning environment that enables learners to engage more in the learning process. Experimental research design in an online language learning marketplace was conducted. The study finds evidence that the mere visibility of social network information positively impacts a learner's learning performance. Learners that engage with social interaction perform better than those that do not. In addition, active social interaction has a stronger impact on learning performance as compared to passive social interaction. The study concludes with implications for platform developers to enable the visibility of social information and engineer the user experience to enhance interactive learning.

INTRODUCTION

Web 2.0 technologies such as e-learning platforms, podcasts, social network sites, mobile applications, and online learning marketplaces are now used as a source of language learning (Godwin-Jones, 2018). Web 2.0 learning tools have helped in making foreign languages more easily accessible and offer endless possibilities for authentic interaction with native speakers in any target language (Sylv & Sundqvist, 2017).

In the past decade, the potential link between Web 2.0 learning tools and language learning has been frequently examined and has been a subject of debate (Alhamami, 2019; Shadiev, Hwang, & Huang, 2017; Y.-F. Yang, 2018). A meta-analysis of this stream of research found that the relationship between the use of Web 2.0 tools and language learning performance is weak and inconclusive in terms of direc-

DOI: 10.4018/978-1-6684-7123-4.ch085

tion and substantial effect (Luo, 2013; Parmaxi & Zaphiris, 2017). On one hand, studies have found that technological innovations can increase learner interest, pleasing value, and motivation (Chang, Chen, & Chiang, 2019; Collins & Halverson, 2018), providing students with increased access to the target language (Ahn & Lee, 2016), providing new learning opportunities for the unfortunate (Schröder, Grüttner, & Berg, 2019), providing increased engagement opportunities (Batanero, de-Marcos, Holvikivi, Hilera, & Otón, 2019), and facilitating peer learning (Lim, Ab Jalil, Ma'rof, & Saad, 2020). On the other hand, studies have found that the use of Web 2.0 learning tools can result in inappropriate input, shallow interaction (Anshari, Almunawar, Shahrill, Wicaksono, & Huda, 2017), inaccurate feedback, frustration with the digital channel (Fisher, Howardson, Wasserman, & Orvis, 2017), and distraction from the learning task (Garcia, Falkner, & Vivian, 2018). With empirical evidence supporting both sides, it is difficult to see the nature of the actual relationship. The findings thus far seem to suggest that different types of Web 2.0 tools, designs, and use relate to differential impacts on learning performance (Parmaxi & Zaphiris, 2017; C. Wang, Fang, & Gu, 2020). Whether or not Web 2.0 learning tools fosters or undermines language learning remains a topic of discussion among scholars (Luo, 2013; Parmaxi & Zaphiris, 2017), and in particular, the design characteristics that promote learning in Web 2.0 learning tools is not yet clear (Gray, Thompson, Sheard, Clerehan, & Hamilton, 2010).

One popular and growing Web 2.0 learning tool is online language learning marketplaces (OLLMs) such as Babbel, Busuu, and Duolingo, where users can teach each other languages. These OLLMs allow for social information visibility. Users' learning network, performance activities of a user and his friends, how well the user is doing against others in the community, along with other related information - is all made visible. This type of information is social information – information about others in one's network. OLLMs have a choice of two broad information-provisioning strategies (Parmaxi & Zaphiris, 2017). These marketplaces can continue to target potential consumers using traditional "non-social" formats such as regular courses, quizzes, etc., or adopt emerging "social formats" such as the visibility of peers' performance, the interaction with peers, the newsfeeds from peers, etc. While firms are actively experimenting with both "social" and "non-social" information-provisioning formats, there is a dearth of research to guide decision making in this context (Chakowa, 2018; Gray et al., 2010). Furthermore, "social" collaboration and interaction on language learning has been examined on mainly Blogs and Wikis (Luo, 2013), studies have not yet examined OLLMs which have altered the level of interaction among users and the number of languages that can be learned. A current meta-analysis has highlighted the need to further investigate such emerging marketplaces (Parmaxi & Zaphiris, 2017). Understanding how social information can impact one's language learning performance in OLLMs remains a wide gap in the existing literature. Furthermore, while interaction has been commonly examined through English as the taught language, how Web 2.0 learning tools respond to less commonly taught languages are largely unknown (Luo, 2013).

The present study seeks to address the gap in the literature by investigating the relationship among the OLLM design characteristics and language learning performance by empirically examining the value of "social information" and social interaction on learning performance. This study seeks to examine the value and impact of "social information"—wherein, a user sees and interacts with the learning activities of her peers—on his language learning proficiency. This study will help academics better understand the relationship between Web 2.0 learning tools and learning effectiveness by examining factors that have been overlooked; the "social" design factor in an understudied emerging marketplace. This study responds to the call for research for such marketplaces, and in particular, for languages other than English (Luo, 2013). The findings of this study will enable e-learning platform providers and Web 2.0 tool designers to value the effectiveness of "social information," and will identify the types of information or viral product design features that impact use, effectiveness, and ultimately sales.

THEORETICAL BACKGROUND

This study draws upon two broad streams of literature. The first relates to research on Web 2.0 learning tools, educational benefits, and language learning. The second relates to social information and its impact on user behavior.

Web 2.0 Education and Language Learning

Digital environments such as weblogs, wikis, online social communities, and online learning marketplaces are providing learners with new opportunities to engage with native speakers through original content and conversations (Gilmore, 2007). Web 2.0 learning technologies has blurred the role of producers and consumers of content and has shifted the learning culture from access to information toward access to other people (Brown & Adler, 2008). Students now take an active role in learning, rather than passively receive information from instructors. Web 2.0 has the potential to create more interactive and powerful learning environments in which learners become knowledge creators (Henry, Carroll, Cunliffe, & Kop, 2018; Richardson, 2010). Web 2.0 technologies facilitate personalized learning and enable the creation of personal learning environments where individuals can take control of and manage their learning and interact with others in the process of learning (Attwell, 2019; Xu, Chan, & Yilin, 2018).

Studies have sought to understand the benefits of Web 2.0 technologies in foreign language teaching and learning, especially in terms of fostering increased learner autonomy and promoting interaction and collaboration (Hung & Huang, 2016; Y. Yang, Crook, & O'Malley, 2014). Studies report increased motivation for learning (Liu et al., 2013; Stevenson & Liu, 2010), and interest in language learning (Chartrand, 2012). Other studies have focused on identifying usability issues and interface design (Stevenson & Liu, 2010). In a study by Brick (2013), language learners were pleased by the unique design features provided by the online learning marketplace to practice their oral skills with native speakers and to receive immediate peer feedback. Prichard (2013) examined the effectiveness of training learners on how to use Facebook safely and effectively for language learning purposes. Another study (Orsini-Jones, Brick, & Pibworth, 2013) reported concern regarding language variety and reliability of user corrections in online learning marketplaces. However, it is still not clear how effective digital instructional tools are (Parmaxi & Zaphiris, 2017); much insight is needed on the facilitative effects of site design for learning (Liu et al., 2013). This study furthers this stream of research by exploring the effectiveness of digital language learning marketplaces and by examining and comparing differing interface design features that promotes learning effectiveness.

Social Information and Social Influence

Social constructivists view learning not just as an individual process, but an ongoing process of knowledge construction within a social environment (Lantolf, 2000). Under this framework, learning is participatory, knowledge is social, and language develops via shared activities (Bronack, Riedl, & Tashner, 2006). This view draws upon social influence theory as a means of learning (Goyal, Bonchi, & Lakshmanan,

2010; Young, 2009). Social influence is when individuals are affected by the opinion and behaviors of others (Kelman, 1958). This study focuses on two closely related streams of research: the first being social information processing theory and the second focusing on how peer effects impact user behavior.

Social Information Processing Theory

Social information processing theory proposes that individuals may be influenced by cues from others about what to attend to, how to value the important dimensions of a phenomenon, and how others evaluate the same phenomena (Salancik & Pfeffer, 1978). Different sources of information have different impacts on outcomes. Social sources of information are more likely to influence a user's attitude than non-social sources of information (Burt, 2017; Leary & Baumeister, 2017). Examining the role of social influence on consumers' pre-purchase search efforts (Y. Wang & Yu, 2017) show that information received from sources that have some personal knowledge about the consumer have more influence than sources that have no personal knowledge about the consumer.

This study seeks to take the social information processing theory a step forward by empirically analyzing the effectiveness of OLLMs through the increase in visibility of social information. The study also examines how different degrees of social information impacts the effectiveness of online language learning.

Peer Effects and Social Interaction

Current advances in technology have significantly increased the importance of consumer social interactions as a market force. There is growing evidence that social media allows firms to engage with customers more efficiently than do traditional marketing channels. Not only are consumers now better able to exchange information, but firms are also gaining the ability to directly initiate and manage consumer social interactions (Ascarza et al., 2018; Wang & Kim, 2017). While advances in technology are creating new opportunities for firms to directly facilitate and manage consumer social interactions, they also impose new challenges. Distinct strategic managerial actions are often necessary for such new social marketplaces. Deciding on the type of information presented to consumers is a crucial decision that will influence a firm's profitability and positioning (Chen, Wang, & Xie, 2011; Kim, Zhu, Xiao, & Lin, 2017).

This study seeks to take the literature on peer effects a step forward by empirically observing and analyzing the reception of peer effects on individual learning performance in an OLLM. The study also examines how the different types of peer effects and social interaction impacts the effectiveness of online language learning.

Research Model and Hypotheses

Figure 1 displays the conceptual research model. Following the research objectives and in line with the social constructivists' view of learning, social information processing theory, and peer effects literature, individuals are influenced by social sources of information and social interaction (Rice & Aydin, 1991; B. Yang, Lei, Liu, & Li, 2017) and are therefore modeled as determinants of learning. Learning performance is used as the outcome variable as it is used to assess the effectiveness of the knowledge attained through assessment and evaluation (Rosenberg & Foshay, 2002; Zhu, 2012).

Figure 1. Conceptual model

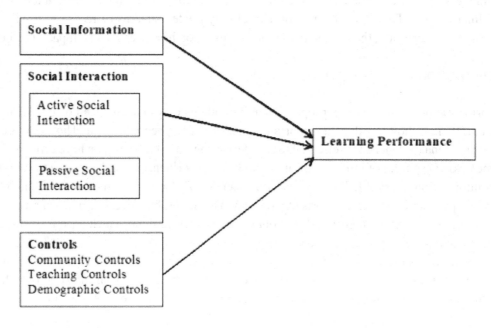

Effects of Social Information on Learning Performance

According to social information processing theory, peer effects, and social constructivist' view of learning, individuals are influenced by social sources of information, as they are perceived to be more trustworthy (B. Yang et al., 2017). The influence of a peer to learn will also be stronger than the influence of a regular platform with no visibility of what other peers are doing (J. Yang, 2016). In networked social spaces, users with different interests are encouraged to improve their abilities and to 'contribute to distributed knowledge' from which everyone in the community can benefit (Gee, 2012). Such networked social spaces allow users to support and encourage each other and socially construct knowledge together (Kelm, 2011). This study proposes that OLLMs that make social information visible will influence a learners' performance more positively towards learning.

Hypothesis 1: Learning performance is higher when social information is presented as compared with the non-presentation of social information in the online language learning marketplace.

Effects of Social Interaction on Learning Performance

Language learners can learn by being the readers, writers, speakers, listeners, and thinkers in the classroom through engagement in social interaction with their peers (Vacca, Vacca, & Mraz, 2016). Learners can learn more when they can talk to one another and be actively involved (Routman, 2005). Social constructivist approaches to language learning and teaching encourage the integration of different language skills through social interaction (Harrison & Thomas, 2009). Within their shared space, learners have the opportunity to offer personal insights and obtain alternative perspectives (Bonk & King, 2012). Learners engage in the co-construction of knowledge during collaborative activities (Duffy & Cunningham, 1996).

This study hypothesizes that social interaction with peers is vital to the learning process. Such that the more a user engages and interacts with peers, the stronger the impact on their learning performance.

Hypothesis 2a: Users that engage in social interaction in the online language learning marketplace are associated with higher learning performance as compared to users that do not engage in social interaction.

Social interaction with peers is of two folds: active and passive (Johansson, 1989; Persson, Wanek, & Johansson, 2001). According to Persson et al. (2001) definition, active social interaction is distinguished from the passive social interaction by the predominance of monitoring tasks. If most of the tasks are monitoring tasks, rather than tasks such a prediction, planning, etc., then the work is considered passive work. The "activeness" of a user is a result of task allocation between the user and the technology. Literature suggests that passive users may face problems in highly automated environments (Cummings, Mason, Shelton, & Baur, 2017; Mitchell, Petter, & Harris, 2017).

Learner control and learner activity in the education workplace has been shown to add more value to knowledge as compared to receiving feedback (Brick, 2013). Learner control and activity may lead to positive results because it is a way of allowing learners to exert their influence on knowledge without trainer control (Chou & Liu, 2005). Such active learning interaction and activity has a stronger impact on learning effectiveness as compared to passive learning interaction and activity.

In this study, active social interaction is when the user is in control of the social interaction such that the user is contributing towards the interaction; while passive social interaction is when there is no control of the social interaction, such that the user is monitoring the interaction rather than contributing towards the interaction. While a user can conduct both active and passive social interaction at the same time, the more active social interaction conducted the higher the learning performance as compared to passive social interaction.

Hypothesis 2b: Active social interaction in the online language learning marketplace will lead to higher learning performance as compared to passive social interaction.

DATA AND METHODOLOGY

The current study collaborated with one of the largest OLLMs to conduct a randomized experiment. This marketplace was founded in 2010 and teaches around 19 different languages. As of 2019, the marketplace has around 200 million active users, with an estimated value of $700 million. One thousand three hundred worldwide users that were interested in learning the Arabic language were randomly chosen from the marketplace to enroll in a free Arabic course. One thousand three hundred emails were sent out and 1032 members enrolled in the free Arabic course. The members were instructed that they had six weeks to complete the course. The course is composed of sub-units, units, and writing exercises. Thirty-two members did not even complete one sub-unit after six weeks and therefore were dropped from the sample.

The members were divided into two groups: a "social" group and a "non-social" group. The "social" group was able to see their "friends" learning performance and interact with them while the "non-social" control group was not able to see any "friends" or interact with them – no social information. Table 1 describes the details of the social information visibility for the groups. The "social" group was instructed to check the profiles of the other users in the course and add them as "friends." There was no limit to the number of "friends" they chose to add.

Table 1. Social information visibility

Social Group	Non-Social Group
Can Add Friends	Cannot Add Friends
Can See Friends Learning Performance (Percentage of Course Completion)	Cannot See Friends Learning Performance
Can Interact With Friends Through Posts and Writing Exercises	Cannot Interact With Friends

The social group had 600 users and the control group 400. The proportion of users assigned to the baseline was chosen in agreement with the community to obtain a population size enough to establish a comparative baseline. There was no significant mean difference between the two groups in terms of age, gender, and education level. The empirical model for the study is shown in the equation below:

Learning Performance = f(Social Information, Social Network Interaction, User Activity in the community, Teaching Performance, Demographics)   (1)

Learning performance is used to assess the effectiveness of the knowledge attained through assessment and evaluation (Rosenberg & Foshay, 2002; Zhu, 2012). Learning performance is measured as lower errors on tests (Chou & Liu, 2005). In the OLLM used in this study, after the completion of a learning unit, the learner needs to pass a short test and complete a writing exercise. Thus, learning performance in this study is measured using two assessment outcome variables: (1) number of completed learning units *(ln_units)* and (2) number of completed writing exercises *(ln_writing)*. The outcome variables were skewed; therefore, the logarithmic transformation was used. Social information is measured using a dummy variable that indicates whether the user can see "friends" *(friend_visibility)*. The ability to see "friends" and their information is social information (Sundararajan, Provost, Oestreicher-Singer, & Aral, 2013). Social interaction is measured using three variables: (1) total number of friends (*ttl_friends*), (2) number of corrections received on writing exercises from friends (*ttl_learn_writingcorrections_received*), and (3) total posts a user corrected for his friends (*ttl_posts_corrected*). The total number of friends (*ttl_friends*) and total posts a user corrects for his friends (*ttl_posts_corrected*) are both considered active social interaction since the user has control over the number of friends being added and is actively participating when posting corrections. On the other hand, the total number of corrections received from friends (*ttl_learn_writingcorrections_received*) is considered passive social interaction as the user has no control over what is being received. Community-related metrics are also controlled for. Table 2 describes the variables used in this study.

To examine the impact of social information visibility, and different types of social interaction on learning performance, multiple regression is conducted. Given that the constructs of the model are single-item variables, it is recommended to use ordinary least squares (OLS) regression method (Nazim & Ahmad, 2013). OLS regressions using STATA version 11 was conducted to examine the impact of social information visibility and social interaction on the learning performance.

Table 2. Variables and description

Variable Name	Description
ln_units	Outcome Variable: Log (Number of completed learning units)
ln_writing	Outcome Variable: Log (Number of writing exercises completed)
friend_visibility	*Independent Variable: Social Information.* Binary, whether friends' performance is visible or not.
ttl_friends	*Independent Variable: Active Social Interaction.* Total number of friends.
ttl_posts_corrected	*Independent Variable: Active Social Interaction.* Total posts corrected for friends.
ttl_learn_writing_corrections_received	*Independent Variable: Passive Social Interaction.* The number of corrections received on writing exercises from friends.
mem_age	*Control Variable: User activity in the community.* Total number of days the member has been in the community.
ttl_group_mem	*Control Variable: User activity in the community.* Total number of community groups the member is part of.
ttl_group_leader	*Control Variable: User activity in the community.* Total number of community groups the member is a group leader of.
lastlogin_todate	*Control Variable: User activity in the community.* Last Login in the community till today's date or the date the data was collected.
ttl_spoken	*Control Variable: Teaching Performance.* Total number of languages spoken.
avg_spoken_lvl	*Control Variable: Teaching Performance.* Average Spoken Level (beginner = 1, intermediate = 2, advanced = 3).
Occupation	*Control Variable: Demographics* Categorical: Student, Working, Other, Undisclosed (Reference)
Age	*Control Variable: Demographics* Age of the member.
Gender	*Control Variable: Demographics* Gender of the member. Male (Reference).
rel_status	*Control Variable: Demographics* Relationship Status Categorical: in a relationship, single, prefer not to say, undisclosed (Reference).
Continent	*Control Variable: Demographics* Geographic Continent Categories: Africa, Asia, Australia, Europe, North America, South America, Undisclosed (Reference).

ANALYSIS AND RESULTS

Table 3 displays the descriptive statistics and their pairwise correlations for the main variables. There are a total of 28 units and 35 writing exercises. The data was taken six weeks later: 71% of the enrolled members completed the course, and the remaining did not complete the complete course. On average, the data finds that the members completed 22 out of the 28 units in the six-week period. On average, each member had 26 writing posts completed.

Table 3. Summary statistics and pairwise correlations on main variables

Variable	Obs	Mean	St. Dev.	Min	Max	(1)	(2)	(3)	(4)	(5)	(6)
(1) ln_units	1000	22.06	3.1	0	28	1					
(2) ln_writing	1000	26.36	3.07	0	35	0.39*	1				
(3) friend_visibility	1000	0.43	0.5	0	1	0.15*	0.14*	1			
(4) ttl_friends	1000	12.36	3.07	0	35	0.16*	0.19*	0.17*	1		
(5)ttl_learn_ writingcorrections_ received	1000	9.32	5.42	0	19	0.05	0.06	0.11	0.09	1	
(6) ttl_posts_corrected	1000	11.12	4.37	0	22	0.13*	0.12*	0.08	0.18*	0.12*	1

* Significant at p<0.001.

Table 4 shows the results of the OLS regression models for the two learning performance variables (*ln_writing* and *ln_units*). The results show that the *ln_writing* model explains around 42% of the variance, and the *ln_units* model explains around 58% of the variance. All independent variables in the model are statistically significant, and the value of AVE (Average Variance Extracted) for all constructs is greater than 0.50 showing that convergent validity was achieved at the required level. Fitness indices also met the required level (F/Chi-Sq= 2885.9) showing construct validity. The correlation between all constructs is lower than 0.85 showing that discriminant validity was satisfied at the required level. The value of Cronbach Alpha is greater than 0.60 showing the internal reliability was achieved at the required level.

The results show that the social information variable, *friend_visibility*, which indicates whether the user can see friends, is positively and significantly associated with learning performance variables ln_writing and ln_units ($\beta = 0.6388, p < 0.01; \beta = 0.5631, p < 0.01$, respectively). The result indicates that a user that can see social information from friends is associated with 63.88% more writing exercises completed and 56.31% more units completed as compared to a user that is not able to see social information from friends. This result highlights the importance of social information from friends in terms of learning performance. This finding indicates that the mere visibility of friends' information is positively associated with learning performance supporting hypothesis one.

The study further finds that the social interaction variables are all positive and significantly associated with learning performance variables. In particular, *ttl_friends* is positively and significantly associated with learning performance variables ln_writing and ln_units ($\beta = 0.1179, p < 0.01; \beta = 0.1158, p < 0.01$, respectively). The total number of corrections received from friends (*ttl_learn_writingcorrections_received*) is also positively and significantly associated with learning performance variables ln_writing and ln_units ($\beta = 0.0153, p < 0.01; \beta = 0.0128, p < 0.01$, respectively). Lastly, the total number of posts corrected by the user (*ttl_posts_corrected*) is also positively and significantly associated with learning performance variables ln_writing and ln_units ($\beta = 0.1199, p < 0.01; \beta = 0.1551, p < 0.01$, respectively). These results show that the group that was able to interact with friends performed better than the group that was not able to interact with friends. Also, the more a user interacts with friends, the higher the learning performance. This result shows the importance of the ability to interact and communicate when it comes to language learning. The more friends a user has to interact with, the higher the performance. Furthermore, the more a user corrects posts and receives corrections from his/her friends, the higher the users' performance, supporting hypothesis two-a.

Table 4. OLS regressions

OLS Regressions	Variable	(1) LN_WRITING	(2) LN_UNITS
Social Information	friend_visibility	0.6388*** (0.2195)	0.5631*** (0.1948)
Social Interaction – Active	ttl_friends	0.1179*** (0.0159)	0.1158*** (0.0152)
Social Interaction – Active	ttl_posts_corrected	0.1199*** (0.0146)	0.1551*** (0.0141)
Social Interaction – Passive	ttl_learn_writing corrections_received	0.0153*** (0.0032)	0.0128*** (0.0028)
Controls			
mem_age		0.1009*** (0.012)	0.0287** (0.0107)
ttl_group_member		-0.1509 (0.0794)	-0.0122 (0.0705)
ttl_group_leader		0.0384 (0.4367)	0.0188 (0.3877)
lastlogin_todate		-0.1202*** (0.0165)	-0.0396** (0.0146)
ttl_spoken		0.3846* (0.1898)	0.0356 (0.1685)
avg_spoken_lvl		0.3092 (0.2063)	0.0364 (0.1832)
Occupation_other		0.0498 (0.4133)	-0.4142 (0.3669)
Occupation_Working		-0.1789 (0.3324)	-0.1016 (0.2951)
Occupation_Student		0.1136 (0.3171)	0.1944 (0.2815)
age		0.0119 (0.0097)	0.0009 (0.0086)
gender_female		0.0258 (0.1739)	-0.0407 (0.1544)
rel_status_inaRelationship		0.2636 (0.3035)	0.3113 (0.2694)
rel_status_PreferNotToSay		0.2538 (0.3254)	0.5861 (0.3889)
rel_status_Single		0.2881 (0.2811)	0.5729 (0.3595)
Continent_Africa		1.1698 (2.7252)	-0.7816 (2.4192)
Continent_Asia		1.6375 (2.7138)	-0.7183 (2.4091)
Continent_Australia		0.3957 (3.0890)	-1.9489 (2.7421)
Continent_Europe		0.8112 (2.6798)	-1.4365 (2.3789)

continues on following page

Table 4. Continued

OLS Regressions	Variable	(1) LN_WRITING	(2) LN_UNITS
Continent_NorthAmerica		0.6105 (2.7085)	-1.7715 (2.4044)
Continent_SouthAmerica		0.8089 (2.6801)	-1.5847 (2.3792)
_cons		18.8465* (8.8385)	10.0476 (7.8461)
No. Observations		1000	1000
R-squared		0.4256	0.5818

*p< 0.10, **p< 0.05, ***p< 0.005. Standard errors shown in parentheses.

The coefficients for active social interaction variables are much higher than the passive social interaction variables for both dependent variables. A unit increase in the number of friends a user has is associated with an 11.79% increase in writing exercises completed and an 11.58% increase in the number of units completed. A unit increase in the number of posts corrected for friends is associated with an 11.99% increase in writing exercises completed and a 15.51% increase in the number of units completed. On the other hand, a unit increase in the total number of writing corrections received is associated with only a 1.53% increase in writing exercises completed and 1.28% in the number of units completed. These results support hypothesis two-b that active social interaction impacts learning performance more than passive social interaction.

DISCUSSION

This study examined the impact of social information and social interaction on language learning performance in the emerging OLLMs. The findings of this study provide interesting insights. The first finding indicates the importance of social information for language learning. The study finds that information attained from peers, particularly relating to information about a user's friends, or social information, significantly influences a user's online language learning performance. This highlights the importance of providing information about peers' performance as well as peers' activity to enhance one's performance. This study further finds that social interaction has an impact on learning performance. In particular, the higher the number of friends using the learning platform, the higher the user's learning performance. This finding highlights the importance of having "friends" and interacting with friends to enhance one's learning performance. Active social interaction has a stronger impact on learning performance as compared to passive social interaction. This result shows that the "activeness" dimension of social interactivity is an important determinant of learning performance in such OLLMs.

The results of this study have interesting implications for firms in managing consumer social interactions and e-learning platforms. The results show that traditional non-social e-learning platforms may no longer be as effective and underscore the importance of the use of social information in e-learning. This study also sheds light on how e-learning platforms can be designed to generate social contagion not only through social information visibility but also by the interactivity of the information (active versus passive). These findings draw attention to the fact that with the increase in information visibility online, e-learning methods should adapt to provide the right type of information to attract and engage consumers. Platform designers should thus optimize the use of social engagement and interaction in such learning environments. This study highlights that learners are not only interested in their performance, but they are also interested in viewing the performance of their peers that also may be a factor in improving their performance.

This study makes several contributions. It is one of the first studies to examine the value of "social information" in an OLLM and the consequences of different social information. Using detailed data from several countries worldwide on different types of "social" and "non-social" information, the study can tease out the differing impacts of "social" and "non-social" information relating to language learning performance. Furthermore, this study is one of the first to identify the effects of the interactive nature of such information on learning performance. More importantly, the study sheds light on the overall impact of IT and Web 2.0 on not only firms, but also on user behavior in the context of the e-learning marketplace, and how a consumer can be used in the e-learning campaign as a "co-creator" of value to the firm. Web 2.0 is shifting the role of a traditional learner to become an active co-creator of one's learning process. As part of the Web 2.0 social phenomenon, the concept of knowledge and how it is created is significantly changing (Lambert, Philp, & Nakamura, 2017). Web 2.0 knowledge seekers take advantage of the web as a platform not only to consume knowledge but also to generate knowledge (Orús et al., 2016). Such user-generated content and mass participation enable new ways of co-constructing ideas leading to "wisdom-of-crowds." This study highlights the impact of the role of a co-creator and sheds light on the debate of what to teach and how to teach with Web 2.0 and the user-generated content movement (Lee & McLoughlin, 2007).

Limitations and Future Research

The current study uses a sample of enrolled members in an OLLM. These users already have an interest in learning a language and are currently using an online platform to learn a language; the current sample does not observe users outside of this community. The generalization of the results is therefore limited to users that already have an interest in learning a language and are users of OLLMs. Future studies can replicate the study and control for this selection bias using a more general sample such that users outside of the community can also enroll.

Furthermore, this study was only able to create two groups for the randomized experiment due to restrictions from the OLLM. Future studies could take this study a step forward and create more experimental groups to strengthen the findings of this study. Also, the study was not able to directly measure the strength of the social tie between users. A fine-grained analysis could be useful to provide additional insight into social information of different "strengths" and their impact on user behavior. A natural question that arises is whether some social information from certain friends is more salient and "influential" than others. The identification of such leaders of social information would be an interesting and important area for future research.

Although social influence is present, the precise mechanism through which social influence exerts itself in this specific context is less understood. This study identified social information as a possibility, but there may be others, and the current analysis does not distinguish between them. More qualitative data via interviews or surveys may shed further light on this issue. Lastly, the current study was limited to a single OLLM; corroboration of these novel findings by subsequent research would be useful. This is especially so as the amount of social information, social interaction, and use of the platform are likely to be contingent on the nature of the platform. Overall, the findings of the study can be generalized to most language e-learning platforms.

CONCLUSION

This study examined the value and impact of social information on language learning proficiency. The study finds that the mere visibility of friends' performance enhances a user's performance. Furthermore, the more friends a user interacts with, the higher the user's performance. The more posts a user corrects for his friends, and the more posts a user receives corrected by his friends, the higher the user's learning performance. Lastly, active social interaction has a stronger impact than passive social interaction in terms of learning performance. These findings indicate the importance of social interaction and the "activeness" dimension when it comes to learning a language. This randomized cross-continental experimental study provides strong indications of the importance of social information in the context of language learning. The results of this study take the social information processing theory a step forward by providing empirical evidence on the impact of increased visibility of social information on user performance in the OLLM.

This study provides empirical evidence on how Web 2.0 has changed the role of the consumer and emphasizes the importance of using consumers and their social information as an essential learning medium. Firms can use the findings to develop guidelines for optimal investments in various social information and interaction methods. The findings of this study would guide platform developers to enable and constrain the visibility of information that operates in their ecosystem and to engineer the user experience to increase sharing, interaction, and virality.

ACKNOWLEDGMENT

This study has been funded by Kuwait University Grant Number IQ01/15. I would like to thank Kuwait University's Research Administration for granting the project and facilitating the research implementation.

REFERENCES

Ahn, T. Y., & Lee, S. M. (2016). User experience of a mobile speaking application with automatic speech recognition for EFL learning. *British Journal of Educational Technology*, *47*(4), 778–786. doi:10.1111/bjet.12354

Alhamami, M. (2019). Learners' beliefs about language-learning abilities in face-to-face & online settings. *International Journal of Educational Technology in Higher Education*, *16*(1), 31. doi:10.118641239-019-0162-1

Anshari, M., Almunawar, M. N., Shahrill, M., Wicaksono, D. K., & Huda, M. (2017). Smartphones usage in the classrooms: Learning aid or interference? *Education and Information Technologies*, *22*(6), 3063–3079. doi:10.100710639-017-9572-7

Ascarza, E., Neslin, S. A., Netzer, O., Anderson, Z., Fader, P. S., Gupta, S., ... Neal, D. (2018). In Pursuit of Enhanced Customer Retention Management: Review, Key Issues, and Future Directions. *Customer Needs and Solutions*, *5*(1-2), 65–81. doi:10.100740547-017-0080-0

Attwell, G. (2019). E-Learning at the Workplace. Handbook of Vocational Education and Training: Developments in the Changing World of Work, 1-25.

Batanero, C., de-Marcos, L., Holvikivi, J., Hilera, J. R., & Otón, S. (2019). Effects of New Supportive Technologies for Blind and Deaf Engineering Students in Online Learning. *IEEE Transactions on Education*, *62*(4), 270–277. doi:10.1109/TE.2019.2899545

Bonk, C. J., & King, K. S. (2012). Searching for learner-centered, constructivist, and sociocultural components of collaborative educational learning tools. In Electronic collaborators. Routledge.

Brick, B. (2013). Social networking sites and language learning. In Technologies, Innovation, and Change in Personal and Virtual Learning Environments. IGI Global.

Bronack, S., Riedl, R., & Tashner, J. (2006). Learning in the zone: A social constructivist framework for distance education in a 3-dimensional virtual world. *Interactive Learning Environments*, *14*(3), 219–232. doi:10.1080/10494820600909157

Brown, J., & Adler, R. (2008). Open education, the long tail, and learning 2.0. *EDUCAUSE Review*, *43*(1), 16–20.

Burt, R. S. (2017). Structural holes versus network closure as social capital. In Social capital. Routledge.

Chakowa, J. (2018). Enhancing Beginners' Second Language Learning through an Informal Online Environment. *Journal of Educators Online*, *15*(1), n1. doi:10.9743/JEO2018.15.1.7

Chang, Y.-S., Chen, Y.-S., & Chiang, C.-W. (2019). The differences in pleasing value and learning performance among different groups using mobile augmented reality system for cultural environment learning. *Multimedia Tools and Applications*, *78*(4), 4965–4986. doi:10.100711042-018-6928-y

Chartrand, R. (2012). Social networking for language learners: Creating meaningful output with Web 2.0 tools. *Knowledge Management & E-Learning: An International Journal*, *4*(1), 97–101.

Chen, Y., Wang, Q., & Xie, J. (2011). Online social interactions: A natural experiment on word of mouth versus observational learning. *JMR, Journal of Marketing Research*, *48*(2), 238–254. doi:10.1509/jmkr.48.2.238

Chou, S. W., & Liu, C. H. (2005). Learning effectiveness in a Web-based virtual learning environment: A learner control perspective. *Journal of Computer Assisted Learning*, *21*(1), 65–76. doi:10.1111/j.1365-2729.2005.00114.x

Collins, A., & Halverson, R. (2018). *Rethinking education in the age of technology: The digital revolution and schooling in America*. Teachers College Press.

Cummings, C., Mason, D., Shelton, K., & Baur, K. (2017). Active learning strategies for online and blended learning environments. In Flipped Instruction: Breakthroughs in Research and Practice. IGI Global.

Duffy, T. M., & Cunningham, D. J. (1996). *Constructivism: Implications for the Design and Delivery of Instruction.* Academic Press.

Fisher, S., Howardson, G., Wasserman, M. E., & Orvis, K. (2017). How do learners interact with e-learning? Examining patterns of learner control behaviors. *AIS Transactions on Human-Computer Interaction, 9*(2), 75–98. doi:10.17705/1thci.00090

Garcia, R., Falkner, K., & Vivian, R. (2018). Systematic literature review: Self-Regulated Learning strategies using e-learning tools for Computer Science. *Computers & Education, 123*, 150–163. doi:10.1016/j.compedu.2018.05.006

Gee, J. P. (2012). *Situated language and learning: A critique of traditional schooling.* Routledge.

Gilmore, A. (2007). Authentic materials and authenticity in foreign language learning. *Language Teaching, 40*(2), 97–118. doi:10.1017/S0261444807004144

Godwin-Jones, R. (2018). Chasing the butterfly effect: Informal language learning online as a complex system. *Language Learning & Technology, 22*(2), 8–27.

Goyal, A., Bonchi, F., & Lakshmanan, L. V. (2010). Learning influence probabilities in social networks. *Proceedings of the third ACM international conference on Web search and data mining.* 10.1145/1718487.1718518

Gray, K., Thompson, C., Sheard, J., Clerehan, R., & Hamilton, M. (2010). Students as Web 2.0 authors: Implications for assessment design and conduct. *Australasian Journal of Educational Technology, 26*(1). Advance online publication. doi:10.14742/ajet.1105

Harrison, R., & Thomas, M. (2009). Identity in online communities: Social networking sites and language learning. *International Journal of Emerging Technologies and Society, 7*(2), 109–124.

Henry, M., Carroll, F., Cunliffe, D., & Kop, R. (2018). Learning a minority language through authentic conversation using an online social learning method. *Computer Assisted Language Learning, 31*(4), 321–345. doi:10.1080/09588221.2017.1395348

Hung, S.-T. A., & Huang, H.-T. D. (2016). Blogs as a learning and assessment instrument for English-speaking performance. *Interactive Learning Environments, 24*(8), 1881–1894. doi:10.1080/10494820.2015.1057746

Johansson, G. (1989). Job demands and stress reactions in repetitive and uneventful monotony at work. *International Journal of Health Services, 19*(2), 365–377. doi:10.2190/XYP9-VK4Y-9H80-VV3K PMID:2714928

Kelm, O. R. (2011). Social media: It's what students do. *Business Communication Quarterly, 74*(4), 505–520. doi:10.1177/1080569911423960

Kelman, H. C. (1958). Compliance, identification, and internalization three processes of attitude change. *The Journal of Conflict Resolution, 2*(1), 51–60. doi:10.1177/002200275800200106

Kim, D.-Y., Zhu, P., Xiao, W., & Lin, D. (2017). Does Customer Network Centrality Matter in Enhancing Supplier Performance? *Academy of Management Proceedings.* 10.5465/AMBPP.2017.17340abstract

Lambert, C., Philp, J., & Nakamura, S. (2017). Learner-generated content and engagement in second language task performance. *Language Teaching Research, 21*(6), 665–680. doi:10.1177/1362168816683559

Lantolf, J. P. (2000). *Sociocultural theory and second language learning* (Vol. 78). Oxford University Press.

Leary, M. R., & Baumeister, R. F. (2017). The need to belong: Desire for interpersonal attachments as a fundamental human motivation. In Interpersonal Development. Routledge.

Lee, M. J., & McLoughlin, C. (2007). Teaching and learning in the Web 2.0 era: Empowering students through learner-generated content. *International Journal of Instructional Technology and Distance Learning, 4*(10), 21-34.

Lim, C. L., Ab Jalil, H., Ma'rof, A. M., & Saad, W. Z. (2020). Assisting Peer Learning Performance Using Online Collaborative Tools in Virtual Learning Environments. In *Preparing 21st Century Teachers for Teach Less, Learn More (TLLM) Pedagogies* (pp. 108–124). IGI Global.

Liu, M., Evans, M., Horwitz, E., Lee, S., McCrory, M., Park, J., & Parrish, C. (2013). *A Study of the Use of Language Learning Websites with Social Network Features By University ESL Students*. Academic Press.

Luo, T. (2013). Web 2.0 for language learning: Benefits and challenges for educators. *International Journal of Computer-Assisted Language Learning and Teaching, 3*(3), 1–17. doi:10.4018/ijcallt.2013070101

Mitchell, A., Petter, S., & Harris, A. (2017). Learning by Doing: Twenty Successful Active Learning Exercises for Information Systems Courses. *Journal of Information Technology Education: Innovations in Practice, 16*, 21-46.

Nazim, A., & Ahmad, S. (2013). A Comparison Between Ordinary Least Square (OLS) And Structural Equation Modeling (SEM) Methods in Estimating The Influential Factors of 8th Grades Student's Mathematics Achievement In Malaysia. *International Journal of Scientific and Engineering Research*.

Orsini-Jones, M., Brick, B., & Pibworth, L. (2013). Practising language interaction via social networking sites: The expert student's perspective on personalized language learning. In Computer-assisted foreign language teaching and learning: Technological advances. IGI Global.

Orús, C., Barlés, M. J., Belanche, D., Casaló, L., Fraj, E., & Gurrea, R. (2016). The effects of learner-generated videos for YouTube on learning outcomes and satisfaction. *Computers & Education, 95*, 254–269. doi:10.1016/j.compedu.2016.01.007

Parmaxi, A., & Zaphiris, P. (2017). Web 2.0 in Computer-Assisted Language Learning: A research synthesis and implications for instructional design and educational practice. *Interactive Learning Environments, 25*(6), 704–716. doi:10.1080/10494820.2016.1172243

Persson, A., Wanek, B., & Johansson, A. (2001). Passive versus active operator work in automated process control—A job design case study in a control centre. *Applied Ergonomics, 32*(5), 441–451. doi:10.1016/S0003-6870(01)00022-9 PMID:11534789

Prichard, C. (2013). Training L2 learners to use SNSs appropriately and effectively. *CALICO Journal, 30*(2), 204–225. doi:10.11139/cj.30.2.204-225

Rice, R. E., & Aydin, C. (1991). Attitudes toward new organizational technology: Network proximity as a mechanism for social information processing. *Administrative Science Quarterly, 36*(2), 219–244. doi:10.2307/2393354

Richardson, W. (2010). *Blogs, wikis, podcasts, and other powerful web tools for classrooms.* Corwin Press.

Rosenberg, M. J., & Foshay, R. (2002). E-learning: Strategies for delivering knowledge in the digital age. *Performance Improvement, 41*(5), 50–51. doi:10.1002/pfi.4140410512

Routman, R. (2005). Writing essentials: Raising expectations and results while simplifying teaching. *Education Review.*

Salancik, G. R., & Pfeffer, J. (1978). A social information processing approach to job attitudes and task design. *Administrative Science Quarterly, 23*(2), 224–253. doi:10.2307/2392563 PMID:10307892

Schröder, S., Grüttner, M., & Berg, J. (2019). Study Preparation for Refugees in German' Studienkollegs'– Interpretative Patterns of Access, Life-wide (Language) Learning and Performance. *Widening Participation and Lifelong Learning: The Journal of the Institute for Access Studies and the European Access Network, 21*(2), 67–85. doi:10.5456/WPLL.21.2.67

Shadiev, R., Hwang, W.-Y., & Huang, Y.-M. (2017). Review of research on mobile language learning in authentic environments. *Computer Assisted Language Learning, 30*(3-4), 284–303. doi:10.1080/09588221.2017.1308383

Stevenson, M. P., & Liu, M. (2010). Learning a language with Web 2.0: Exploring the use of social networking features of foreign language learning websites. *CALICO Journal, 27*(2), 233–259. doi:10.11139/cj.27.2.233-259

Sundararajan, A., Provost, F., Oestreicher-Singer, G., & Aral, S. (2013). Research commentary—Information in digital, economic, and social networks. *Information Systems Research, 24*(4), 883–905. doi:10.1287/isre.1120.0472

Sylv, L. K., & Sundqvist, P. (2017). Computer-assisted language learning (CALL) in extracurricular/extramural contexts. *CALICO Journal, 34*(1), i–iv. doi:10.1558/cj.31822

Vacca, R. T., Vacca, J. A. L., & Mraz, M. E. (2016). *Content area reading: Literacy and learning across the curriculum.* Pearson.

Wang, C., Fang, T., & Gu, Y. (2020). Learning performance and behavioral patterns of online collaborative learning: Impact of cognitive load and affordances of different multimedia. *Computers & Education, 143*, 103683. doi:10.1016/j.compedu.2019.103683

Wang, Y., & Yu, C. (2017). Social interaction-based consumer decision-making model in social commerce: The role of word of mouth and observational learning. *International Journal of Information Management, 37*(3), 179–189. doi:10.1016/j.ijinfomgt.2015.11.005

Wang, Z., & Kim, H. G. (2017). Can social media marketing improve customer relationship capabilities and firm performance? Dynamic capability perspective. *Journal of Interactive Marketing, 39*, 15–26. doi:10.1016/j.intmar.2017.02.004

Xu, X., Chan, F. M., & Yilin, S. (2018). Personal learning environment: An experience with ESP teacher training. *Interactive Learning Environments*, 1–16. doi:10.1080/10494820.2018.1552872

Yang, B., Lei, Y., Liu, J., & Li, W. (2017). Social collaborative filtering by trust. *IEEE Transactions on Pattern Analysis and Machine Intelligence*, *39*(8), 1633–1647. doi:10.1109/TPAMI.2016.2605085 PMID:27608451

Yang, J. (2016). Effects of popularity-based news recommendations ("most-viewed") on users' exposure to online news. *Media Psychology*, *19*(2), 243–271. doi:10.1080/15213269.2015.1006333

Yang, Y., Crook, C., & O'Malley, C. (2014). Can a social networking site support afterschool group learning of Mandarin? *Learning, Media and Technology*, *39*(3), 267–282. doi:10.1080/17439884.2013.839564

Yang, Y.-F. (2018). New language knowledge construction through indirect feedback in web-based collaborative writing. *Computer Assisted Language Learning*, *31*(4), 459–480. doi:10.1080/09588221.2017.1414852

Young, H. P. (2009). Innovation diffusion in heterogeneous populations: Contagion, social influence, and social learning. *The American Economic Review*, *99*(5), 1899–1924. doi:10.1257/aer.99.5.1899

Zhu, C. (2012). Student satisfaction, performance, and knowledge construction in online collaborative learning. *Journal of Educational Technology & Society*, *15*(1), 127.

This research was previously published in the International Journal of e-Collaboration (IJeC), 17(2); pages 72-87, copyright year 2021 by IGI Publishing (an imprint of IGI Global).

Chapter 86

Big Data HE Communities:
Could Twitter Support UK Universities Amid the COVID-19 Transition?

Farag Edghiem

Institute of Management Greater Manchester, University of Bolton, UK

Moheeb Abualqumboz

University of Salford, UK

ABSTRACT

This chapter intends to explore the use of the Twitter social media platform as a microblog to share COVID-19 prescribed knowledge through observing the Twitter accounts of the five most student-populated UK universities. The chapter provides valuable practical insight to UK universities practitioners, students, and concerned stakeholders on the use of Twitter microblogs to share or retrieve knowledge required to cope with the current COVID-19 transition. The chapter sheds light on the unique characteristics of knowledge shared by UK universities through Twitter in relation to the current COVID-19 pandemic. The chapter also highlights the unconventional use of Twitter by UK universities to share COVID-19 prescribed knowledge with their stakeholders.

1. INTRODUCTION

The current Covid-19 pandemic has transformed many sectors in our society. Among the sectors that have been radically affected is the education sector (Devinney & Dowling, 2020). Universities were forced to move entirely from classroom education to virtual education. Although many Universities have resorted to virtual education, other Universities have not been at the same level able to face the crisis in terms of preparedness and facilitate the creation of new or amendments. It is known in crises that the key to success is not only to implement the right strategy, but rather to implement a quick strategy (Elsubbaugh *et al.,* 2004) that responds to the requirements of the seemingly dramatic transition, this necessitates looking up to knowledge resilience.

DOI: 10.4018/978-1-6684-7123-4.ch086

Presently, academics work from their homes, presenting their lectures through different screens and different means of communication to large segments of students, carrying out their research, searching for funding opportunities for their research projects and marking students' assignments and submitting their reports. In addition to the mental burden, the emerging work environment raises questions such as how the relationship now between academics and their workplace looks like? How did academic discourse of knowledge regime changed? What is the future of knowledge infrastructures in universities in the next five years? As the Covid-19 pandemic highlights the stifling nature of our academic work, universities have been forced to reinterpret themselves, their priorities and knowledge infrastructures. Therefore, in our article, we shed light on the Use of Twitter by UK Universities to mark the new shape of knowledge regimes in academia implied by the Covid-19 pandemic.

2. THEORETICAL BACKGROUND

2.1. Managing Knowledge During the Covid-19 Pandemic

One of the prominent classifications of knowledge is the tacit-explicit (Becerra et al., 2008) where explicit knowledge is knowledge stored in physical storage such as books, computers, etc. and tacit knowledge is situational and stored in practices, routines, and feelings (Chuang et al., 2016). The rapid contemporary developments of technology allowed not only storing but communicating, interpreting and assimilating knowledge through *big data* analytics, virtual reality, augmented reality and robotics (Dragicevic et al., 2019). However, we still have to respond to ongoing calls for a better understanding of socio-materiality of knowledge in this digital medium. The conceptualisation of knowledge and technology may couple meaning and matter together (Nova & González, 2016; Orlikowski, 2007; Paananen, 2020). As during a pandemic, communication is critical for organisations to ensure people are reassured, informed, and engaged, communication can take different shapes and forms. In parallel, maintaining the knowledge continuity and restoring the knowledge accumulation would be essential (Shujahat et al., 2019) but failure factors may also hinder knowledge management initiatives (Larsson et al., 1998) as traditional bureaucratic barriers. Social media platforms may effectively help overcome these failure factors and enable communicating knowledge with subscribers to social media accounts where institutions tend to convey messages of various media and meaning to their stakeholder communities, and keep engaged with what the community thinks of and reacts to performance (Magnier-Watanabe et al., 2010).

The socio-materiality of communication is necessarily obvious in this current pandemic due to the radical shift of working patterns i.e. from workplace to home based (Ashcraft et al., 2009). Viewing knowledge as socio-material (Nova & González, 2016; Orlikowski, 2007; Paananen, 2020; Shotter, 2013) should therefore enable us to understand how Universities determine and enact knowledge artefacts to their stakeholders inside and outside of organisational boundaries. In view of the current Covid-19 pandemic developments, the prospective knowledge type that may be essential to Universities' stakeholders is likely to be featured as timely and rapidly dynamic, formalised and explicit as follows:

- Health and wellbeing knowledge in the form of Covid-19 preventative measures and equipment, mental health and personal wellbeing.
- Higher education teaching and assessment adapted processes such as virtual online teaching and assessment.

- Transitional management process to maintain operations and overcome Covid-19 associated difficulties.

In flexible working mode where people can work from anywhere in most institutions, social media allow subscribers to share knowledge that is less formal than organisational channels which Ammirato et al. (2019) and Döring and Witt (2019) argue to provide a platform for collaboration and engagement. However, in a study on software developers' giant discussion forum Stack Overflow, Squire (2015) shed some concerns on how social media is transforming knowledge and information communication. Squire (2015) argued that while knowledge workers found Stack Overflow more efficient in terms of time and quality, some found it restrictive in some of the ways it accepted questions. On a different line of inquiry, Durst and Zieba (2019) summarised risks that face knowledge workers due to social media such as fake and distorted information, fake social media accounts used to troll people, and the distrust atmosphere.

2.2. Knowledge Sharing in the Space of Social Media

Cyber developments such as *Web 2.0* and associated *internet of things* IOT have not only changed the way of social interaction but also resulted in accumulating *big data* and *cloud computing* to connote unprecedented amounts of data (Ali, 2019a; 2018). In relevance to knowledge management, these cyber developments evidently evolved into creating social networking systems to facilitate knowledge exchange (Le et al., 2014). Conventionally, the concept of *social capital* (Nahapiet & Ghoshal, 1998) has been linked to knowledge management and proved to allow knowledge acquisition through social interaction (Inkpen & Tsang, 2005). In essence and in relevance to online social interaction, the two metaphors of *communities of practice* (Kimble & Li, 2010) and *social networks* (Marin & Wellman, 2011) have been extrapolated to online interaction to denote largely the phenomenon of knowledge dispersion through online social networks. Online *communities of practice* are defined as *virtual communities of practice* in which people with common interests, goals or practices interact to share information and knowledge and engage in social interactions (Chiu et al., 2006). In conjunction, the initial research on *social networks* as facilitated through online social media platforms has indicated an efficient use in sharing tacit and explicit organisational knowledge (Wasko & Faraj, 2005).

Fundamentally, there has been an exponential increase of research on social media and knowledge management. For instance, Sundaresan and Zhang (2020) suggested that organisational engagement with social media positively determined how organisations accumulate, manage and transfer knowledge. Heavey *et al.* (2020) also viewed knowledge management in social media context as a social organising of knowledge where people socially learn and engage with others. Previously, Grace (2009) viewed social media as complementary to knowledge management rather than a space where knowledge is managed and argued that its feasibility, ease of access, traceability, and rich content allows for organisations to reap these advantages in the running of efficient knowledge management systems. *Social networking* through online social media may be deemed to be non-mandatory, despite the currently heavy reliance of organisations on it to communicate with their communities (Ammirato *et al.*, 2019; Heavey *et al.*, 2020; Mäntymäki & Riemer, 2016; Sarka & Ipsen, 2017). As a result, two knowledge regimes may appear where one is top-down enforced by organisational policies, strategies and routines, while the other is bottom-up, voluntary and unstructured (Qi & Chau, 2018).

The usefulness of social media seems to encourage organisational leaders to commit to their knowledge dissemination strategies in a less formal environment and as a result reaping the benefit to disseminate real-time knowledge that does not afford formal channels to reach people (Qi & Chau, 2018; Sarka & Ipsen, 2017; Schlagwein & Hu, 2017). In a study of 20 organisations to examine how social media relates to organisational absorptive capacity, Schlagwein and Hu (2017) presented five different uses of social media that organisations resort to: (1) broadcast, (2) dialogue, (3) collaboration, (4) knowledge management and (5) sociability, however, they argued that some types such as dialogue support organisational absorptive capacity and positively improves performance while sociability does seem to have the same impact. In addition, the types of social media platforms varies considerably whereas the focus of this paper would be on Twitter as a microblog platform to share Covid-19 specific knowledge with UK universities' stakeholders. Microblogging platforms such as Twitter, allows institutions to bridge the space between their boundaries and online communities (Sarka & Ipsen, 2017) draws knowledge from subscribers on performance (Sigala, 2012).

2.3. UK Universities' Observed Twitter Interaction

The *netnographic* observation (Kozinets et al., 2014) of UK Universities' online platforms reveals unprecedented activities to disseminate knowledge focused around the current Covid-19 pandemic. The knowledge shared via UK Universities' websites or social media accounts is mainly formalised and explicit and range from Covid-19 research update, advice on health and wellbeing, adapted learning and assessment procedures to operational adaptive measures for staff. This stream of explicit knowledge seem to be directed ultimately towards all the Universities' stakeholders but more specifically staff and students.

UK Universities' Twitter accounts are also observed to undergo dynamic patterns of knowledge sharing in response to the Covid-19 developments of which drew our attention. In addition and as we aim to focus our *netnographic* concern on the Twitter platform, we justify this concern based on two justifications: firstly, social media platforms largely provide the opportunity to interact with the knowledge provider that otherwise not fundamentally available through conventional online mediums. *Secondly,* Twitter has been extensively used by academics and academic institutions to address students, employees and other concerned stakeholders and is observed to remain a useful method to share knowledge in relation to the current Covid-19 pandemic.

Our *netnographic* observation was focused on five UK Universities' Twitter accounts where the prime selection criterion was fundamentally based on the size of the University in terms of students' count. The justification of applying this criterion was determined by the conclusion that the large the students' count will implicate wider stakeholder base and more staff involved, an imminent need for a knowledge exchange, and more knowledge-based interaction with students and staff. In accordance, we have used the Tweetdeck application to observe the sampled Twitter accounts where these accounts consistently contained regular Tweets on Covid-19 related topics of which engaged followers (see Table 1). These curated Tweets mainly resembled formalised explicit knowledge on the Covid-19 pandemic ranging from updates on Covid-19 research to transitional Covid-19 educational and operational measures (see Appendix 1).

*Table 1. UK Universities student count and Twitter accounts followers *Student numbers statistics compiled from Higher Education Statistics Agency*

University	Student Numbers*	Account followers	Covid-19 Tweets' Content
University of London (Including University College London)	101,230 20,005	60,195 76,891	Existent
Open University	113,045	157,966	Existent
University of Manchester	26,855	66,813	Existent
University of Leeds	26,255	105,656	Existent
University of Birmingham	22,940	119,695	Existent

(HESA, 2020)

3. DISCUSSION

The UK's higher education HE sector is experiencing a dramatic phase of transition implied by the Covid-19 pandemic. The HE landscape has encountered a powerful force for change which will introduce new traditions, some of which are yet to be established, tested, publicised and adopted across the sector. Until progress is made by UK Universities in finding out what works best to cope with the current Covid-19 transition, the creation and sharing of knowledge will remain highly dynamic and critically important to maintain Universities' operations and update its varied stakeholders. However, the nature of knowledge in consideration may be mainly formalised, explicit and prescribed to cope with impact of the Covid-19 pandemic. In congruence with the above discussion we make the *proposition* that Twitter as a microblogging social media platform will be utilised extensively by UK Universities to share knowledge amid the Covid-19 pandemic. Not only because Twitter is already used by academics, research communities and universities but also due to its dynamic and interactive characteristics. This proposition conforms with the view of (Sarka & Ipsen, 2017) that emphasises the usefulness of Twitter in allowing institutions to communicate effectively with their associated online communities.

From another perspective, it could be anticipated due to the likely prolonged Covid-19 lockdown limiting conventional professional interaction that *virtual communities of purpose* (Chiu et al., 2006) will be actively created to share knowledge in the form of adaptive measures and experiences of coping with the Covid-19 transition. In the context of UK Universities' Twitter microblogs the creation of *virtual communities of purpose* may be driven by: (1) the need for knowledge in the form of prescribed Covid-19 adaptive measures to guide UK universities' students, staff and other stakeholders during this phase of major transition. There is also a possibility that UK Universities will utilise the Twitter microblog for cross-university knowledge sharing. (2) *knowledge workers* (Squire, 2015) who actively seek and share knowledge; some *knowledge workers,* as academic researchers, may resort to creating and interacting within *virtual communities of purpose* to explore these communities and share knowledge with its subscribers. In line with the aforementioned, we make another *proposition* in agreement with (Chiu et al., 2006) that *virtual communities of purpose* will actively interact via UK universities' Twitter microblogs. In essence, we encourage future research to explore the *virtual communities of purpose* within UK Universities' Twitter microblogs through a *netnographic* research strategy (Kozinets et al., 2014)to enable in-depth investigation of these communities.

4. CONCLUSION

In this paper, we sought to highlight the role that social media (e.g. Twitter) had played as a platform for real-time knowledge-sharing microblog for UK Universities in view of the current Covid-19 pandemic. From a wider perspective, we argue that our awareness of the importance of a University, not only as an educational platform, but also as a boundaryless knowledge ecosystem, stimulates us to think about how Twitter shapes and reshapes university discourse about student numbers and upcoming challenges in light of the current Covid-19 crisis. .

University leaders may foresee that the year 2020 marks a major transition in Universities operations and even real challenges for graduates who will find themselves searching for jobs in a new environment marked by the risk of collapse of many businesses. Twitter as a microblogging platform provides an opportunity in which Universities can share explicit knowledge to engage and inform students, staff and other stakeholders on Covid-19 transitional measures. In line with this argument and based on our observation of sampled UK Universities' twitter accounts, we make two propositions: (1) that Twitter as a microblogging social media platform will be utilised extensively by UK Universities to share knowledge amid the Covid-19 pandemic. (2) That *virtual communities of purpose* will actively interact via UK universities' Twitter microblogs in relevance to the Covid-19 transition.

Finally, this paper's contribution is twofold: *Frist,* as it is a conceptual paper, we hope to stimulate further empirical discussions to understand the changes that the UK HE has gone through during the current crisis. *Secondly,* Twitter as microblog provides an enormous knowledge platform, and for this we hope this paper will stimulate *netnographic* research to investigate in-depth the KS conduct within UK Universities' Twitter pages. For further reading regarding the application of big data systems, cloud systems and social platforms in higher education, refer to the work of industry 4.0 technologies such as IoT and Artificial Intelligence in higher education (Ali, 2021; Ali & Wood-Harper, 2020; Ali, 2019a; 2019b; Ali & Wood-Harper, 2018).

REFERENCES

Ali, M. (2018). The Barriers and Enablers of the Educational Cloud: A Doctoral Student Perspective. *Open Journal of Business and Management, 7*(1), 1–24. doi:10.4236/ojbm.2019.71001

Ali, M. (2019). Cloud Computing at a Cross Road: Quality and Risks in Higher Education. *Advances in Internet of Things, 9*(3), 33–49. doi:10.4236/ait.2019.93003

Ali, M. (2019). Cloud Computing at a Cross Road: Quality and Risks in Higher Education. *Advances in Internet of Things, 9*(3), 33–49. doi:10.4236/ait.2019.93003

Ali, M. B. (2019). Multiple Perspective of Cloud Computing Adoption Determinants in Higher Education a Systematic Review. *International Journal of Cloud Applications and Computing, 9*(3), 89–109. doi:10.4018/IJCAC.2019070106

Ali, M. B. (2021). Internet of Things (IoT) to Foster Communication and Information Sharing: A Case of UK Higher Education. In M. B. Ali & T. Wood-Harper (Eds.), *Fostering Communication and Learning With Underutilized Technologies in Higher Education* (pp. 1–20). IGI Global. doi:10.4018/978-1-7998-4846-2.ch001

Ali, M. B., & Wood-Harper, T. (2020). *The Role of SaaS Applications in Business IT Alignment: A Closer Look at Value Creation in Service Industry*. UKAIS.

Ali, M. B., Wood-Harper, T., & Mohamad, M. (2018). Benefits and challenges of cloud computing adoption and usage in higher education: A systematic literature review. *International Journal of Enterprise Information Systems*, *14*(4), 64–77. doi:10.4018/IJEIS.2018100105

Ammirato, S., Felicetti, A. M., Della Gala, M., Aramo-Immonen, H., Jussila, J. J., & Kärkkäinen, H. (2019). The use of social media for knowledge acquisition and dissemination in B2B companies: An empirical study of Finnish technology industries. *Knowledge Management Research and Practice*, *17*(1), 52–69. doi:10.1080/14778238.2018.1541779

Ashcraft, K. L., Kuhn, T. R., & Cooren, F. (2009). 1 Constitutional Amendments:"Materializing" Organizational Communication. *The Academy of Management Annals*, *3*(1), 1–64. doi:10.5465/19416520903047186

Becerra, M., Lunnan, R., & Huemer, L. (2008). Trustworthiness, risk, and the transfer of tacit and explicit knowledge between alliance partners. *Journal of Management Studies*, *45*(4), 691–713. doi:10.1111/j.1467-6486.2008.00766.x

Chiu, C.-M., Hsu, M.-H., & Wang, E. T. (2006). Understanding knowledge sharing in virtual communities: An integration of social capital and social cognitive theories. *Decision Support Systems*, *42*(3), 1872–1888. doi:10.1016/j.dss.2006.04.001

Chuang, C.-H., Jackson, S. E., & Jiang, Y. (2016). Can knowledge-intensive teamwork be managed? Examining the roles of HRM systems, leadership, and tacit knowledge. *Journal of Management*, *42*(2), 524–554. doi:10.1177/0149206313478189

Devinney, T., & Dowling, G. (2020). Is this the crisis higher education needs to have? *Times Higher Education*. Retrieved 30/5 from https://www.timeshighereducation.com/features/crisis-higher-education-needs-have

Döring, H., & Witt, P. (2019). Knowledge management in family businesses-Empirical evidence from Germany. *Knowledge Management Research and Practice*, 1–13. doi:10.1080/14778238.2019.1621224

Dragicevic, N., Ullrich, A., Tsui, E., & Gronau, N. (2019). A conceptual model of knowledge dynamics in the industry 4.0 smart grid scenario. *Knowledge Management Research and Practice*, 1–15. doi:10.1080/14778238.2019.1633893

Durst, S., & Zieba, M. (2019). Mapping knowledge risks: Towards a better understanding of knowledge management. *Knowledge Management Research and Practice*, *17*(1), 1–13. doi:10.1080/14778238.2018.1538603

Elsubbaugh, S., Fildes, R., & Rose, M. B. (2004). Preparation for crisis management: A proposed model and empirical evidence. *Journal of Contingencies and Crisis Management*, *12*(3), 112–127. doi:10.1111/j.0966-0879.2004.00441.x

Grace, T. P. L. (2009). Wikis as a knowledge management tool. *Journal of Knowledge Management*.

Heavey, C., Simsek, Z., Kyprianou, C., & Risius, M. (2020). How do strategic leaders engage with social media? A theoretical framework for research and practice. *Strategic Management Journal*, *41*(8), 1490–1527. doi:10.1002mj.3156

HESA. (2020). *Where do HE students study?* Higher Education Statistics Agency. Retrieved 27/5 from https://www.hesa.ac.uk/data-and-analysis/students/where-study

Inkpen, A. C., & Tsang, E. W. K. (2005). Social capital, networks, and knowledge transfer. *Academy of Management Review*, *30*(1), 146–165. doi:10.5465/amr.2005.15281445

Kimble, C., & Li, F. (2010). Effective virtual working through communities of practice. In IT Outsourcing: Concepts, Methodologies, Tools, and Applications (pp. 1966-1973). IGI Global.

Kozinets, R. V., Dolbec, P.-Y., & Earley, A. (2014). Netnographic analysis: Understanding culture through social media data. The SAGE handbook of qualitative data analysis, 262-276.

Larsson, R., Bengtsson, L., Henriksson, K., & Sparks, J. (1998). The Interorganizational Learning Dilemma: Collective Knowledge Development in Strategic Alliances. *Organization Science*, *9*(3), 285–305. doi:10.1287/orsc.9.3.285

Le, Q. T., Lee, D. Y., & Park, C. S. (2014). A social network system for sharing construction safety and health knowledge. *Automation in Construction*, *46*, 30–37. doi:10.1016/j.autcon.2014.01.001

Magnier-Watanabe, R., Yoshida, M., & Watanabe, T. (2010). Social network productivity in the use of SNS. *Journal of Knowledge Management*, *14*(6), 910–927. doi:10.1108/13673271011084934

Mäntymäki, M., & Riemer, K. (2016). Enterprise social networking: A knowledge management perspective. *International Journal of Information Management*, *36*(6), 1042–1052. doi:10.1016/j.ijinfomgt.2016.06.009

Marin, A., & Wellman, B. (2011). *Social network analysis: An introduction. In The Sage Handbook of Social Network Analysis*. Sage.

Nahapiet, J., & Ghoshal, S. (1998). Social capital, intellectual capital, and the organizational advantage. *Academy of Management Review*, *23*(2), 242–266. doi:10.5465/amr.1998.533225

Nova, N. A., & González, R. A. (2016). Reframing Coordination in Knowledge Transfer: A Sociomaterial Perspective. *International Joint Conference on Knowledge Discovery, Knowledge Engineering, and Knowledge Management*.

Orlikowski, W. J. (2007). Sociomaterial practices: Exploring technology at work. *Organization Studies*, *28*(9), 1435–1448. doi:10.1177/0170840607081138

Paananen, S. (2020). Sociomaterial relations and adaptive space in routine performance. *Management Learning*, *51*(3), 1350507619896079. doi:10.1177/1350507619896079

Qi, C., & Chau, P. Y. K. (2018). Will enterprise social networking systems promote knowledge management and organizational learning? An empirical study. *Journal of Organizational Computing and Electronic Commerce*, *28*(1), 31–57. doi:10.1080/10919392.2018.1407081

Sarka, P., & Ipsen, C. (2017). Knowledge sharing via social media in software development: A systematic literature review. *Knowledge Management Research and Practice*, *15*(4), 594–609. doi:10.105741275-017-0075-5

Schlagwein, D., & Hu, M. (2017). How and why organisations use social media: Five use types and their relation to absorptive capacity. *Journal of Information Technology*, *32*(2), 194–209. doi:10.1057/jit.2016.7

Shotter, J. (2013). Reflections on sociomateriality and dialogicality in organization studies: From "inter-" to "intra-thinking"… in performing practices. *How matter matters*, 32-57.

Shujahat, M., Sousa, M. J., Hussain, S., Nawaz, F., Wang, M., & Umer, M. (2019). Translating the impact of knowledge management processes into knowledge-based innovation: The neglected and mediating role of knowledge-worker productivity. *Journal of Business Research*, *94*, 442–450. doi:10.1016/j.jbusres.2017.11.001

Sigala, M. (2012). Social networks and customer involvement in new service development (NSD). *International Journal of Contemporary Hospitality Management*, *24*(7), 966–990. doi:10.1108/09596111211258874

Squire, M. (2015). "Should We Move to Stack Overflow?" Measuring the Utility of Social Media for Developer Support. *2015 IEEE/ACM 37th IEEE International Conference on Software Engineering.*

Sundaresan, S., & Zhang, Z. (2020). Knowledge-sharing rewards in enterprise social networks: Effects of learner types and impact of digitisation. *Enterprise Information Systems*, *14*(5), 1–19. doi:10.1080/17517575.2020.1737884

Wasko, M. M., & Faraj, S. (2005). Why should I share? Examining social capital and knowledge contribution in electronic networks of practice. *Management Information Systems Quarterly*, *29*(1), 35–57. doi:10.2307/25148667

This research was previously published in Remote Work and Sustainable Changes for the Future of Global Business; pages 33-44, copyright year 2021 by Business Science Reference (an imprint of IGI Global).

APPENDIX

UK Universities' Curated Tweets

Figure 1. Curated Tweets Image 1

Figure 2. Curated Tweets Image 2

Figure 3. Curated Tweets Image 3

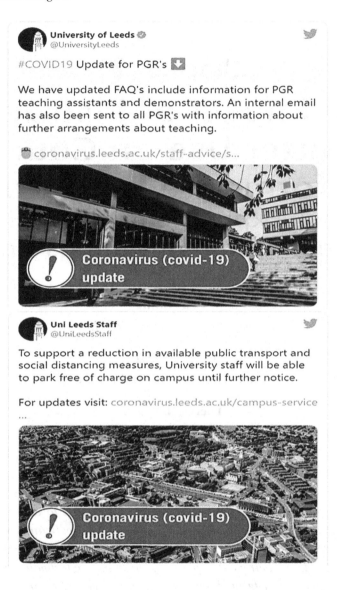

Chapter 87

The Impact of Instructor Twitter Use on Course Performance Indicators:
A Quasi-Experiment within Higher Education Communications Courses

Eric M Fife
James Madison University, USA

C Leigh Nelson
James Madison University, USA

Theresa B Clarke
James Madison University, USA

ABSTRACT

An exploratory quasi-experiment of college-level students was used to examine the difference in a variety of course indicators among instructors when they did not use Twitter as a supplement to their courses, when they moderately used Twitter, and when they used Twitter a great deal in their courses. When instructors used Twitter in their classes, perceived learning via technological mediums, perceived classroom community with regard to technological media, perceived pedagogical affect, perceived course effectiveness, perceived learning performance, and perceived perception of learning from Twitter were all greater than when they did not use Twitter in their courses. Overall results of this study recommend further research and a continued focus on the usage of Twitter in the higher education classroom.

DOI: 10.4018/978-1-6684-7123-4.ch087

INTRODUCTION

In a study of the top technologies to incorporate into the classroom, Tomei (2011) recommended greater inclusion of online technologies by teachers whenever possible. Scholars have conducted research into a variety of ways of incorporating technology into teaching, but research into the use of social networking sites (SNS) was very limited (Nemetz, Aiken, Cooney, & Pascal, 2012) until a recent surge in interest. Scholars have examined the use of online technologies such as blogging (Chang, Liu, & Chang 2011), mobile video blogging (Kim, 2011), and social bookmarking (Gray & Carter, 2012) in an instructional context. Research has also, particularly in the last few years, empirically examined the use of the micro-blogging SNS Twitter (e.g., Clarke & Nelson, 2012; Jacquemin, Smesler, & Bernot, 2014; Kim & Kim, 2016; Lowe & Laffey, 2011; Rinaldo, Tapp, & Laverie, 2011; Tsai, 2016). This chapter adds to that literature by describing an exploratory study in the varying levels of use of Twitter by instructors in the college classroom, noting its impact on several dependent variables, and suggesting possible avenues of future research. Dagada and Chigona (2013) contend that the majority of academics do not fully understand the interrelationships between content, pedagogy, and technologies. Because online technologies carry potential to enrich professional growth (Isman, Gazi, & Aksal, 2012), the value of this chapter is greater insight into effective Web-based teaching methods for academic professionals interested in online learning. As faculty members increasingly search for ways to connect with their students, both within and outside the traditional classroom, Twitter offers another avenue to augment instructional content. As Juhary (2016) notes, "As the way of learning changes day by day, these Digital Natives must be given learning tools that match their demands and expectations" (p. 9).

TWITTER

In the past, Twitter (2013) described itself as "a real-time information network that connects users to the latest stories, ideas, opinions and news about what you find interesting." Now, Twitter (2017) is "what's happening in the world and what people are talking about right now." Despite the slight shift in emphasis, the fundamental Twitter platform has remained virtually unchanged since its inception. The first short message from a user, or "tweet," was sent in 2006 (blog.twitter.com, 2011). In its twelfth year of operation, there are now over 328 million active users of Twitter, including 68 million in the United States (Fiegerman, 2017). Though Twitter user growth is currently somewhat stagnant (Fiegerman, 2017) as other social networking sites, notably Instagram, have exploded in popularity (Constine, 2017), Twitter still occupies a unique and important place in the social media landscape and remains of great interest to scholars. According to Kim and Kim (2016), a recent Google Scholar search for articles including the word "Twitter" in the title yielded approximately 1,150,000 papers. Twitter may be used both by individuals and organizations, none of whom pay a fee or face a limit on the number of "tweets" they can produce per day. Twitter effectively occupies two categories of internet sites researched by scholars, qualifying both as a weblog (specifically, microblogging) site and as an SNS.

A blog, a portmanteau of the phrase web log, is a website containing discrete data entries presented in reverse chronological order. Ebner and Schiefner (2008) attribute what they call "the amazing growth of weblogs" to three factors, which they term "usability, collaboration, and personality" (p. 156). They argue that weblogs are easy to use, encourage connection, and enable someone to assert a unique personality on the Internet. Microblogs, such as Twitter, are those weblogs which limit the content allowed in a single message – in the case of Twitter, to 140 characters often referred to as a "tweet" (Clarke & Nelson, 2012). Uncommonly, Twitter users who want to express their sentiments in a longer message can instead tweet an image of a longer message, or provide a link to a web site or blog. Ebner, Lienhardt, Rohs, and Meyer (2010) noted that there is an ongoing debate as to whether "writing a 140-character statement should be understood as a form of weblog, or whether it indeed represents a new form of communication" (p. 93). Though this question remains unanswered, it is clear that the 140-character limit is an important feature of Twitter in an online instructional context, a point which will be further explored below.

Scholars define a social networking site as "web-based services that allow individuals to (1) construct a public or semi-public profile within a bounded system, (2) articulate a list of other users with whom they share a connection, and (3) view and traverse their list of connections and those made by others within the system" (Boyd & Ellison, 2008, p. 3). Though Twitter does not allow the detailed profile construction of other social networking sites, such as Facebook and Instagram, it does allow posting of a photo and brief biographical information. Users can then view the individuals or organizations both "following" and "followed by" other users. Twitter differs from Facebook, in particular, in its limited privacy settings. While Facebook has a complicated and ever-changing series of privacy settings related to different aspects of a user's profile, Twitter accounts are simply either "protected" or "unprotected." "Protected" Twitter accounts require permission of the user in order to see their tweets. The norm on Twitter appears to be to leave accounts unprotected; thus, individuals can easily examine tweets by others whom they are not officially "following." Though most of the instructional Twitter research has involved unprotected use, a few studies (e.g., Stephens & Gunther, 2016) have used protected accounts as a way of safeguarding student and faculty privacy.

Instructional Research Using Twitter

The last five years has seen a dramatic increase in scholarly research involving classroom use of Twitter, in multiple disciplines and cultures (e.g., Evans 2014; Junco, Elavsky & Heiberger, 2013; Prestridge, 2014). This research involves both hypothetical and actual classroom use of Twitter, and often separates quasi-experimental groups (when they exist) into either "extensive Twitter use" or "no Twitter use," without a middle ground. All of this literature serves both to provide context for the present study, and ultimately to suggest the pragmatic value of using Twitter in an instructional setting.

Some of the instructional advice and extant scholarship for using Twitter focuses on the potential to increase a sense of community in the classroom (Clarke & Nelson, 2012), and consequently one of the concepts which is explored empirically in the present study. Moody (2010) suggests both faculty and students use SNS (including Twitter) in the classroom, asserting that "professors will connect with students and encourage discussions in many formats" (p. 8). Stern (2011) argues that SNS, including Twitter, can help to create a space for a nonthreatening discussion of challenging issues, which might otherwise threaten a sense of classroom community. Because community can be fostered by professor engagement, Dunlap and Lowenthal (2010) note that using Twitter can allow for a faster response – students and faculty members do not have to be logged into Blackboard or other learning management systems to reply, and as they suggest, "Twitter is a helpful tool for addressing student issues quickly" (p. 132). Elavsky, Mislan, and Elavsky (2011) also demonstrated increased engagement through use of Twitter, as their students tweeted comments and questions during a large lecture class.

Other scholars have found more limited effects on classroom community for tweeting faculty. Though students will read and reply to tweets, particularly if required to do so (Junco, Elavsky, & Heiberger,

2013), several studies have suggested that Twitter may not be the most effective tool for facilitating discussion among students (Jacquemin, Smesler, & Bernot, 2014; Prestridge, 2014; Stephens & Gunther, 2016). Thus, while a sense of rapport with an instructor may be increased, overall discussion among students does not always follow. Certain kinds of students, notably those who might be characterized as less likely to speak up in a face-to-face setting, might find Twitter to be a less face-threatening way to participate in class discussion (Tiernan, 2014). Some scholars have also suggested that because students see Twitter as "social" as opposed to academic, they may be less inclined to want to adopt use of that medium for class purposes, and thus discussion is unlikely to be enhanced in that setting (Lin, Hoffman, & Borengasser, 2013). Leslie and Murphy (2008) also found that the primary use of blogging by college students was social.

Scholars also pointed out the symbolic value in the use of Twitter. Moody (2010) noted that faculty "must evolve their coursework to remain relevant to today's students" (p. 1), and using Twitter represents one step in that evolution. As DeGroot, Young and VanSlette (2015) point out, "The use of Twitter may humanize the instructor" for some students (p. 432). Dunlap and Lowenthal (2010) argued that the use of Twitter by students in the classroom can have professional advantages, as well, since social media are increasingly important in a corporate environment, particularly for students in certain academic disciplines. Because Twitter is largely used in fields such as public relations and marketing, exposure to and use of Twitter may be advantageous for those students and others for whom use of Twitter may become a professional necessity.

A number of other studies have explored issues related to instructor credibility when using Twitter Johnson (2011), echoing Moody's advice about "remaining relevant" for today's students, found that a hypothetical instructor who used Twitter for social tweets was seen as more credible than one who used either scholarly and social tweets, or just scholarly tweets. She conceptualized credibility as consisting of three factors: competence, trustworthiness and caring. Unlike the current research project, Johnson used a hypothetical classroom, and did not have an experimental condition in which Twitter was not used. Similarly, DeGroot, Young and VanSlette (2015), also using hypothetical tweeting, found that a hypothetical instructor using generating only professional tweets was seen as more credible than a hypothetical profile which also included social tweets or a mix of professional and social. Overall, DeGroot et al. note that credibility can be impacted by instructor Twitter use in multiple ways, not always positively; as one student said, "It breaks barriers between students and professors, and that can be a good thing or a bad thing" (p. 435). Notably, McArthur and Bostedo-Conway (2012) did not find strong relationships between Twitter usage and perceived faculty credibility – only students who were frequent Twitter users saw frequently tweeting instructors as more credible. Though the present student did not directly address instructor credibility, it has become an important concept in the exiting Twitter scholarship and is indirectly connected to several variables in the current study.

Though credibility, engagement, and the symbolic value of Twitter are all important variables, learning (measured by either perceived learning or actual test scores) should be a central component of classroom Twitter research. Junco, Heibergert, and Loken (2010) found that for multiple sections of the same course, an experimental group which used Twitter extensively for in-class discussions showed both increased engagement and higher grades. For their study, students received an hour-long Twitter training session, and used Twitter as part of their course assignments. Faculty used Twitter as well, producing 301 tweets over the course of the semester. Juhary (2016) also argued that Twitter could be a useful tool in helping students improve their understanding of concepts as measured by a content-based pretest and posttest, though he also acknowledged the limited and exploratory nature of his scholarship.

The existing research on Twitter is helpful, but to our knowledge no study has experimentally explored how varying levels of instructor Twitter usage in different sections of the same classes might influence dependent variables related to student learning. The dependent variables were chosen to indicate a variety of relevant ways in which varying levels of instructor Twitter usage might influence learning outcomes. The conceptual framework of factors affecting learning outcomes, developed by Young, Klemz, and Murphy (2003), is used to capture the multidimensional nature of learning performance. Specifically, we examine overall perceived learning based on traditional and online media and the relationships between different levels of instructor Twitter usage on the students' sense of classroom community, pedagogical affect, and perceptions of learning.

HYPOTHESES

One question which has not been empirically explored in the Twitter literature regards the extent to which students might report learning differentially via various media. Twitter does not have to be more effective than other media to be a useful classroom tool; indeed, as Ebner and Schiefner (2008) suggested, "[microblogging] has to be integrated with other tools" (p. 158). Because instructors who use Twitter will almost always use other online technology as well, it seems reasonable to explore the extent to which varying levels of Twitter use, while other technological use is held constant, might influence perceived learning through technology. Additionally, "traditional" means of learning (i.e., classroom interaction, lectures, textbook, etc.) should also be assessed in classes with varying degrees of Twitter usage – as these more traditional forms of learning also will likely be used along with Twitter in most teaching environments. Thus the following hypotheses are proposed:

H1a: There is a difference in perceived learning from online technological media among students who are exposed to low, medium, and high amounts of instructor Twitter usage.
H1b: There is a difference in perceived learning from traditional means among students who are exposed to low, medium, and high amounts of instructor Twitter usage.

Because the enhancement of classroom community is a perceived benefit associated with social networking sites, as noted by Moody (2010) above, the degree to which students feel as if they are part of a special learning community should vary with the extent of Twitter usage. Again, because traditional means (e.g., lectures, textbook, etc.) also may serve to enhance a sense of community and are utilized along with online technological media (e.g., Blackboard, social media, etc.) in the face-to-face classroom environment, how these means serve to enhance a sense of community should be studied as well. Thus, the following hypotheses are appropriate:

H2a: There is a difference in perceptions of class community with regard to online technological media among students who are exposed to low, medium, and high amounts of instructor Twitter usage.
H2b: There is a difference in perceptions of class community with regard to traditional means among students who are exposed to low, medium, and high amounts of instructor Twitter usage.

Students may feel differently about a course due to the level of Twitter usage employed. Pedagogical affect "represents the positive thoughts or feelings toward the instructional methods deployed in a particular class" (Young, Klemz, & Murphy, 2003, p. 133). To capture the potential educational value of Twitter in a classroom setting, this concept was chosen over similar, but broader ideas, such as affective learning.

H3: There is a difference in perceived pedagogical affect with regard to methods of instruction among students exposed to low, medium, and high amounts of instructor Twitter usage.

If Moody (2010) is correct, and there is a symbolic value to using Twitter in the college classroom, then students might perceive an instructor who integrates Twitter into the course content as more effective generally. Thus,

H4: There is a difference in perceived course effectiveness among groups exposed to low, medium, and high amounts of instructor Twitter usage.

Finally, beyond these fairly specific possible outcomes of Twitter usage in a classroom setting, it would also be important to know whether the students felt instructor Twitter usage helped them better understand course content.

H5a: There is a difference in perceived learning performance among students exposed to low, medium, and high amounts of instructor Twitter usage.
H5b: There is a difference in whether students believe Twitter helps them learn about course content among students exposed to low, medium, and high amounts of instructor Twitter usage.

METHOD

In this quasi-experimental exploration, two higher education instructors who taught the same class in both the fall and spring semester were examined. One instructor taught an interpersonal communication course both semesters (fall n=40, spring n=45) and the other instructor taught a course in integrated marketing communications (fall n=36, spring n=45). The response rates were 75% (fall) and 75.5% (spring) in the interpersonal communications course and 100% (fall) and 97.7% (spring) for the integrated marketing communications course. There were 39 males and 115 females with an average age of 20.86. There were 15 sophomores, 75 juniors, 64 seniors and 1 other student that did not report their class year.

Twitter usage was manipulated by semester over a period of 10 weeks. Neither instructor utilized Twitter during the fall semester. In the spring semester, both instructors utilized Twitter at different frequency levels. Instructors utilized the same teaching methods, same teaching styles, built similar relationships with students, and taught the exact same content as the prior semester. The interpersonal communication instructor used Twitter at a moderate level with an average of two tweets per week of subject-oriented content (e.g., current events, news headlines, or new research on the topic) and one tweet of class-oriented content per week (e.g., reminding students of assignments due that week etc.). The integrated marketing communications professor utilized Twitter at a high level, averaging 4 or more tweets per week on subject matter and 2 or more class-oriented tweets per week. The enrolled students were asked to take an online survey about their experience (which received Institutional Review Board approval) at the end of both semesters.

To measure perceived learning from online technological media, students were asked to assess their agreement on four statements from strongly disagree (coded as a 1) to strong agree (coded as a 5). The statement was "_____ helps me learn about the course content." Blackboard, Facebook, Twitter, and email were the technologies assessed. Cronbach's alpha for this scale was .525.

Perceived learning from traditional means was assessed using the same statement and the same Likert scale utilized above with the following mediums: lectures, course textbook(s)/readings, face-to-face interaction with the instructor, and face-to-face interaction with my classmates. Cronbach's alpha for this scale was .679.

Classroom community with regard to technological media was measured by having participants assess their agreement on four statements from strongly disagree (coded as a 1) to strong agree (coded as a 5). The statement was "_____ helps me become part of the class community." Blackboard, Facebook, Twitter, and email were the technologies assessed. Cronbach's alpha for this scale was .616.

Classroom community derived from traditional means was assessed using the same statement and the same Likert scale utilized above with the following mediums: lectures, course textbook(s)/readings, face-to-face interaction with the instructor, and face-to-face interaction with my classmates. Cronbach's alpha for this scale was .630.

Pedagogical affect with regard to methods of instruction was measured using an adaptation of Mitchell and Olsen's (1981) scale. Young, Klemz, and Murphy (2003) have also used this scale successfully. This seven-point semantic differential scale of four items had a Cronbach's alpha of .77. Items were summed and negatively worded anchors were reversed coded so that a high score represented a high degree of pedagogical affect.

Course effectiveness was measured using a scale developed by Sadera, Robertson, Song, and Midon (2009). This six item five-point Likert scale utilized items that assessed organization, learning outcomes, and enjoyment of the course. Items were summed so that high numbers represented a stronger measure of course effectiveness. Cronbach's alpha for this scale was .886.

Perceived learning performance was assessed with Young, Kelmz, and Murphy's (2003) adaption of Young's (2001) Learning Performance Scale. This six item seven-point scale from very low (coded as a 1) to extremely high (coded as a 7) assessed such issues as knowledge gained, skills, ability to apply material, and understanding. Cronbach's alpha for this scale was .879.

Twitter usage learning was assessed by having participants respond to the single item "Twitter helps me learn course content." Students assessed their degree of agreement with that specific statement on a five-point Likert scale.

RESULTS

Table 1 summarizes key findings for each of the study's hypotheses. The degrees of freedom for dependent variables differ slightly because some participants did not complete all of the scales. To test hypothesis 1a of whether there was a difference in low (M=11.81, SD=2.39), medium (M=13.64, SD=2.23), and high exposure (M=13.69, SD=1.90) to instructor Twitter use and perceived learning via technological mediums, a one-way analysis of variance (ANOVA) was conducted. There was a significant difference among the three groups $F(2,154)=13.673$, $p<.0005$. Utilizing Scheffe testing, there were significant differences between the low and medium groups ($p<.0005$) with medium groups reporting more perceived learning and between the low and high groups (p<.0005) with high groups reporting more perceived learning from online technological media.

Table 1. Summary of key results

	Low Twitter Use	Medium Twitter Use	High Twitter Use	F	p Value
Perceived Learning (Online)	M = 11.81 SD = 2.39	M = 13.64 SD = 2.23	M= 13.69 SD = 1.90	F(2,154)=13.673 Scheffe a, c	.0005*
Perceived Learning (Traditional)	M = 17.28 SD = 2.09	M = 17.28 SD = 2.69	M = 17.58 SD = 1.65		N/S
Classroom Community (Online)	M = 11.80 SD = 2.70	M = 12.85 SD = 2.84	M = 13.02 SD = 2.53	F(2,154)=3.567 Scheffe d	.031*
Classroom Community (Traditional)	M = 15.74 SD = 2.04	M = 16.21 SD = 2.96	M = 15.89 SD = 2.33		N/S
Pedagogical Affect	M = 24.58 SD = 3.68	M = 25.85 SD = 2.63	M = 25.95 SD = 2.54	F(2,150)=3.397 Scheffe d	.036*
Course Effectiveness	M = 24.84 SD = 4.15	M = 27.64 SD = 2.70	M = 25.45 SD = 4.09	F(2,154)=6.995 Scheffe a, b	.001*
Learning Performance	M = 34.08 SD = 4.81	M = 35.82 SD = 4.44	M = 36.09 SD = 3.81	F(2,152)=3.470 Scheffe d	.034*
Twitter usage Learning	M = 1.99 SD = 1.01	M = 3.31 SD = 1.03	M = 2.91 SD = 1.13	F(2,155)=23.417 Scheffe a, c	.0005*

*Significant at *p* < .05 N/S = not significant

Scheffe tests were used to determine significant differences between groups where a = low/medium p < .05, b = medium/high p < .05, c = low/high, d=low/high approached significance p<.08.

Hypothesis 1b which examined whether there was a difference among low (M=17.28, SD=2.09), medium (M=17.85, SD=2.69), and high groups (M=17.58, SD=1.65) of participants exposed to instructor tweets and their perceived learning in the class via traditional means, a one-way analysis of variance was used. There was no difference in perceived learning via traditional means among these groups.

Hypothesis 2a which examined whether there was a difference in classroom community with regard to use of technological media among participants exposed to low (M=11.80, SD=2.70), medium (M=12.85,SD=2.84), and high (M=13.02, SD=2.53) amounts of instructor tweets was assessed utilizing a one-way analysis of variance. The test was significant F(2,154)=3.567, p=.031. Utilizing Scheffe there was no significant difference between individual groups. Although the difference between low and high groups almost achieved significance (p=.06).

To assess hypothesis 2b, a one-way analysis of variance was utilized to determine if there was a difference among low (M=15.74, SD=2.04), medium (M=16.21, SD=2.96), and high (M=15.89, SD=2.33) exposure to instructor Twitter usage and perceptions about classroom community considering traditional means. The test was not significant.

Hypothesis 3 examined whether there was a difference in perceived pedagogical affect with regard to methods of instruction among participants exposed to low (M=24.58, SD=3.68), medium (M=25.85, SD=2.63), and high (M=25.95, SD=2.54), amounts of instructor tweets about the course and the subject area. Using a one-way analysis of variance, there was a significant difference among the groups F(2, 150)=3.397, p=.036. However, again utilizing Scheffe, there was no significant difference among individual groups with the low and medium groups approaching a significant difference (p=.08). Multiple Levene's tests for equality of variances for all ANOVAs indicated that the data overall met the assumption of homogeneity of variance, with the exception of this variable. Therefore, results associated with this ANOVA must be interpreted with caution.

Hypothesis 4 which examined differences among low (M=24.84, SD=4.15), medium (M=27.64, SD=2.70), and high (M=25.45, SD=4.09) exposure to instructor Twitter usage in the course and perceived course effectiveness was tested utilizing a one-way analysis of variance. The test was significant F(2, 154)=6.995, p<.001. Utilizing Scheffe, there was a significant difference between the low and medium groups (p<.001) with the medium group perceiving more course effectiveness and between the medium group and the high group (p=.037) with the medium group perceiving more course effectiveness.

To assess hypothesis 5a which examined whether there was a difference among low (M=34.08, SD=4.81), medium (M=35.82, SD=4.44), and high (M=36.09, SD=3.81) exposure to instructor Twitter usage about the course and perceived learning performance a one-way analysis of variance was utilized. There was a significant difference F(2, 152)=3.470, p=.034 among the groups. However, utilizing Scheffe, only one difference between the low and high groups approached significance (p=.07).

Hypothesis 5b examined whether there was a difference among low, medium, and high exposure to instructor tweets about the course and students' belief that Twitter helps them learn about the course content. A one-way analysis of variance was conducted and the test was significant F(2, 155)=23.417, p<.0005. Using Scheffe, there was a significant difference between the low and medium groups (p<.0005) with the medium group perceiving more learning from Twitter and between the low and high groups (p<.0005) with the high group perceiving more learning from Twitter.

DISCUSSION

Overall, the results of this study argue strongly for a continued focus on the classroom usage of Twitter. In those classrooms with higher Twitter usage, students reported increased learning from technology overall, a greater sense of classroom community, increased pedagogical affect, increased course effectiveness, and improved learning overall. Though the more conservative Scheffe tests were not always able to isolate differences among specific groups, those comparisons which were significant suggested that even a moderate amount of Twitter usage can lead to improved learning outcomes. Thus, this study fits with a growing body of literature suggesting there are some instructional and learning advantages (e.g., Johnson, 2011; Junco, Heigerbert, & Loken, 2010; Ricoy & Feliz, 2016) associated with using Twitter.

Twitter can create an online space for discourse, and engagement, outside the traditional academic environment, in a setting which is very comfortable for today's college students (Moody, 2010). The 140-character maximum does limit the kinds of commentary which are feasible; clearly, students cannot explore ideas in depth, as noted by Ebner, Lienhardt, Rohs, and Meyer (2010). However, as Ebner, Lienhardt, Rohs, and Meyer also point out, microblogging does allow for a range of very valuable shorter messages for both students and instructors, including "facilitation of student group work and getting an impression of the learning climate" (p. 99). Junco, Heigerbert, and Loken (2010) provided a number of examples of student tweets along these lines. Ricoy and Feliz (2016) go so far as to argue that "the restricted number of characters allowed by this tool contributes to sharpen the ingenuity of the participants" (p. 246), a sentiment shared by Hsu and Chang (2012). Clearly, Twitter can have pedagogical value, and further research, as noted below, should explore additional impacts of that relatively new online technology.

Professors should be careful about immediately and thoughtlessly incorporating Twitter, however. As Tomei (2011) pointed out, teachers should infuse technologies into the classroom, but they need to know which technologies work best. Moody (2010) noted several "pitfalls" of unreflective social media use, including the potential to overlook traditional content and teaching in a "top-down" format, if instructor use of social media takes over the course (p. 8). Dunlap and Lowenthal (2010) suggested that Twitter can be addictive, and "possibly even encourage bad grammar" (p. 132). And though privacy is not mentioned as a critical issue in most existing Twitter research, Stephens and Gunther (2016) noted possible privacy concerns and compensated for those by using a protected account.

Limitations

This exploratory, quasi-experimental study had a number of limitations. First, the small sample was predominantly female but this was indicative of the university from which the sample was drawn. Furthermore, the study was only conducted at one university utilizing only two instructors. Another limitation was that there was a disparity in the content of the two classes being examined. One was an interpersonal communication course where Twitter use might not be expected as integral to the course content, and the other course was integrated marketing communications course where Twitter use could have been seen as a necessary technology to understand as part of the course content.

Another limitation was that the fall (no Twitter) and spring (Twitter used) classes may not have been similar. Although in both semesters the students were predominantly Juniors and Seniors, student expectations may differ at certain times of year. Finally, while one of the contributions of this study was the development of multiple new measures pertaining to leaning from social media and enhancing classroom community through social media, such measures should be further developed to reach higher levels of internal consistency.

FUTURE RESEARCH DIRECTIONS

Though most classroom Twitter research has been quantitative, scholars are beginning to use qualitative and mixed methods approaches as well. Adding a qualitative element allows scholars to answer questions related to the rationale for student behavior with and reaction to classroom Twitter usage. For example, Junco, Elavsky and Heiberger (2013) combined quantitative measures with qualitative analysis of tweets, and DeGroot, Young and VanSlette (2015) combined a quantitative approach to consideration of instructor credibility with a thematic analysis of open-ended questions about students' perceptions of tweeting instructors. Prestridge (2014) also used a qualitative analysis of tweets as a way to explore student frustrations with faculty Twitter use, ranging from technological problems to issues related to simultaneous note-taking and tweeting. This kind of research may be quite challenging, however; as Ross, Terras, Warwick, and Welsh (2011) point out, "routinely used textual analysis tools cannot be applied to corpora of Tweets in a straightforward manner, due to the creative and fragmentary nature of language used within microblogging" (p. 214). This concern was echoed by Elavsky, Mislan, and Elavsky (2011), who struggled to code tweets in their attempt to utilize Twitter for the large lecture course. Though clearly difficult, this kind of research project could link more detailed, specific uses of Twitter to instructional outcomes, and thus provide better advice for instructors contemplating its use.

Additionally, scholars should consider increased usage of student perceptions and behaviors as independent variables to measure or qualitative concepts to explore. For example, as noted above, DeGroot, Young and VanSlette (2015) found that students who tweeted more frequently saw frequently tweeting (hypothetical) faculty members as more credible. Other studies have, at least anecdotally, noted that not all students use and view Twitter in the same way, and that these differences could impact how they react to a faculty member using Twitter in the classroom (e.g., Prestridge, 2014); one study also suggested that cultural differences in Twitter usage could contribute to differing perceptions of tweeting faculty (Tur, Marin, & Carpenter, 2017).

Future research also should take into account how the perception of Twitter has changed over time, particularly with regard to other competing social networking sites. Compared to Instagram, for instance, which was largely unknown when this study was conducted, Twitter has experienced minimal growth recently – in short, it is not the "favorite" social networking site of most people. More than twice as many people worldwide use Instagram (Constine, 2017), and still more use Facebook. Future research might instead consider the fascinating visual appeal of Instagram for classroom usage, particularly in those courses with extensive and obvious visual elements (such as art).

Additional research might explore the extent to which other instructionally relevant dependent variables are influenced by Twitter. For example, research might explore the extent to which Twitter usage influences affective learning, a concept explored extensively in communication-based instructional research (e.g., Edwards, Edwards, Torrens, & Beck, 2011; Hsu, 2012). Though Junco, Heigerbert, and Loken (2010) have already demonstrated a substantial difference in GPA for those courses which used Twitter versus those which did not, additional research might further explore differences in actual cognitive learning (as opposed to perceived learning) due to Twitter use.

CONCLUSION

Twitter has the potential to be a powerful online instructional tool, providing advantages related to how both the professor and elements of the course as a whole are perceived by students. Further research is needed to discern more which aspects of Twitter use, in what contexts, contribute positively to instructional and learning outcomes. Additional research might explicitly compensate for some of the limitations noted above, including the nature of the sample. That research should include, at some point, a more thoughtful analysis of the contents of tweets – one which began through the quasi-experimental manipulation of tweeting levels in the study described above.

REFERENCES

Blog.Twitter.com. (2011). *#numbers*. Retrieved March 15, 2012 from http://blog.twitter.com/2011/03/numbers.html

Boyd, D., & Ellison, N. (2008). Social network sites: Definition, history and scholarship. *Journal of Computer-Mediated Communication*, *13*(1), 210–230. doi:10.1111/j.1083-6101.2007.00393.x

Chang, Y., Liu, E. Z., & Chang, M. (2011). Investigating adolescent bloggers from the perspective of creative subculture. *International Journal of Online Pedagogy and Course Design*, *1*(2), 31–45. doi:10.4018/ijopcd.2011040103

Clarke, T. B., & Nelson, C. L. (2012). Classroom community, pedagogical effectiveness, and learning outcomes associated with Twitter use in undergraduate marketing courses. *Journal for Advancement of Marketing Education*, *20*(2), 1–10.

Constine, J. (2017). *Instagram's growth speeds up as it hits 700 million users*. Retrieved September 11, 2017 from https://techcrunch.com/2017/04/26/instagram-700-million-users/

Dagada, R., & Chigona, A. (2013). Integration of E-Learning into curriculum delivery at university level in South Africa. *International Journal of Online Pedagogy and Course Design*, *3*(1), 53–65. doi:10.4018/ijopcd.2013010104

DeGroot, D. M., Young, V. J., & VanSlette, S. H. (2015). Twitter use and its effects on studentperception ofinstructorcredibility. *CommunicationEducation*,*64*(4),419–437. doi:10.1080/03634523.2015.1014386

Dunlap, J. C., & Lowenthal, P. R. (2010). Tweeting the night away: Using Twitter to enhancesocial presence. *Journal of Information Systems Education*, *20*(2), 129–135.

Ebner, M., Lienhardt, C., Rohs, M., & Meyer, I. (2010). Microblogs in higher education – A Chance to facilitate informal and process-oriented learning? *Computers & Education*,*55*(1),92–100. doi:10.1016/j.compedu.2009.12.006

Ebner, M., & Schiefner, M. (2008). Microblogging: More than fun? In I. Sanchez & P. Isaias (Eds.), *Proceedings ofIADIS Mobile Learning Conference*, *2008* (pp. 155-159). Algarve, Portugal: Academic Press.

Edwards, C., Edwards, A., Torrens, A., & Beck, A. (2011). Confirmation and community:The relationships between teacher confirmation, classroom community, student motivation, and learning. *Online Journal of Communication and Media Technologies*, *1*(4), 17–43.

Elavsky, C. M., Mislan, C., & Elavsky, S. (2011). When talking less is more: Exploring outcomes of Twitter usage in the large-lecture hall. *Learning, Media and Technology*, *36*(3), 215–233. doi:10.1080/17439884.2010.549828

Evans, C. (2014). Twitter for teaching: Can social media be used to enhance the process of Learning? *British Journal of Educational Technology*, *45*(5), 902–915. doi:10.1111/bjet.12099

Fiergermon, S. (2017). *Twitter is now losing users in the U.S.* Retrieved September 8, 2017 from http://money.cnn.com/2017/07/27/technology/business/twitter-earnings/index.html

García-Suárez, J., Trigueros, C., & Rivera, E. (2015). Twitter as a resource to evaluate the university teaching process. RUSC. *Universities and Knowledge Society Journal*, *12*(3), 32–45. doi:10.7238/rusc.v12i3.2092

Gray, K., & Carter, M. (2012). "If Many Were Involved": University student self-interest and engagement in a social bookmarking activity. *International Journal of Online Pedagogy and Course Design*, *2*(4), 20–31. doi:10.4018/ijopcd.2012100102

Hsu, C. (2012). The influence of vocal qualities and confirmation of nonnative English-Speaking teachers on student receiver apprehension, affective learning, and cognitive Learning. *Communication Education*, *61*(1), 4–16. doi:10.1080/03634523.2011.615410

Hsu, Y.-C., & Chang, Y.-H. (2012). Mobile microblogging: Using Twitter and mobile devices in an online course to promote learning in authentic contexts. *International Review of Research in Open and Distance Learning*, *13*(4), 211–227. doi:10.19173/irrodl.v13i4.1222

Isman, A., Gazi, Z. A., & Aksal, F. A. (2012). Where time goes: The role of online technology during leisure time learning. *International Journal of Online Pedagogy and Course Design*, *2*(2), 1–10. doi:10.4018/ijopcd.2012040101

Jacquemin, S. J., Smesler, L. K., & Bernot, M. J. (2014). Twitter in the higher education classroom: A student and faculty assessment of use and perception. *Journal of College Science Teaching*, *43*(6), 22–27.

Johnson, K. A. (2011). The effect of Twitter posts on students' perceptions of instructor credibility. *Learning, Media and Technology*, *36*(1), 21–38. doi:10.1080/17439884.2010.534798

Juhary, J. (2016). Revision through Twitter: Do tweets affect students' performance? *International Journal of Emerging Technologies in Learning*, *11*(4), 4–9. doi:10.3991/ijet.v11i04.5124

Junco, R., Elavsky, C. M., & Heiberger, G. (2013). Putting Twitter to the test: Assessing outcomes for student collaboration, engagement and success. *British Journal of Educational Technology*, *44*(2), 273–287. doi:10.1111/j.1467-8535.2012.01284.x

Junco, R., Heibergert, G., & Loken, E. (2010). The effect of Twitter on college student engagement and grades. *Journal of Computer Assisted Learning*, *27*(2), 119–132. doi:10.1111/j.1365-2729.2010.00387.x

Kim, H.-J., & Kim, Y.-H. (2016). Recent researches on application and influence of Twitter. *International Journal of Applied Engineering Research*, *11*(11), 7501–7504.

Kim, P. (2011). "Stay Out of the Way! My Kid is Video Blogging Through a Phone!": A lesson learned from math tutoring social media for children in underserved communities. *International Journal of Online Pedagogy and Course Design*, *1*(1), 50–63. doi:10.4018/ijopcd.2011010104

Leslie, P., & Murphy, E. (2008). Post-secondary students' purposes for blogging. *International Review of Research in Open and Distance Learning*, *9*(3), 1–17. doi:10.19173/irrodl.v9i3.560

Lin, M.-F. G., Hoffman, E. S., & Borengasser, C. (2013). Is social media too social for class? A case study of Twitter use. *TechTrends*, *57*(2), 39–45. doi:10.100711528-013-0644-2

Lowe, B., & Laffey, D. (2011). Is Twitter for the birds? Using Twitter to enhance student learning in a marketing course. *Journal of Marketing Education*, *33*(2), 183–192. doi:10.1177/0273475311410851

McArthur, J. A., & Bostedo-Conway, K. (2012). Exploring the relationship between student-Instructor interaction on Twitter and student perceptions of teacher behaviors. *International Journal on Teaching and Learning in Higher Education, 24*(3), 286–292.

Mitchell, A. A., & Olsen, J. C. (1981). Are product attribute beliefs the only mediators of advertising affects on brand attitude? *JMR, Journal of Marketing Research, 18*(3), 318–332. doi:10.2307/3150973

Moody, M. (2010). Teaching Twitter and beyond: Tips for incorporating social media in traditional courses. *Journal of Magazine and New Media Research, 11*(2), 1–9.

Nemetz, P., Aiken, K. D., Cooney, V., & Pascal, V. (2012). Should faculty use social networks to engage with students? *Journal for Advancement of Marketing Education, 20*(1), 19–28.

Prestridge, S. (2014). A focus on students' use of Twitter – their interactions with each other, content, and interface. *Active Learning in Higher Education, 15*(2), 101–115. doi:10.1177/1469787414527394

Ricoy, M. C., & Feliz, T. (2016). Twitter as a learning community in Higher Education. *Journal of Educational Technology & Society, 19*(1), 237–248.

Rinaldo, S. B., Tapp, S., & Laverie, D. A. (2011). Learning by tweeting: Using Twitter as a pedagogical tool. *Journal of Marketing Education, 33*(2), 193–203. doi:10.1177/0273475311410852

Ross, C., Terras, M., Warwick, C., & Welsh, A. (2011). Enabled backchannel: Conference Twitter use by digital humanists. *The Journal of Documentation, 67*(2), 214–237. doi:10.1108/00220411111109449

Sadera, W. A., Robertson, J., Song, L., & Midon, M. N. (2009). The role of community in online learning success. *Journal of Online Learning and Teaching / MERLOT, 5*(2), 277–284.

Stephens, T. M., & Gunther, M. E. (2016). Twitter, millennials, and nursing education research. *Nursing Education Perspectives, 37*(1), 23–27. doi:10.5480/14-1462 PMID:27164773

Stern, D. M. (2011). You had me at Foucault: Living pedagogically in the digital age. *Text and Performance Quarterly, 31*(3), 249–266. doi:10.1080/10462937.2011.573191

Tiernan, P. (2014). A study of the use of Twitter by students for lecture engagement and discussion. *Education and Information Technologies, 19*(4), 673–690. doi:10.100710639-012-9246-4

Tomei, L. A. (2011). Top Technologies for Integrating Online Instruction. *International Journal of Online Pedagogy and Course Design, 1*(1), 12–28. doi:10.4018/ijopcd.2011010102

Tsai, C.-W. (2016). The use of mobile technology and ubiquitous computing for universal access in online education. *Universal Access in the Information Society, 15*(3), 313–314. doi:10.100710209-014-0389-5

Tur, G., Marin, V. I., & Carpenter, J. (2017). Using Twitter in higher education in Spain and the USA. *Media Education Research Journal, 25*(51), 19–27. doi:10.3916/C-51-2017-02

Twitter.com. (2013). *What is Twitter?* Retrieved May 3, 2013 from https://twitter.com/about

Twitter.com. (2017). *About Twitter*. Retrieved September 14, 2017 from https://about.twitter.com/en_us.html

Young, M. R. (2001). Windowed, wired, and webbed--now what? *Journal of Marketing Education, 23*(1), 45–55. doi:10.1177/0273475301231006

Young, M. R., Klemz, B. R., & Murphy, J. W. (2003). Enhancing learning outcomes: The effects of instructional technology, learning styles, instructional methods, and student behavior. *Journal of Marketing Education, 25*(2), 130–142. doi:10.1177/0273475303254004

This research was previously published in Innovative Applications of Online Pedagogy and Course Design; pages 222-236, copyright year 2018 by Information Science Reference (an imprint of IGI Global).

Chapter 88
Human Attitude Towards the Use of IT in Education:
Academy and Social Media

Silvia Gaftandzhieva

University of Plovdiv Paisii Hilendarski, Bulgaria

Rositsa Doneva

University of Plovdiv Paisii Hilendarski, Bulgaria

ABSTRACT

This chapter aims to explore the human attitude towards the use of IT in education, especially teacher attitudes towards the use of social media in teaching practice. The study is based on a survey questionnaire, which aims to investigate to what extent and for what purposes teachers from different countries from all over the world use social networking in their teaching practice. The chapter presents the method (an exploratory survey using questionnaire for data collection), organization of the study, and thorough analyses of the results in accordance with the study objectives. Finally, summarized results of the survey are presented, depending on the continent where the countries of the participants are located. The analysis of the survey results is presented on the basis of valid responses of 19,987 teachers from 75 countries around the world who participated in the survey.

INTRODUCTION

Students in the 21st century (referred to as the digital generation, digital natives) are growing up constantly connected to the world around them through smartphones, tablets, and computers. Marc Prensky (Prensky, 2001) defines the term "digital native" and applies it to a new group of students enrolling in educational establishments referring to the young generation as "native speakers" of the digital language of computers, videos, video games, social media and other sites on the internet. IT are changing the process of teaching and learning during last decade. IT experts have developed a lot of applications which can be used by teachers and students in the learning process.

DOI: 10.4018/978-1-6684-7123-4.ch088

Millennial learning styles require teachers acquire skills to adapt to digital learning. Nowadays, teachers from all over the world use IT to do and provide students with learning resources, video and audio materials that students can access at any time using their computers, notebooks, smartphones, etc. In order to meet the unique learning needs of digital natives, teachers need to move away from traditional teaching methods that are disconnected from the way students learn today (Morgan, 2014). Students from the digital age thrive on creative and engaging activities, varied sources of information, and a more energetic environment. Teachers are faced with the challenge to understand how they communicate and interact with the world in order to meet the needs of today's students and to teach more effectively.

Nowadays social networking is becoming a more and more powerful tool for communication, sharing of information and discussions on various topics. According to a worldwide survey, approximately 2 billion web surfers are using social networks today (Statista, 2018). The characteristics of social platforms, such as shared content and user-generated content, make them a powerful tool that helps to deliver a quality, personalized and student-centered education. Social networking sites have a significant presence in the contemporary higher education instsitutions and more and more teachers are showing an interest in taking advantage of the possibilities they offer for learning (Hortigüela-Alcalá, Sánchez-Santamaría, Pérez-Pueyo & Abella-García, 2019).

The wide academic and research interest in the use of social networking for educational purposes in higher education is the natural result of the constantly growing popularity of social networking.

According to Pearson (Seaman & Tinti-Kane, 2013), a learning company that promotes the effective use of technology, "A majority of faculty now use social media in a professional context (any aspect of their profession outside of teaching). Use of social media for teaching purposes has lagged even more, but like the other patterns of use, it has increased every year. The number of faculty who use social media in the classroom still does not represent a majority, but teaching use continues its steady year-to-year growth. Faculties are sophisticated consumers of social media. In general, they see considerable potential in the application of social media and technology to their teaching, but not without a number of serious barriers".

Likely the most significant and life changing technologies of the 21st century is the adoption of social media as major components of educational activities (Anderson, 2019). In recent years there has been extensive academic and research interest in the use of social networking for educational purposes (Acharya, Patel & Jethava, 2013; Voorn & Kommers, 2013; Wang, Woo, Quek, Yang & Liu, 2011; Kropf, 2013; Arquero, & Romero-Frías, 2013; Alam, 2018; Carapina, Bjelobrk & Duk, 2013; Ghanem, El-Gafy & Abdelrazig, 2014; Rothkrantz, 2015; Doneva & Gaftandzhieva, 2016; Zancanaro & Domingues, 2018; Awidi, Paynter, & Vujosevic, 2019; Saini & Abraham, 2019; Dommett, 2019; Aleksandrova & Parusheva, 2019; Anderson, 2019; Vivakaran, 2018; Zachos, Paraskevopoulou-Kollia, & Anagnostopoulos, 2018) and the presentation of higher education institutions and courses on social networks (Golubić & Lasić-Lazić, 2012; Golubić, 2017; Zancanaro & Domingues, 2018; Kumar & Nanda, 2019). Some educational institutions use social media educational system to support learning and interaction on campus, foster and encourage active learners' participation in the school system (Azeta et al. 2014).

A number of surveys have been conducted worldwide on the use of social networks by teachers and students (Hendee, 2014; Faculty Focus, 2011; Zanamwe, Rupere, & Kufandirimbwa, 2013; Mardikyan & Bozanta, 2017; Moran, Seaman, & Tinti-Kane, 2011; Kolan & Dzandza, 2018; Abu-Shanab, & Al-Tarawneh, 2015; Prestridge, 2019; Luguetti, Goodyear, & André, 2019; Awidi, Paynter, & Vujosevic, 2019; Saini & Abraham, 2019). The results of these surveys show that teachers do not use social networking sites for communication with their students (Ghanem, El-Gafy & Abdelrazig, 2014; Hendee,

2014; Faculty Focus, 2011) and during lessons (Hendee, 2014). Teachers use social networking sites to share information and resources with educators, to create professional learning communities and to connect with peers and colleagues (edWeb, 2009), to improve students' engagement in their course and their educational experience (Hendee, 2014; Mardikyan & Bozanta, 2017; Rutherford, 2010; Rodriguez, 2011; Junco, Elavsky & Heiberger, 2013; Awidi, Paynter, & Vujosevic, 2019; Saini & Abraham, 2019), to expand their own professional learning opportunities on social media platforms (Prestridge, 2019), to support the development of an authentic sport experience (Luguetti, Goodyear, & André, 2019). These surveys are held within a university or country. Therefore, the summarised results of these surveys do not allow us to draw conclusions about the attitude of teachers towards the use of social networks worldwide.

The chapter aims to explore the human attitude toward the use of IT in education, especially the teachers' attitude towards the use of social media in teaching practice. The study is based on a survey questionnaire, which aims to investigate to what extent teachers from different countries from all over the world use social networking sites in their teaching practice for different purposes on the basis of results from filled questionnaires. The attitude towards the use of social networking in higher education in general is examined. The study is intended to seek dependences between the answers related to the above issues and different teachers' characteristics, on the point of view if the teachers are well informed about social networking sites, or whether they participate in interest groups or research related with social networking and higher education. Finally, summarized results of the survey are presented, depending on the continent where the countries of the participants are located.

The chapter presents the method, organization of the study and thorough analyses of the results in accordance with the study objectives. Some general conclusions about the latest trends in the use of social networking in education are derived.

DESIGN OF THE STUDY

This section describes briefly the process for data collection and analysis, in order to contextualise the sections that follow.

The study´s method is based on an empirical approach – an exploratory survey using questionnaire for data collection. The questionnaire, used for data collection, contains 20 questions divided into three sections (see Appendix 1). It has been used to study the attitude towards the use of social networking in Bulgarian higher education (Doneva & Gaftandzhieva, 2017).

The questions in Section 1. Personal Information for participant (see Appendix 1) aim to determine the profile of respondents: gender, age, degree, title, university, country. This section contains also the question of the degree of awareness of participants about social networking to ensure the reliability of conclusions drawn from the analysis of the inquiry results.

In order to examine teachers' attitude towards the use of social networking for educational purposes, the main part of the questionnaire includes two sections - Opinion on the use of social networks in teaching practice (Section 2, see Appendix 1) and Opinion on the use of social networking for educational purposes in general (Section 3, see Appendix 1). Most of the questions are multiple choice. Respondents should state the extent of their agreement with formulated statements on the 5-point Likert-type scale in which 1 = Strongly Disagree (SD), 2 = Disagree (D), 3 = Neutral (N), 4 = Agree (A) and 5 = Strongly Agree (SA). There is an open-ended question for teachers at the end of the second and third part of the questionnaire. Teachers can indicate how they use social networking in their teaching practice, as well as why they consider that the use of social networks in education has a negative effect (if so).

The questionnaire was sent by email to teachers from different countries from all over the world. After collecting the data through the questionnaires, they were analysed using Microsoft Excel.

FINDINGS AND DISCUSSIONS

Respondents' Profile

The analysis of the survey results is presented on the basis of valid responses of 19 987 teachers from 75 countries around the world who participated in the survey. All countries with participants are marked with a certain color depending on the continent where they are located. Figure 1 presents the number of participants from each continent. 121 teachers did not answer the question about the country in which they work.

Figure 1. Number of participants by continents (Adopted from https://mapchart.net)

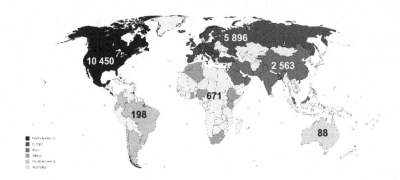

Out of the total number of teachers 49.75% are male and 55.25% are female. The largest group of teachers (28.34%) is above 55 years old, 26.75% of teachers are 45-54 years old and 24.76% of teachers are 35-44 years old. The smallest groups of teachers are 25-34 years old (17.34%) and below 25 years old (2.81%). Half of the teachers have a Ph.D. degree (50.08%) and D.Sc. degree (3.47%). Table 1 presents a summary profile of respondents based on the gathered demographic and other personal data.

Most surveyed teachers are familiar with social networking – 65.49% answered Yes and 29.94% Yes/No to the question "Are you well informed about social networking (e.g. Facebook, Twitter, Google+, Bebo, Myspace, LinkedIn, etc.)?". Figure 2 presents the percentage of answers given by their faculty position and age group.

Table 1. Respondents' profile

Respondent's Information	Total		Male		Female	
	Number	Percent	Number	Percent	Number	Percent
Age						
Below 25	561	2.81%	209	1.05%	352	1.76%
25-34	3 465	17.34%	1 518	7.59%	1 947	9.75%
35-44	4 950	24.76%	2 453	12.27%	2 497	12.49%
45-54	5 346	26.75%	2 475	12.39%	2 871	14.36%
Above 55	5 665	28.34%	3 289	16.45%	2 376	11.89%
Degree						
PhD	10 010	50.08%	6 017	30.10%	3 993	19.98%
D.Sc.	693	3.47%	396	1.98%	297	1.49%
Other	9 284	46.45%	3 531	17.67%	5 753	8.78%
Faculty Position						
Assistant	1 210	6.05%	583	2.92%	627	3.13%
Assistant Professor	4 829	24.16%	2 618	13.10%	2 211	11.06%
Associate Professor	3 487	17.45%	1 969	9.86%	1 518	7.59%
Professor	4 697	23.50%	2 585	12.93%	2 112	10.57%
Other	5 764	28.84%	2 189	10.95%	3 575	17.89%

Figure 2. Percentage of the answers to Question 7 according to teachers' faculty position and age group

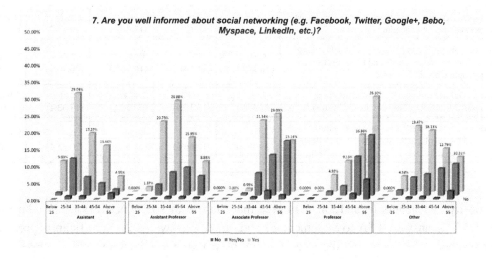

Survey Results

An analysis of the answers given on the statements from Section 2 shows that a significant smaller part of surveyed teachers use the social networking sites to communicate with their students (51.96% answered SD or D, and 18.27% answered N to Statement 8) and participate in online social networking groups for information sharing, discussion and organization of courses (56.80% answered SD or D to Statement 9, and 60.54% answered SD or D to Statement 10). The percentage of teachers who believe that the use of social networking during the lesson increases the engagement of students is even smaller - only 18.40% (see answers to Statement 11). The number of teachers who participate in online groups interested in the use of social networking for educational purposes is also small - 32.63%. 53.03% of the surveyed teachers have a public profile in a social networking site to share research interests and to connect with like-minded people (Statement 13). Finally, when teachers are asked to agree that the use of social networking has a positive effect on student achievement and increases the involvement and interest of students in the training, 39.62% of teachers stated that they are SD or D with Statement 14 and 41.06% of teachers stated that they are SD or D with Statement 15. Table 2 presents summarized results of Section 2.

Table 2. Using of social networking sites in teachers' academic practice

Statement	1=SD	2=D	3=N	4=A	5=SA
8. You often use social networking sites for communication and consultation with your students.	6 919 (34.62%)	3 465 (17.34%)	3 652 (18.27%)	3 608 (18.05%)	2 343 (11.72%)
9. You participate in social networking group/groups with your students for information sharing and discussions on the courses.	7 777 (38.91%)	3 575 (17.89%)	3 454 (17.28%)	3 256 (16.29%)	1 925 (9.63%)
10. You participate in social networking group/groups with your students for organization of the courses.	7 777 (42.38%)	3 630 (18.16%)	3 300 (16.51%)	2 948 (14.75%)	1 639 (8.20%)
11. You use social networking sites during the lesson in order to increase students' involvement and to keep track of their reactions.	9 526 (47.85%)	4 004 (20.11%)	2 717 (13.65%)	2 299 (11.55%)	1 364 (6.85%)
12. You participate in online group/groups interested in the use of social networking for educational purposes.	6 963 (34.84%)	3 091 (15.47%)	3 410 (17.06%)	4 092 (20.47%)	2 431 (12.16%)
13. You have a public profile in some of social networking sites to share yours research interests and to connect with a wide range of people with similar preferences.	3 630 (18.17%)	2 365 (11.84%)	3 338 (16.96%)	5 346 (26.76%)	5 247 (26.27%)
14. The use of social networking sites in your teaching practice has a positive effect on the student achievements.	5 489 (27.46%)	2 431 (12.16%)	6 424 (32.14%)	3 630 (18.33%)	1 980 (9.91%)
15. The use of social networking sites in your teaching practice increases the involvement and interest of students in the training.	5 676 (28.40%)	2 530 (12.66%)	5 720 (28.62%)	4 048 (20.25%)	2 013 (10.07%)

The majority of teachers (see. Table 3.) agree that the use of social networking in education can be useful - 24.71% answered SA to Statement 17 and 36.05% answered A. Significantly greater is the number of teachers who agree that the role of social networking in education will increase – 36.12% answered SA and 37.83% answered A to Statement 18. This shows that despite the relatively low rate of the current use of social networking, the majority of teachers are likely to use social networks in the future. The answers given on Statement 19 show that the low rate of use of social networks at the moment is probably due also to the low level of participation of teachers in research on the use of social networking in education – only 5 764 teachers (28.97%) stated participation in such research.

Table 3. Using of social networking for educational purposes in general

Statement	1=SD	2=D	3=N	4=A	5=SA
17. Social networking sites are/can be useful in education.	1 210 (6.05%)	1 749 (8.75%)	4 884 (24.44%)	7 205 (36.05%)	4 939 (24.71%)
18. The role of social networking sites will increase.	902 (4.52%)	1 001 (5.01%)	3 300 (16.52%)	7 557 (37.83%)	7 216 (36.12%)
19. You participate in research related to the use of social networking sites in education.	7 150 (35.93%)	3 366 (16.92%)	3 619 (18.19%)	3 399 (17.08%)	2 365 (11.89%)

Overall, the survey results show that teachers have a negative attitude towards the use of social networking in their academic practice (an average grade 2.58 on the eight statements from Section 2 of the questionnaire). Although the surveyed teachers do not use social networking sites in their teaching practice now, they believe that social networking sites can be useful for education in general and have a positive attitude towards the use of social networking for educational purposes (an average grade 3.38 on the three statements from Section 3 of the questionnaire). Figure 3 presents the average grades on statements from Section 2 and Section 3 of the questionnaire given by the teachers.

Figure 3. Average grades on statements from Section 2 and Section 3

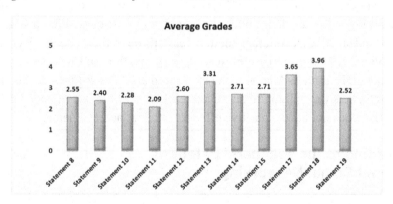

The survey results do not confirm results of the same survey conducted in Bulgaria (Doneva & Gaftandzhieva, 2017) in a full degree. Unlike their colleagues around the world, teachers in Bulgaria are more active in the use of social networking sites for communication with their students. Also small, but relatively larger than in the world, part of the Bulgarian teachers use social networking sites for information sharing, discussions and course organization. Surveyed teachers within this survey are more active than Bulgarian teachers in the use of social networking during lesson, participation in online groups interesting in the use of social networking for educational purposes. Bulgarian teachers gave significant higher grades on statements that the role of social networking in education will increase and social networking can be useful for education, but they are less involved in research related to the use of social networking in education than their colleagues from other countries.

The most results obtained are in line with the findings of other surveys on the use of social networking in education. For example some surveys conducted among teachers (Ghanem, El-Gafy & Abdelrazig,

2014; Hendee, 2014; Faculty Focus, 2011) show that teachers do not use social networks for communication with their students and prefer to use conventional communication channels (email, phone calls, and text messaging respectively). The conclusion that a small number of teachers use social networking during lessons also confirms the results of another survey (Hendee, 2014). The finding that most teachers use social networking sites to share their research interests and to connect with a wide range of people with similar preferences confirms the results of other surveys (edWeb, 2009; Vivakaran, 2018). These surveys concludes that teachers use social networking to share information and resources with educators, to create professional learning communities and to connect with peers and colleagues. Moreover, the positive attitude of the teachers towards the statements that social networking sites can be useful in education and their role in education will increase, substantiates the teachers' expectation to increase their use of social media in the future (Faculty Focus, 2011). However, some of the findings from the current survey do not correspond to those of other studies. This study's conclusions that the use of social networks doesn't increase students' engagement and interest while studying their course differ from the conclusions of other studies, according to which the use of social networks improve students' engagement in their course and their educational experience, on the one hand (Hendee, 2014; Mardikyan & Bozanta, 2017; Rutherford, 2010; Rodriguez, 2011; Junco, Elavsky & Heiberger, 2013; Saini & Abraham, 2019), and peer interaction and students' interaction with faculty members, on the other (Zanamwe, Rupere, & Kufandirimbwa, 2013; Mardikyan & Bozanta, 2017). The findings do not corroborate the results of another studies (Kolan & Dzandza, 2018; Awidi, Paynter, & Vujosevic, 2019; Hortigüela-Alcalá, Sánchez-Santamaría, Pérez-Pueyo & Abella-García, 2019) conducted among the students, according to which the use of social networking increases their understanding of topics discussed in class and improves their grades (Kolan & Dzandza, 2018), encourage them to learn through their Facebook engagement (Awidi, Paynter, & Vujosevic, 2019) and increase both student motivation and involvement, as well as their degree of achievement (Hortigüela-Alcalá, Sánchez-Santamaría, Pérez-Pueyo& Abella-García, 2019). This persuasion contradicts the opinion of surveyed teachers that the use of social networking sites in their teaching practice does not have a positive effect on student achievements.

Analysis According to the Teachers' Extent of Knowledge About Social Networking

The analysis of the answers to Question 7 shows that not all of the surveyed teachers are well informed about social networking. Therefore, it is natural for teachers who are not familiar with social networking sites to use them less often in their academic practice and not to be positive about their use in education. A detailed analysis of the answers to all questions was made to examine the extent to which the use of social networking in the academic practice of the surveyed teachers and their opinion on the use of social networking for education purposes in general are related to the teachers' extent of knowledge about social networking.

Figure 4 and Figure 5 present detailed results in percentage of the answers to the statements from Section 2 and Section 3 in the questionnaire teachers gave according to their extent of knowledge about social networking. The analysis shows that the most positive attitude towards the use of social networks in teaching practice and in education pertains to teachers (answered SA and A to the statements from Section 2 and Section 3) who are familiar with social networking (answered Yes to the Question 7), followed by teachers who are not fully informed about social networking (answered Yes/No to the Question 7). It is interesting to note that even teachers who answered they are unfamiliar with social networking

Figure 4. Percentage of answers to Statements 8-15 according to degree of information about social networking

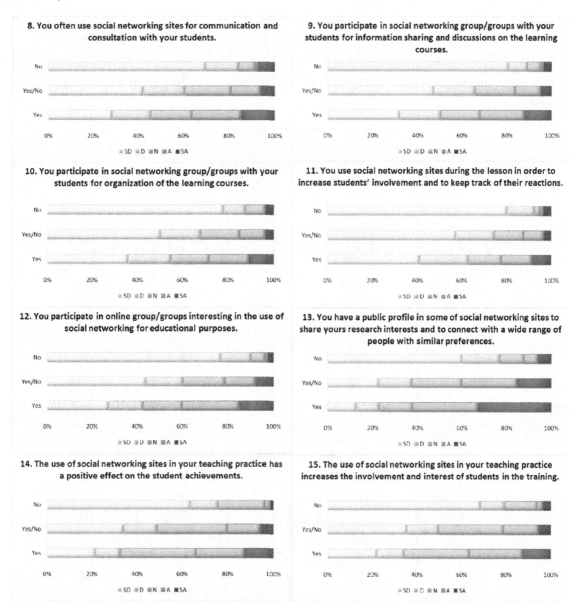

believe that social networking sites can be useful for education and they are convinced that the role of social networks in education will increase (see Figure 5).

The analysis shows that teachers who are familiar with social networking gave the highest average grades (the average of the given answers ranging from 1 to 5), followed by teachers who are not fully informed about social networking and teachers who are not familiar with social networks at all. Overall, teachers from all groups do not use social networking in their academic practice and gave an average grade below 3 to the statements in Section 2. Although teachers do not use social networking sites now and they do not participate actively in research related to the use of social networking sites in education (an average grade below 3 to Statement 19 by all groups of the surveyed teachers), all teachers are positive about the use of social networking in education, believe that social networking sites can be useful for education and they are convinced that their role in education will increase (an average grade above 3 to Statement 17 and to Statement 18 by all groups of the surveyed teachers), see Figure 6.

Figure 5. Percentage of answers to Statements 17-19 according to degree of information about social networking

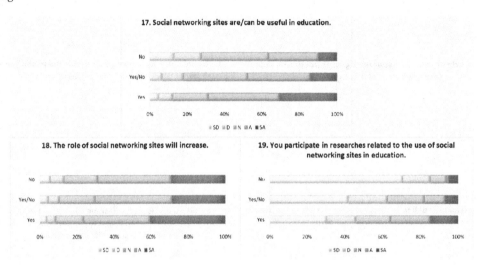

Figure 6. Average grades on statements from Section 2 and Section 3 according to degree of information about social networking

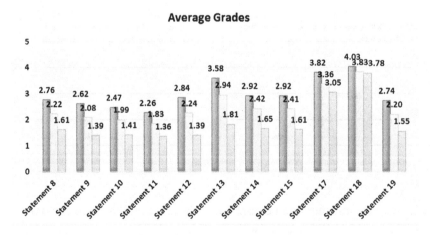

Analysis According to the Teachers' Participation in Groups

A small part of the surveyed teachers participate in groups interested in the use of social networking for educational purposes - only 6 523 (32.64%) of the surveyed teachers answered A or SA to Statement

12. You participate in online group/groups interested in the use of social networking for educational purposes. Significantly higher is the number of teachers who do not participate in groups interested in the use social networks for educational purposes – 10 054 of the surveyed teachers answered SD or D to Statement 12 (50.30%).

Table 4 presents the number of answers given by teachers who do not participate in groups interested in the use of social networking for educational purposes. The results show that teachers who do not participate in such groups rarely use social networking sites in their teaching practice. The analysis of the answers shows that teachers are skeptical towards the use of social networking for communication and consultation with their students, discussions on the studied material and organization of training courses – only 12.03% answered A or SA to Statement 8, 9.73% answered A or SA to Statement 9 and 6.24% answered A or SA to Statement 10. Most teachers are strongly against the use of social networking sites during lessons – only 4.06% of teachers gave answers A or SA to Statement 11. Teachers are skeptical that the use of social networking sites has a positive effect on students' achievements and that it increases their involvement and interest in the training – 9.19% of teachers gave answer A or SA to Statement 14 and 10.06% of teachers gave answer A or SA to Statement 15.

Table 4. Using of social networking sites in teaching practice according to answers on Statement 12 (SD=1 and D=2)

Statement	SD=1	D=2	N=3	A=4	SA=5
8. You often use social networking sites for communication and consultation with your students.	5 511 (54.81%)	2 134 (21.23%)	1 199 (11.93%)	671 (6.67%)	539 (5.36%)
9. You participate in social networking group/groups with your students for information sharing and discussions on the courses.	6 248 (62.14%)	2 035 (20.24%)	792 (7.88%)	671 (6.67%)	539 (3.06%)
10. You participate in social networking group/groups with your students for organization of the courses.	6 765 (67.29%)	1 848 (18.38%)	814 (8.10%)	451 (4.49%)	176 (1.75%)
11. You use social networking sites during the lesson in order to increase students' involvement and to keep track of their reactions.	7 271 (72.56%)	1 958 (19.54%)	385 (3.84%)	286 (2.85%)	121 (1.21%)
13. You have a public profile in some of social networking sites to share yours research interests and to connect with a wide range of people with similar preferences.	3 146 (31.29%)	1 518 (15.10%)	1 485 (14.77%)	2 145 (21.33%)	1 760 (17.51%)
14. The use of social networking sites in your teaching practice has a positive effect on the student achievements.	4 796 (47.70%)	1 496 (14.86%)	2 838 (28.23%)	627 (6.24%)	297 (2.95%)
15. The use of social networking sites in your teaching practice increases the involvement and interest of students in the training.	4 807 (47.81%)	1 672 (16.63%)	2 563 (25.49%)	693 (6.89%)	319 (3.17%)

The teachers who participate in groups interested in the use of social networking for educational purposes are more positive and actively use social networks in their academic practice. Table 5 presents the number of responses from teachers participating in such groups. The analysis of the answers shows that most of the surveyed teachers use social networking for communication and consultation with their students, discussions about the studied material and organization of courses – 56.16% answered SA or A to Statement 8, 52.28% answered A or SA to Statement 9 and 49.92% answered A or SA to Statement 10. A significant part of surveyed teachers have a positive attitude towards the use of social networking sites during lessons – 42.37% of teachers answered A or SA to Statement 11. Most teachers believe that the use of social networking sites has a positive effect on students' achievements and that it increases their involvement and interest in the training – 58.35% of teachers answered A or SA to Statement 14 and 61.89% of teachers answered A or SA to Statement 15.

The analysis of the answers clearly shows (see Figure 7) that teachers who participate in groups interested in the use of social networking sites for educational purposes gave higher average grades of all statements in Section 2. These teachers gave an average grade above 3 to the six statements in Section

Table 5. Using of social networking sites in teaching practice according to answers on Statement 12 (A=4 and SA=5)

Statement	SD=1	D=2	N=3	A=4	SA=5
8. You often use social networking sites for communication and consultation with your students.	770 (11.80%)	781 (11.97%)	1 309 (20.07%)	2 178 (33.39%)	1 485 (22.77%)
9. You participate in social networking group/groups with your students for information sharing and discussions on the courses.	836 (12.82%)	946 (14.50%)	1 331 (20.40%)	2 024 (31.03%)	1 386 (21.25%)
10. You participate in social networking group/groups with your students for organization of the courses.	946 (14.50%)	1 089 (16.69%)	1 232 (18.89%)	1 958 (30.02%)	1 298 (19.90%)
11. You use social networking sites during the lesson in order to increase students' involvement and to keep track of their reactions.	1 375 (21.19%)	1 221 (18.81%)	1 144 (17.63%)	1 650 (25.42%)	1 100 (16.95%)
13. You have a public profile in some of social networking sites to share yours research interests and to connect with a wide range of people with similar preferences.	253 (3.89%)	396 (6.08%)	836 (12.84%)	2 244 (34.46%)	2 783 (42.74%)
14. The use of social networking sites in your teaching practice has a positive effect on the student achievements.	286 (4.38%)	484 (7.42%)	1 947 (29.85%)	2 343 (35.92%)	1 463 (22.43%)
15. The use of social networking sites in your teaching practice increases the involvement and interest of students in the training.	363 (5.56%)	484 (7.42%)	1 639 (25.13%)	2 629 (40.30%)	1 408 (21.59%)

Figure 7. Average grades on statements from Section 2 according to answers on Statement 12

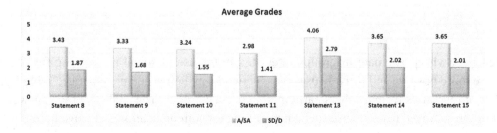

2. Although they have a positive attitude towards social networking in general, a small part of them use social networking sites during lessons - an average grade 2.98 on Statement 11.

Analysis According to the Teachers' Participation in Research for Social Networking

Analysis of the answers to *Statement 19. You participate in research related to the use of social networking sites in education* shows that a significant small part of the teachers participate in research related to the use of social networking sites in education - only 5 764 (28.97%) of the surveyed teachers answered A or SA. More than half of the surveyed teachers do not participate in such research – 10 516 of the teachers answered SD or D to Statement 19 (52.85%) (see Table 3, Statement 19). In order to establish the extent to which the positive attitude towards the use of social networking in education of the surveyed teachers is related to their scientific interests, a detailed analysis of the answers to all statements in Section 3 according to the teachers' participation in social networking research was made.

Table 6 and Table 7 present the analysis of the answers to the statements in Section 3 of the questionnaire according to teachers' participation in research related to the use of social networking sites in education. The analysis of the answers shows that teachers who do not participate in research related to the use of social networking believe that the use of social networking in education can have a positive effect and their role in education will increase – 47.80% answered A or SA to Statement 17 and 66.49% answered A or SA to Statement 18 (see Table 6). Most of the surveyed teachers that participate in such research have a positive attitude towards the use of social networking sites for educational purposes in general – only 330 (5.73%) teachers stated that social networking sites can't be useful in education and 242 (4.20%) teachers stated that their role will not increase (see Table 7).

Table 6. Using of social networking for educational purposes in general according to answers on Statement 19 (SD=1 and D=2)

Statement	SD=1	D=2	N=3	A=4	SA=5
17. Social networking sites are/can be useful in education.	1 034 (9.83%)	1 309 (12.45%)	3 146 (29.92%)	3 256 (30.96%)	1 771 (16.84%)
18. The role of social networking sites will increase.	715 (6.81%)	748 (7.12%)	2 057 (19.58%)	3 839 (36.54%)	3 146 (29.95%)

Table 7. Using of social networking for educational purposes in general according to answers on Statement 19 (A=4 and SA=5)

Statement	SD=1	D=2	N=3	A=4	SA=5
17. Social networking sites are/can be useful in education.	88 (1.53%)	242 (4.20%)	605 (10.50%)	2 519 (43.70%)	2 310 (40.08%)
18. The role of social networking sites will increase.	121 (2.10%)	121 (2.10%)	473 (8.21%)	2 200 (38.17%)	2 849 (49.43%)

Figure 8. Average grades on statements from Section 3 according to answers on Statement 19

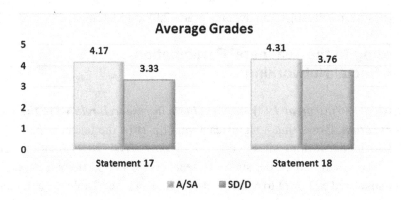

The analysis of the answers clearly shows (see Figure 8) that all teachers gave high average grades (above 3) to Statement 17 and Statement 18. Logically teachers who participate in research related to the use of social networking sites in education are more positive to their use and gave higher average grades (above 4).

Analysis According to the Continent Where Teachers Work

In order to establish the extent to which the attitude towards the use of social networking in education of the surveyed teachers depends on the continent where they are located, a detailed analysis of the answers to all statements according to the continent was made. Figure 9 presents detailed results in percentage of the answers of the statements from Section 2 and Section 3 of the questionnaire given by the surveyed teachers from sixth continents.

Table 8 presents the average grades given by teachers from the sixth continents. The analysis of the answers shows that the surveyed teachers from all countries do not use social networking sites in their teaching practice as a whole (see average grades on Statement 8-15). Teachers from Asia stated that they use social networking sites for communication, consultation and discussions with students (an average grade 3.13 to Statement 8 and 3.12 to Statement 9). Also, they are the most active in groups interested in the use of social networking for educational purposes (an average grade 3.17 to Statements 12), sharing of research interests (the highest average grade to Statement 13). Teachers from Asia have the most positive attitude towards the statement that the use of social networking sites in education has a positive effect on the student achievements (an average grade above 3 to Statements 14). Teachers from Africa have the most positive attitude towards the statement that social networking sites increase the interest and involvement of students in the training, followed by teachers from Asia (an average grade above 3 to Statement 15). Most teachers believe that the use of social networking in education can have a positive effect and their role in education will increase – only teachers from Australia are skeptical about this statement. Teachers from all countries gave average grades above 3 to Statement 18 and Statement 19. Although the answers given and the conviction of teachers for positive effects and the role of social networking, only teachers from Asia, North America and South America participate in research related to the use of social networking for educational purposes (an average grade above 3 to Statement 19).

Figure 9. Percentage of answers to Statement 8-19 according to continent

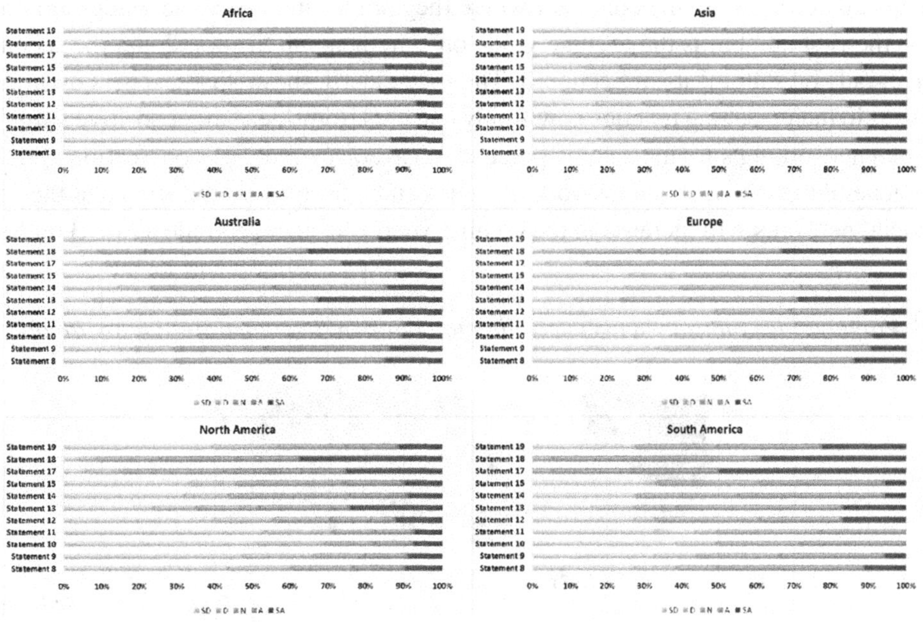

Table 8. Average answers by continents

Statement	Africa	Asia	Australia	Europe	North America	South America
8. You often use social networking sites for communication and consultation with your students.	3.07	3.13	1.88	2.71	2.28	2.94
9. You participate in social networking group/groups with your students for information sharing and discussions on the courses.	2.82	3.12	1.75	2.49	2.15	2.61
10. You participate in social networking group/groups with your students for organization of the courses.	2.59	2.94	1.75	2.40	2.03	2.39
11. You use social networking sites during the lesson in order to increase students' involvement and to keep track of their reactions.	2.39	2.68	1.63	2.00	1.98	2.28
12. You participate in online group/groups interested in the use of social networking for educational purposes.	2.84	3.17	2.00	2.58	2.45	2.94
13. You have a public profile in some of social networking sites to share yours research interests and to connect with a wide range of people with similar preferences.	3.30	3.67	3.25	3.50	3.12	3.33
14. The use of social networking sites in your teaching practice has a positive effect on the student achievements.	3.13	3.22	2.00	2.73	2.55	2.78
15. The use of social networking sites in your teaching practice increases the involvement and interest of students in the training.	3.41	3.22	2.00	2.73	2.55	2.78
17. Social networking sites are/can be useful in education.	3.97	3.82	2.88	3.62	3.60	4.44
18. The role of social networking sites will increase.	4.05	3.99	3.25	3.92	3.98	4.33
19. You participate in research related to the use of social networking sites in education.	3.00	3.14	2.88	2.40	2.39	3.17

Figure 10 presents the average grades of all statements in Section 2 and Section 3 given by the surveyed teachers calculated according to the continent where they are located. Average grades are presented in parentheses – the first number is the average grade on statements in Section 2 and the second number is the average grade on statements in Section 3. The map clearly shows that teachers do not use social networking sites in their teaching practice now – only teachers from Asia have a positive attitude towards the use of social networking sites in teaching practice (an average grade 3.14 on Section 2). All teachers think that in general the use of social networking sites can be useful for education and the educational role of the social networks will increase in the coming years (an average grade above 3 on Section 3).

Figure 10. Average grades on statements according to continent (Adopted from https://mapchart.net)

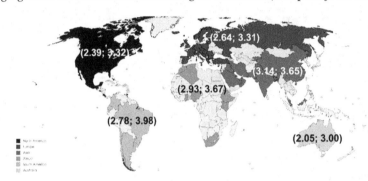

CONCLUSION

Due to the resource constraints the survey does not claim to be representative and has some limitations. The most important limitation is the number of participants. Around 100 000 teachers from all over the world (randomly selected) were asked to participate in the study, but only 19 987 of them filled in the questionnaire. Some of the invited teachers refused to participate because of various reasons - doubts about the reliability of the survey, spam attacks, etc.

The study gives a clear answer to the research questions – what is the extent to which teachers from different countries all over the world use social networking sites in their teaching practice for different purposes and what is their attitude towards the use of social networking in education in general.

The survey results show that teachers do not use social networking for educational purposes in their teaching practice today (an average grade 2.58 on the eight statements from Section 2 of the questionnaire). Only about 30% of the surveyed teachers actually use social networking for the following purposes:

- Communication and consultations;
- Holding discussions on the courses, highlighting of some topics, sharing of lecture notes;
- Increase involvement, cooperation and interest of students;
- Encourage creative writing;
- Sending additional materials and sharing information;
- Guidance for doing assignments/projects and manage progress on projects;
- Organization of the learning activities on specific courses or as a whole and keep students up–to-date on class activities, homework, assignments, midterms;

- Sharing research, best practises and communication with colleagues;
- Publication of events, activities and stories of interest to students;
- Announcement and invitation to workshops, conferences and other professional events;
- Course promotion;
- Contact alumni and former students;
- Open up discussion and exchange of ideas/opinions;
- Building networks between students from different programs or years;
- Help students connect to professionals in their field of interest.

It is natural that teachers who participate in groups interested in the use of social networking sites for educational purposes gave higher average grades of all statements in Section 2 (above 3) than teachers who do not participate in such groups. The average grades of all statements in Section 2 and Section 3 given by the surveyed teachers calculated according to the continent where they are located clearly shows that teachers' attitude towards the use of social networking for educational purposes depends on the continent where teachers are located.

Although the most surveyed teachers do not use social networking sites in their teaching practice now, they agree that the educational role of the social networks will increase in the coming years. Teachers from all continents believe that in general social networking sites can be useful for education (an average grade 3.38 on the three statements from Section 3 of the questionnaire). The answers of the open-ended question at the end of Section 3 show that most teachers today have a negative attitude towards the use of social networking for organizational/teaching activities for the following reasons:

- Distraction of the students and incompatibility to data protection regulations;
- Lack of person-to-person natural and intuitive communication and valuable direct interaction;
- Social networking sites are much informal and give to students too much freedom;
- It requires time to manage it - set up a social network channel for a course, update the social media channel, monitor and comment on it;
- It is hard to stay current with all the different social networking apps that students use;
- Danger of superficiality, lack of a reflective approach to learning;
- Sharing mechanisms blur the boundary between private and public/academic public;
- It is not a reflexive research-tool and does not allow for thorough ethical review process;
- Plagiarism, lack of motivation, laziness of thought and analytical skills, severe drop in communication and presentation skills, etc.;
- Some issues connected to privacy, security, archiving, and ethics;
- In terms of knowledge sharing, it dilutes the information and the objective value is subjected to crowd (mis)interpretation;
- It can blur boundaries between students and instructors;
- It is likely that social media will devalue the role of academics and education;
- Too many boundaries and ethical issues that higher education has yet to address.

The negative attitude of teachers today is related to the fact that not all of them are well informed about social networking and a significant small part of them participate in research related to the opportunities for the use of social networking in education. Teachers who have a positive attitude to the use of social networking for educational purposes believe that their use is quite beneficial if the networking site is created for educational purposes only and if the students are properly targeted to the use of the social networks and have clear guidelines. According to them if social networking is used wisely and properly social networking can enhance the learning experience and enhance the ability of the students to collaborate with others. They think that social networks are one of the channels they can use to communicate effectively with students. According to them social networking can be a useful tool for creation of a sense of community and share resources, for organising and motivating students, for research networking and production. Furthermore, teachers stated that social networking can create interaction and increase the knowledge of the students (especially in language teaching). Some teachers think also that opportunities for research, interaction and collaboration online can play a significant impact on students' achievement and learning. Teachers who do not use actively social networking for organizational/teaching activities today think that all this possibly will change in the next years with new students (with new social media behaviour) coming in.

ACKNOWLEDGMENT

This research was supported by the project "Intelligent Data Analysis for Improving the Learning Outcomes" of the Scientific Research Fund at the University of Plovdiv "Paisii Hilendarski" [grant number MU19-FTF-001] and the project "Digitalization of Economy in a big data environment" funded under the procedure "Creation and development of centres of competence" of Operational Programme "Science and education for smart growth" [grant number BG05M2OP001-1.002-0002-C].

REFERENCES

Abu-Shanab, E., & Al-Tarawneh, H. (2015). The Influence of Social Networks on High School Students' Performance. *International Journal of Web-Based Learning and Teaching Technologies*, *10*(2), 49–59. doi:10.4018/IJWLTT.2015040104

Acharya, V., Patel, Ad., & Jethava, S. (2013). A Survey on Social Networking to Enhance the Teaching and Learning Process. *International Journal of Advanced Research in Computer Science and Software Engineering*, *3*(6), 528–531.

Alam, L. (2018). *Teaching with web 2.0 technologies: Twitter, wikis & blogs*. Retrieved from https://tv.unsw.edu.au/files//unswPDF/CS_Web2_LTTO.pdf

Aleksandrova, Y., & Parusheva, S. (2019). Social Media Usage Patterns in Higher Education Institutions – An Empirical Study. *International Journal of Emerging Technologies in Learning*, *14*(5), 108–121. doi:10.3991/ijet.v14i05.9720

Anderson, T. (2019). Challenges and Opportunities for use of Social Media in Higher Education. *Journal of Learning for Development*, *6*(1), 6–19.

Arquero, J. L., & Romero-Frías, E. (2013). Using social network sites in Higher Education: An experience in business studies. *Innovations in Education and Teaching International*, *50*(3), 238–249. doi:10.1080/14703297.2012.760772

Aviles, M., & Eastman, J. K. (2012). Utilizing technology effectively to improve millennials' educational performance. *Journal of International Education in Business*, 5(2), 96–113. doi:10.1108/18363261211281726

Awidi, I. T., Paynter, M., & Vujosevic, T. (2019). Facebook group in the learning design of a higher education course: An analysis of factors influencing positive learning experience for students. *Computers & Education*, *129*, 106–121. doi:10.1016/j.compedu.2018.10.018

Azeta, A., Omoregbe, N., Ayo, C., Raymond, A., Oroge, A., & Misra, S. (2014). *An anti-cultism social education media system. In Global Summit on Computer & Information Technology* (pp. 1–5). Sousse: GSCIT. doi:10.1109/GSCIT.2014.6970097

Carapina, M., Bjelobrk, D., & Duk, S. (2013). *Web 2.0 tools in Croatian higher education: An overview. In Proceeding of Information & Communication Technology Electronics & Microelectronics (MIPRO 2013)* (Vol. 36, pp. 676–680). Opatija, Croatia: MIPRO.

Dommett, E. (2019). Understanding student use of twitter and online forums in higher education. *Education and Information Technologies*, *24*(1), 325–343. doi:10.100710639-018-9776-5

Doneva, R., & Gaftandzhieva, S. (2017). Social Media in Bulgarian Higher Education: An Exploratory Survey. *International Journal of Human Capital and Information Technology Professionals*, 8(3), 67–83. doi:10.4018/IJHCITP.2017100106

edWeb. (2009). *A Survey of K-12 Educators on Social Networking and Content-Sharing Tools*. Retrieved from https://www.edweb.net/fimages/op/K12Survey.pdf

Faculty Focus. (2011). *Social Media Usage Trends Among Higher Education Faculty*. Retrieved from https://www.facultyfocus.com/free-reports/social-media-usage-trends-among-higher-education-faculty/

Ghanem, A., El-Gafy, M., & Abdelrazig, Y. (2014). Survey of the Current Use of Social Networking in Construction Education. *Proceedings of the 50th ASC Annual International Conference*.

Golubić, K. (2017). *The Role of Social Networks in the Presentation of Croatian Higher Education Institutions* (Unpublished Doctoral Dissertation). University of Zagreb, Croatia.

Golubić, K., & Lasić-Lazić, J. (2012) Analysis of On-line Survey about Need for Presence of Higher Education Institutions on Social Networks: A Step towards Creation of Communication Strategy. *Journal of Computing and Information Technology*, *20*(3), 189-194.

Hendee, C. (2014). *Teachers have mixed feelings on using social media in classrooms*. Retrieved from https://www.bizjournals.com/denver/news/2014/02/11/teachers-have-mixed-feelings-on-using.html

Hortigüela-Alcalá, D., Sánchez-Santamaría, J., Pérez-Pueyo, Á., & Abella-García, V. (2019). Social networks to promote motivation and learning in higher education from the students' perspective. *Innovations in Education and Teaching International*, *56*(4), 412–422. doi:10.1080/14703297.2019.1579665

Junco, R., Elavsky, C. M., & Heiberger, G. (2013). Putting twitter to the test: Assessing outcomes for student collaboration, engagement and success. *British Journal of Educational Technology*, *44*(2), 273–287. doi:10.1111/j.1467-8535.2012.01284.x

Kolan, B., & Dzandza, P. (2018). Effect of Social Media on Academic Performance of Students in Ghanaian Universities: A Case Study of University of Ghana, Legon. *Library Philosophy and Practice (e-journal)*, 1637.

Kropf, D. (2013). Connectivism: 21st Century's New Learning Theory. *European Journal of Open, Distance and e-Learning*, *16*(2), 13-24.

Kumar, V., & Nanda, P. (2019). Social Media in Higher Education: A Framework for Continuous Engagement. *International Journal of Information and Communication Technology Education*, *15*(1), 97–108. doi:10.4018/IJICTE.2019010107

Luguetti, C., Goodyear, V. A., & André, M. H. (2019). That is like a 24 hours-day tournament: Using social media to further an authentic sport experience within sport education. *Sport Education and Society*, *24*(1), 78–91. doi:10.1080/13573322.2017.1292235

Mardikyan, S., & Bozanta, A. (2017). The effects of social media use on collaborative learning: A case of Turkey. *Turkish Online Journal of Distance Education-TOJDE*, *18*(1), 96–110. doi:10.17718/tojde.285719

Moran, M., Seaman, J., & Tinti-Kane, H. (2011). *Teaching, Learning, and Sharing: How Today's Higher Education Faculty Use Social Media*. Boston, MA: Pearson Learning Solutions. Retrieved from https://files.eric.ed.gov/fulltext/ED535130.pdf

Morgan, H. (2014). Using digital story projects to help students improve in reading and writing. *Reading Improvement*, *51*(1), 20–26.

Prensky, M. (2001). Digital Natives, Digital Immigrants. *On the Horizon*, *9*(5), 1–6. doi:10.1108/10748120110424816

Prestridge, S. (2019). Categorising teachers' use of social media for their professional learning: A self-generating professional learning paradigm. *Computers & Education*, *129*, 143–158. doi:10.1016/j.compedu.2018.11.003

Rodriguez, J. (2011). Social media use in higher education: Key areas to consider for educators. *MERLOT Journal of Online Learning and Teaching*, *7*(4), 539–550.

Rothkrantz, L. (2015). How Social Media Facilitate Learning Communities and Peer Groups around MOOCS. *International Journal of Human Capital and Information Technology Professionals*, *6*(1), 1–13. doi:10.4018/ijhcitp.2015010101

Rutherford, C. (2010). Using online social media to support preservice student engagement. *MERLOT Journal of Online Learning and Teaching*, *6*(4), 703–711.

Saini, C., & Abraham, J. (2019). Implementing Facebook-based instructional approach in pre-service teacher education: An empirical investigation. *Computers & Education*, *128*, 243–255. doi:10.1016/j.compedu.2018.09.025

Seaman, J., & Tinti-Kane, H. (2013). *Social Media for teaching and learning*. Boston, MA: Pearson Learning Solutions. Retrieved from https://www.onlinelearningsurvey.com/reports/social-media-for-teaching-and-learning-2013-report.pdf

Statista. (2018). *Most popular social networks worldwide as of January 2018, ranked by number of active users (in millions)*. Retrieved from https://www.statista.com/statistics/272014/global-social-networks-ranked-by-number-of-users/

Vivakaran, M. (2018). Social Media Technologies and Higher Education: Examing its Usage and Penetration Level as Educational Aids in India. *The Online Journal of Distance Education and e-Learning*, *6*(3), 21-29.

Voorn, R. J., & Kommers, P. (2013). Social media and higher education: Introversion and collaborative learning from the student's perspective. *International Journal of Social Media and Interactive Learning Environments*, *1*(1), 59–71. doi:10.1504/IJSMILE.2013.051650

Wang, Q., Woo, H. L., Quek, C. L., Yang, Y., & Liu, M. (2011). Using the Facebook group as learning management system: An exploratory study. *British Journal of Educational Technology*, *43*(3), 428–438. doi:10.1111/j.1467-8535.2011.01195.x

Zachos, G., Paraskevopoulou-Kollia, E., & Anagnostopoulos, I. (2018). Social Media Use in Higher Education: A Review. *Education in Science*, *8*(4), 194. doi:10.3390/educsci8040194

Zanamwe, N., Rupere, T., & Kufandirimbwa, O. (2013). Use of Social Networking Technologies in Higher Education in Zimbabwe: A learners' perspective. *International Journal of Computer and Information Technology*, *2*(1), 8–18.

Zancanaro, A., & Domingues, M. (2018). Massive open online courses (MOOC) for teaching Portuguese for foreigners. *Turkish Online Journal of Distance Education-TOJDE*, *19*(2), 4–20. doi:10.17718/tojde.415602

KEY TERMS AND DEFINITIONS

Digital Native: An individual who was born after the broad adoption of digital technology and grew up with them.

Professional Learning Community: A group of educators, motivated by a shared learning vision, who collaborate to improve teaching skills and the academic performance of students.

Shareable Content: A content with a potential to be transmitted, or shared, by a third party.

Social Media: A website or a software application designed to allow people to communicate and share content quickly, efficiently and in real time on the Internet using a computer or mobile phone or similar.

Social Networking: The process of creating, building and expanding virtual communities and links between people online, often through social media sites such as Facebook, Twitter, etc.

Social Platform: Web-based technology and solutions behind a social media.

User-Generated Content: Any form of content, such as images, blogs, videos, text and audio, that have been created and posted by consumers or end-users on online platforms and is publicly available to others.

This research was previously published in the Handbook of Research on the Role of Human Factors in IT Project Management; pages 501-523, copyright year 2020 by Business Science Reference (an imprint of IGI Global).

APPENDIX

Section 1. Personal Information for Participant

1. What is your gender?
   ○ male ○ female
2. How old are you?
   ○ below 25 ○ 25-34 ○ 35-44 ○ 45-54 ○ above 55
3. What is your scientific degree?
   ○ PhD ○ D.Sc. ○Other
4. What is your academic position?
   ○Assistant ○Assistant Professor ○Associate Professor ○Professor ○Other
5. In which university/institute/academy are you working?
6. In which country are you working?
7. Are you well informed about social networking (e.g. Facebook, Twitter, Google+, Bebo, Myspace, LinkedIn, etc.)?
   ○Yes ○Yes/No ○No

Please, give your opinion on the statement from Section II and Section III by expressing your agreement / disagreement in the following five-point scale:
1. Strongly disagree; 2. Disagree; 3. Neutral; 4. Agree; 5. Strongly agree.

Section 2. Opinion on the Use of Social Networks in Teaching Practice

8. You often use social networking sites for communication and consultation with your students.
   ○1. Strongly disagree ○2. Disagree ○3. Neutral ○4. Agree ○5. Strongly agree.
9. You participate in social networking group/groups with your students for information sharing and discussions on the courses.
   ○1. Strongly disagree ○2. Disagree ○3. Neutral ○4. Agree ○5. Strongly agree.
10. You participate in social networking group/groups with your students for organization of the courses.
    ○1. Strongly disagree ○2. Disagree ○3. Neutral ○4. Agree ○5. Strongly agree.
11. You use social networking sites during the lesson in order to increase students' involvement and to keep track of their reactions.
    ○1. Strongly disagree ○2. Disagree ○3. Neutral ○4. Agree ○5. Strongly agree.
12. You participate in online group/groups interested in the use of social networking for educational purposes.
    ○1. Strongly disagree ○2. Disagree ○3. Neutral ○4. Agree ○5. Strongly agree.
13. You have a public profile in some of social networking sites to share yours research interests and to connect with a wide range of people with similar preferences.
    ○1. Strongly disagree ○2. Disagree ○3. Neutral ○4. Agree ○5. Strongly agree.
14. The use of social networking sites in your teaching practice has a positive effect on the student achievements.
    ○1. Strongly disagree ○2. Disagree ○3. Neutral ○4. Agree ○5. Strongly agree.

15. The use of social networking sites in your teaching practice increases the involvement and interest of students in the training.
    ○1. Strongly disagree ○2. Disagree ○3. Neutral ○4. Agree ○5. Strongly agree.

16. You use social networking sites in your teaching practice in ways other than those stated above – please specify.

Section 3. Opinion on the Use of Social Networking for Educational Purposes in General

17. Social networking sites are/can be useful in education.
    ○1. Strongly disagree ○2. Disagree ○3. Neutral ○4. Agree ○5. Strongly agree.

18. The role of social networking sites will increase.
    ○1. Strongly disagree ○2. Disagree ○3. Neutral ○4. Agree ○5. Strongly agree.

19. You participate in researches related to the use of social networking sites in education.
    ○1. Strongly disagree ○2. Disagree ○3. Neutral ○4. Agree ○5. Strongly agree.

20. You think that the use of social networking sites for educational purposes has a rather negative effect - specify.

Chapter 89

Impact and Usage of Social Media Among the Post Graduate Students of Arts in Alagappa University, Karaikudi, India

P. Pitchaipandi
Alagappa University, India

ABSTRACT

This chapter tries to analyse the impact and usage of social media among the postgraduate students of arts in Alagappa University, Karaikudi, under survey method for the study. The study identified the majority (69.79%) of the respondents under female category, and 72.92% of the respondents belong in the age group between 21 and 23 years. It is observed that 32.29% of the respondents use the social media, preferably YouTube. The plurality (48.96%) of the respondents use smartphone/mobiles compare to iPod, desktop, laptop, and others. 35.42% of the respondents' spent between 1 and 5 hours weekly using social media. Further, the study also observes the positive and negative aspects of using social media in postgraduate students of arts disciplines in the university.

INTRODUCTION

According to P.S. Jeesmitha (2019), the word social media means collection of applications (Facebook, Twitter, Whatsapp, LinkedIn, YouTube. etc.) and websites that link people to share information and aware people about any event through social networking. From the beginning of the 21st century, social media is in progress. People belonging to different age group use social media. Social media plays a vital role in life. Information technology (IT) changed the living standard. These tools provide several ways of interaction and different opportunities to learn foreign languages through worldwide. The world becomes a global village due to social media. Users can connect with other people within seconds and share their ideas and give comments by video conferencing. People of different culture can also talk on

DOI: 10.4018/978-1-6684-7123-4.ch089

any issue. Social media links the people to their culture by showing different documentaries. People also use social media to get information about other countries. Social media influence adolescent's life it has both positive and negative impacts situation.

REVIEW OF LITERATURE

According to Shivarama Rao, K. Subangi, M. C. and Malhan (2019), social software in the Web 2.0 world not only enhances the practical usability in the library but also helps the diminishing librarian's role through value addition to profession itself. In this paper, select cases of social academic networks are described and different perspectives have been given on how academic libraries are participating in this massive social networking drive. Also, an attempt has been made to analyze social media presence of select Indian academic libraries.

A new information landscape is evolving where people largely access information and share ideas from hand held devices and making increasing use of mobile apps and social media tools for their convenience. This new information landscape is shaped by emergence of new web technologies, a variety of knowledge management and data analytic tools and content management software. It offers more convenience and saving of time for new generation of information users. Generation 'Y' is now using Facebook as an alternative to email (E Botha, M Farshid & L Pitt, 2011). And "social networks are now growing with mobile technology that has significantly changed the way in which people stay connected" (Shim *et al.,* 2011). Worldwide, there are over 2.32 billion monthly active users (MAU) of Facebook as of December 31, 2018. This is a 9 percent increase in Facebook MAUs year over year1.52 billion people on average log onto Facebook daily and are considered daily active users (Facebook DAU) for December 2018 (Zephoria, 2019). Institutions require conforming to popular ways of information access for delivery of content.

(Odede Israel,2019) The least used social networking site as indicated by the students is My Space. As regards to the purpose of using social networking sites, the findings indicates that private messaging, photo upload and video sharing were the main purposes for which the students use social networking sites. It is important to state that this study was conducted in a single academic institution; therefore, findings may not be applicable and reasonable to be generalized on all academic institutions. However, students' motivation that will enable students use varieties of social networking sites is highly recommended. In conclusion, students should also be motivated to use social networking sites as platforms for academic discussions such as for assignment and other course related works as well as receive and send academic information among their peers.

This new channel of communication helps to keep more general topics for discussion. It provides various interactive platforms for students to share knowledge and experiences. Hence, various social networking sites are used by students. However, Face book, Twitter and Instagram, are the most popular ones used by students. Others include MySpace, LinkedIn, Mebo, Flickr, Blogs, Wikis, Youtube Google+, Tumblr, 2go, Skype etc. Students are known to be dedicated users of one or more of these social networking sites, many of whom have been made to use these sites as daily for communication and other activities. Charnigo and Barnett-Ellis (2013) stated that Face book is currently the largest online social network targeted for the academic environment, while Muruli and Kumar (2013) asserts it is the most popular and successful of its kind as it is very user-friendly and interactive website for connection. Social network sites enable students to establish and maintain an academic relationship with one another where issues pertaining to academics can be discuss with the aim of learning and assisting each other. Students also use social networking sites as a medium of making useful connections with their lecturers as well as course mates.

The use of Social Networking Sites among students have been recognized as advantageous in terms of enhancing communication, collaboration and the potential for the promotion of and support for learning (Junco, 2011). Thus, Hussain (2012) indicated that social networking sites seemed to have a greater impact in higher education than other levels of education. This is evident in a study on social networking sites usage involving selected students from all the colleges at the University of New Hampshire in the United States of America that showed 96% (1,082) of the surveyed students being regular users of social networking sites especially Face book (Martin, 2009). Also, Research conducted by Blaschke (2014) supports that students could benefit from social networking sites usage throughout their college years. It could also mold them into a better learner as well. In the classroom, tools such as YouTube enhanced learning by connecting students both with external experts and novel educational content. Outside the classroom, Twitter, face book and other applications sustained and augmented learning conversations, enabling real-time dialogue to take place among students. This new way of communication enhances sharing of dynamic experience.

OBJECTIVES OF THE STUDY

1. To observe the Gender- wise respondents of the study in Alagappa University.
2. To analyzed the social demographic data on the respondents of the University
3. To find out the department wise distribution of the respondents in Alagappa University
4. To analyse the respondents opinion among using Social Medias and web browser.
5. To find out the different browsers and tools for using the Social Medias by the respondents.

METHODOLOGY

The study undertaken by the researcher attempted to collect the data among the postgraduate students of Arts in Alagappa University. A total number of 100 questionnaires were distributed among the students out of seven departments in the faculty of Arts. The filed questionnaire of received from the respondents. Further the study applying the percentage analysis wherever applicable to the study.

SAMPLING TECHNIQUES

For this study convenience Random sampling method was adopted for collecting primary data. A sample including Postgraduate Students of Arts in Alagappa University, Karaikudi. A total number of 100 questionnaires were distributed and 96 properly field questionnaires were received back. Hence selected 96 questionnaires are used for analysis of data.

ANALYSIS AND INTERPRETION

The Research concerned with the use of "Impact and Usage of Social Medias among the Postgraduate Students of Arts in Alagappa University, Karaikudi". This analysis is based on the data collected through questionnaire among postgraduate students of Arts in Alagappa University, Karaikudi.

DISTRIBUTION OF GENDER WISE RESPONDENTS

Table 1 shows the gender wise distribution of respondents. In this study, 29(30.21%) of the respondents belong to the category of male, whereas 67(69.79%) of the respondents belong to the category of female (Fig.1).

Table 1. Distribution of gender wise respondents

S. No	Gender	No. of Respondents	Percentage
1	Male	29	30.21
2	Female	67	69.79
Total		96	100

Source: Primary data

Figure 1. Distribution of gender wise respondents

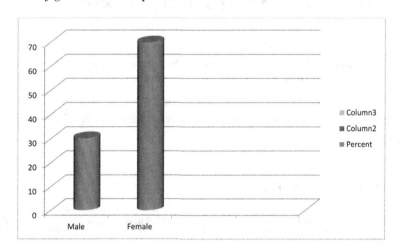

DISTRIBUTION OF AGE WISE RESPONDENTS

Table 2 reveals the distribution of age-wise respondents of the study. It shows that 13.54% of the respondents belong to the category of age18-20 out of 96 respondents. It followed by 72.92% of the respondents belong to the category of age 21-23, and 8.33% respondents belong to the category of age 24-26 and 5.21% of the respondents belong to the category of age a above 27 (Fig.2).

Table 2. Distribution of age wise respondents

S. No	Age	No. of Respondents	Percentage
1	18-20	13	13.54
2	21-23	70	72.92
3	24-26	8	8.33
4	A bove-27	5	5.21
Total		96	100

Source: Primary data

Figure 2. Department wise distribution of respondents

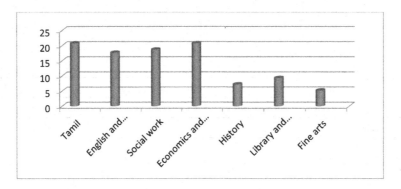

DEPARTMENT WISE DISTRIBUTION OF RESPONDENTS

Table 3 reveals the department-wise distribution of Respondents. In this study 20(20.83%) respondents belong to Tamil department, 17(17.71%) respondents belong to departments of English and foreign languages, 18(18.75%) respondents belong to Social work, 20(20.83%) respondents belong to Economics and rural development department, 7(7.29%) respondents belong to History department, 9(9.38%) respondents belong to Library and information science department and 5(5.21%) respondents belong to Fine arts department respectively.

Table 3. Department wise distribution of respondents

S. No	Department	No. of Respondents	Percentage
1	Tamil	20	20.83
2	English and foreign languages	17	17.71
3	Social work	18	18.75
4	Economics and rural development	20	20.83
5	History	7	7.29
6	Library and information science	9	9.38
7	Fine arts	5	5.21
	Total	96	100

Source: Primary data

DEPARTMENT WISE DISTRIBUTION OF RESPONDENTS

Table 4 highlights the location from where the social media mostly accessed by the students 25(26.04%) access the social media from Home, 28(29.17%) access the social media from department/Hostel, 17(17.71%) access the social media from the central Library, 10 (10.42%) access the social media from Friends/ Relatives house, 7(7.29%) access the social media from the Cybercafé and 9(9.38%) respondents access the social media from the other location.

Table 4. Place of access social medias

S. No	Place of Access	No. of Respondents	Percentage
1	Home	25	26.04
2	Department /Hostel	28	29.17
3	Central library	17	17.71
4	Friends/ Relatives house	10	10.42
5	Cybercafé	7	7.29
6	Other places	9	9.38
Total		96	100

Source: Primary data

TIME SPENT IN SOCIAL MEDIAS THE WEEK

Table 5 Shows the opinions on time spend in social media. In this study, 19(19.79%) respondents spend time Below one hours, 34(35.42%) respondents time spend in 1-5 hours, 10(10.42%) respondents 5-10 hours, 14(14.58%) respondents 10-15 hours, 5(5.21%) respondents 15-20 hours, 14(14.58%) respondents time spend in more than 20 hours.

Table 5. Time spent in social medias the week

S. No	Time Spent	No. of Respondents	Percentage
1	Below one hours	19	19.79
2	1-5 hours	34	35.42
3	5-10 hours	10	10.42
4	10-15 hours	14	14.58
5	15-20 hours	5	5.21
6	More than 20 hours	14	14.58
Total		96	100

Source: Primary data

USE OF SOCIAL MEDIAS TOOLS

Table 6 Shows the opinion about using social media tools 4(4.17%) respondents use Tablet computer, 25(26.04%) respondents use of Laptop,12(12.5%) respondents use Desktop,47(48.96%) respondents use of Smart phone/mobiles and 8(8.33%) respondents use I pad.

Table 6. Use of social medias tools

S .No	Type of Tools	No. of Respondents	Percentage
1	Tablet computer	4	4.17
2	Laptop	25	26.04
3	Desktop	12	12.5
4	Smart phone/mobiles	47	48.96
5	I pad	8	8.33
	Total	96	100

Source: primary data

TYPES OF BROWSER USING FOR SOCIAL MEDIAS

Table 7 Shows the opinion an using social media sites Browser 9(9.38%) respondents use Internet Explorer, 7(7.29%) respondents use of Mozilla fire fox, 72(75%) respondents use Google chrome and 8(8.33%) respondents use opera.

Table 7. Types of browser using for social medias

S .No	Types of Browser	No. of Respondents	Percentage
1	Internet Explorer	9	9.38
2	Mozilla fire fox	7	7.29
3	Google chrome	72	75
4	Opera	8	8.33
	Total	96	100

Source: primary data

USING SOCIAL MEDIAS BY THE RESPONDENTS

Table 8 shows the opinion an using social media sites 8(8.33%) respondents use of face book, 3(3.13%) respondents use of Twitter, 31(32.29%) respondents use YouTube, 9(9.38%) respondents use of Tumbler/ Messenger,25(26.04%) respondents use of What Sapp,13(13.54%) respondents use of Google + and 7(7.29%) respondents use Instagram.

Table 8. Using social medias by the respondents

S .No	Social Media	No. of Respondents	Percentage
1	Face book	8	8.33
2	Twitter	3	3.13
3	YouTube	31	32.29
4	Tumbler/Messenger	9	9.38
5	What Sapp	25	26.04
6	Google +	13	13.54
7	Instagram	7	7.29
	Total	96	100

Source: primary data

PERIOD OF USE SOCIAL MEDIAS BY THE RESPONDENTS

Table 9 revels that the opinion on period of uses Social Media. In this study 23(23.96%) respondents Less than one year,26(27.08%) respondents 1 year- 2 year,12(12.5%) respondents 2 year -3 year, 17 (17.71%) respondents using period of 3 year -4 year,13(13.54%) respondents using period of 4 year - 5 years,5 (5.21%) respondents using period of More than 5 years.

Table 9. Period of use social medias by the respondents

S. No	Period	No. of Respondents	Percentage
1	Less than one year	23	23.96
2	1 year- 2 year	26	27.08
3	2 year -3 year	12	12.5
4	3 year -4 year	17	17.71
5	4 year - 5 years	13	13.54
6	More than 5 years	5	5.21
Total		96	100

Source: Primary data

PURPOSE OF USE SOCIAL MEDIAS

Table 10 reveals that the 12(12.50%) respondents use the Social Media services for Lesson writing Purpose, 19(19.79%) respondents' services for Assignment preparation, 11(11.46%) respondent's service for Listening subject ideas,25(26.04%) respondent's service for Sharing general information and, 29(30.21%) respondent's service for Preparing for conference / seminars.

Table 10. Purpose of use social medias

S. No	Purpose	No. of Respondents	Percentage
1	Lesson writing	12	12.50
2	Assignment preparation	19	19.79
3	Listening subject ideas	11	11.46
4	Sharing general information	25	26.04
5	Preparing for conference / seminars	29	30.21
Total		96	100

Source: Primary data

CONCLUSION

The study discussed above the use of Social Networks and Medias among the Post Graduate students in the Faculty of Arts of Alagappa University, Karaikudi, India. The results of the study finds, 29(30.21%) of the respondents belong to the category of male, whereas 67(69.79%) of the respondents belong to the category of female. age-wise respondents of the study. It shows that 13.54% of the respondents belong to the category of age18-20 out of 96 respondents. 20(20.83%) respondents belong to Tamil department, 17(17.71%) respondents belong to departments of English and foreign languages. mostly accessed by the students 25(26.04%) access the social media from Home. 28 (29.17%) access the social media from department/Hostel. 19 (19.79%) respondents spend time Below one hours, 34 (35.42%) respondents time spend in 1-5 hours, 10 (10.42%) respondents 5-10 hours. 9 (9.38%) respondents use Internet Explorer, 7 (7.29%) respondents use of Mozilla fire fox, 72 (75%) respondents use Google chrome and 8(8.33%) respondents use opera. 23(23.96%) respondents Less than one year, 26 (27.08%) respondents 1 year- 2 year,12(12.5%) respondents 2 year -3 year.

ACKNOWLEDGMENT

This article has been written with the financial support of RUSA phase 2.0 grant sanctioned vide letter No. F24-51, 2014 U Policy (TN Multi-Gen0, Dept. of Edn, Govt. of India, Dt. 09.10.2018.

REFERENCES

Blaschke, L. M. (2014). Using Social Media to Engage and Develop the Online Learner in Self-Determined Learning. *Research in Learning Technology*, 22.

Botha, E., Farshid, M., & Pitt, L. (2011). How sociable? An exploratory study of university brand visibility in social media. *South African Journal of Business Management*, *42*(2), 43–51. doi:10.4102ajbm.v42i2.494

Charnigo, L., & Barnett-Ellis, P. (2013). Checking out Facebook.com: The impact of a digital trend on academic libraries. *Information Technology and Libraries*, *26*(1), 23–34. doi:10.6017/ital.v26i1.3286

Hussain, I. (2012). A Study to Evaluate the Social Media Trends among University Students. *Social and Behavioral Sciences, 64*(1), 639–645.

Jeesmitha, P. S. (2019). The Impact of Social Media. *International Journal of Scientific Research and Engineering Development, 2*(1), 229–235.

Junco, R. (2011). Too much face and not enough books: The relationship between multiple indices of Face book use and academic performance. *Computers in Human Behavior, 28*(1), 187–198. doi:10.1016/j.chb.2011.08.026

Shim, J.P., Dekleva, S., Guo, C., & Mittleman, D. (2011). *Twitter, Google, iPhone/iPad, and Facebook (TGIF) and Smart Technology Environments. How Well Do Educators Communicate with Students via TGIF?* Academic Press.

Shivarama Rao, K., Subangi, M. C., & Malhan, I. V. (2019). Social Networks as a Platform for Academic Interaction: Possibilities and Challenges for Indian Academic Libraries. *Asian Journal of Information Science and Technology, 9*(1), 6–10.

Zephoria. (2019). *Facebook demographic update.* Retrieved from: https://zephoria.com/top-15-valuable-facebook-statistics/

This research was previously published in Measuring and Implementing Altmetrics in Library and Information Science Research; pages 99-110, copyright year 2020 by Information Science Reference (an imprint of IGI Global).

Chapter 90

Asia–Pacific Students' Awareness and Behaviour Regarding Social Networking in the Education Sector

Tomayess Issa
Curtin University, Perth, Australia

Sulaiman Alqahtani
Curtin University, Perth, Australia

Theodora Issa
Curtin University, Perth, Australia

Noorminshah A. Iahad
Universiti Teknologi Malaysia (UTM), Johor Bahru, Malaysia

Peldon Peldon
Jigme Dorji Wangchuck National Referral Hospital, Thimphu, Bhutan

Sooyoung Kim
Seoul Women's University, Seoul, South Korea

Samant Saurabh
Indian Institute of Technology, Jharkhand, India

Sumaiya Pervaizz
Curtin University, Perth, Australia

Sun Joo Yoo
Seowon University, Cheongju, South Korea

ABSTRACT

Social networking (SN) technology has been presented to human beings as a means of communicating, collaborating, connecting, and cooperating to exchange knowledge, skills, news, chat, and to maintain contact with peers world-wide. This article examines SN awareness in the Asia-Pacific (AP) education sector (ES) with a specific focus on the advantages and disadvantages of SN; and investigated whether AP culture influences SN adoption by the ES. An online survey was distributed to 1014 AP students and a total of 826 students responded. Several new advantages of adoption emerged from the data analysis. SN enabled students to accomplish their study tasks more quickly; it allowed them to communicate and collaborate with peers world-wide; and it fostered sustainability. The disadvantages perceived by students include depression, loneliness, and distraction, lack of interest in pursuing traditional activities, and security and privacy concerns. Finally, culture does influence SN adoption by ES institutions in AP countries.

DOI: 10.4018/978-1-6684-7123-4.ch090

1. INTRODUCTION

Social networking in the education sector's assessment and teaching activities has been adopted and integrated as an essential tool in recent curricula to promote students' personal and professional skills for their current studies and their future in the workforce. The use of SN in the education sector encourages students to study independently while allowing them to collaborate with their peers locally and globally. Students have begun to use SN to gain more knowledge about other countries, communities, issues and news, and to share their thoughts and opinions with their peers. This type of interaction will allow students to develop several skills including personal skills such as motivation, leadership, negotiation, communication, problem solving, time management, and reflection, and professional skills such as reading, writing, research, search, critical thinking, decision making, digital oral presentations, diagrammatic representations such as concept maps, and teamwork. Such skills can improve and enrich students' learning in their current studies and will be indispensable to them in the workforce. On the other hand, the use of SN has several associated disadvantages including a deterioration of basic skills such as reading and writing, depression, loneliness, distraction from studies, and lack of concentration. These disadvantages should be tackled promptly to prevent or minimize their potential harm to students. SN has transformed education systems. Classrooms have become more collaborative; this helps to create a more relaxed atmosphere among students and between them and their lecturer, since this platform encourages students to contribute their comments, concept maps, PowerPoint slides and documents. However, the use of SN in the education sector is associated with several disadvantages in terms of cognitive skills, socio-physical development, and security. This study aims to examine students' attitudes toward SN use, and to determine whether culture can influence SN adoption by students in Asia-Pacific countries (Australia, Bhutan, India, Malaysia, Pakistan and South Korea). An online survey was conducted to examine and address the research questions and aims. This paper is organized as follows: 1) Introduction; 2) Social Networking in the Higher Education; 3) SN Advantages; 4) SN Disadvantages; 5) SN use in Asia Pacific; 6) Asia-Pacific -Cultural Orientation based on Hofstede's cultural framework; 7) Research Method and Questions; 8) Participants; 9) Results, Discussion; 10) New Theoretical Findings and Contribution; 1) Limitations, and 12) Conclusion.

2. SOCIAL NETWORKING IN THE HIGHER EDUCATION

In the 21st century, SN has become an essential tool that allows stakeholders ranging from individuals to organisations to communicate, connect, collaborate and cooperate with their peers, colleagues or community both locally and globally in order to exchange knowledge and useful information. Social networking websites and services include Myspace, Facebook, YouTube, LinkedIn, Twitter, Wikis, Blogs and Podcasts, Instant Messaging, Mashups and Virtual World. They allow stakeholders to interact, intermingle, share and communicate, and to exchange opinions, advice and philosophies regarding numerous subjects (De-Marcos, Domínguez, Saenz-de-Navarrete, & Pagés, 2014; DeKay, 2009; Holmes & O'loughlin, 2014; Park, Kee, & Valenzuela, 2009; Waters, Burnett, Lamm, & Lucas, 2009).

The education sector in the Asia-Pacific region has started to integrate SN especially in assessments and learning/teaching activities. One reason for this implementation is that it allows students to become independent learners and enhance their professional and personal skills which are needed for their current studies and for their future in the workforce. Furthermore, the most important reason for this implementation is that SN can make classes more interactive, creative and engaging, fostering a friendly and close rapport between students and lecturer.

By the same token several authors (Durak, 2017; Gülbahar, Rapp, Kilis, & Sitnikova, 2017) indicate that using SN in higher education will enhance communication, collaboration, participation and sharing information and discussion with colleagues and peers. Furthermore, SN will promote and enhance critical thinking and decision making and facility personalized learning.

Furthermore, several studies (Chugh & Ruhi, 2018; Peruta & Shields, 2017) point out that SN adoption in the higher education has shifted the way communication and collaboration take place between the students and academics to exchange knowledge, ideas, thoughts and opinions in an informal way, and SN use is significant to attract and retain students. Students can easily interact with SN technology, since the SN interface is efficient, effective, and easy to learn, remember and use. Students can upload their work in various formats including PDF, video, PowerPoint slides, concept maps, and images. These formats allow students to comment on and provide feedback regarding the contents, style and layout. Furthermore, communication, collaboration and cooperation will be developed between the students themselves and the lecturer.

Our teaching experience indicates that this type of collaboration makes the learning and teaching activities more innovative, imaginative and engaging. The current literature (Blatt, 2015; Dillenbourg, 1999; Frydenberg, 2008; Kontos, Emmons, Puleo, & Viswanath, 2010; Ku, Tseng, & Akarasriworn, 2013; Langheinrich & Karjoth, 2010; Lin & Lu, 2011; McCarroll & Curran, 2013; Minocha & Thomas, 2007; Moreno & Kolb, 2012; Pan, Xu, Wang, Zhang, Ling, & Lin, 2015; Tharp, 2010; Tsinakos, 2006; Wang, 2008) indicates that SN applications are essential in any sector including that of education, as these applications inspire the learning process and collaboration among the students and lecturers, as students can share their knowledge, understanding and experiences and sentiments. Integrating SN in the education sector will improve students' self-confidence, facilitate knowledge transfer and problem solving, and enhance the effectiveness of learning and teaching activities. Therefore, academics should take this opportunity, and commence to incorporate SN in assessments and activities. They need to know how to integrate SN correctly by employing learning theories and models to improve students' learning outcomes.

3. SN ADVANTAGES

Several studies have indicated (Din, Yahya, Suzan, & Kassim, 2012; Forrester Research, 2010; Issa, 2016; Kelin, 2008; Kiehne, 2004; Lin & Lu, 2011; Mathew, 2014; McCarroll & Curran, 2013; McKenna, 2010; Moreno & Kolb, 2012; Oh, Ozkaya, & LaRose, 2014; Pempek, Yermolayeva, & Calvert, 2000; Zhu, Chang, Luo, & Li, 2014) that SN applications offer several advantages: sharing of cutting edge knowledge; collaboration; inter-crossing relationships; communication skills; environment-friendly and new acquaintances can be made. Figure 1 shows the advantages of SN applications in greater detail.

Figure 1. SN advantages in detail – prepared by researchers

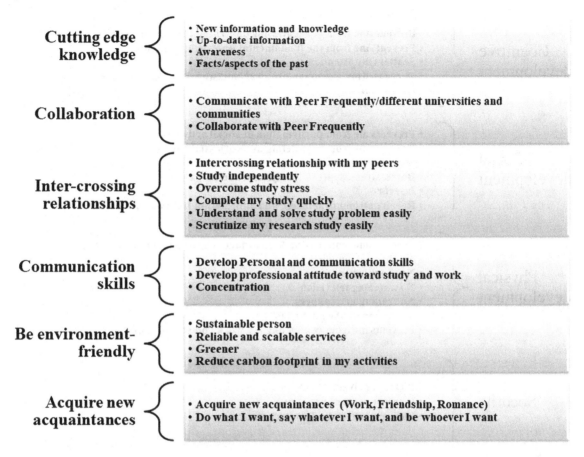

4. SN DISADVANTAGES

The use of SN applications in the education sector can create some disadvantages concerning students' cognitive, social and physical development, and security. Figure 2 shows the major disadvantages of SN applications in details, while Figure 4 illustrates the SN disadvantages in more detail (Clarke, 2010; Din et al., 2012; Fox & Moreland, 2015; Issa, 2016; Johnson & Knobloch-Westerwick, 2014; Kontos et al., 2010; Langheinrich & Karjoth, 2010; Mathew, 2014; Moreno & Kolb, 2012; Steinfield, DiMicco, Ellison, & Lampe, 2009 ; Velasquez, Graham, & McCollum, 2009). Finally, Figure 1 and 2 present the online survey questions.

5. SN USE IN ASIA PACIFIC

SN applications are common in the education sector in some countries such as Australia, but in other Asia-Pacific countries, they are still in the initial stages. Currently, countries in the Asia-Pacific region are using the Internet, social networking and mobile technology intensively.

Figure 2. SN disadvantages in detail– prepared by researchers

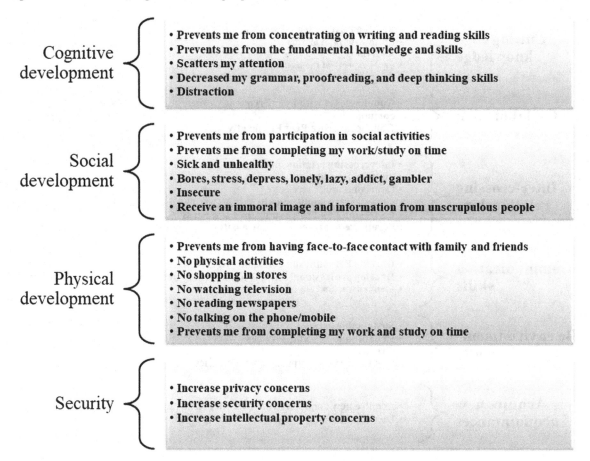

According to Kepios (2017), in Australia, more than two million in a population of 24 million are actively engaged in social networking; while in Bhutan it is more than 70 thousand from one million. In India more than 61 million from 1.3 billion are using social networking; whereas in Malaysia, more than four million from 31 million are active SN users. Moreover, in Pakistan three million from 193 million are using social networking. Finally, in South Korea, one million from 51 million are active in social networking.

The Asia-Pacific studies (Abdulahi, Samadi, & Gharleghi, 2014; Heller Baird & Parasnis, 2011; Kuzma, 2010; Lipp, Davis, Peter, & Davies, 2014; Miller & Lammas, 2010; Peluchette & Karl, 2008; Peng & Zhou, 2005; Phua & Jin, 2011; Shin & Harman, 2009; Sigman, 2009; Tariq, Mehboob, Asf, & Khan, 2012; Trusov, Bucklin, & Pauwels, 2009) discuss the Internet and SN technology use on marketing, among individuals and Internet and technology in the education sector to improve students' interaction and collaboration among their colleagues and unit-coordinator.

To the best of our knowledge, none of the research from the Asia-Pacific discussed the SN inspiration for students from the awareness, advantages, disadvantages, and culture, especially from the education sector perspective. Therefore, the current literature review in the AP is limited to examining students' reaction toward Internet and SN use. However, this study aims to examine the AP students' perspective, behaviour and performance regarding the use of SN in the education sector and students' awareness of sustainability.

Therefore, in order to integrate this technology in the education sector, especially in the Asia-Pacific region, specific standards and guidelines need to be followed by academics and teaching and learning departments in order to maximise the advantages and mitigate or eliminate the disadvantages.

Finally, SN usage in the education sector globally or in the Asia-Pacific region will bring several advantages to students, as mentioned previously. Hence, the appropriate introduction and implementation of technology in tertiary institutions will ensure that students, unit coordinators and the administration will benefit, and that the associated disadvantages will be mitigated.

6. ASIA-PACIFIC - CULTURAL ORIENTATION BASED ON HOFSTEDE'S CULTURAL FRAMEWORK

From the cultural perspective, several studies (Clark, 2010; Heydari & Laroche, 2017; Hudson, Huang, Roth, & Madden, 2016; Lowry, Zhang, Zhou, & Fu, 2010; Ngai, Tao, & Moon, 2015; Papacharissi, 2010; Stump & Gong, 2017; Wallace & Brooks, 2015) have examined and assessed how cultural contexts shape the use of technology including social networking. From the marketing perspective, studies have investigated consumer–brand relationships, technology adoption, and the self-control effect of difference in terms of the six dimensions of Hofstede's cultural framework (Hofstede, 1984, 2003) (i.e., power distance, long-term orientation, individualism, masculinity, indulgence, and uncertainty avoidance).

To the best of our knowledge, none of the studies has examined the use of social networking in the Asia-Pacific education sector, particularly in regard to its advantages and disadvantages. Therefore, this study aims to identify and determine if the Asia-Pacific culture will be influenced by SN adoption in the education sector by examining if the Asia-Pacific students are sharing same advantages or disadvantages by using the SN.

Therefore, to examine and assess the cultural orientation in the Asia-Pacific countries chosen for this study, the researchers applied Hofstede's cultural framework comprising six dimensions by comparing the six countries in this study using the Hofstede Insights (2018) website.

Figure 3 indicates that the power distances for Malaysia and Bhutan are very high compared to those in India, South Korea, Pakistan and Australia. This is significant since low power distance allows students to participate in decisions that affect them.

Australia has a high score for Individualism compared to other countries; this means that Australians are expected to take care of themselves and their immediate families. On the other hand, Pakistan, South Korea and Malaysia have the lowest scores. Collectivism is the descriptive term applied to a group that has a low score for Individualism; members of this group strive to develop and consolidate relationships with their extended families and others within the group. Moreover, they are expected to support each other when challenged by risks and conflicts.

Furthermore, a high score for the Masculinity dimension indicates that the society will be driven by competition. Figure 3 shows that Australia, India, Malaysia, Pakistan scored 61, 56, 50 and 50 percent respectively, compared to South Korea and Bhutan with scores of 39 and 32 respectively. A low score for the Masculinity dimension means that the dominant values in that society emphasize the care of others and the quality of life.

Figure 3. Comparison of Asia-Pacific countries - adopted from the Hofstede Insights website. Prepared by researchers.

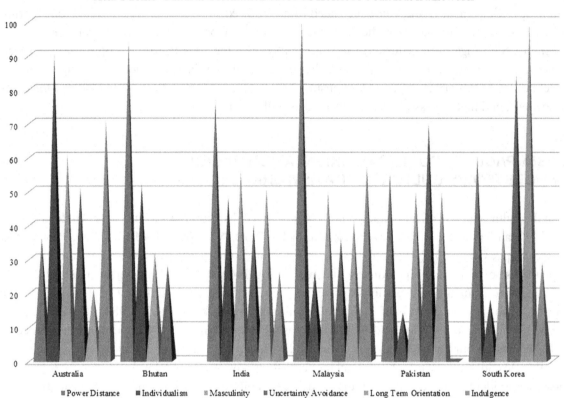

Regarding the Uncertainty Avoidance dimension, Pakistan and South Korea had the highest scores compared to other countries. These cultures are industrious and productive, so innovation and security are significant elements of individual enthusiasm.

For the Long-Term Orientation dimension, South Korea scored 100 percent compared to Australia with 21 percent. This means that low-scoring countries prefer traditions and norms, while countries with high scores encourage a robust and innovative education system as a way of preparing for the future.

Finally, for the Indulgence dimension, Australia scored 71 percent. This indicates that Australian people tend to give in to their impulses and desires with regard to enjoying life and having fun. However, those countries with low indulgence scores are considered to be restrained, meaning that individuals and society in general (e.g. India and South Korea) control and overcome their desires by means of strict social norms (Hofstede, 1984, 2003; Hofstede Insights, 2018; Matusitz & Musambira, 2013).

Finally, this study contributes new significance and findings to the current literature by examining students' attitudes toward and opinions about the use of SN, thereby identifying new advantages and disadvantages from the perspective of the Asia-Pacific education sector. In addition, this study will confirm whether the cultural contexts of Asia-Pacific nations will influence SN adoption, especially in the education sector in terms of Hofstede's cultural framework.

7. RESEARCH METHOD AND QUESTIONS

This study aims to answer these questions: "What are the advantages and disadvantages of SN use in ES institutions in Asia-Pacific countries? How can Asia-Pacific cultures influence SN adoption by tertiary students in this region? In order to answer these questions, an online survey was developed based on the literature. The survey comprised three sections: background of the respondents, perceived benefits of SN, and perceived disadvantages of SN. For the benefits section, the main researcher developed twenty-five statements based on the literature review. These statements related to cutting edge knowledge, collaboration, inter-crossing relationships, communication skills, being environment-friendly and making new acquaintances. For the disadvantages section, the main researcher developed thirty statements based on the literature review. These statements concerned cognitive development, social development, physical development, and security.

A five-point Likert scale was used for each part of the online survey to "examine how strongly subjects agree or disagree with statements" (Sekaran, 2003, p. 197). The five-point Likert scale range was: Strongly Disagree, Disagree, Neutral, Agree, and Strongly Agree (Likert, 1932). Likert scale is used in the online survey to measure the strength of a respondent's perceived agreement or disagreement to statements. In the Five Likert scale the value three is the neutral position, while one and five are the two extremes. (Sohmee & Oppeniander, 2010, p. 15)

In the online survey, the main researcher provided clear instructions at the top of the page and a progress bar along the bottom to indicate to participants their proximity to the finishing point. Finally, the main researcher presented three questions per page to minimize scrolling, and a 'thank you' message was presented at the end to acknowledge the respondents' participation. The online survey was distributed via email, Facebook, WhatsApp, LinkedIn and the university portal system. The survey received ethics approval from the main researcher's university, and was distributed to the researchers in Bhutan, India, Malaysia, Pakistan and South Korea. The data for Australia was collected via Qualtrics within three weeks. The online survey results were analyzed using SPSS version 24. The online survey data was collected for a period of six to eight months from the AP countries.

General speaking, the online survey is considered the most sophisticated tool for collecting participants' responses, but in order to collect a high rate of responses, researchers should provide accurate guidelines and instructions to the participants, and a follow-up message should be sent after the first distribution phase. Online surveys are easy, inexpensive and anonymous. On the other hand, due to technical issues such as viruses and hacking, the response rate may be less than anticipated (Couper, Traugott, & Lamias, 2001; Dillman, D, 2007; Dillman, D, Glenn, Tortora, Swift, Kohrell, Berck, & Messer, 2009; Dillman, Reipus, & Matzat, 2010; Dillman, 2017; Fan & Yan, 2010; Smyth, Dillman, Christian, & O'Neill, 2010; Toepoel & Dillman, 2008; Umbach, 2004).

8. PARTICIPANTS

This study targeted several countries in the Asia-Pacific region, namely Australia, Bhutan, India, Malaysia, Pakistan and South Korea. This study selected these countries since they are located in the same region, and some countries are sharing the same culture and attitude. An online survey was distributed to tertiary students. Of the 1014 Asia-Pacific students, 826 completed the whole survey, with response rates of 100%, 80%, 52%, 68% 82% and 96% respectively. The online survey was distributed via several channels including email and social networking sites such as Facebook, LinkedIn, What's up and other facilities; however, the data for Australia was collected via Qualtrics. Table 1 shows the statistics for Gender, Age, Qualifications, number of hours spent daily on social networking (not including email), number of hours per day spent on the Internet for email, and finally, the participants' reason(s) for using the Internet. Table 1 indicates that Pakistan had the highest number of male respondents 75% (139 respondents) while South Korea had the highest number of female respondents 75% (180 respondents).

Table 1. Online survey statistics Asia Pacific - prepared by researchers

Number and Percentage of Online Survey	Australia	Bhutan	India	Malaysia	Pakistan	South Korea
Questionnaires Distributed	153	163	162	109	186	241
Questionnaires Returned	153	130	85	74	153	231
Response Rate	100%	80%	52%	68%	82%	96%
Gender						
Male Respondents	63 (41%)	93 (57%)	125 (77%)	55 (50%)	139 (75%)	61 (25%)
Female Respondents	90 (59%)	70 (43%)	37 (23%)	54 (50%)	47 (25%)	180 (75%)
Age						
18-22	21(14%)	83 (51%)	54 (31%)	43 (39%)	93 (50%)	116 (48%)
22-32	44 (29%)	64 (39%)	84 (48%)	50(46%)	78 (42%)	112 (47%)
32-42	42 (27%)	14 (9%)	29 (17%)	15 (14%)	12 (14%)	7 (3%)
42-52	46 (30%)	1 (1%)	7 (4%)	1 (1%)	1 (1%)	5 (2%)
Over 52	0	1 (1%)	1 (1%)	0	2 1(%)	0
Qualifications						
Primary Education	57 (39%)	1(0.7%)	18 (11%)	0	4 (2%)	0
Higher Secondary /Pre-University	13 (9%)	34 (22.5%)	6 (4%)	13 (13%)	21 (12%)	187 (78%)
Professional Certificate	18 (12%)	5 (3.3%)	13 (8%)	1 (1%)	7 (4%)	0
Diploma	6 (4%)	53 (35.1%)	20 (12%)	2 (2%)	8 (5%)	0
Advanced/Higher/Graduate Diploma	36 (25%)	0	11 (7%)	3 (3%)	7 (4%)	0
Bachelor's Degree	4 (3%)	53 (35.1%)	55 (33%)	50 (51%)	105 (60%)	50 (21%)
Post Graduate Diploma	11 (8%)	3 (2.0%)	9 (5%)	2 (2%)	5 (3%)	1 (0.42%)
Master's Degree	0	2 (1.3%)	33 (20%)	27 (28%)	18 (10%)	1 (0.42%)
PhD	0	0	0	0	0	0
Others	0	0	0	0	0	0
Hours you spend on the social networking daily, not including email (per day).						
Less than an hour	81 (53%)	91 (61%)	84 (61%)	23 (24%)	93 (54%)	89 (37%)
Up to five hours	52 (34%)	51 (34%)	50 (36%)	49 (52%)	58 (34%)	126 (53%)
Five to ten hours	11(7%)	7 (5%)	2 (1%)	18 (19%)	12 (7%)	19 (8%)
Ten to twenty hours	7 (5%)	0	1 (1%)	3 (3%)	7 (4%)	4 (2%)
Over twenty hours	2 (1%)	1 (1%)	0	1 (1%)	3 (2%)	0

continues on following page

Table 1. Continued

Number and Percentage of Online Survey	Australia	Bhutan	India	Malaysia	Pakistan	South Korea
Hours you spend on the Internet for email (per day).						
Less than an hour	82 (54%)	118 (79%)	100 (73%)	67 (71%)	136 (79%)	207 (87%)
Up to five hours	53 (35%)	24 (16%)	25 (18%)	15 (16%)	26 (15%)	29 (12%)
Five to ten hours	14 (9%)	4 (3%)	11 (8%)	9 (10%)	5 (3%)	0
Ten to twenty hours	1 (1%)	2 (1%)	1 (1%)	2 (2%)	3 (2%)	1(0.4%)
Over twenty hours	3 (2%)	2 (1%)	0	1 (1%)	3 (2%)	0
You use the Internet to: (you can choose more than one option)						
Email	139 (18%)	96 (20%)	123 (16%)	83(17%)	134 (19%)	133 (13%)
Play Games	54 (7%)	30 (6%)	29 (4%)	26 (5%)	53 (7%)	49 (5%)
Study	65(8%)	121 (25%)	119 (15%)	88 (18%)	136 (19%)	190 (18%)
Work	65(8%)	57 (12%)	70 (9%)	46 (9%)	92 (13%)	45 (4%)
Shop Online	96 (12%)	2 (0.4%)	86 (11%)	29 (6%)	32 (4%)	149 (14%)
Chat	54 (7%)	107(22%)	95 (12%)	63 (13%)	117 (16%)	56 (5%)
Research Hobbies	64 (8%)	41 (8%)	62 (8%)	33 (7%)	43 (6%)	134 (13%)
Bank Online	102 (13%)	6 (1%)	65 (8.4%)	50 (10%)	29 (4%)	72 (7%)
Buy goods or services	78 (10%)	1 (0.2%)	43(6%)	23 (5%)	28 (4%)	107 (10%)
Buy stocks or investing online	14 (2%)	0	7 (1%)	3 (1%)	11(2%)	9 (1%)
Make or research travel information or reservations	55 (7%)	13 (3%)	65(8%)	44 (9%)	25(3%)	70 (7%)
Others – Please specify	7 (1%)	10 (2%)	8 (1%)	5 (1%)	15 (2%)	38 (4%)

Furthermore, most of the participants ranging in age from 18-22 were from Bhutan, Pakistan and South Korea at 83 (51%), 93(50%) and 116(48%) respectively. While the ages range from 22-32 were from India, Pakistan and South Korea at 84 (48%), 78(42%) and 112(47%) correspondingly. Australia had the highest in age range 32-42 and 42-52 at 42 (27%) and 46 (30%) respectively. In regard to the participants' qualifications, South Korea had the greatest number of participants in the higher secondary/pre-university level with 187 (78%) participants, Australia had the highest number for the advanced higher graduate diploma with 36(25%) participants; and Pakistan had the highest number of participants with the bachelor's degree with 105(60%) participants. Finally, India had the highest number of participants with a master's degree. The online survey results indicated that participants from Pakistan, Bhutan, and South Korea spend less than an hour on social networking with 93 (54%), 91(61%) and 89(37%) participants correspondingly. However, 126 (53%) participants from South Korea spend up to five hours on social networking. On the other hand, participants in South Korea, Pakistan, and Bhutan spend less than an hour using the Internet for email (per day) at 207(87%), 136(79%) and 118(79%) respectively. Furthermore, Australia had the highest number (53 (35%)) of participants spending up to five hours per day on the Internet for email use. Furthermore, the majority of participants indicated that they used the Internet for email, study, shop online, chatting, research and banking online; as for the "other" option, participants indicated that they used the Internet for watching movie, TV and YouTube, and listening to music.

9. RESULTS AND DISCUSSION

In this section, results, discussion and limitations will be presented and discussed to determine whether or not the study aims were achieved. Both Tables 2 and 3 show the results of Cronbach's Alpha, KMO and Barlett's test for the social networking advantages and disadvantages. For the advantages, the Cronbach's Alpha for all 25 variables was .961, .950, .904, .919, .938, .888 and .926 for Australia, Bhutan, India, Malaysia, Pakistan, South Korea and all countries in the Asia-Pacific region, respectively. The Alpha result indicates an excellent internal consistency of the items in the scale (Bland & Altman, 1997; Bravo & Potvin, 1991; Connelly, 2011; Tavakol & Dennick, 2011). Kaiser-Meyer-Olkin measures of sampling adequacy of .920, .912, .804, .732, .873, .843, and .919 were obtained for Australia, Bhutan, India, Malaysia, Pakistan, South Korea, respectively; hence, all countries, had a good sample size for the analysis, and since the KMO was .9 and above, .8 and .7, this indicated that an adequate sample was obtained for the analysis, and the KMO was interpreted as a 'marvelous,' 'meritorious,' and 'middling' result (Frohlich & Westbrook, 2001; Hill, 2012). Regarding the disadvantages, the Cronbach's Alpha for all 30 variables was .970, .948, .941, .944, .950, .909 and .935, for Australia, Bhutan, India, Malaysia, Pakistan, South Korea and the total of all the Asia-Pacific countries in this study respectively, indicating the excellent internal consistency of the items in the scale (Bravo & Potvin, 1991; Gliem & Gliem, 2003). A Kaiser-Meyer-Olkin measure of sampling adequacy of .924, .868, .799, .821, .900, .857, and .916 obtained for Australia, Bhutan, India, Malaysia, Pakistan, South Korea and all countries in Asia-Pacific, respectively, indicated a good sample size was obtained for the analysis, and since the KMO was .9 and above, .8 and .7 this was considered a 'marvellous', 'meritorious' and 'middling' result (Hill, 2012; Williams, Onsman, & Brown, 2010). Furthermore, the Bartlett's test of sphericity for the advantages was highly significant for Australia, Bhutan, India, Malaysia, Pakistan, South Korea, as well as for all the Asia-Pacific countries chosen for this study, as the items of the scale were sufficiently correlated for factors to be found (Burns & Burns, 2008; Schaefer, Larson, Davidson, & Coan, 2014). Finally, Bartlett's test of sphericity for the Disadvantages aspects was highly significant for Australia, Bhutan, India, Malaysia, Pakistan, South Korea, as well as for the total of all Asia-Pacific countries in this study, indicating that the items in the scale were sufficiently correlated for factors to be found (Burns & Burns, 2008; Das, Dash, Sahoo, & Mohanty, 2017; Dziuban & Shirkey, 1974; Tobias & Carlson, 1969).

Table 2. Advantages – Cronbach's Alpha, KMO and Bartlett's test - prepared by researchers

Advantages			
Country	**Cronbach's Alpha**	**KMO**	**Bartlett's Test**
Australia	.961	.920	$\chi^2 = 3420.299$, df = 300, p < .000
Bhutan	.950	.912	$\chi^2 = 1981.573$, df = 300, p < .000
India	.904	.804	$\chi^2 = 1242.529$ *df* = 300, *p* < .000
Malaysia	.919	.732	$\chi^2 = 1234.436$ df = 300, p < .000
Pakistan	.938	.873	$\chi^2 = 2434.196$ df = 300, p < .000
South Korea	.888	.843	$\chi^2 = 2387.333$ df = 300, p < .000
Total all Countries	.926	.919	$\chi^2 = 8581.140$ df = 300, p < .000

Table 3. Disadvantages – Cronbach's Alpha, KMO and Bartlett's test - prepared by researchers

Disadvantages			
Country	**Cronbach's Alpha**	**KMO**	**Bartlett's Test**
Australia	.970	.924	$\chi^2 = 4498.143$, df = 435, p < .000
Bhutan	.948	.868	$\chi^2 = 2620.397$, df = 435, p < .000
India	.941	.799	$\chi^2 = 1964.200$, df = 435, p < .000
Malaysia	.944	.821	$\chi^2 = 1989.899$, df = 435, p < .000
Pakistan	.950	.900	$\chi^2 = 3165.904$, df = 435, p < .000
South Korea	.909	.857	$\chi^2 = 3460.030$, df = 435, p < .000
Total all Countries	.935	.916	$\chi^2 = 11274.267$, df = 435, p < .000

Furthermore, to access the regression coefficients (i.e. slopes), factor loading was carried out to examine the advantages and disadvantages for social networking in Asia-Pacific, the factor loadings for both advantages and disadvantages were high enough to be considered as important (Costello & Osborne, 2005). Several items were excluded under factors where the factor loading was below 0.5 based on the rule of thumb of Stevens (1992) for a sample size above 100. The results which were produced from SPSS (version 24) generated two to three new advantages for each country as well as for all countries (see Table 4). It came to our attention that Asia-Pacific students indicated that SN assists them to make new acquaintances, acquire cutting edge knowledge and awareness locally and globally, encourages them to study independently and makes them sustainable people. Furthermore, communication and collaboration with peers are increased as SN usage is considered an essential tool for study and research, especially for students in South Korea. The most interesting results from this study came from students in Australia and Malaysia who indicated that via SN use, they have become more sustainable and greener; on the other hand, South Korean students expressed that SN helped to form romantic attachments. These new advantages justified the study aims, and answered the first research question: that using SN in education sector in Asia-Pacific countries will make students more aware of news and information locally and globally, and facilitates communication and collaboration with peers. This study confirmed findings in the current literature (Issa, 2014; Kearns & Frey, 2010; Kontos et al., 2010; Lanning, Brickhouse, Gunsolley, Ranson, & Willett, 2011; Vereecken, Van Heddeghem, Colle, Pickavet, & Demeester, 2010; Waycott, Bennett, Kennedy, Dalgarno, & Gray, 2010) as the use of SN assists students with both their studies and social life.

Furthermore, the study results confirmed that the individual cultures of Asia-Pacific countries can influence the adoption of SN by HE students in this region. It came to our attention that Bhutan and India students perceived the same advantages - that SN allows students to have more communication and collaboration with their peers, and encourages them to complete their study tasks independently. On the other hand, Bhutan, India and Malaysia shared a new factor which is communication and collaboration with their peers; while South Korea and Australia shared the new advantage namely, the making of new acquaintances. Students in Australia, Bhutan, India, Malaysia, and Pakistan indicated that SN enables them to study independently. These results confirmed that culture can influence SN adoption; despite students living in different countries, they are living in the same region; therefore, they share the same attitudes and thoughts regarding the use of SN. This outcome answered research question two, and confirmed findings in the current literature (Lowry et al., 2010; Papacharissi, 2010; Wallace & Brooks,

2015). Finally, we combined the results from all the countries (see Table 4), and SPSS generated two new advantages related to SN use by Asia-Pacific students. These advantages are: study tasks can be facilitated and accomplished quickly; and SN enables students to communicate and collaborate with peers worldwide.

Table 4. Social networking advantages - prepared by researchers

Advantages	
Country	**Label /Advantages**
Australia	• Independent study and sustainable person • Make new acquaintances • Acquire local and global knowledge and information
Bhutan	• Accomplish my study independently • Communication and collaboration with my peers
India	• Independent study • Communication and collaboration with my peers
Malaysia	• Directed study and sustainability • Communication and collaboration among my peers
Pakistan	• Conclude study rapidly • Awareness and communication locally and globally
South Korea	• Tool for study and research • Cutting edge and awareness locally and globally • Attain new romance acquaintances
All the Countries in this study	• Support and accomplish study swiftly; • Communicate and collaborate with peers world-wide

Figures 4, 5,6,7,8, and 9 indicate the new advantages for Australia, Bhutan, India, Malaysia, Pakistan and South Korea regarding SN use among Asia-Pacific students. Each variable and factor loading is assigned a different color.

Figure 4. Australia – New advantages - prepared by researchers

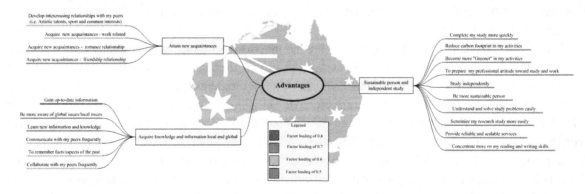

Figure 5. Bhutan – new advantages - prepared by researchers

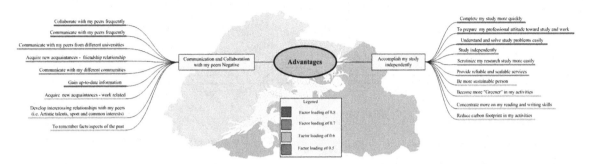

Figure 6. India – new advantages - prepared by researchers

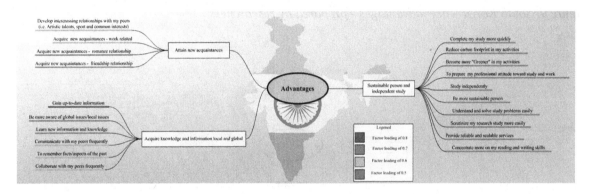

Figure 7. Malaysia – new advantages - prepared by researchers

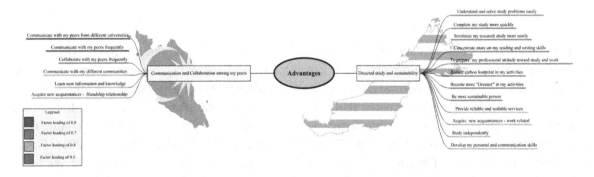

Furthermore, the researchers investigated whether the use of SN has any disadvantages; by examining the online survey, the SPSS generated two to three disadvantages for some countries (see Table 5). These disadvantages were, namely, depression and gambling, lack of concentration, security and privacy, loneliness, and preventing students from using the traditional media. Furthermore, the SPSS results indicated that students from several countries perceive the same disadvantages: students in Australia, India, Pakistan and South Korea mention depression and depression and anxiety; while the majority of the students in Australia, Bhutan, Pakistan and South Korea are concerned about security and privacy issues associated with SN. Finally, students in India, Malaysia and South Korea believe that SN prevents students from obtaining information via traditional media such as television and newspapers.

Figure 8. Pakistan – new advantages – prepared by researchers

Figure 9. South Korea – new advantages - prepared by researchers

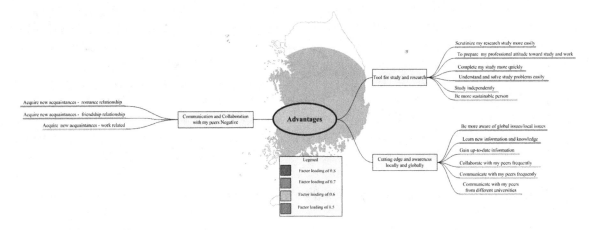

Finally, the online survey data for all countries were combined to examine the new disadvantages that emerged for the six countries. The SPSS generated three disadvantages, namely: depression and loneliness; SN prevents students from engaging in traditional activities, most importantly, they are concerned about security and privacy particularly when sharing personal details with others. First of all, by listing these disadvantages the research questions were answered and confirmed the literature findings (Andrzejczak & Liu, 2010; Dalbudak, Evren, Aldemir, Coskun, Ugurlu, & Yildirim, 2013; Fox & Moreland, 2015; Frison & Eggermont, 2015; Grabher & König, 2017; Martínez-Alemán & Wartman, 2008; Mueller, Mitchell, Peterson, Faber, Steffen, Crosby, & Claes, 2011; Selfhout, Branje, Delsing, Bogt, & Meeus, 2009 ; Young & Rodger, 1998).

However, these new disadvantages alerted the researchers and academics to the likelihood that students' incorrect or inappropriate use of SN will lead to several problems (see Table 5). Therefore, a suitable and appropriate model should be adopted especially regarding assessment and learning activities of students, to prevent or at least minimize the disadvantages. These problems should be tackled promptly by introducing a new social networking model: Social Networking and Education Model (SNEM) (Issa, Isaias, & Kommers, 2016). The aim of SNEM is to assist academics and researchers to implement SN in the education sector successfully by reducing the disadvantages and increasing the benefits associated with SN. The SNEM contains five elements namely: Teaching Methods, Learning, Technology Design and Psychological Aspects.

Figures 10, 11, 12, 13, 14, and 15 indicate the new disadvantages for Australia, Bhutan, India, Malaysia, Pakistan and South Korea regarding SN use by Asia-Pacific students. Each variable and factor loading is assigned a different color.

Table 5. Social networking disadvantages - prepared by researchers

Disadvantages	
Country	**Label /Disadvantages**
Australia	• Depression and gambling • Privacy and Security
Bhutan	• Lack of concentration and social activities • Security and privacy
India	• Depression and Loneliness • Dispersing and Distraction • Avert using the traditional media
Malaysia	• Failing and distraction to study on time • Prevent using the traditional media
Pakistan	• Depression and loneliness • Lack of concentration • Security and Privacy
South Korea	• Loneliness, depression and anxiety • Prevent using the traditional media • Security and privacy
All the Countries in this study	• Depression and Loneliness • Prevent using the traditional activities • Security and Privacy

Figure 10. Australia – new disadvantages – prepared by researchers

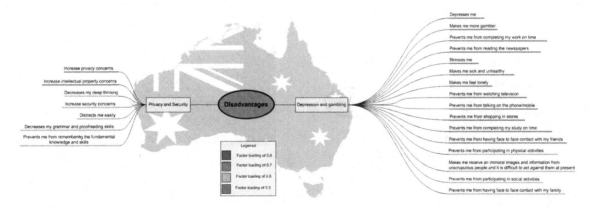

Figure 11. Bhutan – new disadvantages – prepared by researchers

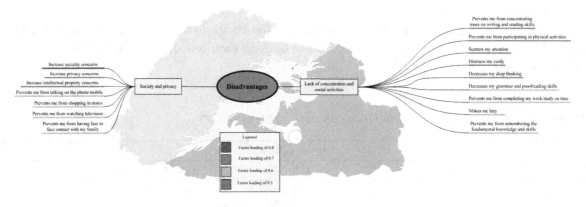

Figure 12. India – new disadvantages – prepared by researchers

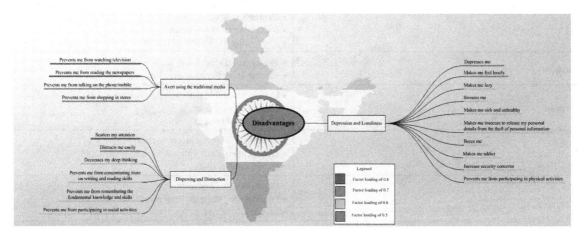

Figure 13. Malaysia – new disadvantages – prepared by researchers

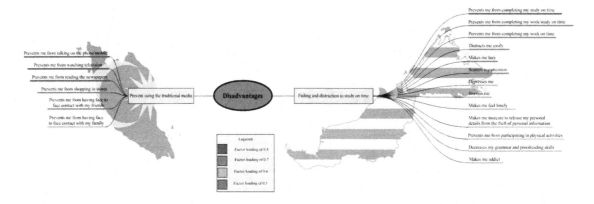

Figure 14. Pakistan– new disadvantages – prepared by researchers

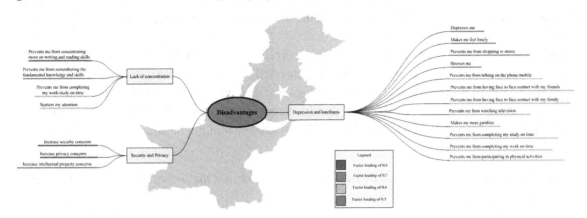

Figure 15. South Korea – new disadvantages – prepared by researchers

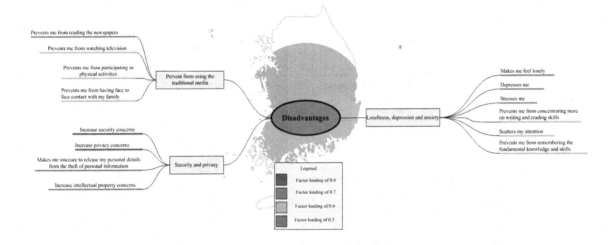

10. NEW THEORETICAL FINDINGS AND CONTRIBUTION

This study has made numerous theoretical contributions to the current literature, especially regarding SN awareness and specifically the advantages and disadvantages associated with social networking, specifically in the Asia-Pacific region. Tables 4 and 5 list the advantages and disadvantages for each country and for the All the Countries chosen for this study, respectively. This study will assist researchers to recognize students' attitudes toward SN for study or work especially in AP. SN provides several advantages, but can also produce disadvantages. Therefore, this study confirmed the research aims, as it generated new advantages and disadvantages of SN use among AP students. Consequently, researchers and academics should work very closely locally and globally to minimize the disadvantages and increase the advantages for students world-wide, and especially in the Asia-Pacific region.

Furthermore, this study confirmed that although students are living in different countries, they perceive the same advantages and disadvantages of SN; this means that culture is capable of influencing the adoption of SN by Asia-Pacific students since they are living in the same region and share the same attitudes and mind-set regarding SN adoption in the education sector. Table 6 illustrates the relationship between Hofstede's cultural framework and the use of SN from the perspective of the Asia-Pacific sample obtained for this study.

Table 6 lists the advantages and disadvantages perceived by AP students who are using SN in the education sector based on Hofstede's cultural framework. It was noted that students in some AP countries share the same opinion regarding the advantages and disadvantages in terms of Hofstede's cultural framework. However, some advantages and disadvantages are missing from Hofstede's cultural framework, although this issue is outside the scope of this study and will not be addressed.

Table 6. Relationship between Hofstede's cultural framework and the use of SN from the Asia-Pacific perspectives

Hofstede's Cultural Framework	AP Countries Comparison (Figure 5)	SN Advantages	AP Country Based on this Study	SN Disadvantages	AP Country Based on this Study
Power Distance		N/A	N/A	N/A	N/A
Individualism	Australia	Independent study	Australia *Bhutan* *India* *Malaysia*	N/A	N/A
Collectivism	South Korea Pakistan Malaysia	Communication and collaboration with my peers	*Bhutan* *India* Malaysia		N/A
Masculine	Australia India Malaysia Pakistan	N/A	N/A	N/A	N/A
Femininity	South Korea Bhutan	Sustainability	*Australia* *Malaysia*	N/A	N/A
Uncertainty avoidance	Pakistan South Korea	Cutting edge and awareness locally and globally	Australia Pakistan South Korea	Security	*Australia* *Bhutan* Pakistan South Korea
Long Term Orientation	South Korea	Tool for study and research	South Korea	Loneliness, depression and anxiety	*Australia* *India* *Pakistan* South Korea
Indulgence	Australia	Make new acquaintances	Australia *South Korea*	N/A	N/A
Restraint	India South Korea			Prevents use of traditional media	India *Malaysia* South Korea

This study confirmed the cultural contexts based on Hofstede's cultural framework. However, some countries shift from one dimension to another (the new countries are in italics). For example, regarding the Individualism dimension, in Bhutan, India and Malaysia, students in the higher education sector prefer to study independently by using SN technology. As indicated in Figure 5, these countries have a more collectivist culture. For example, from this study, Australia and Malaysia are part of the Femininity dimension, since Australian and Malaysian students are using SN tool as a tool fostering sustainability, since they are concerned about sustainability and our natural resources similar to South Korea and Bhutan as depicted in Figure 5.

In regard to the Uncertainty Avoidance dimension, according to this study, Australia is added to this dimension, as the Australian participants are keen to know about cutting edge technology and awareness locally and globally. AP students in Australia, Bhutan, North Korea and Pakistan regard the issue of security as a disadvantage. As for the Long Term Orientation dimension, South Korea is keen to use modern education methods to enhance the teaching and learning for the future. South Korean participants confirmed that the use of SN in the education sector was beneficial for study and research. However, for the same dimension, South Korean, Australian, Indian and Pakistani students believed that the use of SN can lead to loneliness, depression and anxiety. As for the Indulgence dimension, Australian students are using SN to make new acquaintances, and this is one of the advantages also perceived by the South Korean students. Finally, the Restraint dimension indicated that the use of SN technology prevented students from India, South Korea and Malaysia (a new country added to this dimension) from using traditional media.

Figure 16. Asia-Pacific countries chosen for this study - advantages – prepared by researchers

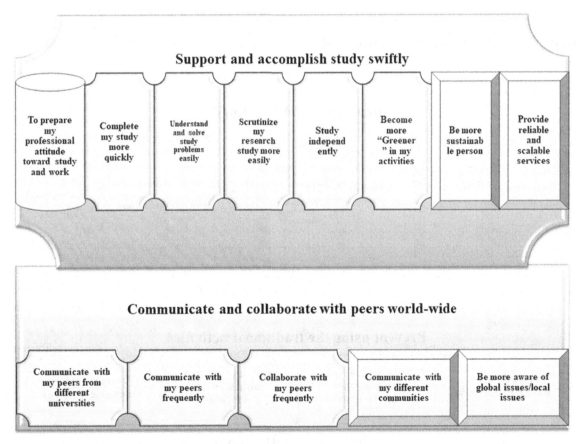

This study confirmed that culture influences the use of SN in AP countries, as students from various AP countries have the same opinion about the SN advantages and disadvantages. Moreover, the new findings from this study match AP countries comparison based on Hofstede's cultural framework; while some AP countries are added to different dimensions in the Hofstede's cultural framework based on students' attitudes toward SN use, this means, this study added new findings and significance to the current literature.

As mentioned previously, the researchers examined the Asia-Pacific results as a whole. Figures 16 and 17 show the advantages and disadvantages for all the Asia-Pacific countries used for this study; the cylindrical shape indicates a factor loading of .8, the plague shape shows a .7 factor loading and the rectangle shape indicates a .6 factor loading.

Finally, this study raised the awareness of the advantages and disadvantages of the use of SN in the Asia-Pacific education sector as the new generation world-wide considers this as an essential tool that enables students to improve their personal and professional skills, which are needed for their current studies and the workforce in future. Therefore, researchers and academics should take the lead in encouraging teaching and learning departments in education sector institutions to integrate SN principles in the curriculum, pedagogy and teaching principles, especially in the assessments and learning/teaching activities by implementing the SNEM model in the integration in order to increase the advantages and reduce or eliminate the disadvantages of SN use by Asia-Pacific students.

Figure 17. Asia-Pacific countries chosen for this study - disadvantages – prepared by researchers

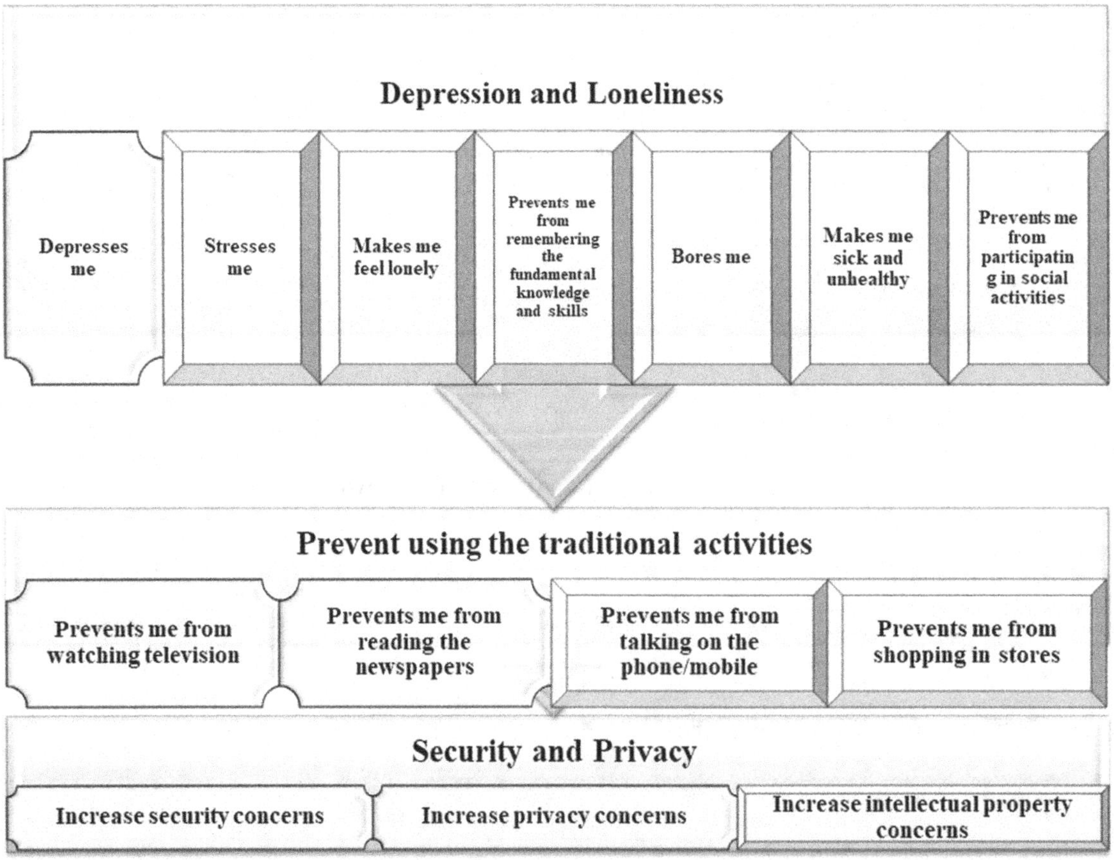

11. LIMITATIONS

This study's investigation was limited to six countries in the Asia-Pacific region and was intended to determine students' attitudes to SN. The results obtained from the 826 valid responses generated new advantages and disadvantages from the Asia-Pacific students' perspective. Moreover, the relation between learning styles and the social networking use were not analyzed in this study. Therefore, further research will be carried out in the future to examine the SN use in other Asia-Pacific countries to collect further data to strengthen the goals research conclusions.

12. CONCLUSION

This study examined the Asia-Pacific students' attitudes and behaviours regarding the use of SN in their studies, and whether their culture influences their use of SN. A total of 826 students were recruited for this study from six countries in the Asia-Pacific region, namely Australia, Bhutan, India, Malaysia, Pakistan, and South Korea; the data was collected over 6 to 8 months. The online survey outcomes indicated several advantages and disadvantages associated with SN use by Asia-Pacific students. Namely, it encouraged more communication and collaboration with peers, made them more sustainable; enabled them to acquire local and global knowledge and information; enabled them to establish new romantic attachments, and SN helped them to finish their study tasks quickly. On the other hand, there were several disadvantages including depression and gambling, privacy and security concerns, loneliness, and less utilization of traditional media such as TV and newspapers. These disadvantages sent a warning to researchers and academics to tackle these problems by implementing an appropriate model such as SNEM to minimise the disadvantages and extend the advantages. Moreover, this study confirmed that culture had an influence on SN adoption, since students in different Asia-Pacific countries perceived the same advantages and disadvantages concerning SN use, since they are living in the same region and have the same attitudes and behaviours. Furthermore, some AP countries are added to different dimensions in the Hofstede's cultural framework based on students' attitudes toward SN use, this means, this study added new findings and significance to the current literature. Finally, further research will be carried out in the future to examine SN use in other Asia-Pacific countries to collect further data to consolidate the research outcomes and objectives.

REFERENCES

Abdulahi, A., Samadi, B., & Gharleghi, B. (2014). A study on the negative effects of social networking sites such as Facebook among Asia Pacific University scholars in Malaysia. *International Journal of Business and Social Science*, *5*(10).

Andrzejczak, C., & Liu, D. (2010). The effect of testing location on usability testing performance, participant stress levels, and subjective testing experience. *Journal of Systems and Software*, *83*(7), 1258–1266. doi:10.1016/j.jss.2010.01.052

Bland, J., & Altman, D. G. (1997). Statistics notes: Cronbach's alpha. *BMJ (Clinical Research Ed.)*, *314*(7080), 572. doi:10.1136/bmj.314.7080.572 PMID:9055718

Blatt, A. J. (2015). *Collaborative Mapping. In Health, Science, and Place* (pp. 63–75). Springer.

Bravo, G., & Potvin, L. (1991). Estimating the reliability of continuous measures with Cronbach's alpha or the intraclass correlation coefficient: Toward the integration of two traditions. *Journal of Clinical Epidemiology*, *44*(4-5), 381–390. doi:10.1016/0895-4356(91)90076-L PMID:2010781

Burns, R., & Burns, R. (2008). Business Research Methods and Statistics Using SPSS. *Sage (Atlanta, Ga.)*.

Chugh, R., & Ruhi, U. (2018). Social media in higher education: A literature review of Facebook. *Education and Information Technologies*, *23*(2), 605–616. doi:10.100710639-017-9621-2

Clark, A. (2010). How to create change in a conservative culture. *Green Economy*. Retrieved from http://greeneconomypost.com/how-to-create-green-change-in-a-conservative-culture-9086.htm

Clarke, M. (2010). Controlling privacy on social networking services. *UXmatters*. Retrieved from http://www.uxmatters.com/mt/archives/2010/04/controlling-privacy-on-social-networking-services.php

Connelly, L. M. (2011). Cronbach's Alpha. *Medsurg Nursing*, *20*(1), 44–45. PMID:21446295

Costello, A., & Osborne, J. (2005). Best practices in exploratory factor analysis: Four recommendations for getting the most from your analysis. *Practical Assessment, Research & Evaluation*, *10*(7), 1–9.

Couper, M. P., Traugott, M. W., & Lamias, M. J. (2001). Web survey design and administration. *Public Opinion Quarterly*, *65*(2), 230–253. doi:10.1086/322199 PMID:11420757

Dalbudak, E., Evren, C., Aldemir, S., Coskun, K. S., Ugurlu, H., & Yildirim, F. G. (2013). Relationship of internet addiction severity with depression, anxiety, and alexithymia, temperament and character in university students. *Cyberpsychology, Behavior, and Social Networking*, *16*(4), 272–278. doi:10.1089/cyber.2012.0390 PMID:23363230

Das, J. R., Dash, M., Sahoo, M. A., & Mohanty, A. K. (2017). An empirical study on customers' internet banking behavior. International Journal of Management, *7*(7). Retrieved from http://www.ijmra.us

De-Marcos, L., Domínguez, A., Saenz-de-Navarrete, J., & Pagés, C. (2014). An empirical study comparing gamification and social networking on e-learning. *Computers & Education*, *75*, 82–91. doi:10.1016/j.compedu.2014.01.012

DeKay, S. (2009). Are business-oriented social networking web sites useful resources for locating passive jobseekers? Results of a recent study. *Business Communication Quarterly*, *72*(1), 101–105. doi:10.1177/1080569908330378

Dillenbourg, P. (1999). *What do you mean by collaborative learning?* Oxford: Elsevier.

Dillman, D. A. (2007). *Mail and Internet Surveys "The Tailored Design Method"* (2nd ed.). USA: John Wiley & Sons, Inc.

Dillman, D. A., Phelps, G., Tortora, R., Swift, K., Kohrell, J., Berck, J., & Messer, B. L. (2009). Response rate and measurement differences in mixed-mode surveys using mail, telephone, interactive voice reponse (IVR) and the Internet. *Social Science Research*, *38*(1), 1–18. doi:10.1016/j.ssresearch.2008.03.007

Dillman, D. A., Reipus, U. D., & Matzat, U. (2010). Advice in Surveying the general public over the Internet. *International Journal of Internet Science*, *5*(1), 1–4.

Dillman, D. A. (2017). The promise and challenge of pushing respondents to the Web in mixed-mode surveys. *Survey Methodology*, *43* (1).

Din, N., Yahya, S., Suzan, R., & Kassim, R. (2012). Online Social Networking for Quality of Life. *Procedia: Social and Behavioral Sciences*, *35*, 713–718. doi:10.1016/j.sbspro.2012.02.141

Durak, G. (2017). Using Social Learning Networks (SLNs) in higher education: Edmodo through the lenses of academics. *The International Review of Research in Open and Distributed Learning*, *18*(1). doi:10.19173/irrodl.v18i1.2623

Dziuban, C. D., & Shirkey, E. C. (1974). When is a correlation matrix appropriate for factor analysis? Some decision rules. *Psychological Bulletin*, *81*(6), 358–361. doi:10.1037/h0036316

Fan, W., & Yan, Z. (2010). Factors affecting response rates of the web survey: A systematic review. *Computers in Human Behavior*, *26*(2), 132–139. doi:10.1016/j.chb.2009.10.015

Forrester Research. (2010). *Social Networking in The Enterprise: Benefits and Inhibitors*. USA: Forrester Research.

Fox, J., & Moreland, J. J. (2015). The dark side of social networking sites: An exploration of the relational and psychological stressors associated with Facebook use and affordances. *Computers in Human Behavior*, *45*(0), 168–176. doi:10.1016/j.chb.2014.11.083

Frison, E., & Eggermont, S. (2015). The impact of daily stress on adolescents' depressed mood: The role of social support seeking through Facebook. *Computers in Human Behavior*, *44*(0), 315–325. doi:10.1016/j.chb.2014.11.070

Frohlich, M. T., & Westbrook, R. (2001). Arcs of integration: An international study of supply chain strategies. *Journal of Operations Management*, *19*(2), 185–200. doi:10.1016/S0272-6963(00)00055-3

Frydenberg, M. (2008). Wikis as a Tool for Collaborative Course Management. *MERLOT Journal of Online Learning and Teaching*, *4*(2), 169–181.

Gliem, J. A., & Gliem, R. R. (2003). Calculating, Interpreting, and Reporting Cronbach's Alpha Reliability Coefficient for Likert-Type Scales. *Paper presented at the 2003 Midwest Research to Practice Conference in Adult, Continuing and COmmunity Education.*

Grabher, G., & König, J. (2017). *Performing network theory? Reflexive relationship management on social network sites. In Networked Governance* (pp. 121–140). Springer.

Gülbahar, Y., Rapp, C., Kilis, S., & Sitnikova, A. (2017). Enriching higher education with social media: Development and evaluation of a social media toolkit. *The International Review of Research in Open and Distributed Learning*, *18*(1). doi:10.19173/irrodl.v18i1.2656

Baird, H. (2011). From social media to social customer relationship management. *Strategy and Leadership*, *39*(5), 30–37. doi:10.1108/10878571111161507

Heydari, A., & Laroche, M. (2017). Cross-Cultural Study of Social Media-Based Brand Communities: An Abstract. *Paper presented at the Academy of Marketing Science Annual Conference.*

Hill, B. D. (2012). *Sequential Kaiser-Meyer-Olkin Procedure As an Alternative for Determining The Number of Factors in Common-Factor Analysis: A Monte Carlo Simulation* [Doctoral dissertation]. Oklahoma State University.

Hofstede, G. (1984). *Culture's consequences: International differences in work-related values.* sage.

Hofstede, G. (2003). *Culture's consequences: Comparing values, behaviors, institutions and organizations across nations.* Sage Publications.

Hofstede Insights. (2018). Country comparison. Retrieved from https://www.hofstede-insights.com/country-comparison/pakistan,south-korea/

Holmes, K. M., & O'loughlin, N. (2014). The experiences of people with learning disabilities on social networking sites. *British Journal of Learning Disabilities, 42*(1), 1–5. doi:10.1111/bld.12001

Hudson, S., Huang, L., Roth, M. S., & Madden, T. J. (2016). The influence of social media interactions on consumer–brand relationships: A three-country study of brand perceptions and marketing behaviors. *International Journal of Research in Marketing, 33*(1), 27–41. doi:10.1016/j.ijresmar.2015.06.004

Issa, T. (2014). Learning, Communication and Interaction via Wiki: An Australian Perspective. In H. Kaur & X. Tao (Eds.), *ICTs and the Millennium Development Goals: A United Nations Perspective* (pp. 1–17). Boston, MA: Springer US. doi:10.1007/978-1-4899-7439-6_1

Issa, T. (2016). Social Networking in Australia: Opportunities and Risks. In T. Issa, P. Isaias, & P. Kommers (Eds.), *Social Networking and Education Global Perspectives* (pp. 17–39). USA: Springer. doi:10.1007/978-3-319-17716-8_2

Issa, T., Isaias, P., & Kommers, P. (2016). Social Networking and Education Model (SNEM). In T. Issa, P. Isaias, & P. Kommers (Eds.), *Social Networking and Education Global Perspectives* (pp. 323–345). USA: Springer. doi:10.1007/978-3-319-17716-8_20

Johnson, B. K., & Knobloch-Westerwick, S. (2014). Glancing up or down: Mood management and selective social comparisons on social networking sites. *Computers in Human Behavior, 41*(0), 33–39. doi:10.1016/j.chb.2014.09.009

Kearns, L., & Frey, B. (2010). Web 2.0 Technologies and Back Channel Communication in an Online Learning Community. *TechTrends, 54*(3), 41–54.

Kelin, K. (2008). Are Social Networking Sites Useful for Business? *Bloomberg.* Retrieved from http://www.bloomberg.com/bw/stories/2008-08-06/are-social-networking-sites-useful-for-business-businessweek-business-news-stock-market-and-financial-advice

Kepios. (2017). Digital in Asia-Pacific in 2017 Retrieved from https://kepios.com/blog/apac2017

Kiehne, T. (2004). Social Networking Systems: History, Critique, and Knowledge Management Potentials Retrieved from https://www.ischool.utexas.edu/~i385q/archive/kiehne_t/kiehne%282004%29-sns.pdf

Kontos, E., Emmons, K., Puleo, E., & Viswanath, K. (2010). Communication Inequalities and Public Health Implications of Adult Social Networking Site Use in the United States. *Journal of Health Communication, 15*(S3), 216–235. doi:10.1080/10810730.2010.522689 PMID:21154095

Ku, H.-Y., Tseng, H. W., & Akarasriworn, C. (2013). Collaboration factors, teamwork satisfaction, and student attitudes toward online collaborative learning. *Computers in Human Behavior, 29*(3), 922–929. doi:10.1016/j.chb.2012.12.019

Kuzma, Joanne. (2010). Asian government usage of Web 2.0 social media. *European Journal of ePractice*(9), 1-13.

Langheinrich, M., & Karjoth, G. (2010). Social networking and the risk to companies and institutions. *Information Security Technical Report, 15*(2), 51–56. doi:10.1016/j.istr.2010.09.001

Lanning, S. K., Brickhouse, T. H., Gunsolley, J. C., Ranson, S. L., & Willett, R. M. (2011). Communication Skills Instruction: An Analysis of self, peer-group, student instructors and faculty assessment. *Patient Education and Counseling, 83*(2), 145–151. doi:10.1016/j.pec.2010.06.024 PMID:20638816

Likert, R. (1932). A Technique for the Measurement of attitudes. *Archives de Psychologie, 22*(140), 55.

Lin, K. Y., & Lu, H. P. (2011). Why people use social networking sites: An empirical study integrating network externalities and motivation theory. *Computers in Human Behavior, 27*(3), 1152–1161. doi:10.1016/j.chb.2010.12.009

Lipp, A., Davis, R. E., Peter, R., & Davies, J. S. (2014). The use of social media among health care professionals within an online postgraduate diabetes diploma course. *Practical Diabetes, 31*(1), 14–17a. doi:10.1002/pdi.1821

Lowry, P. B., Zhang, D., Zhou, L., & Fu, X. (2010). Effects of culture, social presence, and group composition on trust in technology-supported decision-making groups. *Information Systems Journal, 20*(3), 297–315. doi:10.1111/j.1365-2575.2009.00334.x

Martínez-Alemán, A. M., & Wartman, K. L. (2008). *Online social networking on campus: Understanding what matters in student culture.* Routledge.

Mathew, B. (2014). Using a social networking tool for blended learning in staff training: Sharing experience from practice. *Journal of Neonatal Nursing, 20*(3), 90–94. doi:10.1016/j.jnn.2014.03.005

Matusitz, J., & Musambira, G. (2013). Power distance, uncertainty avoidance, and technology: Analyzing Hofstede's dimensions and human development indicators. *Journal of Technology in Human Services, 31*(1), 42–60. doi:10.1080/15228835.2012.738561

McCarroll, N., & Curran, K. (2013). Social Networking in Education. *International Journal of Innovation in the Digital Economy, 4*(1), 1–15.

McKenna, B. (2010). Social networking: The 'what not to do' guide for organisations. *Infosecurity, 7*(5), 22–24. doi:10.1016/S1754-4548(10)70086-3

Miller, R., & Lammas, N. (2010). Social media and its implications for viral marketing. *Asia Pacific Public Relations Journal, 11*(1), 1–9.

Minocha, S., & Thomas, P. (2007). Collaborative Learning in a Wiki Environment: Experiences from a Software Engineering Course. *New Review of Hypermedia and Multimedia*, *13*(2), 187–209. doi:10.1080/13614560701712667

Moreno, M. A., & Kolb, J. (2012). Social Networking Sites and Adolescent Health. *Pediatric Clinics of North America*, *59*(3), 601–612. doi:10.1016/j.pcl.2012.03.023 PMID:22643167

Mueller, A., Mitchell, J. E., Peterson, L. A., Faber, R. J., Steffen, K. J., Crosby, R. D., & Claes, L. (2011). Depression, materialism, and excessive Internet use in relation to compulsive buying. *Comprehensive Psychiatry*, *52*(4), 420–424. doi:10.1016/j.comppsych.2010.09.001 PMID:21683178

Ngai, E. W., Tao, S. S., & Moon, K. K. (2015). Social media research: Theories, constructs, and conceptual frameworks. *International Journal of Information Management*, *35*(1), 33–44.

Oh, H. J., Ozkaya, E., & LaRose, R. (2014). How does online social networking enhance life satisfaction? The relationships among online supportive interaction, affect, perceived social support, sense of community, and life satisfaction. *Computers in Human Behavior*, *30*(0), 69–78. doi:10.1016/j.chb.2013.07.053

Pan, Y., Xu, Y., Wang, X., Zhang, C., Ling, H., & Lin, J. (2015). Integrating social networking support for dyadic knowledge exchange: A study in a virtual community of practice. *Information & Management*, *52*(1), 61–70. doi:10.1016/j.im.2014.10.001

Papacharissi, Z. (2010). *A networked self: Identity, community, and culture on social network sites*. Routledge.

Park, N., Kee, K. F., & Valenzuela, S. (2009). Being immersed in social networking environment: Facebook groups, uses and gratifications, and social outcomes. *Cyberpsychology & Behavior*, *12*(6), 729–733. doi:10.1089/cpb.2009.0003 PMID:19619037

Peluchette, J., & Karl, K. (2008). Social networking profiles: An examination of student attitudes regarding use and appropriateness of content. *Cyberpsychology & Behavior*, *11*(1), 95–97. doi:10.1089/cpb.2007.9927 PMID:18275320

Pempek, T., Yermolayeva, Y., & Calvert, S. (2000). College Students' social networking experieences on Facebook. *Journal of Applied Developmental Psychology*.

Peng, M. W., & Zhou, J. Q. (2005). How network strategies and institutional transitions evolve in Asia. *Asia Pacific Journal of Management*, *22*(4), 321–336. doi:10.100710490-005-4113-0

Peruta, A., & Shields, A. B. (2017). Social media in higher education: Understanding how colleges and universities use Facebook. *Journal of Marketing for Higher Education*, *27*(1), 131–143. doi:10.1080/08841241.2016.1212451

Phua, J., & Jin, S.-A. A. (2011). 'Finding a home away from home': The use of social networking sites by Asia-Pacific students in the United States for bridging and bonding social capital. *Asian Journal of Communication*, *21*(5), 504–519. doi:10.1080/01292986.2011.587015

Schaefer, H. S., Larson, C. L., Davidson, R. J., & Coan, J. A. (2014). Brain, body, and cognition: Neural, physiological and self-report correlates of phobic and normative fear. *Biological Psychology*, *98*, 59–69. doi:10.1016/j.biopsycho.2013.12.011 PMID:24561099

Sekaran, U. (2003). *Research Methods for Business "A Skill Building Approach"* (4th ed.). MA, USA: John Wiley & Sons.

Selfhout, M., Branje, S., Delsing, M., Bogt, T., & Meeus, W. (2009). Different types of Internet use, depression, and social anxiety: The role of perceived friendship quality. *Journal of Adolescence, 32*(4), 819–833. doi:10.1016/j.adolescence.2008.10.011 PMID:19027940

Shin, J. C., & Harman, G. (2009). New challenges for higher education: Global and Asia-Pacific perspectives. *Asia Pacific Education Review, 10*(1), 1–13. doi:10.100712564-009-9011-6

Sigman, A. (2009). Well connected. *Biologist (Columbus, Ohio), 56*(1), 14–20.

Smyth, J. D., Dillman, D. A., Christian, L. M., & O'Neill, A. C. (2010). Using the internet to survey small towns and communities: Limitations and Possibilities in the early 21st Century. *The American Behavioral Scientist, 53*(9), 1423–1448. doi:10.1177/0002764210361695

Sohmee, J., & Oppeniander, J. E. (2010). *JMP Means Business Statistical Models for Management.* USA: SAS Institute Inc.

Steinfield, C., DiMicco, J., Ellison, N., & Lampe, C. (2009). Bowling Online: Social Networking and Social Capital Within the Organization. *Paper presented at the C & T '09*, University Park, Pennsylvania, USA.

Stevens, J. P. (1992). *Applied multivariate statistics for the social sciences.* Hillsdale, NJ: Erlbaum.

Stump, R. L., & Gong, W. (2017). Social networking sites: An exploration of the effect of national cultural dimensions on country adoption rates and usage patterns. *International Journal of Electronic Business, 13*(2-3), 117–142. doi:10.1504/IJEB.2017.083288

Tariq, W., Mehboob, M., Khan, M. A., & Ullah, F. (2012). The Impact of social media and social networks on education and students of Pakistan. *International Journal of Computer Science Issues, 9*(4), 407.

Tavakol, M., & Dennick, R. (2011). Making sense of Cronbach's alpha. *International Journal of Medical Education, 2*, 53–55. doi:10.5116/ijme.4dfb.8dfd PMID:28029643

Tharp, T. L. (2010). "Wiki, Wiki, Wiki-What?" Assessing Online Collaborative Writing. *English Journal, 99*(5), 40–46.

Tobias, S., & Carlson, J. E. (1969). Brief report: Bartlett's test of sphericity and chance findings in factor analysis. *Multivariate Behavioral Research, 4*(3), 375–377. doi:10.120715327906mbr0403_8 PMID:26745847

Toepoel, V., & Dillman, D. (2008). Words, Numbers and Visual Heuristics in Web Surveys: Is there a Hierarchy of Importance?

Trusov, M., Bucklin, R. E., & Pauwels, K. (2009). Effects of word-of-mouth versus traditional marketing: Findings from an internet social networking site. *Journal of Marketing, 73*(5), 90–102. doi:10.1509/jmkg.73.5.90

Tsinakos, A. (2006). Collaborative Student Modelling - A new Perspective using Wiki. *WSEAS TRANS on Advance in Engineering Education, 6*(3), 475–481.

Umbach, P. D. (2004). Web Surveys. *Best PracticesNew Directions for Institutional Research*, (121), 23–38. doi:10.1002/ir.98

Velasquez, A., Graham, C., & McCollum, K. (2009). Online Social Networking Used to Enhance Face to Face and Online Pre-Servicve Teacher Education Courses. *Paper presented at the Society for Information Technology and Teacher Education International Conference.*

Vereecken, W., Van Heddeghem, W., Colle, D., Pickavet, M., & Demeester, P. (2010). Overall ICT Footpring and Green Communication Technologies. *Paper presented at the Proceedings of the 4th International Symposium on Communications, Control and Signal Processing, ISCCSP 2010*, Limassol. 10.1109/ISCCSP.2010.5463327

Wallace, C. S., & Brooks, L. (2015). Learning to Teach Elementary Science in an Experiential, Informal Context: Culture, Learning, and Identity. *Science Education*, *99*(1), 174–198. doi:10.1002ce.21138

Wang, H. (2008). Wiki as a Collaborative Tool to Support Faculty in Mobile Teaching and Learning. *Paper presented at the Society for Information Technology & Teacher Education International Conference 2008*, Las Vegas, NV. Retrieved from http://www.editlib.org/p/27658

Waters, R. D., Burnett, E., Lamm, A., & Lucas, J. (2009). Engaging stakeholders through social networking: How nonprofit organizations are using Facebook. *Public Relations Review*, *35*(2), 102–106. doi:10.1016/j.pubrev.2009.01.006

Waycott, J., Bennett, S., Kennedy, G., Dalgarno, B., & Gray, K. (2010). Digital divides? Student and staff perceptions of information and communication technologies. *Computers & Education*, *54*(4), 1202–1211. doi:10.1016/j.compedu.2009.11.006

Williams, B., Onsman, A., & Brown, T. (2010). Exploratory factor analysis: A five-step guide for novices. *Australasian Journal of Paramedicine*, *8*(3).

Young, K., & Rodger, R. (1998). The relationship between depression and Internet addiction. *Cyberpsychology (Brno)*, *1*(1), 25–28. doi:10.1089/cpb.1998.1.25

Zhu, D. H., Chang, Y. P., Luo, J. J., & Li, X. (2014). Understanding the adoption of location-based recommendation agents among active users of social networking sites. *Information Processing & Management*, *50*(5), 675–682. doi:10.1016/j.ipm.2014.04.010

This research was previously published in the Journal of Global Information Management (JGIM), 27(4); pages 119-146, copyright year 2019 by IGI Publishing (an imprint of IGI Global).

Chapter 91
Exploring the Role of Facebook Pages During the Mass Student Protest for Road Safety in Bangladesh

Shahla Shahnaz Dyuti
The Queen's University of Belfast, UK

ABSTRACT

The mass student protest for road safety in Bangladesh started in the capital city Dhaka after the death of two students by a road accident. Focusing on the event during 2018, this paper analyses the comments and memes of selected Facebook pages to find out the reactions by netizens towards the protest. Although there are several studies based on protest and social media in different nations, in Bangladesh it remains an under-researched field. Data were collected from four selected public Facebook pages using the thematic analysis method. Through the analysis of the data, it became clear that netizens wanted to express their feelings and thoughts freely in this open space as new media offers them an almost censor-free platform. The findings contribute to understanding how social media plays a role in providing an open platform of freedom of expression.

INTRODUCTION AND BACKGROUND OF THE STUDY

Nowadays, the world is experiencing an era of digital communication. Apart from mainstream media, social or digital media are gaining public support and popularity. These types of media help to spread important information, videos, recordings and documents within a moment. According to Gerbaudo, "the importance of the struggle for public space in contemporary social movements invites us to rethink the way in which we understand the role of new media and social media in particular" (2012, p. 11). As the raw data is written by the participants themselves, they can be directly accessed from the social media platform, eliminating the potential bias of eliminating or adding data in traditional interview transcription etc. (Halaweh, 2018; Hewson et al., 2016). Like some other countries, Bangladesh is no exception to

DOI: 10.4018/978-1-6684-7123-4.ch091

the global trend of the youth movement, as was most observable during the protest for road safety, that overwhelmed the entire country. Most importantly it was the very first contemporary massive protest by teenage students in this country which had been taken into account by various international media.

In Dhaka, the capital city of Bangladesh, two high school students were killed by a speedy unlicensed bus on 29 July 2018. After the killing, thousands of students mostly in their mid-teens (The Guardian, 2018) poured into the street demanding justice for the incident. The protest then spread outside Dhaka. During the protest, students kept the highways blocked and checked the valid license of all public, private transports. Gradually many people of various age groups started demonstrating solidarity and joined with the pupils and also numerous citizens including the protestors were posting updates on social media. The demand for improved road safety protest was held from 29 July to 7 August 2018. At that time traditional media houses did not publish all the updates of the protest but Facebook and other forms of social media did. To quell the protest Bangladesh police and security forces launched a massive crackdown on protesters. In that protest social media, particularly Facebook, played a key role in raising support by letting the netizens comment on news-related posts, posting schedules of meetings, work plans and encouraged people to join with the protesters. Simultaneously, this platform was also reportedly used to spread rumours and misinformation, including false reports of students being raped and killed (Mahmud, 2018).

This study explored the role that was played by Facebook pages by analysing comments and memes posted on the protest-related videos of two news media pages and two satire pages. All these pages were generated from Bangladesh and all data related to the protest were collected and analysed in the three months. The main aim was to find out netizen's tendency to say whatever they think in this media that has freedom of expression by studying their comments and memes. By analysing the data through thematic analysis method, this study identifies five themes that have been posted frequently by netizens: - movement support; strong demand for safer roads and punishment; the reflection of dissatisfaction with the government; Facebook as a platform for dissenting views; Facebook as a tool to spread rumours. An important point to be noted is that this research did not study the activity by the protesters either offline or online, but rather tried to identify and analyse the characteristics of the online posts (comments and memes).

Young people will determine the future of a country and its system, so it is important to gain an in-depth understanding of their engagement in social protest on serious national issues like road accidents. There has been previous research led on student movements or student participation in a mass movement and its association with social media in different nations between 2008-2015. Among them, the following examples are- The Candlelight protests in South Korea (Chang and Yun, 2011); The South African Student Movement (Millham, 2016); The Sunflower Movement in Taiwan (Lin, 2015) and The Umbrella Movement in Hong Kong (Li and Suh, 2015). Except for Millhams' (2016), none of these studies had a specific focus on the reactions (comments or memes) in social media toward the students and their protest. However, as there is no literature on the student movement for safer roads in Bangladesh and youth participation in social protest is prominent in different countries, it is important to build work and expand scholarly knowledge of this contemporary phenomenon.

Data such as comments and memes have been analysed and represented via a thematic analysis method. Themes were developed that were generated straight from the data to gain an in-depth insight into the point of view held by the general public as well as, attitudes and modes of engagement with this issue.

Facebook and Facebook Memes

For Bock & Figueroa (2018), social media sites constitute a special type of online text as multiple stake-holders contribute to content that creates community besides delivering information. The internet started its journey long ago but Web 2.0 enhanced opportunities for observation of the interactive behaviour online (Hewson et al., 2016). The term "web 2.0" was coined in 2005 and as the word·"social" features prominently in the term 'social media' that ensures participation, users contribution, control of one's data, rich users experience etc. (Fuchs, 2014). According to Statista (Clement, 2020), Facebook is the most popular social network based on global audience size. Facebook allows people to like/react, share, comment, post videos, text, images, memes, stickers, emojis etc. Several studies have been conducted to understand Facebook use and its connection to behaviour. For example, Lang and Barton (2015) represented several methods by which individuals managed undesirable Facebook photos to maintain their self-images. However, Jin et al. (2015) suggested that the popularity of a community on Facebook, as well as its message styles, can impact perceived source credibility and information value. For instance, Facebook users prefer popular pages that have a high number of "likes" and informational messages from experts over less popular pages and testimonial messages from other users (Jin et al., 2015). Buddy Media (2012 cited in Kim et al. 2016), found that the most frequently visited Facebook pages were News Feed (27%) and Timeline (21%). The News Feed page, also known as the Home Page, is a list of updated stories from people who are followed and pages. From this point of view, the highest liked four Facebook pages have been considered for this research to analyse people's activity and behaviour.

Whereas, in this research, the memes of the two highest liked Bangladeshi Facebook fun pages have been analysed which portrayed the then situation of the country by creating satire illustrations that supported the protestors but represented authorities' failure. Memes are usually individual user or page created still images, animated GIFs, and videos typically intended as a joke (Davison, 2012). Börzsei (2013) argued that memes are not meant to be beautiful or visually appealing, and instead focus on delivering an ideological message. Shifman (2011) included that meme phenomena should be considered according to cultural-aesthetic and social logics. Scholars have argued that memes can be an effective way to increase political participation and construct a collective identity (Gal et al., 2016; Milner, 2013). Memes may also serve as a social anchor for the communities that form around them (Prochazka, 2018).

Social Media and Protests

In contemporary movements organisers increasingly rely on digital technology and social media became a 'mundane tool' to facilitate the protests (Nielsen 2011, Nielsen 2013 cited in Suh et al., 2017). In general, studies have tended to find a positive relationship between the frequency of social media use and protest behaviour, in line with existing research on the digital media. For example: during candlelight protests in South Korea, the researchers (Chang and Yun, 2011) addressed that 'internet's powerful role' influenced teenagers' political participation. While during the Arab Spring (2011) Smidi & Shahin's (2017) survey research on this movement shows that 'social networking sites made citizens believe they had a 'say' in public affairs'. In the case of the umbrella movement in Hong Kong the researchers showed, respondents think Facebook pages allow them to write 'opinionated message' in a 'transparent manner' unlike mainstream media (Li & Suh, 2015). Another study on the occupy wall street movement demonstrates the 'repression-mobilisation relationship' as well as the digital media allowance for protesters to 'disseminate diverse depictions of police aggression' (Suh et al., 2017). On the other hand, during the Indignados protest Facebook can support new forms of alternative politics inspired by more participatory modes of engagement and Facebook also reinforces civic talk through activists' digital story telling (Papa, 2017). Whereas, on the Shahbag movement in Bangladesh demanding death sentence of a war criminal, twitter activities always increased when something special happened around Shahbag area and also many new account were created then for protest purposes (Raychoudhury et al., 2015). Moreover, another study based on the student protest in South Africa showed some examples of the most used themes developed during the protest on Twitter (Millham, 2016). So from the aforementioned studies, it is clear that social media ease the way of freedom of expression in sensitive issues like a protest. Users feel free to say whatever they are thinking and support the protest virtually by creating groups or profiles in social media. Generally, due to censorship rules, freedom of speech of mass people regarding protest-related issues is almost impossible in traditional media. So obviously social media has opened a unique dimension by letting people speak.

These considerations may lead us to hypothesise that:

1. There is a relationship between the Facebook/social media users and their tendency to express opinions related to protest issue as such new media offer them a platform with freedom of expression.
2. And thus they have the willingness to express on Facebook during the student protest for road safety in Bangladesh. Frequent Facebook users are more likely to take part in this unprecedented issue virtually such as giving and exchanging opinions, learning information etc.

METHODOLOGY

Content Selection

A timeframe between June 29, 2018- August 7, 2018, was chosen as these continuous 10 days were considered as 'the rise and silencing' of the student protest (The Daily Star, 2018). A total of four public Facebook pages have been selected for this research based on the high number of likes that they received, a high rate of likes indicates that a large number of people follow the pages. As the research question focused on the role of Facebook pages during the protest, only Facebook generated data or extant documents were considered for this study. The two top liked news media pages were selected by consulting Afroz (2018), 1. A Facebook page of a leading daily Bengali newspaper (14,302,164 likes) named The Daily Phothom Alo that has both a print and online version. 2. A Facebook page of BBC News Bangla (12,595,965 likes). This is a regional Bengali version of the British Broadcasting Corporation. But there is no existing study based on the top liked national Facebook fan pages. So we made a random list of five popular satire pages and selected the first two pages according to the highest number of likes as a final sample. The first one named 'earki' (@earkidotcom) with a total of 405,225 likes. Earki is a Bengali word meanings 'Joke'. In this page, they introduced themselves as 'a satire platform that provides a different lens on current affairs and local news'. The second one named 'Bengal Beats' (@TheBengalBeats) with 370,253 likes. Although they address themselves as 'a viral publisher that creates and provides ENGAGING, and SHAREABLE high-quality stories (contents) for the INTERNET GENERATION of BANGLADESH'.

All accessible and visible comments of each video of the news pages; memes and its comments of the satire pages during the given period were considered as a final sample of this research on the Bangladesh student movement. The comments of the total 20 videos from the daily Prothom Alo; 10 videos from the BBC news Bangla; 3 memes from the Bengal Beats page and 36 memes from the earki page collected for analysis. Samples collected manually from the archive section of each Facebook pages. Videos are recorded from the Dhaka city only were considered for this research, as the student movement took place in the capital city of Dhaka mainly. Only text materials that included the memes with text and only the comments of each video and memes were considered for analysis.

Data Analysis

This project's aim was to explore the role of Facebook pages during the teen student movement of Bangladesh in 2018, by interpreting the comments and memes made by participants in four social media pages. Thematic analysis according to Braun and Clarke's (2006) six guidelines were considered as the method of qualitative data analysis. According to the guidelines, the researcher first establishes a relationship with the data by reading and rereading. Then the interesting features of the data were coded systematically from the entire data set and a total of 298 initial codes were conducted manually by going on with the data and according to the actions rather than applying pre-structured categories. Third, the researcher searched for themes by organising the initial codes into potential themes. 15 potential themes were conducted that appeared more frequently and deemed to be more significant among the initial coding. Fourth, the potential themes were cross-examined with the data to establish codes and a total of five core themes were finally selected for analysis. Fifth, each theme was given a label and sub-themes according to necessity. Finally, a report was produced through distinguishing the necessary examples (comments and memes) for each theme. The extant texts, such as- comments of a total of 30 videos and 39 memes were coded through the initial coding process. While analysis, codes and themes identified recorded and formatted into tables.

Ethics

'One important view expressed by researchers is that information shared on public social media platforms without password or membership restrictions can be used for research without the need for informed consent' (Sloan & Quan-Haase, 2017:58). In this research, only public comments/videos/memes of the four Facebook pages have been collected. According to API and related tools, public information, its collection and use do not require ethical value or special consideration (Bruns et al., 2014), because consent is necessary to obtain when data is collected from private or closed online platforms (Sloan & Quan-Haase, 2017). User consent was determined to be not required in this case, however, in the result section, the comments from the videos and memes were rephrased to prevent any possibilities to discover user's identities by searching with the comments. Therefore, the participant information was securely stored and shared with anonymity here.

Result

In the following section, the constructed categories are presented to give an understanding of how Facebook played a unique role during the protest.

Movement Support

This theme consists of three subcategories. The student movement for road safety is the first-ever protest that was generated and organised by teen students in Bangladesh. For this reason, people throughout the country witnessed an unprecedented event.

Defining Them as the Pioneers

During the protest, the students were professionally controlling the vehicles. They organised different lanes for each type of vehicles, and also created an emergency lane for an ambulance which is rare in the city (Sadeque, 2018). That is why people called them a pioneer to turn the transport system to what it was supposed to. Despite what was essentially a road blockade that caused delays to reach the workplace, most people truly wanted to solve the burning problem- road accident:

Definitely, they (the students) deserve admiration for maintaining the traffic such an organised way, creating an emergency lane, checking papers etc. (Comment: earki)

This generation knows how to maintain honesty, punctuality with strong discipline. Maybe we have passed our dark time. (Comment: BBC Bangla)

These comments indicate that young students did their best in the movement. They also suggest that students were able to run the protest following their plan and discipline to achieve a high level of support.

Expressing Support for Pointing Out the Mismanagements

Although road accidents and traffic jams, currently the most frequently occurring problems in Bangladesh, there has not been a protest mobilisation of that size from the mass of people before. It was because of that reason that the teen students' protest gained nationwide popularity. People in Facebook appeared to be happy and satisfied with the actions that were taken by the students to minimise the mismanagements in the transport sector:

We are with you always. (Comment: earki)

Salute to you all. (Comment: The Phothom Alo)

There are no buses from the morning. It delayed me to reach my workplace but still, I am strongly supporting them (the students) and want the solution of public transport mismanagements. (Comment: The Prothom Alo)

The students are doing the right things. We all are supporting you. (Comment: BBC Bangla)

It can be said the comments captured an indication of their eagerness to get rid of this deadly and intense situation happening in this country.

Labelling Them as 'Generation-Police'

Some memes called them 'generation police' because they were checking licences, creating an emergency lane for ambulances etc. As Bangladesh's transport sector is widely perceived as corrupt, unregulated and dangerous (Al Jazeera, 2018), people appeared to be impressed by and grateful to the students for their protest action:

Dhaka is now under the control of generation-police. Keep your papers ready. (Meme: earki)

The aforementioned comment also implied that teen students in Bangladesh have the potential to gain mass support if they can do an effective and productive job.

Strong Demand for Safer Roads and Punishment

This theme contained five subcategories. Each of these represented the dimensions of strong demand and justice for the bus driver who killed the two students. Although, the primary demands of the students were to ensure safe roads and punishment for the accused bus driver, while analysing the collected data it became clear that people in Facebook were also claiming similar things.

Demanding Fitness of All Public Transport

The students had nine demands for the government to fulfil. Ensuring the fitness of all public transport was one of them. Facebook comments and memes, also highlighted that some people were also demanding the same confirmation. They were claiming that most of the public buses had no fitness at all and that caused accidents:

We would rather walk but do not want to ride that buses dangerous to us, please destroy all of them. (Comment: The Pothom Alo)

This comment indicates peoples were ready for temporal suffering but wanted certainty of safer roads and transports. And most importantly, their earnest demand for the safe road was expressed widely along with the students during the protest.

Demanding Valid Licences for All Public-Private Vehicles

From the beginning of this protest, students were checking registration certificates and licences of all private and public transports. Surprisingly they have found police officers, Navy officials, and several other general commuters without the possession of valid driving licences or a registration certificate of vehicles (The Daily Star, 2018). Along with the student protesters, netizens were also posting comments and expressing their demand for a valid licence of every vehicle:

I am strongly suggesting the students mark the unlicensed vehicles with a permanent marker. (Comment: BBC Bangla)

We do not want any cars without licence and fitness. Drivers, please keep the licences with you. Youngsters are now checking; you have no place to hide. (Comment: The Prothom Alo)

Checking licence should be the duty of police but sadly some of them did not have one. A young student was asking a policeman in a series of memes:

The kid student:

Uncle (police), please show your licence? (Then the policeman was laughing and offering a candy instead)

The kid student:

Show your licence first, then give me a candy. (Memes: Bengal Beats)

By analysing peoples' comments and memes, it was clear that most people were are truly demanding transparency. Their comments and support with each demand of the students indicating their strong claim for a better transport system of Bangladesh.

Demanding Educational Qualification and Drug Test of Each Driver

People were also expressing their opinion regarding the necessity for a certain level of education and diving certificate before appointing him/her as a driver. Drug tests were also another high in demand as transport workers usually abused drugs that helped them to remain awake for a long time but these drugs also reduced their capacity to make right decisions while driving (The New Age. 2019). Facebook memes compared these drivers' recklessness as:

Rejected air force pilots became the bus drivers afterwards! (Meme: earki)

Despite the metaphoric exaggeration of this meme, reckless driving is indeed another reason for peoples' anxiety of being killed by accident.

Demanding the Punishment of the Accused Bus Driver

Their (the protesters') demand was widely acceptable to the people who commented in the news videos and creating memes:

We are always with you dear youngsters. Please continue the peaceful movements until you get justice. (Comment: The Prothom Alo)

If we cannot ensure the punishment of the killer, we will die in road crash one day. (Meme: earki)

Time for protest has passed, now it's time for prevention. (Comment: earki)

We want justice at any cost. (Comment: The Phothom Alo)

Although ensuring punishment of all accused drivers was supposed to be the first and foremost duty of the authorities, the volume of the Facebook users' comments in videos and memes represented the uncertainty of what can be an appropriate and right punishment to the driver.

Ensuring the Importance of Personal Awareness First

Whilst, this particular issue was not raised by the students during the analysis, it was a noticeable comment. The commenters were telling the importance of maintaining signal lights, using foot over bridges and zebra crossings because road accidents might happen due to unconsciousness and not obeying the traffic rules.

Brother, you have to be aware first if you want to correct others. (Meme: earki)

No traffic law or protest can change anything; we have to be conscious and sensible first. (Comment: The Prothom Alo)

This dimension of online reaction opened another window of expression. That is, people were aware of their awareness besides pointing out the governmental mismanagements.

This Movement Reflected Dissatisfaction With the Government

Several data sections encapsulated this issue, especially after the attack on the student protesters during the seventh day of their protest. The following three focused codes reflected netizens' anger, malice and frustration.

Blaming the Attackers

According to BBC News (2018), although it was not clear who attacked the student, the local media blamed a student group linked to the ruling party named Bangladesh Chattra League (BCL). Nonetheless, people brought up their anger and claimed the BCL attack on Facebook:

Except for the brainwashed BCL, everyone is with the protest. (Comment: BBC Bangla)

It is true that BCL first started the attack on innocent students. (Comment: earki)

I have read the history of Bangladesh, that students fought for our language, our motherland. But in 2018 they are protesting for justice and our people are attacking them (police and BCL). Do they have any humanity? (Comment: The Prothom Alo)

However, from the Facebook users' point of view, they directly blamed the governments' student wing behind the attack on the teen students along with the police.

Demanding the Resignation of the Transport Minister

As road accidents had been occurring in this country regularly and no effective measures and preventions were take to stop it, people showed their anger and distrust to the then transport minister. They directly demanding his resignation:

To the honourable prime minister, I am requesting you to replace Mr Shahjahan Khan (the then transport minister) from his post. There is no necessity to keep him in your parliament. Most people in Bangladesh do not like him...... The illiterate and arrogant bus-truck drivers have turned wild because of his indulgence. (Comment: The Prothom Alo)

As the minister was smiling in a press conference while declaring the death of the two students. His smile (intentional or unintentional) on this sensitive issue was provoking people to make comments against him:

One smile that creates forever hatred. (Meme: earki)

Expressing Anger Against the Decision of 'Small' Punishment for the Accused Driver

However, the police arrested the bus driver right after the protest began. The government also approved the law of five years' jail as the highest punishment for all the accused drivers. But most of the netizens were demanding the death sentence for killing people with their reckless driving:

These drivers should be hanged to death. (Comment: The Prothom Alo)

If these drivers get a death sentence, then the other would come under control. (Comment: The Prothom Alo)

Five years is too short; it should be at least 12 years of jail. (Comment: BBC Bangla)

No doubt, their collective anger, expression against the decision by the government has not grown in one day.

Facebook as a Platform for Dissenting Views

Facebook users not only were acting as a supporter of the protest overall; it was also playing a role as a platform for expressing different views. Not huge, but several people also gave dissent opinion about the students and their protest. Moreover, most of these dissent views were posted after the governments' verbal assurance of acceptance of the nine demands that were put forward by the protesters. This unique characteristic of social media or Facebook inspired the construction of this as a core category.

Requesting the Students Not to Damage the Vehicles and Go Back to Their Home

Social media or Facebook experiences lack of gatekeeping (with some restrictions in the use of abusive, homophobic language or any language that a user finds offensive), that is why freedom of speech is practised here. This characteristic of Facebook was observable in this study. While most of the people were supporting the students on Facebook, several netizens showed an opposite behaviour:

Please do not damage the buses, now go back home. (Comment: The Prothom Alo)

Dear children, you should go back home now. Otherwise, you all will be sick. Not all people are guilty but you are harassing everyone in the road... Now you should only focus on your study and be a sensible person. You will lead this country in future. (Comment: BBC Bangla)

They were expressing their concern about the vandalism that was allegedly committed by the students. Also, that body of netizens was trying to say that this outrage was not expected from them.

Expressing Annoyance With the Students and Their Movement

Similarly, some people were also expressing an explicit annoyance with the movement. For that group, there was no rationality to continue the movement after the assurances that were given by the government:

Don't agree (the demand for justice) because accidents can happen anytime. (Comment: The Prothom Alo)

I want a safe road and the students proved that they can handle it. But they do not know what they have done. It will create another problem which will be dangerous to our country. So please stop everyone before it becomes a political issue. Please remember, we all want to be safe. (Comment: BBC Bangla)

A safer transport system will not be created overnight. So, this movement is now annoying. (Comment: BBC Bangla)

Is their (the students) movement against the people? We are suffering from them. The school students are breaking the glasses of public transports, forcing people to get down from the buses, women and children are facing insecurity. They would rather go against the ministers than causing sufferings of mass people. (Comment: BBC Bangla)

However, most of these dissent views were posted 5/6 days after the protest. It seemed the students were losing support gradually at the end of the movement.

Facebook as a Tool to Spread Rumours

With the absence of gatekeeping, netizens either intentionally or unintentionally posted comments that were not only false but dangerous. The following two codes had been used to represent how netizens used Facebook as a tool to spread rumours at that time.

Spreading Rumours of Raping and Killing

There was a rumour spread through peoples' comments that, teen protesters were raped and killed by the counter-protesters. Those spreading the rumour were also encouraging (via comment) to share this information. The authorities were asked to ignore the misinformation of killing and raping as fake news but as it happens some people were not believing the warning by the authorities. Most importantly, the commenters (that were spreading the rumours) were also claiming the involvement of BCL (governments' student wing) men in the raping and killing. The same people also appeared to believe that more than two students were killed by a road crash on the same day and the government did not publish the actual number.

A total of five students died in the road crash that day, not only two. (Comment: BBC Bangla)

Why do the government is silent now? BCL men are raping female students, killing them. (Please spread the post). (Comment: The Prothom Alo)

The comments containing rumours were highly noticeable on the two news media pages rather than the two satire pages. Moreover, the satire pages created memes to make people aware about the rumours:

Do not share, if you are not sure. (Meme: earki)

It was hard to determine original sources of the rumours, but it was not difficult to understand that several people or netizens shared and were trying to provoke other people to share the rumours.

Blaming the Journalists for Not Publishing the So-Called Information (Rumours)

Apart from sharing, those people also requested that the journalists of BBC Bangla and The Prothom Alo publish the information (rumours). When they realised that the news pages were not posting any videos that supported the rumours, they were enraged and that was manifested by a continuous blaming of the journalists at that time:

You are a stupid journalist! A total of 7 students were killed not 2. Why you people are not publishing the exact news? (Comment: BBC Bangla)

The students are beaten by the police and BCL leaders, not a single reporter is here. (Comment: The Prothom Alo)

Netizens' freedom of delivering speeches full of hate and wrath on Facebook was observable during the development of this code.

DISCUSSION AND CONCLUSION

This study aimed to explore the role of Facebook during the student movement for road safety in Bangladesh and how people switch from one reaction to others along with the protest itself. The findings of this study show how the integration of Facebook into everyday life is altering how people interact with and experience information. This study illustrates the contrasts and variety of sentiments of people towards teen students' activity that reflect both communal and individual experiences in which people interact with the broad diversity of information within Facebook content. This study points to three main ways Facebook is altering the nature of how people connect, communicate and use information in a crisis period like a protest.

Firstly, from the analysis, it was evident that besides a large volume of support, number of people were also against the protest. Interestingly, both views were expressed at the same time and same place. This experience was, closely linked to the two identified themes in this study- *'Movement support'* and *'Facebook as a platform for dissent views'*. Before the invention of social media, it was not easy and common practice to express our thoughts freely in an open platform but Facebook (and other forms of social media) have brought this dramatic change in the field of movement like the students' protest that we examined here.

Studies (Millham, 2016; Papa, 2017) on social media and protest found out peoples' spontaneous participation on social media could facilitate a movement and reinforce debate on Facebook by developing themes. However, these studies also did theme-based analysis but mostly focused on the participation and use of social media by the protesters, but this study only worked with the language that was used in comments and memes. Moreover, during the student protest for road safety in Bangladesh, Facebook played a unique role by creating an open field for discussion and debate. It can also be said that the protesters may have been influenced by the commenters' and meme creators' huge support and encouragement. The same can be argued about the 'internet's powerful role' on other movements with a social media input, such as the umbrella movement (Taiwan), the sunflower movement (Hong Kong), the candlelight protest (South Korea) where students played an active role and gained support by the masses like this protest for road safety (Lin, 2015; Chang and Yun, 2011).

Secondly, through creating a harmless discussion forum to express the dissatisfaction or anger toward the authority or ruling political party. Such as conversing freely, delivering own opinion without the fear of censorship, being dependent and self-regulating. The two themes *'Strong demand for safer roads and punishment'* and *'the reflection of the dissatisfaction with the government'* linked together in this experience. However, the protesters indicated some failures of the ruling political party such as delaying bringing to justice the accused drivers, no visible steps to reduce road accidents, the inappropriate behaviour of the transport minister. Their offline reactions towards the government were similar to their online comments and memes. People disclosed their inner thoughts widely on Facebook. Thoughts that they could not express in traditional media so easily in the past. We considered that by accepting that Facebook could be also used as an alternative media for expressing dissatisfactions toward the government or related authority during the protest.

Thirdly, through creating almost a filter less platform that allows the entering of harmful data and misinformation such as rumours. This experience directly linked to the last theme *'Facebook as a tool to spread rumours'* and also considered as a disadvantage of social media during protest mobilisations. As described in the result section the news pages were also a source of rumours at that time. By creating an open platform, on one hand, Facebook is providing the chance to speak freely but on the other, it also allows the entry of misinformation. It can be said that, unlike the mainstream media where professional journalists check information sources before publication, the shortage of reliable information in Facebook (or other social media) may be more likely to allow promoted fabrications.

Facebook creates a special and alternative atmosphere during new social movements where netizens are willing to express their own opinion without any fear and some of them also deliver information without crosschecking. In other words, we observe a relationship between the Facebook users and their tendency to express opinions related to protest issues and thus they have the willingness to express on Facebook during the student protest for road safety in Bangladesh as such new media offer them an almost censor-free platform. In Bangladesh, currently, social media is the only medium without the lack of gatekeeping. So the above mentioned discussion is showing the positive reflections of the hypotheses.

This research is not beyond limitation. One of the major limitations within this study was that this researcher worked with only four Facebook pages after considering time and cost. Besides, as the sample was limited, findings cannot be generalized and need to be compared with other contexts. Several recommendations can be made for future research. The expectation is, this research will play a role as a direction for future researchers in this underrated field. Moreover, there are no other existing studies based on the student protest for road safety in Bangladesh. Therefore, considering more samples, the same type of research can be done in the future. Secondly, this study was based on the comments posted by all netizens and memes. Future research can be focused on teen protesters' online activities during the movement to find out their role in social media.

REFERENCES

Afroz, R. (2018, Oct. 1). Top liked Facebook pages in Bangladesh. *Business Inquiries*. https://developmentbd.com/top-liked-facebook-page-in-bangladesh/

Bangladesh: Mass student protests after deadly road accident. (2018, August 2). *Al Jazeera*. https://www.aljazeera.com/news/2018/08/bangladesh-mass-student-protests-deadly-road-accident-180802174519088.html

Bock, A. M., & Figueroa, J. E. (2018). Faith and reason: An analysis of the homologies of Black and Blue Lives Facebook pages. *New Media & Society*, *20*(9), 3097–3118. doi:10.1177/1461444817740822

Bock, A. M., & Figueroa, J. E. (2018). Faith and reason: An analysis of the homologies of Black and Blue Lives Facebook pages. *New Media & Society*, *20*(9), 3097–3118. doi:10.1177/1461444817740822

Börzsei, L. K. (2013). Makes a meme instead: A concise history of internet memes. *New Media Studies Magazine*, *7*, 152–189.

Braun, V., & Clarke, V. (2006). Using thematic analysis in psychology. *Qualitative Research in Psychology*, *3*(2), 77–101. doi:10.1191/1478088706qp063oa

Bruns, A. (2014). A topology of Twitter research: Disciplines, methods, and ethics. *Aslib Journal of Information Management*, *66*(3), 250–261. doi:10.1108/AJIM-09-2013-0083

Chang, Y. W., & Yun, S. (2011). New Media and Political Socialization of Teenagers: The Case of the 2008 Candlelight Protests in Korea. *Asian Perspective*, *35*(1), 135–162. doi:10.1353/apr.2011.0019

Clement, J. (2020). *Social Media- Statistics and Facts*. Retrieved December 5, 2020 from https://www. statista.com/topics/1164/social-networks/#dossierSummary__chapter5

Davison, P. (2012). The language of internet memes. In M. Mandiberg (Ed.), *The Social Media Reader* (pp. 120–134). New York University Press.

Fuchs, C. (2014). *Social Media a critical introduction*. SAGE Publications. doi:10.4135/9781446270066

Gal, N., Shifman, L., & Kampf, Z. (2016). It gets better: Internet memes and the construction of collective identity. *New Media & Society*, *18*(8), 1698–1714. doi:10.1177/1461444814568784

Gerbaudo, P. (2012). *Tweets and the Streets: Social Media and Contemporary Activism*. Pluto press.

Hewson. (2016). *Internet Research Methods* (2nd ed.). SAGE Publications. doi:10.4135/9781473920804

Jin, S. V., Phua, J., & Lee, K. M. (2015). Telling stories about breastfeeding through Facebook: The impact of user-generated content (UGC) on pro-breastfeeding attitudes. *Computers in Human Behavior*, *46*, 6–17. doi:10.1016/j.chb.2014.12.046

Kim, H. D. (2016). Are you on Timeline or News Feed? The roles of Facebook pages and construal level in increasing ad effectiveness. *Computers in Human Behaviour*, *56*, 312-320. https://doi-org.queens. ezp1.qub.ac.uk/10.1016/j.chb.2015.12.031

Lang, C., & Barton, H. (2015). Just untag it: Exploring the management of undesirable Facebook photos. *Computers in Human Behavior*, *43*, 147–155. doi:10.1016/j.chb.2014.10.051

Li, R., & Suh, A. (2015). Factors Influencing Information credibility on Social Media Platforms: Evidence from Facebook Pages. *Procedia Computer Science*, *72*, 314–328. doi:10.1016/j.procs.2015.12.146

Lin, S. S. (2015). Sunflowers and Umbrellas: Government Responses to Student-led Protests in Taiwan and Hong Kong. *The Asian Forum*. http://www.theasanforum.org/sunflowers-and-umbrellas-government-responses-to-student-led-protests-in-taiwan-and-hong-kong/

Mahmud, F. (2018). *Bangladesh ramps up efforts to monitor social media after months of student-led agitations*. Scrool.in. https://scroll.in/article/891011/bangladesh-ramps-up-efforts-to-monitor-social-media-after-months-of-student-led-agitations

Millham, R. (2016). *Theme evolution and structure in Twitter: A case study of South African student protests of 2015*. Paper presented at IEEE International Conference on Big Data Analysis (ICBDA), Hangzhou, China. https://doi-org.queens.ezp1.qub.ac.uk/10.1109/ICBDA.2016.7509828

Milner, R. M. (2013). Pop polyvocality: Internet memes, public participation, and the Occupy Wall Street movement. *International Journal of Communication*, *7*(34), 2357–2390. https://ijoc.org/index.php/ijoc/article/view/1949

Papa, V. (2017). To activists: Please post and share your story: Renewing understandings on civic participation and the role of Facebook in the Indignados movement. *European Journal of Communication*, *32*(6), 583–597. doi:10.1177/0267323117737953

Prochazka, O. (2018). A chronotopic approach to identity performance in a Facebook meme page. *Discourse Context and Media*, *25*, 78-87. https://doi-org.queens.ezp1.qub.ac.uk/10.1016/j.dcm.2018.03.010

Raychoudhury, V. (2015). *Shahbag movement: The tweeted perspective.* Paper presented at the 2015 7th International Conference on Communication Systems and Networks (COMSNETS), Bangalore, India.

Sadeque, S. (2018). Angered by Traffic Deaths, Students Began to Direct Traffic in Bangladesh. *NPR News.* https://www.npr.org/sections/goatsandsoda/2018/08/07/635981133/angered-by-traffic-deaths-students-began-to-direct-traffic-in-bangladesh?t=1563398153770

Shifman, L. (2011). An anatomy of a YouTube meme. *New Media & Society, 14*(2), 187–203. doi:10.1177/1461444811412160

Sloan, L., & Quan-Haase, A. (Eds.). (2017). The SAGE Handbook of Social Media Research Methods. London: SAGE Publications.

Smidi, A., & Shahin, S. (2017). Social Media and Social Mobilisation in the Middle East: A Survey of Research on the Arab Spring. *India Quarterly. Journal of International Affairs, 73*(2), 96. 10.1177%2F0974928417700798

Suh, C. S., Vasi, I. B., & Chang, P. Y. (2017). How social media matter: Repression and the diffusion of the Occupy Wall Street movement. *Social Science Research, 65,* 282–293. doi:10.1016/j.ssresearch.2017.01.004 PMID:28599778

The Daily Star. (2018a, August 2). *Students check licenses, discipline traffic.* Retrieved December 5, 2020 from https://www.thedailystar.net/city/students-checking-licenses-disciplining-traffic-safe-road-demand-in-dhaka-bangladesh-1614910

The Daily Star. (2018b, August 10). *The rise and silencing of the mass student movement.* Retrieved December 5, 2020 from https://www.thedailystar.net/news/star-weekend/cover-story/the-rise-and-silencing-mass-student-movement-1618390

The New Age. (2018, February 17). *Arrangement needed for driver dope test.* Retrieved December 5, 2020 from http://www.newagebd.net/article/65039/arrangement-needed-for-driver-dope-test

This research was previously published in the International Journal of Social Media and Online Communities (IJSMOC), 12(2); pages 61-82, copyright year 2020 by IGI Publishing (an imprint of IGI Global).

APPENDIX A

For Reviewers Only

Table 1. Initial codes of all comments of the videos

Comments from BBC Bangla and the Prothom Alo	Date of the videos	Initial Codes
1. BBC (2854 comments)	August 7, 2018.	• Saying to unite the residents of Dhaka- Protect the students- No more prevention- It is time for revenge; • Claiming the student movement are now going toward other direction- Opposition political party (BNP) is trying to take advantages; • Defining the govt. as an ethics less ruler- The transport minister doesn't confess his fault; • Not arresting the attackers- People are busy with FB rumours (rape of the female students); • Not publishing rape related news by the BBC journalists- Defined them (journalists) as servants of the govt.; • Students point out the irregularities- Need solution and their safety; • Army needed; • Every political party is selfish; • Only 5 years of jail is not enough; • The students have been attacked by police and BCL, BCD (repeated many time); • The Almighty will punish; • PM could console the students; • Denial of BCL attackers; 18. All are rumours; • Demand of resignation of all ministers; • Rejecting the need of student movement anymore; • Countrywide more train lines needed; • More participation in the movement needed; • Media is hiding the truth; • Demanding safe road
2. BBC (332 comments)	August 6, 2018.	• Considering the absence of democracy; • 5 years of jail is not enough; • Denial of independent BD; • Being supportive for the architects (who made a human chain and showed solidarity with the students); • Govt. didn't punish the teen students- But beating the adults; • Govt. did not let them (architects) to protest- No protests were successful yet- Demanding safe road is everyone's claim; • Not only drivers are guilty but our lack of awareness; • Claiming foreign power behind the govt.; • Unnecessity of this protest- Importance of discussion with the govt. instead; • Demanding safe road; • The architects should protest earlier- When the students were in the field; • General people always protest in BD; • Fitness of all vehicles should check first; • Absence of corruption should ensure in all sectors; • Defining this protest unnecessary- the government accepted their claims; • Being occupied the busy road is not appropriate for demanding safe road; • Importance of signal lights; • Defining justification for accidents in a populated country;

continues on following page

Table 1. Continued

Comments from BBC Bangla and the Prothom Alo	Date of the videos	Initial Codes
3. BBC (2266 comments)	August 6, 2018.	• Claiming attack on the student of two private universities (repeated many times); • Claiming transport ministers' influence behind the drivers' strike; • Demanding the highest punishment for drivers; • Claiming the truth of reckless driving on the highway; • Skilled drivers needed with valid licence; • Claiming the fault of all transport related organisations; • Only 5 years of jail (repeated the highest); • Being optimistic for the ruling govt.; • Demanding death sentence of accused driver; • Demanding implementation of the law; • Demanding drug test of all drivers; • Defining the student protest as wrong; • Claiming polices' torture toward students; • Demanding safety of life; • Claiming the govt. as liar; • Asking educational qualification of bus drivers; • Claiming the vehicles are unfit;
4. BBC (352 comments)	August 5, 2018.	• Claiming the protest is not no longer on students' hand- others are playing behind- students might fall in danger; • Claiming govt. and BCL as the criminal; • Accusing the protesters for being around PMs' office- Not happy for students' activities; • Claiming, the students should clean their own home instead of road; • Govt. has already given them word- they should stop the protest; • Requesting the students to go back before dark- They might be under attack; • Sounding like road-blocking protest is 'meaningless' now- Expressing botheration (repeated); • Claiming govt. has lost trust from mass people;
5. BBC (2402 comments)	August 3, 2018.	• Demanding safe road- justice (repeated); • Expressing distrust toward the govt.- transport minister; • Showing support and solidarity for students; • Demanding punishment for drivers; • Claiming govt. did not act like trustworthy;
6. BBC (3127 comments)	August 2, 2018.	• Supporting the students strongly (repeated); • Claiming BCL are attacking the students; • Expressing hate speech toward police force, govt.; • Demanding safe road (repeated); • Claiming govt. is seating silence; • Claiming the students are so brave • Demanding drivers' literacy.
7. BBC (186 comments)	August 2, 2018.	• Showing strong support, respect and solidarity with the students (repeated); • Also demanding safe transport for females; • Demanding valid licence of each car; • Expressing supportiveness in spite of transport crisis; • Again mistrust for govt.; • Showing pity for the drivers- directing students not to harm them;
8. BBC (16341 comments)	August 2, 2018.	• Demanding safe road (repeated); • Expressing tremendous support and respect toward Ilias Kanchan (covered most of the comments); • Demanding implementation of proper law; • Demanding proper driver; • Demanding resign of the minister;

continues on following page

Table 1. Continued

Comments from BBC Bangla and the Prothom Alo	Date of the videos	Initial Codes
9. BBC (480 comments)	August 1, 2018.	• Expressing joy for publishing the issue in international media; • Expressing support (repeated); • Demanding valid licence- literate drivers- drug test-safe road (repeated); • Claiming the protest is not only for student but the nation; • Expressing hate speech toward BCL; • Claiming the protest as non-political • Demanding resign of the minister; • Demanding school bus in every institution;
10. BBC (355 comments)	August 1, 2018.	• Expressing hate speech toward the leguna driver (repeated); • Claiming traditional media didn't cover the true story but fb did; • Demanding resign of the minister; • Expressing the need of ethical development as well as personal awareness;
11. Prothom alo (92 comments)	July 30, 2018	• Demanding safe road-justice (repeated); • Showing support to the teens (repeated); • Demanding resign of the minister (repeated); • Demanding army rule; • Demand valid licence; • Claiming the accident as killing; • Demanding their parents' involvement; • Spreading hate speech for the minister (repeated); • Demanding whole new traffic management system; • Demanding killing of more than 2 (repeated rumour);
12. Prothom alo (427 comments)	July 31, 2018	• Claiming more than 2 students were killed (rumour repeated frequent); • Demanding justice for the accused driver- Valid licence; • Supporting the students (repeated); • Ensuring self-awareness first; • Showing distrust toward the law and the govt.; • Not showing support to the teens in terms of damaging the car (repeated few);
13. Prothom alo (61 comments)	July 31, 2018	• Demanding death sentence. • Demanding resign of the minister. • Demanding more students were killed.
14. Prothom alo (2571 comments)	August 1, 2018	• Showing support and solidarity (repeated). • Not showing support.
15. Prothom alo (356 comments)	August 1, 2018	• Demanding justice- showing support (repeated); • Claiming the transport system as the worst; • Demanding military rule; • Claiming more students were killed (repeated); • Advising to change the transport rule;
16. Prothom alo (57 comments)	August 2, 2018	No New Codes found.
17. Prothom alo (70 comments)	August 2, 2018	• Showing support; • Demanding resign of the minister; • Demanding army rule; • Demanding justice for invalid licence holder;
18. Prothom alo (384 comments)	August 2, 2018	• Sowing support; • Demanding resign of the minister; • Demanding valid licence; • Demanding safe road; • Advising to renew the transport system;
19. Prothom alo (51 comments	August 2, 2018	• Supporting the protest;

continues on following page

Table 1. Continued

Comments from BBC Bangla and the Prothom Alo	Date of the videos	Initial Codes
20. Prothom alo (90 comments)	August 2, 2018	• Advising the teens to stop the protest. • Expressing pessimist view toward govt.;
21. Prothom alo (120 comments)	August 3, 2018	• Demanding valid licence; • Expressing hate speech toward BCL and the govt.
22. Prothom alo (95 comments)	August 4, 2018	No New Codes Found.
23. Prothom alo (126 comments)	August 4, 2018	• Some believes students should go back to home; • Spreading rumours of being raped and beaten (frequently repeated);
24. Prothom alo (126 comments)	August 4, 2018	No New Codes Found.
25. Prothom alo (760 comments)	August 4, 2018	No New Codes Found.
26. Prothom alo (60 comments)	August 4, 2018	No New Codes Found.
27. Prothom alo (80 comments)	August 5, 2018	• Supporting as well as requesting them to stop now; • Frequent hate speech for BCL and the govt.
28. Prothom alo (122 comments)	August 5, 2018	No New Codes Found.
29. Prothom alo (224 comments)	August 6, 2018	No New Codes Found.
30. Prothom alo (474 comments)	August 6, 2018	No New Codes Found.

Table 2. Initial codes of the memes and its comments

Memes and Comments	Date	Initial Codes
1. Bengal Beats (no comments)	August 4, 2018	• A school boy Requesting a traffic police to show the licence
2. Bengal Beats (no comments)	August 4, 2018	No New Codes Found.
3. Bengal Beats (no comments)	August 4, 2018	No New Codes Found.
4. Earki (8 comments)	August 7, 2018	• Number of vehicles is double than the registered licence; • Making fun by saying each parson has two cars; • Rest of them are bearing car (fun)
5. Earki 10 comments	7 August 2018	• Blaming BCL; • Demanding safe road;
6. Earki 11 comments	7 August 2018	• Demanding safe road for pet animals also.
7. Earki 25 comments	6 August 2018	• Mocking police and BCL attackers by 'call of duty' game.
8. Earki 66 comments	6 August 2018	• Mocking attackers style of attack with spinners; • Commenters making fun of them with Lasith Malinga etc.
9. Earki 19 comments	5 August 2018	• Making comment against the students; • Showing support to the attackers.
10. Earki 42 comments	4 August 2018	• Requesting not share any rumours; • Commenters mostly denying the rumours of rape and killing;
11. Earki 5 comments	4 August 2018	• Telling the PM to ensure safe road for in order to cross her highway of development (metaphor); • Some commenters assuming to be dead to cross it.

continues on following page

Table 2. Continued

Memes and Comments	Date	Initial Codes
12. Earki 5 comments	3 August 2018	• Telling not to insult the teens. • Claiming they have already proof their maturity in terms of culture, anti-communalism, patriotism etc.
13. Earki 10 comments	3 August 2018	• Expressing the teens deserve 100/100 in terms of their transport maintenance ability; • Asking to open an online complain system for mass people- their complains will be discussed with the ministers. • Demanding total rejection of power practice
14. Earki 2 comments	3 August 2018	• The lightness of ensuring valid licence comparing other countries;
15. Earki 23 comments	2 August 2018	• The meme is a parody of a popular Bengali rhyme; • Showing gratitude to the students for maintaining the transport system; • Blaming the other for not controlling the traffic like them;
16. Earki 10 comments	2 August 2018	• Meme illustrated the picture of organised vehicles- claiming by spending millions of money the authority did not organise that way before; • Supporting the students for doing it.
17. Earki 3 comments	2 August 2018	• Expressing the students' courage for pointing out the mismanagement
18. Earki 2 comments	2 August 2018	• Defining the govt. supposed to ensure safe road at the time of the protest;
19. Earki 5 comments	2 August 2018	• Illustrated a New York picture where a mother cat was crossing the road with kitten- the traffic sergeant ensured the safety; • Expressing even human has no safety in road here.
20. Earki 12 comments	2 August 2018	• Illustrated a picture of the transport minister smiling while talking about the dead students; • Spreading hate speech for him
21. Earki 0 comments	2 August 2018	• Govt. declared holyday in order to save the police and no licenced cars (mocking)
22. Earki 0 comments	2 August 2018	• Defining Dhaka is now under control of 'generation-police'- requesting to keep licence
23. Earki 1 comments	2 August 2018	• Police and security forces are now keeping licence-
24. Earki 1 comments	2 August 2018	• Defining courage and honesty is the most necessary virtue now.
25. Earki 2 comments	2 August 2018	No New Codes Found.
26. Earki 151 comments	2 August 2018	• Expressing solidarity with Ilias Kanchan; • Expressing tremendous support for him; • Claiming him to be the transport minister.
27. Earki 7 comments	2 August 2018	No New Codes Found.
28. Earki 1 comments	2 August 2018	• Mocking the minister by defining only two useful ministers in the chess board.
29. Earki 2 comments	2 August 2018	• Illustrated stomach ache did not come today for teens;
30. Earki 5 comments	1 August 2018	No New Codes Found.
31. Earki 48 comments	1 August 2018	• Defining the roads are under construction by the students;
32. Earki 12 comments	1 August 2018	• Defining Bangladesh has gone back to its teen age; • Claiming they are creating history.
33. Earki 28 comments	1 August 2018	• Expressing fake fear for posting such memes.
34. Earki 31 comments	1 August 2018	• Claiming adults should learn from the teenagers;
35. Earki 3 comments	1 August 2018	• Claiming the word 'justice' as joke.
36. Earki 66 comments	31 August 2018	• Expressing surprise for police attack on the teen students; • Expressing hate speech toward the police. • Claiming this attach as child abuse.
37. Earki 5 comments	31 August 2018	• Expressing how the student could study when their friends are killed.
38. Earki 6 comments	31 August 2018	No New Codes Found.
39. Earki 5 comments	31 August 2018	No New Codes Found.

APPENDIX B

Some Memes Described in the Result Section

Figure 1. The transport minister was smiling while declaring the death of two student

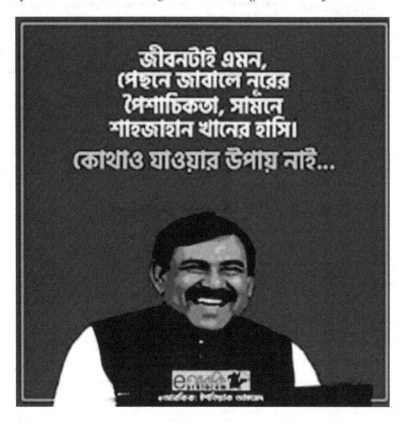

Figure 2. Illustrates the emergency lane created and organised by the teen students

Figure 3. A teen student was checking the licence and this meme declared them as 'generation police'

Figure 4. Do not share if you are not sure

Chapter 92
Perception of Social Media Use by Distance Learners in Nigeria

Airen Edale Adetimirin

https://orcid.org/0000-0001-5958-0597
University of Ibadan, Ibadan, Nigeria

Jide Ayoola
University of Ibadan, Ibadan, Nigeria

ABSTRACT

Perceived ease of use (PEOU) and perceived usefulness (PU) of social media by distance learners may affect its acceptance for learning. These constructs were investigated among 341 distance learners in two universities, the University of Ibadan- UI and the National Open University- NOUN in Nigeria using a questionnaire and was analyzed using frequency and percentages. The main purpose and use of social media in UI and NOUN was to share information (100% and 100%) and for group discussion (96.3% and 100%) respectively. WhatsApp was used daily in NOUN (100%) and UI (91.3%). The PEOU by the respondents in NOUN and UI were both high: requiring a lot of mental effort (100%) and promoting distance interactions between learners and lecturers outside the lecture room (96.9%), while PU in NOUN and UI was also high: it decreased travel expenses (100%) and improved academic performance (100%). Therefore, the high perception of social media use (PEOU and PU) by distance learners should be sustained by facilitators through the adoption of social media for all their courses.

INTRODUCTION

A distance learning program broadens access to education, which gives opportunity for continuous and life-long learning for individuals. Jimoh (2013) averred that distance learning affords learners the privilege of being free from the time constraints, limited place and offers flexible opportunities of learning for anybody who has the inclination for higher education. Through a distance learning program, students have access to higher education which otherwise would have been hindered due to their employment

DOI: 10.4018/978-1-6684-7123-4.ch092

status, marital status, family responsibilities, distance, and expenses incurred with traditional education (Hannay & Newvine, 2006).

The physical distance between the learners and instructors makes it necessary to use information and communication technologies (ICT) for delivery of learning resources such as the Internet. Universities have been able to cater for the educational needs of distance learners through social media platforms which may ensure learners learn and become equipped at their own pace. Selwyn (2012) suggested that in recent years, the wide-scale uptake of these ICT tools has transformed the ways in which the Internet is experienced and used by most students due to the presence of social media tools. Social media is becoming a major form of communication, interaction and provides information access and generation for people globally. The use of social media by undergraduates is now a global trend (Wickramanayake & Jika, 2018; Leyrer-Jackson & Wilson, 2018; Al-rahmi, Zeki, Alias, & Saged (2017).

Social media is described as an "application that allows users to converse and interact with each other; create, edit and share new forms of textual, visual and audio content, and categorise, label and recommend existing forms of content" (Boateng & Amankwaa, 2016, p. 3). Social media enables individuals to meet new people and friends, have discussions with one another through the use of text and exchange information carrying content they both understand. Social media is characterized by active participation on the part of distance learners as it provides a forum for learners to share knowledge, provide clarification to questions, disseminate information, and engage in group discussion. These social media environments can be very useful for e-learning purposes, being a potential communication channel where distance learners can collaborate with lecturers for educational purposes.

Some social media sites include Facebook, Wikipedia, Twitter, Blogs, LinkedIn, YouTube, MySpace, Yahoo, Answers, Google+, Pinterest. Social media site allows distance learners to engage in wall posting, video sharing, tagging, photo uploading, making comments, podcasting, blogging for the purpose of learning. The use of social media sites allows "students and faculty members interact, express their views, and share resources by constantly maintaining their profiles and creating groups on social media sites such as Facebook, Twitter, Blogs, Google docs, YouTube and others" (Beltran-Cruz & Cruz, 2013, p. 69).

Beltran-Cruz and Cruz (2013) affirmed that "social media sites are now being used by universities as alternative spaces wherein students can adapt to the university lifestyle through interacting online with peers and faculty" (p. 69). Presently universities around the world are harnessing the advantages that social media offers to improve the delivery of teaching and learning practices to distance learners. Gulbahar (2014) reported that students in Turkey were using social media for collaboration and knowledge sharing. According to Adamson (2012), social media enable students to collaborate and share information with their lecturers and the entire world at large at any time convenient to them and from any place in the world. This also encourages peer sharing, which offers students the opportunity to learn from each other in the content they produce. Al-rahmi, Othman, and Musa (2014) reported that "one of the most commonly cited benefits of social media by scholars is its ability to facilitate collaborative learning and communication among peers and with people outside academia" (p. 179).

Social media could be used by distance learners for personal and educational purposes as it contributes significantly to the development of their learning related activities and also provides a flexible opportunity for teaching and learning. The frequency of social media use by distance learners could vary as a result of their different commitments to other day to day activities. Distance learning students may use social media daily, weekly, monthly or as often as they have the opportunity to (Olowu & Seri, 2012). Social media like Facebook, WhatApps, Line and others have been frequently used to communicate, upload articles and update profile.

Social media has been recognized as an important facilitator for teaching and learning among distance learners, however some factors may hinder its maximum use for learning based on a learner's intention in either to accept or reject such use in their higher educational pursuits. These factors may include: perceived ease of use (PEOU) and perceived usefulness (PU). There are two key components that have made the Technology Acceptance Model (TAM) (Figure 1) one of the most influential research models related to understanding information technology usage and acceptance (Perceived Ease of Use and Perceived Usefulness).

Figure 1. Technology acceptance model 1

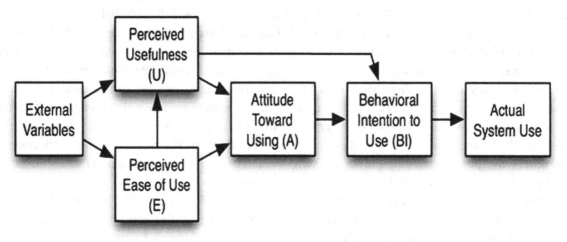

Perceived Ease of Use

Davies (1989) as cited in Sago (2013) stated that perceived ease of use (PEOU) and perceived usefulness (PU) determine attitude towards a technology, which in turn impacts the adoption and use of a new information technology (p. 3). Perceived ease of use and usefulness may affect attitude towards the use of social media and shapes learners' intentions to use it for learning activities. Perceived ease of use (PEOU) is the degree to which distance learners believe or think that using a particular system would be free from difficulty or great effort. Social media acceptance by distance learners may be based on its ease of use, clarity and ability to speed up the rate of learning activities.

Distance learners may desire a learning platform (social media) provided by universities to be less tedious and difficult to use to carry out their learning activities using technology. PEOU has an influence on attitudes and behavior on how frequently they will use social media for learning purposes. It contributes to a better performance, as effort saved due to ease of use may enable the individual to accomplish more tasks (Al-rahmi et al., 2014).

Distance learners' perceived ease of use of social media may have an influence on attitude towards usage for learning activities. The less difficulty distance learners encounter when using social media gives them the opportunity to adequately explore the different tools to enhance qualitative learning experiences. The use of social media by distance learners for academic purposes may depend on the ease with which these learners find the social media.

Perceived Usefulness

Perceived usefulness (PU) is defined as to what degree the new technology or system would contribute to increase of an individual's job (or learning) performance (Saritas, Yildiz, & Senel, 2015). Social media is perceived useful in a learning environment when it is capable of being used advantageously to increase the learning participation of distance learners. Based on the characteristics of distance learners (physical absence from the university campus, use of ICT to access learning resources), distance learners will use social media for learning when they perceive that using it for classroom activities will help them to achieve the desired academic excellence. A system high in perceived usefulness, in turn, is one for which a user believes in the existence of a positive use-performance relationship (Abeka, 2012).

Perceived usefulness may affect the use of social media since distance learners want to achieve their desired result with a technology that is reliable and caters for all learning related activities. The use of social media is assumed to provide learners the opportunity of taking control at any time for their learning task within a shorter time which may lead to effectiveness in their learning performance. As learners perceive social media to be useful and easy to use, they develop a positive attitude toward this technology and accept it for their learning tasks. Perceived ease of use and perceived usefulness explains that users' behavioural intention shapes their actual use of the technology. If distance learners have an intention to use a specific technology, then such technology (social media) will be used.

Statement of the Problem

Social media has been used by universities to increase the efficiency of providing quality education to distance learning students. It provides an avenue for them to get higher education with no barrier in geographical area and also expands the university market. However, it has been observed by some researchers (Beltran-Cruz & Cruz, 2013) that students which include distance learners use social media mostly for social and entertainment purposes, but not as much for academic purpose, where the frequency of use is lower. This may be due to their perceived ease of use and perceived usefulness of social media for learning which have an impact on the behavioural intention in accepting or rejecting social media to facilitate their learning activities. This study investigated the perception of social media use for learning among distance learning students in University of Ibadan, Ibadan and National Open University, Ibadan campus, both in Oyo state, Nigeria.

Research Questions

The following are the research questions used for the study:

1. What is the purpose of use of social media by distance learning students?
2. What is the frequency of use of social media by distance learning students?
3. What is the level of perceived ease of use of social media for learning among distance learners?
4. What is the level of perceived usefulness of social media for learning among distance learners?

METHODOLOGY

The descriptive survey was the research design employed for the study. The target population was 20,335 undergraduate distance learning students of two universities in Oyo State: University of Ibadan (16, 683 students) and National Open University, Ibadan (3,652 students) in the 2017/2018 academic year. Purposive sampling technique was used to select only faculties that were common to both universities and three major faculties were selected (Arts, Education and Social Sciences). A sampling fraction of 2% was used to select the sample size for each of the faculties giving a total of 341 (Table 1). The justification of a sampling fraction of 2% is confirmed by Sudman (1976) who averred that "a sampling fraction of 2% or less has the same degree of confidence as that of a higher fraction" (p. 15).

Data was collected using a questionnaire having four sections: Demographic information of the respondents; Social media use which had subsections for purpose of use and frequency of use were self-designed. The Perceived Ease of Use and Perceived Usefulness of Social media sections had questions that were adapted from previous study on perceived ease of use and perceived usefulness by Davis (1989) and Cowen (2009). The reliability of the questionnaire was carried out by pre testing on thirty distance learning students from the Faculty of Science, University of Ibadan, using Cronbach Alpha method and the results of the psychometric test for the sections are as follows: Social media use ($\alpha = 0.81$), Perceived Ease of Use ($\alpha = 0.87$) and Perceived Usefulness ($\alpha = 0.88$), all exceeding the threshold of 0.70, which indicates a good level in terms of reliability (Hair, Black, Babin, & Anderson, 2010).

Table 1. Population and sample size of the study

UNIVERSITY OF IBADAN (UI)			NATIONAL OPEN UNIVERSITY OF NIGERIA (NOUN)		
Faculties	**Population**	**Sample**	**Faculties**	**Population**	**Sample**
Arts	1,860	37	Arts and Social Science	886	18
Education	4,568	91	Education	393	8
Social Sciences	9,341	187			
TOTAL	**15,769**	**315**	**TOTAL**	**1279**	**26**

A four point Likert scale was adopted for measuring purpose of social media use, perceived ease of use and perceived usefulness with the following parameters SA- Strongly Agree, A-Agree, D-Disagree, SD-Strongly Disagree with four (4) representing the positive end of the scale and one (1), the negative. The copies of the questionnaire were administered randomly to the students during the face to face interactive sessions with their facilitators and a total of 303 copies were found useful and used for analysis giving a response rate of 88.9%. Data was analysed using frequency count and test of norm.

RESULTS AND DISCUSSION

Demographic Characteristics of the Respondents

There were more females (57.2%) than males (42.8%) in University of Ibadan, while the reverse was the case in NOUN, although with variation (Males: 52.0%, Female: 48.0%). Majority of the distance learners in both universities were in the age range 21- 25 years (UI: 46.4%; and NOUN: 60.0%).

Research Question One: What is the Purpose of Use of Social Media by the Distance Learning Students?

The major purposes for using social media by the distance learners varied. The four-point Likert scale were merged to become agree and disagree for ease of presentation in Table 2. In both universities, respondents used the social media mostly for sharing information and connecting, interacting, chatting with friends (Table 2). In UI, respondents revealed sharing information (97.8%); using it as a communication network (97.1%); surfing for useful information (96.0%) and connecting, interacting and chatting with friends (96.0%) as the major purpose for social media use (Table 2). The major purposes for using social

Table 2. Purpose of social media use by distance learners

| Purpose of Social Media Use | University of Ibadan | | | | NOUN | | | |
| | Agree | | Disagree | | Agree | | Disagree | |
	N	%	N	%	N	%	N	%
Chat with new and existing friends	262	94.2	16	5.8	24	96.0	1	4.0
Sharing files (music, videos, pictures, software)	254	91.4	24	8.6	22	88.0	3	12.0
Group discussions	263	94.6	15	5.4	22	88.0	3	12.0
Ask questions related to course topic	263	94.6	15	5.4	24	96.0	1	4.0
Surfing for useful information	267	96.0	11	4.0	23	92.0	2	8.0
Submission of assignment	240	86.3	38	13.7	22	88.0	3	12.0
Blogging	185	66.5	93	33.5	16	64.0	9	36.0
Download course materials	256	92.1	22	7.9	24	96.0	1	4.0
As a communication network (with family)	270	97.1	8	2.9	23	92.0	2	8.0
Reading news update	248	89.2	30	10.8	25	100.0	-	-
Political participation	180	64.7	98	35.3	20	80.0	5	20.0
Post inspirational link	227	81.7	51	18.3	24	96.0	1	4.0
Search for updates about events	257	92.4	21	7.6	23	92.0	2	8.0
Publicise events	242	87.1	36	12.9	23	92.0	2	8.0
Religious propagation	222	79.9	56	20.1	21	84.0	4	16.0
Share information	272	97.8	6	2.2	25	100.0	-	-
Connect, interact, chat with friends	267	96.0	11	4.0	25	100.0	-	-
Business empowerment	245	88.1	33	11.9	17	100.0	-	-

media by all the respondents in NOUN were: sharing information; connecting, interacting, chatting with friends; reading news update and business empowerment (Table 2).

The findings of this study confirmed that the distance learners in both universities used social media for different purposes such as sharing information; connecting, interacting, chatting with friends; as a communication network (with family) and reading news update. This could be because social media enhances communication between people irrespective of their geographical location. This finding is corroborated by Owusu-Acheaw and Larson (2015) who stated that "social media provide tools by which students can communicate, share information, and create new relationships" in a study carried out on Koforidua Polytechnic students in Ghana (p. 97). Thus, distance learning students used social media for both academic purposes and building relationships.

Research Question Two: What is the Frequency of Use of Social Media by the Distance Learners?

Table 3 presents the response rate on the frequency of social media use by the distance learners. The scales used for frequency of social media use by distance learning students in the university were; daily (D), twice a week (TW), weekly (W), monthly (M), occasionally (O), and never (N). Findings from Table 3 revealed that the daily use of WhatsApp, Facebook and Instagram were common to respondents in both universities, although with a higher percentage for respondents in NOUN for the three social media platforms. MySpace, Pinterest and Line were the social media platforms never used by most of the respondents in both universities. In the University of Ibadan, respondents that never used these social media platforms were: Pinterest (60.1%), Line (58.6%) and MySpace (50.4%), while those in NOUN were: MySpace (52.0%), Line (48.0%) and Pinterest (40.0%).

There were similarities in the frequency of use of social media for learning by the respondents in both universities as majority of the undergraduates posited that they make daily use of WhatsApp. With WhatsApp messenger, communication through mobile phones has become easier, faster and cheaper as it an application that supports instant messenger. This finding agrees with those of Hrastinski and Agahee (2006) who in their investigation of how students are using the social media discovered that all but one of the students interviewed are frequent social media users and use such media roughly every day. The findings confirmed Sheldon (2008) study that more than 50% of college students go on a social networking sites several times a day.

On the contrary, over 40% of distance learning students never used LINE. This could be as a result of low awareness of its use for learning activities among respondents. However, the result is in variance with those of van De Bogart and Wichadee (2015) who examined how undergraduates at the University of Thailand accepted LINE using it for classroom-

related activities (e.g., submit homework, follow up course information queries, download materials) and explored the factors that might affect their intention to use it. They discovered that when students were asked to identify the kinds of social networks they were using, the findings revealed that LINE was chosen by a majority (95.8%) of the Thai students. In addition, the results indicated that LINE was the most effective tool for communicating with teachers that students perceived (76.4%).

Table 3. Frequency of social media use by distance learners

Social Media Types	UI Frequency of Use										NOUN Frequency of Use									
	D		W		M		O		N		D		W		M		O		N	
	F	%	F	%	F	%	F	%	F	%	F	%	F	%	F	%	F	%	F	%
MySpace	72	25.9	18	6.5	8	2.9	40	14.4	140	50.4	2	8.0	8	32.0	1	4.0	1	4.0	13	52.0
Facebook	160	57.6	57	20.5	13	4.7	42	15.1	6	2.2	20	80.0	3	12.0	1	4.0	1	4.0	-	-
Imo	57	20.5	59	21.2	13	4.7	43	15.5	106	38.1	7	28.0	4	16.0	1	4.0	3	12.0	7	28.0
Academia.edu	154	55.4	35	12.6	6	2.2	22	7.9	61	21.9	18	72.0	4	16.0	1	4.0	-	-	2	8.0
Twitter	71	25.5	46	16.5	15	5.4	49	17.6	97	34.9	8	32.0	7	28.0	2	8.0	3	12.0	5	20.0
WhatsApp	253	91.0	7	2.5	3	1.1	11	4.0	4	1.4	25	100	-	-	-	-	-	-	-	-
Instagram	126	45.3	58	20.9	10	3.6	28	10.1	56	20.1	18	72.0	5	20.0	-	-	1	4.0	1	4.0
YouTube	75	27.0	72	25.9	18	6.5	56	20.1	57	20.5	9	36.0	8	32.0	1	4.0	3	12.0	4	16.0
Blogs (Tumbir, Blogger)	48	17.3	48	17.3	24	8.6	55	19.8	103	37.1	7	28.0	5	20.0	1	4.0	3	12.0	9	36.0
Skype	26	9.4	48	17.3	14	5.0	65	23.4	125	45.0	2	8.0	9	36.0	2	8.0	7	28.0	5	20.0
BBM	112	40.3	36	12.9	7	2.5	58	20.9	65	23.4	14	56.0	5	20.0	1	4.0	2	8.0	3	12.0
Google+	132	47.5	50	18.0	7	2.5	59	21.2	30	10.8	16	64.0	5	20.0	-	-	2	8.0	2	8.0
Pinterest	14	5.0	38	13.7	21	7.6	38	13.7	167	60.1	3	12.0	5	20.0	3	12.0	4	16.0	10	40.0
LINE	46	16.5	26	9.4	10	3.6	33	11.9	163	58.6	5	20.0	3	12.0	2	8.0	3	12.0	12	48.0

Research Question Three: What is the Level of Perceived Ease of Use of social Media for Learning by the Distance Learners?

The perceived ease of use (PEOU) of social media by the distance learners is presented in Table 4 with the response format as agree and disagree. To determine the level of perceived ease of use of social media by the distance learners, a test norm was used with the following categorisation: Low (0 - 33%), Average (34 - 66%) and High (67 – 100%).

Out of the seventeen statements in Table 4, fourteen showed that respondents in UI have high PEOU scores for the use of social media, while three statements indicated average PEOU scores for the use of social media by the respondents (55.0 – 63.7%). The statements for average PEOU are: I rarely make errors when using it for learning (63.7%); I need assistance to effectively use (62.2%) and I find it easy to use it for learning (55.0%). In NOUN, respondents' scores for PEOU of social media were found to be relatively high (72.0 – 100%) with only two items falling in the average level: I need assistance to effectively use (64.0%) and I find it easy to use it for learning (56.0%). This implies that in both universities, the distance learners perceived the use of social media as easy.

The findings agree with those of Shen, Laffey, Lin, and Huang (2006) who reported that online learning through social media has become a common educational tool used by universities and their students globally, due to its flexibility of time and place. Based on this perception, social media is accepted as a means of learning among the respondents.

Table 4. Perceived ease of use of social media by distance learners

	Statements on PEOU	UI				NOUN			
		Agree		Disagree		Agree		Disagree	
		N	%	N	%	N	%	N	%
1	I find it easy to use it for learning	153	55.0	125	45.0	14	56.0	11	44.0
2	It provides helpful and easy guidance in performing learning centered activities	244	88.8	34	12.2	22	88.0	3	12.0
3	Enhance creativity in learning	255	91.7	23	8.3	25	100.0	-	-
4	It is easy to become skillful when using it	248	89.2	30	10.8	24	96.0	1	4.0
5	I need assistance to effectively use it	173	62.2	105	37.8	16	64.0	9	36.0
6	It gives control over learning	221	79.5	57	20.5	22	88.0	3	12.0
7	Provides academic support	259	93.2	19	6.8	24	96.0	1	4.0
8	Promote distance interactions	264	95.0	14	5.0	24	96.0	1	4.0
9	It has a user-friendly interface for learning	258	92.8	20	7.2	25	100.0	-	-
10	It has catchy options	233	83.8	45	16.2	24	96.0	1	4.0
11	It promotes interaction between learners and lecturers outside the lecture room	256	92.1	22	7.9	24	96.0	1	4.0
12	It is easy to obtain learning resources for studies	259	93.2	19	6.8	25	100.0	-	-
13	Its use does not require a lot of mental effort	225	80.9	53	19.1	23	92.0	2	8.0
14	It is flexible to use for learning activities	262	94.2	16	5.8	24	96.0	1	4.0
15	I rarely become confused when using it for learning	195	70.1	83	29.9	21	84.0	4	16.0
16	I rarely become frustrated when using it for learning	210	75.5	68	24.5	19	76.0	6	14.0
17	I rarely make errors when using it for learning	177	63.7	101	36.3	18	72.0	7	28.0

Key: A –Agree, D- Disagree

Research Question Four: What is the Level of Perceived Usefulness of Social Media for Learning by the Distance Learners?

The result on the perceived usefulness (PU) of social media by distance learners is presented in Table 5.A test norm was used to determine the level of perceived usefulness of social media as follows: Low (0 - 33%), Average (34 - 66%) and High (67 – 100%). The distance learners' perceived usefulness of social media in both universities was high (above 84%) with those from UI having a range of 85.6 - 94.4% and those from NOUN with a range of 84- 100% (Table 5).

The findings revealed that the most rated PU indicated by the respondents in University of Ibadan was: it enhances efficiency in learning activities (94.2%) and enhances effectiveness on communicating with group members (94.2%). All the respondents in NOUN indicated it increases their satisfaction; encourages active participation in learning and speeds up acquisition of knowledge (Table 5) as the highest rated perceived usefulness of social media. This supports the findings of Caraher and Braselman (2010) who surveyed more than 1,000 college students in the United States and reported that 64% used social media to connect with classmates and study or work on class assignments at least several times per month. Twenty-seven percent used it to connect with faculty to study or work on class assignments, at least several times in a month.

Table 5. Perceived usefulness of social media by distance learners

	Statements on PU	UI				NOUN			
		Agree		Disagree		Agree		Disagree	
		N	%	N	%	N	%	N	%
1	It saves time	238	85.6	40	14.8	23	92.0	2	8.0
2	It improves my academic performance as I get	249	89.6	29	10.3	24	96.0	1	4.0
3	It supports quick accomplishment of academic tasks	253	91.0	25	9.0	24	96.0	1	4.0
4	Learning activities are not difficult when using it	253	91.0	25	9.0	24	96.0	1	4.0
5	It enhances effectiveness on communicating with group members	262	94.2	16	5.8	24	96.0	1	4.0
6	Reading the lecture materials through it clarifies some points and improves understanding of the lectures	246	88.5	32	11.5	23	92.0	2	8.0
7	It decreases travel expenses	253	91.0	25	9.0	22	88.0	3	12.0
8	It provides equal opportunity as learning in lecture rooms	240	86.3	38	13.7	21	84.0	4	16.0
9	It increases my satisfaction	243	87.1	35	12.6	25	100.0	-	-
10	It encourages active participation in learning	245	88.1	33	11.9	25	100.0	-	-
11	It speeds up acquisition of knowledge	254	91.4	24	8.6	25	100.0	-	-
12	It provides immediate feedback for learning interaction	256	92.1	22	7.9	24	96.0	1	4.0
13	It enhances effectiveness in learning activities	254	91.4	24	8.6	24	96.0	1	4.0
14	It enhances efficiency in learning activities	262	94.2	16	5.8	24	96.0	1	4.0
15	It is useful for my study	256	92.1	22	7.9	22	88.0	3	12.0
16	It increases my productivity in studying	254	91.4	24	8.6	23	92.0	2	8.0
17	It enhances working together as a group on social media sites	250	89.9	28	10.1	23	92.0	2	8.0
18	It would make it easier to study for tests and assignments	239	86.0	39	14.0	21	84.0	4	16.0

Limitations

The study was only carried out on distance learners in faculties that were common to both universities (Arts, Education and Social Science) using purposive sampling and samples not selected from all the faculties found in each of the universities. This result is therefore limited in generalization, as only distance learning students from the three faculties were used in both universities.

CONCLUSION

Distance learners in University of Ibadan and National Open University, both in Ibadan, Oyo State, Nigeria use social media frequently for academic purposes and this has a lot of advantages for distance learners for academic achievement in universities. Perceived ease of use and perceived usefulness have been identified as factors that affect the use of social media for learning among distance learners globally, including Nigeria. However, the perception about social media ease of use and usefulness determines distance learning students' acceptance and effective use of social media for learning. The distance learners had a high level of perception of use of social media for academic activities. To sustain and invariably increase this high perception of social media use, lecturers should deploy social media for all their courses as this will optimise its use by the distance learners.

REFERENCES

Abeka, S. O. (2012). Perceived usefulness, ease of use, organisational and bank support as determinants of adoption of Internet banking in East Africa. *International Journal of Academic Research in Business and Social Sciences, 2*(10), 97–112.

Adamson, C. (2012). The role of social media in education. ICWE. Retrieved from http://www.icwe.net/oeb_special/OEB_Newsportal/the-role-of-social-and-mobile-media-in-education

Al-rahmi, W., Othman, M., & Musa, M. (2014). The improvement of students' academic performance by using social media through collaborative learning in Malaysian higher education. Asian Social Science. *Canadian Center of Science and Education, 10*(8), 177–204.

Al-rahmi, W., Zeki, A. M., Alias, N., & Saged, A. A. (2017). Social Media and its Impact on Academic Performance among University Students. *The Anthropologist, 28*(1-2), 52–68.

Beltran-Cruz, Maribel; Cruz, Shannen Belle B. (2013). The Use of Internet-Based Social Media as a Tool in Enhancing Student's Learning Experiences in Biological Sciences. *Higher Learning Research Communications, 3*(4), 68–80.

Boateng, R. O., & Amankwaa, A. (2016). The impact of social media on student academic life in higher education. *Global Journal of Human Social Science Research, 16*(4), 1–9.

Caraher, K., & Braselman, M. (2010). *The 2010 21st-Century campus report: Campus 2.0.* CDW Government LLC. Retrieved from http://webobjects.cdw.com/webobjects/media/pdf/newsroom/CDWG-21st-Century-Campus-Report-0710.pdf

Cowen, J. B. (2009). *The influence of perceived usefulness, perceived ease of use, and subjective norm on the use of computed radiography systems: A pilot study.* Retrieved from https://kb.osu.edu/dspace/bitstream/handle/1811/36983/FinalSubmitted.pdf?sequence=1

Davis, F. D. (1989). Perceived usefulness, perceived ease of use and user acceptance of information technology. *Management Information Systems Quarterly, 13*(3), 319–339. doi:10.2307/249008

Gulbahar, Y. (2014). Current state of social media for education: Case of Turkey. *Journal of Social Media Studies, 1*(1), 53–69. doi:10.15340/2147336611763

Hair, J. F., Black, W. C., Babin, B. J., & Anderson, R. E. (2010). Multivariate data analysis (7thed.). New Jersey: Prentice Hall.

Hannay, M., & Newvine, T. (2006). Perceptions of distance learning: A comparison of online and traditional learning. *MERLOT Journal of Online Learning and Teaching, 2*(1), 1–11.

Hrastinski, S., & Aghaee, N. (2012). How are campus students using social media to support their studies? An explorative interview study. *Education and Information Technologies, 17*(4), 451–464. doi:10.100710639-011-9169-5

Jimoh, M. (2013). An appraisal of the open and distance learning programme in Nigeria. *Journal of Education and Practice, 4*(3), 1–8.

Wickramanayake, L. & Jika, S. M. (2018). Social media use by undergraduate students of education in Nigeria: A survey. *The Electronic Library, 36*(1), 21-37.

Leyrer-Jackson, J. M., & Wilson, A. K. (2018). The associations between social-media use and academic performance among undergraduate students in biology. *Journal of Biological Education, 52*(2), 221–230. doi:10.1080/00219266.2017.1307246

Olowu, A. O., & Seri, F. O. (2012). A study of social network addiction among youths in Nigeria. *Journal of Social Science and Policy Review, 4*, 62–71.

Owusu-Acheaw, M., & Larson, A. G. (2015). Use of social media and its impact on academic performance of tertiary institution students: A study of students of Koforidua Polytechnic, Ghana. *Journal of Education and Practice, 6*(6), 94–101.

Sheldon, P. (2008). Student favorite: Facebook and motives for its use. *Southwestern Mass Communication Journal, 23*(2), 39-53.

Sago, B. (2013). Factors influencing social media adoption and frequency of use: An examination of Facebook, Twitter, Pinterest and Google+. *International Journal of Business and Commerce, 3*(1), 1–14.

Saritas, M. T., Yildiz, E., & Senel, H. C. (2015). Examining the attitudes and intention to use synchronous distance learning technology among pre-service teachers: A qualitative perspective of Technology Acceptance Model. *American Journal of Educational Research, 3*(10A), 17–25. doi:10.12691/education-3-10A-3

Selwyn, N. (2012). Social media in higher education. In *The Europa World of Learning*. Education Arena. Retrieved from http://www.educationarena.com/pdf/sample/sample-essay-selwyn.pdf

Shen, D., Laffey, J., Lin, Y., & Huang, X. (2006). Social influence for perceived usefulness and ease-of use of course delivery systems. *Journal of Interactive Online Learning, 5*(3), 270–282.

Sudman, S. (1976). *Applied Sampling*. New York: Academic Press.

Van De Bogart, W., & Wichadee, S. (2015). Exploring students' intention to use LINE for academic purposes based on technology acceptance model. *The International Review of Research in Open and Distributed Learning, 16*(3), 1–21. doi:10.19173/irrodl.v16i3.1894

This research was previously published in the International Journal of Online Pedagogy and Course Design (IJOPCD), 10(2); pages 37-47, copyright year 2020 by IGI Publishing (an imprint of IGI Global).

Chapter 93

Social media and Increased venture creation tendency with innovative ideas:
The case of female students in Asia

Syed Far Abid Hossain
(iD) https://orcid.org/0000-0003-0729-1456
Xi'an Jiaotong University, China

Xu Shan
Xi'an Jiaotong University, China

Mohammad Musa
Shaanxi Normal University, China

Preethu Rahman
Shaanxi Normal University, China

ABSTRACT

The purpose of this chapter is to ascertain the contemporary role of social media in increased venture creation tendency along with innovative ideas. The key objective of this study is to discover the tendency of female students' innovativeness in venture creation in China. A random sampling method was used to conduct a survey in different universities in China to identify the scenario of innovativeness in venture creation. Findings from primary data collection indicated that the female students in China are highly involved with social media marketing with innovative ideas. As a result, apart from traditional marketing, society is involved with contemporary marketing where innovativeness with social media and smartphones are the key factors. Innovative ideas in venture creation may generate additional earning for people with low income in society. Future studies with mixed methodology and respondents who use different social media as a tool to innovate new venture may shed light on the undiscovered phenomenon of social media marketing in the context of the mobile phone.

DOI: 10.4018/978-1-6684-7123-4.ch093

INTRODUCTION

Although entrepreneurial tendency with the help of social media which can be expressed as media entrepreneurship, is poorly investigated so far (Khajeheian, 2013), it has potential market due to social networking, trust, and online reviews. A recent survey revealed that 88% of total online buyers either review, read or trust online reviews (Chen, Luo, & Wang, 2017) which enhance the probability to make a final buying decision. Systematic mobile device usage (Hossain et al., 2019) recently is the main motivation for innovative business ideas. The broad objective of this chapter is to ascertain the contemporary role of social media in increased venture creation tendency along with innovative ideas. The specific objective of this study is to discover the tendency of female students' innovativeness in venture creation with a special focus of China because of its large population and recent development in online shopping. The role of mobile phones in media entrepreneurship is investigated with social networking (Hossain, 2019). However, the role of social media in generating innovative business idea is an undiscovered phenomenon. This study is an attempt to shed light on it. This chapter focused on related data from significant and relevant literature and finally provided a basis for further research in the next sections. The following sections describe the methodology of the study, Review of literature, result, discussion, limitations, conclusion and further research direction.

BACKGROUND OF THE STUDY

Social media and venture creation have a strong relationship. Social media helps to create new ventures. The venture creation phenomenon heavily influenced by the social media and media industries as long as they, in their very nature, fall into the culture and creativity-related businesses. The crucial distinctiveness of the venture creation activities such as creation, innovation, and original ways of thinking are critical in making business success. "Media particularly social media also plays an important role in influencing the venture creation phenomenon, by making a talk that transmits qualities and pictures credited to venture creation, by giving a transporter advancing innovative practices, and by empowering a pioneering soul in the society. Through these methods, media and venture creation have a reciprocal impact" (Khajeheian, 2013). The qualities of the social media items are particularly adjusted to the elements of the pioneering procedure, for example, self-sufficiency, ingenuity, hazard taking, star liveliness, and focused forcefulness. These measurements speak to the enterprising introduction of the firm, which can be characterized as the processes, practices, and decision-making activities that lead firms to choose to enter another market or dispatch another product. Media and companies are urged to be particularly risk-taking and innovative. The entrepreneurial approach they have to develop is without a doubt extremely important (Hang & VanWeezle, 2007). The goal of social media in venture creation must be to build a bridge between the general discipline of venture creation and the specificities of the media industry and social media (Achtenhagen, 2008).

As expressed by Fruhling and Digman (2000), online life can upsurge the client base and piece of the overall industry, which thus can encourage the development methodologies of a business. Coherently, a two-path correspondence between the clients and the business can give data and thoughts, to upgrade the nature of the business' market contributions and to urge them to improve. The stage in this way can give chances to draw in potential clients and hold existing ones, constructing a more grounded connection between the gatherings included (Mangold & Faulds, 2009). Social media can help to provide "promoting that is increasingly compelling, new correspondence and dissemination channels, shorter time to showcase, redid items, 24-hour online specialized help, and online intuitive network" (Mukolwe & Korir, 2016). The reason organizations are exploiting the long-range informal communication destinations is that there is another age of purchasers whose purchasing conduct is altogether different from the past gatherings of clients. This development of a completely new economy on the Internet is the result of purchasers looking for more comfort in shopping, better correspondence, greater commitment, and capacity to choose (Tigo, 2012; Perju, 2015; Tosifyan & Tosifyan, 2017). Business people consider internet-based life a helpful device since it energizes the ID of chances in the business condition (Park & Sung, 2017). There are changing perspectives about "pioneering opportunity"; where Schumpeter (1932) expressed that one must search for new data accessible in the market so as to make a chance, Kirzner (1997) then again contended that a business must utilize the current data to find a chance. Web-based life is such a stage, that has now empowered business visionaries to find and make openings by surveying both existing and new data by conveying and interfacing with friends on the system (Park & Sung, 2017) and variety seeking (Hossain et al., 2019)

RESEARCH METHODOLOGY

First, the study utilized a literature review in the arena of social networking, innovation, media entrepreneurship and device usage in shopping. In addition, the authors used a case study from a real entrepreneur to represent the real scenario in China. Finally, a total number of 42 female students were interviewed in China. They all are involved directly with media entrepreneurship with the help of social networking. Most of the students are from 18-25 years old, studying at the university level in business, social science, and engineering majors. The total number of 42 students were asked questions about the perception of social media, value co-creation, target customers and difficulty handling.

Table 1. Electronic database used for the literature review

Source	online access
Science Direct	http://www.sciencedirect.com/
Emerald Insight	http://www.emeraldinsight.com/
Scopus	http://www.scopus.com/
Springer	http://link.springer.com/
Web of Science	https://apps.webofknowledge.com
ACM Digital Library	http://dl.acm.org/

REVIEW OF LITERATURE ON SOCIAL MEDIA AND VENTURE CREATION

Throughout the decades, various patterns have been knowledgeable about the business condition and got shriveled in the blink of an eye by any stretch of the imagination. Once in a while, the entry of certain marvels holds the ability to change and impact the business condition, as it were, one such wonder is web-based social networking, which is frequently reciprocally utilized with the term Web 2.0 (Kadam & Ayarekar, 2014). There are assortments of internet-based life stages extending from informal organizations, private interpersonal organizations, to web journals and miniaturized scale online journals (Shabbir et al., 2016). A portion of the well-known and generally-utilized, long-range informal communication destinations include Facebook, LinkedIn, Instagram, Twitter, Skype, WhatsApp, Viber, WordPress, YouTube, Flikr, Google+, Pinterest, Quora, Reddit and Snapchat (Bajaj, 2017; Mehra, 2017; Maina, 2018). In spite of its origin in 1997 (Shabbir et al., 2016), there was a blast in internet-based life in the year 2000, when a noteworthy increment was found in the quantity of long-range interpersonal communication destinations (Kadam & Ayarekar, 2014). Thus, the manner in which clients and businesspeople impart changed in light of the fact that this stage enabled organizations to have more noteworthy access to a more extensive scope of target groups of onlookers; grasp their shifting needs and needs; improve and enhance items and benefits; and support client commitment with the business (Smith & Taylor, 2004; Jagongo & Kinyua, 2013). Be that as it may, among all the web-based life destinations, the most generally utilized online life stage by organizations and advertisers is Facebook (Driver, 2018). As indicated by the reports of Statista (2018), the main web-based life stages for advertisers everywhere throughout the world incorporate Facebook (94%), Instagram (66%), Twitter (62%), LinkedIn (56%), YouTube (half), Pinterest (27%) and Snapchat (8%). So also, in Bangladesh, most of the online retailers go through Facebook (Gilchrist, 2018). Because of the different points of interest of working together via web-based networking media, it has reshaped the regular promoting techniques in the nation. Presently many, beginning from understudies to housewives can initiate a start-up via web-based networking media since it doesn't require physical space or tremendous labor (Farhin, 2018). As expressed by Fruhling and Digman (2000), online life can upsurge the client base and piece of the pie, which thusly can encourage the development procedures of a business. Sensibly, a two-route correspondence between the clients and the business can give data and thoughts, to upgrade the nature of the business' market contributions and furthermore to urge them to improve. The stage can, in this way, give chances to draw in potential clients and hold existing ones, constructing a more grounded connection between the gatherings included (Mangold & Faulds, 2009). Web-based life can help give "promoting that is increasingly compelling, new correspondence and circulation channels, shorter time to showcase, modified items, 24 hours online specialized help, and online intelligent network" (Mukolwe & Korir, 2016). The reason organizations are exploiting the long-range informal communication destinations is on the grounds that there is another age of purchasers whose purchasing conduct is altogether different from the past gatherings of clients. This rise of a completely new economy on the Internet is the result of customers looking for more comfort in shopping, better correspondence, greater commitment and capacity to choose (Tigo, 2012; Perju, 2015; Tosifyan & Tosifyan, 2017). Business visionaries consider web-based social networking a valuable apparatus since it empowers distinguishing proof of chances in the business condition (Park & Sung, 2017). There are shifting perspectives about "enterprising chance"; where Schumpeter (1932) expressed that one must search for new data accessible in the market so as to make a chance, Kirzner (1997) then again contended that a business must utilize the current data to find a chance. Web-based life is such a stage, that has now empowered businesspeople to find and make openings by evaluating both existing and new data by conveying and collaborating with companions on the system (Park & Sung, 2017).

Social media has without a doubt opened up windows of new opportunities for people (Mukolwe & Korir, 2016). Another type of online businesspeople has surfaced who are not just reassuring new companies on

Internet-based life, but at the same time are utilizing the stage to upgrade the current organizations and make systems of clients more than ever (Fischer & Reuber, 2011). There is no satisfactory data, on what number of individuals are enlisting their organizations via web-based networking media every year, or how are their organizations performing, however. In any case, numerous analysts investigating the field of enterprise, unveil that internet-based life has made better approaches for working together and organizing feasible for people (Genç & Oksüz, 2015; Cesaroni et al., 2017; Mukolwe & Korir, 2016; Upkere et al., 2014; Melissa et al., 2013; Oke, 2013). A portion of the common advantages have been separated from the discoveries of investigates led on the connection between online networking and business visionaries in the creating nations (Melissa et al., 2013; Upkere et al., 2014; Vivakaran & Maraimalai, 2016; Cesaroni et al., 2017), which are referenced as pursues:

- Social media has enabled people to perceive pioneering opportunity through selling on the web and understand that their time can be utilized in profitably to acquire benefit from an enormous potential market.
- There are a low venture and working costs engaged with an internet-based life start-up that in the long run propels youthful businesspeople.
- Since numerous ladies can maintain their organizations from home and at their own comfort, this has helped them to have a superior work-life balance, where they can successfully oversee both their expert and individual lives at the same time.
- It is leeway that in most of the organizations via web-based networking media does not require an abnormal state of innovative proficiency, which decreases the start-up intricacy.
- Some different advantages incorporate practical advancement; access to a more extensive target group of onlookers; item improvement and upgrade; the foundation of outer networks of a client who might share their encounters; and the extent of better teaching clients (Baghdadi, 2013; Brengman & Karimov, 2012; Cesaroni et al., 2017).

As opposed to the preferences examined, subjective research led by Genç and Oksüz (2015) uncovered a few challenges business visionaries face while working together via web-based networking media. Some of the serious issues recognized were: impersonation of work, proficient disappointment, trouble in distinguishing explicit target gathering of people, more extensive spread-out of piece of the pie, and unreasonable challenge. In spite of the fact that a couple of creators have investigated the impact of web based life on businesspeople with regards to creating nations (Cesaroni et al., 2017), there is next to no scholarly proof on how internet based life have quickened enterprise. Various writing has been separated in importance to businesspeople (Afroze et al., 2014; Ahammad & Moudul-Ul-Huq, 2013; Islam & Ahmed, 2016), yet none of those showed the effect online life has on them, or the degree to which it has added to the development of potential business visionaries.

TENDENCY OF FEMALE STUDENTS USING SOCIAL MEDIA IN ASIAN REGION

Needless to say, in many regions of Asia, females are deprived and have less opportunity for work due to innumerable reasons. Sometimes, the work opportunity is not sufficient enough and sometimes culture is a factor which restricts women to do a certain type of work. For example: from a traditional Muslim family from Pakistan or Bangladesh, women may not work as a sales executive or in the marketing department. This is not the case in all the Asian region, however, this is a common phenomenon in many Asian regions. That is why now a day, women are using social media to do something for themselves. Till date, many of them are conducting a kind of little business by themselves with very short manpower and limited resources. However, the attraction or intention to conduct business is very high.

VENTURE CREATION OPPORTUNITY WITH SOCIAL MEDIA

Regardless of the type of social media, venture creation usually depends on the circle of friends of a motivated entrepreneur. For example: If someone wants to start selling goods via an online platform, the important issue is to determine the social media platform used by his or her circle of friends and well-known people. This is the first stage of motivation and individual can be pursued or initiated by a kind of self-confidence level that the circle of friends may help. In real life, this is true most of the time, however, if the seller can't maintain the reputation or fail to serve properly, the circle of friends can't help for a long time. So, there is tremendous opportunity to create venture due to the availability and affordability of social media and smartphones in particular. This process even works faster rather than other traditional techniques of selling. For example: From production to consumption, there are the complexity of intermediaries and promotional activities as well as cost, so, usually, it takes time to make the product known to the potential customers. But, in social media people trust friends and known-people and they can decide faster without hesitation. This is one of the reasons why social media is attracted by many people in the contemporary era.

Figure 1. Venture creation opportunity with social media

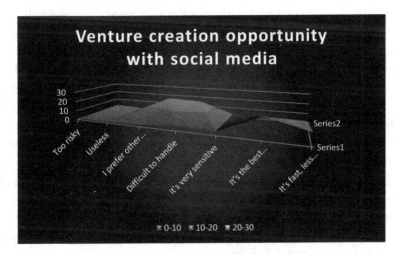

CASE STUDY

Although social media is used by so many people, the innovativeness is always unique. Especially, in China the market is huge, the buyers are unlimited and the competition is tremendous. As a result, in-novativeness is a crucial issue in China. A few months ago, one of the authors of this study was invited for lunch by a Chinese language teacher. The author had no idea about any business talk. The Chinese teacher who invited the author was actually a new entrepreneur with a social media marketing platform and she was trying to enhance her channel. She cordially ordered some dishes with due respect to her guest and started a normal conversation. All on a sudden, she revealed the main purpose of that meeting. Actually, she was involved with a new kind of social media platform where members can sell goods to their known people and earn profit without investing anything. The platform is simply a mobile Apps. Anyone can register with a phone number and enjoy shopping. The only difference between regular online shopping and this innovative new platform is earning profit by the person who introduces others to buy from this platform. Although it is hard to say that it is not a kind of real entrepreneurship where people conduct business activities by themselves, however, this is a platform generated by the third party, sellers enjoy the advantage of mobile technology and conduct social media marketing activities to boost-up the sales. This is not a job because there is no work time and no salary. So it is purely a kind of start-up from a different perspective which is an example of innovative entrepreneurship practice in China.

THE BLESSING OF TECHNOLOGY IN INNOVATION

The importance of social networking was acknowledged by Ardichvili et al. (2000), who claimed that social networks are one of the main factors influencing the core process of opportunity recognition. Fischer & Reuber (2011) also stated that, in order to answer complex business issues that arise, business industries are likely to interact with other people to discuss their options to come to a decision as well as cooperative partnerships. For these, they often lead to new business insights and therefore new goals to attain. Social networks can be identified with the more popular term, social media. The role of social media has been researched in various fields already (Fischer & Reuber, 2011; Greve & Salaff, 2003). Therefore, in this book tries to discover the influence of national culture on new business processes, there is also the aim to discover what kind of role there is for social media platforms in the business decisions. The research of Fischer and Reuber (2011) discovered that social media platforms such as Twitter can help businesses to create and follow opportunities. Fischer and Reuber (2011) aim to propose social media as a "corridor for opportunity creation and exploration", yet they state that there are several factors to be taken into account.

De Carolis, Litzky, and Eddleston (2009) state that research has indicated the importance of networks and social capital during the process of creating a new venture. More specific, new venture creation appears to be the result of the social network of the entrepreneur combined with their cognitive biases. De Carolis et al. (2009) found out that cognitive bias could even explain why social capital has a greater effect on the progress of creating a new venture for some. However, research on the intersection of the concepts of social networks, new venture creation, and effectuation is lacking. Fischer and Reuber (2011) claim that the use of effectual thinking processes by businesses can increase the efficacy of new ventures. Also, costs of business failure have proven to be reduced, due to earlier failure and lower levels of investment of effectual firms compared to causational ones. Besides, the level of expertise correlates with the usage of effectual logic by industries. Prior research has indicated that using of effectual logic is forced to make decisions within an uncertain business environment, relating to the fact that they shape the market instead of treating the market as a given fact. This relates inevitably to one of the most important concepts in business processes, namely the recognition of opportunities.

NEW CONCEPT DEVELOPMENT FOR VENTURE CREATION

The technological innovation of new products and concepts can be seen as a key driver of competitive advantage and commercial success. The number of worldwide social media users is increasing every day, which becomes a great opportunity for businesses to reach their online audience through social networks. One of the advantages of the social network is that it enables businesses to reach a worldwide customer population so that customers can survey, select, and purchase products and services from businesses around the world (Al Kailani & Kumar, 2011). In particular, peer communication through social media, a new form of consumer socialization, has profound impacts on consumer decision making and thus marketing strategies. Consumer socialization theory predicts that communication among consumers affects their cognitive, effective, and behavioral attitudes (Ward, 1974). Nowadays, the analysis of consumer behavior is central to marketing success, especially since most potential consumers are using the internet and different online socializing tools. The online audience is a booming market worldwide, however giving its globalized nature a level of segmentation is needed cross-culturally. The unique aspects of social media and its immense popularity have revolutionized marketing practices such as advertising and promotion (Hanna, Rohm, & Crittenden, 2011). Social media has also influenced consumer behavior from information acquisition to post-purchase behavior such as dissatisfaction statements or behaviors (Mangold & Faulds, 2009) and patterns of Internet usage (Ross et al., 2009; Laroche et al., 2012). Other functions of social media involve affecting and influencing perceptions, attitudes and end behavior (Williams & Cothrell, 2000) while bringing together different like-minded people (Hagel & Armstrong, 1997). In an online environment, Laroche (2012) pointed out that people like the idea of contributing, creating, and joining communities to fulfill needs of belongingness, being socially connected and recognized or simply enjoying interactions with other like-minded members.

In recent years, social networking sites and social media have increased in popularity, at a global level. For instance, Facebook has more than a billion active users (as of 2012) since its beginning in 2004. Indeed, online social networks have profoundly changed the propagation of information by making it incredibly easy to share and digest information on the internet (Akrimi & Khemakhem, 2012). Marketing through social media can help increase brand recognition, it is cost-effective, and it helps improve brand dependability and power. We can talk about Facebook marketing here. Nearly any kind of brand can be promoted through Facebook, turning potential customers into active fans who follow news of promotions and developments and share the news with their own circle. For successful marketing through Facebook, a business needs a clear goal and strategy, stay active in online with regular posts, encourage comments and reply quickly, nurture relationships with customers and frequent online promotions.

LOWER RISK AND LIMITED INVESTMENT USING SOCIAL MEDIA

Social networks can be used as a great tool and effective platform (Jain & Sinha, 2018) for people who typically share a common interest or activity. They provide a variety of ways for users to interact with each other. Every person, who wants to join a social networking site he must create his own profile. This profile describes his interests, needs, and wishes. Through that profile, we can know his friends who have similar interests. These networks offer a unique opportunity for highly targeted marketing. The use of social network can contribute to the success of the company. The Internet-based applications have the advantage that they are actively working with the customers and can get feedback directly from there.

Figure 2. New concept development

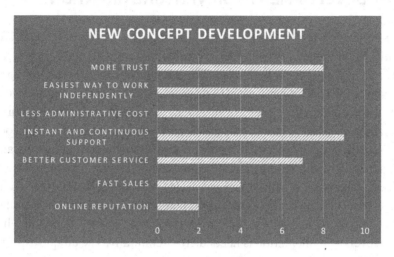

Social network marketing can be very advantageous for businesses as it has lower risk and limited investment options for investors. Establishing communities around products and services is a potential strategy to build brand loyalty, establishing exit barriers, and facilitating viral marketing through self-emergent customer testimonials. Such communities can also be a source of innovation by soliciting consumer input, and customer suggestions. Social networking can find new customers, and help conduct brand intelligence and market research with that the company can make its advertising in a social network. The communication in the social network gets shoppers to listen to one another, review ratings for products and services, and provide product knowledge and personal information. Social networks protect users from interaction with the outside world and keep information and interaction away from strangers. Social marketing can be an inexpensive way to promote a company rather than putting together a huge marketing team or a prohibitive budget. While using social media as a business promoter business must be especially careful in the market research and advertising laws not to cross legal borders. The advertisement in a social net brings danger to product brands. Social networks are user-generated contents where end users about their experiences with products, services, and customer service, etc. The contents sometimes can be critical to the product, and societies have very little control in which end users share in their social network. The supervision of the general perception of brands of the online community and directing problems discussed online is extremely important for brands of the product and service. We must not forget the most important thing through social marketing there is an opportunity to collect consumer data; however, these compilations of data cannot just be trapped in it. Social network users are more careful regarding sharing their private data. To have access to the consumer Information, a business must build products and applications which will require that a user divides at least some personal data.

OPPORTUNITY TO EXPAND BUSINESS

In recent years, a change in the relationship between companies and customers has revealed. The customer has received more and more control over and through regarding the company and its products through the goal to achieve sustainable business development (Oskam, Bossink & de Man, 2018). The core of

Figure 3. Handling difficulty

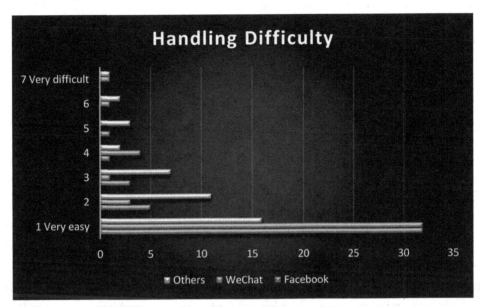

any business is the customers, and social networking represents an opportunity to build even closer and more profitable relationships with customers, which brings unlimited opportunity to expand the business. Therefore, the company must respond to this change. In fact, companies can gain benefits through using social networking in marketing: they can achieve a better understanding of the customer needs and can build better relationships with customers. For companies to achieve measurable commercial benefits, they must plan their activities in social networks for better control and measurement. The correct behavior can also change the way in how the companies consider their customers. This is the area for the use of customer relationship management to intersect with social networks, and customers, and social networks, which are looking for ways to deal with the companies in connection. Whenever the coordination between social networking and marketing is achieved, companies can more easily follow their clients, achieve their requirements, control, and measure their activities. Social-networking tools may provide a better introduction mechanism for accounts with higher conversation rates. Social networking sites are the source of almost inexhaustible views of clients and situations, and the challenge is to control this information in an appropriate manner and in a meaningful way for the company and that brings real benefits for them. Social networking is also a suitable framework for core activities in marketing on the Internet. Strategically, establishing communities around products and services has been a well-known method of building brand loyalty, establishing exit barriers, and facilitating viral marketing through self-emergent customer testimonials. One of the key success factors of social marketing is involving its customers and determining their needs on a personal level by encouraging consumers to participate enthusiastically and listening to their desires. Burt (1992) states that relations with colleagues, friends, and clients can create opportunities that the business can turn into a success by successfully using their financial and human capital (to finance and create the product). It is, therefore, the final arbiter of competitive success. Coleman (1988) agrees with this point of view. He defends that there are different functions and purposes assigned to the concept of social capital. He adds that an important form of social capital is

Figure 4. Target customers

the potential for information, which gives the access to the information that may make investors exploit more opportunities or create more opportunities and find ways to expand business gradually.

IMPLICATIONS, LIMITATIONS AND FUTURE RESEARCH

Feedback from the customers is a tool to come up with innovativeness in social media marketing and it also can help to make a good relationship (Lin, Luo, Cheng, & Li, 2019). Customers sometimes have latent demand which is complicated to understand sometimes for the marketer. As the social media marketing procedure is very direct and contact with the customer is easily reachable, sellers can get more feedback from buyers and come up with more innovative ideas to satisfy them and retain them for a longer period of time. Also, the feedback from the customers works as a tool to boost up the business or bring new customers. Word-of-mouth or e-word of mouth is a very crucial factor in this regard. It is true that all the customers are not satisfied with the same product always, however, the majority is an issue. If the majority of customers provide positive feedback, the others could take it positively and reach a final decision without enough hesitation. In China, people usually read comments from other users before buying a particular product online. As there is no chance to touch or feel the product in real, comments or feedback from other users motivate the potential buyers to go ahead and make purchases. As a result, feedback from customers is a very crucial factor in social media marketing in achieving innovativeness in business. This study was limited to collect data from only one Asian country. Future research may go in depth with more scientific research in broad scale.

CONCLUSION

In the contemporary era, people are fascinated with change and focus on sustainable business development (Naranjo-Valencia et al., 2018). New and innovative ideas attract people and excite them as well. Innovativeness is observed in various industries in the market especially in fashion and clothing, jewelry, travel, film, and food industry. Innovativeness is appreciated by consumers over the years and made them happy and satisfied. If the new venture is innovative, people will be automatically attracted to it. They will be curious to know about it. Apart from that, innovative venture creation is a tool to compete with the other existing competitors within the same industry in the market. In some restaurants, innovative interior decoration attracts customers. Some people go there just for the innovative interior or service such as eating inside an airplane or customers enjoy the variation when waitresses serve the food wearing a nurse uniform in some restaurants. It is easily arguable that all the innovative venture may not be accepted by the customers, however, innovativeness could be either a primary or secondary tool to face the competitors and survive in the market. In addition, a venture can grow fast due to innovativeness.

REFERENCES

Achtenhagen, L. (2008). Understanding entrepreneurship in traditional media. *Journal of Media Business Studies*, 5(1), 123–142. doi:10.1080/16522354.2008.11073463

Afroze, T., Alam, K., Akther, E., & Jui, S. N. (2014). Women Entrepreneurs in Bangladesh-Challenges and Determining Factors. *Journal of Business and Technology (Dhaka)*, 9(2), 27–41. doi:10.3329/jbt. v9i2.26194

Ahammad, I. & *Moudud-Ul- Huq, S.* (2013). Women Entrepreneurship Development in Bangladesh Challenges And Prospects. *International Journal of Innovative Research and Development*, (pp. 41–48). Retrieved from http://www.ijird.com/index.php/ijird/article/view/36096/29238

Akrimi, Y., & Khemakhem, R. (2012). What Drive Consumers to Spread the Word in Social Media? *Journal of Marketing Research & Case Studies*, 1–14. doi:10.5171/2012.969979

Al Kailani, M., & Kumar, R. (2011). Investigating Uncertainty Avoidance and Perceived Risk for Impacting Internet Buying: A Study in Three National Cultures. *International Journal of Business and Management*, 6(5), 76–92. doi:10.5539/ijbm.v6n5p76

Baghdadi, Y. (2013). From E-commerce to social commerce: A framework to guide enabling cloud computing. *Journal of Theoretical and Applied Electronic Commerce Research*, 8(3), 12–38. doi:10.4067/ S0718-18762013000300003

Bajaj, R. (2017). Top 10 Most Popular Social Sites and Apps in 2017. Retrieved from https://www. linkedin.com/pulse/top-10-most-popular-social-networking-sites-apps-2017-rajiv-bajaj

<bok>Mukolwe, E., & Korir, J. (2016). Social Media and Entrepreneurship: Tools, Benefits, and Challenges. A Case Study of Women Online Entrepreneurs on Kilimani Mums Marketplace on Facebook. International Journal of Humanities and Social Science, 6(8), 248–256.</jrn>

Brengman, M., & Karimov, F. P. (2012). The effect of web communities on consumers' initial trust in B2C e-commerce websites. *Management Research Review*, 35(9), 791–817. doi:10.1108/01409171211256569

Burt, R. S. (1992). The social structure of competition. In N. Nohria, & R. Eccles (Eds.), *Networks and Organizations: Structure, Form and Action* (pp. 57–91). Boston, MA: Harvard Business School Press.

Cesaroni, F. M., Demartini, P., & Paoloni, P. (2017). Women in business and social media: Implications for female entrepreneurship in emerging countries. *African Journal of Business Management*, *11*(14), 316–326. doi:10.5897/AJBM2017.8281

Chen, K., Luo, P., & Wang, H. (2017). An influence framework on product word-of-mouth (WoM) measurement. *Information & Management*, *54*(2), 228–240. doi:10.1016/j.im.2016.06.010

Coleman, J. S. (1988). Social Capital in the Creation of Human Capital. *American Journal of Sociology*, *94*, Supplement: Organizations and Institutions: Sociological and Economic Approaches to the Analysis of Social Structure, S95-S120.

De Carolis, D. M., Litzky, B. E., & Eddleston, K. A. (2009). Why Networks Enhance the Progress of New Venture Creation: The Influence of Social Capital and Cognition. *Entrepreneurship Theory and Practice*, *33*(2), 527–545. doi:10.1111/j.1540-6520.2009.00302.x

Driver, S. (2018, Oct. 15). Social Media for Business: A Marketer's Guide. Business News Daily. Retrieved from https://www.businessnewsdaily.com/7832-social-media-for-business.html

Farhin, N. (2018, Jan. 9). How small businesses use Facebook to promote products and services. Dhaka Tribune. Retrieved from https://www.dhakatribune.com/ business/2018/01/09/small-businesses-use-facebook-promote-products-services

Fischer, E., & Reuber, A. R. (2011). Social interaction via new social media: (How) can interactions on Twitter affect effectual thinking and behavior? *Journal of Business Venturing*, *26*(1), 1–18. doi:10.1016/j.jbusvent.2010.09.002

Fruhling, A. L., & Digman, L. A. (2000). The Impact of Electronic Commerce on Business-Level Strategies. *Journal of Electronic Commerce Research*, *1*(1), 13–22.

Genç, M., & Oksüz, B. (2015). A fact or an Illusion: Effective social media usage of female entrepreneurs. *Procedia: Social and Behavioral Sciences*, *195*, 293–300. doi:10.1016/j.sbspro.2015.06.345

Gilchrist, K. (2018, July 17). Facebook and 3 millennials are changing the start-up scene in Bangladesh. CNBC. Retrieved from https://www.cnbc.com/2018/07/17/shopup-bangladesh-start-up-uses-facebook-to-help-micro-entrepreneurs.html

Greve, A., & Salaff, J. W. (2003). *Social Networks and Entrepreneurship, Entrepreneurship Theory and Practice*, (Fall): 1–22. doi:10.1111/1540-8520.00029

Hagel, J., & Armstrong, A. G. (1997). *Net gain: Expanding markets through virtual communities*. Boston, MA: Harvard Business School Press.

Hang, M., & Van Weezle, A. (2007). Media and entrepreneurship: A survey of the literature relating both concepts. *Journal of Media Business Studies*, *4*(1), 51–70. doi:10.1080/16522354.2007.11073446

Hanna, R., Rohm, A., & Crittenden, V. L. (2011). We're all connected: The power of the social media ecosystem. *Business Horizons*, *54*(3), 265–273. doi:10.1016/j.bushor.2011.01.007

Hossain, S. F. A. (2019). Social Networking and Its Role in Media Entrepreneurship: Evaluating the Use of Mobile Phones in the Context of Online Shopping–A Review. [JMME]. *Journal of Media Management and Entrepreneurship*, *1*(1), 73–86. doi:10.4018/JMME.2019010105

Hossain, S. F. A., Nurunnabi, M., Hussain, K., & Saha, S. K. (2019). Effects of variety-seeking intention by mobile phone usage on university students' academic performance. *Cogent Education*, *6*(1). doi:10.1080/2331186X.2019.1574692

Hossain, S. F. A., Ying, Y., & Saha, S. K. (2019). Systematic Mobile Device Usage Behavior and Successful Implementation of TPACK Based on University Students Need. In *Science and Information Conference* (pp. 729-746). Cham, Switzerland: Springer.

Islam, N., & Ahmed, R. (2016). Factors Influencing the Development of Women Entrepreneurship in Bangladesh. doi:. doi:10.2139/ssrn.2851786

Jain, S., & Sinha, A. (2018). Social Network Analysis: Tools, Techniques, and Technologies. In Social Network Analytics for Contemporary Business Organizations (pp. 1-18). Hershey, PA: IGI Global.

Kadam, A., & Ayarekar, S. (2014). Impact of Social Media on Entrepreneurship and Entrepreneurial Performance: Special Reference to Small and Medium Scale Enterprises. *SIES Journal of Management*, *10*(1), 3–11.

Khajeheian, D. (2013). New Venture Creation in Social Media Platform; Towards a Framework for Media Entrepreneurship. Handbook of Social Media Management Value Chain and Business Models in Changing Media Markets, 125-142. doi:10.1007/978-3-642-28897-5_8

Khajeheian, D. (2013). New venture creation in social media platform; Towards a framework for media entrepreneurship. In *Handbook of social media management* (pp. 125–142). Berlin, Germany: Springer. doi:10.1007/978-3-642-28897-5_8

Kirzner, I. M. (1997). Entrepreneurial discovery and the competitive market process: An Austrian approach. *Journal of Economic Literature*, *35*(1), 60–85.

Laroche, M., Habibi, M. R., Richard, M. O., & Sankaranarayanan, R. (2012). The effects of social media based brand communities on brand community markers, value creation practices, brand trust and brand loyalty. *Computers in Human Behavior*, *28*(5), 1755–1767. doi:10.1016/j.chb.2012.04.016

Lin, J., Luo, Z., Cheng, X., & Li, L. (2019). Understanding the interplay of social commerce affordances and swift guanxi: An empirical study. *Information & Management*, *56*(2), 213–224. doi:10.1016/j.im.2018.05.009

Maina, A. (2018). 20 Popular Social Media Sites Right Now. Retrieved from https://smallbiztrends.com/2016/05/popular-social-media-sites.html

Mangold, W. G., & Faulds, D. J. (2009). Social media: The new hybrid element of the promotion mix. *Business Horizons*, *52*(4), 357–365. doi:10.1016/j.bushor.2009.03.002

Mehra, G. (2017). 105 Social Networks Worldwide. Retrieved from https://www.practicalecommerce.com/105-leading-social-networks-worldwide

Melissa, E., Hamidati, A., & Saraswati, M. S. (2013). Social Media Empowerment: How Social Media Helps to Boost Women Entrepreneurship in Indonesian Urban Areas. *The IAFOR Journal of Media, Communication and Film*, 1(1), pp. 77-90.

Naranjo-Valencia, J. C., Calderón-Hernández, G., Jiménez-Jiménez, D., & Sanz-Valle, R. (2018). Entrepreneurship and innovation: Evidence in Colombian SMEs. In Handbook of Research on Intrapreneurship and Organizational Sustainability in SMEs (pp. 294–316). Hershey, PA: IGI Global. doi:10.4018/978-1-5225-3543-0.ch014

Oke, D. F. (2013) The Effect of Social Network on women entrepreneurs in Nigeria: A case study of Ado-Ekiti Small scale Enterprise. *International Journal of Education and Research, 1*(11), pp. 1-14.

Oskam, I., Bossink, B., & de Man, A. P. (2018). The interaction between network ties and business modeling: Case studies of sustainability-oriented innovations. *Journal of Cleaner Production, 177*, 555–566. doi:10.1016/j.jclepro.2017.12.202

Park, J. Y., & Sung, C. S. (2017). Does Social Media Use Influence Entrepreneurial Opportunity? A Review of its Moderating Role. *Sustainability, 9*(1593), 1–16. doi:10.3390u9091593

Perju, A. (2015). Gender Differences in Modeling the Influence of Online Marketing Communication on Behavioral Intentions. *Procedia Economics and Finance, 27*, 567–573. doi:10.1016/S2212-5671(15)01034-5

Schumpeter, J. A. (1932). *The Theory of Economic Development*. London, UK: Transaction Publishers.

Shabbir, M. S., Ghazi, M. S., & Mehmood, A. R. (2016). Impact of Social Media Applications on Small Business Entrepreneurs. *Arabian Journal of Business and Management Review*6(203), pp. 1-3. doi:. doi:10.4172/2223-5833.1000203

Smith, P., & Taylor, J. (2004). Marketing Communications: An Integrated Approach. London, UK: Kogan Page.

Jagongo, A., & Kinyua, C. (2013). The Social Media and Entrepreneurship Growth (A New Business Communication Paradigm among SMEs in Nairobi). *International Journal of Humanities and Social Science, 3*(10), 213–227.

Tigo, M. (2012). Revisiting the Impact of Integrated Internet Marketing on Firms' Online Performance: European Evidences. *Procedia Technology, 5,* pp. 418-426.

Tosifyan, M., & Tosifyan, S. (2017). A Research on the effect of social media on tendency to entrepreneurship and business establishment (Case Study: Active Iranian Entrepreneurs in Social Media). *Italian Journal of Science & Engineering, 1*(1), pp. 43-48.

<unknown>Assaad, W., & Gómez, J. M. (2011). Social Network in marketing (social media marketing) opportunities and risks. International Journal of Managing Public Sector Information and Communication Technologies (IJMPICT), 2(1). Retrieved from http://www.seokursu.com.tr/social-network-in-marketing.pdf</eref>

<unknown>Statista. (2018). Leading social media platforms used by marketers worldwide as of January 2018. Retrieved from https://www.statista.com/statistics/259379/social-media-platforms used-by-marketers-worldwide/</eref>

<unknown>Upkere, C. L., Slabbert, A. D., & Upkere, W. I. (2014). Rising Trend in Social Media Usage by Women Entrepreneurs across the Globe to Unlock Their Potentials for Business Success Mediterranean Journal of Social Sciences, 5(10), 551–559.</jrn>

Vivakaran, M. V., & Maraimalai, N. (2016). Feminist pedagogy and social media: A study on their integration and effectiveness in training budding women entrepreneurs. *Gender and Education,* pp. 1-21. doi:10.1080/09540253.2016.1225008

Ward, S. (1974). Consumer Socialization. *The Journal of Consumer Research, 1*(2), 1–14. doi:10.1086/208584

Williams, L., & Cothrell, J. (2000). Four smart ways to run online communities. *Sloan Management Review, 41*, 81–91.

This research was previously published in the Handbook of Research on Managerial Practices and Disruptive Innovation in Asia; pages 194-209, copyright year 2020 by Business Science Reference (an imprint of IGI Global).

Chapter 94

Impact of Social Media Usage on Information Retrieval Among Undergraduate Students in Faculty of Management Sciences, University of Ilorin

Evelyn Olakitan Akinboro
University of Ilorin, Nigeria

Taylor Morenikeji Olayinka
University of Ilorin, Nigeria

ABSTRACT

The chapter examined the impact of social media on information retrieval among undergraduate students in Faculty of Management Science, University of Ilorin. It determined the social media network that undergraduate students are more exposed to for retrieving information, identifying the differences in undergraduate students' usage of social media network for information retrieval based on gender and age brackets, exploring preference for social media compared to other sources of information retrieval system available for students, exploring the types of information retrieved from social media network, and identifying the challenges faced by undergraduates in the use of social media networks. The population of the study was comprised of 3,634 students out of which a sample of 360 was chosen through stratified random technique. A self-designed questionnaire was used to collect data. Five research questions were developed and answered by the study. The findings revealed that undergraduate students' exposure to social media is very high.

DOI: 10.4018/978-1-6684-7123-4.ch094

BACKGROUND

The social media tools where students exposure is high is WhatsApp application compared to any other social media platform. Students prefer using social media platforms to retrieve information than using conventional resources like textbooks, journals, etc. There is a negligible difference between social media exposure level of Male gender and Female gender. Furthermore, the study revealed that undergraduates' level of exposure varies by age brackets while those within age bracket 21-25years have the highest level of exposure. The study also demonstrated that a higher percentage of students like using social media platforms to retrieve Information on the latest update of school activities and to gratify their need in entertainment. The major challenge faced by students is the high cost of access to social media platforms (subscription).

INTRODUCTION

Social media provides an easy way to receive feedback and communicate with peers, young adults attitudes of themselves can be affected by using social media networks (Pempek, Yermolayeva & Calvert 2009). Social media sites empower users to take an active role in their own socialization process and in constructing their own self-identity (Urista,2009). A personal profile is the way users present themselves; they can include as much information as desired about themselves, including posting pictures. Due to digital technology, users can show considerable information about themselves and their friends. This self-disclosure is a way to open up their own identities of how they want others to perceive them (Pempek et al., 2009). Intimate self-disclosures help produce greater intimacy in computer-mediated communication than in face-to-face contacts (Jiang, Bazarova, & Hancock, 2011). Producing an attractive personal profile for others to admire is a way to improve self-concept. It has been suggested that individuals partake in selective self-presentation on social media sites so they may appear to want to impress others (Jiang et al., 2011). This is especially true for college students as they self-disclose frequently during this exploratory period. In accordance with Arnett's theory, emerging adulthood (18-25 years old) is a time when there is a period of freedom and independence in a young person's life (Arnett, 2000). Self-disclosure is an identity challenge in emerging adulthood (Pempek et al., 2009). Self-disclosure helps by getting feedback from peers that helps develop a sense of self and strengthens existing relationships as well (Pempek et al., 2009). Many individuals use social network sites to feel popular, trying to add as many "friends" as possible so they appear to be more admired. Young adults reported an average of 358 Facebook friends (Pempek et al., 2009). Another study reported a mean of 200 Facebook friends, almost all of which they had met in person prior to the internet connection (West, Lewis, & Currie, 2009). According to Peter (2015), a direct relationship exists between Social media usage and the academic performance of students in universities. However the darker side within technological evolution has resulted in dilemmas such as the setback of real values of life especially among students who form the majority of users interacting through the use of social networking sites. Online social networking sites focus on building and reflecting social associations among people who share interests and or activities. With so many social networking sites displayed on the internet, students are tempted to abandon their homework and reading times in preference for chatting online with friends. Many students are now addicted to the online rave of the moment, with Facebook, Twitter etc. Today most youths and students possess Facebook accounts. The reason most of them perform badly in school might not be far- fetched. While many minds might be quick to blame the poor quality of teachers, they might have to think even harder, if they have not heard of the Facebook frenzy (Oche & Aminu 2010). Olubiyi (2012) noted that these days' students are so engrossed in the social media that they are almost 24 hours online. Even in classrooms and lecture theatres, it has been observed that some students are always busy pinging, going or Facebooking, while lectures are on. Times that ought to be channeled towards learning, academic research and innovating have been crushed by the passion for meeting new friends online, and most times busy discussing trivial issues.

Apart from the negative way of using social media by youths especially students in tertiary institutions, the platform can be used for information retrieval. Information has become the most significant source of our day-to-day life. Information available on internet may create some confusion among its users because of its diversity. Information leads to confirmation but when information is processed and internalized it becomes knowledge. Today, lots of information is available in print and non-print format thereby leading to information overload. Internet is one of the vital sources of information. Sometimes it becomes impossible for the users to understand the available information or they do not understand where to find it or they are unable to access the right information. These factors lead to their stress, delay in decision making, waste of time etc. Social networks are very popular these days, and it facilitates search and retrieval of information through internet. One of the best examples of information retrieval system (IRS) is library system where information is stored, processed, organized and retrieved on demand of its users. However, social media is now serving as an avenue for retrieving information. Availability of information is not synonymous to usage. Information can be available but not being accessed by users especially undergraduate students. There is a need to know whether students are accessing information on social media and how the available information has been impacting these students. Hence, the study will be undertaken on impact of Social media usage on information retrieval among undergraduate students in the University of Ilorin, Kwara State.

Everybody needs information, however the kind of information needed may differ. Advancement in technology has really advanced information retrieval. Information users now access information through various means. Information now resides everywhere including the 'cloud'. Most of the available sources of information on the web have social links on their sites as an alternative way of access to information. One would not question the incorporation of social links in most of these information providers because social media has turn to a "household concept". Everybody wants to be online! Many people, especially students in tertiary institutions make use of at least one social media platform. The benefit of the existing social media sites cannot be overestimated. Information materials for academic can be found in many, if not all, of these social media sites. Since most of the students in tertiary institutions are using social media, it is expected that the platform will go a long way in helping them to seek their information needs easily and as at when due. In University of Ilorin, it was observed closely that almost all students in use social media sites for different activities like for academic purpose, entertainment purpose, religious purpose, e.t.c.

However, the researchers have observed that despite the benefits of social media identified in the literature such as providing opportunities to connect with friends and loved ones, sharing academic information, collaboration with academic colleagues etc,; research that focus on the impact of social media on undergraduate students information retrieval seems to have been ignored. Not this alone research that examine use of social media and its impact on access to and retrieval of information particularly among the undergraduate students of the University of Ilorin, Nigeria is currently lacking. Most researchers have reviewed the various uses of social media networking site but majority of the researchers focused only on the usage and purpose of social media sites. These are gaps in knowledge that need to be filled. Hence, the study examined the impact of social media usage on information retrieval among undergraduate students in Faculty of Management science, University of Ilorin.

Objectives of the Study

The broad objective of this study is to examine the impact of social media usage on information retrieval among undergraduate students in Faculty of Management Science, University of Ilorin. The specific objectives are to:

1. determine the social media network that undergraduate students' in Faculty of Management science, University of Ilorin are more exposed to for retrieving information;
2. identify the differences in undergraduate students' usage of social media network for information retrieval based on gender and age brackets;
3. determine the students preference for social media compare to other sources of information retrieval system available to students in Faculty of Management Science, University of Ilorin;
4. Identify the types of information retrieved from social media network by undergraduates in Faculty of Management Science, University of Ilorin; and
5. identify the challenges faced by undergraduates in Faculty of Management science, University of Ilorin in the use of Social Media Networks to retrieve information.

Research Questions

In order to achieve the objectives of this study, the following research questions are formulated accordingly:

1. What social media are used to retrieve information by the undergraduate students in Faculty of Management science, University of Ilorin?
2. What differences exist in the Faculty of Management science, University of Ilorin undergraduate students' usage of social media network for information retrieval in terms of gender and age brackets?
3. What is the undergraduate students' in Faculty of Management science, University of Ilorin preference for social media platform to retrieve information compared to other sources of information retrieval system available?
4. What are the types of information retrieved by undergraduates in Faculty of Management science, University of Ilorin with the aid of social media networks?
5. What are the problems encountered by undergraduates in Faculty of Management science, University of Ilorin in the use of Social Media Networks to retrieve information for their respective information needs?

LITERATURE REVIEW

Concept of Social Media

Social media is a phenomenon that has been developing in a rapid pace. Different scholars have described in different ways, to Jacka & Scott (2011) there is no single recognized definition of social media. However, Drury (2008) defines social media as "online resources that people use to share content: video, photos, images, text, ideas, insight, humor, opinion, gossip, news". Safko & Brake (2008) further defined social media as "activities, practices, and behaviors among communities of people who gather online to share information, knowledge, and opinions using conversational media. Conventional media are Web-based applications that make possible for one to create and easily transmit content in the form of words, pictures, videos, and audios (Safko & Brake, 2008).

Lewis (2009) defines social media as the platforms that link people together in order to provide a means which will allow them to create and share content with others. According to Choi & Kang (2014), social media can be categorized into two: those (Facebook, Twitter, Pinterest, YouTube, Flikr) for social networking and those (Wikis, Blogs, Discussion Boards, Online Forums) for learning activities. Social media is that means that employs mobile and web based technology to create highly interactive platforms via which individuals and community share, co-create, discuss and modifies user generated content (Kietzmannn, 2012). Social networks are online services, platforms or sites that focus building and reflecting social relations among people, who, for example, share interests and activities. Social networking sites are websites that allow those who have account with them to communicate with a selected group of friends (Awake, 2011). According to Eke (2014), most of the social networks are web-based and provide means for their users to interact via the Internet, such as e-mail and instant messaging; social networks allow activities, events and interact within their individual networks. Social media, as defined by Bryer & Zavatarro (2011) are technologies that facilitate social interaction, make possible collaboration, and enable deliberation across stakeholders. These technologies now include blogs, wikis, media (audio, photo, video, text) sharing tools, networking platforms, and virtual worlds.

Alican & Saban (2013) defined the Social Networks as the web sites that provides people with an environment for creating profile with personal information, developing new friendships from all over the World, maintaining existing friendships in an online environments, sharing and commenting on something and organizing events. Parr (2010) defines social media as the use of electronic and Internet tools for the purpose of sharing and discussing information and experiences with other human beings in more efficient ways. Social Media Online (2011) defined social media as primarily internet-and mobile-based tools for sharing and discussing information by users. The term, according to Andreas and Michael (2010) refers to a group of Internet-based applications that build on the ideological and technological foundations of Web 2.0 and that allow the creation and exchange of user-generated content. Web 2.0 was coined by Darcy DiNucci in 1999 to describe interactive social websites which allow users to interact and collaborate with each other in a social media dialogue. Kietzmannn, Silverstre, McCarthy and Leylan (2012) describe social media as the platform that employs mobile and web based technology to create highly interactive platforms via which individuals and community share, co-create, discuss and modifies user generated content. Social media is a platform that facilitates information sharing and participation from users of the media in order to create and/or distribute the content (Steenkamp & Hyde-Clarke, 2014). These platforms have shifted the emphasis of Internet services from being consumption-based towards becoming more interactive and collaborative, thereby creating new opportunities for interaction between organizations and the public (Henderson & Bowley, 2010).

By contrast, the foundation of social media is based on user generated content (UGC), that is, various forms of media content created by internet users and available on the web based on Web 2.0 technology (Kaplan & Haenlein, 2010). Social media applications include blogs and micro blogs (logger & twitter), wikis (Wikipedia), social networking (e.g. Facebook, LinkedIn), multimedia sharing services (YouTube), content syndication (e.g. RSS feeds), podcasting and content tagging services (Hansen, Shneiderman, & Smith, 2010).

Categories of Social Media

Social media are classified based on the nature of their communities; which include social news, social measuring, micro blogging, video, sharing, photo sharing, professional networks, niche communities, social E-mail, comment communities, broadcasting communities, blog networks, product-based, networks, presentation sharing and review and recommendation sites (Jason, 2010).

According to Mayfield (2008), there are basically seven kinds of social media, including social networks, blogs, wikis, podcasts, forums, content communities and microblogging. In the same vein, Kaplan & Haenlein (2010) classified social media into six different classes as follows; collaborative project (Wikipedia); blogs and micro blogs (Twitter); content communities(Youtube); social networking site (Facebook. 2go, BB chat); virtual game world (world of war craft); and virtual second world (second life).

Types of Social Media Students Are Exposed to for Information Retrieval

Facebook

Facebook is the most popular social networking sites (Rainie, Smith, & Duggan, 2013), followed by Twitter (Brenner & Smith, 2013) and LinkedIn (Duggan & Brenner, 2012). Facebook allows users to set up a profile and post updates, links, photos, conversations, and the like. Christopher (2010) opined that some social networking websites such as Facebook, fall in the "general, category, they accommodate folks of all interest and backgrounds on this type of social networking websites. Members can after include their interest and then locate members with similar interests by searching for key words and key phrases. The main purpose of general social networking websites is to serve as a special platform where people can reunite with old friends; stay connected with current ones, and even make new acquaintances. Morseo, Sponcil & Gitimu (2007) reported that 88.5% recognized Facebook as their preferred social media site. Wang, Chen, & Liang (2011) reported that students spend roughly 100 minutes per day on Facebook. In 2007, 92% of college students reported that they had a Facebook account. By 2008, 99% of students had an account on Facebook (Wang, Chen, &Liang, 2011). Also, Williams & Merten (2008) found that university students are often obsessed with their Facebook and Twitter profile. A study by Pempek, Yermolayeva, &Calvert (2009) showed that students spend an average of 28 minutes a day on Facebook (p. 231). Student researchers from the Whitmore School of Economics and Business found that younger students tend to use Facebook more frequently than older students to keep in touch with friends from high school or from their home town (Pempek, Yermolayeva, & Calvert, 2009). Many individuals use social network sites to feel popular, trying to add as many "friends" as possible so they appear to be more admired. Young adults reported an average of 358 Facebook friends (Pempek, Yermolayeva, &

Calvert, 2009, p. 236). Quan-Haase & Young (2010) found that 82% of college students reported logging into Facebook several times a day.

Twitter

Twitter allows users to send out short messages or "tweets" about what they are doing or links to resources of interest. People can choose to "follow" selected users' tweets and they can retweet or repost someone's tweet for others to see. It is an online version of text-messaging with the capability of sending the same message to several thousand people all at once (Ezumah, 2013). As a social network, Twitter revolves around the principle of followers. When you choose to follow another Twitter user, his/her tweets appear in reverse chronological order on your main Twitter page (Olaniran, 2014).

Linkedin

Linkedin is targeted at professionals interested in professional networking. Each user sets up a profile similar to a resume and then can link to other people that they know. Having been created in 2003, LinkedIn is one of the oldest social networks. However, this particular site is relatively new to younger generations. Facebook, Twitter and Linkedin are being joined by a complete new line of competitors in the social media business. LinkedIn is a strictly professional site that focuses on business and professional relationships. Its mission statement attests to a commitment to "connect the world's professionals to make them more productive and successful" (LinkedIn, 2012). The social network platforms Snapchat, Instagram, Pinterest, and YouTube have become the new gateway for the expression for today's college generation.

MySpace

MySpace's founder, Tom Anderson, capitalized on a rumor that Friendster networks (social networking sites that helped people maintain their offline relationship online and provided a dating forum as well) might be asking for a fee. Andersen lured Friendster users to this new site with an offer for free membership. At the same time, the Indie-rock band from Los Angeles was expelled from Friendster for violation of some regulation and MySpace extended a welcoming hand to them as well. They found their new home on MySpace site (Boyd & Ellison, 2008; Newman, 2008). Certain features such as the ability to build one's front page and profile, advertising, a forum for interaction between bands and their fans, and complying with user-demands especially requests for personalizing pages including background designs, and uploading information links—were great advantages of and for MySpace (Boyd & Ellison, 2008). MySpace reached its peak in popularity when it attracted News Corp. to pay $580 million in 2005 for its acquisition (BusinessWeek, 2005). Ironically, as soon as News Corp. acquired MySpace (which was considered the summit of its existence), the site met a downward spiral in terms of popularity, revenue, and membership due to incidences of sexual predators and abusers. This was a serious issue that compelled Connecticut Attorney General, Richard Blumenthal to call for more stringent control and regulations on MySpace (Oser, 2006).

Snapchat

Snapchat is an application for iPhones, iPads and Android devices. It allows subscribers to send to other subscriber's photos that expire in one to ten seconds. There are an estimated 100 million daily active users of Snapchat, about 70% of whom are women (Smith, 2015). Wagner (2014) found that more than 77% of college students use Snapchat at least once per day. The most popular Snapchat use was for creativity (73%) followed by keeping in touch (27%). About one-fourth of the college student respondents (23%) reported that Snapchat is easier to use than texting (n.p.). Instagram. Instagram is an application that allows users to take pictures and videos and share them on a variety of social networking platforms. It is owned by Facebook.

Pinterest

Pinterest is a personalized media platform which allows registered users to "pin" and organize media content into collections called pin-boards. Users can also browse the content of others in their feed.

YouTube

Youtube is a video sharing website. It is owned by Google. Unregistered users can watch videos and registered users can upload videos.

Uses of Social Media by Undergraduate Students

Social networking sites have become excellent tools for education and can be used socially and collaboratively between learners and teachers as well as amongst students. Asabere (2012) notes that "current ICT trends are providing accessibility to online services such as social networks and this enable collaboration amongst students and contribute a lot to social learning activities. Students of tertiary institutions in Nigeria are keying into the limitless opportunities". Social media technologies provide to their user's adequate freedom of what they do with them (Wilson, 2012).

As social media platforms are many, so also their functions and uses are. Osatuyi (2013) elaborated social networks are classified based on how people use them. For instance, Social Networking Sites such as MySpace, Facebook are used to share and update message, Microblogs such as Twitter is used for short messages, Wikis are mainly used for educational and informational purposes, Blogs are usually personal or collaborative online publishing diary, while Online Forums are interactive space where participants discuss issues which are posted on a discussion board.As a communication platform, many undergraduate students use the Internet with its various applications such as social media like Facebook, Twitter, YouTube, etc. for different purposes. According to Adelabu (2011), social media is on daily basis creating new culture which is geared towards sharing information and being surprised by the experiences, knowledge, and voices of others. For undergraduate students, there are various reasons for the usage of social media, Gross (2004) noted that 'students use social networking sites not only for leisure and personal socialization but also as a platform for more meaningful and serious deliberations, and students are using social networking for making friends, sharing links, online learning, finding jobs to accomplish their economic, educational, political and social being. Bilandzic, Patriarche &Traudt (2012) introduced three main "Social Use of Media" as: interactivity, recognition, and participation. People use social media for either hard or soft issues or both. For instance, some people use social media to play online games, while others use it to negotiate, establish, maintain, and participate in a political and cultural issue. Therefore, the popularity, availability, and accessibility of social media technologies make their usage in almost every aspect of life. Osatuyi (2013) listed that, people use social networks to organize campaigns (political or non-political), create awareness, social interaction, sharing of information, marketing, healthcare activities. But the list of its usage goes beyond that. In institutions of learning, social media are used as tools for instructions, students' engagement, and peer review (Choi & Kang, 2014). In higher institutions in Nigeria, Asemah & Edegoh (2013) asserted that, many students are assumed to be using social networks.Tınmaz (2013) explained that todays' youth utilize social networks with very different purposes, such as establishing new friendships, keeping in touch with existing friends and being accessible all the time. According to Richter and Koch (2008), social networking sites provide users with the opportunities for identity management and for keeping in touch with other users.

Specifically, Minocha (2009) opines that social networking enhances a student's sense of community, sharing and collaboration brings an additional responsibility and workload, which some students find inflexible and rather "forced". For instance, Konetes and McKeague (2011) reported that students are using Facebook and other channels to develop their identities, beliefs and stances on various issues such as politics, religion, economy and works, as well as to pioneer and develop intimate relationships. Also, Gross (2004) noted that students use social networking sites not only for leisure and personal socialisation but also as a platform for more meaningful and serious deliberations, and students are using social networking for making friends, sharing links, online learning, finding jobs to accomplish their economic, educational, political and social being.According to Nicole (2007), students and teenagers have especially recognized these social media platforms to be able to contact their peers, share information, reinvent their personas and showcase their social live.

Social media according to Onuoha, Unegbu and Lasisi (2012) creates an avenue for undergraduates to network with one another irrespective of time or space. The introduction of Facebook, twitter and other digital media, according to Levine (2012), has opened up a whole new world of social interaction, and potential distraction in the office environment. Kim, Yoo-Lee and Sin (2011) in their study pointed out that as social media are gaining popularity, and some of them seem to be playing an important role as an information sources, it is crucial to understand what kinds of social media are used as information sources.

Tukru et al. (2013) reported that university students in Turkey use Facebook more for communicating with friends, getting information about people and events, entertainment and relaxing as well as messaging. Oluwatoyin (2011) stated that users of SNSs spend an average of two to six hours studying while non-users spent between eight and seventeen hours studying per week. Schulten (2000) opines that Student spend an average of 40 to 50 minutes a day surfing on Facebook. Many students find that they actually spend 3 to 4 minutes during each visit to check updates, making several visits a day and others spend 8 hours a day on the website (Rouis, Limayen & Sangari, 2011).

Preferred Social Media by Undergraduate Students

In the view of Ahsan & Chand (2012) the most favorite social networking sites are Facebook, Twitter, LinkedIn, WhatsApp among the lot. According to the study, about 87.5% of students of both genders have Facebook accounts and consume equal time on the internet. The study observed further that male students have a lot of Facebook companions but female students consume much of their time on Facebook. Kanagarathiam (2014) undertook a study on the impact of social networking sites on the academic performance of adolescents in Coimbatore City India, and disclosed that students used Facebook, Skype, WhatsApp and YouTube than any other sites. In the study, Google+ and LinkedIn were reported as the least used sites among the participants. Mazman & Usluel (2010), indicated that Facebook is the popular social-networking site due to its educational usefulness, information sharing, its structure and multiple uses. In the view of Lenhart,A., Purcell, K.,Smith, A., & Zickuhr, K. (2010) females are more likely than males to have a personal profiles on Facebook, but males are more likely than females to sustain a profile on LinkedIn. According to Moran, Seaman, & Tinti-Kane (2012), YouTube is the most frequently used social media tool in the classroom. Students can watch videos, answer questions and discuss content and additionally, create videos to share with others.

Another survey found that the users of Facebook were unlikely to look for information through their network on Facebook. However, they still thought that useful information was given to them by that site (Lampe, et al., 2012). It showed that more information was encountered than sought (Lampe, et al., 2012). Another study showed that social networking was about interaction with friends and not news (Wilson, T., 2012). Sharing of news was found to be more on Twitter. The motivations for the sharing three kinds of information on Twitter were investigated. These were posts from friends, breaking news and information related to the intrinsic use of the user. Breaking news was found to be the most popular information shared (Xu, et al., 2012). Twitter was also found to be a significant source of news at the times of political or natural disasters well as crisis (Mansour, 2012). It was also revealed that Twitter had a powerful ability to collect information from the scenes of disaster and visualizing it for decision making on relief work. Disaster relief information could also be broadcast using Twitter (Gao, 2012).

Concept of Information Retrieval

Information resources as a variable play a role in the way libraries are utilized. Information resources are not only acquired but organized in such a way they can be easily accessed and retrieved by users. Information retrieval is concerned with the exploitation and extraction of information and other contents of documents from different information sources (Akanwa & Udo-Anyanwu, 2017). Retrieval tools are crucial for retrieving information for educational outcomes. Information retrieval tools according to Edom (2012) are the simple mechanisms or apparatuses that aid the library user to locate, retrieve and use the needed documents from the library or information from a book or document. He further outlined the tools to include; bibliographies, indexes and abstracts, catalogues, computer filing or websites, subject index, title index, directories, OPAC, CD-ROMS, online databases, internet search engines, etc. Presently, there are various tools at students' disposal to aid them in access the information they need. In addition, Nnadozie (2007) listed the library information retrieval tools to include: reading list, index, abstract, library catalogue, search engine, OPAC, bibliography, shelf guides, web-based information retrieval systems which are presently, at students' disposal to aid them in accessing information.

Influence of Gender in the Use of Social Media

A study on the gender of users of social networking sites appears to have some impact on the online information behaviour. Globally, male students tend to use internet sources more frequently than females (Li & Kirkup, 2007). In a similar study by Nadkarni &Hofmann, (2012) concerning media use, social networking sites emerge to be used by female rather than male students.

A study carried out by Raacke & Bonds-Raacke (2008) indicated that although females and males are both likely to have SNS accounts, the purposes for creating the accounts may vary based on gender. For females, social networking sites are primarily to reinforce pre-existing friendships; for males, the networks also offer a way for sexual activities and making new friends (Raacke & Bonds-Raacke, 2008).

Giles & Price (2008) revealed that females use social media for chatting and downloading music. Rafferty (2009) opined that the primary purposes female use social networks platform are to post pictures of themselves and also to discuss sex issues on these public fora. Merten & Williams (2009) reported that females are more likely to share their personal information on SNSs which is a public platform than their male counterparts. Merten & Williams (2009) emphasized that about 55% of females shared their private issues such as depression, anxiety, and relationship problems on SNSs, while 15% of males shared any personal information besides their hobbies, interests, and friendships. According to Boneva et al., (2001) sending and receiving emails with friends and family was one of the dominant online activities for females, while males tended to spend more time on reading online news, engaging in task-oriented work, or visiting websites of governmental departments (Na, 2002).

Challenges in the Use of Social Media for Information Retrieval

Farkus, et al (2012) opined that some of the challenges associated with use of social media stem from the risks inherent in student internet usage. They went on to argue that internet exposes students to inappropriate material, unwanted adult interactions, and bullying from peers. Similar remarks were made by Romero-Frías & Montaño (2012) that, Web 2.0 is also a source of concern regarding issues such as, privacy, authorship and ownership rights, digital divide in the classroom or time management issues. Additionally, Benito-Ruiz (2009) cited information overload as another challenge whereas, Keen (2007), lamented quality of content as a major concern. Since social networking sites are part of Web 2 technologies the challenges raised here are also true of social networking sites.

Generally, Oluwalanu et al (2014) identified the following as some of the challenges in the use of social media in Nigeria.

- **Lack of Basic Amenities:** Nigeria, like many Third World countries constantly battle outage of power across the country so much that even when the learner has the means to access information through these social sites, the unavailability of power supply has always had a debilitating effect on the desire to source for information on the internet.
- **Lack of Conducive Environment**: Again, because there are no constant power supply, learners may not have access to the site as and at when due; and when they do they may be doing so at internet cafe which may not be conducive for learning purpose. Access to computers: despite the prevalence of computers in the Nigerian market, not many Nigerians have access to computers, and when they do it is but for a few working hours except for few who have laptops and modems at home.

RELATED STUDIES

Baym, Zhang, & Lin (2004) studied social interactions of college students across all media. Their results indicated that 64% still prefer face-to-face interaction, 18.4% prefer the telephone, and only 16.1% prefer the internet for making social contacts. The internet interactions reported showed that e-mail was by far the most dominant form of contact, followed by chat and instant-messaging (Baym et al., 2004). Of the 51 participants in the study, 49 reported conducting their social life contacts through at least two, and often three, methods on any given day (Baym et al., 2004). Similarly, one study reported that over 27% of young adults used a social networking site every day in 2009 (Lenhart, Purcell, Smith, & Zickuhr, 2010).

Idubor (2015) investigated social media usage and addiction levels among undergraduates in University of Ibadan, Nigeria. The study revealed that majority of the respondents attested to making friends 651 (78.2%), getting news 566 (67.9%), communication 554 (66.5%) and online learning 450 (54.0%) as the major purposes for which they make use of social media networks. This implies that undergraduate students in University of Ibadan make use of social media network mainly for the purposes of making friends, getting news, communication and online learning.

Asemah & Edegoh (2013) examined the influence of social media on the academic performance of the undergraduate students of Kogi State University. The rationale behind the study is to find out whether the exposure of the students to social media has effect on their academic performance. The survey research method was adopted, employing the questionnaire as an instrument of data collection. The findings show that undergraduate students of Kogi State University, Anyigba, Nigeria, have access to social media and that their exposure to social media is to a very great extent. Findings also showed that exposure to social media has effect on the students and that the effect is negative. Findings also showed that Facebook is the most used social media by undergraduate students of Kogi State University. Based on the findings, the paper concludes that exposure to social media by the undergraduate students of Kogi State University has negative effect on their academic performance. Eke, Omekwu and Odoh (2014) in their study on the use of social networking sites among the undergraduate students of University of Nigeria, Nsukka. They found out that those students use social media for communicating with friends, online learning, finding friends online, academic purpose etc. Khan (2010) carried out a study on the impact of social networking websites on students. The study sampled 168 participants and out of this number, 101 were males, while 67 were females. Findings of the study reported that majority of male students use social networking sites than their female counterpart and their purpose is for searching knowledge.

According to Lenhart et al., (2010), about 57% of social network users are 18-29 years old and have personal profiles on multiple social media websites. In a study by Pempek, Yermolayeva, & Calvert (2009), the amount of time spent daily on social network sites varied greatly. However, an analysis of the data indicated most participants spent approximately thirty minutes a day socializing, mostly during the evening hours between 9p.m to 12a.m students spent an average of forty seven minutes a day on Facebook. More than 50% of college students go on social networking sites several times a day (Sheldon, 2008).A study undertook by Lin & Subrahmanyam (2007) reported that males have been online more than their female's counterparts in the past decades because of earlier forms of technology such as video or computer games. Thompson & Lougheed (2012), found that more females are "heavy users" of Facebook and that they spend more than 1 hour a day on the site than their male counterparts. According to Lenhart, Purcell, Smith, & Zickuhr (2010), 72% of all college students have a social media profile with 45% of college students using a social media site at least once a day. In the study of Sheldon (2008) about 50% of college students go on a social networking site several times a day.

Shen and Khalifa (2010) carried out a study on gender differences in relation to Facebook among Arabic students. The study found that Arabic females spend fewer hours on Facebook than their male's counterparts as the females consider too much time on Facebook as time wasting. Budden, Anthony, Budden, and Jones (2007), carried out a survey study using 272 undergraduate and graduate students. The research found that females spent more time on social networking sites such as Facebook and MySpace than males, though, these differences were not found to be statistically significant. In a similar study by Foregger (2008) it came out that female freshmen and female juniors spent most of their time on Facebook, while male juniors and male seniors spent lesser amount of time on the site.

Ndaku (2013) investigated the impact of social media on students' academic performance. The aim of the study was to analyze the impact of social media on the student's academic performance Respondents were drawn from the University of Abuja, using the simple random sampling technique and purposive sampling. Four research questions guided the study. Research findings showed that a great number of students in University of Abuja, had access to the internet. To this end, the researcher recommended that sites should be created for educational purposes as well. This is to create a balance between social networking and academic activities of students to avoid setbacks in the academic performance of the students.

From the above studies it could be articulated that modern technology in correspondence undoubtedly has transformed the whole world into a "Worldwide Village". Be that as it may, modernization like two sides of a coin, carry with it both the negative and positive sides. This implies that although social media is a very good tool that improve educational upbringing of students if used appropriately, it also has a negative aspect if students over indulge themselves to it. Social networking sites are considered to play an active role in younger generation's daily lives (Lenhart, 2009), as most of the active users are students of tertiary institutions. No wonder, Oblinger & Oblinger (2005) called them 'the most wired and connected generation in human history', 'Digital Natives', and 'the Net Generation'. Against this backdrop, The rapid growth of this technology has improved and enabled collaborative and learning activities especially because of its high level of interactivity, accessibility and affordability. However, exposure and use of these networks tend to have both positive and negative implications on the student. David, Helou and Rahim (2012) buttressed this in their assertion emanating from their findings that "as a result of more time being dedicated to the use of social networking sites for non-academic usage and less time to academic usage by students, it tells considerably on what becomes their academic output". In view of this, the use of social networking sites has raised dust among researchers. Some see it as distraction to learning for the student as it involves multitasking, while others attest to the potentials of Social networking sites for learning. There are also those who argue that young adult learners view and use Social networking sites as platforms for socializing more than learning. Burke (2010) conducted a study on social network activity and social well-being and revealed that females spend more time on social network sites and use them more actively than their male's counterparts. The study of Tufekci (2008) confirmed that majority of the females were four to five times more likely than males to use social networking sites.

The reviewed literature has shown the importance and the collaborative usage of social media among undergraduate students. Specifically, the reviewed studies showed that social media are primarily used by undergraduate for academic related activities. The reviewed literature also showed that there is a great usage of social media among undergraduate students with preference for Facebook coupled with heavy usage among the male students compare to female.

More so, the reviewed literature showed that social media can have both negative and positive effect on the academic performance of undergraduate students; however, undergraduate students are recommended to use the platform for the benefits of their academics. Information overload coupled with information retrieval skill are found to be the major challenges of using social media for information retrieval. To the best of the knowledge of the researchers, there is dearth of literature on the impact of social media on information retrieval among undergraduate students. It is on this note that this study sough to investigate the impact of social media on information retrieval among undergraduate students of the Faculty of Management Sciences, University of Ilorin.

METHODOLOGY

Research Design

The research design adopted for this study was survey method. This method was the most appropriate for the study because it involves gathering data on a target population. Ifidon and Ifidon (2007) posited that survey research gathers data from a population in order to determine the status of that population with respect to one or more variables. However, it is characterized by selecting sample from a population and the findings obtained can be used in the generalization of the population. It is believed to be the best research type to get facts about social media usage for information retrieval by undergraduates in University of Ilorin.

Population of the Study

The target population in this research is all the full time undergraduate students in the Faculty of Management Sciences, University of Ilorin in 2017/2018 academic session. Faculty of Management Sciences comprises of six departments, with population indicated in Table 1.

Table 1. Population of the study

S	Name of Department	Population
1	Accounting	819
2	Finance	847
3	Business Administration	557
4	Marketing	450
5	Industrial relations and Personal management	553
	Public Administration	550
	TOTAL	3,634

Source: Academic planning office unilorin (2018)

The total population (**3,634**) comprised undergraduate full time students (COMSIT, 2018).

Sampling and Sample Size

The sampling technique adopted in this study is simple random sampling and stratified random sampling. Simple random sampling is considered suitable for this study because it gave respondents equal chance of being part of the study. Sampling and sample size are crucial issues in quantitative research. This is to enable statistically based generalizations from the study results to the entire population.To generalize in this way, it is essential that the sampling method used and the sample size is appropriate, such that the results are representative, and that the statistics can discern associations or differences within the results of a study. Sample represents a smaller group of the elements or members, drawn through some definite procedure from a specified population. In order to determine the required sample for the population,

Slovin's formula was used to calculate the sample size for the population (3,634). The sample size for this research is 360 going by:

Slovin's formula, where:

n= Number of sample size
N= Total population size
e= Acceptable error value/tolerance

(Error of tolerance 95%=0.05)

$n=N \div (1+Ne^2)$

$n=3,634 \div (1+3,634 \times 0.05 \times 0.05) = 360$. (See table 2)

Table 2. Population and sample size selection

S/N	Name of Department	Population	Sample
1	Accounting	819	60
2	Finance	847	60
3	Business Administration	557	60
4	Marketing	450	60
5	Industrial relations and Personal management	553	60
6	Public Administration	550	60
	Total	**3,634**	**360**

A total of 360 questionnaires were administered to the six department in faculty of management science (60 questionnaire per department).

Source: Academic planning office unilorin (2018)

The total population (3,634) comprised undergraduate full time students (COMSIT, 2018).

Instrument(s) for Data Collection

A structurally designed questionnaire was used for the collection of data in this study. The instrument was designed to reflect the purpose of the study. The choice of questionnaire for the collection of data in this study was based on the fact that most related studies reviewed in chapter two adopted the use of questionnaire for the collection of data. The instrument comprised of sections A and B. Section A required the respondents" bio-data information including name, gender, age, and education level. Section B contained the items based on the purpose of the study. A check list response format was used for the items. This consisted of Yes (2) and No (1) response format.

Procedure for Data Collection

The questionnaire was administered to the undergraduate students in Faculty of Management Sciences, University of Ilorin. The administration of questionnaire to respondents was done within a period of five days (9th of July 2018 to 13th of July 2018).

Validity and Reliability of the Instrument(s)

To ensure the validity of the questionnaire used in this study, lecturers from the department of Library and Information Science, University of Ilorin, reviewed the questionnaire. The advice and suggestions given by these lecturers led to the modification of the items in the questionnaire. All the items in the instrument were judged to be relevant to what is being measured thereby ensuring both the content and face validity of the instrument. The questionnaire was subjected to pilot test. Split half method of reliability was used in order to establish that the data is consistent, stable and reliable. Reliability of the instrument was determined by calculating the Cronbach's alpha coefficient. According to Ary et al. (2006), an instrument must have a Cronbach's Alpha Value of 0.7 or above to be considered to have adequate internal consistency and reliable for use with a given population. The items on the questionnaire structured for this study had an average Cronbach's value of 0.766 for the all the items on the questionnaire (excluding demographics). This means that the research instrument (questionnaire), have relatively good internal consistency. According to Warmbrod (2001), if Cronbach's Alpha is greater than 0.7, the instrument is good and it is reliable. Based on B the alpha coefficient value of this instrument is 0.746 (Cronbach's Alpha), the instrument can be adopted repeatedly.

Data Analysis Technique

Descriptive statistics is the major method adopted in the course of analyzing the data gathered through the administration of Questionnaire. Data collected were analyzed using frequency counts and percentages for variables such as age and gender, level or year of study and department. Questionnaire was used to gather data from respondent. This Questionnaire was generated from the research questions which include section A and B. Section A requires the respondents' bio-data information including name, gender, age, and education level. Section B contained items based on the purpose of the study. Descriptive and inferential statistics are the major methods adopted in the course of analyzing the data gathered.

Ethical Considerations

In order to get quality research work, some research ethics are considered in the course of study. The researchers give priority to honesty, confidentiality and informed consent. Also, that none of the copyright law is violated. Every work are cited and referenced accordingly. None of the reviewed literature is plagiarized. All works used are acknowledged.

RESULTS AND DISCUSSION

This section presents the analysis of data gathered from the respondents in this study which focused on "Impact of Social Media Usage on information retrieval among Undergraduate Students in University of Ilorin". The data was gathered using a self-administered face-to-face questionnaire to Undergraduate students in Faculty of Management Science, University of Ilorin.

Data Analysis

Demographics of Respondents

All the respondents for this study vary by different demographic characteristics. Their varying demographic characteristics were based on department, gender, academic level, and age brackets (See Table 4). In faculty of Management Science where the data was gathered, the departments surveyed were department of Accounting, Business Administration, Finance, Public Administration, Marketing and departments of Industrial Relations and Personnel Management (IRPM). Responses rate from each of this department are shown in Table 3.

Table 3. Distribution of respondents by departments

Departments	Frequency	Percent (%)
1. Accounting	59	16.7
2. Business Administration	59	16.7
3. Finance	60	17.0
4. Public Administration	59	16.7
5. Marketing	58	16.4
6. IRPM	58	16.4
TOTAL	353	100.0

Source: Author's survey, 2018

Out of 353 respondents, 59 of them each are from the departments of Accounting, Business Administration and Public Admin with each representing 16.71% of the total respondents. Also 60 of the respondents which represents 17.0% of the total respondents are from department of Finance while frequencies of 58 each which 16.43% of the total respondents are from the department of IRPM and Marketing. Apart from departments, the respondents have specific demographics. Table 4 shows the demographics of the respondents in respect to gender, academic level and age bracket. Data gathered in these categories are shown in Table 4.

As shown in Table 4, responses from Male gender have frequency of 170 which represents 48.2% of the total population while responses from Female gender have frequency of 183 representing 51.8% of the total population. In terms of academic level, 66 students representing 18.8% of the respondents are 100Level students while 115 of them representing 32.6% of the total respondents are from 200Level. In the same category, there are 77 respondents from 300Level which represents 21.8% of the total respondents;

while those from 400Level have a frequency of 95 representing 26.9% of the total respondents. In the age bracket category, respondents 16-20years of age have a frequency of 126 representing 35.7% of the total sampled while between 21-25years has a frequency of 195 representing 55.2% of total respondents. Also, sampled undergraduates between ages 26-30years are 23 in number which represents 6.5% of the total sampled while only 1 respondents representing 0.3% of the total sampled is between 31-35years and 8 of them above 35years representing 2.3% of the total respondents. These demographics mean that there are more female respondents than the female respondents although with just 3.6% difference. Most of the respondents are from 200Level while majority of the respondents are from ages16-25years.

Table 4. Demographics of respondents

Demographic Variables		Frequency	Percent (%)
Gender	Male	170	48.2
	Female	183	51.8
	Total	**353**	**100%**
Academic Level	100 Level	66	18.7
	200 Level	115	32.6
	300 Level	77	21.8
	400 Level	95	26.9
	Total	**353**	**100%**
Age Bracket	16-20 years	126	35.7
	21-25 years	195	55.2
	26-30 years	23	6.5
	31-35 years	1	.3
	Above 35 years	8	2.3
	Total	**353**	**100%**

Source: Author's survey, 2018

Exposure of Respondents to Social Media

Table 5 shows various existing social media networks. The exposure of respondents was measured using some specified social media platforms. The social media platform specified was WhatsApp, Facebook, Twitter, YouTube, Instagram, LinkedIn, Skype and Blogs. Respondents' level of exposure was measured using Friedman's Mean Rankings.

The rankings of respondents based on their level of exposure are arranged in shown in Table 5 (arranged in descending order). From the results, WhatsApp has the highest mean rank followed by Facebook (6.59), Instagram (6.52), Twitter (6.36), Blogs (6.25), YouTube (5.96), LinkedIn (4.88), followed by Skype which has the lowest mean ranking of 4.66. This result means that undergraduate are more exposed to WhatsApp than any other social media platform.

Table 5. Distribution of respondents based on exposure to social media

Social Media Platforms	YES		NO		Mean Rank
	Freq.	Perc. (%)	Freq.	Perc. (%)	
1. WhatsApp	349	98.9	4	1.1	**7.84**
2. Facebook	269	76.2	84	23.8	**6.59**
3. Instagram	264	74.8	89	25.2	**6.52**
4. Twitter	254	72.0	99	28.0	**6.36**
5. Blogs	247	70.0	106	30.0	**6.25**
6. YouTube	228	64.6	125	35.4	**5.96**
7. LinkedIn	159	45.0	194	55.0	**4.88**
8. Skype	145	41.1	208	58.9	**4.66**

Note: No other social media platform(s) was indicated apart from the ones specified

Source: Author's survey, 2018

Differences in Respondents' Social Media Usage for Information Retrieval Based on Gender

The differences between respondents' exposure to social media based on gender are shown in Table 6 Mean of each gender (Male and Female) are compared with different social media platforms used for information retrieval by undergraduates in the faculty of management science, university of Ilorin.

Table 6. Mean differences between social media usage and genders (Male and Female)

Social Media Platforms	Male			Female		
	Mean	N	Std. Dev	Mean	N	Std. Dev
WhatsApp	**.98**	170	.152	**1.00**	183	.000
Facebook	**.84**	170	.367	**.69**	183	.464
Twitter	**.72**	170	.449	**.72**	183	.452
YouTube	**.59**	170	.493	**.69**	183	.462
Instagram	**.63**	170	.484	**.86**	183	.350
LinkedIn	**.56**	170	.497	**.34**	183	.476
Skype	**.44**	170	.498	**.38**	183	.487
Blogs	**.71**	170	.454	**.69**	183	.464

Source: Author's survey, 2018

In Table 6, Male respondents who use WhatsApp have a mean value of 0.98 while Female respondents using WhatsApp have a mean value of 1.00. Male gender using Facebook have mean of 0.84 while female gender have mean of 0.69. There are equal mean values of 0.72 each for those that use Twitter by both genders. YouTube users have 0.59 mean values for male gender and 0.69 for female gender. For Instagram, 0.63 and 0.86 mean values were recorded for Male and Female gender respectively. There is 0.56 mean values for LinkedIn users by Male genders while there are 0.34 mean value for female gender users. Subsequently, Skype users have 0.44 and 0.38 mean values for Male and Female genders respectively while Blogs users have 0.71 mean for Male gender and 0.69 mean for female gender. These results imply that there is just a slight difference in social media usage between Male and Female gender in the faculty of management science, university of Ilorin.

Preference for Social Media Compared to Other Information Retrieval System

Social media platforms are greatly used by the respondents as a result of their high exposure to most of the platforms. Since other information retrieval exists apart from social media, respondents preferences for other social media platforms was measured using Friedman's Test as shown in Table 7. The Mean rankings in the test were used to measure the degree of respondents' preference. The Table only shows the frequency of those that "prefer" social media networks than other information retrieval systems out of the 353 respondents.

Table 7. Social Media Preference of respondents compared to other information retrieval systems N=353

Social Media Preferred	Frequency	Mean Rank
1. WhatsApp	342	7.82
2. Facebook	258	6.51
3. Twitter	240	6.23
4. YouTube	237	6.18
5. Instagram	235	6.15
6. Blogs	232	6.10
7. LinkedIn	165	5.06
8. Skype	127	4.47

Note: No other social media platform(s) was preferred apart from the ones specified
Source: Author's survey, 2018

Table 7 shows the descending order of preference of respondents with social media platform than other information retrieval systems. From the results, WhatsApp has the highest mean rank of 7.82 followed by Facebook (6.51), Twitter (6.23), YouTube (6.18), Instagram (6.15), Blogs (6.10), followed by Skype which has the lowest mean ranking of 4.47. This result indicates that undergraduate students surveyed preferred all the specified social media platforms than other retrieval systems except for Skype which has a low Mean Ranking.

Types of Information Retrieved Through Social Media

It has been established that the respondents prefer using social media to retrieve information than other information retrieval systems. The type of information retrieved through social media networks by these respondents are shown in Table 8. Only the frequencies of those that agreed to the statements are shown in Table 8. The mean values of each type of information are also shown in the Table 8 which serves as a determinant for acceptance or rejection of the statements used to measure the type of information they (respondents) preferred

From Table 8, 345 with a mean value of 0.98 retrieved Information about the latest update on school activities; 306 of the total respondents with 0.87 mean value retrieve information on courses undertaken; while 269 of them having 0.67 mean value make use of the social media to broaden their horizon. In the same vein, 248 of them with 0.70 Mean value use it to acquire new skills; 281 with 0.80 mean use it for clarification while 213 of them having 0.60 mean use it to know more about language, ethics and values. Also, 268 of the total respondents with a mean value of 0.76 use it to know the latest trends in the media while 332 of them with 0.94 mean value use it for entertainment and 217 of them with a mean value of 0.61 use it to retrieve information on Relationship and Marriage. Also in Table 8, it was gathered that 207 of the undergraduate student sampled with a mean values of 0.59 search information related to politics on social media while 241 of them with 0.68 Mean value use it for Health; and 253 of them having 0.72 use it for Job purposes. For Agriculture related information, 196 respondents with a mean value of 0.56 indicated that they use it for that purpose while 234 with a mean value of 0.66 use it to retrieve information about latest technology 221 of the total respondents use it for retrieving information relating to Religion with a Mean value of 0.63.

Table 8. Distribution of respondents based on Types of Information Retrieved through Social Media

Statements	Freq.	X	Decision
1. Information about the latest update on school activities	345	0.98	Accepted
2. Information related to one of the courses undertaken in the department	306	0.87	Accepted
3. Information to broaden my horizon	269	0.67	Accepted
4. Information on how to acquire new skills	248	0.70	Accepted
5. Information for more clarifications of things taught in class	281	0.80	Accepted
6. Information about language, ethics and values	213	0.60	Accepted
7. Information about latest trends on social media	268	0.76	Accepted
8. Information related to entertainment	332	0.94	Accepted
9. Information on relationship and marriage	217	0.61	Accepted
10. Information about politics	207	0.59	Accepted
11. Information about health	241	0.68	Accepted
12. Information related to job	253	0.72	Accepted
13. Information related to agriculture	196	0.56	Accepted
14. Information about the latest technology	234	0.66	Accepted
15. Information on religion	221	0.63	Accepted

Note: No other types of information was indicated order than the specified ones
Source: Author's survey, 2018

Challenges Faced in the Use of Social Media Networks for Information Retrieval

Respondents' high exposure and preference for social media networks are not without challenges. The challenges faced by the surveyed undergraduate students in the faculty of management science are shown in Table 9.

Table 9. Challenges faced in the use of social media networks for information retrieval

Statements	Yes		No		Remark
	Freq.	Perc.(%)	Freq.	Perc.(%)	
1. Information over load (too much of information on social media networks)	243	68.8	110	31.2	High
2. Distraction in the course of retrieving information	240	68.0	113	32.0	High
3. Existence of information that is not authentic	248	70.3	105	29.7	Very High
4. Existence 5. of plagiarism on some of the retrieved information	241	68.3	112	31.7	High
6. Source credibility is lacking in some of the information available on social media networks	213	60.3	140	39.7	High
7. Digital divide i.e. technology has created gap between those that know about technology and those that do not know	192	54.4	161	45.6	Moderate
8. Confidentiality is a big issue	222	62.9	131	37.1	High
9. High cost of access to the social media	291	82.4	62	17.6	Very High

Note: No other types of information was indicated order than the specified ones
Source: Author's survey, 2018

As shown in Table 9 challenges faced varied and the remarks were given based on the scale of "very high", "High" and "Moderate" in order to have a general overview of the weight of each challenge. It was gathered that 243 representing 68.8% of the respondents indicated that *information overload* is a challenge while 240 of them covering 68.0% total sampled stated that *Distraction* is a challenge and 248 of them representing 70.3% stated that *the existence of information that is not authentic in social media* is also a challenge while 241 of them (68.3%) stated that existence of *plagiarism* in some retrieved information through social media is a challenge. Subsequently, 213 respondents representing 68.3% of the total respondents stated that *source credibility is lacking* in some information materials available on social media while 192 of them (54.4%) believe that digital divide is a challenge. It was also gathered that 222 respondents representing 62.9% of the respondents indicates confidentiality as an issue while 291 of them (82.5%) indicates high cost of access to social media as a challenge. From the results, it can be deduced that the challenges highly faced by the respondents in the use of social media for retrieving information are cost of accessing social media and inauthentic information on the social media.

Discussion of Findings

All the departments in the faculty of Management science were almost evenly represented based on the data collected. The findings of the study are dominated by more female gender, and more of them are in 200Level. More of the responses of the analyzed data were from those within the age of 21-25years. It is assumed that any students in this age category is mature enough to give valid answer to the center focus of this research project. It was found that undergraduate students in the faculty of Management Science are well exposed to various social media networks. Perhaps this was as a result of the assertion of Boyd (2007) who stated that Social networking sites provide an outlet for teens to express themselves in their own unique ways. Almost all of them (98.9%) are exposed to WhatsApp (See Table 6). This is not surprising because youths of this present age are very exposed to WhatsApp and WhatsApp is allows for expressiveness which was indicate by Boyd (2007).. Apart from WhatsApp, undergraduate students studied are also very exposed to Facebook, Twitter, YouTube, Instagram and Blogs. Meanwhile, more than half of the respondents are not aware about LinkedIn and Skype. Findings of this study also showed that there is just a slight difference between undergraduates' social media exposure and gender (See Table 5). The difference in the exposure level of Male gender to female gender is negligible. In other words, there is no significant difference between the level of exposure by male gender and level of exposure by female gender. This is similar to the findings of Perin (2015) that women and men use social media at similar rates.

To a very large extent, majority of the respondents prefer to use social media to retrieve needed information than other information retrieval systems. However, their rate of preference (see Table 7) is closely related to their level of exposure to social media (See Table 6). This means that their preference for social media was greatly influenced by their level of exposure and it may also be vice versa. The Undergraduate Students studied make use of social media to retrieve Information about the latest update on school activities; subject undertaken; broadening of horizon; acquiring of new skills; clarification; learning of language, ethics and values; following latest trends in the media; entertainment; information on Relationship and Marriage; Politics; Health; Job Search; Agriculture; Technology; and Religion. In all, the three main types of information mostly retrieved online are information based on the assignment given in class; Entertainment; and subject undertaken in the department respectively.

Despite the exposure, preference and gratification of social media by the undergraduates studied, it was gathered that there are some challenges they faced in the course of retrieving information through social media platforms. Some of the challenges they faced include information overload, distraction, plagiarized materials, source credibility problem, digital divide, confidentiality and high cost of access to social media platforms. From all these challenges, high cost of access to social media platforms is the major challenge indicated by almost all the surveyed undergraduate students.

CONCLUSION

This study provides findings that can inform future researcher, Lecturers, scholars, family care agencies, educational institutions, and social work agencies on the Social Media Usage for the Retrieval of Information among Undergraduate Students in University of Ilorin.

Students in the Faculty of Management Science, University of Ilorin are very exposed to social media. They also prefer social media than the conventional way of getting information. Hence, their preference level is a function of their level of exposure. This make social media network to be greatly used among the undergraduate students for the retrieval of information.

RECOMMENDATIONS

Since there were shortcomings in the areas of study and based on the research focus, there is a need to suggest ways by which the shortcomings can be resolved. Therefore, the following recommendations were proffered based on the findings of this study:

1. Students should not have a bias preference for social media platforms than the conventional sources of information like textbooks and journals because the conventional sources of information had been adjudged to contain more quality information than the ones on the social media platforms.
2. The management of the institution should endeavor to put in place strong Internet connectivity for her students in order to have access to social media since high cost of subscription is a challenge to these students.
3. Students should control their high exposure to social media in order to prevent them from being addicted to social media networks

REFERENCES

Adelabu, O. (2011). The role of social media in democratic mobilization in Nigeria. In *Media, terrorism and political communication in a multicultural environment conference proceedings*.

Ahsan, U., & Chand, S. (2012). The pattern of facebook usage and its impact on academic performance of university students: A gender based comparison. *Bulletin of Education and Research, 34*(2), 19–28.

Alican, C., & Saban, A. (2013). Ortaokul ve lisede öğrencim gören öğrencilerin sosyal medya kullanımına ilişkin tutumları: Ürgüp Örneği. *Sosyal Bilimler Enstitüsü Dergisi, 35*(2), 1–14.

Arnett, J.J. (2000). Emerging adulthood: A theory of development from the late teens through the twenties. *American Psychologist, 55*(5), 469-480. doi: 066x.55.5.469 doi:10.1037/0003

Asabere, N. Y. (2012). *A research analysis of online social networking sites (SNSs) and social behaviour at University of Ghana (UG)*. Legon, Accra, Ghana. In International Journal of Science and Technology.

Asemah, E. S., & Edegoh, L. O. N. (2013). Influence of social media on the academic performance of the undergraduate students of Kogi State University, Anyigba, Nigeria. *Journal of Research in Humanities and Social Sciences, 3*(12), 90–91.

Bachchhav, K. P. (2016). *Information Retrieval: search process, techniques and strategies*. Retrieved on 29th of July from: www.ijnglt.com

Baker, L. R., & Oswald, D. L. (2010). Shyness and online social networking services. *Journal of Social and Personal Relationships, 27*(7), 873–889. doi:10.1177/0265407510375261

Barker, V. (2009). Older adolescents' motivations for social network site use: The influence of gender, group identity, and collective self-esteem. *Cyberpsychology & Behavior, 12*(2), 209–213. doi:10.1089/cpb.2008.0228 PMID:19250021

Baym, N. K., Zhang, Y. B., Kunkel, A., Ledbetter, A., & Mei-Chen, L. (2007). Relational quality and media use in interpersonal relationships. *New Media & Society, 9*(5), 735–752. doi:10.1177/1461444807080339

Baym, N. K., Zhang, Y. B., & Lin, M. (2004). Social interactions across media. *New Media & Society, 6*(3), 299–318. doi:10.1177/1461444804041438

Bilandzic, H., Patriarche, G., & Traudt, P. J. (Eds.). (2012). *The social use of media: cultural and social scientific perspectives on audience research*. Intellect Books.

Bonds-Raacke, J., & Raacke, J. (2008). MySpace and facebook: Applying the uses and gratifications theory to exploring friend-networking sites. *Cyberpsychology & Behavior, 11*(2), 169–174. doi:10.1089/cpb.2007.0056 PMID:18422409

Boneva, B., Kraut, R., & Frohlich, D. (2001). Using e-mail for personal relationships: The difference gender makes. *The American Behavioral Scientist, 45*(3), 530–549. doi:10.1177/00027640121957204

Bowen, G. (2008). Preventing school dropout: The eco-interactional developmental model of school success. *Prevention Researcher, 16*, 3–8.

Boyd, D. M., & Ellison, N. B. (2008). Social network sites: Definition, history, and scholarship. *Journal of Computer-Mediated Communication, 13*(1), 210–230. doi:10.1111/j.1083-6101.2007.00393.x

Brenner, J., & Smith, A. (2013). *72% of online adults are social networking site users*. Washington, DC: Pew Internet & American Life Project.

Bryant, J. A., Sanders-Jackson, A., & Smallwood, A. (2006). IMing, text messaging, and adolescent social networks. *Journal of Computer-Mediated Communication, 11*, 10. Retrieved from http://jcmc.indiana.edu/vol11/issue2/Bryant.html

Bryer, T. A., & Zavattaro, S. M. (2011). Social media and public administration: Theoretical dimensions and introduction to the symposium. *Administrative Theory & Praxis, 33*(3), 325–340. doi:10.2753/ATP1084-1806330301

BusinessWeek. (2005). MySpace: WhoseSpace? *BusinessWeek*.

Cabral. (2011). Is Generation Y Addicted to Social Media? *The Elon Journal of Undergraduate Research in Communications, 2*(1), 5-14.

Choi, J., & Kang, W. (2014). A dynamic examination motives forusing social media and social media usage among undergraduate students. A latent class analysis. *Procedia: Social and Behavioral Sciences, 131*, 202–210. doi:10.1016/j.sbspro.2014.04.105

Christopher, S. G. K. (2010). Issues in Information behavior in social media. *Libers., 24*(2), 75–96.

Coyle, C., & Vaughn, H. (2008). summer). Social networking: Communication revolution or evolution. *Bell Labs Technical Journal, 13*(2), 13–17. doi:10.1002/bltj.20298

David, O. N., Helou, A. M., & Rahim, N. Z. A. (2012). Model of perceived influence of academic performance using social networking. *International Journal of Computers and Technology, 2*(2a), 24–29. doi:10.24297/ijct.v2i1.2612

De Souza, Z., & Dick, G. (2008). Information disclosure on myspace- the what, the why and the implications. *Pastoral Care in Education*, 26(3), 143–157. doi:10.1080/02643940802246427

Domizi, D. P. (2013). Microblogging to foster connections and community in a weekly graduate seminar course. *TechTrends*, 57(1), 43–51. doi:10.100711528-012-0630-0

Drury, G. (2008). Opinion piece: Social media: Should marketers engage and how can it be done effectively. *Journal of Direct. Data and Digital Marketing Practice*, 9(3), 274–277. doi:10.1057/palgrave.dddmp.4350096

Duggan, M., & Brenner, J. (2013). *The demographics of social media users, 2012* (Vol. 14). Washington, DC: Pew Research Center's Internet & American Life Project.

Edom, B. O. (2012). *Principles of the use of the library*. Owerri: Springfield Publishers Ltd.

Eick, C. J., & King, D. T. (2012). Non-science majors' perceptions on the use of YouTube video to support learning in an integrated science lecture. *Journal of College Science Teaching*, 42(1), 26–30.

Eke, H., N., Omekwu, C., O., & Odoh, J., N., (2014). The use of social networking sites among the undergraduate students of University of Nigeria, Nsukka. *Library Philosophy and Practice*, 1195.

Farkus, G. (2010). *Final report on Saugus Union School District's SWATTEC Program," Saugususd.org*. Irvine, CA: University of California.

Fewkes, A., & McCabe, M. (2012). Facebook: Learning Tool or Distraction? *Journal of Digital Learning in Teacher Education*, 28(3). Retrieved on 24th of July, 2018 from http://eric.ed.gov/?id=EJ972449

Gao, L., Luo, T., & Zhang, K. (2012). Tweeting for learning: A critical analysis of research on microblogging in education published in 2008- 2011. *British Journal of Educational Technology*, 43(5), 783–801. doi:10.1111/j.1467-8535.2012.01357.x

Geach, N., & Haralambous, N. (2009). Regulating harassment: Is the law fit for the Social networking age. *Journal of Criminal Law*, 73(3), 241–257. doi:10.1350/jcla.2009.73.3.571

Gee, J. P. (2005). Semiotic Social Spaces and Affinity Spaces: From The Age of Mythology to Today's Schools. In D. Barton & K. Tusting (Eds.), Beyond communities of practice: Language, power and social context (pp. 214–232). Academic Press. doi:10.1017/CBO9780511610554.012

Giles, G., & Price, I. R. (2008). Adolescent computer use: Approach, avoidance, and parental control. *Australian Journal of Psychology*, 60(2), 63–71. doi:10.1080/00049530701829896

Greenfield, P., & Subrahmanyam, K. (2008). Online communication and adolescent relationships. *The Future of Children*, 18(1), 119–140. doi:10.1353/foc.0.0006 PMID:21338008

Gross, E. (2004). Adolescent Internet use: What we expect, what teens report. *Journal of Applied Developmental Psychology*, 25(6), 633–649. doi:10.1016/j.appdev.2004.09.005

Hansen, D. L., Shneiderman, B., & Smith, M. A. (2010). *Analyzing social media networks with NodeXL: Insights from a connected world*. Morgan Kaufmann.

Henderson, A., & Bowley, R. (2010). Authentic dialogue? The role of "friendship" in a social media recruitment campaign. *Journal of Communication Management, 14*(3), 237–257. doi:10.1108/13632541011064517

Idubor, I. (2015). Investigating social media usage and addiction levels among undergraduates in University of Ibadan, Nigeria. *British Journal of Education, Society &. Behavioral Science, 7*(4), 291–301.

Itodo, D. S. (2012). Nigeria: Youths and Social Networking Obsession. Retrieved from AllAfrica.com/stories/20110140376.html

James. (2005). *The Wisdom of Crowds.* Anchor Books.

Jason, R. (2006). *Types of social networking sites.* Academic Press.

Jeong, T.G. (2005). The effect of internet addiction and self-control on achievement of elementary school children. *Korean Journal of Yeolin Education, 5*(3).

Jiang, L. C., Bazarova, N. N., & Hancock, J. T. (2011). The disclosure-intimacy link in computer-mediated communication: An attributional extension of the hyperpersonal model. *Human Communication Research, 37*(1), 58–77. doi:10.1111/j.1468-2958.2010.01393.x

Jonah, A. (2013). *Social networking: the new Nigeria.* The Bug, p. 2.

Junco, R., Heiberger, G., & Loken, E. (2011). The effect of Twitter on college student engagement and grades. *Journal of Computer Assisted Learning, 27*(2), 119–132. doi:10.1111/j.1365-2729.2010.00387.x

Kaplan, A. M., & Haenlein, M. (2010). Users of the world, unite! The challenges and opportunities of Social Media. *Business Horizons, 53*(1), 59–68. doi:10.1016/j.bushor.2009.09.003

Keen, A. (2007). *The cult of the amateur: How the democratization of the digital world is assaulting our economy, our culture, and our values.* New York: Doubleday Currency.

Kietzmann, J. H., Silvestre, B. S., McCarthy, I. P., & Pitt, L. F. (2012). Unpacking the social media phenomenon: Towards a research agenda. *Journal of Public Affairs, 12*(2), 109–119. doi:10.1002/pa.1412

Kietzmannn, J., Silverstre, B., Mccarthy, I., & Leyland. (2012). Unpacking the social media phenomenon: towards a research agenda. *Journal of Public Affairs, 12*(2), 109-119.

Kuppuswamy, S., & Narayan, P. (2010). The Impact of Social Networking Websites on the Education of Youth. *International Journal of Virtual Communities and Social Networking, 2*(1), 67–79. doi:10.4018/jvcsn.2010010105

Kuss D. J., & Griffiths M. D. (2011). Online Social Networking and Addiction-A Review of the Psychological Literature. *Int. J. Environ. Res. Public Health, 8*, 3528-3552. . doi:10.3390/ijerph8093528

Lenhart, A., Purcell, K., Smith, A., & Zickuhr, K. (2010). *Social Media & Mobile Internet Use among Teens and Young Adults. Millennials.* Pew internet & American life project.

Li, N., & Kirkup, G. (2007). Gender and cultural differences in Internet use: A study of China and the UK. *Computers & Education, 48*(2), 301–317. doi:10.1016/j.compedu.2005.01.007

Lin, G., & Subrahmanyam, K. (2007). Adolescents and the net: Internet use and wellbeing. *Adolescence*, *42*(168), 659–675. Retrieved from http://findarticles.com/ p/articles/ mi_m2248/ is_168_42 / ai_n27483301/ PMID:18229503

Livingstone, S. (2008). Taking risky opportunities in youthful content creation: Teenagers' use of social networking sites for intimacy, privacy and self-expression. *New Media & Society*, *10*(3), 393–411. doi:10.1177/1461444808089415

Livingstone, S. (2008). Taking risky opportunities in youthful content creation: Teenagers' use of social networking sites for intimacy, privacy and self-expression. *New Media & Society*, *10*(3), 393–411. doi:10.1177/1461444808089415

Lui, X., & LaRose, R. (2008). Does using the internet make people more satisfied with their lives? The effects of the internet on college students' school life satisfaction. *Cyberpsychology & Behavior*, *11*(3), 310–320. doi:10.1089/cpb.2007.0040 PMID:18537501

Mayfield, A. (2008). *What is social media?* Academic Press.

Mazman, S. G., & Usluel, Y. K. (2010). Modeling educational usage of Facebook. *Computers & Education*, *55*(2), 444–453. doi:10.1016/j.compedu.2010.02.008

Merten, M., & Williams, A. (2009). Adolescents' online social networking following the death of a peer. *Journal of Adolescent Research*, *24*(1), 67–90. doi:10.1177/0743558408328440

Mesch, G. (2009). Parental mediation, online activities, and cyberbullying. *Cyberpsychology & Behavior*, *12*(4), 387–392. doi:10.1089/cpb.2009.0068 PMID:19630583

Minocha, S. (2009). Role of social software tools in education: A literature review. *Education + Training*, *51*(5/6), 353–369. doi:10.1108/00400910910987174

Morahan-Martin, J., & Schumacher, P. (2000). Incidence and correlates of pathological Internet use among college students. *Computers in Human Behavior*, *16*(1), 13–29. doi:10.1016/S0747-5632(99)00049-7

Moran, M., Seaman, J., & Tinti-Kane, H. (2012). Blogs, wikis, podcasts and Facebook: How today's higher education faculty use social media. Boston, MA: Pearson Learning Solutions.

Na, Y. E. (2002). Gender differences in new media use and values mobile phones and the internet. *Korean Journal of Broadcasting and Telecommunication Studies*, *16*, 77–115.

Nadkarni, A., & Hofmann, S. G. (2012). Why do people use Facebook? *Personality and Individual Differences*, *52*(3), 243–249. doi:10.1016/j.paid.2011.11.007 PMID:22544987

Newman, E. (2008). Airwalk print lauds MySpace celebrities. *Brandweek*, *49*(10), 5.

Nicole, E. (2007). The benefits of Face book "Fiends;" Social Capital and College Students' Use of Online Social Network Sites. *Journal of Computer-Mediated Communication*.

Nnadozie, A. C. (2006). Collection development activities in selected academic Libraries in Nigeria. *Nigerbibilios*, *17*(1&2), 22–27.

Obi, N. C., Bulus, L. D., Adamu, G. M., & Sala'at, A. B. (2012). The Need for Safety Consciousness among Youths on Social Networking Sites. *Journal of Applied Science and Management, 14*(1).

Oblinger, D. G., & Oblinger, J. L. (2005). *Educating the net generation*. Retrieved from www.educause.edu/educatingthenetgen/

Ogedebe, P. M., Emmanuel, J. A., & Musa, Y. (2012). A survey on Facebook and Academic Performance in Nigeria Universities. *International Journal of Engineering Research and Applications, 2*, 788–797.

Olaniran, S. (2014). Social media and changing communication patterns among students: An analysis of twitter use by University of Jos students. *Covenant Journal of Communication, 2*(1).

Oluwatoyin, A. E. (2011). ICT, CGPA: Consequences of Social Networks In An Internet Driven Learning Society. *International Journal of Computer Trends and Technology, 2*(2), 11–32.

Osatuyi, B. (2013). Information sharing on social media sites. *Computers in Human Behavior, 29*(6), 2622–2631. doi:10.1016/j.chb.2013.07.001

Oser, K. (2006). MySpace, big audience, big risks. *Advertising Age, 77*(8), 3–25.

Parr, B. (2008). *Ben Parr's Entrepreneurial Musings*. Retrieved from http://benparr.com/2008/08/its-time-we-defined-social-media-no-more-arguing-heres-the-definition/

Pempek, T. A., Yermolayeva, Y. A., & Calvert, S. L. (2009). College students' social networking experiences on Facebook. *Journal of Applied Developmental Psychology, 30*(3), 227–238. doi:10.1016/j.appdev.2008.12.010

Pempek, T. A., Yermolayeva, Y. A., & Calvert, S. L. (2009). College students' social networking experiences on facebook. *Journal of Applied Developmental Psychology, 30*(3), 227–238. doi:10.1016/j.appdev.2008.12.010

Peter, J., Schouten, A., & Valkenburg, P. (2006). Friend networking sites and their relationship to adolescents' well-being and social self-esteem. *Cyberpsychology & Behavior, 9*(5), 584–590. doi:10.1089/cpb.2006.9.584 PMID:17034326

Peter, J., & Valkenburg, P. (2009). Social consequences of the internet for adolescents: A decade of research. *Psychological Science, 18*(1), 1–4. PMID:19152536

Quan-Haase, A., & Young, A. L. (2010). Uses and gratifications of social media: A comparison of facebook and instant messaging. *Bulletin of Science, Technology & Society, 30*(5), 350–361. doi:10.1177/0270467610380009

Raacke, J., & Bonds-Raacke, J. (2008). MySpace and Facebook: Applying the uses and gratifications theory to exploring friend-networking sites. *Cyberpsychology & Behavior, 11*(2), 169–174. doi:10.1089/cpb.2007.0056 PMID:18422409

Rafferty, F. (2009). Boys should be Boys-is it that Simple? *Education Journal, 116*, 32–33.

Rainie, L., Smith, A., & Duggan, M. (2013). *Coming and going on Facebook*. Pew Research Center's Internet and American Life Project.

Rapacki, S. (2007). Social networking sites: Why teens need places like myspace. *Young Adult Library Services*, 28-30. Retrieved on 24th of June, 2018 from http://files.eric.ed.gov/fulltext/EJ991339.pdf

Roblyer, M. D., McDaniel, M., Webb, M., Herman, J., & Witty, J. V. (2010). Findings on Facebook in higher education: A comparison of college Faculty and student uses and perceptions of social networking sites. *Internet and Higher Education*, *13*(3), 134–140. doi:10.1016/j.iheduc.2010.03.002

Romero-Frías, E & Arquero Montaño, L. J (2012). *Exploring the use of social network sites on accounting education: a social constructivist approach*. Academic Press.

Rouis, S., Limayem, M., & Salehi-Sangari, E. (2011). *Impact of Facebook Usage on Students´ Academic Achievement: Role of self-regulation and trust*. Academic Press.

Safko, L., & Brake, D. K. (2009). *The social media bible: Tactics, tools, and strategies for business success*. John Wiley & Sons.

Schulten, K. (2000). *The learning network blog*. Retrieved June 10 208 from learning blogs: nytimes.com/2009/12/21

Scott, P. R., & Jacka, J. M. (2011). *Auditing social media: A governance and risk guide*. John Wiley & Sons.

Sheldon, P. (2008). Student favorite: Facebook and motives for its use. *Southwestern Mass Communication Journal*, *23*(2), 39–53.

Sherer, P., & Shea, T. (2011). using online video to support student learning engagement. *College Teaching*, *59*(2), 56–59. doi:10.1080/87567555.2010.511313

Siibak, A. (2009). Constructing the self through the photo selection- Visual impression management on social networking websites. *Journal of Psychological Research on Cyberspace*, *3*(1), 1–6. Retrieved from http://www.cyberpsychology.eu/view.php

Sin, S. C. J., & Kim, K. S. (2013). International students' everyday life information seeking: The informational value of social networking sites. *Library & Information Science Research*, *35*(2), 107–116. doi:10.1016/j.lisr.2012.11.006

Smith, A. (2010). Social media & mobile internet use among teens and young adults. *Pew Research Center's Internet & American Life Project*, 1-37. Retrieved from http:// web.pewinterne t.org/~/ media/ Files /Reports/2010/PIP_Social _Media_and_Young_Adults_Report_Final_with_toplines.pdf

Social Media Online. (2011). *Social Media*. Accessed: www.creativemediafarm.com/information/glossary

Sorav, J. (2010). *Most Popular Social Networking Sites of the World*. Retrieved 28 January 2011 from: http://socialmediatoday.com/soravjain/195917/40-mostpopular-socialnetworking-sites-world

Sponcil, M., & Gitimu, P. (2013). Use of social media by college students: Relationship to communication and self-concept. *Journal of Technology Research*, *4*, 1.

Tınmaz, H. (2013). *Sosyal Ağ Web Siteleri ve Sosyal Ağların Eğitimde Kullanımı*. Kürşat Çağıltay ve Yüksel.

Trusov, M., Bucklin, R., & Pauwels, K. (2009). Effects of word of-mouth versus traditional marketing: Findings from an internet social networking site. *Journal of Marketing*, *73*(5), 90–102. doi:10.1509/jmkg.73.5.90

Tufekci, Z. (2008). Grooming, gossip, facebook, and myspace. *Information Communication and Society*, *11*(4), 544–564. doi:10.1080/13691180801999050

Tufekci, Z. (2008). Grooming, gossip, facebook, and myspace. *Information Communication and Society*, *11*(4), 544–564. doi:10.1080/13691180801999050

Turkle, S. (2004). Preference for online social interaction. *The Chronicle of Higher Education*.

Urista, M. A., Dong, Q., & Day, K. D. (2009). Explaining why young adults use myspace and facebook through uses and gratifications theory. *Human Communication*, *12*(2), 215–229.

Wang, Q., Chen, W., & Liang, Y. (2011). *The effects of social media on college students*. Academic Press.

West, A., Lewis, J., & Currie, P. (2009). Students' facebook 'friends': Public and private spheres. *Journal of Youth Studies*, *12*(6), 615–627. doi:10.1080/13676260902960752

Williams, Boyd, Densten, Chin, Diamond, & Morgenthaler, (2009). Social Networking Privacy Behaviors and Risks. In *Proceeding of CSIS Research Day*. Seidenberg School of CSIS, Pace University.

Wilson, T. (2012). *Community Reporting and Citizens Journalism: A Venn Diagram*. Discussion Paper from the Institute of Community Reporters- June 2012 Part of People's Voice Media Charity.

KEY TERMS AND DEFINITIONS

Media: Are all those media technologies that are intended to reach a large audience by mass communication. "They are messages communicated through a mass medium to a number of people.

Social Media: They are forms of electronic communication which facilitate interactive base on certain interests. Social media includes web and mobile technology.

Social Networking: The use of internet to make information about yourself available to other people especially people you share an interest with to send messages to them.

Social Networking Sites: A website where people put information about them and can send to others.

Tweets: A short message posted on Twitter (a micro blog).

This research was previously published in the Handbook of Research on Digital Devices for Inclusivity and Engagement in Libraries; pages 406-436, copyright year 2020 by Information Science Reference (an imprint of IGI Global).

Chapter 95

Impact of Social Networking Sites Among College Students With Special Reference to Rural Areas in India

T. Balamurugan

Department of Library and Information Science, Alagappa University, India

M. Aravinthan

Library and Information Science, Annamalai University, India

ABSTRACT

Social networking sites over the years have changed from a few user-based sites into a phenomena that has become a platform for a huge number of users. However, the growth and development of social networking sites have brought great concerns on parents and educational authorities with respect to potential risks that are facing the university students as they use online social networking frequently for gathering information. The use of social networking sites among the university students requires much attention with increasing number of students creating profile and feeding their personal information into the sites. The increasing activity on the sites by student community can negatively impact the normal activity of students' lives. This can also become a hindrance to the academic development as well as social engagement of students. Therefore, there is a need to study, assess, and evaluate the issues revolving the usage of social networking sites among the student community. The study shows that the distribution of respondents according to their influence of SNS. It shows both section-wise distribution and their composite scores. Also, the table shows the respective mean scores and standard deviation. It may be inferred that 77.50% of the respondents have stated that the influence of SNS are high, 18.55% of the respondents have stated that the influence of SNS is moderate, and 3.95% of the respondents have stated that the influence of SNS is low. However, the composite mean score (2.72), standard deviation (0.530) depicts that the respondents have stated that the influence of SNS is high.

DOI: 10.4018/978-1-6684-7123-4.ch095

INTRODUCTION

Social Networking Sites have been instrumental in contracting the world more than other innovative improvements. Social networking websites like Facebook, MySpace, WhatsApp and YouTube are winding up increasingly prominent and has progressed toward becoming an integral part of regular day to day existence for an expanding number of individuals. In view of their highlights, youngsters are pulled in towards these Social Networking Sites. Modem, broadband, remote and satellite a synchronous email, texting, and transport through interactive media, students have grown up socialized into a world formed by the web and display local and idle instincts and understandings of web innovation obscure to past generations.

The contemporary time frame has been named as the Information Age, Communication Age and the present Networking Age. The web offers a wide assortment of specialized instruments. Billions of individuals use offices like search engines, emails, web pages, e-journals, e-books, e-mails, e-newspapers, internet telephony, multi-media sharing, conferencing, internet banking, blogging, shopping, gaming and online news rooms and all the more imperatively, social networking. Today web is a basic correspondence medium in expert and in addition individual life.

Among the different devices that web has brought our direction Social Networking has turned into a worldwide wonder. A large number of individuals currently use web to take part in social networks. There are in excess of 300 Social Networking Sites (Also known as SNS) and the aggregate number of individuals utilizing Social Networking Sites the world over is 1.73 billion of every 2013 and it will increment to 2.55 billion by 2017. Lately, usage of Social Networking Sites has developed quickly. It took 38 years to pull in 50 million audience members for remote radio framework, 13 years for TV to draw in 50 million watchers; yet in just 4 years the web has pulled in 50 million surfers. Actually, IPods took 3 years to achieve 50 million clients; however Facebook, one of the main Social Networking Sites, included more than 200 million clients in only a year. This demonstrates the entrance limit and prevalence of Social Networking Sites.

PURPOSES OF SOCIAL NETWORKING SITES

The fame of social networks develops quickly continuously. These social sites have turned out to be successful (to a degree) methods for conveying thoughts and sentiments among their clients. Therefore, they are starting to get more consideration from instructive establishments. Gardner (2009) opined that organizations are finding a way to instruct students on the utilization of the sites, particularly in the zones of the protection, lawful issue and potential financial and mental threats. Also, social networking upgrades a student's feeling of network, sharing and joint effort, brings an extra obligation and remaining burden, which a few students find unbendable and rather "forced". This innovation utilizes web cams or voice-just delicate product to hold virtual courses on the web. This is amazingly helpful for coordinated efforts where the accomplices live in various parts of the globe.

Using social networking sites students can convey what needs be impart and gather profiles that feature their ability and experience. According to Konetes and McKeague in 2011, thought of specific disclosures about the employments of the social networking sites particularly, Facebook, the researchers announced that, ''students are utilizing Facebook and different channels to build up their personalities, convictions and positions on different issues, for example, governmental issues, religion, economy and work, and additionally to pioneer and create suggest connections.

Uses and Gratification Theory

"Utilizations and Gratification Theory" researches about what individuals do with the media which is the driven idea of this investigation as well. The investigation is endeavoring to know the usage of social networking sites by the students. Since, it is seen that there is falsehood colossal fame among SNS clients as their four straightforward necessities proposed by scholar are fulfilled at a more prominent degree:

- "Diversion": People will in general have some redirection from their day by day schedule and ob-ligations. To spruce up their brain or unwind now and then subsequently, social networking sites are a free, simple to get to and engaging stage for them to escape from routine work.
- "Personal Relationship": Man cannot make due in forlornness. He needs individuals around to see the energy of society. With quick life it is hard to invest genuine energy with companions and relatives. Social Networking Sites gives a virtual time chance to create connections by joining companions on the web and numerous social gatherings.
- "Personality Identity": One's identity is made out of thought, emotions and conduct. Through SNS an individual can look for introduction to different occasions as indicated by his inclina-tion prompting advancement of an attractive identity of the prosperity. This helps in discovering increasingly about oneself and associating with more individuals of similar identities. No other medium can interface alike the social networking sites.
- "Surveillance": Surveillance is a quality embraced and drilled by all being ideal from their initial age. This causes them in learning etiquettes, social conduct, educate to learn and respond. SNS helps finding, breaking down, responding to various wonder circling the surroundings of a man. He isn't just restricted to his environment however anything at worldwide dimension is open to him through SNS. For e.g. "Aleppo Tragedy, 2016"; "Nirbhaya Case, 2012" "Middle Easterner Spring, 2011" and some more. With the help of this theory it could be comprehended that Social Networking Sites is a prevalent medium among the students and it is going about as a facilitator in building up their frame of mind and conduct.

REVIEW OF LITERATURE

Eyrich, Padman and Sweetser (2008) viewed social media to comprise of various tools like intranets, blogs, podcasts, photo sharing, video sharing, social networks, gaming, wikis, virtual universes, micro blogging/presence applications, content informing, video conferencing, PDAs, text talk, social occasion/ logbook frameworks, social bookmarking, news total/RSS and email.

Lau (2017) stated that upshot of social media use and social media performing various tasks impact the scholarly execution of university students. The exploration found that utilizing social media for scholarly reasons for existing was not an imperative indicator of educational execution as estimated by total review point normal, though utilizing social media for non-academic purposes (video gaming specifically) and social media performs multiple tasks essentially adversely anticipated academic performance.

Thanuskodi (2013) academic libraries cater to the diverse needs of scholars, scientists, technocrats, researchers, students, and others personally and professionally invested in higher education. Due to advancements in information and communication technologies (ICT), the vision and mission of academic libraries are changing in developing countries.

Mahadi, et al., (2016) directed an examination on the effect of social media on Art students' frame of mind from Art and Design Faculty in University Technology Mara, Perak campus. The result uncovers that the greater part of students are progressively associated with social media and they understood the effect of social media in their day by day life and also their demeanour.

Alwagait, Shahzad and Alim (2015) inspected the effect of inordinate social media use on scholastic execution. They also decide out which social network site is the most popular and liked among Saudi students, the thing that students thought about their social media utilization and factors other than social media use which contrarily influence academic performance. The result is invertebrate that there was no direct connection between social media use in a week and GPA score. Students hued that also social media use; time the executives is an angle which influences students 'considers contrarily. The discoveries of the investigation can be utilized to propose the viable plans for enhancing the scholarly execution of the students so that equalization in the unwinding, data trade and scholastic execution can be kept up.

Li and Sakamoto (2014) stated how aggregate conclusion may impact the apparent honesty and the sharing probability of wellbeing related articulations on social media. It was exposed that, when surveying the unwavering quality of an announcement, members embraced the mutual honesty rating associated with the announcement. In like manner, experimentation two demonstrated that the probability that members would share an announcement pursued the aggregate sharing opportunity associated with the announcement. These social effects were boundless, occurring for explanation suspected as questionable, true and false. This result contributed new experiences into how individuals perceive and share data on social media and in addition how aggregate conclusion may influence the nature of data on social media.

Salvation and Azharuddin (2014) opined that Social system sites (SNS) draws in impressive consideration among adolescents and youthful grown-ups who will in general associate and offer basic intrigue. The investigation was structured in approaches to break down the effect of social system sites on students' scholastic execution in Malaysia, utilizing a theoretical methodology. The investigation presumed that more students incline toward the utilization of Facebook and twitter in scholarly related exchanges in supplementing ordinary classroom instructing and learning process.

Maria Paramo, et al., (2014), dissected the degree to which diverse sources and subjective/emotional parts of apparent social help anticipated explicit regions of change in an example of 300 first-year Spain University students. The example achieved the Social Support Questionnaire (SSQ), the Perceived Acceptance Scale (PAS) and the Student Adaptation to College Questionnaire (SACQ). Relapse examination uncovered that apparent social help was a decent indicator of change to school. The affiliation was tough for companions bolster than family bolster once University section review point normal and gender were controlled for. The association between the quantity of accessible others when required and the fulfilment with accessible help with modification was intermediated by apparent feeling of acknowledgment.

Tayseer et al., (2014) in their examination analyzed the impact of use of social networks on students' commitment in both scholarly and social viewpoints. The examination uncovered that students utilize social networks for social purposes more than the scholastics. Students consider social media as amusement networks and it lessens pressure and influences them to disregard scholastics.

Mahat (2014) Lot of writing is accessible now days on the social networking sites and their effect on the youth of any country, youngsters, adolescence and families as amid the most recent 5 years, utilization of such sites has expanded among preadolescents and teenagers. Out of 75% of young people owning mobile phones, 25% use them for social media, 24% use them for texting and 54% use them for messaging. Positive out originates from these advances as employments found through LinkedIn or political activities sorted out by means of Facebook.

Thanuskodi (2013) the present study evaluates the use of library facilities and information resources in university libraries in Tamil Nadu. A survey of 518 students from 5 universities in Tamil Nadu was conducted through a set of questionnaires. The collected data covers the use of library resources, services, (e.g. reference services, photocopying services), etc. The chapter concludes that the main intention for the use of libraries has been the academic interest of the students.

De Andrea, et al., (2012) gave an account of a student focused social media site intended to improve students' view of social help preceding their landing on grounds. Result demonstrated that site utilization enlarged students' discernments that they would have assorted social encouraging group of people amid their first semester at college.

Jahan and Ahmed (2012) considered view of scholarly utilization of social networking sites (SNSs) by the students of University of Dhaka, Bangladesh. That review shows an uplifting demeanour towards scholarly utilization of SNSs by the students. In spite of the fact that there are a few contrasts as far as students' assessments on scholarly uses of SNSs, these distinctions are to a great extent because of the way that the utilization of these sites in scholastic settings is not all around characterized. The higher scholastic establishments need to devise fitting arrangements and methodologies on how they can use social networking sites to help training and learning past the classroom.

Kindi and Alhasmi (2012) lead an investigation "Use of Social networking among Shinas college of Technology students in Oman". The investigation found that the significant purposes behind incessant utilization of SNSs are discovering data and sharing news. The investigation demonstrated that absence of experience and lacking time and IT abilities are viable variables of not utilizing SNSs. At long last, the examination found that Google Groups, Facebook and Yahoo! 360 are the most well known SNSs utilized by SHCT students.

Zhang (2012) investigated undergrads' utilization of social networking sites for wellbeing and health data. Thirty-eight undergrads were met. The meeting transcripts were dissected utilizing the subjective substance investigation strategy. Generally, members were incredulous about the nature of data. In light of the outcomes, a model of students' acknowledgment of social networking sites for wellness and health data was proposed and suggestions for planning social stages to all the more likely help wellbeing request were talked about Using social networking sites for wellbeing and health data is certifiably not a famous conduct among college students in this investigation.

Thanuskodi (2009) India has noteworthy favourable circumstances in the 21st century information race. It has a vast advanced education segment – the third biggest on the planet in student numbers, after China and the United States. By China, India is the most populated nation on the planet. The reason for training is balanced advancement. Students require a mix of expressions, software engineering, science, and humanities or writing courses to accomplish this sort of improvement. A well-managed and well-equipped library is the establishment of present day instructive structure. It is said that training without library administrations resembles a body without soul, a vehicle without a motor, and working with blocks yet no concrete.

Zohoorian-Fooladi and Abrizah (2014) mentioned about the social media nearness in Malaysian scholastic libraries setting and furthermore found that the custodians are utilizing social media for advancing library administrations, sorting out learning and for getting criticism from clients against their data sources.

Church and deOliveira (2013), discusses WhatsApp as a cross-stage texting application for advanced mobile phones. It empowers clients to send and get area data, pictures, video, sound and instant messages progressively to people and gatherings of companions at no expense.

Paul, Baker and Cochran, (2012) in their exploration on impact of online social networking on students' scholarly execution found that there is factually inconsequential negative connection between time spent by students on online social networking and their scholastic execution.

Chen, et al., (2012) ponder concentrated on how libraries can make cooperation with clients by utilizing social networking sites. This investigation further worried on necessities for libraries to organize different kinds of SNSs as to enhance the proficiency of communicating with clients on social networking sites.

Jacobson (2011) estimated the utilization of Facebook as a library device whether it meets expected objectives of a library with respect to receiving as well as actually using Facebook. He explored the sustainable utilization of social media especially with regards to marketing libraries.

Banquil and Chua (2009) concocted an end that social networking sites do influence one's scholastic execution antagonistically. It specifically causes the progressive drop of evaluations of students. It specifically influences students' scholarly execution if the student puts his time in social networking sites rather than his investigations. Scholastic execution is a multifaceted develop made of three measurements, along these lines, students' attributes, educators'/instructors' skills and the helpfulness of the scholarly condition. The student's viewpoint is the way they manage their investigations and how they adapt to or achieve learning circumstances

Charnigo and Barnett-Ellis (2007) led an investigation into the take-up of Social Networking Sites, specifically Facebook. They reviewed various administrators, some of whom were supportive of Facebook being utilized in libraries to advance administrations and occasions, while most of the libraries were not for Facebook having a presence in libraries by any stretch of the imagination. The after effects of the Charnigo and Barnett-Ellis study might be a sign that the utilization of Social Networking Sites increments as age diminishes, and that albeit no age of the custodians met is referenced in the investigation, that as new curators move into libraries, so the take-up and acknowledgment of Social Networking Sites will increment. This investigation encourages us to discover a utilization design SNS with regards to age.

Ahn (2012), secondary school students are likewise progressively associated with their locale when they take part in social network sites. He presumes that juvenile who utilizes social network sites will likewise report larger amounts of social capital (both holding and connecting). In spite of the way that a great part of the media and training exchanges centre on the negative parts of SNSs, especially the manners by which adolescents utilize these apparatuses to menace their friends. He further composes that while young people may discuss fundamentally with known companions in SNSs, they are additionally presented to the bigger world through their associations. As individuals share connections, thoughts, and media, they are associated with an expansive exhibit of data. As past researchers have estimated, it is conceivable that young person's utilization of SNSs causes them feel associated with the more extensive world past their school and home. Such relationships are identified with the idea of connecting social capital.

Steinfield et al (2012) explained that bonding social capital is found between people in close relationships, for example, family and dear companions. Holding social capital speaks to the sorts of advantages that emerge from close relationships inside an elite gathering - family and dear friends - and is connected to passionate and social help and additionally substantive unmistakable help like financial loans.

Ahmed and Qazi (2011) mentioned that technological powers like those of developments are solid powers that have shaken up everything, particularly the web in all circles of individual, social and professional human life. Appropriate from the insignificant methods for communication to the running of enormous frameworks, we are using the accommodations given by the presence of web. Innovation is changing the manner in which those individuals communication or interact. New innovations are furnishing more approaches to speak with others and particularly among the young people.

RESEARCH OBJECTIVES

- To know the significance of social networking sites among the students generation.
- To analyze the causal relationship among the study variables identified in the study.
- To provide suggestions for development of students through social networking sites.

SEM Hypotheses

- $H_{01.1}$ Interactive has no impact on Knowledge management.
- $H_{01.2}$ Socialization has no impact on Knowledge management.
- $H_{01.3}$ Information Sharing has no impact on Knowledge management.
- $H_{01.4}$ Social Awareness has no impact on Knowledge management.
- $H_{01.5}$ Facilitation has no impact on Knowledge management.
- $H_{02.1}$ Interactive has no impact on SNS Threat.
- $H_{02.2}$ Socialization has no impact on SNS Threat.
- $H_{02.3}$ Information Sharing has no impact on SNS Threat.
- $H_{02.4}$ Social Awareness has no impact on SNS Threat.
- $H_{02.5}$ Facilitation has no impact on SNS Threat.
- $H_{03.1}$ Knowledge management has no impact on Students' Achievement.
- $H_{03.2}$ SNS Threat has no impact on Students' Achievement.

Analysis and Discussion

It can be seen from Table 1 that "Gender" obtained the following ratings: 70.2% respondents are male and 29.8% respondents are female.

Table 1. Gender – wise distribution of respondents

Particulars	Number of Respondents	Percentage (%)
Male	342	70.2
Female	145	29.8
Total	**487**	**100.0**

Source: Primary Data

It can be seen from Table 2 that "Age" obtained the following ratings: 14.4% respondents are below 20 years, 33.7% respondents are between 20 – 22 years, 48.9% respondents are between 23 – 25 years and 3.1% respondents are above 25 years.

Table 2. Age- wise distribution of respondents

Particulars	Number of Respondents	Percentage (%)
Below 20 years	70	14.4
20 – 22 years	164	33.7
23 – 25 years	238	48.9
Above 25 years	15	3.1
Total	**487**	**100**

Source: Primary Data

It can be seen from Table 3 that "SNS helps in spend time on sharing information with students having common interest" Obtained the following ratings: 6.6% respondents rated strongly disagree, 6% respondents rated disagree, 11.9% respondents rated neutral, 49.9% respondents rated agree and 25.7% respondents rated strongly agree.

Table 3. Time spent on sharing information with students having common interest

Particulars	Number of Respondents	Percentage (%)
Strongly Disagree	32	6.6
Disagree	29	6.0
Neutral	58	11.9
Agree	243	49.9
Strongly Agree	125	25.7
Total	**487**	**100.0**

Source: Primary Data

It can be seen from Table 4 that "Sharing of learning outcome through SNS" Obtained the following ratings: 6.2% respondents rated strongly disagree, 5.7% respondents rated disagree, 12.7% respondents rated neutral, 45.4% respondents rated agree and 30% respondents rated strongly agree.

It can be seen from Table 5 that "SNS enables rapid exchange of knowledge" Obtained the following ratings: 9% respondents rated strongly disagree, 15% respondents rated disagree, 23.6% respondents rated neutral, 32.9% respondents rated agree and 19.5% respondents rated strongly agree.

It can be seen from Table 4.26 that "SNS provides collaborative communication through text, audio and video" Obtained the following ratings: 12.5% respondents rated strongly disagree, 2.5% respondents rated disagree, 21.4% respondents rated neutral, 45.2% respondents rated agree and 18.5% respondents rated strongly agree.

Table 4. Sharing of learning outcome through SNS

Particulars	Number of Respondents	Percentage (%)
Strongly Disagree	30	6.2
Disagree	28	5.7
Neutral	62	12.7
Agree	221	45.4
Strongly Agree	146	30.0
Total	**487**	**100.0**

Source: Primary Data

Table 5. SNS enables rapid exchange of knowledge

Particulars	Number of Respondents	Percentage (%)
Strongly Disagree	44	9.0
Disagree	73	15.0
Neutral	115	23.6
Agree	160	32.9
Strongly Agree	95	19.5
Total	**487**	**100.0**

Source: Primary Data

Table 6. SNS Provides collaborative communication through text, audio and video

Particulars	Number of Respondents	Percentage (%)
Strongly Disagree	61	12.5
Disagree	12	2.5
Neutral	104	21.4
Agree	220	45.2
Strongly Agree	90	18.5
Total	**487**	**100.0**

Source: Primary Data

It can be seen from Table 4.27 that "SNS acts as a platform for sharing knowledge and creative ideas" Obtained the following ratings: 22.2% respondents rated strongly disagree, 22% respondents rated disagree, 12.9% respondents rated neutral, 33.9% respondents rated agree and 9% respondents rated strongly agree.

It can be seen from Table 4.28 that "SNS helps in promoting social message" Obtained the following ratings: 25.5% respondents rated strongly disagree, 18.7% respondents rated disagree, 13.1% respondents rated neutral, 29.6% respondents rated agree and 13.1% respondents rated strongly agree.

Table 7. SNS acts as a platform for sharing knowledge and creative ideas

Particulars	Number of Respondents	Percentage (%)
Strongly Disagree	108	22.2
Disagree	107	22.0
Neutral	63	12.9
Agree	165	33.9
Strongly Agree	44	9.0
Total	**487**	**100.0**

Source: Primary Data

Table 8. SNS helps in promoting social message

Particulars	Number of Respondents	Percentage (%)
Strongly Disagree	124	25.5
Disagree	91	18.7
Neutral	64	13.1
Agree	144	29.6
Strongly Agree	64	13.1
Total	**487**	**100.0**

Source: Primary Data

It can be seen from Table 9 that "Social and economic issues are actively supported through SNS" Obtained the following ratings: 10.9% respondents rated strongly disagree, 18.5% respondents rated disagree, 36.6% respondents rated neutral, 23% respondents rated agree and 11.1% respondents rated strongly agree.

It can be seen from Table 10 that "People have used SNS to raise their voice against the bad elements harming people's culture" Obtained the following ratings: 22% respondents rated strongly disagree, 18.3% respondents rated disagree, 12.5% respondents rated neutral, 35.3% respondents rated agree and 11.9% respondents rated strongly agree.

Table 9. Social and economic issues are actively supported through SNS

Particulars	Number of Respondents	Percentage (%)
Strongly Disagree	53	10.9
Disagree	90	18.5
Neutral	178	36.6
Agree	112	23.0
Strongly Agree	54	11.1
Total	**487**	**100.0**

Source: Primary Data

Table 10. People have used SNS to raise their voice against the bad elements harming people's culture

Particulars	Number of Respondents	Percentage (%)
Strongly Disagree	107	22.0
Disagree	89	18.3
Neutral	61	12.5
Agree	172	35.3
Strongly Agree	58	11.9
Total	**487**	**100.0**

Source: Primary Data

It can be seen from Table 11 that "Students are socially active and possess social consciousness through social networking sites" Obtained the following ratings: 8% respondents rated strongly disagree, 10.3% respondents rated disagree, 14.8% respondents rated neutral, 41.3% respondents rated agree and 25.7% respondents rated strongly agree.

It can be seen from Table 12 that "SNS helps in developing lot of job opportunities for students graduating from universities" Obtained the following ratings: 8.2% respondents rated strongly disagree, 11.3% respondents rated disagree, 15.6% respondents rated neutral, 48.3% respondents rated agree and 16.6% respondents rated strongly agree.

Table 11. Students are socially active and possess social consciousness through social networking sites

Particulars	Number of Respondents	Percentage (%)
Strongly Disagree	39	8.0
Disagree	50	10.3
Neutral	72	14.8
Agree	201	41.3
Strongly Agree	125	25.7
Total	**487**	**100.0**

Source: Primary Data

Table 12. SNS helps in developing lot of job opportunities for students graduating from universities

Particulars	Number of Respondents	Percentage (%)
Strongly Disagree	40	8.2
Disagree	55	11.3
Neutral	76	15.6
Agree	235	48.3
Strongly Agree	81	16.6
Total	**487**	**100.0**

Source: Primary Data

It can be seen from Table 13 that "Able to connect easily with my friends" Obtained the following ratings: 8% respondents rated strongly disagree, 9.7% respondents rated disagree, 15.2% respondents rated neutral, 45.2% respondents rated agree and 22% respondents rated strongly agree.

Table 13. Able to connect easily with friends

Particulars	Number of Respondents	Percentage (%)
Strongly Disagree	39	8.0
Disagree	47	9.7
Neutral	74	15.2
Agree	220	45.2
Strongly Agree	107	22.0
Total	**487**	**100.0**

Source: Primary Data

It can be seen from Table 14 that "SNS is the source of recreation" Obtained the following ratings: 6.6% respondents rated strongly disagree, 11.3% respondents rated disagree, 14.4% respondents rated neutral, 45.4% respondents rated agree and 22.4% respondents rated strongly agree.

Table 14. SNS is the source of recreation

Particulars	Number of Respondents	Percentage (%)
Strongly Disagree	32	6.6
Disagree	55	11.3
Neutral	70	14.4
Agree	221	45.4
Strongly Agree	109	22.4
Total	**487**	**100.0**

Source: Primary Data

It can be seen from Table 15 that "Social Networking Sites allow users to manage, build and represent their social networks" Obtained the following ratings: 11.7% respondents rated strongly disagree, 15.2% respondents rated disagree, 21.6% respondents rated neutral, 34.1% respondents rated agree and 17.5% respondents rated strongly agree.

It can be seen from Table 16 that "Social networking site enables us to stay connected despite the hindrances of distance and time." Obtained the following ratings: 18.1% respondents rated strongly disagree, 16.8% respondents rated disagree, 16.4% respondents rated neutral, 34.3% respondents rated agree and 14.4% respondents rated strongly agree.

Table 15. Social networking sites allow users to manage, build and represent their social networks

Particulars	Number of Respondents	Percentage (%)
Strongly Disagree	57	11.7
Disagree	74	15.2
Neutral	105	21.6
Agree	166	34.1
Strongly Agree	85	17.5
Total	**487**	**100.0**

Source: Primary Data

Table 16. Social networking site enables us to stay connected despite the hindrances of distance and time

Particulars	Number of Respondents	Percentage (%)
Strongly Disagree	88	18.1
Disagree	82	16.8
Neutral	80	16.4
Agree	167	34.3
Strongly Agree	70	14.4
Total	**487**	**100.0**

Source: Primary Data

It can be seen from Table 17 that "Social media poses a liberal environment for students to discuss share their views and opinions easily freely" Obtained the following ratings: 7.8% respondents rated strongly disagree, 11.1% respondents rated disagree, 16.2% respondents rated neutral, 42.9% respondents rated agree and 22% respondents rated strongly agree.

It can be seen from Table 18 that "Social medial can be associated with an increased tendency for students to multitask" Obtained the following ratings: 6.2% respondents rated strongly disagree, 8.2% respondents rated disagree, 13.6% respondents rated neutral, 43.1% respondents rated agree and 29% respondents rated strongly agree.

Table 17. Social media poses a liberal environment for students to discuss share their views and opinions easily freely

Particulars	Number of Respondents	Percentage (%)
Strongly Disagree	38	7.8
Disagree	54	11.1
Neutral	79	16.2
Agree	209	42.9
Strongly Agree	107	22.0
Total	**487**	**100.0**

Source: Primary Data

Table 18. Social medial can be associated with an increased tendency for students to multitask

Particulars	Number of Respondents	Percentage (%)
Strongly Disagree	30	6.2
Disagree	40	8.2
Neutral	66	13.6
Agree	210	43.1
Strongly Agree	141	29.0
Total	**487**	**100.0**

Source: Primary Data

It can be seen from Table 19 that "SNS is safe place for college students to display personal information" Obtained the following ratings: 6.2% respondents rated strongly disagree, 9.7% respondents rated disagree, 15% respondents rated neutral, 46.2% respondents rated agree and 23% respondents rated strongly agree.

It can be seen from Table 20 that "Students have on-line discussion about your subject" Obtained the following ratings: 4.7% respondents rated strongly disagree, 6.8% respondents rated disagree, 14.8% respondents rated neutral, 50.1% respondents rated agree and 23.6% respondents rated strongly agree.

Table 19. SNS is safe place for college students to display personal information

Particulars	Number of Respondents	Percentage (%)
Strongly Disagree	30	6.2
Disagree	47	9.7
Neutral	73	15.0
Agree	225	46.2
Strongly Agree	112	23.0
Total	**487**	**100.0**

Source: Primary Data

Table 20. Students have on-line discussion about your subject

Particulars	Number of Respondents	Percentage (%)
Strongly Disagree	23	4.7
Disagree	33	6.8
Neutral	72	14.8
Agree	244	50.1
Strongly Agree	115	23.6
Total	**487**	**100.0**

Source: Primary Data

It can be seen from Table 21 that "Social Networking technology uses web cams or voice-only software to hold virtual seminars online" Obtained the following ratings: 9.4% respondents rated strongly disagree, 17.9% respondents rated disagree, 10.5% respondents rated neutral, 43.7% respondents rated agree and 18.5% respondents rated strongly agree.

Table 21. Social networking technology uses web cams or voice-only software to hold virtual seminars online

Particulars	Number of Respondents	Percentage (%)
Strongly Disagree	46	9.4
Disagree	87	17.9
Neutral	51	10.5
Agree	213	43.7
Strongly Agree	90	18.5
Total	**487**	**100.0**

Source: Primary Data

It can be seen from Table 22 that "Students use social media in different manners to enhance and strengthen their learning, through reflection and collaborative activities" Obtained the following ratings: 9.4% respondents rated strongly disagree, 11.1% respondents rated disagree, 9.2% respondents rated neutral, 49.1% respondents rated agree and 21.1% respondents rated strongly agree.

Table 22. Students use of social media in different manners to enhance and strengthen their learning, through reflection and collaborative activities

Particulars	Number of Respondents	Percentage (%)
Strongly Disagree	46	9.4
Disagree	54	11.1
Neutral	45	9.2
Agree	239	49.1
Strongly Agree	103	21.1
Total	**487**	**100.0**

Source: Primary Data

It can be seen from Table 23 that "SNS promotes learning, exchanges information and extends moral support" Obtained the following ratings: 10.1% respondents rated strongly disagree, 9% respondents rated disagree, 10.5% respondents rated neutral, 47.6% respondents rated agree and 22.8% respondents rated strongly agree.

Table 23. SNS promotes learning, exchanges information and extends moral support

Particulars	Number of Respondents	Percentage (%)
Strongly Disagree	49	10.1
Disagree	44	9.0
Neutral	51	10.5
Agree	232	47.6
Strongly Agree	111	22.8
Total	**487**	**100.0**

Source: Primary Data

It can be seen from Table 24 that "Students uses social media as a platform of discussions for their assignment and other course work" Obtained the following ratings: 8.4% respondents rated strongly disagree, 9.4% respondents rated disagree, 15.4% respondents rated neutral, 46.8% respondents rated agree and 19.9% respondents rated strongly agree.

Table 24. Students uses social media as a platform of discussions for their assignment and other coursework

Particulars	Number of Respondents	Percentage (%)
Strongly Disagree	41	8.4
Disagree	46	9.4
Neutral	75	15.4
Agree	228	46.8
Strongly Agree	97	19.9
Total	**487**	**100.0**

Source: Primary Data

TESTING OF HYPOTHESES

Research Question 1 (RQ1): Does the dimensions viz. Interactive, Socialization, Information Sharing, Social Awareness and Facilitation have an impact on Knowledge management?

$H_{01.1}$Interactive has no impact on Knowledge management.

Analysis: It can be seen from Table. No 4.64, the p value is greater than the significance level, hence the null hypothesis is accepted.

Result: Interactive has a negative impact on Knowledge management.

$H_{01.2}$Socialization has no impact on Knowledge management.

Analysis: It can be seen from Table. No 4.64, the p value is lesser than the significance level, hence the null hypothesis is rejected.

Result: Socialization have a positive impact on Knowledge management.

$H_{01.3}$ Information Sharing has no impact on Knowledge management.

Analysis: It can be seen from Table. No 4.64, the p value is greater than the significance level, hence the null hypothesis is accepted.

Result: Information Sharing has a negative impact on Knowledge management.

$H_{01.4}$ Social Awareness has no impact on Knowledge management.

Analysis: It can be seen from Table. No 4.64, the p value is lesser than the significance level, hence the null hypothesis is rejected.

Result: Social Awareness has a positive impact on Knowledge management.

$H_{01.5}$ Facilitation has no impact on Knowledge management.

Analysis: It can be seen from Table. No 4.64, the p value is lesser than the significance level, hence the null hypothesis is rejected.

Result: Facilitation has a positive impact on Knowledge management.

Table 25. Path analysis (SEM)

Dimensions	Path	Dimensions	SE	P Value	Result
Knowledge management	<---	Interactive	.049	0.826	Not significant
Knowledge management	<---	Socialization	.049	0.000	Significant
Knowledge management	<---	Information Sharing	.060	0.565	Not significant
Knowledge management	<---	Social Awareness	.061	0.007	Significant
Knowledge management	<---	Facilitation	.050	0.000	Significant

**Significant at 0.01

Research Question 2 (RQ2): Does the dimensions viz. Interactive, Socialization, Information Sharing, Social Awareness and Facilitation have an impact on SNS Threat?

$H_{02.1}$ Interactive has no impact on SNS Threat.

Analysis: It can be seen from Table. No 4.65, the p value is greater than the significance level, hence the null hypothesis is accepted.

Result: Interactive has a negative impact on SNS Threat.

$H_{02.2}$ Socialization has no impact on SNS Threat.

Analysis: It can be seen from Table. No 4.65, the p value is lesser than the significance level, hence the null hypothesis is rejected.

Result: Socialization have a positive impact on SNS Threat.

$H_{02.3}$ Information Sharing has no impact on SNS Threat.

Analysis: It can be seen from Table. No 4.65, the p value is lesser than the significance level, hence the null hypothesis is rejected.

Result: Information Sharing has a positive impact on SNS Threat.

$H_{02.4}$Social Awareness has no impact on SNS Threat.

Analysis: It can be seen from Table. No 4.65, the p value is greater than the significance level, hence the null hypothesis is accepted.

Result: Social Awareness has a negative impact on SNS Threat.

$H_{02.5}$Facilitation has no impact on SNS Threat.

Analysis: It can be seen from Table. No 4.65, the p value is lesser than the significance level, hence the null hypothesis is rejected.

Result: Facilitation has a positive impact on SNS Threat.

Table 26. Path analysis (SEM)

Dimensions	Path	Dimensions	SE	P Value	Result
SNS Threat	<---	Interactive	.055	0.661	Not significant
SNS Threat	<---	Socialization	.055	0.006	Significant
SNS Threat	<---	Information Sharing	.068	0.000	Significant
SNS Threat	<---	Social Awareness	.069	0.463	Not significant
SNS Threat	<---	Facilitation	.056	0.000	Significant
Students' Achievement	<---	Knowledge management	.043	0.000	Significant
Students' Achievement	<---	SNS Threat	.040	0.001	Significant

**Significant at 0.01

Research Question 3 (RQ3): Does the dimensions viz. Knowledge management and SNS Threat have an impact on Students' Achievement?

$H_{03.1}$Knowledge management has no impact on Students' Achievement.

Analysis: It can be seen from Table. No 4.65, the p value is lesser than the significance level, hence the null hypothesis is rejected.

Result: Knowledge management has a positive impact on Students' Achievement.

$H_{03.2}$SNS Threat has no impact on Students' Achievement.

Analysis: It can be seen from Table. No 4.65, the p value is lesser than the significance level, hence the null hypothesis is rejected.

Result: SNS Threat has a positive impact on Students' Achievement.

Model Fit Indices Summary: The important fit indices are presented in the Table below.

Interpretation: It can be seen from Table 27 the Goodness of Fit Index (GFI) value was 0.967, Adjusted Goodness of Fit Index (AGFI) value was 0.919 and Comparative Fit Index (CFI) value was 0.966. All these values are (greater than 0.9) indicating a very good fit. It was found that Root Mean Score Error of Approximation (RMSEA) value was 0.043 (lesser than 0.06) and Root Mean Square Residual (RMR) value was 0.014 (lesser than 0.02).

Table 27. Models fit indices summary

Parameters	Acceptable Values for Good Fit	Research Model Values
GFI	>0.9	0.967
AGFI	>0.9	0.919
CFI	>0.9	0.966
RMSEA	<0.06	0.043
RMR	<0.02	0.014

Source: Primary Data, SPSS AMOS output, Haier et al. (2009); Hooper et al. (2008); Steiger (2007); Hu and Bentler (1999).

Suggestions

Students can be encouraged to utilize SNS appropriately since it advances good communication with their teachers in regards to class work and related educational activities. Social Networking Sites should be utilized for self-improvement, where these sites help in upgrading individuals in their desired fields. Moreover, social sites act as a platform in enabling people to share information on topics with people having common interests.

SNS is highly useful for sharing and trading data and accordingly, it should be utilized to make awareness among individuals in a general public and to associate groups in regards to social issues. The Social Networking Sites can be utilized for the reasons for exchanges on social issues and furthermore to share their very own thoughts and contemplations in addition to creating groups on Social Networking Sites to enhance their academic performance along with entertainment.

Tools that will enable the user to expel their records and also alter their very own posts on the other individuals' must be watched carefully. Automated separating instruments for deciding the authentic substance should be used. Tools for controlling the labeling of pictures delineating them must be utilized by every user. New security programming, for example, perception devices for expanding the usage of protection choices by giving clear portrayals of social networks, companion vicinity, and accessibility of profile highlights. The quality of confirmation technique changes from SNS to SNS. Notwithstanding, so as to keep away from fake and troublesome users, the validation component should be further fortified utilizing extra confirmation factors, for example, using Captchas as double-check validation.

Users should be increasingly cognizant about the data they uncover through their own profiles in online social networks. They additionally need to precisely keep up their profiles through periodical survey and fundamental alteration of the profile substance to guarantee proper exposure of data. Government should start distinctive instructive and awareness raising efforts to illuminate the users to make the reasonable utilization of the Social Networking Sites and in addition to urge the suppliers to create and review security aware with corporate approaches.

CONCLUSION

The use of social networking sites among the university students requires much attention with increasing number of students creating profile and feeding their personal information into the sites. The increasing activity on the sites by student community can negatively impact the normal activity of students' life. This can also become a hindrance to the academic development as well as social engagement of students. Therefore, there is a need to study, assess and evaluate the issues revolving the usage of social networking sites among the student community. The study shows that the distribution of respondents according to their influence of SNS. It shows both section – wise distribution and their composite scores. Also, the table shows the respective mean scores and standard deviation. It may be inferred that, 77.50% percent of the respondents have stated that, the influence of SNS are high, 18.55% of the respondents have stated that, the influence of SNS is moderate and 3.95% of the respondents have stated that, the influence of SNS is low. However, the composite mean score (2.72), standard deviation (0.530) depicts that the respondents have stated that, the influence of SNS is high.

Based on the findings of the study the faculty members should assist the students with making significant utilization of social networking sites by joining them into their exercises. This should be possible by acquainting the students with the social networking sites that are entirely for scholarly work and research. Both the parents and faculty members should attempt endeavors to urge the students to invest more energy studying their books than on social networking sites. Social Networking Sites ought to be utilized for self-improvement, where these sites upgrade IT abilities and help students to stay in contact with their experts. SNS are the most amazing media for sharing and trading data and accordingly, it ought to be utilized to make mindfulness among individuals in a general public and to associate bunches in regards to social issues. The Social Networking Sites ought to be utilized for the reasons for exchanges on social issues and furthermore to share their very own thoughts and contemplations. The ministry of information and Technology, Government of India should draft regulatory measures to control the workings of social networking sites that are accessible by Indian students.

ACKNOWLEDGMENT

This article has been written with the financial support of RUSA – Phase 2.0 grant sanctioned vide Letter No. F.24-51 / 2014-U, Policy (TNMulti-Gen), Dept. of Edn. Govt. of India, Dt.09.10.2018

REFERENCES

Ahmed, Q. (2011). Retrieved from http://californiawatch.org/dailyreport/social-networkinghelpsstudents-perform-better-professor-says-12292

Ahn, J. (2012). Teenagers' experiences with social network sites: Relationships to bridging and bonding social capital. *The Information Society*, *28*(2), 99–109. doi:10.1080/01972243.2011.649394

Alwagait, E., Shahzad, B., & Alim, S. (2015). Impact of social media usage on students' academic performance in Saudi Arabia. *Computers in Human Behavior*, *51*, 1092–1097. doi:10.1016/j.chb.2014.09.028

Banquil, K., & Chua, N. A. (2009). Social Networking Sites affects one's academic Performance adversely. *UST College of Nursing*, 1-42. Retrieved from http// www.Scribd. Com/ doc/2891955

Charnigo, L., & Barnett-Ellis, P. (2007). The Impact of a Digital Trend on Academic Libraries. *Information Technology and Libraries*, *26*(1), 23–33. doi:10.6017/ital.v26i1.3286

Chen, D. Y. T., Chu, S. K. W., & Xu, S. Q. (2012). How do libraries use social networking sites to interact with users. *Proceedings of the American Society for Information Science and Technology, 49*(1), 1–10. doi:10.1002/meet.14504901286

Church, K., & de Oliveira, R. (2013). What's up with WhatsApp? Comparing Mobile Instant Messaging Behaviours with Traditional SMS. In *Proceedings of the 15th international conference on Human-computer interaction with mobile devices and services* (pp. 352-361). ACM.

DeAndrea, D. C., Ellison, N. B., LaRose, R., Steinfield, C., & Fiore, A. (2012). Serious social media: On the use of social media for improving students' adjustment to college. *The Internet and higher education, 15*(1), 15–23. doi:10.1016/j.iheduc.2011.05.009

Eyrich, N., Padman, M. L., & Sweetser, K. D. (2008). PR practitioners' use of social media tools and communication technology. *Public Relations Review, 34*(4), 412–414. doi:10.1016/j.pubrev.2008.09.010

Jacobson, T. B. (2011). Facebook as a library tool: Perceived vs. actual use. *College & Research Libraries, 72*(1), 79–90. doi:10.5860/crl-88r1

Jahan, I., & Ahmed, S. (2012). Students' perceptions of academic use of social networking sites: A survey of university students in Bangladesh. *Information Development, 28*(3), 235–247. doi:10.1177/0266666911433191

Kindi, S., &Alhashmi, S. M. (2012). Use of Social Networking Sites among Shinas College of Technology Students in Oman. *Journal of Information & Knowledge Management, 11*(1), 1250002-1-1250002-9.

Lau, W. W. (2017). Effects of social media usage and social media multitasking on the academic performance of university students. *Computers in Human Behavior, 68*, 286–291. doi:10.1016/j.chb.2016.11.043

Li, H., & Sakamoto, Y. (2014). Social impacts in social media: An examination of perceived truthfulness and sharing of information. *Computers in Human Behavior, 41*, 278–287. doi:10.1016/j.chb.2014.08.009

Mahadi, S. R. S., Jamaludin, N. N., Johari, R., & Fuad, I. N. F. M. (2016). The Impact of Social Media among Undergraduate Students: Attitude. *Procedia: Social and Behavioral Sciences, 219*, 472–479. doi:10.1016/j.sbspro.2016.05.022

Mahat, S. (2014). Impact of social networking Sites (SNS) on the youth. In *National conference on Innovations in IT and Management* (pp. 978-81). Academic Press.

Nielit, S. G., & Thanuskodi, S. (2016). E-discovery components of E-teaching and M-learning: An overview. In *E-Discovery Tools and Applications in Modern Libraries* (pp. 240–248). Academic Press. doi:10.4018/978-1-5225-0474-0.ch013

Paramo, M. F. (2014). The impact of perceived social support in first- year Spanish college students' adjustment. *Journal of International Scientific Publications, 12*, 289–300.

Paul, J. A., Baker, H. M., & Cochran, J. D. (2012). Effect of Online Social Networking on Student Performance. *Computer in Human Behaviors, 28*(b).

Salvation and Adzharuddin. (2014). The Influence of Social Network Sites (SNS) upon Academic Performance of Malaysian Students. *International Journal of Humanities and Social Science, 10*(1).

Steinfield, C., Ellison, N., Lampe, C., & Vitak, J. (2012). Online social network sites and the concept of social capital. In F. L. Lee, L. Leung, J. S. Qiu, & D. Chu (Eds.), *Frontiers in New Media Research* (pp. 115–131). New York: Routledge.

Tayseer, Z., & Alcheikh, A. (2014). Social Network: Academic and Social Impact on College Students. *ASEE 2014 Zone I Conference.*

Thanuskodi, S. (2009). The Environment of Higher Education Libraries in India. *Library Philosophy and Practice*, 278.

Thanuskodi, S. (2013). *Challenges of academic library management in developing countries.* Academic Press. doi:10.4018/978-1-4666-4070-2

Thanuskodi, S. (2016). Awareness and use of e-resources among social scientists of alagappa university and its affiliated colleges. *Library Philosophy and Practice, 2016*, 1–28.

Thanuskodi, S., & Meena, M. (2013). Use of e-journals by the faculty members, researchers, and students in the faculty of engineering and technology, annamalai university: A survey. In Challenges of Academic Library Management in Developing Countries (pp. 218–225). Academic Press. doi:10.4018/978-1-4666-4070-2.ch016

Yan, Z. (2012). College students' uses and perceptions of social networking sites for health and wellness information. *Information Research, 17*(3), 3.

Zohoorian-Fooladi, N., & Abrizah, A. (2014). Academic librarians and their social media presence a story of motivations and deterrents. *Information Development, 30*(2), 159–171. doi:10.1177/0266666913481689

ADDITIONAL READING

Balamurugan, T., & Thanuskodi, S. (2019). Use of social networking sites among the college students in Tamil Nadu, India. *Library Philosophy and Practice, 2019*. Retrieved from Scopus.

Jacobson, T. B. (2011). Facebook as a library tool: Perceived vs. actual use. *College & Research Libraries, 72*(1), 79–90. doi:10.5860/crl-88r1

Jahan, I., & Ahmed, S. (2012). Students' perceptions of academic use of social networking sites: A survey of university students in Bangladesh. *Information Development, 28*(3), 235–247. doi:10.1177/0266666911433191

Kindi, S., &Alhashmi, S. M. (2012). Use of Social Networking Sites among Shinas College of Technology Students in Oman. *Journal of Information & Knowledge Management, 11*(1), 1250002-1-1250002-9.

Kumar, A., & Thanuskodi, S. (2015). Using social network sites for library services in public libraries: Possibilities and challenges. In Handbook of Research on Inventive Digital Tools for Collection Management and Development in Modern Libraries (pp. 53–68). doi:10.4018/978-1-4666-8178-1.ch004

Lenhart, A., Madden, M., Macgill, A.R., & Smith, A. (2007). Teens and social media, Pew internet American life project.

Mahajan, P., Singh, H., & Kumar, A. (2013). Use of SNSs by the researchers in India. *Library Review*, *62*(8/9), 525–546. doi:10.1108/LR-11-2012-0119

Thanuskodi, S. (2011). *Use of ICT among faculty members of self financing engineering colleges in the changing higher education environment. Library Philosophy and Practice, 2011(AUGUST)*. Retrieved from Scopus.

Thanuskodi, S. (2012). Assessing the efficacy of library services of district central libraries in tamil nadu from users perception. *DESIDOC Journal of Library and Information Technology*, *32*(6), 485–492. doi:10.14429/djlit.32.6.2845

KEY TERMS AND DEFINITIONS

Facebook: Currently Facebook is the fifth most trafficked site on the internet worldwide and second most trafficked social media site on the world. It was first founded by Mark Zuckerberg in 2004. These are interactive allowing visitors to leave comments, message each other via widgets on the blogs and it is the interactivity that distinguishes them from other static websites. It has affected the social life and activity of people in various ways.

Social Media Hermit: Is an individual who avoids any form of online sharing. With the increasing societal pressures to be searchable on social media platforms, the number of social media hermits is constantly declining. One of the headwinds facing social media hermits is the trend for recruiters and human resource professionals to rely on online networks such as LinkedIn to send out new postings, as well as the new emphasis on social media experience in many professional jobs.

Social Network: Social network is a broad term used to denote the blogs, user created videos and wikis. A social networking is an online service, platform or site that focuses on building and reflecting of social network or social relations among people who share interests and activities.

Social Networking Sites: Social networking site functions like an online community of internet users. People use social networking sites for communication personally as well as professionally to contact with others. Social networking sites like Facebook provides new venues for young LIS Professionals to express themselves and to interact with one another.

Twitter: Fast and sometimes furious, certain businesses really thrive on Twitter. If your business is related to entertainment, sports, politics, or marketing, you stand to earn tremendous engagement on Twitter. On Twitter, brands have an opportunity to craft and hone their voice – there's room to be clever and personable in addition to informative and helpful.

This research was previously published in the Handbook of Research on Digital Content Management and Development in Modern Libraries; pages 124-147, copyright year 2020 by Information Science Reference (an imprint of IGI Global).

Chapter 96

Using Twitter to Form Professional Learning Communities:

An Analysis of Georgia K–12 School Personnel Discussing Educational Technology on Twitter

Mete Akcaoglu
Georgia Southern University, USA

Charles B. Hodges
iD https://orcid.org/0000-0003-3918-9261
Georgia Southern University, USA

Lucas John Jensen
Georgia Southern University, USA

ABSTRACT

Social media has become an important tool for informal teacher professional development. Although there is a growing body of research investigating issues across the US, there is a lack of research on teacher professional development taking place on Twitter in Georgia, USA. In this research, the authors applied digital methods to analyze 5,425 entries from educators participating in a state-level, weekly, synchronous chat about educational technology (#TECHTalkGA) on the social media platform Twitter. Findings include that participants utilized the chat for organization, planning, and classroom technologies, with a predilection toward specific hardware and software topics. Limitations and implications for future research are discussed.

DOI: 10.4018/978-1-6684-7123-4.ch096

INTRODUCTION

Teachers are required to maintain their professional knowledge, and the process of maintaining current professional knowledge often is described as *professional development*. Professional development can be categorized as formal or informal (Hodges, 2015). Formal professional development often is experienced in traditional formats such as face-to-face workshops, conference sessions, or webinars led by an expert or experts. Informal professional development may take many forms, but increasingly online social networking tools are utilized. Professional development was the most common educational purpose for social networking identified in the reviewed literature (Galvin & Greenhow, 2020, p. 21).

In addition to formal forms of teacher professional development, teachers have accepted informal professional development experiences such as EdCamp meetings or online professional learning networks (e.g. Carpenter, 2014; Trust et al., 2014). One platform for informal online professional development has been through communicating (e.g., sharing resources) through social media (Rosenberg et al., 2016; Greenhalgh et al., 2020). These informal professional development experiences are typically not led by a single expert, but are led by teachers, for teachers. The focus of this paper is a specific use of the free-to-access online service Twitter (http://www.twitter.com) as a professional learning network by education professionals. .

BACKGROUND

Online Education and Online Professional Learning

In the last two decades, the mainstream growth of the Internet has led to transformative change in education, particularly higher education, as the Internet has provided new opportunities for online and distance learning (Allen & Seaman, 2010; Shea & Bidjerano, 2010). Commensurate with this change has been a rise in the sphere of online activity known as social media – networks of users tied together via Web 2.0-based applications that offer individuals an opportunity to generate and share content of their own (Kaplan & Haenlein, 2010). Noting that the term *social media* is hard to define in a world where almost all technologies feature a social component, Kaplan and Haelein (2010) defined *social media* as "a group of Internet-based applications that build on the ideological and technological foundations of Web 2.0, and that allow creation and exchange of user generated content" (p. 61). Examples of social media are large social networks like Twitter, Facebook, Tumblr, or sites like Instagram and YouTube, which focus on one type of media.

Online education has been steadily growing, and as of 2008, nearly 4.6 million students were enrolled in some form of online education (Gabriel, 2010). Recent economic downturns have driven millions of people to look online for new learning opportunities and careers. Between 2007 and 2010, online education enrollment increased 25% (Allen & Seaman, 2010; Shea & Bidjerano, 2010). Universities – whether public, private, or for profit – are increasingly pushing online education as part of their curricula (Gabriel, 2010). In some cases, online education is considered necessary for these institutions' long-term survival (Gabriel, 2010; Kaya, 2010). As universities and other institutions of higher education move to implement more online education, they also struggle with the quality of the education (Kaya, 2010). Lack of engagement and motivation is seen as one of the central problems in the current landscape of online education. Online education – sometimes known as e-learning – offers significant advantages in flexibility, individuality of instruction, and fewer geographic and temporal limitations; it has also been shown to have significant drawbacks, such as student isolation, the need for tutors, and lack of participation (Wu, Tennyson, & Hsia, 2010; Wu, Tennyson, Hsia, & Liao, 2008; Yang & Liu, 2007). Research has shown that online learning can be a disengaging experience (Barbour & Plough, 2009; Palloff & Pratt, 2007). The flexibility and convenience of taking a class online is an enticing prospect to many students, but staying engaged in an online course, whether synchronous or asynchronous, requires a high level of motivation (Barbour & Plough, 2009).

Online Communication, Social Media, and Personal Learning Environments

The pedagogical concept of Personal Learning Environments (PLEs) challenges the dominance of learning management system (LMS) usage in online courses, bringing a student-centered and bottom-up perspective to online education. The concept of PLEs is relatively recent and, as such, no central, agreed-upon definition of a PLE exists, though some key common elements appear in the literature. McElvaney and Berge (2010) defined a PLE as "the sum of websites and technologies that an individual makes use of to learn" (para. 18). This definition is a broad, inclusive one, but it is an acknowledgment that online learning can, and does, take place in spheres beyond the typical LMS-housed world of online education. To be sure, LMSs are included in this definition, but so are social media like Facebook or Twitter, blogs, video sharing sites, and informational clearinghouses like Wikipedia, to name a few. In much the same manner as students learn outside of the face-to-face classroom context, so, too, do online students. Online students might learn from articles posted by friends on Facebook, have heated debates replying to posts using a political Twitter hashtag, or share home renovation ideas on Pinterest. These are all learning activities, however removed they are from the formality of an online classroom. In a sense, all people engaged in online activity have their own personal online environment made up of the websites they frequent, including social media sites that employ hashtags.

The thinking behind PLEs has been that instruction should be situated in an environment more congruent with the learners' typical technology usage for their personal lives (Attwell, 2007). In a PLE, each online learner may create her and his own personal learning environment and can choose to engage with the course materials and assignments using the tools more closely aligned with each learner's non-academic life (Sclater, 2008; Van Harmelen, 2008), including social media like Facebook, Instagram, Twitter, and Pinterest. In this type of learning environment, students have more choice about how they engage with the material and can use tools with which they are more comfortable. Students rarely encounter environments like LMSs in their personal online lives, yet many of them spend time traversing the Internet, tweeting, social networking, posting photos to Instagram, putting videos on YouTube and TikTok, and engaging in online discussions. These active online personal lives stand in contrast to the lesser-motivated online educational lives of students.

The PLE concept could be a benefit to teachers and students alike, as it allows, almost mandatorily, for differentiated teaching as it moves between online platforms. Students receive more variety in their instruction and teachers have more control over which technologies, tools, and platforms they use to create and deploy the content. As Mott (2010) describes, an ideal PLE features student choice, meaning that they can select tools that most match their needs and interests. However, this approach might be more fractious and decentralized than an LMS, with content and communication possibly happening in multiple places. This might prove confusing and complicated for inexperienced faculty and students, and there could also be privacy and FERPA issues for the use of some of the tools (Mott, 2010). It could also be time-consuming and costly to maintain the disparate tools needed to teach a course, and the data is not always available or connects with institutional systems like online grade books and class roles (Mott, 2010). Technical support is also split up between tools and platforms, meaning little control over outages and technical issues and splintered support apparatus between providers (Mott, 2010). PLEs support modular, student-centered, constructivist approaches that offer teachers and students the choice to engage with content and course technology in a manner that more meets their needs and interests, but this combination of creative possibility for teachers means multiple tools and non-standardized technology usage from student to student. This could be highly rewarding and offer lots of pedagogical possibilities, but it might require extra time and effort.

To understand the concept of the PLE and the contrast between personal and academic online activity, it is important to also understand the development of the Web 2.0 paradigm. Web 2.0 has been a philosophical shift as much as a technological one, representing a change in how people create and share content on the Internet, moving from developer-generated to user-generated and shared content (Cormode & Krishnamurthy, 2008; Greenhow, Robelia, & Hughes, 2009; Ravenscroft, 2009). In the early Internet days of the 1990s, retroactively known as the era of "Web 1.0," content was delivered in a top-down manner by a limited number of content providers (Cormode & Krishnamurthy, 2008; Greenhow et al., 2009). Although Web 1.0 was touted as being "interactive," beyond its e-commerce role, it functioned as little more than a repository of knowledge, akin to an encyclopedia or dictionary, or a series of news articles generated by the major media (Cormode & Krishnamurthy, 2008; Greenhow et al., 2009). This version of the Internet mirrored traditional educational practices, expert-driven and top-down, with users functioning as passive receptors of information (Dede, 2008; Greenhow et al., 2009). Most user-generated content was relegated to communication-based communities, like message boards, chat rooms, and bulletin boards, and posting content online required knowledge of programming hypertext markup language, otherwise known as HTML (Greenhow et al., 2009). In the late 1990s, and even more so in the early 2000s, the top-down paradigm of content generation started to shift toward the user, as new tools – dubbed Web 2.0 – helped users generate and post content to the Web themselves (Greenhow et al., 2009). Websites and tools like blogs, YouTube, wikis, Twitter, and social networking sites all accurately represent the movement in user-generated content that characterizes Web 2.0.

What is Twitter?

Twitter is an online social media platform that allows users to communicate publicly. Twitter can be accessed with a variety of digital devices through web browsers or dedicated apps. The unique structure of Twitter allows for synchronous or asynchronous conversations on various topics from news, culture to education (Greenhalgh, et al., 2020). Communication with Twitter centers around sending out tweets to one's followers and receiving tweets from the individuals (or entities) they follow in their timeline. A *tweet* is a message consisting of text (up to 280 characters) and media files such as images, animations, or videos can be attached with each message. It is common to identify tweets with special keywords called *hashtags*. For example, a hashtag identifying a tweet as relevant to teachers would be "#teachers." Galvin and Greenhow (2020) noted that the use of hashtags and synchronous chats have been repeatedly found to be important to teachers, and that Twitter has been found to be the most popular social networking service for K-12 teachers. Use of hashtags has been found to be similar to "affinity spaces" (Greenhalgh & Koehler, 2017), which helps organize the conversation and context of the discussions.

How is Twitter Used by Educators?

Twitter is utilized for various purposes in education. Teachers find it to be an efficient, accessible, and interactive tool for staying on top of novel ideas, education advances, trends, and educational technology (Carpenter & Krutka, 2015). New teachers have used it to form mentoring networks (Risser, 2013). It has been integrated into the learning process to enhance the linguistic competence of secondary school students (i.e. Cano, 2012), and it has been embraced by educators as a way to form professional learning networks (Carpenter & Krutka, 2014; Coleman et al., 2018; Davis, 2015). In an analysis of several thousand tweets from teachers, Fischer et al. (2019) observed that "Twitter reflects aspects of high-quality professional development" (para. 1). Educators use Twitter to share information and resources with colleagues all around the world, thus possibly alleviating feelings of isolation experienced by some teachers (Carpenter & Krutka, 2014; Trust et al., 2016; Tucker, 2019). It also has been used as just-in-time teacher professional development in response to (tragic) current events (Greenhalgh & Koehler, 2017), and as a way to connect teachers during pandemic-related school closings (Hogan, 2020). Researchers have noted that state-level Twitter chats involving educators are thriving, but also that there is more to be known about these chats (Greenhalgh, 2020; Rosenberg et al., 2016).

The #TechTalkGA hashtag is an informal hashtag created by educators who work and live in Georgia, USA to share resources and thoughts about the use of educational technologies. It was formed by educators who are interested in using technology in their classrooms, professionals who work in school libraries, and other district professionals who are involved and interested in increasing the effective usage of technology in schools. Due to its informal and voluntary nature, information regarding its founders, founding date, or other elements that defines its structure does not exist by design (Rosenberg et al., 2016). In fact, the non-existence of this information is what defines these spaces: they are shared and not owned.

Theoretical Framework

To structure our investigation, we used the *Enriching Professional Learning Networks* (EPLN) framework introduced by Krutka, Carpenter, and Trust (2017). The EPLN framework describes a teacher professional learning network as consisting of people, spaces, and tools. Within EPLN, questions are asked such as: **Who** are the people in the PLN?, **Which spaces** are conducive to professional growth?, and **What tools** are acquired by participating in the PLN? Applying EPLN as our lens for this investigation provides a structure for our two research questions.

The Present Study

To address the need to know more about state-level Twitter chats, the focus of the present research is examining K12 educators' use of the Twitter hashtag, #TECHtalkGA, the Georgia-centered Twitter professional learning network with a specific focus on using technology for teaching and learning. #TECHtalkGA functions as both a weekly online chat and an asynchronous portal for educators in Georgia focusing on topics related to technology in education. Our purpose in this study was to examine this network for Georgia educators to fill the gap in the literature about state-level Twitter chats and investigate the nature of the conversation in this hashtag. Two research questions guided our examination of the hashtag data:

1. What is the nature of the activity of the Twitter discussions using the #TECHtalkGA hashtag?
   a. How is #TechTalkGA used across time?
   b. What types of Twitter interaction types were present across time?
2. What is the nature of the content discussed using the Twitter hashtag #TECHtalkGA?

Methods

Digital methods were utilized for the present research. Rosenberg et al. (2016) note that "digital methods are new research techniques that have been built around the collection and analysis of data coming from Twitter and similar sources" (p. 27). While we have applied newer tools and techniques to our data, the use of public data mining has been "an emerging research method for the past two decades" (Kimmons & Veletsianos, 2018, p. 492) and other researchers have established the appropriateness and utility of automated digital methods for quantitative content analysis (e.g. Greenhalgh, 2020). Digital methods may include setting up automations to collect and store publicly available data in Google Spreadsheets. For example, in this study, by using a script we were able to collect a large amount of public data (Tweets) in a Google Spreadsheet and analyze them using computational tools. This exploratory data analysis is "a different approach to analysis that can generate valuable information and provide ideas for further investigation" (Pertl & Hevey, 2010, p.456).

Data Sources and Collection

From January 2019 to April 2020, by using a publicly available script, Twitter Archiving Google Sheet (TAGS; Hawksey, 2014), we collected and stored a total of 5425 tweets by automatically searching for the hashtag #TechTALKGA at every hour and save them to a Google Sheet. Greenhow, Galvin, and Staudt Willet (2019) note that studying these tweets as "digital traces" (p. 181) allows researchers "opportunities to conduct authentic and useful research of social media behavior, in the contexts where it actually occurs, to better inform practice and policy" (p. 182).

Once the tweets were stored in the spreadsheet, it was exported as a data frame to be analyzed using quantitative and computational qualitative methods. We did not find unwanted tweets to be a problem in the data we collected, but data sets should be examined for possible spam entries (Carpenter, Willet, Koehler, & Greenhalgh, 2019). Using the *tidytags* R package (Staudt Willet & Rosenberg, 2021) we were able to remove deleted or private tweets.

Data Analysis and Procedures

To prepare the data for analysis, we followed the following steps. First, using tidytags R package (Staudt Willet & Rosenberg, 2021), we cleaned the data off of the protected and deleted tweets. Although tidytags can pull numerous variables for each tweet (e.g., location, urls, etc.), due to the nature of our research questions we were only interested in time, interaction, and tweet text data. Using the built-in functions inside tidytags, we created an edgelist to identify the usage types (e.g., retweet, quote tweet, etc.). This allowed us to perform analyses on the tweet data regarding the usage frequency and types that were investigated the first research question.

In addition to providing basic descriptive statistics, we also analyzed the content of the Tweets using the *Quanteda* package in R (Benoit, et al., 2018). Quanteda allows researchers to analyze the content of the Tweets using a corpus-centered approach to understand overall trends. Corpus here refers to the text, in other words the content of each tweet. By creating a corpus from the tweets, we created a data that is composed of each word of each tweet. Using this corpus data, we were able to clean up the words that would not contribute to the findings (e.g., http, #TechTalkGA, personal pronouns, etc.) or were a regular part of the tweets sent to this hashtag (e.g., "A1" for answering tweets to questions asked during weekly chats). In order to understand the content discussed in #TECHtalkGA, our initial analysis was to take a look at the most frequently used words in the hashtag.

To prepare the data for the corpus analyses, first we converted the tweet text data into Quanteda corpus. Using the built-in functions in the package we were able to conduct "dictionary analysis, exploring texts using keywords-in-context, computing document and feature similarities, and discovering multi-word expressions through collocation scoring" (para. 1). After removal of the stopwords, and creation of the corpus text data, we analyzed both the nature of activity (using regular statistics), and also explored the frequency of certain keywords, as well as how the content of the tweets were related to each other (i.e., textplot networks). To prepare the figures, we used ggplot2 package available in tidyverse (Wickham et al., 2019).

Findings

The findings are organized by research questions.

Research Question 1: What is the nature of the activity of the Twitter discussions using the #TECHtalkGA hashtag?

First, we examined the activity on #TechTalkGA over time as seen in Figure 1. The data showed that from January 2019 to April 2020 the highest levels of activity (i.e., number of Tweets) for #TECHtalkGA occurred mostly on synchronous chat nights (Monday evenings), when the regularly scheduled chat occurred. During this period, users frequently tagged (i.e., @ mentions, n = 7346), retweeted (n = 1152), sent direct responses to each other (n = 943), and quoted other tweets (n = 672), as seen in Figure 2. Periods of relatively low activity are during winter and summer breaks.

Next, we analyzed the dataset to determine the most active participants in terms of the number of tweets they sent and received. We found that participation was skewed: only four users had been power users of the hashtag, accounting for almost half the number of tweets (n = 2401). The most sought out member was the organizer of the weekly Twitter chats associated with the hashtag. The top sender list was highly similar to the top receiver list.

Research Question 2: What is the content discussed using the Twitter hashtag #TECHtalkGA?

Our analysis revealed that there were a total of 5399 unique words identified, after grouping similar words by the first four letters. The most frequently used word was "tech," (n = 940) being followed by "teac," (n = 911) and "lear" (n = 688). Using these letter combinations allowed us to capture various forms of words. For example, using "teac" captures words like "teach", "teaching", and "teacher".

Figure 1. Hashtag Activity January 2019 - April 2020*
Note. Green points are days with more than the number of average Tweets.

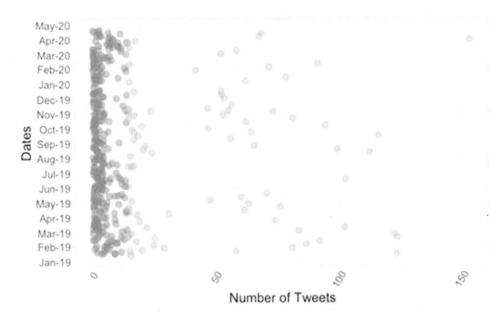

Figure 2. Interaction Types Across the Timeline

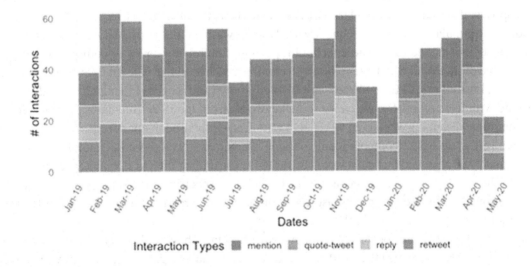

As can be seen in Figure 3, the most frequently used words reflect the main components of educational technology: learning, teachers, students, time, school. The frequency of words technology, edtech (n = 518), and google (n = 422), indicate that technology was a central focus of the PLN (34%). It also is evident that the hashtag served some social functions, as indicated by the frequency of the words "share" and "friend" in the most frequently used words.

Figure 3. Word Frequency January 2019 - April 2020

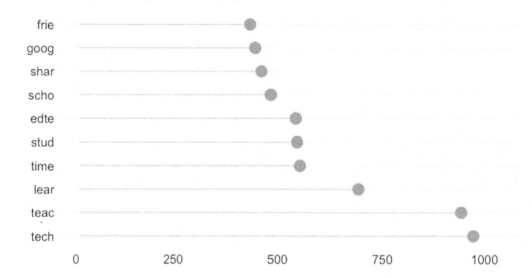

As it can be seen in Table 1, friend and share were usually used in the context of inviting others to the weekly chats or introducing themselves during these chats. The words school, edtech, student, teach, learn, and tech were contextualized within educational technology where the participants talked about the use of technology for teaching and learning purposes. Google was used to talk about Google-specific tools and apps, and indicates the popularity of Google tools in schools.

In addition to populating the most frequently used topics, we ran a follow-up analysis to see how much the users talked about some of the more technology integration related topics in comparison to topics that relate to the overall design and integration of technology-rich learning. The International Society for Technology in Education (ISTE) publishes various, well-known and accepted standards related teaching and learning with technology. So, we chose some keywords from the ISTE Standards for Educators as well as other more technology-centered words that were frequently used in our corpus: "empow", "construct", "innovat", "design", "computational", "think", "creative", "collabor","technology", "google", "tool", "digital". We observed that most words in our ISTE vocabulary did not frequently occur in tweets tagged with the hashtag of focus, especially some of the more specific words such as "computational" or "constructionism" (Figure 4). In contrast, the technocentric words relating to specific software or hardware more frequently occurred in the corpus.

Finally, to get a sense of the conversation involving the hashtag, above and beyond stand-alone words, we analyzed the context in which the words co-occurred. This analysis gave us a sense of which words were used in the context of the others, enabling us to make some conjectures about the content of the conversation. Using the feature co-occurrence matrix (FCM) created through Quanteda, we created a text network plot. First, using the topfeatures function, we selected the most frequently used 30 words. Next, we created a network plot depicting the frequency of occurrence and co-occurrence (the minimum threshold was set to .85). In our network plot, the size of the words and the links between them represent their proportional frequency. In other words, if a word occurs more frequently or two words appear in the same context more frequently their text size and link width would be proportionally bigger.

Table 1. Sample Tweets for the most frequent keywords in TechTalkGA tweets

Keyword	Tweet
friend	Get ready for tonight's #TECHtalkGA at 9pm (EST), sharing our best WFH tips! **Remember to invite a friend!**
google	#TECHtalkGA A4: Most recently, I've been "teaching" more & more ppl about **Google** Meet, Microsoft Teams, Flipgrid, and Screencastify!
share	Q1: Welcome to #TECHtalkGA! **Share** your name/dist/role and where you were in 2009!
school	#TECHtalkGA A3: I am so incredibly proud to work in **@FCSchoolsGA**! We have some of the best Ts ever, who truly care about Ss; who are working harder than ever to design "qual learning exps" for Ss from afar with ZERO prep! They are amazing!! Never been prouder!
edtech	#TECHtalkGA Q2: What's the number one thing you think Ts need to understand about using **#edtech** in the classroom?
student	#techtalkga A4: I've done the flipped classroom several years, and I'm often asked to speak about it. Just like other tech, a flipped classroom won't fix bad teaching. But, it can be a technique that can turn class time a more **student-centered** environment.
time	You guys! #GaETC19 is THIS WEEK! I'm so pumped! If you are attending, be sure to join in the #TECHtalkGA chat tonight at 9pm to talk about how to get the most out of our **time** at the conference!
learn	#TECHtalkGA A4: Some the recommendations from the authors were things like "keep your lessons engaging" That's easy to say, but difficult to do if you haven't seen it WITH TECH. Be purposeful about how Ss use it. Teach them how to use it to **learn**. Model it for learning.
teach(er)	#TECHtalkGA returns to our normal format tonight focusing on how we support students, **teachers**, and each other! Come share; join the convo at 9pm!
tech(nology)	@iste Regional chat: #TECHtalkGA on Mondays at 9pm! For #ETCoaches, MSs, and anyone passionate about **technology** in education! All are welcome, even if you're not in GA!

Figure 4. Frequency of Combined Keywords in #TECHtalkGA

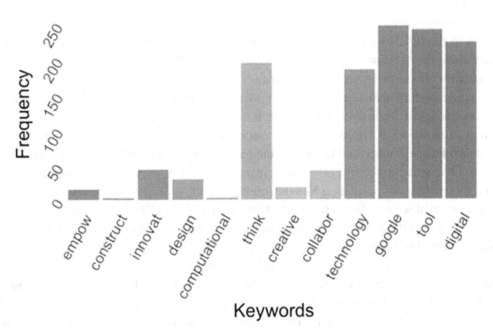

As seen in Figure 5, we were able to group the discourse into three categories: planning, organization, and classroom technology. Organization included conversations such as organizing the synchronous chat hour the next week, while planning seems to focus on planning to attend an upcoming conference (GAETC19), and classroom technology included using technology to teach and learn.

Figure 5. Co-occurrence Matrix

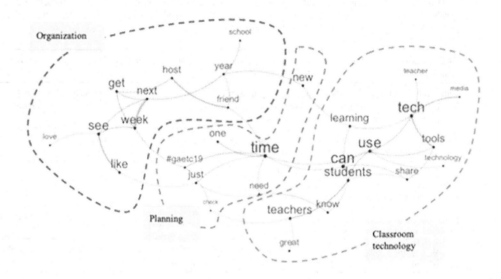

DISCUSSION

With respect to the EPLN framework, our investigation of the data related to research question 1 revealed answers to the questions, *Who are the people in the PLN?,* and *Which spaces are conducive to professional growth?* First, it seems like the answer to the *who* question is that there were relatively few people active in the discussion and the most involved member was the organizer of the discussion. As for spaces conducive to professional growth, it must be noted that the *space* consists of the online discussion utilizing the #TECHtalkGA hashtag, but it may be considered in two parts: the synchronous chat held on Monday evenings, and the use of the hashtag asynchronously at other times of the week. For maximum engagement with the other participants in the PLN, participants should plan to join the chat during its synchronous portion on Monday nights.

Our observation of seeing a few participants dominating the #TECHtalkGA discussions is consistent with the "low active participation, yet high professional value seems to define the typical Twitter PD experience" observed by (Galvin & Greenhow, 2020, p. 18). We observed in particular that the use of the hashtag was mostly during the typically scheduled Monday night synchronous chats and that there were comparatively lower levels of activity with the hashtag outside of the synchronous chats and on breaks in the school year (i.e. summer). Based on this finding, we can argue that teachers use the hashtag during the school year, and tend to engage more during times that allow for more interaction. As identified by Greenhalgh et al. (2020), there is a difference between the participation during chat and non-chat times in terms of tweets' content (e.g., more work-related discussions during non-chat contexts).

The chat and the synchronous communication seem to serve social purposes more, but attract a small number of participants.

In the weekly non-chat contexts we observed that there was a smaller group of individuals who dominated the communication in terms of contributing original content, and active participation in the discussion consisted mostly of retweets or mentioning another user than replies or quoting tweets. This conforms with Greenhalgh et al.'s (2020) findings in that non-chat use of the Twitter hashtags for informal PLN's tend to lend themselves to more passive participation, as well as acts that aim to share and disseminate content. The acts of retweeting and mentioning require less cognitive involvement with the conversation than replying and tweeting, which may explain the frequency of the types of interactions that we observed. The results may also indicate that the majority of users may view the hashtag as a source of information to be read or quickly shared more than a community for active discussion.

With respect to the EPLN framework, our investigation of the data related to research question 2 revealed answers to the question, *What tools are acquired by participating in the PLN?* Our analysis of the content of the conversation showed that the hashtag was centered on technology hardware and software and associated planning and organization for hardware and software, and much less so on concepts related to leveraging the power of technology for student learning. That is, the conversation was most often focused on specific technology products (e.g. Chromebooks or Google tools) instead of established models of technology integration. Still, the observed conversations are clearly within the categories of teacher professional learning observed by Greenhow, Galvin and Staudt Willet (2019) of resource exchange, community building, and individualized needs. This suggest that #TechTalkGA as a PLN platform serves its purpose by allowing its participants to share and disseminate knowledge. The content of the conversation reflects the issues that immediately the teachers have to tackle more than issues that require more deliberation and longer-term planning. Ideally topics regarding issues in educational technology, which would be a focus on concepts of student empowerment, design, creativity, etc., would be covered, more, but our data is valuable in that it reflects what the participating teachers worry about in their day to day teaching. Veletsianos (2017) notes that "the hashtag becomes a tool to serve the needs of its users" (p. 290), and in this case #TechTalkGA's users' needs seem to focus on more technology-use related and practical issues.

Although it is impossible for the authors to gain deep understanding of PLNs mutual engagement, joint enterprise, and shared repertoire (Wenger, 1998) using the digital methods gave us a powerful new way to understand large volumes of conversation happening very quickly and efficiently. Such approaches show promise and will give researchers more analysis power as the software is developed further, especially given the fact that these are open-source and free tools.

LIMITATIONS

This research is not without a few limitations. The major limitations are related to the research methods used. First, it is impossible with the quantitative methods used to know the intentions and desires of the PLN members regarding what they perceive as the purpose of the PLN. The author's interpretations of the PLN discussion were based on their own notions of what the participants should be discussing. Interviewing or survey some participants may negate some of those notions, leading to different interpretations. Also, it is common in Twitter chats to comment and reply with non-text content like memes, videos, etc. These elements were present in the #TECHtalkGA tweets but could not be analyzed with our chosen digital methods, which analyzed text only. The lack of ability to analyze the non-text responses has been noted in previous literature (i.e. Greenhow, Galvin, & Staudt Willet, 2019). While these are viewed as limitations, the chosen methods allowed us to perform analysis on a large dataset that would be practically impossible to analyze in a timely or reliable manner using more traditional approaches to analysis.

CONCLUSIONS AND FUTURE RESEARCH

This paper provides an example of new methods to analyze state-level teacher professional development conversations using digital traces as data and digital methods, gaining some insights into what teachers are discussing and the terminology they are using. All cited resources in this article and software used are open-source and have user-guides as well as well-documented examples. We hope that these methods could easily be applied to other hashtags for other communities of educators. Based on the observations made in the present paper one can determine that at the state-level, teachers will participate in a synchronous Twitter chat organized by a particular hashtag and that they will share information on professionally relevant ideas such as planning, organization, and classroom technology. As Greenhalgh (2020) notes, regional educational Twitter hashtag spaces "are defined by different practices, different social dynamics, and presumably different goals" (p. 18). Depending on the participating teachers' needs and motivations, they may find participation in this or similar discussions to be what Krutka, Carpenter, and Trust (2017) describe with their framework for *enriching professional learning networks*.

Some questions for future research studies worth pursuing would include: What are researchers and teacher educators to do with the observations from the present study? Is it appropriate for them to join this, or similar PLNs, and attempt to drive the conversation to issues they may view as more important? Should teacher professional learning or graduate degrees for teachers use the findings to revise their preparation programs either to focus more on what in-service teachers are discussing, or to determine what concepts are not being discussed and to enhance teacher preparation curriculum in those areas? Would it be beneficial to encourage pre-service teachers to participate in the PLN as a form of informal mentoring and inclusion in genuine conversations as described in Sheridan and Young (2016)? And finally, it would be worthwhile to investigate the teachers' use of Twitter as a PLN during the school closings of the COVID pandemic of 2019, if any, and if they did in what ways they found use for it (socially and academically).

REFERENCES

Benoit, Watanabe, Wang, Nulty, Obeng, Müller, & Matsuo. (2018). quanteda: An R package for the quantitative analysis of textual data. *Journal of Open Source Software, 3*(30), 774. doi:10.21105/joss.00774

Cano, E. V. (2012). Mobile learning with Twitter to improve linguistic competence at secondary schools. *The New Educational Review*, *29*(3), 134–147. http://www.educationalrev.us.edu.pl/dok/volumes/tner_3_2012.pdf#page=134

Carpenter, J. P. (2016). Unconference professional development: Edcamp participant perceptions and motivations for attendance. *Professional Development in Education, 42*(1), 78–99. doi:10.1080/19415 257.2015.1036303

Carpenter, J. P., & Krutka, D. G. (2014). How and why educators use Twitter: A survey of the field. *Journal of Research on Technology in Education, 46*(4), 414–434. doi:10.1080/15391523.2014.925701

Carpenter, J. P., & Krutka, D. G. (2015). Engagement through microblogging: Educator professional development via Twitter. *Professional Development in Education, 41*(4), 707–728. doi:10.1080/19415 257.2014.939294

Carpenter, J. P., Willet, K. B. S., Koehler, M. J., & Greenhalgh, S. P. (2019). Spam and educators' Twitter use: Methodological challenges and considerations. *TechTrends*, 1–10. doi:10.100711528-019-00466-3

Coleman, J. M., Rice, M. L., & Wright, V. H. (2018). Educator communities of practice on Twitter. *Journal of Interactive Online Learning, 16*(1), 80–96. https://www.ncolr.org/issues/jiol/v16/n1/5/

Davis, K. (2015). Teachers' perceptions of Twitter for professional development. *Disability and Rehabilitation, 37*(17), 1551–1558. doi:10.3109/09638288.2015.1052576 PMID:26030199

Fischer, C., Fishman, B., & Schoenebeck, S. Y. (2019). New contexts for professional learning: Analyzing high school science teachers' engagement on Twitter. *AERA Open, 5*(4). doi:10.1177/2332858419894252

Galvin, S., & Greenhow, C. (2020). Educational networking: A novel discipline for improved K-12 learning based on social networks. In A. Peña-Ayala (Ed.), *Educational Networking* (pp. 3–41). Springer. doi:10.1007/978-3-030-29973-6_1

Greenhalgh, S. P. (2020). *Differences between teacher-focused twitter hashtags and implications for professional development. Italian Journal of Educational Technology.* doi:10.17471/2499-4324/1161

Greenhalgh, S. P., & Koehler, M. J. (2017). 28 days later: Twitter hashtags as "just in time" teacher professional development. *TechTrends, 61*(3), 273–281. doi:10.100711528-016-0142-4

Greenhow, C., Galvin, S. M., & Staudt Willet, K. B. (2019). What should be the role of social media in education? *Policy Insights from the Behavioral and Brain Sciences, 6*(2), 178–185. doi:10.1177/2372732219865290

Hodges, C. B. (2015). Professional development tools and technologies. In J. M. Spector (Ed.), *The SAGE encyclopedia of educational technology* (pp. 590–593). SAGE Publications, Inc. doi:10.4135/9781483346397. n246

Hogan, J. (2020). *How Twitter can serve as a COVID-19 school resource.* Retrieved April 9, 2020 from: https://blog.nassp.org/2020/03/24/how-twitter-can-serve-as-a-covid-19-school-resource/

Kimmons, R., & Veletsianos, G. (2018). Public internet data mining methods in instructional design, educational technology, and online learning research. *TechTrends, 62*(5), 492–500. doi:10.100711528-018-0307-4

Krutka, D. G., Carpenter, J. P., & Trust, T. (2017). Enriching professional learning networks: A framework for identification reflection and intention. *TechTrends, 61*(3), 246–252. doi:10.100711528-016-0141-5

Malik, A., Heyman-Schrum, C., & Johri, A. (2019). Use of Twitter across educational settings: A review of the literature. *International Journal of Educational Technology in Higher Education, 16*(1), 36. doi:10.118641239-019-0166-x

Mott, J. (2010). Envisioning the Post-LMS Era: The Open Learning Network. *EDUCAUSE Quarterly, 33*(1).

Pennebaker, J. W., Boyd, R. L., Jordan, K., & Blackburn, K. (2015). *The development and psychometric properties of LIWC2015*. University of Texas at Austin.

Pertl, M. M., & Hevey, D. (2010). Exploratory data analysis. In N. J. Salkind (Ed.), *Encyclopedia of research design* (pp. 455–458). SAGE. doi:10.4135/9781412961288.n143

Risser, H. S. (2013). Virtual induction: A novice teacher's use of Twitter to form an informal mentoring network. *Teaching and Teacher Education, 35*, 25–33. doi:10.1016/j.tate.2013.05.001

Rosenberg, J. M., Greenhalgh, S. P., Koehler, M. J., Hamilton, E. R., & Akcaoglu, M. (2016). An investigation of state educational Twitter hashtags (SETHs) as affinity spaces. *E-Learning and Digital Media, 13*(1-2), 24–44. doi:10.1177/2042753016672351

Sheridan, L., & Young, M. (2016). Genuine conversation: The enabler in good mentoring of pre-service teachers. *Teachers and Teaching, 22*(3), 293–314. doi:10.1080/13540602.2016.1218327

Staudt Willet, K. B., & Rosenberg, J. M. (2021). *tidytags: Simple collection and powerful analysis of Twitter data (Version 0.1.2)* [R package]. https://github.com/bretsw/tidytags

Trust, T., Krutka, D. G., & Carpenter, J. P. (2016). Together we are better: Professional learning networks for teachers. *Computers & Education, 102*, 15–34. doi:10.1016/j.compedu.2016.06.007

Tucker, L. (2019). Educational professionals' decision making for professional growth using a case of twitter adoption. *TechTrends, 63*(2), 133–148. doi:10.100711528-018-0346-x

Veletsianos, G. (2017). Three cases of hashtags used as learning and professional development environments. *TechTrends, 61*(6), 284–292. doi:10.100711528-016-0143-3

Wenger, E. (1998). *Communities of practice: Learning, meaning, and identity*. Cambridge University Press. doi:10.1017/CBO9780511803932

Wickham, Averick, M., Bryan, J., Chang, W., McGowan, L., François, R., Grolemund, G., Hayes, A., Henry, L., Hester, J., Kuhn, M., Pedersen, T., Miller, E., Bache, S., Müller, K., Ooms, J., Robinson, D., Seidel, D., Spinu, V., ... Yutani, H. (2019). Welcome to the tidyverse. *Journal of Open Source Software, 4*(43), 1686. doi:10.21105/joss.01686

ADDITIONAL READING

Benoit, K., Watanabe, K., Wang, H., Nulty, P., Obeng, A., Müller, S., & Matsuo, A. (2018). quanteda: An R package for the quantitative analysis of textual data. *Journal of Open Source Software, 3*(30), 774. doi:10.21105/joss.00774

Cho, V., Dennen, V., Fishman, B., & Greenhow, C. (2019). Education and social media: Research directions to guide a growing field. *Teachers College Record*, *121*(14), 1–22.

Greenhalgh, S. P., & Koehler, M. J. (2017). 28 days later: Twitter hashtags as "just in time" teacher professional development. *TechTrends*, *61*(3), 273–281. doi:10.100711528-016-0142-4

Jocker, M. L. (2014). *Text Analysis with R for Students of Literature*. Springer., doi:10.1007/978-3-319-03164-4

Kimmons, R., Carpenter, J. P., Veletsianos, G., & Krutka, D. G. (2018). Mining social media divides: An analysis of K-12 US School uses of Twitter. *Learning, Media and Technology*, *43*(3), 307–325. doi:10.1080/17439884.2018.1504791

Lantz-Andersson, A., Lundin, M., & Selwyn, N. (2018). Twenty years of online teacher communities: A systematic review of formally-organized and informally-developed professional learning groups. *Teaching and Teacher Education*, *75*, 302–315. doi:10.1016/j.tate.2018.07.008

Rosell-Aguilar, F. (2018). Twitter: A professional development and community of practice tool for teachers. *Journal of Interactive Media in Education*, *2018*(1), 1. doi:10.5334/jime.452

Staudt Willet, K. B. (2019). Revisiting how and why educators use Twitter: Tweet types and purposes in# Edchat. *Journal of Research on Technology in Education*, *51*(3), 273–289. doi:10.1080/15391523.2019.1611507

This research was previously published in the Handbook of Research on Advanced Research Methodologies for a Digital Society; pages 510-525, copyright year 2022 by Information Science Reference (an imprint of IGI Global).

Section 6
Managerial Impact

Chapter 97
Social Media in Tertiary Education: Considerations and Potential Issues

Ann M. Simpson
Unitec Institute of Technology, New Zealand

ABSTRACT

Social media use is prevalent throughout the world and is now commonplace in higher education. The devices, support technologies, and social media applications used in higher education are in a constant state of change. Using social media in education creates new and sometimes challenging issues for institutions, instructors, and students. This chapter attempts to address some of the considerations and potential issues that impact our use of social media in the higher education classroom. It examines social media as an educational tool in higher education, possible pedagogies for social media use, potential educational contexts, and privacy concerns raised by social media use in educational environments. This chapter also provides a possible definition for social media and introduces some themes that will be explored in further detail in the following chapters.

INTRODUCTION

This introductory chapter introduces the potential for social media as an educational tool in higher education, possible pedagogies for social media use, potential educational contexts and privacy concerns raised by social media use in educational environments. Beginning with a brief account of the extensive current use of social media applications throughout the world, the chapter discusses a variety of meanings for social media. Possible pedagogies for social media use are explored and potential educational contexts investigated. Some privacy concerns about the use of social media in educational environments are raised. This chapter also provides a possible definition for social media and introduces themes that will be explored in further detail in the following chapters. In addition, throughout this book, there are vignettes, case studies, or examples of how social media has been used in educational contexts which will assist in describing the content as well as providing potential examples for practitioners to experiment with.

DOI: 10.4018/978-1-6684-7123-4.ch097

BACKGROUND

Social media use around the world has increased at a phenomenal rate. The Global social media research summary, 2017 states that the number of Facebook active users alone stands at 1.8 billion users (Chaffey, 2017). At the time of writing, the total world population sits at 7.5 billion people (United Nations, 2017); this means that approximately 24% of the world's population is actively using Facebook daily (Chaffey, 2017). In addition, WhatsApp and Facebook Messenger and other popular social media platforms have approximately 1 billion active users each (Chaffey, 2017). Instagram has 600 million active users, Twitter has 317 million active users, and SnapChat and Skype both have 300 million active users respectively (Chaffey, 2017). WeChat and QQ, applications popular in China, have more than 850 million active users each (Chaffey, 2017). From the sheer volume and number of social media application users, it is undeniable that social media use is prevalent, worldwide, and will continue to grow. Although worldwide statistics on active student use of social media applications are not readily available, it is possible to surmise that many students' personal use of social media is included in those numbers. That is, some students will have experienced social media for personal use, business use, or both.

WHAT IS SOCIAL MEDIA?

At the core of social media is what Miller et al. call 'scalable sociality' (2016); two scales that describe the way in which people associate with each other to form social interactions or relations through social media (Miller et al., 2016). The first scale allows users to control the level of privacy for a group or audience "from the most private to the most public" (Miller et al., 2016, p. 3). The second scale allows users control over group size "from the smallest group to the largest group" (Miller et al., 2016, p. 3). These two scales can operate separately or together to determine the privacy and size of the group used for its purpose. They also describe the basic general function of social media applications and platforms in terms of the scope and size of the intended audience and how students can control and govern their audiences. Since the technologies utilized for social media will no doubt change in the future, the scales assist in describing the nature of social media regardless of the underlying technologies used in its creation. In terms of educational context, the scales can assist in describing and determining the size and scope of educational activity. They can also assist in the description of the difference between teacher- created, student-led and student self-created educational activities. While these scales assist in the description of what makes media social, they do not define it.

In many cases, social media is defined through example such as blogs, wikis, multi-media platforms and social networking sites (Selwyn, 2012; Tess, 2013). Social media enables collective user communities to generate, harness and share content for others (Selwyn, 2012). Defining social media is difficult because it changes constantly as the technologies that support it are changing (Tess, 2013). For the purposes of this book, social media is defined as any program or website that enables social interaction amongst an audience of users. The audience is determined by its users and the privacy of the content can be dictated by the collective users as well as the individuals.

Table 1. Augmented reality and art? A true story

The following vignette describes how augmented reality incited the author's interest in social media for higher education. One evening, my teenage daughter came up to me to show me her newest 'version' of herself. She showed me two photos she had taken of herself with her iPhone using Instagram; it applied a 'filter' over her image and she stated, "This is what I have to draw for my art class. What do you think? Which one, this one or the other one?"

Figure 1. Augmented reality: Filter 1	*Figure 2. Augmented reality: Filter 2*

Source: A.M. Simpson	Source: A.M. Simpson

After laughing hysterically, I helped her choose one. I began to think how much her teenage years were different than mine because of social media. I found myself in astonishment that a social media tool, one designed to engage in interactive and social activities with others, was used for an art project. Even more interesting, was that this forced her to think about how she is portraying herself to her peers and teacher (her selected audience). This was an assigned task and not a self-generated one. While I use social media frequently, and not always in a classroom setting, I never thought it could be used for an art project in school. This experience started my personal quest for a better understanding of social media and how it could be applied through my work in the tertiary sector.

THE EDUCATIONAL CONTEXT

Many students today have grown up knowing only a life of Wi-Fi connectivity and social media (Selwyn, 2012). For institutions and instructors alike, a drive exists to embrace these technologies to connect with students using the tools they are most likely to know and use (Selwyn, 2016). For example, many institutions now utilize social media to communicate with and recruit potential students (Hrastinski & Dennen, 2012). As these technologies change, the need for teaching and learning and pedagogical foundations in the use of these technologies will continue. Institutions, teachers and students will continue to connect, communicate and engage in educational activities and dialogues based on pedagogical foundations (Wegerif, 2007). As students continue to learn there will always be a need for them to discuss and connect with their teachers, peers and others to facilitate their learning. It is the modalities of how students connect with others and the advance of affordances in web technologies that will continue to change.

Use of social media tools in everyday life is different from use in an educational context (Selwyn, 2012). Carr suggests that social media users in daily life seem to possess the ability to pick and choose snippets of knowledge to forward on to their social networks without developing a deeper knowledge or comprehension of that information (2010). If this is the case, how can this behavior be harnessed to engage students in educational activities? It is up to the teacher to determine how pedagogically-informed activities are designed and used to scaffold learning within the course and to guide the students through the appropriate use of the media for their activities. Some researchers, however, feel that this way of using social media in education is artificial and inherently flawed, as it reflects the traditional top-down teaching approach (Selwyn, 2012; Tess, 2013). For those researchers social media should be used from a grass roots, bottom-up approach in which content is generated by and for the students without instructor mandate.

The case study in Table 2 describes how an instructor implemented Blogging as a research tool for students in her class.

Table 2. Case study: Blog as a research tool

"To show that research had been done over a period of time and had been thought about by students"   *The lecturer wanted a place for students to accumulate and collate their research over a period of time. She felt that many students were conducting cursory research at the last minute and spending little time critically examining their research issue. By collecting a variety of material over several weeks the lecturer hoped that students would research in more depth and have more time to critically evaluate their material.*   *To encourage this collection of resource material over a period of time, the lecturer added blog posting as an assessment item. For this, students were marked on the number of their posts and given top marks for this item if they posted every day. To encourage variety another item measured diversity of posts and students were encouraged to find a wide range of material that related to their research topic.*   "*(they had to) post every day for a month. A variety: from academic to general websites, newspapers, position papers, government websites, academic journal articles, magazines, podcasts, cartoons, music, photos, self-made -own videos, observations and personal reflections. This led to judgements, personal reflection".*   *The lecturer was also interested in giving the students a voice and privileging their knowledge, and encouraging both formal and informal postings, allowing students to discuss their knowledge and point of view. In addition, she wanted the students to be "seduced into enjoying their work" and to discover that the more their effort the better their final product.*   *Students were able to like each other's posts but, as there was no comment function available with Tumblr, Pinterest, and blogs, others couldn't comment on posts unless they imported the post to their own page. The lecturer felt that students had to think about what they wrote as they had to own anything they re-blogged onto their own page. She also thought this reduced the negativity experienced on some social media. 'Likes' also meant students experienced positive reinforcement only from each other, creating a positive group atmosphere. This blogging achieved the goal of more and deeper research, more in depth consideration of that research, improved students' presentation content and seemed to increase engagement.*   "*(Students) enjoyed using it and usually made over 30 posts ...seeing students really engage, a nice buzz. (it was) student directed, the lecturer scaffolds. It was a great low stakes/ early reward assessment for early in the course."*

Blended Learning

Blended learning (BL) provides opportunities for increased interaction amongst students and teachers, flexibility in the environments used and potential for increased student engagement (Vaughan, 2007). Blended learning is defined as the combination of the digital and physical classroom environments; digital environments can include the use of a learning management system such as Moodle in combination with other digital tools such as social media. The physical environments involve the physical spaces that the face to face sessions are conducted in. The 2017 New Media Consortium report on Technology in Higher Education notes that the inclusion of BL in tertiary institutions is a currently a high priority for many academic institutions internationally (Jaramillo, 2017; Spring, Graham, & Hadlock, 2017). Social media has increased opportunities for students in blended learning environments and has allowed a shift from the traditional top down approach to student-centered learning. That is learning that is generated by the students themselves to share with each other through collaborative discourse and interaction via social media.

The rise of social media use in higher education has led to a dramatic shift away from conventional classroom-based learning (Adams Becker, Cummins, et al., 2017). There has been a growth in interest towards student-centered pedagogy and the role of students in course design, content generation and delivery. The broad conceptualization of student-centered pedagogy holds that teaching strategies adhere to "a participatory mode of decision-making in all aspects of learning" and focus on "uncovering the excitement in intellectual and emotional discovery" (Motschnig-Pitrik & Holzinger, 2002, p. 162). Student-centered pedagogy, then, appears to describe learning and teaching in social media settings. Hoffman and Novak state that student-centered pedagogy enables its users to "...connect, create, consume, and control", key elements in social media use (2011, p. 5). Social media can provide educators with specific social contexts and resources that "exist outside the formal spaces of the institution" creating "opportunities for authentic learning that is personally meaningful and relevant" (McLoughlin & Lee, 2010, p. 31). What must be considered is that social media can potentially reinforce student-centered teaching practices by presenting alternative ways to knowledge acquisition and giving students more power and control over their learning.

Changing Learning Environments

Traditional lecture style classrooms across the world are slowly being replaced with modern innovative spaces. A modern innovative learning space is one that contains moveable and configurable seating arrangements, equipment and sometimes partitions or walls. For example, a modern innovative learning space can involve moveable computers that display on large screens alongside moveable, modular desks that can be clustered together to form groups or separated for individual work. The classroom space design and resources available within reconfigured learning spaces can potentially change the way teachers and students interact and engage in their teaching and learning. Research suggests that the ways in which students interact with each other using the tools available to them, both digital and physical, can potentially impact how they learn (Carvalho, Goodyear, & de Laat, 2017). That is, a modern learning space can change the way the students and instructor engage in learning activities and dialogues based on their proximity, the social aspects of their in-class relationships and the resources they use in the classroom, with potential for improved learning (Goodyear, Carvalho, & Dohn, 2016; Ravelli & McMurtrie, 2016). Social media and other technologies can be mobile and can be utilized across the digital and physical classroom spaces and can provide significant opportunities for learning activities.

In the past 12 years, blended learning environments have been contextualized and described as learning networks (Goodyear, 2005; Yeoman, 2015). A learning network, as the word network implies, focuses on the connections of things and people in a learning environment (Thibaut, Curwood, Carvalho, & Simpson, 2015). The 'things' in a learning environment, sometimes referred to artefacts, can be either digital or physical and consist of anything that is utilized for learning purposes such as whiteboards, learning management systems like Moodle, handouts, books and social media tools. The people in a learning network consist of the students, instructors, or other individuals (guest speakers or librarians, for example) who participate in the learning network. A learning network is defined as "...a heterogeneous assemblage of people and things connected in activities that have learning as an explicit goal or as a significant side effect" (Goodyear et al., 2016, p. 93). Learning and activities in the learning network are "… mediated across agents, tools, and spaces" (Thibaut et al., 2015, p. 459). That is, learning activities occur through the connections of the people involved, the things or artefacts they use to assist in learning and the digital and physical spaces in which learning can occur. For example, the social media tools such as Facebook or Twitter, can be viewed and utilized as tools to provide connection and networking opportunities for students and others in a learning network. In this instance, social media can play a role in learning networks.

Real-world learning is becoming more important to students as they obtain qualifications to become job ready in both vocational and higher education settings (Adams Becker et al., 2017). Real-world learning fosters connections between what they are learning and the real-world experience. Of benefit in trades or vocational training is the use of e-portfolios utilizing a wide of array of technologies including, social media tools, digital photos, videos, and recordings and links to resources to document skills or tasks. Nore (2015) found students could document their skills and tasks through creating videos with their devices while on site at work and share them for assessment and skills evidence for potential employers. In this case, Nore created a learning environment that enabled the extension of the learning into the students' work environments.

Cochrane, Narayan and Oldfield, in their study on authentic contexts of mobile social media use in New Zealand, analyzed three case studies from three different institutions in New Zealand (2014). Each case study was implemented with the same methodology informed by nine authentic learning principles (Cochrane et al., 2014). They include "…real-life, authentic tasks, access to expert performances and modelling processes, multiples roles and perspectives, construction of knowledge, reflection, articulation, coaching and scaffolding, and authentic assessment" (Cochrane et al., 2014, pp. 127–128). 'Authentic context and tasks' refers to how the learning or knowledge gained will be used in life or work, for example using a lathe in a construction workshop. 'Access to expert performances or modelling processes' describes how students can be shown how social media, if relevant, is used in their targeted work environment such as Xero for on-site invoicing for a tradesperson, as well to potentially video or post images of learning or task achievements, such as a kitchen installation (Cochrane et al., 2014, pp. 127–128). In addition, 'Multiple roles and perspectives' means that students are able to construct knowledge and content across 'formal and informal' learning contexts relevant to their authentic learning contexts (Cochrane et al., 2014, pp. 127–128). 'Collaborative construction of knowledge' refers to the fact that the students and instructors as well as any others involved in the students learning can collaborate and co-construct knowledge together, such as user forums (Cochrane et al., 2014, pp. 127–128). 'Reflection' refers to the self-reflective opportunities potentially present in the authentic context and social media tools can provide a potential modality for this expression such as blogging or keeping a diary (Cochrane et al., 2014, pp. 127–128). 'Articulation' refers to the different modalities of presentation that can be utilized with mobile social media, for example links to Piktochart or Prezi, infographics presentation tools in an authentic learning context (Cochrane et al., 2014, pp. 127–128). 'Coaching and scaffolding' provides opportunities for students to teach and learn from each other, their instructors, and anyone from their social learning communities (Cochrane et al., 2014, pp. 127–128). Finally, 'authentic assessment' describes that the assessment activities created should utilize the affordances of the mobile technologies available, such as taking a formative quiz through Kahoot, an online interactive quiz tool (Cochrane et al., 2014, pp. 127–128).

These nine principles can act as a useful guide to assist in the generation of authentic contexts in which social media can be used. Authentic contexts and use of social media and in many cases the potential mobile devices and their affordances can facilitate more opportunities for students to engage in their learning networks. Research into social media and its use in blended learning environments, learning networks and authentic environments will need to continue, since the technologies constantly change, students' requirements change, and teaching and work environments change.

Digital Divide

With the advancement of mobile devices, learning can take place in a mobile way. As Parsons suggests, mobile learning is an extension of e-learning and distance learning and offers additional affordances through the newer mobile technologies, such as learning in specific contexts, creating shared resources, the affordances of Web 2.0 technologies, and more opportunities for student self-ownership of learning (2014). While the potentials of the technologies are considerable, there remains a gap for the few who do not have access or skills required to use the technologies. Wei, Teo, Chan, and Tan suggest there are three potential digital divides: access to digital technologies, the capability of using digital technologies, and the outcomes based on the capabilities of the individuals using the technologies (2011). In terms of access to technologies, the ECAR study of Undergraduate Students and Information Technology 2016 report surveyed 71,641 students from 183 countries and 37 U.S. states on undergraduates' use and access to information technology in tertiary education (Brooks, 2016). The research found that over half of students surveyed owned one of each of the three major pieces of device technology, including a laptop, a tablet and a smartphone (Brooks, 2016). The study found despite the high rates of device ownership that 1% of students did not own any (Brooks, 2016). This showed that technology access for some students continues to remain an issue around the world (Brooks, 2016; Selwyn, 2012, 2016). However, to assist this issue, many institutions offer loan computers or computer labs as well as software and IT skills training support to minimize disadvantage to those that do not have access (Wei et al., 2011).

Aside from personal device ownership, another potential barrier for students is lack of access to the Internet. The 2016 UNESCO's Annual World Education Report suggests that internet access is not always readily available in developing countries and is largely dependent upon a combination of factors, including the institution's geographic location, ability to pay for internet access, and the country's telecom infrastructure (2016). For example, in 2012, the Mongolian government provided funding to their schools to ensure Internet connectivity continued to be available to students regardless of the cost (Unesco, 2016). For both developed and developing nations, the digital divide continues to be an issue for some students and must not be discounted at the government, institutional and course levels (Adams Becker et al., 2017; Brooks, 2016; Unesco, 2016). Institutions and instructors should continue to provide alternative modes of access and training for students to provide equal opportunities for device access and digital literacy in social media use.

International Students and Cultural Inclusivity

Many attempts in current research have been made to identify specific possibilities of social media for international education and culturally relevant practices. The questions have been asked with regard to social media use in learning and teaching of international students. Concerning challenges associated with study abroad, the research has been focusing on the extent to which social media may help students to overcome cultural and academic differences. For example, with regard to the role of social media in supporting international students' adjustment to new educational and social environments, some research-ers highlight that it has a "positive effect on students" grades, engagement and motivation" (Saw, Abbott & Donaghey, 2013, p. 3). In the same vein, Lin, Peng, Kim, Kim and LaRose (2012) found that social networking sites contribute to international students' "online bridging capital and social adjustments" (p. 436). In the Australian Journal of Educational technology, McCarthy reports on results of a two-year study on the use of Facebook in combination with face to face lectures and tutorials that involved not only local, but international students. The author holds the view that "the blending of real and virtual environments increased peer interaction and academic engagement" and enhanced students' first year experience overall (McCarthy, 2010, p. 738).

Another aspect is the growing prominence of the effectiveness of social media within a cross-cultural educational context. Although there are no universally accepted teaching practices specifically designed for the international classroom integrating social media, some researchers have defined principles of pedagogy for online learning environments. For instance, McLoughlin (2006) states that to effectively teach in cross-cultural online settings there is a need for culturally inclusive pedagogy and curriculum that "are flexible, adaptable and relevant to students from a diverse range of cultural and language back-grounds" (p. 7). In response to the continuing internationalization of tertiary education, there seems to be one reasonable clear-cut approach to ensure quality in the international classroom – to create learning experiences for international students that are responsive to their personal learning needs and goals, and allow to showcase their existing skills and knowledge. In this respect, social media can potentially serve as a tool to support and enhance learning experiences for students, more specifically international ones.

Privacy Anyone?

Today, many higher education institutions use learning management systems to create and govern their online courses. One of the many advantages of learning management systems is that they usually offer a myriad of social media tools for students and staff to use in their courses. LMSs' are usually self-contained within their institutional networks and can insure privacy of student information and data. Social media applications, on the other hand, are controlled and governed by corporate entities, thus creating privacy concerns for students. Should therefore an academic institution prevent students from utilizing social media software programs due to privacy issues?

Commercial social media sites are backed by incredible amounts of corporate investment and because they are businesses they seek ways to continue to increase profits. One way they accomplish this is through selling user information. As soon as an individual signs up for 'free' access to a commercially driven social media site, the individual agrees to the site's' terms and conditions; this means, in many cases, the individual has potentially forfeited his or her personal information for the corporation to resell to others (Jacobsson, 2010). In addition, the individual has given permission to the corporation to monitor his or her onsite behavior for the purposes of targeted marketing (DeMers, 2017). For example, if an individual looked up traveling to Thailand on Facebook, a mathematical formula, an algorithm, will be activated and advertisements on traveling to Thailand will 'suddenly' display on the user's Facebook homepage or 'feed'. Based on how students utilize Facebook in class, content will be served to the students through Facebook advertisers. The institution and the instructor do not have control over the advertising content. For some researchers, the commercial presence in commercial social media sites negatively impacts the sites' potential affordances for learning and teaching (Friesen & Lowe, 2012).

Alternatively, non-commercial social media sites, ones that do not feature in Global Social Media Statistics Summary, usually consist of user- created and monitored content (Zheng, Niiya, & Warschauer, 2015). Non-commercial sites do not resell an individual's information. They do not have the financial backing that corporate giants do to attract and maintain the number of individual users that commercialized sites can. In some cases, this can mean limited program functionality when compared to the commercialized sites. When asking students to use commercial social media websites, we must inform them about threats to their personal information when we endeavor to engage them in using social media applications and activities. Institutions, instructors and students should inform students of what happens with their personal information when they utilize corporate social media sites, so they can make informed choices about their participation in educational social media activities.

Another potential concern is how other users in the social media community disseminate content. Cain and Fink illustrate this through the metaphor of email (Cain & Fink III, 2010). Emails, like letters, are private until opened or viewed (Cain & Fink III, 2010). Once the email is opened it is up to the discretion of the recipient to choose how he or she utilizes the information. That is, once social media content has been posted or viewed, the audience or individual chooses how to engage with the content afterward; this typically includes copying and pasting or re-sharing the content with others (Cain & Fink III, 2010). In many instances, students will have pre-existing accounts, for example on Facebook, that contain highly private information which is deemed personal and not appropriate for a classroom page. How students portray themselves in social media sites forms another potential concern. It is suggested that for educational purposes students create a generic account for their educational persona. Or as described in further detail in Chapters 3 and 4 of this book, students can watch and learn what appropriate protocols and behavior are according to the culture of the form. Alternatively, and perhaps most optimal, let the class decide the rules of appropriate behavior in the digital space, in digital citizenship, in the classroom and how they will conduct themselves in this shared collaborative group environment as suggested in Chapters 2 and 5. It is extremely important for institutions, teachers and students to work together to establish guidelines and rules around online behavior, privacy and the ethical practice and use of content dissemination of social media in the educational context.

FUTURE RESEARCH DIRECTIONS

While a phenomenal amount of research already exists into the social media landscape and how it is currently being utilized in higher education, further research is warranted to gain a better understanding on how the technologies impact institutional responsibilities in terms of student information and privacy as well as instructor and student support. The digital support structures that enable access to the Internet and social media technologies will continue to open possibilities for social interaction and potential learning opportunities. Further research into the international classroom and cultural contexts for students and classes continues to be needed. While blended learning seems to be gaining wider acceptance and adoption, further research into blended learning that focuses on the new technological affordances and tools is warranted. Also, further research into learning networks could provide more clarity on social media use in the digital and physical spaces of modern or refurbished learning environments and how it impacts the students and teachers involved in terms of the learning opportunities, tools utilized and the artefacts created.

CONCLUSION

The increase in technological advances in software, devices and infrastructures impact opportunities for learning networks, the changing nature of the learning environments and potential learning opportunities for students to engage with. Social media is part of daily life for many students worldwide and there are many potential opportunities to embrace it in the higher education. Because of this fact, cultural contexts and sensitivity should be considered for students who choose to obtain their education outside of their home countries. While device use and access is increasing and common place for many students, for others the digital divide continues to remain an important issue in terms of access, skillset and outcomes. In addition, privacy issues continue to be a concern for institutions, instructors and students alike. However, the opportunities for social collaborative learning are enormous and research in this area must continue to explore its potential, despite the challenges for students and social media use in higher education.

As the ancient Greek philosopher Heraclitus taught his students, the only constant in life is change (Kirk, 1951). This constant state of change aptly describes the state of social media use in higher education today. This book covers a relevant, in the moment view of the state of social media use in various contexts used in New Zealand. The following chapters address a series of pedagogical concepts related to students in the international classroom, culturally relevant practices of social media, teachers' experiences with social media implementation in the tertiary environment, and emergent social media trends and possibilities for higher education. It is hoped that it will provide further understanding about the dynamic nature of social media use and provide examples and ideas for potential implementation.

REFERENCES

Adams Becker, S., Cumins, M., Davis, A., Freeman, A., Hall Giesinger, C., & Ananthanarayanan, V. (2017). *NMC horizon report: 2017 higher education edition* (p. 60). Austin, TX: The New Media Consortium. Retrieved from http://cdn.nmc.org/media/2017-nmc-horizon-report-he-EN.pdf

Brooks, D. C. (2016). *ECAR study of undergraduate students and information technology*. Retrieved from https://library.educause.edu/resources/2016/6/~/media/files/library/2016/10/ers1605.pdf

Cain, J., & Fink, J. L. III. (2010). Legal and ethical issues regarding social media and pharmacy education. *American Journal of Pharmaceutical Education*, 74(10), 1–8. doi:10.5688/aj7410184 PMID:21436925

Carr, N. (2010). The web shatters focus, rewires brains. *Wired.Com, 24*. Retrieved from http://aplangandcomp.blogs.rsu1.org/files/2010/06/the-shallows.pdf

Carvalho, L., Goodyear, P., & de Laat, M. (Eds.). (2017). *Place-based spaces for networked learning*. New York: Routledge, Taylor and Francis Group. Retrieved from http://ezproxy.massey.ac.nz/login?url=http://massey.eblib.com.au/patron/FullRecord.aspx?p=4579047

Chaffey, D. (2017, April 27). *Global social media statistics summary 2017*. Retrieved September 14, 2017, from http://www.smartinsights.com/social-media-marketing/social-media-strategy/new-global-social-media-research/

Cochrane, T., Narayan, V., & Oldfield, J. (2014). 11 emerging technologies in New Zealand. In Activity Theory, Authentic Learning and Emerging Technologies: Towards a Transformative Higher Education Pedagogy (pp. 126–143). Academic Press.

DeMers, J. (2017, January 23). *Does your social media app know too much about you?* Retrieved October 26, 2017, from https://www.forbes.com/sites/jaysondemers/2017/01/23/does-your-social-media-app-know-too-much-about-you/

Friesen, N., & Lowe, S. (2012). The questionable promise of social media for education: Connective learning and the commercial imperative. *Journal of Computer Assisted Learning*, 28(3), 183–194. doi:10.1111/j.1365-2729.2011.00426.x

Goodyear, P. (2005). Educational design and networked learning: Patterns, pattern languages and design practice. *Australasian Journal of Educational Technology*, 21(1), 82–101. doi:10.14742/ajet.1344

Goodyear, P., Carvalho, L., & Dohn, N. B. (2016). Artefacts and Activities in the Analysis of Learning Networks. In *Research, Boundaries, and Policy in Networked Learning* (pp. 93–110). Cham: Springer. doi:10.1007/978-3-319-31130-2_6

Hew, K. F., & Cheung, W. S. (2013). Use of Web 2.0 technologies in K-12 and higher education: The search for evidence-based practice. *Educational Research Review*, 9, 47–64. doi:10.1016/j.edurev.2012.08.001

Hoffman, D. L., & Novak, T. P. (2011). Marketing communication in digital era. *Marketing Management*, 20(3), 36–43.

Hrastinski, S., & Dennen, V. (2012). Social media in higher education: Introduction to the special issue. *The Internet and Higher Education*, 15(1), 1–2. doi:10.1016/j.iheduc.2011.11.004

Jacobsson, S. (2010, May 20). *Social networking sites may be sharing your info with advertisers*. Retrieved October 26, 2017, from https://www.pcworld.com/article/196869/Social_Network_Privacy.html

Jaramillo, S. G. (2017). Horizon Report-2017 Higher Education Edition. *CUADERNO ACTIVA*, 9(9), 171.

Kirk, G. S. (1951). Natural Change in Heraclitus. Oxford University Press.

Lin, J.-H., Peng, W., Kim, M., Kim, S. Y., & LaRose, R. (2012). Social networking and adjustments among international students. *New Media & Society*, 14(3), 421–440.

McCarthy, J. (2010). Blended learning environments: Using social networking sites to enhance the first year experience. *Australasian Journal of Educational Technology*, 26(6), 729–740.

McLoughlin, C. (2006). Inclusivity and alignment: Principles of pedagogy, task and assessment design for effective cross-cultural online learning. *Distance Education*, 22(1), 7–29. doi:10.1080/0158791010220102

McLoughlin, C., & Lee, M. J. W. (2010). Personalised and self-regulated learning in the Web 2.0 era: International exemplars of innovative pedagogy using social software. *Australasian Journal of Educational Technology*, 26(1). doi:10.14742/ajet.1100

Miller, D., Costa, E., Haynes, N., McDonald, T., Nicolescu, R., Sinanan, J., … Wang, X. (Eds.). (2016). What is social media? In *How the World Changed Social Media* (Vol. 1, pp. 1–8). UCL Press. Retrieved from http://www.jstor.org/stable/j.ctt1g69z35.8

Motschnig-Pitrik, R., & Holzinger, A. (2002). Student-centered teaching meets new media: Concept and case study. *Journal of Educational Technology & Society*, *5*(4), 160–172.

Parsons, D. (2014). The future of mobile learning and implications for education and training. In *Increasing access through mobile learning* (Vol. 217, pp. 217–229). Vancouver, Canada: Commonwealth of Learning (COL); Athabasca University. Retrieved from http://oasis.col.org/bitstream/handle/11599/558/pub_Mobile%20Learning_web.pdf#page=234

Ravelli, L. J., & McMurtrie, R. J. (2016). Networked places as communicative resources. *Place-Based Spaces for Networked Learning*, 111–130.

Saw, G., Abbott, W., & Donaghey, J. (2013). *Social media for international students – it's not all about Facebook*. Library Management. Retrieved from http://epublications.bond.edu.au/library_pubs/35

Selwyn, N. (2012). Social Media in Higher Education. *The Europa World of Learning*, 1–10.

Selwyn, N. (2016). Digital downsides: Exploring university students' negative engagements with digital technology. *Teaching in Higher Education*, 1–16. doi:10.1080/13562517.2016.1213229

Spring, K. J., Graham, C. R., & Hadlock, C. A. (2017). The current landscape of international blended learning. *International Journal of Technology Enhanced Learning*, *8*(1), 84–102. doi:10.1504/IJ-TEL.2016.075961

Tess, P. A. (2013). The role of social media in higher education classes (real and virtual) – A literature review. *Computers in Human Behavior*, *29*(5), A60–A68. doi:10.1016/j.chb.2012.12.032

Thibaut, P., Curwood, J. S., Carvalho, L., & Simpson, A. (2015). Moving across physical and online spaces: A case study in a blended primary classroom. *Learning, Media and Technology*, *40*(4), 458–479. doi:10.1080/17439884.2014.959971

UNESCO. (Ed.). (2016). *Education for people and planet: creating sustainable futures for all* (2nd ed.). Paris: UNESCO.

United Nations. (2017). *World population prospects: The 2017 revision, key findings and advance tables* (No. ESA/P/WP/248). Retrieved from https://esa.un.org/unpd/wpp/Publications/Files/WPP2017_Key-Findings.pdf

Vaughan, N. (2007). Perspectives on blended learning in higher education. *International Journal on E-Learning*, *6*(1), 81–94.

Wegerif, R. (2007). *Dialogic, Education and Technology: Expanding the space of learning* (Vol. 7). Exeter, UK: Springer Science & Business Media. doi:10.1007/978-0-387-71142-3

Wei, K.-K., Teo, H.-H., Chan, H. C., & Tan, B. C. Y. (2011). Conceptualizing and testing a social cognitive model of the digital divide. *Information Systems Research*, *22*(1), 170–187. doi:10.1287/isre.1090.0273

Yeoman, P. (2015, October 28). *Habits and habitats: An ethnography of learning entanglement*. The University of Sydney, Australia. Retrieved from http://trove.nla.gov.au/work/199277646?q=pippa+yeoman&c=book&versionId=218342152

Zheng, B., Niiya, M., & Warschauer, M. (2015). Wikis and collaborative learning in higher education. *Technology, Pedagogy and Education*, *24*(3), 357–374. doi:10.1080/1475939X.2014.948041

KEY TERMS AND DEFINITIONS

Authentic Learning Principles: Authentic, real, life-like learning is based upon the following nine principles: real-life, authentic tasks, access to expert performances and modelling processes, multiples roles and perspectives, construction of knowledge, reflection, articulation, coaching and scaffolding, and authentic assessment.

Blended Learning: Described as the combination of the digital and physical classroom environments, digital environments can include the use of a learning management system such as Moodle in combination with other digital tools such as social media.

Digital Divide: Described as a skills gap for the students who do not have access to or the skills required to use technologies.

Digital Privacy: A term used to describe the privacy of an individual's information through the social media tools used. Privacy is determined by the scalable sociality (defined above) set by the individual.

Learning Networks: A connected network of agents (students, teachers, and other individuals), tools (artefacts, blogs, whiteboards, Facebook pages, wikis, etc.), and spaces (both physical classroom spaces and digital spaces) who use the network for a learning purpose.

Modern Learning Environments or Spaces: A learning environment or space that contains moveable and configurable seating arrangements, equipment, and sometimes partitions or walls.

Real-World Learning: Learning that occurs in real-life contexts, such as a construction apprentice learning on the job at a building site.

Scalable Sociality: Two scales that describe the nature of the way in which people associate with each other to form social interactions or relations available through social media. The first scale describes privacy control from private to public and the second scale describes the size of the audience from the smallest group to the largest group.

Social Media: Any program or website that enables social interaction amongst an audience of users. The audience is determined by its users and the privacy of the content can be dictated by the collective users as well as the individuals.

Chapter 98
The Integration of Social Networking Services in Higher Education:
Benefits and Barriers in Teaching English

Lenny Marzulina
State Islamic University of Raden Fatah, Palembang, Indonesia

Akhmad Habibi
Jambi University, Jambi City, Indonesia

Amirul Mukminin
Jambi University, Jambi City, Indonesia

Deta Desvitasari

State Islamic University of Raden Fatah, Palembang, Indonesia

Mohd Faiz Mohd Yaakob
University Utara Malaysia, Kuala Lumpur, Malaysia

Doni Ropawandi
National University of Malaysia, Bangi, Malaysia

ABSTRACT

Social networking services (SNSs) have been popular and essential media to increase lecturer-student interaction, collaboration, and communication as well as lecturers' supervision in Indonesian universities including in teaching English as a foreign language (EFL). This mixed method study utilized a survey and interview as the techniques of data collection which specifically explored the lecturers' perspectives on the use SNSs for personal and educational purposes as well as demographic information related to the experience and frequency using SNSs, ownership (possession) of SNSs, and SNSs popularity. The findings revealed that the participants had much knowledge and experiences with SNSs. Even though most participants found some benefits of SNSs in EFL classes including easing communication, supervision and evaluation, time flexibility, and creativity. There were two barriers that have emerged, including lack of skill and cost to use. Implications and future research are offered to improve technology integration in higher education.

DOI: 10.4018/978-1-6684-7123-4.ch098

INTRODUCTION

Technology has provided eases, applications, approaches, and strategies in education with its features. The success of technology integration in any educational programs is dependent on users' attitudes and perceptions. The establishment of new technology integrations for the improvement of education has been a significant issue to have influences on how education is perceived, implemented, and evaluated. This integration has been an interesting object of research in higher education (e.g., Hamshire & Cullen, 2014; Georgina & Olson, 2008; Mncube, Dube, & Ngulube, 2017; Beldarrain, 2006). One of many technologies which are integrated in higher education is Social networking services (SNSs). Robbin and Singger (2014) informed the utilities of the examples of SNSs such as massaging (WhatsApp, BBM, Telegram), images sharing (Instagram, Snapchat, Pinterest), videos sharing (Vine, YouTube), audios sharing (iTunes, Sticher), micro blogging, (Facebook, Twitter, Google Plus, Path), blogging (Tumblr, Blogger, WordPress), professional sharing (LinkedIn), and academic sharing (Google Scholar, Academia, ResearchGate).

Although, SNSs establishment was firstly proposed to establish a social interaction, the purpose has currently become popular in higher education (Greifeneder, Pontis, Blandford, Attalla, Neal, & Schlebbe, 2018) which has values on supporting relationships between lecturers and their students for learning, educators' professional development, and content and knowledge sharing (Manca & Ranieri, 2013, 2016). Despite many educational values of SNSs in higher education, barriers in using SNSs for university lecturers have also emerged (Habibi, Mukminin, Riyanto, Prasojo, Sulistiyo, Saudagar, & Sofwan, 2018; Manca & Ranieri, 2013; Prasojo, Habibi, Mukminin, Muhaimin, Ikhsan, Taridi & Saudagar, 2017; (Hadiyanto, Mukminin, Arif, Fajaryani, Failasofah, & Habibi, 2017).

In addition to the SNSs establishment in higher education, they also become a thought-provoking topic for a foreign language pedagogy including teaching English as a foreign language (EFL) where many EFL researchers conducted research in this area (Fewell, 2014; Kaplan & Haenlein, 2010; Prasojo, Habibi, Mukminin, Muhaimin, Ikhsan, Taridi & Saudagar, 2017). Mondahl and Razmita (2014) informed that foreign language learning is a collaborative and individual learning process that can be mediated through the use of SNSs. SNSs have been widely integrated in supporting language teaching and learning since they have decreased other responses of physical activities offering limitless opportunities for communication (Fewell, 2014).

For the Indonesian context, the studies on SNSs in educational settings of higher education informed various benefits and barriers viewed from students' perspectives (Habibi et al., 2018; Prasojo et al., 2017). However, research on the SNSs integration from the perspectives of universities lecturers is limited and to fill the gap, this study was done to answer the following questions:

1. How popular are SNSs among Indonesian EFL university lecturers?
2. How do the lecturers perceive the benefits of SNSs use in higher education?
3. What barriers do they face in line with the integration of SNSs?

LITERATURE REVIEW

Social Networking Services

Social networking services (SNSs) used by people around the world are available in various forms (Hamid, Waycott, Kurnia, & Chang, 2014). Experts in literatures have proposed various definitions of SNSs. For example, Bartlett-Bragg (2006) defines SNSs as a range of internet-based applications augmenting group or peer interactions and as spaces for social connections, collaboration, communication, and information exchanges. The SNSs concept is a way on how to conceptualize social groupings, which emphasize interactions emerging through SNSs. Comparably, Park et al. (2015) define SNSs as web-based services provided to facilitate online-based interactions in the form of social interaction and communication. In conclusion, these definitions highlight that SNSs function as social relation and interaction tools.

However, one definition that has been mostly quoted by the majority of researchers is the one that is offered by Boyd and Ellison (2008). They defined SNSs as web-based services allowing individuals to establish public and semi-public profiles with a bounded system, to enunciate a list of other SNSs users whom they have connection and interaction with, to browse and navigate the connection lists created by other users within the system. This definition is different from other definitions, which mostly define SNSs from the perspectives of their functionality.

SNSs in Education: Benefits and Barriers

Facebook according to some researchers on the SNSs integration in education (Akçayır & Akçayır, 2016; Junco et al., 2011; Lim & Richardson, 2016; Khan et al., 2014) is the most SNS used with more than 1.65 billion users across the world. Twitter, a type of micro blogging that facilitates a combination between messaging and blogging (Pervaiz, 2016) is also popular among students and educators who use it in teaching and learning process. YouTube as a video sharing media provides users with vast videos containing information, sharing facility, and entertainment. Apart from those types of SNSs, other various SNSs applications have been used in education such as WhatsApp (Habibi et al., 2018), Instagram (Akhiaar, 2017), and BBM (Rooyen, 2015).

In addition, in higher education, there have been plenty of research conducted on SNSs integration with various methodologies; quantitative, qualitative, and mixed methods (Brady, Holcomb, & Smith, 2010; Habibi et al., 2018; Jones, et al., 2010; Tess, 2013). Habibi et al. (2018) revealed the benefits of the use of SNSs in an Indonesian university from students' perspectives. There were positive attitudes and perception of the students on the capacity of Ning, an SNS that allows users to make their own communities and social links within specific interests with their own design of visual, features choice, and member data to build communication (Brady, Holcomb, & Smith, 2010). Tess (2013) published a literature review article on SNSs studies and informed that most research explored learning outcomes and student achievements improvement in relation to SNSs use at a university level. Beside the positive outcomes revealed by those studies, there were also negative results or findings related to the SNSs use such as a study done by Jones et al. (2010) which indicated that students did not always utilize SNSs in their educational activities. In addition, Tess (2013) confirmed that there was no enough evidence to show whether or not SNSs are efficient in education.

The positive and negative attitudes and perceptions on the use of SNSs in education both from students and educators or lecturers as presented in the literature indicate that not all students and lecturers are in favor of using or integrating SNSs in their teaching and learning processes. For those who have negative attitudes and perception on the use of SNSs in education, it might result from difficulties or barriers that they might face to use SNSs in teaching and learning processes. Lack of skills and knowledge to integrate SNSs in teaching and learning might be one of the reasons why some students and educators or lecturers are reluctant to use SNSs in education. Another reason might be due to the lack of facilities such as electricity for those who live in remote areas that prevent them from using SNSs in in teaching and learning processes. Additionally, ages might be one of the reasons for some lecturers who do not like using SNSs in their classrooms. Older lecturers might not be interested in integrating SNSs in their teaching processes because of their lack of knowledge with new technologies.

SNSs in English Language Teaching

In English language teaching, TESOL/TEFL, researchers have informed that the SNSs use (micro blogging, blogging, massaging, images sharing, and video sharing) has a significant contribution in English language teaching and learning (Kabilan, Ahmad, & Abidin, 2010; Mondahl & Razmerita, 2014; Prasojo et al., 2017; Suthiwartnarueput & Wasanasomsithi, 2012). Facebook, as the most popular SNS has been used as a tool to improve reading and writing skills, promotes interactions among students, and develops a sense of socializing through internet-based applications (Prasojo et al., 2017; Kabilan, Ahmad, & Abidin, 2010).

In addition, Twitter has contributed beneficial effects to community of learning to help maintain motivation and learning activities and to promote a social cohesion (Fewell, 2014). Other SNS, Wikis, online publishing tools used to share knowledge allowing users to edit pages, have been integrated into English language teaching (Zorko, 2009; Kessler, 2010; Chik & Breidbach, 2011). They have a significant influence on the process of teaching and learning. The combination of Wikis, Facebook, and Skype can also be a good platform to establish multimodal texts in language teaching (Chik & Breidbach, 2011).

SNSs Among University Lecturers

Comprehending and exploring educators' perceptions on SNSs as types of technology are critical in improving their rationale and knowledge in order to use technology meaningfully in their teaching activities (Bozalek et al., 2013; Gorder, 2008; Murire & Chilliers, 2017; Kirkwood & Price, 2013). Such comprehension and exploration can also help to broaden opportunities for students' authentic learning. Additionally, the comprehension and exploration of educators' perceptions on SNSs can help them deal with challenges in professional practices into learning process (Bozalek et al., 2013). An examination on the beliefs of educators underpinning the appraisal of effective academic uses of new technologies is also critical to overcoming unreliable findings of the effectiveness of technology (Kirkwood & Price, 2013). It serves academic institutions to design effective trainings in order to accomplish educators' teaching objectives (Gay, 1997). It is critical to challenge the perspectives on the technology integration by seeking explanations about the effectiveness of SNSs in education.

Educators' perceptions on the SNSs integration are shaped by their teaching context, benefits, and barriers that SNSs present as well as the educators' general experiences with these technologies (McCarthy, 2012; Scott, 2013; Veletsianos, 2013). The educators' view on social media ranges from positive ones to negative ones. From a positive point of view, literature informs that SNSs integration in education contributes to change educators' perceptions on their teaching activities from a provision of learning resources to students' collaboration, interaction, and communication (Scott, 2013), from teaching content to international collaborations (McCarthy, 2012), and from personal work to groups of online scholars to enact pedagogy and visible practices (Veletsianos, 2013). However, Educators' negative perceptions and attitudes of the emerging of SNSs integration have also been reported. The reports have emphasized barriers on the fast pace of emerging SNSs developments. SNSs are considered to bringing feelings of inadequacy and triggering defensive behaviors about the need of SNSs integration in education in general and in their teaching activities (Herrington & Parker, 2013), concerning of privacy violations (Dahlstrom, 2012), and perceiving lack of control of educators on SNSs platform (Ng'ambi, 2013) and allegations of plagiarism by students. Educators also face other barriers such as lack of the best type of SNSs use and institutional guidelines for effective integrations (Ng'ambi, 2013).

METHODOLOGY

This study was a mixed-method study which was aimed at examining phenomenon within the research context using various data sources (Creswell & Clark, 2007) and developing both reliability and validity of the research findings (Borrego, Douglas, & Amelink, 2009; Mukminin et al., 2017a, 2017b; Azkiyah & Mukminin, 2017). Through this method, we investigated the use of SNSs, popularity, benefits, and barriers in education among EFL lecturers in Jambi and Palembang, two cities located in Southern Sumatra Island, Indonesia.

The study was conducted from August to December 2017 as part of a larger study examining Indonesian higher education technology integration. Multiple data collection methods, such as observation, interviews, document analysis, and questionnaires are significant in a mixed-method study (Patton & Appelbaum, 2003). With the significance of multiple data sources according to Stake (1995), we applied two primary sources of data collection, a survey and semi-structured interview. Saunders et al. (2007) claimed that the method for the collection of data relates to research approaches. The two data collection methods are important to provide full and detail information in this study. Convenience sampling was used due to its appropriateness in a mixed method study (Fraenkel & Wallen, 2009).

Quantitative Data

We collaborated with six Indonesian universities in two cities; Jambi and Palembang where participants were 239 EFL lecturers (55 males and 184 females) aged between 25 and 55 years old. Their teaching experience varied from one year to more than thirty years (see Table 1).

This study used the instruments developed by Lim and Richardson (2016) adapted to fit the context in line with the university lecturers' perspectives on SNSs integration in education in EFL. Validity of this study was facilitated through the content analysis where an expert panel consisted of five faculty members specializing on ICT and pedagogy were asked to review the items or statements of the proposed questionnaire. The final decision of the survey included four sub-categories (see Table 7 in the Appendix). The questions were established to be more specific to achieve the aims of the study. For instance, 'Using SNSs for educational purposes would be convenient', was changed to 'Using SNSs for teaching in higher university was convenient.' The final survey was composed of 24 questions. The reliability of the survey was .89 (good). To collect the data through the questionnaire, we utilized a Google form (an online form that Google programs provide for users to collect any kinds of data) and hardcopies in the distribution of the questionnaire. We applied descriptive statistics by using SPSS 22 software for the data analysis and measured the frequency, percentage, mean, and standard deviation of the data to either counter or support the qualitative data. Descriptive statistics is summary statistics which describes features of a group of information (Ross, 2010).

Table 1. Participants' information

Variables	Sub-Variable	The Respondents (n. 239)	
		F (%)	
Gender	Male	55 (23.01%)	
	Female	184 (76.99%)	
Age (years)	25-35	99 (48.23%)	
	36-45	87 (43.41%)	
	46-55	53 (7.72%)	
Teaching experience (years)	1-10 11-20 21-30 +30	95 (39.75) 84 (35.15) 64 (26.78) 4 (1.67)	

Qualitative Data

To seek university lecturers' opinions regarding SNSs, benefits and barriers in EFL, we held interview sessions. For this aim, we set a semi-structure interview, which the questions were adapted from the survey items. Semi-structured interviews were used to understand how interventions work and how they are improved allowing interviewers to discuss issues that may not be included in the other study data collection method (Creswell, 2009; Mukminin & McMahon, 2013; Mukminin, 2012a, 2012b; Patton, 2002). In the survey, we provided participants with a statement if every participant was willing to participate in the interview sessions. Fifteen lecturers agreed to be interviewed. However, only six lecturers were finally willing to be interviewed due to several reasons such as some of them had no free time or some were busy with their activities. All of interviewees' names were masked through the use of pseudonyms (Andy, Kylie, Susan, Goerge, Dina, and Dorothy). Among the interviewees were two male and four female lecturers. Their ages were between 25 and 55 years old and their teaching experiences were between 2 and 35 years. We emailed, called, and texted all chosen participants willing to give their opinions in the interviews. These interviews were held in order to obtain in-depth information related to the purposes of the research. Each interview lasted from 35 to 40 minutes in participants' mother tongue, Indonesian language, to get more in-depth information aiming to answer the research problems.

In the very beginning step of the qualitative data, we applied what Miles and Huberman (1994) called "within case analysis." We conducted interviews with participants by audio-taping them with smartphones, we then transcribed the data. We analyzed and categorized "open coding" the transcripts of the interviews into the categories (benefits and barriers) and this process was repeated until the last participant, the sixth participant. We translated the analyzed data into English before presenting the data. We all read each English translation of each participant line-by-line independently, and once again marked relevant chunks of statements, put relevant chunks of statements into fixed categories. Data collection and data analysis happen in a random way since they mutually influence each other (Creswell, 2009; Mukminin Ali, & Ashari, 2015; Patton, 2002).

For the consideration of ethics and protection of the rights of human participants, we hid the participants' name through the application of pseudonyms (Mukminin et al., 2017a, 2017b). Their decision to get involved in the interview sessions in this study was voluntary as we facilitated them with informed-consent forms. In order to ensure the trustworthiness, validity and reliability, of the data (Lincoln & Guba, 1985) of the study, we delivered verbatim examples from the transcribed interviews and conducted a member checking (Johnson & Christensen, 2008; Creswell, 2009; Habibi et al., 2017). We checked and rechecked not only with all participants of the interviews but also with co-researchers that served as member checking processes. In this type of steps, we returned back all the interview data and our findings to participants in order to obtain their feedback and agreement. This step was done to convince readers that our data were not bias. We were keen to ensure that the participants agreed with the finding presented in this study (Johnson & Christensen, 2008). In brief, the participants informed that they agreed we use the data for our research purpose.

FINDINGS

In this part, popularity and daily uses of SNSs among lecturers (ownership (possession) of SNSs accounts, types of SNSs use, and time in using SNSs/day) and the use of SNSs in EFL are presented. First we present the popularity and daily uses of SNSs among Lecturers. We think that it is also important to give our readers a picture on the backgrounds of our participants in using SNSs not only for teaching and learning English but also for the use of SNSs for general purposes. In the second part, we present the use of SNSs in EFL. In this part, we provide readers with the lecturers' opinions on the SNSs use in EFL classes.

Popularity and Daily Use of SNS Among Lecturers

The data for the use of SNSs among EFL lecturers which include the ownership (possession) of SNS, years of SNSs use, types of SNSs use, and frequency using SNSs a day are shown in Table 2. All lecturers (100%) reported that they owned SNSs accounts. Most lecturers (68.20%) had used SNSs from six to ten years. Only 15 lecturers (6.28%) had less than a three-year experience using SNSs. Facebook was the most popular SNSs owned by 231 lecturers (96.65%). This was followed by WhatsApp (98.7%), and Youtube (94.85%). We also explored time the lecturers spent on SNSs/day. Most lecturers (41.00%) spent their time using SNSs from two hours to three hours. Meanwhile, 15 lecturers (6.28%) spent less than 30 minutes a day using SNSs.

Data from the survey for the use of SNSs in daily life revealed that majority of the university lecturers (82.43) frequently used SNSs to keep in touch with their friends and families. The next frequent uses of SNSs were to obtain new information (64.85%), to share some information (46.86%), and to connect with people I have lost touch with (51.46%). While the least frequent use of SNSs was to let others know what is happening in their life (20.08%) (see Table 3).

The findings from qualitative data (interview with the six lecturers) indicated similar results of SNSs purposes among university lecturers revealed in the survey part. In the interview, the participants reported that they used SNSs in order to keep in touch with friends and families, to obtain some new information, to share some information, to do career networking, to connect with people I have lost touch with, and let others know what is happening in my life (see Table 4). From the interview, there were two emerging purposes were not informed from the survey as the evidence that the use of SNSs develops and expands. The two purposes were to buy online, and join group pages of personal hobby.

Table 2. University lecturer's use of SNS (n. 239)

	N	%
Ownership (possession) of SNSs accounts		
Yes	239	100
No	0	0
Years of SNSs use		
0-2	0	0
3-5	61	25.52
6-8	84	35.15
8-10	79	33.05
More 10 years	15	6.28
Types of SNSs use		
Instagram	158	66.11
Facebook	231	96.65
WhatsApp	229	95.82
Line	57	23.85
YouTube	219	91.63
Facebook messenger	201	84.10
BBM	45	18.83
Others	89	37.24
Time spent using SNSs/day		
0-30 minutes	15	6.28
31 minutes -1+ hours	95	39.75
2 hour- 3+ hours	98	41.00
4 hour or more than 4 hours	31	12.97

Table 3. Lecturers' general purpose of SNSs

Purposes	n	%
To keep in touch with friends and families	197	82.43
To obtain some new information	155	64.85
To share some information	112	46.86
To do career networking	75	31.38
To connect with people I have lost touch with	123	51.46
To let others know what is happening in my life	48	20.08

Table 4. Purposes and sample statements on the use of SNSs for general purposes

Using SNSs to...	Statements
keep in touch with friends and families	Kylie; "I use SNSs to get connected with my family and friends where we could communicate limitlessly using our smartphones".
obtain new information	Goerge; "I read and watch current news using social media...the social media always provide users with latest information and headlines."
share information	Dina; "It is an effective platform to share information. I use social media to share information to my family and friends such as job vacancy, wedding invitation, and other information".
do career networking	Dorothy; "Facebook and WhatsApp are two media that I often use to establish my professional activity and build networking"
connect with people whom I lost contact with	Susan; I use Facebook to look for my childhood friends. It is nice when you get connected to them and share experience and memories".
let others know what is happening in my life	Andy; "I am happy when my facebook friends or instagram followers give likes and comments on pictures or status I share. It shows their attention to what I do".
buy and sell online	Dina; "I love buying things online from fashion products to)
have entertainment (games, music, and videos)	Dina: "Youtube is the best application when you get bored with your daily routines. Watching vlogs and cooking show are two of my favorite programs
join group pages of personal hobby	Andy; "I join groups of WhatsApp where we have time to discuss about cars and bikes. It is very useful to know more about what I like".

The Use of SNSs in EFL

In order to explore lecturers' opinions on the SNSs use in EFL classes, we presented the survey data through descriptive statistics which involved frequency, percent, mean, and standard deviation. In the survey, we had 10 positive perspective statements and two negative perspective statements. We informed the data through complete information, frequency, percentage, mean, and standard deviation for each item (see Table 5).

From the mean scores, it indicated that lecturers' agreement on questionnaire's positive statements was in "agree category", for example, using SNSs for EFL teaching was convenient (3.35), SNSs supported EFL face-to-face teaching (3.35), and using SNSs for EFL teaching increased motivation to learn English (3.28). However, one positive statement that is not in the category "agree" was statement "I felt more comfortable using SNSs as a discussion medium with students than using traditional method" with a mean of 2.92 which indicates that most lecturers still preferred traditional teaching method when holding a discussion. The negative items of the survey resulted in lower mean scores. They disagreed that SNSs would invade their privacy if their course and SNSs overlapped (2.32) and with the statement, "they don't care one way or the other about SNSs being used for their EFL course" (2.25).

We categorized the data from the interviews through the data analysis processes into two salient themes; benefits and barriers. The participants, university lecturers teaching English for specific purposes reported four benefits of SNSs in EFL courses in positive statements while they talked about two barriers in the SNSs. Our data analysis of the interviews reported four sub-themes emerged which we classified as benefits of SNSs in EFL classes; communication, supervision and evaluation, time flexibility, creativity. SNSs use eased not only communication between lecturers and their students in EFL classes but also supervision on the tasks or assignment given by the lecturers. The use of SNSs such Facebook and WhatsApp messenger as a means of communication has provided a virtual conversation giving easiness in terms of time and space for lecturers to communicate with their students. The result also pointed that SNSs ease the supervision such as efficient sharing medium of workload discussion where both lecturer and students had freedom to discuss the tasks. SNSs gave lecturers flexible time during the courses. Applications such as a WhatsApp group gave lecturers and students freedom of time to discuss course materials in their EFL teaching. Students also had improved their creativity using SNSs in the teaching and learning processes when one lecturer applied YouTube for teaching a speaking course in English, the students had some ways recording, editing, and presenting their activity in YouTube (see Table 6).

Table 5. The use of SNSs in EFL (n: 239)

Question	Strongly Disagree	Disagree	Neither Agree/ Disagree	Agree	Strongly Agree	M	Std. Dev.
	n (%)	*n (%)*	*n (%)*	*n (%)*	*n (%)*		
Using SNSs for EFL teaching was convenient	12 (5.02)	59 (24.69)	37 (15.48)	96 (40.17)	35 (14.64)	3.35	1.147
SNSs supported EFL face-to-face teaching	13 (5.44)	57 (23.85)	38 (15.90)	101 (42.26)	30 (12.55)	3.35	1.009
Using SNSs for EFL teaching increased motivation	15 (6.28)	55 (23.01)	41(17.15)	103(43.10)	25 (10.46)	3.28	1.12
Using SNSs for class made me feel more connected to my EFL students	12 (5.02)	60 (25.10)	39(16.32)	110 (46.03)	18 (7.53)	3.26	1.07
I felt more comfortable using SNSs as a discussion mode with students than using traditional method	14 (5.86)	95(39.75)	38(15.48)	78(32.64)	14 (5.86)	2.92	1.09
SNSs were effective media to share EFL materials to the students	14(5.86)	56(23.43)	40 (16.74)	95(39.75)	34 (14.23)	3.30	1.16
SNSs were educational platforms in EFL facilitated better rapport of students	16(6.69)	54(22.59)	36(15.06)	102(41.84)	31(12.97)	3.33	1.15
SNSs were effective tool to collaborate with colleagues in EFL course	16(6.69)	55(23.01)	38(15.90)	97(40.59)	33 (13.81)	3.32	1.16
SNSs were an effective to communicate with students	19 (7.95)	52(21.76)	34(14.23)	104(43.51)	30(12.55)	3.31	1.16
I felt that my privacy was invaded when SNSs integrated in my EFL classes	37 (15.48)	96(40.17)	35(14.64)	62(25.94)	9(3.77)	2.62	1.13
I don't care one way or the other about SNSs being used for my EFL course	39(16.32)	93(38.91)	34(14.23)	65(27.20)	8(3.34)	2.62	1.14

Regardless all of the benefits, the interview data also revealed some barriers emerged on the SNSs integration in EFL classes. There were two interesting sub-themes coded from the interview data; lack of skill and costly to use. Some senior university lecturers had difficulties in using SNSs since they were not accustomed to using them. Therefore, it is considered as a main barrier in the SNSs integration in EFL classes. They also thought that SNSs was costly to use either for students or for new lecturers. Due to limitation of the wireless access of the Internet, either the students or the lecturers need to buy Internet data from Indonesian providers that cost them extra money.

Table 6. Themes, subthemes, and sample statements of the interview

Themes	Sub-Themes	Statements
Benefits	Communication	Dorothy; "As a means of communication, Messengers such as Facebook and WhatsApp certainly ease our communication because there was no limitation of time and places. I also used Facebook group as an upload media and it was so functional to actively engage students to discuss and argue where I could easily supervise."
	Supervision and evaluation	Dina; "I love Facebook group in teaching writing because I could check their writing easily. It really helps me do supervision and evaluation."
	Time flexibility	Kylie; "You can share materials, deliver tasks, observe and evaluate the students with flexible time. It helps a lot to plan our activity in classrooms or outside classrooms."
	Creativity	Goerge; "I once used Youtube teaching speaking for juniors and gave an assignment "self-introduction It was nice to see the students had improved their creativity posting their speaking tasks through Youtube."
Barriers	Lack of skill	Susan; "I am too old to use some technological devices. They are not for me. I am not using it in my classroom since I have lack of skill. I just know some of them such Facebook and WhatsApp messenger."
	Costly to use	Dina; "Using SNSs is certainly costly since you have to buy internet data all the time. It is a problem not only for students but also for new lecturers since we earn little."

DISCUSSION

The article explored EFL university lecturers' use of SNSs and adoption of social media into their teaching practices in six Indonesian universities. The results of the study informed that EFL university lecturers in Indonesian higher education institutions used SNSs on a daily basis where more than 66% of the lecturers had owned SNSs accounts from six to ten years. The most popular SNS among the lecturers in the study was Facebook which was owned by almost all of the lecturers (96.65%). Most of the lecturers (41.00%) spent their time using SNSs between two and more than three hours a day. These findings are consistent with the findings reported by Akçayır and Akçayır, (2016); Kabilan, Ahmad, and Abidin, (2010); Lim & Richardson, (2016); Murire and Chilliers (2017); Prasojo et al., (2017) who investigated SNSs use in education informed that Facebook was the most popular SNS and all participants on their study were conversant with the use of SNSs. Data from the survey showed that most lecturers frequently used SNSs to keep in touch with their friends and families (82.43%). It was followed by "to obtain new information" (64.85%) and "to share some information" (46.86%). While the least frequent use of SNSs among the lecturers was to let others know what is happening in their life (20.08%). These results agree with other previous findings (Akçayır, 2017; Kirkwood & Price, 2013; Lim & Richardson, 2016) informing that the main users who were related to education SNSs were to communicate and obtain information. However, there were emerging goals of SNSs use in the lecturers' daily life from the interview; to buy online and to join group pages of personal hobby. These two findings of this research revealed that majority of the lecturers and students used SNSs especially Facebook owned by all lecturers providing an opportunity to integrate the technology into instructions. Therefore, Indonesian lecturers and students in various environments can improve their SNSs use in educational setting without being required to adapt with the SNSs' basic functionalities.

In addition to the popularity and daily use of SNSs among lecturers, we also investigated the SNSs use in education carried out by the lecturers. From the mean scores, it is informed that lecturers' agreement on questionnaire's positive statements were in agree category such as using SNSs for EFL teaching was convenient (3.35) and SNSs supported EFL face-to-face teaching (3.35). On the other hand, one positive statement had low mean is "I felt more comfortable using SNSs as a discussion with students than using traditional method" indicating that most lecturers prefer traditional teaching than using SNSs in class discussion. The negative items resulted in lower mean scores; "SNSs would invade their privacy if their course and SNSs overlapped" (2.32) and "they don't care one way or the other about SNSs being used for their EFL course" (2.25). The findings are similar to the study by Akçayır (2017) and Lim and Richardson (2016). Besides the survey results, we presented benefits of SNSs in EFL classes qualitatively from the perspectives of the lecturers which include eases on communication, supervision and evaluation, time flexibility, creativity (Murire & Chilliers, 2017; Kirkwood & Price, 2013).

Regardless all of the benefits informed both by the survey and by the interview, some barriers emerged on the SNSs integration in EFL classes. There are two barriers emerged from the interview with the university lecturers, lack of skill and costly to use. One senior lecturer stated that she was too old to use some technological devices and the devices were not for her. So that, she was not using it in her classroom. Another lecturer who was a new-recruited educator informed that using SNSs was certainly costly for her since she had to buy internet data all the time. The problem was not only for students but also for new lecturers since they earn little. These two emerging findings agree with some parts of the study results stating cost and skill were problems in SNSs integration in education (Hamid et al., 2011; Murire & Chilliers, 2017; Prasojo et al., 2017).

In brief, the results of this study informed that most lecturers were familiar with kinds of SNSs and always used them for in their daily life. This study also revealed lecturers' agreement on most positive statements regarding the use of SNSs in education. More benefits than barriers were discussed in the interview with the lecturers that reflect that social networking services have latent qualities or abilities to improve higher education teaching and learning process especially in teaching English as foreign language classes. Along with previous studies (Akçayır & Akçayır, 2016; Kabilan, Ahmad, & Abidin, 2010; Lim & Richardson, 2016; Murire & Chilliers, 2017; Prasojo et al., 2017) and our own findings, it is safe to inform that integrating SNSs for educational environment purposes is an actual possibility as media to tackle some educational issues for instance as isolation or lack of community of face-to-face learning, given continued cutting edge in SNSs functionality. However, the question emerges whether these study findings also play significant roles for online learning environments situated in Indonesia as a developing country where the Internet is still limited in big city as we originally aimed to discover. The participants were from universities EFL lecturers. However, further research is needed to determine EFL learners perceived of SNSs in Indonesian higher education context to promote a quality education (Luschei, 2018; Yusuf, Yusuf, Yusuf, & Nadya, 2017; Abrar, Mukminin, Habibi, Asyrafi, Makmur, & Marzulina, 2018).

IMPLICATIONS

Implications for practice, policy, and future research are offered in this part. Firstly, because the lecturers' perceptions and opinions of the SNSs use for educational purposes were mostly positive despite some barriers emerged, Indonesian students, instructors, teachers or lecturers are recommended to integrate SNSs in their education, curriculum, and instructional designs in order to improve learning and teaching experiences (Lim & Richardson, 2016), to establish collaboration and discussion (Prasojo et al., 2017), and to foster engagement in education (Habibi et al., 2018).

Policy makers in higher education institutions should carefully evaluate lecturers' barriers in SNSs integration in education that include cost and skills. To provide supporting infrastructures of connection of the internet for all stakeholders in higher education institutions especially for developing countries would lower the cost of SNSs integration in those countries (Habibi et al., 2018; Prasojo et al., 2017). Internet providers are also suggested to offer lower prices of internet packages for students and lecturers to support the integration of technology especially social networking services as well as broaden the internet broadband access across the countries. Sustainable trainings for some lack-skilled lecturers are also suggested to conduct since many lecturers still have difficulties to integrate technology in education. Future research is recommended to conduct to investigate Indonesian senior lecturers in integrating technology in Indonesia where there are lack of studies discussing this issue. there are limited sources of infrastructures and human resource. In addition, studies on policy makers' opinions, expectations, and concerns are needed regarding educational uses of SNSs (Akçayır, 2017).

REFERENCES

Abrar, M., Mukminin, A., Habibi, A., & Asyrafi, F, Makmur, M. & Marzulina, L. (2018). "If our English isn't a language, what is it?" Indonesian EFL student teachers' challenges speaking English. *Qualitative Report*, *23*(1), 129–145.

Akçayır, G., & Akçayır, M. (2016). Research trends in social network sites' educational use: A review of publications in all SSCI journals to 2015. *Review of Education*, *4*(3), 293–319. doi:10.1002/rev3.3075

Akhiar, A., Mydin, A., & Kasuma, S.A.A (2017). Students' perceptions and attitudes towards the use of Instagram in English language writing. *Malaysian Journal of Learning and Instruction (MJLI)*, 47-72.

Azkiyah, S. N., & Mukminin, A. (2017). In search of teaching quality of student teachers: The case of one teacher education program in Indonesia. *Center for Educational Policy Studies Journal*, *7*(4), 105–124.

Bates, A. W., & Poole, G. (2003). *Effective teaching with technology in higher education: Foundations for success*. Jossey-Bass.

Beldarrain, Y. (2006). Distance education trends: Integrating new technologies to foster student interaction and collaboration. *Distance Education*, *27*(2), 139–153.

Borrego, M., Douglas, E. P., & Amelink, C. T. (2009). Quantitative, qualitative, and mixed research methods in engineering education. *Journal of Engineering Education*, *98*(1), 53–66. doi:10.1002/j.2168-9830.2009.tb01005.x

Boyd, D. M., & Ellison, N. B. (2008). Social network sites: Definition, history, and scholarship. *Journal of Computer-Mediated Communication, 13*(1), 210–230. doi:10.1111/j.1083-6101.2007.00393.x

Bozalek, V., Gachago, D., Alexander, L., Watters, K., Wood, D., Ivala, E., & Herrington, J. (2013). The use of emerging technologies for authentic learning: A South African study in higher education. *British Journal of Educational Technology, 44*(4), 629–638. doi:10.1111/bjet.12046

Brady, K., Holcomb, L., & Smith, B. (2010). The use of alternative social networking sites in higher education settings: A case study of the e-learning benefits of Ning in education. *Journal of Interactive Online Learning, 9*(2), 151–170.

Chik, A., & Breidbach, S. (2011). Online language learning histories exchange: Hong Kong and German perspectives. *TESOL Quarterly, 45*(3), 553–564. doi:10.5054/tq.2011.256795

Creswell, J. W. (2009). *Research design: Qualitative, quantitative, and mixed methods approaches.* Thousand Oaks, CA: Sage.

Creswell, J. W., & Clark, V. L. P. (2007). *Designing and conducting mixed methods research.* Thousand Oaks, CA: Sage.

Dahlstrom, E. (2012). *ECAR study of undergraduate students and information technology. (Research report).* Louisville, CO: EDUCAUSE Center for Applied Research.

Davis, F. D., Bagozzi, R. P., & Warshaw, P. R. (1992). Extrinsic and intrinsic motivation to use computers in the workplace. *Journal of Applied Social Psychology, 22*(14), 1111–1132. doi:10.1111/j.1559-1816.1992. tb00945.x

Fewell, N. (2014). Social networking and language learning with Twitter. *Research Papers in Language Teaching and Learning, 5*(1), 223–234.

Fraenkel, J., & Wallen, N. (2009). *How to design and evaluate research in education.* New York, NY: McGraw-Hill.

Gay, S. (1997). Teaching with technology: a case study of teachers' perceptions of implementing computers into the classroom. [Doctoral thesis]. University of Nebraska, Lincoln, NB.

Georgina, D. A., & Olson, M. R. (2008). Integration of technology in higher education: A review of faculty self-perceptions. *The Internet and Higher Education, 11*(1), 1–8. doi:10.1016/j.iheduc.2007.11.002

Gorder, L. (2008). A study of teacher perceptions of instructional technology integration in the classroom. *Delta Pi Epsilon Journal, 50*(2), 63–76.

Greifeneder, E., Pontis, S., Blandford, A., Attalla, H., Neal, D., & Schlebbe, K. (2018). Researchers' attitudes towards the use of social networking sites. *The Journal of Documentation, 74*(1), 119–136. doi:10.1108/JD-04-2017-0051

Habibi, A., Mukminin, A., Riyanto, Y., Prasojo, L. D., Sulistiyo, U., Saudagar, F., & Sofwan, M. (2018). Building an online community: Student teachers' perceptions on the advantages of using social networking services in a teacher education program. *Turkish Online Journal of Distance Education, 19*(1), 46–61. doi:10.17718/tojde.382663

Hadiyanto, M. A., Arif, N., Fajaryani, N., Failasofah, & Habibi, A. (2017). In Search of quality student teachers in a digital era: Reframing the practices of soft skills in teacher education. The Turkish Online Journal of Educational Technology, 16(3), 71-78.

Hamid, S., Kurnia, S., Waycott, J., & Chang, S. (2011). Exploring Malaysian students' perspectives of Online Social Networking (OSN) use for higher education. *Paper presented at the 22nd Annual Conference ISANA International Education Association (ISANA) 2011*, Hobart, Tasmania.

Hamshire, C., & Cullen, W. R. (2014). Providing students with an easystart to higher education: The emerging role of digital technologies to facilitate students' transitions. *International Journal of Virtual and Personal Learning Environments*, 5(1), 15. doi:10.4018/ijvple.2014010105

Herrington, J., & Parker, J. (2013). Emerging technologies as cognitive tools for authentic learning. *British Journal of Educational Technology*, 44(4), 607–615. doi:10.1111/bjet.12048

Johnson, R. B., & Christensen, L. B. (2008). *Educational research: Quantitative, qualitative, and mixed approaches* (3rd ed.). Thousand Oaks, CA: Sage.

Jones, C., Ramanau, R., Cross, S., & Healing, G. (2010). Net Generation or Digital Natives: Is There a Distinct New Generation Entering University? *Computers & Education*, 54(3), 722–732. Retrieved from https://www.learntechlib.org/p/67144/ doi:10.1016/j.compedu.2009.09.022

Junco, R., Heiberger, G., & Loken, E. (2011). The effect of Twitter on college student engagement and grades. *Journal of Computer Assisted Learning*, 27(2), 119–132. doi:10.1111/j.1365-2729.2010.00387.x

Kabilan, M. K., Ahmad, N., & Abidin, M. J. Z. (2010). Facebook: An online environment for learning of English in institutions of higher education. *Internet and Higher Education*, 13(4), 179–187. doi:10.1016/j.iheduc.2010.07.003

Kaplan, A. M., & Haenlein, M. (2010). Users of the world, unite! The challenges and opportunities of Social Media. *Business Horizons*, 53(1), 59–68. doi:10.1016/j.bushor.2009.09.003

Kessler, S. (2010). *The case for social media in the schools*. Retrieved from http://mashable.com/2010/09/29/social-media-in-school

Khan, M. L., Wohn, D. Y., & Ellison, N. B. (2014). Actual friends matter: An internet skills perspective on teens' informal academic collaboration on Facebook. *Computers & Education*, 79, 138–147. doi:10.1016/j.compedu.2014.08.001

Kirkwood, A., & Price, L. (2013). Examining some assumptions and limitations of research on the effects of emerging technologies for teaching and learning in higher education. *British Journal of Educational Technology*, 44(4), 536–543. doi:10.1111/bjet.12049

Lim, J., & Richardson, J. C. (2016). Exploring the effects of students' social networking experience on social presence and perceptions of using SNSs for educational purposes. *The Internet and Higher Education*, 29, 31–39. doi:10.1016/j.iheduc.2015.12.001

Lincoln, S. Y., & Guba, G. E. (1985). *Naturalistic inquiry*. New York, NY: SAGE Publications.

Luschei, T. (2017). 20 years of TIMSS: Lessons for Indonesia. *Indonesian Research Journal in Education, 1*(1), 6-17.

Manca, S., & Ranieri, M. (2013). Is it a tool suitable for learning? A critical review of the literature on Facebook as a technology-enhanced learning environment. *Journal of Computer Assisted Learning, 29*(6), 487–504. doi:10.1111/jcal.12007

Manca, S., & Ranieri, M. (2016). "Yes for sharing, no for teaching!": Social media in academic practices. *The Internet and Higher Education, 29,* 63–74. doi:10.1016/j.iheduc.2015.12.004

McCarthy, J. (2012). International design collaboration and mentoring for tertiary students through facebook. *Australasian Journal of Educational Technology, 28*(5), 755–775. doi:10.14742/ajet.1383

Miles, M. B., & Huberman, A. M. (1994). *Qualitative data analysis: An expanded sourcebook*. San Francisco, CA: Sage.

Mncube, L. S., Dube, L., & Ngulube, P. (2017). The role of lecturers and university administrators in promoting new e-learning initiatives. *International Journal of Virtual and Personal Learning Environments, 7*(1), 11. doi:10.4018/IJVPLE.2017010101

Mondahl, M., & Razmerita, L. (2014). Social media, collaboration and social learning–a case-study of foreign language learning. *Electronic Journal of E-Learning, 12*(4), 339–352.

Mukminin, A. (2012a). *From east to west: A phenomenological study of Indonesian graduate students' experiences on the acculturation process at an American public research university.* Unpublished Doctoral Dissertation, Florida State University, Tallahassee, FL.

Mukminin, A. (2012b). Acculturative experiences among Indonesian graduate students in US higher education: Academic shock, adjustment, crisis, and resolution. *Excellence in Higher Education Journal, 3*(1), 14–36. doi:10.5195/EHE.2012.64

Mukminin, A., & Ali, Rd. M., & Fadloan, M.J. (2015). Voices from within: Student teachers' experiences in english academic writing socialization at one Indonesian teacher training program. *Qualitative Report, 20*(9), 1394–1407.

Mukminin, A., Kamil, D., Muazza, M., & Haryanto, E. (2017b). Why teacher education? Documenting undocumented female student teachers' motives in Indonesia: A case study. *The Qualitative Report (USA), 22*(1), 309–326.

Mukminin, A., & McMahon, B. J. (2013). International graduate students' cross-cultural academic engagement: Stories of Indonesian doctoral students on American campus. *Qualitative Report, 18*(69), 1–19.

Mukminin, A., Rohayati, T., Putra, H. A., Habibi, A., & Aina, M. (2017a). The long walk to quality teacher education in Indonesia: Student teachers' motives to become a teacher and policy implications. *Elementary Education Online, 16*(1), 35–59.

Murire, O. T., & Cilliers, L. (2017). Social media adoption among lecturers at a traditional university in Eastern Cape Province of South Africa. *South African Journal of Information Management, 19*(1), a834. doi:10.4102ajim.v19i1.834

Ng'ambi, D. (2013). Effective and ineffective uses of emerging technologies: Towards a transformative pedagogical model. *British Journal of Educational Technology, 44*(4), 652–661. doi:10.1111/bjet.12053

Patton, E., & Appelbaum, S. H. (2003). The case for case studies in management research. *Management Research News, 26*(5), 60–71. doi:10.1108/01409170310783484

Patton, M. Q. (2002). *Qualitative research & evaluation methods*. London: Sage.

Pervaiz, S. (2016). The advantages and risks of using social networking in higher education in Pakistan. In T. Issa, P. Isaias, & P. Kommers (Eds.), *Social networking and education: Global perspectives* (pp. 83–97). Cham: Springer. doi:10.1007/978-3-319-17716-8_6

Prasojo, L. D., Habibi, A., & Mukminin, A. (2017). Managing Digital Learning Environments: Student Teachers' Perception on the Social Networking Services Use in Writing Courses in Teacher Education. *The Turkish Online Journal of Educational Technology, 16*(4), 42–55.

Robbins, S. P., & Singer, J. B. (2014). From the editor – The medium is the message: Integrating social media and social work education. *Journal of Social Work Education, 50*(3), 387–390. doi:10.1080/10 437797.2014.916957

Rogers, D. L. (2000). A paradigm shift: Technology integration for higher education in the new millennium. *AACE Journal, 1*(13), 19–33.

Rooyen, A. V. (2015). Distance education accounting students' perceptions of social media integration. *Procedia: Social and Behavioral Sciences, 176*, 444–445. doi:10.1016/j.sbspro.2015.01.495

Ross, S. M. (2017). *Introductory statistics*. Academic Press. doi:10.1016/B978-0-12-804317-2.00031-X

Saunders, M., Lewis, P., & Thornhill, A. (2007). *Research Methods for Business Students* (6th ed.). London: Pearson.

Scott, K. (2013). Does a university teacher need to change e-learning beliefs and practices when using a social networking site? A longitudinal case study. *British Journal of Educational Technology, 44*(4), 571–580. doi:10.1111/bjet.12072

Stake, R. E. (1995). *The Art of case study research*. Thousand Oaks: Sage.

Tess, P. A. (2013). The Role of Social Media in Higher Education Classes (Real and Virtual)—A Literature Review. *Computers in Human Behavior, 29*(5), A60–A68. doi:10.1016/j.chb.2012.12.032

Veletsianos, G. (2013). Open practices and identity: Evidence from researchers and educators' social media participation. *British Journal of Educational Technology, 44*(4), 639–651. doi:10.1111/bjet.12052

Yusuf, Q., Yusuf, Y., Yusuf, B., & Nadya, A. (2017). Skimming and scanning techniques to assist EFL students in understanding English reading texts. *Indonesian Research Journal in Education, 1*(1), 43–57.

Zorko, V. (2009). Factors affecting the way students collaborate in a wiki for English language learning. *Australasian Journal of Educational Technology, 25*(5), 645–666. doi:10.14742/ajet.1113

This research was previously published in the International Journal of Virtual and Personal Learning Environments (IJVPLE), 8(2); pages 46-62, copyright year 2018 by IGI Publishing (an imprint of IGI Global).

APPENDIX

Table 7. Survey questions

Sub-Categories	Descriptions
Q1–Q3 (Demographic information)	Demographic information (gender, age, and teaching experience)
Q4–Q7 (general information about SNSs ownership (possession) and popularity)	Ownership (possession) of SNSs, years of using SNSs, types of SNSs being used time spending on SNSs a day
Q8-Q13 (Questions for general information on the use of SNSs)	General purposes of SNSs
Q14–Q24 (5-point Likert-scale, 1 *strongly disagree*- 5 *strongly agree*)	University lecturers' perceptions using SNSs in EFL.

Chapter 99
Using Social Media to Facilitate Instruction and Increase Marketing in Global Higher Education

Michael D. Richardson
Columbus State University, USA

Sarah G. Brinson
Albany State University, USA

Pamela A. Lemoine
Columbus State University, USA

ABSTRACT

The technological revolution of the past two decades has changed global higher education, particularly with the impact of social media. There are two primary functions of social media in higher education: instruction and marketing. Social media offers higher education students an array of options to socialize, network, stay informed, and connected, but technology proficiency may not be the same for instructors. As social media use by students becomes more established, educators in higher education pursue methods to parlay expertise in instruction into increased opportunities to advertise and market higher education institutions. Social media's impact of instruction in higher education is undeniable. The next major focus is on social media as a robust recruiting instrument to increase enrollment in global higher education.

DOI: 10.4018/978-1-6684-7123-4.ch099

INTRODUCTION

Educators in global higher education are exploring alternative means of instruction including social media tools designed for ease of use, convenience, instructional freedom, and constant online discussions (Bartosik-Purgat, Filimon & Calli, 2017; Yu, Tian, Vogel & Kwok, 2010). Social media is commonly defined as any medium used to integrate technology into the lives of people to facilitate communication (DeAndrea, Ellison, LaRose, Steinfield, & Fiore, 2012; Ituman, 2011; Veletsianos, 2011). As social media has proliferated in society, more higher education institutions are using social media tools such as social networking, wikis, blogs, or video, to interact with or engage students for instructional purposes (Elmannai, Odeh & Bach, 2013; Veletsianos, 2010). Increased engagement has been advocated as a critical component in increasing student learning and retention (Gupta, 2015). Therefore, social media has the potential to enhance student participation and improve academic performance (Buzzetto-More, 2012; Chen & Bryer, 2012; Kirschner & Karpinski, 2010; Mastrodicasa & Metellus, 2013).

Although social networks have increased exponentially in recent years there is some controversy over the imbedded nature of social media in educational settings (Chang, Yu & Lu, 2015; Ferguson & Tryjankowski, 2009; Greaves, Hayes, Wilson, Gielniak & Peterson, 2010). Social media sites enable users to link to others, to send messages, to connect with friends and colleagues, to send mail and instant messages, to meet new people, to share pictures and information, and to post personal information profiles (Gikas & Grant; 2013; Greenhow, Robelia & Hughes, 2009; Junco, 2011; Junco, Heibergert, & Loken, 2010). However, some researchers speculate that such openness of communication could lead to security problems when used in higher education (Lemoine, Hackett & Richardson, 2016).

Technology's Transformation of Higher Education

During the past 15 years methods of communicating and sharing have changed drastically (Bjerede, Atlins & Dede, 2012; Griesemer, 2012). Today higher education professors facilitate the acquisition of knowledge through technologies that necessitates a paradigm shift --teaching students how to think (Greenhow, 2011). Instead of imparting knowledge the focus is on teaching students to understand where and how to find knowledge and information (Hoffman & Novak, 2011; Kezar, 2014; Lemoine & Richardson, 2013; Records, Pritchard & Behling, 2011). Students must be able to find the information they need, analyze it appropriately, and not just regurgitate facts (Junco, 2014; Lane, Kehr & Richardson, 2010). Changing traditional higher education approaches to education from the acquisition of short-term skills to proactive life-long learning attitudes are of paramount importance as colleges and universities prepare students for the 21st century's global society (Hemmi, Bayne & Land, 2009; Lederer, 2012).

Technology, like all innovations, is only as efficient and effective as the persons who use it (Evans, 2014; Wamba & Carter, 2014). Technology can give the instructor the ability to function more efficiently and effectively; however, professors must understand the capabilities and limitations inherent in the technology (Tadros, 2011; Tess, 2013). Technology can be the means to improving the curriculum, the delivery system and student achievement (Ferguson & Tryjankowski, 2009; Smith & Kukulaks-Hulme, 2012).

The use of social networking and other forms of technology illustrate the global reach of wireless technology for everyone, and is especially critical for those teaching in today's changing global educational environment (Hussain, Guliez & Tahirkheli, 2012; Shih & Waugh, 2011; Teclehaimanot & Hickman, 2011). Online higher education avenues expand daily (Clark & Wagner, 2017). Some researchers have suggested that students using online learning resources outperform students in traditional face-to-face teaching settings (Allen & Seaman, 2010; Lemoine, Hackett & Richardson, 2016). They have also speculated that online learning experiences meet individual student learning needs (Baran, Correia & Thompson, 2011). With the requirement that 21st century student skills include the necessity to access and use information effectively, social media provides higher education faculty access to different methods for teaching and learning (Dede, 2011; Lumauag, 2017).

Social Media for Instruction

One of the largest technology developments over the past few years has been the global rise in online social networking (Booth & Esposito, 2011; Khanna, Jacob & Yadav, 2014). Typically, students are very familiar with social media and how they use it to learn on their own, but can social media be incorporated into formal instruction (Hemmi, Bayne & Land, 2009)? Higher education faculty can use social media to customize their teaching methods to meet the individual needs of students thus allowing students to learn at their own speed at their own time (Baran, Correia & Thompson, 2011; Bart, 2010). Social media can be a catalyst for the 21st century educator to increase instructional presentation and learning activities that can directly influence student productivity (Arnold & Paulus, 2010). The increasing use of social networking in higher education demonstrates a generational shift now permeating global higher education institutions (Allen & Seaman, 2010; Hung & Yuen, 2010; Mahmud, Ramachandiran & Ismail, 2016).

Integrating social media in instruction at the post-secondary level allows for many significant benefits in student learning (Anagnostopoulou, Parmar & Priego-Hernandez, 2009; Barnes & Lescault, 2011; Benson, 2014). Social media provides a method to increase the level of interactivity and engagement among learners because it is essentially a hands-on enterprise (Booth & Esposito, 2011). Social media also provides students with realistic preparation for their careers as it is now, and will continue to be, an integral tool in the future (Mathieson & Leafman, 2014). With the requirement that 21st century student skills include the necessity to access and use information effectively, social media provides higher education faculty access to different methods for teaching and learning and empowers learners to take more responsibility for their own learning (Dede, 2011; Nafukho, 2015).

Twenty-four/seven access to digital technologies can facilitate new media for professional learning through interactive technology (Benson, 2014). The use of social media as educational tools presents professors with the possibilities of using technology means with students to facilitate access to information for research, creativity and collaboration (Smith & Kukulska-Hulme, 2012). However, adding social media tools to instruction requires professors to restructure 20th century pedagogies to leverage 21st century opportunities for learning (Pechenkna & Aeschliman, 2017). For professors and students, once isolated to their own individual classrooms with limited print resources, social media promotes access, communication, tools for collaboration and analysis, and the ability to interactively share their knowledge (Blacher-Wilson, Mense & Richardson, 2011; Junco, 2011).

Social media allow professors to expand their messages and listen to what students want (Taylor, Mulligan & Ishida, 2012). Not only is it important that professors communicate to students, but it is important that the students transmit their needs to professors and administrators (Teclehaimanot & Hickman, 2011; Waters, 2011). Access to social media for higher education instructors has also resulted in a change for education delivery systems (Moran, Seaman, & Tinti-Kane, 2011, 2012). Social media permit students to become more active participants in their learning and explore new learning opportunities (Bullen, Morgan & Qayyum, 2011; Piotrowski, 2015; Rambe, 2012). Social media permit students and teachers to have instant access to news, information, and interactive experiences through computers, tablets, and smartphones (Toole, Khetaguri & Zangaladze, 2015). The key concept behind utilizing social media in higher education instruction is the ability to improve communication within the class, and the voice of each individual student (Hemmi, Bayne, & Land, 2009; Reid, 2014). Social media also provides the benefit of increased collaboration, which can be applied in many contexts and subjects (Hrastinski & Aghaee, 2012).

Technology for learning in a digital age is not going to go away; therefore, higher education is adapting to the changing culture (Dabbah & Kitsantas, 2012). The challenge for higher education is to move beyond traditional teaching methods and provide students with social media skills and strategies in take charge of their own learning (Kukulska-Hulme, 2012). The use of social media may not be a panacea, but it is a technique that can change learning in global higher education institutions (Toyin & Harerimana, 2017; Gulbahar & Center, 2014). Professors and administrators are challenged to use social media as one technique for increasing cyberlearning (Lemoine & Richardson, 2013) and to collaboratively ensure the best learning opportunities for 21st century students (George & Dellasega, 2011). Cyber learning is the key to current and future learning but social media is often the force driving the innovation (Barbour & Plough, 2009; Kukulska-Hulme, 2012; Lemoine & Richardson, 2013; Moran, Seaman & Tinti-Kane, 2012; Neier & Zayer, 2015; Tinti-Kane, 2013).

Focus on Student Learning

Social media allows professors to expand their messages and listen to what students want (Taylor, Mulligan & Ishida, 2012). Not only is it important that professors communicate with students, but it is important that the students transmit their needs to professors and administrators (Teclehaimanot & Hickman, 2011; Westerman, Daniel & Bowman, 2016). Access to social media for higher education instructors has also resulted in a change for education delivery systems (Moran, Seaman & Tinti-Kane, 2011, 2012). Social media permit students to become more active participants in their learning and explore new learning opportunities (Chen & Bryer, 2012; Evans, 2014; Koseoglu & Mercan, 2016; Leafman & Mathieson, 2013; Rambe, 2012).

Differentiating instruction may also describe faculty attempts to use social media for instruction (Turner, Solis & Kincade, 2017). The differentiation of instruction has many benefits both to the learner and to the instructor and social media is a key tool (Dosch & Zidon, 2014). When used by faculty, social media promotes engagement, facilitates motivation, and helps students make the connection between the formal instruction to the things they value outside of class (Purvis, Rodgers & Beckingham, 2016). When such connections are made explicit by the faculty, students tend to improve in their retention of the learning (Logan, 2011). In addition, differentiation using social media can encourage students to discover new interests both in formal instruction and also outside the class (Kahenya, 2017). Turner, Solis and Kincade (2017) posited the following additional advantages: students recognize that they are the focal point of the instructional process; it provides faculty flexibility in assigning learning tasks while giving students flexibility in how to report their learning; it encourages faculty to respect the differences between student needs and preferred learning modalities; and, it levels the field for students to demonstrate their learning.

Diversity is another concept in student learning that deserves attention, meaning that the traditional one-size-fits all, teacher-centered model of lecture-style teaching sets students up for failure (Balakrishnan, Teoh, Pourshafie & Liew, 2017; Dosch & Zidon, 2014). Social media can help faculty creatively differentiate the instruction to meet the individual and collective needs of students (Wandera, James-Waldon, Bromley & Henry, 2016). Some instructors assume their job is to tell students the information or provide it online without explanation. Telling or presenting is not effective pedagogy for students in higher education (Lemoine, Hackett & Richardson, 2016). The more proficient faculty teach in such a manner that students find both the learning and skills meaningful (Wang, Scown, Urquhart & Hardman, 2014)). Social media can help faculty make the connections in the learning for current and later application. The use of social media provides greater student engagement and greater student interest while also allowing students to take more control and more responsibility of their individual learning (Al-Mukhini, Al-Qayoudhi & Al-Badi, 2014).

Higher education faculty are being forced to adopt and to rethink their teaching approaches while using the new technologies and taking into consideration the challenges of the knowledge society (Dore-Natteh & Ussiph, 2017). Learners are likely to reject higher education institutions that do not integrate technology into the curriculum because of the perceived negative impact on their employability after graduation if they are not exposed to the use of technology (Ituma, 2011). An institution that deliberately shuns technology and places great emphasis on small group teaching, with a low student-teacher ratio, is likely to be a very expensive and hence highly exclusive institution (Kirwin & McGuckin, 2013).

Universities face major challenges in providing access and devices for every student and educator (Groeger & Buttle, 2014; Woodard, Shepherd, Crain-Dorough & Richardson, 2011). Three current challenges are evident for higher education: (1) the struggle to keep up with the latest technology (Pucciarelli & Kaplan, 2016); (2) the fight to find enough money for the technology (Woodard, Shepherd, Crain-Dorough & Richardson, 2011); and (3) the difficulty in getting faculty to adopt new technology (Kahenya, 2017; Leafman & Mathieson, 2015; Tinti-Kane, 2013). Social media advocates would argue that learning and learning opportunities are fluid; not confined to the classroom or to the university setting (Kirwan & McGukin, 2013). They propose that learning can manifest itself across settings, and informal or formal techniques, such as social media, can enhance learning (McEwan, 2012; Qureshi & Nair, 2015). Faculty must understand that learning is truly a life-long process, for them just as much as for their students (Roblyer, McDaniel, Webb, Herman, & Witty, 2010; Seaman & Tinti-Kane, 2013).

To establish effective instruction that uses social media, professors must listen and learn from current conversations with students and participate in the use of social media to become familiar with students' needs (Bullen, Morgan & Qayyum, 2011; Hrastinski & Aghaee, 2012; Waters, 2011). Communication forms the basic framework of social media (Nafukho, 2015). In fact, because its usage has reached such epic proportions in people's daily lives, global society has entered the age of social media (Hall, Delello & McWhorter, 2017; Rambe, 2012; Schroeder, Minocha & Schneider, 2010). As a result, many faculty in higher education institutions are now commonly adopting and integrating social media in their instructional design strategies (Hagler, 2015; Pham, 2012).

Social Media for Marketing

Social media is the current instrument of choice for building relationships between people and organizations (Wadhwa, 2017). Social media has revolutionized modern communication by creating a totally new culture based on the open movement of information. People engage in social media to express themselves and socialize with their friends and networks. Higher education institutions that insert themselves into these conversations are perceived as more personal, concurrently allowing potential students and parents to learn about the institution and to share their interests and opinions (Vuori, 2015). Higher education marketing is focused on putting the right message in front of the right target group at the right time, instead of striving to generate general awareness like traditional marketing strategies (Trefzger & Dunfelder, 2016).

The social media platform has become the new trend for marketing especially to the younger generation. Higher education is rapidly becoming more aware of this trend in order to use the right social media tool to market and compete for local and international students at a minimal cost (Assintakopooulos, Antoniadis, Kayas & Dvizac, 2017). Social media is an instant medium that can reach millions of people all around the world through likes and sharing links. Higher education is tapping into social media that allows them to reach a global audience and increase their enrollments (Biczysko & Jablonska, 2016). Student recruitment has become very competitive among universities, forcing them to find efficient and effective means of providing information to its potential students, reduce recruitment costs and increase student retention (Clark, Fine & Scheuer, 2017). Competition for top student talent has changed marketing strategies and the global environment has been revolutionized by social media (Constantinide & Zinck-Stagno, 2011).

Today's potential students, and to a certain extent their parents, require immediate access to information at their convenience (Faubet & Thomas, 2017)). Potential students or their parents are looking to have a conversation with someone online about a particular university. They will be increasingly unforgiving of institutions that seem out of touch with developments in the *real* world (Kuznetsov, Yugay, Muslimova, Dami & Nasridinov, 2016).

University brand is the identity of the higher education institution as a potential destination for students. A positive brand helps higher education institutions to be seen as a school of choice while a negative brand one will substantially reduce the opportunity for reaching the right candidates in the fight for talent. (Hope, 2015) To be competitive the institution should reflect reality as accurately as possible. Accuracy will help prospects to better understand the institution, its culture, values and programs (Bolat & O'Sullivan, 2017). Social media has become the "always on" operational environment for communicating the university brand to all those concerned (Iosub, Ivanov & Smedescu, 2016). Social media now radically changed the game, as it is where the potential students increasingly spend their time and energy searching for an institutional fit for them and their future education (de Haan, 2015). Now that social media has become a linchpin channel for not only social networking, but searching for information and sharing referrals and reviews, it is causing most institutions to significantly change their approach to recruitment. Consequently, institutions are adapting every part of their marketing strategy, and for some institutions even changing the product itself, to make them more relevant and to connect with more potential clients (Jan, 2016; Tuten, 2014).

There are basically two marketing strategies used by higher education institutions. Some delegate marketing decisions to their departments, especially when university is a large structure and departments are financially quasi-independent. Other universities unite departments under one coherent marketing strategic, which is typical for smaller universities. Marketing promotions by universities to students are almost identical to marketing promotions in any customer service environment (Akar & Topcu, 2011). However, academics face revolutionary changes in technology, financing and student recruitment (Bienkowska & Klofsten, 2012)). Additionally, universities are moving away from traditional marketing and demonstrating a strategic approach to their online communications using various platforms of social media (Tantivorakulchia, 2015). Regardless of the strategy, higher education institutions are forced to adopt marketing in order to differentiate their offering from competitors (Melchiorre & Johnson, 2017). The use of social media content as "advertising" is based on the accepted view that word-of-mouth communications are the most persuasive and create the strongest of all consumer triggers – the personal recommendation (Taecharungroj, 2017).

CONCLUDING THOUGHTS FOR CONSIDERATION

Since 2010, technical innovations have altered the skills and knowledge needed to succeed in the workplace and society (Bjerede, Atlins & Dede, 2012). Preparing technically educated and skilled individuals is of great economic importance to most counties and requires significant attention from both educators and employers (Al-Mukhaini, Al-Qayoudhi & Al-Bade, 2014). As a direct result, universities are using social media platforms to share their missions, market, and engage in conversations with future and current students (Barnes & Lescault, 2011).

However, higher education institutions may be missing a great opportunity to use their prowess using social media applications in instruction to convince potential students of their desirability as a university of choice for technologically savvy students (Akar & Topcu, 2011; Blacher-Wilson, Mense & Richardson, 2011). Higher education institutions face with a quandary: a rational need to become more dependent on market–oriented status driven by purely financial motivation (Bienkouska & Klofsten, 2012; Constantinides & Zinck-Stagno, 2011; Vuori, 2015). However they also want to become independent of market requirements to preserve their "pedagogical purity" (de Haan, 2015). As a result, colleges and universities are rapidly redefining their interaction with all of their stakeholders (Benson & Morgan, 2015; Hope, 2015), particularly through social media which defines the dual realities of improving instruction and increasing enrollments (Iosub, Ivanov & Smedescu, 2016; Junco, 2014).

REFERENCES

Akar, E., & Topcu, B. (2011). An examination of the factors influencing consumers' attitudes toward social media marketing. *Journal of Internet Commerce, 10*(1), 35–67. doi:10.1080/15332861.2011.558456

Al-Mukhaini, E. M., Al-Qayoudhi, W. S., & Al-Badi, A. H. (2014). Adoption of social networking in education: A study of the use of social networks by higher education students in Oman. *Journal of International Education Research, 10*(2), 143.

Allen, E., & Seaman, J. (2010). *Class differences: Online education in the United States, 2010.* Needham, MA: Sloan Consortium.

Anagnostopoulou, K., Parmar, D., & Priego-Hernandez, J. (2009). An exploration of perceptions of learning and e-learning held by students who withdraw and those who persist with UK higher education. *E-Journal of Learning and Teaching, 2*(4).

Arnold, N., & Paulus, T. (2010). Using a social networking site for experiential learning: Appropriating, lurking, modeling and community building. *The Internet and Higher Education, 11*(2), 71–80.

Assimakopoulos, C., Antoniadis, I., Kayas, O. G., & Dvizac, D. (2017). Effective social media marketing strategy: Facebook as an opportunity for universities. *International Journal of Retail & Distribution Management, 45*(5), 532–549. doi:10.1108/IJRDM-11-2016-0211

Balakrishnan, V., Teoh, K. K., Pourshafie, T., & Liew, T. K. (2017). Social media and their use in learning: A comparative analysis between Australia and Malaysia from the learners' perspectives. *Australasian Journal of Educational Technology*, *33*(1).

Baran, E., Correia, A. P., & Thompson, A. (2011). Transforming online teaching practice: Critical analysis of the literature on the roles and competencies of online teachers. *Distance Education*, *32*(3), 421–439. doi:10.1080/01587919.2011.610293

Barbour, M., & Plough, C. (2009). Social networking in cyberschooling: Helping to make online learning less isolating. *TechTrends*, *53*(4), 56–60. doi:10.100711528-009-0307-5

Barnes, N. G., & Lescault, A. M. (2011). *Social media soars as higher-ed experiments and reevaluates its use of new communications tools.* Retrieved from: http://www. umassd.edu/media/umassdartmouth/cmr/studiesandresearch/higherEd.pdf

Bart, M. (2010). Social media usage among college faculty. *Trends in Higher Education, Faculty Focus.* Retrieved from http://www.facultyfocus.com/articles/trends-in-higher-education/social-media-usage-among-college-faculty

Bartosik-Purgat, M., Filimon, N., & Calli, M. K. (2017). Social media and higher education-An international perspective. *Economia e Sociologia (Evora, Portugal)*, *10*(1), 181.

Benson, V. (Ed.). (2014). *Cutting-edge technologies and social media use in higher education.* Hershey, PA: IGI Global. doi:10.4018/978-1-4666-5174-6

Benson, V., & Morgan, S. (2015). *Measuring the social impact: How social media affects higher education institutions.* Hershey, PA: IGI Global. doi:10.4018/978-1-4666-7401-1.ch009

Biczysko, D., & Jablonska, M. R. (2016). Social media marketing tools among Polish public higher education institutions. *European Journal of Educational & Social Sciences*, *1*(1).

Bienkowska, D., & Klofsten, M. (2012). Creating entrepreneurial networks: Academic entrepreneurship, mobility and collaboration during PhD education. *Higher Education*, *64*(2), 207–222. doi:10.100710734-011-9488-x

Bjerede, M., Atlins, K., & Dede, C. (2012). *Ubiquitous mobile technologies and the transformation of schooling.* Retrieved from: http://www.qualcomm.com/media/documents/files/ubiquitous-mobile-technologies- and-the-transformation-of-schooling.pdf

Blacher-Wilson, F., Mense, E. G., & Richardson, M. D. (2011). Marketing services globally: The benefits of e-learning. In S. Mukerji & P. Tripathi (Eds.), *Cases on innovations in educational marketing: Transnational and technological strategies* (pp. 313–326). Hershey, PA: IGI. doi:10.4018/978-1-60960-599-5.ch019

Bolat, E., & O'Sullivan, H. (2017). Radicalising the marketing of higher education: Learning from student-generated social media data. *Journal of Marketing Management*, *33*(9-10), 742–763. doi:10.1080/0267257X.2017.1328458

Booth, M., & Esposito, A. (2011). Mentoring 2.0 – High tech/high touch approaches to foster student support and development in higher education. In L. A. Wankel & C. Wankel, C. (Eds.), Higher education administration with social media (Cutting-edge technologies in higher education, Volume 2). (pp. 85-103). London: Emerald Group Publishing Limited.

Bullen, M., Morgan, T., & Qayyum, A. (2011). Digital learners in higher education: Generation is not the issue. *Canadian Journal of Learning and Technology*, *37*(1), 1–24. doi:10.21432/T2NC7B

Buzzetto-More, N. (2012). Understanding social media. In C. Cheal, J. Coughlin, & S. Moore (Eds.), *Transformation in teaching: Social media strategies in higher education* (pp. 1–18). Santa Rosa, CA: Informing Science Press.

Chang, Y. T., Yu, H., & Lu, H. P. (2015). Persuasive messages, popularity cohesion, and message diffusion in social media marketing. *Journal of Business Research*, *68*(4), 777–782. doi:10.1016/j.jbusres.2014.11.027

Chen, B., & Bryer, T. (2012). Investigating instructional strategies for using social media in formal and informal learning. *International Review of Research in Open and Distance Learning*, *13*(1), 1–10. doi:10.19173/irrodl.v13i1.1027

Clark, K. R., & Wagner, J. B. (2017). Using social media and hashtags to engage medical imaging students. *Radiologic Technology*, *88*(5), 564–567. PMID:28500102

Clark, M., Fine, M. B., & Scheuer, C. L. (2017). Relationship quality in higher education marketing: The role of social media engagement. *Journal of Marketing for Higher Education*, *27*(1), 40–58. doi:10.1080/08841241.2016.1269036

Constantinides, E., & Zinck Stagno, M. C. (2011). Potential of the social media as instruments of higher education marketing: A segmentation study. *Journal of Marketing for Higher Education*, *21*(1), 7–24. doi:10.1080/08841241.2011.573593

Dabbagh, N., & Kitsantas, A. (2012). Personal learning environments, social media, and self-regulated learning: A natural formula for connecting formal and informal learning. *Internet and Higher Education*, *15*(1), 3–8. doi:10.1016/j.iheduc.2011.06.002

de Haan, H. H. (2015). Competitive advantage, what does it really mean in the context of public higher education institutions? *International Journal of Educational Management*, *29*(1), 44–61. doi:10.1108/IJEM-07-2013-0115

DeAndrea, D. C., Ellison, N. B., LaRose, R., Steinfield, C., & Fiore, A. (2012). Serious social media: On the use of social media for improving students' adjustment to college. *Internet and Higher Education*, *15*(1), 15–23. doi:10.1016/j.iheduc.2011.05.009

Dede, C. (2011). Reconceptualizing technology to meet the necessity of transformation. *Journal of Curriculum and Instruction*, *5*(1), 4–16. doi:10.3776/joci.2011.v5n1p4-16

Dore-Natteh, D., & Ussiph, N. (2017). Adaptation and effects of social media in teaching and learning at the second cycle institution level in Ghana. *International Journal of Computers and Applications*, *166*(3).

Dosch, M., & Zidon, M. (2014). "The Course Fit Us": Differentiated instruction in the college classroom. *International Journal on Teaching and Learning in Higher Education, 26*(3), 343–357.

Elmannai, W., Odeh, A., & Bach, C. (2013). Academic use of online social networks. *International Journal of Innovation and Applied Studies, 32*, 337–345.

Evans, C. (2014). Twitter for teaching: Can social media be used to enhance the process of learning? *British Journal of Educational Technology, 45*(5), 902–915. doi:10.1111/bjet.12099

Faubet, R., & Thomas, M. (2017). Branding and communications on social media within higher education. *Journal of Education Advancement & Marketing, 1*(4), 302–312.

Ferguson, J., & Tryjankowski, A. M. (2009). Online versus face-to-face learning: Looking at modes of instruction in Master's-level courses. *Journal of Further and Higher Education, 33*(3), 219–228. doi:10.1080/03098770903026149

George, D. R., & Dellasega, C. (2011). Social media in medical education: Two innovative pilot studies. *Medical Education, 45*(11), 1158–1159. doi:10.1111/j.1365-2923.2011.04124.x PMID:21939449

Gikas, J., & Grant, M. M. (2013). Mobile computing devices in higher education: Student perspectives on learning with cellphones, smartphones & social media. *The Internet and Higher Education, 19*, 18–26. doi:10.1016/j.iheduc.2013.06.002

Greaves, T., Hayes, J., Wilson, L., Gielniak, M., & Peterson, R. (2010). *Technology factor: Nine keys to student achievement and cost-effectiveness.* Retrieved from: http://www.projectred.org/uploads/PREP11/ProjectREDPreview.pdf

Greenhow, C. (2011). Online social networking and learning. *International Journal of Cyber Behavior, Psychology and Learning, 1*(1), 36–50. doi:10.4018/ijcbpl.2011010104

Greenhow, C., Robelia, B., & Hughes, J. (2009). Learning, teaching, and scholarship in a digital age – Web 2.0 and classroom research: What path should we take now? *Educational Researcher, 38*(4), 246–259. doi:10.3102/0013189X09336671

Griesemer, J. A. (2012). Using social media to enhance students' learning experiences. *Quality Approaches in Higher Education, 3*(1), 8–12.

Groeger, L., & Buttle, F. (2014). Word-of-mouth marketing influence on offline and online communications: Evidence from case study research. *Journal of Marketing Communications, 20*(1-2), 21–41. doi:10.1080/13527266.2013.797736

Gülbahar, Y., & Center, D. E. (2014). Current state of usage of social media for education: Case of Turkey. *Journal of Social Media Studies, 1*(1), 53–69. doi:10.15340/2147336611763

Gupta, A. (2015). Scope and implications of social media in the context of higher education: Review of researches. *MIER Journal of Educational Studies, Trends and Practices, 4*(2).

Hagler, B. E. (2013). Value of social media in today's classroom. *The Journal of Research in Business Education, 55*(1), 14.

Hall, A. A., Delello, J. A., & McWhorter, R. R. (2017). Using Facebook to supplement instruction in online and hybrid courses. *International Journal of Innovation and Learning, 22*(1), 87–104. doi:10.1504/IJIL.2017.085250

Hemmi, A., Bayne, S., & Land, R. (2009). The appropriation and repurposing of social technologies in higher education. *Journal of Computer Assisted Learning, 25*(1), 19–30. doi:10.1111/j.1365-2729.2008.00306.x

Hoffman, D. L., & Novak, T. P. (2011). Marketing communication in a digital era. *Marketing Management, 20*(3), 36–43.

Hope, J. (2015). Incorporate inbound marketing into your recruitment strategy. *Recruiting & Retaining Adult Learners, 17*(8), 1–7. doi:10.1002/nsr.30045

Hrastinski, S., & Aghaee, N. M. (2012). How are campus students using social media to support their studies? An explorative interview study. *Education and Information Technologies, 17*(4), 451–464. doi:10.100710639-011-9169-5

Hung, H.-T., & Yuen, S. C.-Y. (2010). Educational use of social networking technology in higher education. *Teaching in Higher Education, 15*(6), 703–714. doi:10.1080/13562517.2010.507307

Hussain, I., Gulrez, N., & Tahirkheli, S. (2012). *Academic use of social media: Practices and problems of university students.* Paper presented at International Conference on Education and Management Innovation, Singapore.

Iosub, I., Ivanov, A., & Smedescu, D. (2016). Social-media platforms and marketing of higher education institutions. *Journal of Emerging Trends in Marketing and Management, 1*(1), 328–338.

Ituma, A. (2011). An evaluation of students' perceptions and engagement with e-learning components in a campus based university. *Active Learning in Higher Education, 12*(1), 57–68. doi:10.1177/1469787410387722

Jan, M. T., & Ammari, D. (2016). Advertising online by educational institutions and students' reaction: A study of Malaysian Universities. *Journal of Marketing for Higher Education, 26*(2), 168–180. doi:10.1080/08841241.2016.1245232

Junco, R. (2011). The relationship between frequency of Facebook use, participation in Facebook activities, and student engagement. *Computers & Education, 58*(1), 162–171. doi:10.1016/j.compedu.2011.08.004

Junco, R. (2014). *Engaging students through social media: Evidence-based practices for use in student affairs.* San Francisco, CA: John Wiley & Sons.

Junco, R., Heiberger, G., & Loken, E. (2010). The effect of Twitter on college student engagement and grades. *Journal of Computer Assisted Learning, 27*(2), 119–132. doi:10.1111/j.1365-2729.2010.00387.x

Kahenya, N. P. (2017). The use of social media to facilitate real-time e-learning. In *Handbook of research on transformative digital content and learning technologies* (pp. 171–183). Hershey, PA: IGI Global. doi:10.4018/978-1-5225-2000-9.ch010

Kezar, A. (2014). Higher education change and social networks: A review of research. *The Journal of Higher Education, 85*(1), 91–125. doi:10.1080/00221546.2014.11777320

Khanna, M., Jacob, I., & Yadav, N. (2014). Identifying and analyzing touchpoints for building a higher education brand. *Journal of Marketing for Higher Education, 24*(1), 122–143. doi:10.1080/08841241 .2014.920460

Kirschner, P. A., & Karpinski, A. C. (2010). Facebook and academic performance. *Computers in Human Behavior, 26*(6), 1237–1245. doi:10.1016/j.chb.2010.03.024

Kirwan, G., & McGuckin, C. (2013). Professional reputation and identity in the online world. *International Review of Information Ethics, 19*, 41–58.

Köseoglu, P., & Mercan, G. (2016). The educational use of Facebook as a social networking site in animal physiology classes. *World Journal on Educational Technology: Current Issues, 8*(3), 258–266.

Kukulska-Hulme, A. (2012). How should the higher education workforce adapt to advancements in technology for teaching and learning? *The Internet and Higher Education, 15*(4), 247–254. doi:10.1016/j. iheduc.2011.12.002

Kuznetsov, V., Yugay, O., Muslimova, D., Dami, A., & Nasridinov, A. (2016). An assessment of university attractiveness using social media. *Advanced Science Letters, 22*(9), 2339–2347. doi:10.1166/asl.2016.7839

Lane, K. E., Kehr, G. A., & Richardson, M. D. (2010). The paradox of productivity measurement in higher education. *Academe: Journal of Leadership and Management in Higher Education, 1*(3), 23–39.

Leafman, J. S., & Mathieson, K. (2015). Online instructor perceptions of social presence and educational use of social media. *Advances in Social Sciences Research Journal, 2*(11).

Leafman, J. S., Mathieson, K. M., & Ewing, H. (2013). Student perceptions of social presence and attitudes toward social media: Results of a cross-sectional study. *International Journal of Higher Education, 2*(1), 67. doi:10.5430/ijhe.v2n1p67

Lederer, K. (2012, September 19). Pros and cons of social media in the classroom. *Campus Technology*. Retrieved from http://campustechnology.com/Articles/2012/01/19/Pros-and-Cons-of-Social-Media-in-the-Classroom.aspx?m=2&Page=2

Lemoine, P. A., Hackett, P. T., & Richardson, M. D. (2016). The impact of social media on instruction in higher education. In *Handbook of research on mobile devices and applications in higher education settings* (pp. 373–401). Hershey, PA: IGI Global. doi:10.4018/978-1-5225-0256-2.ch016

Lemoine, P. A., & Richardson, M. D. (2013). Cyberlearning: The impact on instruction in higher education? *The Researcher, 26*(3), 57–83.

Logan, B. (2011). Examining differentiated instruction: Teachers respond. *Research in Higher Education, 13*, 1–14.

Lumauag, R. G. (2017). Learners' accessibility and adaptability to technology. *Asia Pacific Higher Education Research Journal, 4*(1).

Mahmud, M. M., Ramachandiran, C. R., & Ismail, O. (2016). Social media and classroom engagement: Students' perception. *Journal of Media Critiques, 2*(8), 197–207. doi:10.17349/jmc116214

Mastrodicasa, J., & Metellus, P. (2013). The impact of social media on college students. *Journal of College and Character, 14*(1), 21–30. doi:10.1515/jcc-2013-0004

Mathieson, K., & Leafman, J. S. (2014). Comparison of student and instructor perceptions of social presence. *Journal of Educators Online, 11*(2). doi:10.9743/JEO.2014.2.3

McEwan, B. (2012). Managing boundaries in the Web 2.0 classroom. *New Directions for Teaching and Learning, 131*(131), 15–28. doi:10.1002/tl.20024

Melchiorre, M. M., & Johnson, S. A. (2017). Finding new ways to reach older students: Creating a social media marketing plan for professional and continuing higher education programs. *The Journal of Continuing Higher Education, 65*(2), 73–81. doi:10.1080/07377363.2017.1320178

Moran, M., Seaman, J., & Tinti-Kane, H. (2011). *Teaching, learning, and sharing: How today's higher education faculty use social media.* Boston, MA: Pearson Learning Solutions.

Moran, M., Seaman, J., & Tinti-Kane, H. (2012). *Blogs, wikis, podcasts and Facebook: How today's higher education faculty use social media.* Boston, MA: Pearson Learning Solutions and Babson Survey Research Group.

Nafukho, F. M. (Ed.). (2015). *Handbook of research on innovative technology integration in higher education.* Hershey, PA: IGI Global. doi:10.4018/978-1-4666-8170-5

Neier, S., & Zayer, L. (2015). Students' perceptions and experiences of social media in higher education. *Journal of Marketing Education, 37*(3), 133–143. doi:10.1177/0273475315583748

Pechenkina, E., & Aeschliman, C. (2017). What do students want? Making sense of student preferences in technology-enhanced learning. *Contemporary Educational Technology, 8*(1), 26–39.

Pham, H. L. (2012). Differentiated instruction and the need to integrate teaching and practice. *Journal of College Teaching and Learning, 9*(1), 13–20. doi:10.19030/tlc.v9i1.6710

Piotrowski, C. (2015). Pedagogical applications of social media in business education: Student and faculty perspectives. *Journal of Educational Technology Systems, 43*(3), 257–265. doi:10.1177/0047239515570575

Pucciarelli, F., & Kaplan, A. (2016). Competition and strategy in higher education: Managing complexity and uncertainty. *Business Horizons, 59*(3), 311–320. doi:10.1016/j.bushor.2016.01.003

Purvis, A., Rodger, H., & Beckingham, S. (2016). Engagement or distraction: The use of social media for learning in higher education. *Student Engagement and Experience Journal, 5*(1).

Qureshi, R., & Nair, S. (2015). The role of higher education in emerging knowledge society. *Global Journal on Humanities and Social Sciences, 1*(1), 543–548.

Rambe, P. (2012). Constructive disruptions for effective collaborative learning: Navigating the affordances of social media for meaningful engagement. *The Electronic Journal of e-Learning, 10*(1), 132-146.

Records, H., Pritchard, J., & Behling, R. (2011). Exploring social media as an electronic tool in the university classroom. *Issues in Information Systems, 12*(2), 171–180.

Reid, P. (2014). Categories for barriers to adoption of instructional technologies. *Education and Information Technologies, 19*(2), 383–407. doi:10.100710639-012-9222-z

Roblyer, M. D., McDaniel, M., Webb, M., Herman, J., & Witty, J. V. (2010). Findings on Facebook in higher education: A comparison of college faculty and student uses and perceptions of social networking sites. *The Internet and Higher Education, 13*(3), 134–140. doi:10.1016/j.iheduc.2010.03.002

Schroeder, A., Minocha, S., & Schneider, C. (2010). The strengths, weaknesses, opportunities and threats of using social software in higher and further education teaching and learning. *Journal of Computer Assisted Learning, 26*(3), 159–174. doi:10.1111/j.1365-2729.2010.00347.x

Seaman, J., & Tinti-Kane, H. (2013, October). *Social media for teaching and learning.* Boston, MA: Pearson Learning Solutions and the Babson Survey Research Group.

Shih, C., & Waugh, M. (2011). Web 2.0 tools for learning in higher education: The presence of blogs, wikis, podcasts, microblogs, Facebook and Ning. In M. Koehler & P. Mishra (Eds.), *Proceedings of Society for Information Technology & Teacher Education International Conference 2011* (pp. 3345-3352). Chesapeake, VA: AACE.

Smith, M., & Kukulska-Hulme, A. (2012). Building mobile learning capacities in higher education: E-books and iPads. In M. Specht, J. Multisilta, & M. S. Sharples (Eds.), *11ᵗʰ World Conference on Mobile and Contextual Learning* (pp. 298-301). Helsinki, Finland: CELSTEC & CICERO Learning.

Tadros, M. (2011). A social media approach to higher education. *Educating Educators with Social Media, 1*, 83–105. doi:10.1108/S2044-9968(2011)0000001007

Taecharungroj, V. (2017). Higher education social media marketing: 12 content types universities post on Facebook. *International Journal of Management Education, 11*(2), 111–127.

Tantivorakulchai, K. (2015). Thai students'destination choice for higher education: A comparative study on US, UK and Australia. *AU Journal of Management, 12*(2).

Taylor, S. A., Mulligan, J. R., & Ishida, C. (2012). Facebook, social networking, and business education. *American Journal of Business Education (Online), 5*(4), 437. doi:10.19030/ajbe.v5i4.7121

Teclehaimanot, B., & Hickman, T. (2011). Student-teacher interaction of Facebook: What students find appropriate. *TechTrends, 55*(3), 19–30. doi:10.100711528-011-0494-8

Tess, P. A. (2013). The role of social media in higher education classes (real and virtual) – A literature review. *Computers in Human Behavior, 29*(5), A60–A68. doi:10.1016/j.chb.2012.12.032

Tinti-Kane, H. (2013, April 1). Overcoming hurdles to social media in education. *EDUCAUSE Review Online.* Retrieved from http://www.educause.edu/ero/article/overcoming-hurdles-social-media-education

Toole, T., Khetaguri, T., & Zangaladze, M. (2015). An evaluation of e-Learning in Eastern and Western Europe. *The Journal of Educational Innovation, Partnership and Change, 1*(1).

Toyin, A. O., & Harerimana, J. P. (2017). A comparative study of use of social media for instruction among pre-service teachers in Nigeria and Rwanda. *European Journal of Education Studies, 3*(4).

Trefzger, T. F., & Dünfelder, D. (2016, July). Unleash your brand! Using social media as a marketing tool in academia. In *International Conference on Social Computing and Social Media* (pp. 449-460). New York, NY: Springer International Publishing. 10.1007/978-3-319-39910-2_42

Turner, W. D., Solis, O. J., & Kincade, D. H. (2017). Differentiating instruction for large classes in higher education. *Executive Editor*, *29*(3), 490–500.

Tuten, T. L., & Solomon, M. R. (2014). *Social media marketing*. Thousand Oaks, CA: Sage.

Veletsianos, G. (2011). Designing opportunities for transformation with emerging technologies. *Educational Technology*, *51*(2), 41–46.

Vuori, J. (2015). Excellent prospects for beautiful minds: Marketing international education. *International Journal of Educational Management*, *29*(5), 582–595. doi:10.1108/IJEM-10-2013-0156

Wadhwa, R. (2017). Social media, information processing and potential clients in international higher education market. *Asian Journal of Research in Social Sciences and Humanities*, *7*(7), 382–396. doi:10.5958/2249-7315.2017.00393.8

Wamba, S. F., & Carter, L. (2014). Social media tools adoption and use by SMEs: An empirical study. *Journal of Organizational and End User Computing*, *26*(2), 1–17. doi:10.4018/joeuc.2014040101

Wandera, S., James-Waldon, N., Bromley, D., & Henry, Z. (2016). The influence of social media on collaborative learning in a cohort environment. *Interdisciplinary Journal of e-Skills and Lifelong Learning, 12*, 123-143.

Wang, R., Scown, P., Urquhart, C., & Hardman, J. (2014). Tapping the educational potential of Facebook: Guidelines for use in higher education. *Education and Information Technologies*, *19*(1), 21–39. doi:10.100710639-012-9206-z

Waters, J. K. (2011). Social networking: Keeping it clean. *T.H.E. Journal*, *38*(1), 52–54.

Westerman, D., Daniel, E. S., & Bowman, N. D. (2016). Learned risks and experienced rewards: Exploring the potential sources of students' attitudes toward social media and face-to-face communication. *The Internet and Higher Education*, *31*, 52–57. doi:10.1016/j.iheduc.2016.06.004

Woodard, H. C., Shepherd, S. S., Crain-Dorough, M., & Richardson, M. D. (2011). The globalization of higher education: Through the lens of technology and accountability. *I-manager's Journal of Educational Technology*, *8*(2), 16–24.

Yu, A. Y., Tian, S. W., Vogel, D., & Kwok, R. C. (2010). Can learning be virtually boosted? An investigation of online social networking impacts. *Computers & Education*, *55*(4), 1494–1503. doi:10.1016/j.compedu.2010.06.015

This research was previously published in Marketing Initiatives for Sustainable Educational Development; pages 226-245, copyright year 2018 by Information Science Reference (an imprint of IGI Global).

Chapter 100

Social Media Integration in Educational Administration as Information and Smart Systems:
Digital Literacy for Economic, Social, and Political Engagement in Namibia

Sadrag Panduleni Shihomeka
University of Namibia, Namibia

Helena N. Amadhila
University of Namibia, Namibia

ABSTRACT

The proliferation and access to social media platforms that allow easy access to information systems and services, content creation, and sharing, in a convenient form, has taken education administration and management by storm. Facebook is one of the many online media that can let education administrators and managers interact with each other or their subordinates by sharing information about themselves or any topical community issue via personal profiles or institutional profiles. Furthermore, it is noted that social media applications by their nature have the capabilities of educating, informing, entertaining (leisure), and socializing the audience. The research revealed that there are various groups on Facebook where youthful education administrators can use to post educational information and discuss pertinent issues concerning their institutions. Indeed, social media are being used as channels to foster economic, social, and political development education among Namibian educational administrators.

DOI: 10.4018/978-1-6684-7123-4.ch100

INTRODUCTION

In recent years, the education systems have been facing alternatives in learning and teaching activities with new and multi-use of technologies in which they transformed learning environments (Durnalı, Orakcı, & Aktan, 2019). School administration and management experts (e.g. Erçetin, Akbaşlı and Durnalı, 2018; Durnalı, 2013;2019) have been debating on the adverse effect of digitalisation and how it can enhance administrative services of schools, tertiary institutions and relevant departments from primary to tertiary educational level. This led to discussions and academic conversations among educational administration researchers around the globe. Several studies (Raja, 2018; Raut & Patil, 2016) revealed that the emergence of social media platforms brought positive changes to administration and management as school leaders, Heads of Departments, inspectors, Directors of education both in urban and rural areas can now virtually manage their functional units with easy. It came to light that some educational managers created Facebook pages for their schools or institutions of higher learning; departments, classes or probably staff members. In other cases, they have created WhatsApp groups to enhance and fasten their communications with their subordinates. This did not only economically benefit the institution as it is now spending less money on organising offline meetings, but it is accelerating the decision making processes at that institution.

Though this was supposed to be a good opportunity for e-governance in educational administration, there are some individuals that have created their own social media platforms and pages depicting institutional names. However, these platforms to certain extend are not used wisely and are mostly accused of spreading Fake News and misinformation about policies, incidences and overall management of educational systems in developing world. We are currently facing numerals challenges in this and as educational administrators, we need to be vigilant and become digital literate to ensure that our digital actions, space and efforts are not compromised by the most digital literate members of the society aimed at causing chaos in education. These technological advancements such as education 4.0, society 5.0 calls for greater efforts from us as educational administrators to upgrade our digital competencies on social and cultural ethics of these platforms. Additionally, this also require our systems, policies and systems to be reformed, revisited and re-engineered to be digitally ready for all the good and bad effects of virtual administration. The arrival of these digital platforms serve as an extension that can make education as a lifelong learning opportunities for administrators for continuous acquisition of knowledge and skills. Our local educational legislations as well as school policies are also demanding contemporary soft and technical skills that we all need to have to make sure that activities are digitised to the benefits of our learners and students. During the integration process we should also not forget that the digital divide is partly claimed to be a crippling factor the integration and utilisation of various technologies in the administration of educational institutions be it at primary, secondary or tertiary levels. Namibia is one of those countries that is trying by all means to narrow this gap through public private partnership agreements. Therefore, utilisation of social media as a virtual public, where social, economic and political education takes place became now a pressing issue for all educational administrators and managers.

BACKGROUND

Facebook is one of the emerging technological advancement tool for social, economic and political debates. Due to the mushrooming of affordable smartphones from various Indian and Chinese shops, the majority of Namibians have access to social media (Shihomeka & Arora, 2018). Additionally, the free and pre-loaded data given by various telecommunications providers such as Mobile Telecommunication (MTC), also increases the number of Facebook users in Namibia. Currently we have over 570 000 Facebook users in Namibia. The arrival of Information and Communication Technologies which allows for easy access to information systems and services in a convenient form, have taken the globe in a storm fashion. Facebook also have a group of applications which can allow users to share their common interests by providing a common space where users can meet others that are interested in a specific topic, disseminate information about that topic, and have public discussions relevant to that topic (Conroy, Feezell & Guerrero, 2012). The use of these technologies enables easier accessibility and retrieval of information from anywhere and anytime. Social media technologies have become a conventional, modified personal relationship enabled individuals to contribute and engage in a number of issues and open up new avenues and encounters for economic, social and political development education among Namibian people. Furthermore, it is noted that social media technologies by their nature have the capabilities of educating, informing, entertaining and socialising the audience if used ethically.

The proliferation of internet access and an increase in mobile phone subscriptions in Namibia and globally, necessitated assumptions, debates and enabled greater digital participation of youth and adults in the political sphere. Social media can be defined as interactive computer-mediated technologies or websites and applications that enable users to create and share content or to participate in social networking and virtual communities, share information, ideas, personal messages and other contents such as videos and audios. Some of the popular social media platforms are Facebook, Twitter, WhatsApp, Instagram and LinkedIn. All these platforms can be accessed via mobile phones. Some studies reported that over 500,000 Namibians are on these platforms. The presence of youth on social media platforms is said to be higher than the elders' online presence. Although Namibia is characterised by a high national unemployment rate at 34% especially among the youth, which stands at 43%, the majority of the youth in Namibia own mobile phones for easy communication purposes (NSA, 2017). There are reportedly more mobile phones than the size of our population. It is said that more males own mobile phones than their female counterparts. It is very interesting that, even the youth from marginalised communities have access and own mobile phones. There are two groups of mobile phone owners in Namibia: those that own smart phones that can enable them to have access to internet services including mobile social media such as Facebook, Twitter, Instagram, WhatsApp and others and non-smart phone owners. This can be attributed to affordable phones available at Indian and various Chinese shops around the country. Interestingly, Social Media are currently praised for creating digital publics whereby citizens from different corners can meet at their convenience to debate, discuss, share and educate each other on various issues that affect their lives regardless of their political affiliation, social class, ethnicity, age, education level or employment status.

Our latest observation on various platforms in Namibia is that, citizens create social media pages on Facebook or other platforms to serve as meeting and discussion points of various political, social, economic and technological issues. This can best be described by the increasing and mushrooming of various Facebook pages and WhatsApp groups joined by citizens especially the youth depicting names of various school institutions. Fascinatingly, University graduates, youth from well-off families and grade 12 school leavers tend to dominate these digital platforms than any other group. Mostly youthful educational administrators in urban and semi-urban areas are more on social media than others due to the digital divide that cripples the democratic digital sphere. Therefore, these platforms can be a source of information retrieval, political conversation and economic development education for our country.

Problem Statement

Most people adapt easily to social media and like to interact with their friends and other people this way. Many Namibians are seeing a great deal of success by using social media in particular Facebook as a means of communicating, educating and sharing information with other Namibians. In the process, digital literacy is now a common issue on various public platforms. School managers and administrators are not an exception in this as they are looking for digital avenues to manage their schools and other relevant institutions digitally. Digitalisation brought a number of great benefits to school administrators as they can manage their schools and educate the society from the comfort of their offices of houses. It is observed that, there is still lack of Social media into economic, social and political education. Additionally, many schools and educational institutions have advanced technological systems and facilities, but the digital readiness of school administrators and other staff members is believed to be an obstacle to their full integration in e-administration of schools or tertiary institutions in Namibia. Therefore, this chapter explored the use and integration of Social Media (SM) as Information and smart systems for economic, social and political education in Namibia. Additionally, how social media can be integrated in the Namibian educational curriculum to offer cross –curricular issues to the society. The aim is to have an empowered society which does not only rely on education that takes place inside the classroom. Social Media are becoming complementary lifelong learning platforms for a digital economy.

Research Questions

The study was designed to address three questions which were central to exploring social media as information systems and services for economic, social and political development education in Namibia. The study was guided by the following questions:

- In what ways do young administrators and managers in the education system use Facebook as a social tool in Namibia?
- How can Facebook be used as an information system and services economically by the youthful school administrators and managers?
- To what extend does Facebook can be regarded as a political information system for educational administration and development?

SOCIAL MEDIA AS AN E-DEMOCRACY TOOL FOR YOUTH ENGAGEMENT IN NAMIBIA

Lately, there has been a decline of youth presence and attendance in offline political and non-political activities in Namibia (The Namibian Newspaper, November 2017, p.14). This came to light as the youth view traditional political gatherings as not addressing their unique problems and situations. Although youth participation in national elections such as the national assembly and presidential elections is reported to be relatively high in the previous elections, there is a grave concern of youth participation in regional and local authority elections. Some studies reported that youth are not taking part in elections, disengaged, not members of political parties and find it difficult to communicate with their fellows in various political organisations (Archambault, 2013; Asgarkhani, 2005; Chadwick & May, 2003). We observed that during election campaign rallies, the presence of youth at these gatherings tend to be lower than that of adults and children. Apart from party politics, youth are also not seen at community meetings/gatherings such as constituency councillors'/village headmen's meetings. This trend of less engagement of youth in regional, local politics and civic duties in Africa, particularly in Namibia is associated and linked to a number of challenges, including old guards (ageing politicians) across the political spectrum clinging to power, and the lack of youth representation in political leadership positions. It is believed that youth feel that the current politics in Namibia is for older politicians that are not inclusive, self-centred and not accommodative when it comes to youth empowerment and capacity building. Youth also claim that going to those offline meetings or gatherings is only a waste of time rather than staying at home and do some other constructive activities. They have cited a number of reasons such that at those meetings, speakers tend to focus more on political history and liberation struggle issues which are less important to nowadays youth. Youth further stated that offline community meetings and gatherings are highly politicised, characterised by restrictive political protocols that need to be followed and youth do not feel free to express themselves in front of the elders as they may be seem to be violating cultural norms and values (Gökçe-Kızılkaya & Onursal-Beşgül, 2017; Kruikemeier & Shehata, 2016; Papacharissi, 2016). They also said they are more interested in socio-political discussions that can pave way for improved standard of living for the youth in Namibia, especially addressing the high unemployment rate, land distribution, youth empowerment projects, do away with political favouritism, tribalism and politics of the belly.

Political participation in the eyes of old politicians, especially those that participated in the liberation struggle of the Namibian independence has been regarded as active attendance and presence of citizens at political rallies, meetings, conferences, and other gatherings like that. This has been declining as citizens particularly the youth opt not to attend these meetings as they can also participate digitally. In recent years, reports have surfaced on the political engagement practices among civic and political leaders in regional and local authorities in Sub-Saharan Africa, particularly in Namibia (Kruikemeier & Shehata, 2016; Papacharissi, 2016). They are accused by the youth of not involving their citizens actively in public debates, political activities and community projects. Citizens have complained that their government representatives are not easily accessible and available to listen to their needs, aspirations and the wants of their community members. This has led to some of the youth to find politics less engaging and interesting. This prevails, despite the Namibian government's efforts to construct regional councillors' offices in all the constituencies around the country, in addition to the provision of mobile phones, phone allowances, internet connectivity and a car to reach communities, regardless of the geographic location of the villages. It became clear that youth and political leaders rarely use these facilities as provided by the government to interact in order to strengthen inclusive digital democracy.

With an increase in mobile phone subscriptions in Namibia, civic and political leaders' engagement practices are expected to leverage the newly created public sphere by these media to be as inclusive as possible to provide equal opportunities for all the citizens to debate matters concerning their regions or constituencies. A recent research that we conducted recently reveals that, although, mobile phone numbers for regional politicians were made available publicly, the youth still found it difficult to talk directly to the politicians as their calls were either not being answered or they were instructed by the assistants in the councillors' offices, who usually answered the politicians' phones when they were in meetings, to make appointments. Given that, leaders are not reachable on their mobiles and most of the youth own mobile phones that enables them to use social media platforms, they came up with various e-democracy initiatives that serve as their digital platforms to discuss issues that affect their lives (Gökçe-Kızılkaya

& Onursal-Beşgül, 2017). They created various social media pages and account that make it easier for them to meet anytime. Not only the youth created digital platforms, but some regional politicians also created social media accounts as engagement platforms. Therefore, the implementation of a social media policy and implementation plan by the Namibian government may address some of these digital engagement practices. However, we are cautioning that the government really need to provide effective training on social media ethics and practices to the employees and the community at large. Failure to do this, this policy will not yield the intended outcomes as majority of the people, including some political leaders are digital illiterate and have a negative attitude towards the use of social media platforms as engagement platforms. Based on findings there is less inclusivity as anticipated with the mobile phone emergence and social media in the political sphere especially at regional and local authority level. We are recommending that, proper and continuous social media trainings should be conducted throughout the country, regional councils should appoint a trained and qualified digital media/social media officer for effective implementation and interaction with local citizens. We are also suggesting that, the appointed social media officer should be political neutral and free from political hallucination. Finally, we of the opinion that each region should have a social media center/department. At the end we need to enhance digital participatory democracy and promote digital inclusiveness among our citizens.

Integrated Knowledge Management Cycle

The chapter used the Integrated Knowledge Management Cycle (IKMC) to explain how individuals are being developed economically, socially and politically through social media technologies. Dalkir (2005) proposed the integrated knowledge management cyclce comprising of three major stages:

- Knowledge capture and /or creation.
- Knowledge sharing and disseemination.
- Knowledge acquisition and application.

Figure 1. Integrated Knowledge Model (Source: Dalkir, 2005)

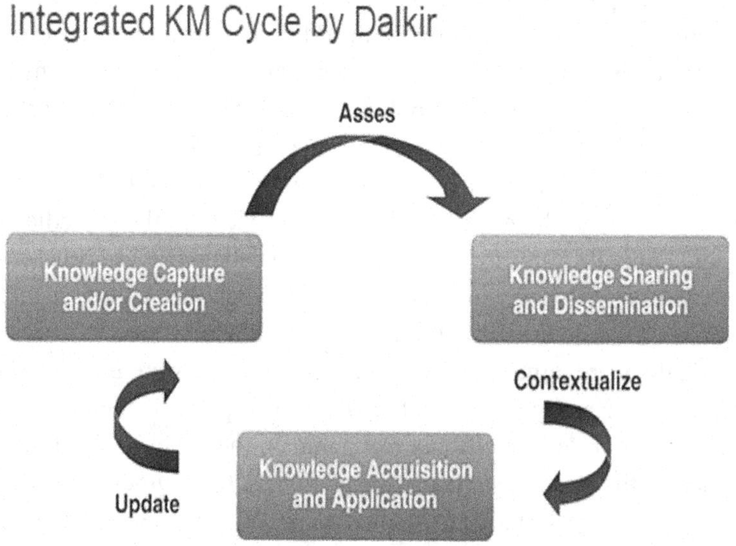

In the transition from knowledge capture/ creation to knowledge sharing and dissemination, creation of knowledge is critical to provide lifelong learning opportunities for educational administrators. Knowledge is then contextualised in order to be understood (acquisition) and used (application) by the users. This stage feeds back into the first one in order to update the knowledge content. The application of the IKMC to the study at hand is that through Facebook groups' knowledge is being captured, shared, disseminated and assessed. Knowledge is further contextualised to national and local situations, understood and used to develop an individual economically, socially and politically. These stages further used to update the initial knowledge content.

Facebook is an online medium that lets users interact with each other by sharing information about various topics of interests and concerns. Although initially focused on sharing information via personal profiles, Facebook introduced the "group" application in September 2004 as additional basic features. Users share their information by creating public and closed groups and allow others to join the groups to be able to post and comment on what others have posted, which made it to be one of the biggest educational platforms globally. Groups also have the ability to connect individuals who are not friends, yet share common political, social and economic interests. Individuals who would not be normally connected to on Facebook are networked together in these groups based on their shared interests. Groups are unique in the sense that they have a powerful networking ability. Groups also allow members to directly converse with each other over one-on-one private messages, which signifies the powerful potential of groups to facilitate political and social communication. Social media in general, and Facebook in particular, provided new sources of information the regime could not easily control and were crucial in shaping how citizens made individual decisions about participating.

MATERIALS AND METHODS

The chapter employed qualitative content analysis to analyse information shared on six Facebook groups for economic, social and political development. This comprised of two public groups and four closed groups. Digital ethnography was done over a period of 3 weeks (24 July 2017 to 13 August 2017). Qualitative content analysis provided a better understanding of the type of information and discourse to be found among these Facebook groups. See the table that follow:

Table 1. Facebook groups/pages

Group name	Type of group	Members	Admin	Link
Affirmative Repositioning AR- we want land	Public group	134,642	7	https://www.facebook.com/groups/1495977557293810/
Youth in politics	Closed group	33,087	5	https://www.facebook.com/groups/youthsinpolitics/
Political Watch Namibia	Closed group	73,043	6	https://www.facebook.com/groups/politicswatch/
Namibian Entrepreneurs	Closed group	10,370	1	https://www.facebook.com/groups/426930034018693/
Property Namibia- Buy/sell and rentals	Public group	35 620	5	https://www.facebook.com/groups/249455075182569/
Namibians in democracy	Closed group	12 783	5	https://www.facebook.com/groups/415856851838689/

Source: Facebook pages (Online)

In order to understand how the youth, use mobile social media platforms, such as: Facebook and WhatsApp for political and civic participatory education in Namibia, we have conducted a three weeks online ethnographic work on two public groups and four closed groups. We participated in the discussions on different FB pages and WhatsApp groups in the region, especially, those one that are targeting the youth and under the regional youth forum. We kept on asking follow up questions on issues raised on these pages and groups but we kept it minimal to avoid driving members to the intended type of responses. Fieldwork was undertaken from 24 July 2017 to 13 August 2017. One particular advantage of ethnographic research on media, is that it enables scholars to place media forms and practices in context, and consider the human tensions, negotiations and beliefs that are embedded in the everyday interaction with media technologies.

As we subsequently reveal, ethnographic research can provide many important insights that can enable a deeper understanding of social media and of their political potential, and encourage scholars to distance themselves from techno-deterministic assumptions of their effects. The ethnographic analysis was also enriched with qualitative textual analysis of online discussions. Every status update provided by each member was scraped using the *netvizz* software system, along with every comment made by any Facebook or WhatsApp friend or member on these pages. Once texts were scraped, they were exported to a database and entered into the text-based sentiment software, WordStat. This program made it possible to track the most common key words, terms, and phrases. After that, we used ATLAS-ti software to code the data and we used an inductive analyses of qualitative data where the main purpose is to allow themes to emerge from constant comparison, dominant or significant themes inherent in raw data, without the restraints imposed by a more structured theoretical orientation. Each interview, Facebook and WhatsApp group word document was constantly compared with other group or page document to see if there are themes emerging until all themes are exhausted. To protect the identity of participants, the names of participants and those of Constituencies they represent were changed. Where Constituency names are mentioned, then it is based on the researcher's observation or Census results.

FINDINGS AND DISCUSSIONS OF THE RESULTS

This study represents one of the first studies that explored Social Media and Technologies as Information Systems and Services for Economic, Social and Political Development in Namibia. The results are categorised in various categories to provide a clear understanding of social media technologies usage among young Namibians.

Facebook As An Economic Generating Tool

Namibians use Facebook to buy, sell or rent properties in Namibia. A public group called Property Namibia-buy/sell and rentals are created for advertising products, properties, services and events in Namibia. The research revealed that there are various groups on Facebook where people can post their goods on sale in search of customers, economic advancement and other information aimed at educating and awakening citizens to be more informed and aware of things hindering their economic freedom and emancipation.

The posts below talks to the statement above.

YOUNG FRIENDS, from Friday to yesterday, we registered at total of 385 Delegates, visitors and observers for the #GenerationalAssembly on the National Youth MANIFESTO. All these delegates received documentation pack containing the Discussion Guide providing Clarity of Objectives. They also got identification and all other material they can take home for further mobilization. As expected, the Assembly was a success and exceeded our expectations. While the detailed statements will be released, it is necessary to be informed that the Generational Assembly RESOLVED that in September, a NATIONAL CONSULTATIVE MEETING ON WHAT IS TO BE DONE REGARDING THE SME BANK CORRUPTION be convened. All delegates from 14 Regions and majority of the constituency endorse and acknowledge AR as an Organic Organizational tool for Economic Freedom in general and our Generational in particular. We are building a consciousness from bellow - full of Rhythm and SPIRIT. When the National Youth MANIFESTO is eventually released, it will become clear that Elite Rhetorics, POSTPONEMENT and CONTAINMENT of the Youth as FUTURE leaders is nothing but narratives and tales of Greedy and Self-Glorifying Elites, full of sound and furry Signifying FOKOL. There is no YOUTH organization that is as well organized as the AR MOVEMENT. AR is, therefore, the Zeigists Movement of Revolutionary Change in Namibia. OUR YOUTH Will awaken! (Facebook Member 11, 2017.Affirmative Repositioning).

This post proved to be liked by many Namibians with a total likes of 352 and 6 love. However, the group targeted in this research – Property Namibia-buy/sell and rentals was rarely used despite the group being a public group with 35 620 members and 5 admin.

The research also found out that another group called Namibian Entrepreneurs is not actively in use despite boosting 10 370 members and 1 admin. For the 3 weeks digital ethnography only one post was posted in the group and attracted on like only.

The post read as follow:

Hi everybody. I am looking for long term business partners who can be interested in working with me on a Media project that will operate in the following SADC countries, Botswana, Namibia, Zambia, Swaziland, Mozambique, South Africa and Malawi.

Interested parties should be able to commit financially as well as ready to come down to Gaborone to meet and discuss the operation. Character and integrity counts.

Inbox me for further details and arrangements.

One would expect a post of nature to attract more likes, sharing and comments seeing that there is a high number of unemployment in Namibia.

Facebook as a Social and Communication Advancement Tool

Social media is praised to be the largest pool of applications that enable thousands of people in the world to communicate, meet friends, share problems and ideas, and advice each other. It is also a very nice platform where the youth usually meet to discuss political matters that affect their daily lives in the constituencies, villages or regions. Based on our ethnographic research in Namibia recently, most of the people in rural areas do not have access to social media daily, however, they all indicated that, they occasionally access social media in one way or the other once they go to towns. However, this supports the findings of some studies which claim that despite the digital divide and network access in some countries, young people are actively using mobile internet to access social media for political and civic participation (Dawson, 2014; García-Albacete, 2014). It is concluded that social media is a good platform educational administrators to interact in politics. The findings for our study additionally informed us that social media platforms are used by the youth, politicians, non-politicians, and others in the region as information sharing and debating places. It can be seen that both youth and political leaders interact with one another without any time limit on these platforms. This is a good sign of political intimacy between the citizens and government representatives as citizens feel ownership of the region (García-Albacete, 2014). This engagement alerts the political leadership of the concerns of the youth and how the youth would like to have certain challenges addressed in the region. This is part of the direct democracy. It is also concluded that mostly the discussions are taking place after working hours or during weekends. This shows that both youth and politicians are using their free time to access, share and discuss topical issues in the region. Additionally, this means that private time is used constructively by both the youth and political leaders for the benefit of the region to ensure that there is change and growth. With this, we can conclude that there is leisure-oriented political will among the citizens (García-Albacete, 2014).

Another major lesson is the capitalisation of digital resources and digital literacy. Youth are using Facebook and WhatsApp to provide advice to others or to ask questions that they do not have answers to since they have a lot of professionals online. The explored social media platforms show that, participants mainly share pictures of documents, either vacancies in the public sector from the newspapers or take pictures of the advertised posts at the constituency offices and share them. A very interesting point is the issue of some of the political leaders who are actively sharing vacancies and other important messages on these platforms. It should be noted that not all the political leaders in Namibia are on these platforms and also not all the youth are on these platforms. While research data reveal that primarily urban and educated males have usurped these online forums, the efforts by the leaders of the forums at using their phone plans, free vouchers, sending SMS's and calling their rural members make for a more complex narrative. It makes the case of how we need to assess digital participation not just through direct means as online participation and presence but also through indirect measures as we have seen above that involves traditional and old technologies. This pushes us to expand what constitutes as digital inclusion and helps evaluate strategies to reduce the digital divide gap through the bridging of the old and new media (García-Albacete, 2014). We are suggesting that political advocacy groups and lifelong learning opportunities for marginalised communities on mobile social media should be initiated and get funded by the state and private sector to ensure that digital democracy is a reality in Namibia.

Digital Political Education and Development

Additionally, they also post on various groups for them to advance their political development, share their political knowledge and contribute to democracy in the country. Recently there have been political unrest in the country which saw some politicians losing their political home and ground. Namibian citizens took to social media technologies to air their views. One notable post stated that:

KUKU IS MORE THAN TRIBALISM

I have nothing much to say about this Kuku VS Swapo sopa opera cos I've been enjoying watching from afar (because tribalism will take us nowhere), but I want to add sauce by reminding my fellow Owambos that Menas Kame is the same one who insulted us directly as "aafyoona";

Also, Kuku has absolutely nothing to lose, neither is his voice and freedom of speech cut, for he can be voted back into that National Assembly with his own political party.

This is the scatteredization of SWAPO votes!

The contradiction is measured when the Party says they hadn't expelled the Honourable from the Party, yet the judged statements would automatically cause a resignation: "If they recall me from Swapo, immediately, 30 seconds later I'll resign from Swapo"

Kuku's remarks are brutal truth, and a matter of fact that must be analyzed by every individual in their own tribal capacity and thirst for ownership of land; they'll realise that this is more than tribalism, and all tribes shall come to salute Hon.Kuku in unity;

This is about having a vibrant and young political party in the National Assembly with a few seats, voted and representing not only Namas, Damaras, San or Khoisan, but also Kavangos, Hereroes, Himbas and Owambos in the Memberships of Parliament wearing orange overalls.

This is going to be a crucial point of debates, discussions and overlooks on this land issue at Parly level, being once Deputy Minister of Land Resettlements, Hon. Kuku has the right paperwork to thrive in this intellectual war.

Stay tuned to the sopa opera, we might just have a youtube channel on Namibian Parliamentary debates, Come 2019(Facebook Member 12, 2017, Politics Watch Namibia).

Although some view this as bad others are supporting the posts as one member said: *Viva Kuku well educated u loose nothing walk the talk bra (Facebook Member 13, 2017).*

Dehumanisation of Political Leaders

The analysis shows that some Facebook members are mocking political leaders based on what they heard via social media technologies. Few comments made are

Gossiping mongers...normally it's women on the forefront now is men overtaking women. In the picture on the right stand miss Uutapi "Governor Tuka" and his second run up Ms "Partner Peka" on his left.

Just like we know that, the house of the loud talker, leaks.

1. Great minds discuss ideas.
2. Average minds discuss events.
3. Small minds discuss people

And on number three: Governor Tuka and Partner Peka (Facebook Member 1, 2017 Affirmative Repositioning –we want land group)

This post had 89 comments most of them mocking and belittling the governor in various areas such as intellectual, manhood and insults. The post has 198 likes, 48 ha ha, 6 wow, 2 loves and 2 angry:

Honourable gossiper (Facebook Member 2, 2017)

Useless guy (Facebook Member 3, 2017)

Shameless Gay ... argh I mean guy (Facebook Member 4, 2017)

Tuka must take his ARVs on time and leave the Ndongas and Kwanyamas alone. Facebook Member 5, 2017)

Some Namibians felt that there were some individuals who are pressing too much Tuka and one posted like *Kani Kuni leave Tuka alone. We also don't know what you use to discuss with your friends behind doors. Omunanufu ino yola mukweni a nya, ngula ongwee... continue to fight for land access. We want land and I suppose that's the reason you were kicked out from SPYL. So watch what you say, why you say it, to whom that matters. Please stick to good use. Stick to AR. Fight for the landless.... I rest my case Facebook Member, 2017).*
 This status has 53 comments with 173 likes, 14 ha ha, 11 love, 2 wow and 1 sad

Digital Counselling and Sympathetic Educational Platform

The findings show that Namibian citizens care about each other in times of trouble. This is shown by digital counselling and sympathy shown and given to those perceived to be offenders.

I think at MTC there is a spy placed there... I doubt whether she is really the one. We all gossip and the Hon Governor is also human please. There audio isn't sensitive either...Those mentioned should forgive and forget the honourable remarks. This post was liked by nine people.

You people,, its fine now ooo... (Facebook Member 6, 2017.)

The Governor is right in his observation of this so-called Peka. I've listen to the recording and I have come to the very same conclusion. She was the lead actor in that conversation and the Governor simply played along (Facebook Member 7, 2017).

Political Remorseful /Apologetic

Our study reveals that, most of the citizens are using social media for political remorsefulness. For instance, the following:

Accept apology or leave it.... we were once called peasants clap hand at a packed stadium and it was live on TV...

But now this personal little thing is being followed..go beat up him for your anger to go away (Facebook Member 8, 2017). This posts generated 117 likes, 6 ha ha, 5 love and 2 sad. further, the posts received 48 comments and was shared for 63 times. Other members went on to say: Well-done governor. For me its just good (Facebook Member 9, 2017). I like the way our Governor responded to the media, that shows that he is a great leader (Facebook Member 10, 2017).

Omusati governor Tuka on the morning of 24 July 2017 apologised to the nation for private remarks he made regarding the Aandonga people, among others. The governor has been under fire on social media for reportedly making tribal utterances against the Aandonga people and some politicians. He denied being a tribalist, saying he was trapped. "Towards the end of June2017, I received a telephone call from Peka, whereby we had a private conversation. During this conversation, Peka had probing questions, with ulterior motives, whereby she specifically tried to lead me into that particular discussion, with her questions as set, which led to me innocently answering without knowing that I was being trapped for a specific reason, to portray me as a tribalist, which I am not," said Tuka. "At some point during the conversation I intended to stop the conversation but she continued with her probing questions"(Facebook Member 10, 2017).

The posts attracted 106 likes, 9 haha, 4 loves 2 angry and 1 sad. 102 comments were made and 2 people shared the posts. This shows that people liked the apology. The posts was shared twice and generated 102 comments.

SOLUTIONS AND RECOMMENDATIONS

Solutions

Analysis of few social media pages in Namibia revealed that political parties, government agencies, youth and ministries have created these platforms, however there is less engagement and interactions with the grassroots level. These are commendable e-democracy initiatives by citizens to create political and social networks for inclusivity and social coherence. While others gain and benefit through digital literacy and information sharing, others go so low by discrediting others, calling others different names, vilifying and blackmailing others, destroying their personal identities and that of their relatives/families, revealing private and confidential issues, recording personal and private mobile conversations and share them on social media, share their half-naked or sexual revealing pictures on social media, expressing their anger and frustration on these platforms rather than seeking clarifications and advises from appropriate and relevant offices or experts; judging and crucifying elders publicly which is against our cultural norms as Africans. All these issues led to societal morality being questioned.

RECOMMENDATIONS

We are recommending that, proper and continuous social media trainings should be conducted throughout the country, regional councils should appoint a trained and qualified digital media/social media officer for effective implementation and interaction with local citizens. We are also suggesting that, the appointed social media officer should be political neutral and free from political hallucination. Finally, we of the opinion that each region should have a social media center/department. At the end we need to enhance digital participatory democracy and promote digital inclusiveness among our citizens.

Observations and analysis also revealed that, social media is slowly taking over traditional media's role as media platforms that inform and notify the public in a timely manner about any issue in the country. It has become clear that we have different categories of people on social media: self-proclaimed experts and defenders, such as digital political evangelists, political hallucinators, affective and displaced lovers, social entertainers and I do not care type of people, the lost and found digitizers. Therefore, it is very important for you to categorize your friends based on their social closeness and digital behavior on social media. Many a time, digital political evangelists and political hallucinators tend to dominate these platforms as they are seeking support, comfort, votes, and sympathizers for their ill-gotten behaviors. Although, social media was initially seen as a platform that citizens in any economy could use for leisure and socialization, lately, these platforms have become avenues for political infighting and struggles, vilification, blackmailing and character assassination. This can be better understood in the latest incidents whereby, citizens' insults, discredit, shame and vigilantism others. Incidents such as the Aandonga issue, sex video circulation, photos and SMSs sharing, political shaming and circulation of private and confidential documents. Other examples include information, sharing of learners' papers or recorded videos by teachers for learners that are not fluent in the official language or not well taken care of, sharing unofficial confirmed accident pictures and videos. These incidents do not only destroy the characters of those mentioned in those videos or messages. But also show the level of education, maturity and literacy of the one who shares and posts the messages on these platforms. All this leads to social disorder and social disharmony. Equally, these actions by some citizens can lead to provocations and marriage break-downs. There is a misunderstanding of these platforms as many youth look at them as unregulated platforms where they can say or write anything they feel like writing. As a social media researcher, we have to caution that, posting insulting, vilifying and character assassinating messages on digital platforms raises ethical concerns and also moral obligations as a digital citizen in that country or village or constituency. We also end up sending the wrong message to our fellow citizens that are not yet on social media platforms as they only look at them as avenues for gossip, sex scandals, vigilantism and others. However, there are laws and regulations that control this, ranging from the constitution, and other parliamentary laws. As a dutiful citizen, you need to familiarize yourself with these country and international laws to avoid committing serious digital offences. One of the ethical dilemma that we have is the leakage of very confidential conversations and documents from very private and public offices. Our citizens tend to ignore our traditions, culture, values and norms that shape our well-being and existence on earth. Many of the young people are using these platforms as money making schemes where they blackmail others and threaten to expose them if they do not give them certain amounts. This defeats the purpose of these platforms.

Our advice to those that fall victim to these type of digital crimes and offences is to report these issues to the nearest police station or CRAN. Being attacked, insulted or discussed on social media has some of the following effects: it discourages and labels people and leads to moral decay. Spiritual questioning and tradition and may lead to suicides or contribute to gender-based violence, which is growing at an alarmingly high rate now in Namibia. Below we are offering the do's and don't's of social media from my personal experience as a regular social media user and researcher:

The do's of social media:

- *Share social constructive news, information or ideas.*
- *Share scholarships, vacancies, educational videos, any other pertinent information.*
- *Ask the online community to assist you with explanations on assignments or projects that you are working on.*
- *Share and post pictures that are relevant and deemed fit to be on the public platform.*
- *Share successes (but be extra careful that not everybody is happy about your success).*
- *Protect your pictures, statuses, and any other documents on your social media page.*
- *Accept friend requests from people that you have a lot of mutual friends with.*
- *Block those that irritate or remove yourself from some groups on social media.*
- *Always update your location when you are no longer in that location or town.*
- *Have a purpose driven aim of posting messages or sharing ideas on social media.*
- *Aim at digitally educating others and advise and warn others when they are abusing or misbehaving on social media.*
- *Stand by what you believe in when posting or commenting.*
- *Be sensitive and put yourself in the shoes of others.*

The don'ts of social media:

- *Do not share private issues such as having problems with your partner or family or boss/supervisor at work on social media.*
- *Do not share sensitive and pornographic videos BUT rather report them to Facebook or any other authority as sharing them means you are promoting the act.*
- *Do not accept friend requests from unknown people that you do not have mutual friends with (though you have mutual friends, check which ones and how close you are).*
- *Do not forget where you come from, your culture, profession, industry, norms and values. Always log out.*
- *Do not use your work PC or time for your own private social networking activities.*
- *Do not share your password.*

Consequently, our behaviour and attitude on Social Media makes many people to hate us and deactivate their accounts from social media. Be as friendly as possible; be an observer, read and understand posts and statuses before commenting and liking; use emotions correctly and appropriately to avoid offending others and be sensitive. We are suggesting that, we need to have a national education program focusing on Social Media Ethics and Practices country-wide urgently. Our people, be it the educated or less educated are now becoming a public shame by displaying and showing their digital illiteracy skills and knowledge on social media platforms. Many of them became laughing stocks in their communities while they thought they were becoming public figures and increasing their popularity. Additionally, we need to establish a state funded Institute of Digital Literacy to promote digital literacy and social media literacy among our citizens. So, while social media rises our opportunities to interact digitally increase it is equally leading to a fall in social and cultural morals. Above all, take note that today it is you that exposes and insults others on social media, and the following day it will be you or your relative who will be crucified. Let's build a responsible, digitally inclusive house.

FUTURE RESEARCH DIRECTIONS

We strongly believe that, future research and policy directions should focus on digital literacy as well as digital divide in the Global South. Additionally, more focus should be given to the following:

Digital Literacy: Lies, Fake News, Misinformation, Digital Footprint and digital ethics on Mobile Phones and Social Media

Though Mobile phones were expensive in the early 2000's, there are now different manufacturers and suppliers of various mobiles and data access in the country. There are Smart Phones and Non-smart phones and their prices differs from the type of specifications in that phone. Some mobiles can be as affordable as NAD120.00 especially in the Chinese and Indian Shops country wide. This made it easier and affordable for the unemployed and employed citizens to acquire mobile phones. The smart phones can allow citizens to have access to various social media applications such as Facebook, Instagram, WhatsApp, Twitter and LinkedIn. These applications are now more popular than ever, and some citizens spend more time on these platforms viewing, reading, posting and sharing various contents and networking with their friends outside the country (*Mobile Phones and Social Media Addiction*). In as much as these platforms have advantages, there has been a societal outcry necessitated by the way citizens conduct themselves digitally. Most of the time citizens are using these platforms to insults, gossip, vilify, dehumanise and call each other names. Additionally, there has been reports of confidential documents that were shared on these platforms as most of the smartphones have those features that can enable a user to record or take a picture and share it on any social media platform or their friends. This raised a social concern with regards to moral obligations of citizens. This is one of the issues to be explored in this era, *on digital lies, fake news, misinformation and digital ethics*.

Mobile Phones and Social Media Deception: Culture, Religion and Political Values

Another issue that came with the increased mobile phones acquisition is that, businesses and other individuals, especially entrepreneurs are now using these platforms as advertising platforms to access more potential clients or customers for their products or services. However, there are grave concerns by which these business oriented people deceive their customers or individuals deceive each other as they share unrealistic pictures of products or themselves. Many people fell victims of digital romance just by viewing pictures of their digital friends and end up having affairs with the people that they do not know. However, the end results are always not in good faith for our society. Therefore, *Mobile phones and Social Media Deception* is another issues to be explored further.

Digital Evangelism: Leadership and Membership Literacy-Phase 3

Similarly, some churches also owned mobile phones and created social media accounts where they share posts/status about meetings, Sunday services or any testimonies from their churches. However, it is reported that, some people are only watching these digital videos and do not go to offline services. The project will also focus on *Digital evangelism* and contemporary phenomenon and how mobile phones as well as social media are used during church services.

Social Media: Use of Indigenous Languages

Most of mobile phones applications are in different languages other than our indigenous languages in Namibia. But you can see that users even those that cannot read and write English can make use these platforms and participate in digital discussions. A project that will do assessment on the use of indigenous languages on social media and how digital literacy (mobile phones, social media) can contribute to effective digital engagement for the benefit of the society is needed.

Digital Romance and Counselling

Though citizens buy mobile phones and access social media platforms for communication and interactions, it is also used for romantic relationships where citizens meet their new lovers and romantise each other. There are reports that some couples are already in marriages and they only met on these platforms until they meet face to face. Additionally, for those that have problems such as marriage up and downs, family break downs and disappointed ones, they access these platforms to get what they call *digital counselling*. To some extend they either get what they want to they get more disappointed than before. Hence, further research should look at these issues try to come up with *digital literacy program* for all the citizens.

CONCLUSION

Analysis of few social media pages in Namibia revealed that political parties, government agencies and ministries have created these platforms, however there is less engagement and interactions with the grassroots level. Many of these sites are not updated regularly. These are commendable e-democracy initiatives by citizens to create political and social networks for inclusivity and social coherence. While others gain and benefit through digital literacy and information sharing, others go so low by discrediting others, calling others different names, vilifying and blackmailing others, destroying their personal identities and that of their relatives/families, revealing private and confidential issues, recording personal and private mobile conversations and share them on social media, share their half-naked or sexual revealing pictures on social media, expressing their anger and frustration on these platforms rather than seeking clarifications and advises from appropriate and relevant offices or experts; judging and crucifying elders publicly which is against our cultural norms as Africans. All these issues led to societal morality being questioned.

ACKNOWLEDGMENT

This research received no specific grant from any funding agency in the public, commercial, or not-for-profit sectors.

REFERENCES

Archambault, J. S. (2013). Cruising through uncertainty: Cell phones and the politics of display and disguise in Inhambane, Mozambique. *American Ethnologist, 40*(1), 88–101. doi:10.1111/amet.12007

Asgarkhani, M. (2005). Digital government and its effectiveness in public management reform: A local government perspective. *Public Management Review, 7*(3), 465–487. doi:10.1080/14719030500181227

Chadwick, A., & May, C. (2003). Interaction between states and citizens in the age of the Internet: 'E-government' in the United States, Britain, and the European Union. *Governance: An International Journal of Policy, Administration and Institutions, 16*(2), 271–300. doi:10.1111/1468-0491.00216

Conroy, M., Feezell, J. T., & Guerrero, M. (2012). Facebook and political engagement: A study of online political group membership and offline political engagement. *Computers in Human Behavior, 28*(5), 135–1546. doi:10.1016/j.chb.2012.03.012

Dalkir, K. (2005). *Knowledge management in theory and practice.* Oxford, UK: Elservier/Butterworth Heinemann.

Dawson, H. (2014). Youth politics: Waiting and envy in a South African informal settlement. *Journal of Southern African Studies, 40*(4), 861–882. doi:10.1080/03057070.2014.932981

Durnalı, M. (2013). The contributions of E-School, a student information management system, to the data process, environment, education, and economy of Turkey. In *Proceedings of the International Academic Forum (IAFOR) Official Conference: The Third Asian Conference on Technology in the Classroom 2013,* (pp. 170–84). Osaka, Japan: Ramada Hotel.

Durnalı, M. (2019). Technological leadership behavior level of secondary schools principals according to teachers' views. *Journal of Theoretical Educational Science, 12*(2), 401-430. doi: keg.449484 doi:10.30831/aku

Durnalı, M., Orakcı, Ş., & Aktan, O. (2019). The smart learning potential of Turkey's Education System in the context of FATIH Project. In A. Darshan Singh, S. Raghunathan, E. Robeck, & B. Sharma (Eds.), *Cases on Smart Learning Environments* (pp. 227–243). Hershey, PA: IGI Global. doi:10.4018/978-1-5225-6136-1.ch013

Erçetin, Ş. Ş., Akbaşlı, S., & Durnalı, M. (2018). Dijital Teknolojilere Erişim Motivasyonu Ölçeğinin Türkçe'ye uyarlanmasi: Geçerlik ve güvenirlik çalişmasi. *Sakarya University Journal of Education, 8*(4), 75–88. doi:10.19126uje.431126

García-Albacete, G. (2014). *Young people's political participation in Western Europe: Continuity or generational change?* Basingstoke, UK: Palgrave Macmillan. doi:10.1057/9781137341310

Gökçe-Kızılkaya, S., & Onursal-Beşgül, Ö. (2017). Youth participation in local politics: City councils and youth assemblies in Turkey. *Southeast European and Black Sea Studies, 17*(1), 97–112. doi:10.10 80/14683857.2016.1244239

Kruikemeier, S., & Shehata, A. (2016). News media use and political engagement among adolescents: An analysis of virtuous circles using panel data. *Political Communication,* 1–22.

Papacharissi, Z. (2016). Affective publics and structures of storytelling: Sentiment, events and mediality. *Information Communication and Society, 19*(3), 307–324. doi:10.1080/1369118X.2015.1109697

Raja, T. (2018). *Social Media on Education.* Retrieved from https://www.researchgate.net /publication/322636174_Social_Media_on_Education/citation/download

Raut, V., & Patil, P. (2016). Use of Social Media in Education: Positive and Negative impact on the students. *International Journal on Recent and Innovation Trends in Computing and Communication, 4*(1), 281–285. Retrieved from https://ijritcc.org/download/conferences /ICRRTET_2016 /ICRRTET_Track/1455261816_12-02-2016.pdf

Shihomeka, S. P., & Arora, P. (2018). Mobile social media and digital political inclusion among Namibia's rural youth. *Proceedings at the International Communication Association.*

The Namibian Newspaper. (2017). The Youth and Politics. *The Namibian (Windhoek).* Retrieved from https://www.namibian.com.na/171223/archive-read/The-Youth-and-Politics

Tufekci, Z., & Wilson, C. (2012). Social Media and the Decision to Participate in Political Protest: Observations From Tahrir Square. *Journal of Communication, 62*(2), 363–379. doi:10.1111/j.1460-2466.2012.01629.x

ADDITIONAL READING

Habermas, J. (1989). *The Structural Transformation of the Public Sphere.* Cambridge: Polity Press.

Kahne, J., Hodgin, E., & Eidman-Aadahl, E. (2016). Redesigning Civic Education for the Digital Age: Participatory Politics and the Pursuit of Democratic Engagement. *Theory and Research in Social Education, 44*(1), 1–35. doi:10.1080/00933104.2015.1132646

Kang, S., & Gearhart, S. (2010). E-Government and Civic Engagement: How is Citizens' Use of City Web Sites Related with Civic Involvement and Political Behaviors? *Journal of Broadcasting & Electronic Media, 54*(3), 443–462. doi:10.1080/08838151.2010.498847

Mpofu, S. (2013). Social media and the politics of ethnicity in Zimbabwe, Ecquid Novi: *African. Journalism Studies, 34*(1), 115–122.

Paˇtruț, B., & Paˇtrut, M. (Eds.). (2014). *Social Media in Politics. Public Administration and Information Technology 13.* Switzerland: Springer International Publishing; doi:10.1007/978-3-319-04666-2_1

Quintelier, E., & Vissers, S. (2008). The Effect of Internet Use on Political Participation: An Analysis of survey Results for 16-year-old in Belgium. *Social Science Computer Review*, 26(4), 411–427. doi:10.1177/0894439307312631

Van Belle, J., & Cupido, K. (2013). Increasing Public Participation in local government by means of Mobile Phones: The View of South African youth, *The Journal of Community Informatics,* 9(4), Available: http://ci-journal.net/index.php/ciej/article/view/983/1054, Accessed: 14 November 2016.

Wasserman, H. (2011). Mobile Phones, Popular Media, and Everyday African Democracy: Transmissions and Transgressions. *Popular Communication*, 9(2), 146–158. doi:10.1080/15405702.2011.562097

KEY TERMS AND DEFINITIONS

Digital Evangelism: A situation whereby citizens access or use digital devices to spread convincing news among their fellows or attracting more likes and comments for their own benefits.

Digital Literacy: Ability of an individual to use digital devices at his/her disposal constructively and for the good benefit of the society.

Digital Romance: A situation whereby an individual falls in love with a person that met on digital platform without them meeting face to face.

E-Democracy: Initiatives by local citizens created using digital devices with the main aim of making sure that all people in their community are taking part in social, economic and political processes without any favour.

Political Participation: Refers to actions of citizens to take part in election campaigns rallies, decision making processes, town hall meetings/public meetings using their digital devices.

Social Media Deception: A situation whereby citizens use social media platforms to sell or advertise unrealistic products or services.

This research was previously published in Utilizing Technology, Knowledge, and Smart Systems in Educational Administration and Leadership; pages 203-223, copyright year 2020 by Information Science Reference (an imprint of IGI Global).

Section 7
Critical Issues and Challenges

Chapter 101

Making Social Media More Social:
A Literature Review of Academic Libraries' Engagement and Connections through Social Media Platforms

Elia Trucks
 https://orcid.org/0000-0003-1951-8902
University of Denver, USA

ABSTRACT

This chapter explores how academic libraries have used social media for broadcasting information, responsive communication, and engagement. Many libraries focus on the marketing aspect of social media, since it is a successful method of promoting events, services, and resources. However, exclusively using social media as a marketing tool ignores the best part of social media: the connections it fosters between people. The online community is just an extension of the in-person community that the academic library serves. This chapter examines the state of the literature on libraries' use of social media through the lens of increasing engagement and connections with the community as the key to successful social media.

INTRODUCTION

Social media is ubiquitous and pervasive on the digital landscape today, including in higher education and academic libraries. One only has to turn on the television to see any commercial promoting the company's Facebook presence or website for details. Despite the differences among the multitude of social media platforms, the main commonality they share is that they are used to connect people with other people. Facebook, Twitter, Instagram, and YouTube are among the many tools people use to reach out to old friends, make new friends over a shared interest, and learn more about hot topics and current events.

DOI: 10.4018/978-1-6684-7123-4.ch101

The massive scale of the Internet has made it necessary for academic libraries to have an online social media presence to meet users where they are. The biggest social media platform in use at the time of this writing is Facebook, with 2.196 billion active users monthly. Other major platforms include YouTube with 1.9 billion users, Instagram with 1 billion users, and Twitter with 336 million users (We Are Social, n.d.). This chapter will focus on Facebook and Twitter as the primary networks that libraries are using or can use to reach their communities, but the rising popularity of Instagram and YouTube will also be discussed. There are many different networks currently in use by public, academic, and special libraries. Gonzalez, Marks, and Westgate (2018) launched a Social Media Directory of Academic Libraries that lists accounts associated with various academic libraries across the globe, along with contact information for the librarian or representative responsible for the accounts. At the time of this writing, the directory includes 173 libraries on Facebook, 157 libraries on Twitter, 128 libraries on Instagram, and 101 libraries on YouTube.

The boundaries between online and offline have blurred significantly since the Internet has become a pervasive influence in society. A library's community exists in both online and offline spaces simultaneously, and it is necessary to bridge the gap between these spaces to create a holistic experience for the community. Young and Rossmann (2015) emphasize the need to integrate the offline presence of the library into the online world. Social media is "a tool that enables users to join together and share in the commonalities of research, learning, and the university community" (p. 22). Social media can bring together individuals in a community, and libraries must learn to use these tools more effectively to bridge the gaps.

This crossover between the digital and physical worlds has become even more enmeshed with the rise of mobile technology. The Pew Research Center (2018, February 5) reports that 95% of Americans own a cellphone, and 77% own smartphones. This instant connection to social media, news, businesses, and information has changed behaviors. New Media Consortium's (2017) Horizon Report indicates that mobile learning is a major trend for higher education. Convenience and communication drive this trend, and ease of access can improve learning outcomes for students all over the world (Adams Becker, et al, 2017).

This chapter's objectives are to determine how academic libraries have used social media in less than effective ways, how they are using social media for communication or engagement with their communities, and how to incorporate best practices for readers to improve user engagement on social media. This narrative literature review examines the state of academic libraries' social media presence and their use for engagement with students. A search of the Library Information Science and Technology Abstracts database (LISTA) with the keywords "social media" and "libraries" brings back over 2,800 results. A search adding the keyword "engagement" to the previous search string returns only 141 results. A further limitation using the search string "social media AND academic libraries AND engagement," reflecting the focus of this review, returned only 31 articles. Focusing on these articles and examining their references for relevant materials became the basis for this chapter. The search was limited to articles published between 2011 and 2018, but relevant references cited by more than one paper were also examined and included for context. College and Research Libraries News offers additional resources of interest, since many of these are not "scholarly" peer review articles but focus on trends in the field that are important for working professionals. A similar search of "social media" on the College and Research Libraries News archive returned 262 items, comprising many "how-to" articles, strategy tips, and descriptions of successful campaigns or promotions.

In order to share a common vocabulary, the following are some definitions of popular terms used at length in this chapter:

- **Content**: Material created for and shared through social media networks including but not limited to images, text, and videos;
- **Platform**: The website or technology upon which a social network is built;
- **Social Media**: Social networking websites that allow users to follow, "friend," or interact with chosen people. This chapter primarily discusses Facebook and Twitter;
- **Users**: People in the community of a specific library, often the target audience of a marketing strategy, including students, faculty, staff, and community members;
- **User Engagement**: "The emotional, cognitive, and behavioural connection that exists, at any point in time and possibly over time, between a user and a resource" (Attfield, Kazai, Lalmas, & Piwowarski, 2011).

BACKGROUND

Since its inception, the Internet has continuously grown and developed. The concept of Web 2.0 has influenced how libraries utilize the Internet and social media for many years. O'Reilly (2005) coined the term Web 2.0 as a new, interconnected version of Internet technologies focusing on community-driven participation that, while not quite idealized in its utopian form, influenced the way social media networks were built and utilized. O'Reilly emphasizes interactivity between companies and users, including "trusting users as co-developers [and] harnessing collective intelligence" (p. 5) as core competencies for these websites. Academic libraries led the adoption and use of Web 2.0 applications like blogs, RSS feeds, instant messaging, social networking services, wikis, and social tagging (Chua & Goh, 2010).

Early goals of using these networks were to forge connections and share information between users and librarians (Chua & Goh, 2010). These goals have remained relatively static through the years, even as the tools have changed. An examination of social media policies at academic libraries found that most libraries' goal for using social media is to "engage the community in conversations and to share information" (p. 403).

While the goals have not changed, opinions about the usage of social media have. In the mid-2000s, many librarians did not see the value of having libraries participate with social media. An Online Computer Library Center (OCLC) study by De Rosa, Cantrell, Havens, Hawk and Jenkins (2007) explored librarians' viewpoints on aspects of the networked world including sharing information, privacy concerns, and future involvement. The study revealed that librarians did not see a place for the library on social media. Twitter, Facebook, and YouTube were still in their infancy, the possibilities still unseen. Librarians reported using social bookmarking sites like Delicious, sharing videos on YouTube, and maintaining individual blogs for themselves or their libraries. The librarians were not necessarily wrong. Koerwer (2007), a 19-year-old college sophomore, wrote a column about his experiences and described how seeing librarians on Facebook "seemed like another instance of adults arriving too late to a fad, like a soccer mom wearing a Pikachu T-shirt" (p. 40). He goes on to say there may be opportunities for librarians to ingratiate themselves gracefully, but with strict limitations.

Attitudes have changed since 2007, and many articles have explored librarians' social media preferences, usage, and presence. More recently, Chu and Du (2013) surveyed librarians on their perceptions of various social networking tools. The majority of their 38 respondents currently use or plan to use social networking. Librarians value the promotion and marketing features, the convenient dissemination of news, and the possibility of engagement with users. These benefits outweigh the costs, which they describe as little to none; however, they face challenges of inadequate time and training, and a relatively unengaged user base. Social media platforms had saturated the market by this point in 2013, and many more librarians have become more familiar with how these networks work.

LIBRARIES' USE OF SOCIAL MEDIA

Broadcasting

As opinions about social media in academic libraries changed, its goals and uses remained static. Librarians feel most comfortable using social media platforms for promotion and advertising, or broadcasting. Broadcasting most accurately describes the practice of posting on social media to share information and raise awareness, but without engaging in conversation or deeper online responses. This one-way communication can be effective for just-in-time messages, but without user interactions it can feel like shouting into the void. Broadcasting is the current status quo for libraries who use social media, and it can be an ineffective method for communicating, engaging, and bridging the gap between the online and offline worlds. The literature explores in great detail the history of how librarians use social media for broadcasting, and the benefits and challenges of the practice.

One of the earliest studies of libraries' social media posting habits examined Twitter use in libraries. Aharony (2010) collected tweets from 30 public and academic libraries in the United States between August and October 2009. These tweets revealed similarities in the content that each created. Aharony labeled tweets in five major categories: "library, information about, miscellaneous, technology, and general information" (p. 345). Seven years later, Harrison, Burress, Velasquez, and Schreiner (2017) analyzed the social media habits of six Midwestern academic libraries and found very similar themes in the types of postings, falling into the categories "Make community connections, create an inviting environment, and provide content." Considering the time that elapsed between the two previous studies, the content that libraries are publishing has not changed much. Providing basic information about the library itself and promoting resources and events are basic elements of social media.

The most popular use for social media is to promote services or resources at the library. Surveys of librarians in the U.S. and internationally show that librarians recognize the utility of social media as a marketing tool, the most important aspect of their usage (Ayu & Abrizah, 2011; Hendrix, Chiarella, Hasman, Murphy, & Zafron, 2009; Omeluzor, Oyovwe-Tinuoye, & Abayomi, 2016). The Mansfield Library Archives and Special Collections developed a program to feed into Instagram's Application Program Interface to create a dynamic embedded feed of images from their collection (Wilkinson, 2018). Their content promoted rare, interesting, and light-hearted materials, selected to create "user delight."

In addition to the surveys of librarians, studies of the social media postings themselves confirm that librarians use social media for promotion purposes. Since social media platforms have a wide reach and little monetary cost except for time, it is a cost-effective method of marketing. Many librarians explore the uses and effectiveness of social media as a marketing tool in libraries, as well as in other businesses (Sachs, Eckel, & Langan, 2011; Sriram, 2016; Thomsett-Scott, 2014).

Understandably, there is little literature from librarians describing why this is an ineffective method of social media use. Young and Rossman (2015) at Montana State University Library struggled with their social media presence prior to their engagement strategy. An analysis of their tweets determined that the majority of their postings about workshops, library spaces, and event promotion yielded very low interaction rates. This prompted a new approach, which is discussed later in this chapter.

Responsive Communication

Some librarians have determined that broadcasting their messages does not help them reach their users. They have begun to ask their users exactly what they want and to build strategies around their particular preferences. This strategy can be considered "responsive communication," the practice of determining what kinds of messages, platforms, and methods users prefer, and strategizing to take account of those preferences.

Users have a variety of information-retrieval methods, and it is necessary to understand the preference of the library's audience before making general assumptions about the best way to reach them. The librarians who have written about their experiences with responsive communication emphasize the importance of each individual library looking at its specific population, since results vary so much.

A survey undertaken by Booker and Bandyopadhyay (2017) asked library users about their social media habits and preferences. The majority of respondents use social media platforms and think it is important for the library to have a social media presence. However, they do not prefer to get their information about the library from social media, but rather the email and flyers in the library. Users under age 35 prefer to get information from the library webpage or the newsletter before social networking sites. They still feel that the library should be present on social media platforms, but not mainly for promotion. Similarly, Gustafson, Sharrow, and Short (2017) created and disseminated a survey to gauge how the campus community preferred to receive information. This informed a marketing strategy used by the authors to promote events and services. Social media was found to be less useful than email or posters, but useful for "instant gratification and just-in-time communication" (p. 429).

Stvilia and Gibradze (2017) created a survey to determine the perceived value of different types of library tweets. They asked 120 undergraduate students to rate which library services they valued most and how important different categories of social media postings were to them. Students stated overwhelmingly that they value the library as a place to study (90%), and the next highest ranked service was access to information and resources (58%). The social media postings they most valued were operations updates, study support, and event information.

Some libraries include reference assistance as a goal of for their social media presence, assuming that a reference interview requires conversation and engagement between a librarian and a user. Sachs, Eckel, and Langan (2011) at Western Michigan University created a social media policy with this as one of their goals. However, a survey of their users revealed that users were not seeking to interact with the library on social media and would likely not use that service. Their social media management team took this preference into consideration and dropped the goal from their social media policy.

The major takeaway from the literature is that each library's users have different preferences, and every author emphasizes the importance of learning about your own users before creating a social media presence. Responding to users' preference is important, but is it engagement? As Attfield et al. (2011)

describe, user engagement is the connection between a user and a resource. Crafting a social media approach to cater to the library's population can lead to user engagement, but it requires strategic tactics that move beyond responsive communication.

Moving Beyond Responsiveness: Engagement or Active Communication

Libraries that use social media platforms to engage with their users participate in active communication, in which libraries initiate conversations that can move from the online world into the offline world by affecting policy, bringing people into the library space, or providing assistance. Historically, libraries have not been very successful in this endeavor. A study of academic-library Twitter accounts found that few accounts were using social media for conversation or engagement: "Most of the libraries were not being mentioned by their followers; in fact, only four library Twitter accounts had more than ten mentions" (Del Bosque, Leif, & Skarl, 2012, p. 209). However, some librarians have successfully developed their social media presence to build connections with their users.

As mentioned earlier in this chapter, Young and Rossmann (2015) created a social media group that analyzed the Twitter activity and usage at Montana State University Library and developed methods to focus on building community rather than one-way broadcasting and promotion. Their target audience was students at their university, and their goal was to increase interaction rates as measured by favorites, retweets, and mentions. Their most popular topics before beginning their new strategy included workshops, library spaces, and events, common themes found frequently on many library social media accounts. The community-focused approach included more personality in the tone of tweets, focusing on topics their community wanted to hear about such as student life or local community, and quick responses:

We prioritized responsiveness, availability and scholarship with the goal of connecting with students and building a sense of community. . . . By creating personality-rich content that invites two-way interaction, our strategic social media program has helped form a holistic community of users around our Twitter activity. (Young & Rossmann, 2015, p. 30)

Their plan worked, and their Twitter account saw a 366% increase in student followers.

Stewart, Atilano, and Arnold (2017) developed a "Social Listening" strategy. The Thomas G. Carpenter Library at the University of North Florida used a customer relationship management concept to connect with students, gauge their interest, and make their social media presence more engaging. Social listening, a process more prominent in private businesses than in libraries, focuses on listening and responding to users' input rather than broadcasting and marketing. The social media team prioritized social listening on their social media platforms rather than creating original content. They observed any "mention" of the library, "check in" at their location, and popular hashtags related to the university, and responded to every comment. Regardless of the sentiment of the comment, whether it was complaining about noise or gratitude for study rooms, librarians responded. Librarians note that this method has worked. User engagement has increased, their Twitter impressions rose to 15,000 per month, and they receive feedback from their users. By building reciprocity and trust between their students and the library, they in turn receive more feedback from their students and provide more help.

Another practice to improve engagement is to work with students directly to create resources and marketing strategies. Luo, Wang, and Han (2013) created a video series called "Falling in Love with the Library" that they developed, created, and executed in partnership with students. They looked at specific social media sites that their students were using, to determine where they could best reach their target audience and make the most impact. Youku, the Chinese version of YouTube, seemed a likely candidate. Librarians worked together with students to create and promote the video series, which was a smash hit. The authors identify four factors contributing to their success: content, style, venue, and partnership with students. The authors note that this last factor, partnership with students, is the most important, as it ensured that the previous three would be relevant and engaging for other students on campus.

In an attempt to create engagement with their campuses, some libraries interact heavily with other departments or units at the same school. This can be useful, as many student life or official university accounts have more activity, followers, and interactions than library accounts. By interacting with other institutional accounts, library postings and presence can find a wider audience of users still connected to the university or college. Stewart and Walker (2018) examined 16 Historically Black Colleges and Universities (HBCU) library social media accounts to see if patrons are engaging with them, by focusing on hashtags, retweets, and sentiment analysis. Retweets showed only 11% of followers engaged with library content. A majority of interaction came from other institutional accounts or non-followers engaging with posts related to institutional boosterism, the practice of creating content that focuses on the school's culture or events in a positive manner. These tweets focused on sports, campus activities, and popular culture, and usually contain slogans, mascots, or other university events. The authors found an over-representation of campus culture on library twitter feeds rather than original content, promotion of library events or services, or focus on the library as a place. They found that "library-centric content, at its best, appears rather generic in tone and did not evoke transcendent and enthusiastic engagement with followers" (p. 123). The Twitter accounts they studied did not encourage two-way communication; rather those accounts used the platform as a broadcasting service focusing on the campus culture. The HBCUs they examined made attempts at engagement but fell short.

One major challenge to improving engagement with social media is that many people use social media passively. Passive social media use is when a person observes, rather than interacting with others using the platform (Zhu & Bao, 2018). Students reported privacy concerns, the desire to control and manage their impression on other users, and social network fatigue as contributing factors to passively using social media networks. These factors are not addressed in library literature, but can explain why engagement, which requires active participation, can be a challenge. Prior to the rise of social media, passive use of message boards and other online communities was a recognized issue. Jakob Nielsen (2006) examined internet communities and coined the 90-9-1 rule: 90% of users are "lurkers" who read or observe without contributing to the discussion, 9% of users contribute occasionally, and 1% of users participate greatly and account for the majority of the content. Reference services on social media may be depressed for this reason. Sachs, Eckel, and Langan (2011) found this to be the case when trying to add reference assistance to their social media.

Despite this challenge, other fields within higher education successfully use social media to create connections and further engagement. Academic libraries can look to models created by colleagues in classroom instruction and student life for inspiration in their social media usage. Chugh and Ruhi (2018) examine how Facebook has functioned as a powerful tool, used to engage in after-class discussion groups, seek assistance outside the formal classroom setting, and foster learning communities among students and instructors. Junco, Heiberger, and Loken (2011) used Twitter in their freshman seminar for in-class discussions and coursework and found that student and faculty engagement increased. Discussions that could not have achieved depth in a one-hour seminar found rich answers and connections between students, study groups formed for other classes, and students who discovered mutual interests that formed the basis of new relationships. Harris (2016) describes ways in which other campus departments and entities can use social media to support Student Life initiatives. Athletics, student affairs, community relations, and campus safety all have unique relationships with students, and social media can enhance interactions. The examples given by each of these authors can provide guidelines or ideas for academic librarians, and even if we may not have the exact same goals, there are correlations that can be implemented.

SOLUTIONS AND RECOMMENDATIONS

Best Practices for Engagement

Developing a strategy is key for a cohesive and effective social media experience. There are many articles and books about how to develop marketing strategies or marketing plans for libraries. Even if advertising is not high on the priority list for the library's social media presence, these strategies can be used to reach the target audience, plan content, and develop better relationships. Creating a strategic marketing plan can focus and streamline social media efforts. Deploying an unfocused series of social media posts or platforms can feel unorganized and chaotic to the user, so having a strategy is important (Chua & Goh, 2010).

Libraries can take a cue from business and marketing professionals when considering their strategy. Potter's (2012) *The Library Marketing Toolkit* lays out the marketing cycle and provides methods to design a plan based on these stages. Libraries can use this step-by-step plan for their social media approach to improve their engagement. The marketing cycle is as follows:

1. Decide on your goals;
2. Market research;
3. Segmentation;
4. Set objectives;
5. Promotional activities;
6. Measurement;
7. Evaluation; and
8. Modification.

Set Goals

The first step in creating a social media presence is to determine a purpose and set goals. One might frame one's goals by answering the question, "Why are we doing this, and what do we hope to gain from it?" (Burkhardt, 2010). The answers to these questions will help to inform the kind of platforms to use, the messages to put out, the content to produce, and the target audience.

Social media policies can help to set goals and create a strategic presence. Policies can be instrumental in making sure all stakeholders understand the priorities, mission, and limits of using social media. Johnson and Burclaff (2013) examined academic library policies regarding social media, and found that very few academic libraries have such policies. Many share the general social media policy created by the larger university without adapting it to fit the library's specific needs. The authors recommend considering the library's mission and goals and crafting a policy that aligns with those priorities. "The library mission should drive the library's activities and should therefore be present in these guiding policies" (p. 404).

Creating goals for a library's social media account can vary. Popular goals include raising awareness about the library, reaching a certain number of people in a time frame, or creating original content. Strategies that support engagement often move beyond these goals. Young and Rossman (2015) developed goals to "connect with students and build community" with the activity focus of "information sharing [and] social interaction," with specifics for "tone and tenor, posting frequency, posting categories, and posting personnel" (p. 26). Each component contributed to the overall goal, and created a cohesive strategy for their team to follow.

Market Research and Segmentation

Market research is the process of analyzing the market and where one sits in it (Potter, 2012). This can involve looking at similar institutions and studying the demographics of a community. There is no one-size-fits-all approach to all users that will work for every library. Focusing on meeting the library's users where they are will eliminate costly diversions to platforms that do not work for them. Look at the age group of the community's user base. If the library's social media target audience is freshmen, part of the Gen Z cohort, they may be using different platforms than most librarians have ever used. The 18-to-24-year-olds embrace a wide variety of platforms, including Snapchat, Instagram, and YouTube, and they are leaving Facebook at a rapid pace (Pew Research Center, 2018, March 1). Other populations have different preferences as well, so consider adult learners, international students, transfer students, and other user groups that may be overlooked. Consider different strategies for reaching those populations and develop specific goals for them.

The first step is to identify the target audience for a social media platform, and find out if they are responsive to social media connections with the library. Many of the surveys looking at student preferences examine how students want to receive marketing or advertising from the library (Gustafson, Sharrow, & Short, 2017; Booker & Bandyopadhyay, 2017). Look back at the goals for one's social media presence and determine if one's audience will be receptive.

Set Objectives

Based on the goals determined at the beginning of this process, objectives are measurable and attainable benchmarks that can determine if one is progressing toward meeting those goals.

Objectives can be a simple measure of analytics, such as "obtaining 60 followers within the first four months of using the service and using multiple likes per image" (Ramsey & Vecchione, 2014). Other objectives can include posting a certain number of unique items within a time frame, creating an amount of original content, or sharing a certain number of links back to library resources. For engagement, different goals are needed. Stewart, Atilano, and Arnold (2018) established goals focusing on content creation and awareness of the library in their first iterations of their social media policy, but as they developed their Social Listening strategy, their goal shifted to "seeking out opportunities to reply to, connect with, and encourage library customers to reach out to the library" (p. 54). Their objectives focused on responding to every mention and check-in at the library, which led them to achieve their overall goal.

Libraries should create a team to manage their social media presence. This will alleviate the pressure on a librarian or staff member and has multiple benefits. A team can create a calendar and update more regularly, make sure that each department or subject is represented fairly, and set bigger goals that align with other marketing objectives (Jansen, 2017). Librarians who use a variety of social media platforms can get bogged down or overwhelmed by producing content for each channel. Having a team, a strategy, and a plan can help to avoid this.

Time is a major concern for librarians using social media, especially for those interested in building relationships with their users. Posting several times per day can be daunting and takes a great deal of time. Librarians must set aside time to learn the platforms; update their knowledge of constant changes on the platforms in the face of user requests and technical fixes; respond to users' queries or comments quickly; and create content that is interesting and engaging. One major concern for librarians using these platforms is the cost of their time (Chu & Du, 2013; Dickson & Holley, 2010).

Promotional Activities

Creating unique content that fits user preferences is an integral and sometimes difficult part of maintaining a social media presence. Graphics, pictures, and visual media are the most popular posts on many of these platforms. A survey of the target population will help guide decisions about the kind of content of most interest or use to them, and those preferences should guide the goals, strategy, and content. From their survey results, Stvilia and Gibradze (2017) learned that students prefer operations updates, study support, and event information. Content that caters to these themes may better engage them than faculty and staff profiles or collections updates.

In addition to creating content for each platform, it is also important to respond to users who interact with an account. Stewart, Atilano, and Arnold (2017) used "social listening" to improve engagement. Students felt heard by the library and that built trust between them. This responsiveness, in addition to content that appeals to them, can generate goodwill and develop relationships.

Looking at other libraries' postings and modifying them to fit the library's vision can be easy and inspirational; however, this can lead to homogeneity in its overall social media presence. Harrison, Burress, Velasquez, and Schreiner (2017) found overwhelmingly similar postings in their analysis of six Midwestern universities, despite differences in sizes, populations, and strategies. Adherence to mimicking other successful posts might overshadow analyzing the effectiveness of posting.

Measurement, Evaluation, and Modification

Assessment of social media can be a challenge for librarians. Clearly defined and measurable goals can improve the experience for managers. In the early days of social media, quantitative data about the effectiveness and success of these platforms was not readily available (Dickson & Holley, 2010). However, in recent years a plethora of tools and methods has become available to librarians.

One easy way to measure engagement is to look at followers, retweets, and replies. Counting mentions, retweets, shares, likes, or comments on various platforms can be a quick tool for measurement. Kim, Abels, and Yang (2012) examined 10 academic libraries' tweets to find out who was sharing their content, and found that university organizations and students are the two largest groups who retweet library accounts. Stvilia and Gibradze (2014) analyzed tweets from six major university libraries to measure the most popular topics and effectiveness of those themes. The most popular categories of tweets include event, resource, and community building. Retweets and favorites determined which content was most effective, and study support was the most popular category by far, followed by community building and resources. Some of the most frequently used words in the "community building" category included "learning, hope, great, student, luck, best, follow, awesome" (p. 139). Based on their description of the category and these kinds of words, this would relate to engagement and building connections with users.

Native tools on each platform can be powerful. Facebook has a sophisticated suite of tools called Page Insights that can provide information about who is engaging with posts, the volume of people, and common traits that may help provide better understanding of the audience. The key terms for these metrics include "impressions," the number of times a post is shown; "reach," the number of unique users who have seen a post; and "frequency," the average number of times a user sees an ad (Nonprofits on Facebook, n.d). Using these tools can help align the target audience with the people actually interacting with posts, determine what days and times are most successful for increasing engagement, and develop new methods and strategies (Ramsey & Vecchione, 2014; Vucovich, Gordon, Mitchell, & Ennis, 2013). Twitter, Instagram, and YouTube also have their own programs that measure algorithms and audiences to provide similar sophisticated information (Twitter for Business, n.d.; Instagram, n.d.; Youtube Creator Academy, n.d.). Many of the tools provided by these companies focus on advertising revenue, which may not be relevant for libraries who do not purchase ad space from them. Third-party tools also provide assessment capabilities if the native tools or individual measurements do not provide enough information. Klout, SumAll, and StatCounter are three alternatives with similar functions.

The marketing cycle requires continuous adaptation and updating. Once the assessment data has been analyzed, determine if the goals made at the outset have been met or if they need to be tweaked in order to reach a desirable outcome. This can lead to improving strategies and developing new goals based on the information one has obtained, which begins the cycle anew.

CONCLUSION

One major issue in the literature about academic libraries' social media use is the privacy of users. Privacy has been discussed in terms of what information universities and colleges collect about students, what corporations collect, and what private information is freely available, but this topic has not been studied in terms of what academic libraries collect from social media. When a library follows or friends a user, any manager on the account can usually see a great deal of information about that user unless they have strict privacy settings. This can give the library much more information than the amount with which the user may feel comfortable. Assessment tools such as Page Insights and Twitter Analytics can provide even more information in the aggregate about the user base. Librarians must consider the implications of collecting that much data about students or the community. Dickson and Holley (2010) considered privacy in their research, but few others have recently looked at social media use through this lens.

Even with all of the analytics tools available to librarians today, these may not be sufficient for measuring engagement. Assessment and evaluation are an important aspect of the marketing cycle, and libraries currently can't determine outcomes that may be more complicated than reach or impressions. Engagement is about connection with individuals, and a gap exists for measuring engagement in social media.

Another issue that carries with it an opportunity is the concept of using social media to incorporate participatory culture for collective knowledge creation. One promise of Web 2.0 was that users could communally build knowledge together. A participatory culture is one that breaks down the hegemonic imposition of cultural and structural barriers on knowledge. Deodato (2014) discusses how libraries are considered the organizers of knowledge, but through collection development, classification, and restriction of access, they are actually creators of knowledge that support, or choose to subvert, the cultural hegemony. The proliferation of Web 2.0 was thought to subvert the top-down hierarchical creation of knowledge by letting users become involved in that creation. For example, websites like Yahoo Answers allow for the creation of collective knowledge where users can post questions, answer others' questions, and rate answers. This could be possible in social media, allowing for more participation from users in the communal creation of knowledge, growing beyond engagement into something more inclusive.

The rapid growth of social media over the past decade has created new opportunities for academic libraries to bridge the gap between the online and offline realms. At the moment, libraries that incorporate engagement into their social media strategies are one-off success stories rather than trends that are taking off. This is an opportunity for libraries to move beyond broadcasting our promotional messages into the social media void, while considering the questions surrounding privacy, assessment, and participatory culture. Building connections and having conversations with students, faculty, and the community to develop relationships, improve real-world services and resources, affect policy, and meet target goals can improve the social media experience for librarians, patrons, and the community.

REFERENCES

Adams Becker, S., Cummins, M., Davis, A., Freeman, A., Hall Giesinger, C., & Ananthanarayanan, V. (2017). *NMC Horizon Report: 2017 Higher Education Edition*. Austin, TX: The New Media Consortium.

Aharony, N. (2010). Twitter use in libraries: An exploratory analysis. *Journal of Web Librarianship*, *4*(4), 333–350. doi:10.1080/19322909.2010.487766

Attfield, S., Kazai, G., Lalmas, M., & Piwowarski, B. (2011, February). Towards a science of user engagement (position paper). *WSDM workshop on user modelling for Web applications*. Retrieved from: http://www.dcs.gla.ac.uk/~mounia/Papers/engagement.pdf

Ayu, A. R., & Abrizah, A. (2011). Do you Facebook? Usage and applications of Facebook page among academic libraries in Malaysia. *The International Information & Library Review*, *43*(4), 239–249. doi: 10.1080/10572317.2011.10762906

Booker, L., & Bandyopadhyay, S. (2017). How academic libraries can leverage social networking to popularize their services: An empirical study. *Journal of the Indiana Academy of the Social Sciences*, *16*(2), 129–146. Retrieved from https://digitalcommons.butler.edu/jiass/vol16/iss2/12/

Burkhardt, A. (2010, January). Social media: A guide for college and university libraries. *College & Research Libraries News*. Retrieved from https://crln.acrl.org/index.php/crlnews/article/view/8302/8391

Chu, S. K. W., & Du, H. S. (2013). Social networking tools for academic libraries. *Journal of Librarianship and Information Science*, *45*(1), 64–75. doi:10.1177/0961000611434361

Chua, A. Y., & Goh, D. H. (2010). A study of Web 2.0 applications in library websites. *Library & Information Science Research*, *32*(3), 203–211. doi:10.1016/j.lisr.2010.01.002

Chugh, R., & Ruhi, U. (2018). Social media in higher education: A literature review of Facebook. *Education and Information Technologies*, *23*(2), 605–616. doi:10.100710639-017-9621-2

De Rosa, C., Cantrell, J., Havens, A., Hawk, J., & Jenkins, L. (2007). *Sharing, privacy, and trust in our networked world: A report to the OCLC membership*. Dublin, OH: OCLC Online Computer Library Center. Retrieved from https://www.oclc.org/content/dam/oclc/reports/pdfs/sharing.pdf

Del Bosque, D., Leif, S. A., & Skarl, S. (2012). Libraries atwitter: Trends in academic library tweeting. *RSR. Reference Services Review*, *40*(2), 199–213. doi:10.1108/00907321211228246

Deodato, J. (2014). The patron as producer: Libraries, Web 2.0, and participatory culture. *The Journal of Documentation*, *70*(5), 734–758. doi:10.1108/JD-10-2012-0127

Dickson, A., & Holley, R. P. (2010). Social networking in academic libraries: The possibilities and the concerns. *New Library World*, *111*(11), 468–479. doi:10.1108/03074801011094840

Gonzalez, C., Marks, G. J., & Westgate, H. (2018). *Social media directory of academic libraries*. Retrieved from: https://sites.google.com/wpunj.edu/nj-social-media-directory/home

Gustafson, J. C., Sharrow, Z., & Short, G. (2017). Library marketing on a small liberal arts campus: Assessing communication preferences. *Journal of Library Administration*, *57*(4), 420–435. doi:10.1080/01930826.2017.1300459

Harris, P. (2016). Drinking from the fire hose: Social media on campus. *Security Technology Executive*, 32-34. Retrieved from: https://search-proquest-com.du.idm.oclc.org/docview/1777246161?accountid=14608

Harrison, A., Burress, R., Velasquez, S., & Schreiner, L. (2017). Social media use in academic libraries: A phenomenological study. *Journal of Academic Librarianship*, *43*(3), 248–256. doi:10.1016/j.acalib.2017.02.014

Hendrix, D., Chiarella, D., Hasman, L., Murphy, S., & Zafron, M. L. (2009). Use of Facebook in academic health sciences libraries. *Journal of the Medical Library Association: JMLA*, *97*(1), 44–47. doi:10.3163/1536-5050.97.1.008 PMID:19159005

Instagram. (n.d.). *What are Instagram Insights?* Retrieved from: https://help.instagram.com/788388387972460

Jansen, A. (2017). Likes, shares and follows: Launching a Facebook page for your academic library. *JLAMS, 13*(1), 1-12. Retrieved from: https://scholarsarchive.library.albany.edu/jlams/vol13/iss1/6/

Johnson, C., & Burclaff, N. (2013, April). Making social media meaningful: Connecting missions and policies. In *Imagine, innovate, inspire: Proceedings of the ACRL 2013* (pp. 10–13). Conference. Retrieved from http://www.ala.org/acrl/sites/ala.org.acrl/files/content/conferences/confsandpreconfs/2013/papers/JohnsonBurclaff_Making.pdf

Junco, R., Heiberger, G., & Loken, E. (2011). The effect of Twitter on college student engagement and grades. *Journal of Computer Assisted Learning*, *27*(2), 119–132. doi:10.1111/j.1365-2729.2010.00387.x

Kim, H. M., Abels, E. G., & Yang, C. C. (2012). Who disseminates academic library information on Twitter? *Proceedings of the American Society for Information Science and Technology, 49*(1), 1–4. doi:10.1002/meet.14504901317

Koerwer, S. (2007). Commentary—One teenager's advice to adults on how to avoid being creepy on Facebook. *Computers in Libraries, 27*(8), 40. Retrieved from https://search-proquest-com.du.idm.oclc.org/docview/231113980?accountid=14608

Luo, L., Wang, Y., & Han, L. (2013). Marketing via social media: A case study. *Library Hi Tech, 31*(3), 455–466. doi:10.1108/LHT-12-2012-0141

Nielsen, J. (2006). *The 90-9-1 rule for participation inequality in social media and online communities.* Retrieved from: https://www. nngroup. com/articles/participation-inequality

Nonprofits on Facebook. (n.d.). *Page insights.* Retrieved from: https://nonprofits.fb.com/topic/page-insights/

O'Reilly, T. (2005). *What is Web 2.0: design patterns and business models for the next generation of software.* Retrieved from: https://www.oreilly.com/pub/a/web2/archive/what-is-web-20.html

Omeluzor, S. U., Oyovwe-Tinuoye, G. O., & Abayomi, I. (2016). Social networking tools in library service delivery: The case of academic libraries in South-East Zone of Nigeria. *DESIDOC Journal of Library and Information Technology, 36*(5), 269–277. doi:10.14429/djlit.36.5.10174

Pew Research Center. (2018, February 5). *Mobile fact sheet.* Retrieved from: http://www.pewinternet.org/fact-sheet/mobile/

Pew Research Center. (2018, March 1). *Social media use in 2018.* Retrieved from: http://www.pewinternet.org/2018/03/01/social-media-use-in-2018/

Potter, N. (2012). *The library marketing toolkit.* London: Facet Publishing. doi:10.29085/9781856048897

Ramsey, E., & Vecchione, A. (2014). Engaging library users through a social media strategy. *Journal of Library Innovation, 5*(2), 71–82. Retrieved from http://citeseerx.ist.psu.edu/viewdoc/download?doi=10.1.1.679.6263&rep=rep1&type=pdf

Sachs, D. E., Eckel, E. J., & Langan, K. A. (2011). Striking a balance: Effective use of Facebook in an academic library. *Internet Reference Services Quarterly, 16*(1-2), 35–54. doi:10.1080/10875301.2011.572457

Sriram, V. (2016). Social media and library marketing: Experiences of KN Raj Library. *DESIDOC Journal of Library and Information Technology, 36*(3), 153–157. doi:10.14429/djlit.36.3.9810

Stewart, B., & Walker, J. (2018). Build it and they will come? Patron engagement via Twitter at historically black college and university libraries. *Journal of Academic Librarianship, 44*(1), 118–124. doi:10.1016/j.acalib.2017.09.016

Stewart, M. C., Atilano, M., & Arnold, C. L. (2017). Improving customer relations with social listening: A case study of an American academic library. *International Journal of Customer Relationship Marketing and Management, 8*(1), 49–63. doi:10.4018/IJCRMM.2017010104

Stvilia, B., & Gibradze, L. (2014). What do academic libraries tweet about, and what makes a library tweet useful? *Library & Information Science Research*, *36*(3-4), 136–141. doi:10.1016/j.lisr.2014.07.001

Stvilia, B., & Gibradze, L. (2017). Examining undergraduate students' priorities for academic library services and social media communication. *Journal of Academic Librarianship*, *43*(3), 257–262. doi:10.1016/j.acalib.2017.02.013

Thomsett-Scott, B. C. (Ed.). (2013). *Marketing with social media: A LITA guide*. Chicago: American Library Association.

Twitter for Business. (n.d.). *How to use Twitter Analytics*. Retrieved from: https://business.twitter.com/en/analytics.html

Vucovich, L. A., Gordon, V. S., Mitchell, N., & Ennis, L. A. (2013). Is the time and effort worth it? One library's evaluation of using social networking tools for outreach. *Medical Reference Services Quarterly*, *32*(1), 12–25. doi:10.1080/02763869.2013.749107 PMID:23394417

We Are Social. (n.d.). Most popular social networks worldwide as of July 2018, ranked by number of active users (in millions). *Statista—The Statistics Portal*. Retrieved from https://www.statista.com/statistics/272014/global-social-networks-ranked-by-number-of-users/

Wilkinson, J. (2018). Accessible, dynamic web content using Instagram. *Information Technology and Libraries*, *37*(1), 19–26. doi:10.6017/ital.v37i1.10230

Young, S. W. H., & Rossmann, D. (2015). Building library community through social media. *Information Technology and Libraries*, *34*(1), 20–37. doi:10.6017/ital.v34i1.5625

Youtube Creator Academy. (n.d.). *Get insights with Youtube Analytics*. Retrieved from: https://creatoracademy.youtube.com/page/course/analytics-series?hl=en

Zhu, X., & Bao, Z. (2018). Why people use social networking sites passively: An empirical study integrating impression management concern, privacy concern, and SNS fatigue. *Aslib Journal of Information Management*, *70*(2), 158–175. doi:10.1108/AJIM-12-2017-0270

ADDITIONAL READING

Bess, M., Wu, S. K., & Price, B. (2015). 49er alerts: Utilizing mobile marketing technology for library outreach. *Public Services Quarterly*, *11*(4), 291–299. doi:10.1080/15228959.2015.1088816

Brookbank, E. (2015). So much social media, so little time: Using student feedback to guide academic library social media strategy. *Journal of Electronic Resources Librarianship*, *27*(4), 232–247. doi:10.1080/1941126X.2015.1092344

Collins, G., & Quan-Haase, A. (2014). Are social media ubiquitous in academic libraries? A longitudinal study of adoption and usage patterns. *Journal of Web Librarianship*, *8*(1), 48–68. doi:10.1080/19322909.2014.873663

Cuddy, C., Graham, J., & Morton-Owens, E. G. (2010). Implementing Twitter in a health sciences library. *Medical Reference Services Quarterly*, *29*(4), 320–330. doi:10.1080/02763869.2010.518915 PMID:21058176

Gardois, P., Colombi, N., Grillo, G., & Villanacci, M. C. (2012). Implementation of Web 2.0 services in academic, medical and research libraries: A scoping review. *Health Information and Libraries Journal*, *29*(2), 90–109. doi:10.1111/j.1471-1842.2012.00984.x PMID:22630358

Garofalo, D. (2013). *Building communities: Social networking for academic libraries*. Cambridge, UK: Chandos Publishing. doi:10.1533/9781780634012

Grieve, R., Indian, M., Witteveen, K., Tolan, G. A., & Marrington, J. (2013). Face-to-face or Facebook: Can social connectedness be derived online? *Computers in Human Behavior*, *29*(3), 604–609. doi:10.1016/j.chb.2012.11.017

Palmer, S. (2014). Characterizing university library use of social media: A case study of Twitter and Facebook from Australia. *Journal of Academic Librarianship*, *40*(6), 611–619. doi:10.1016/j.acalib.2014.08.007

Phillips, N. K. (2011). Academic library use of Facebook: Building relationships with students. *Journal of Academic Librarianship*, *37*(6), 512–522. doi:10.1016/j.acalib.2011.07.008

Swanson, T. (2012). *Managing social media in libraries: Finding collaboration, coordination, and focus*. Cambridge, UK: Chandos Publishing. doi:10.1533/9781780633770

Tarantino, K., McDonough, J., & Hua, M. (2013). Effects of student engagement with social media on student learning: A review of literature. *The Journal of Technology in Student Affairs*, *1*(8), 1–8. Retrieved from http://studentaffairs.com/ejournal/Summer_2013/EffectsOfStudentEngagementWithSocialMedia.html

Tomcik, L. (2015). Tying it all together: Utilizing market research to inform a marketing plan and further library branding. *Public Services Quarterly*, *11*(1), 59–65. doi:10.1080/15228959.2014.995856

Wan, G. (2011). How academic libraries reach users on Facebook. *College & Undergraduate Libraries*, *18*(4), 307–318. doi:10.1080/10691316.2011.624944

Wright, J. (2015). Assessment of social media in the library: Guidelines for administrators. *Journal of Library Administration*, *55*(8), 667–680. doi:10.1080/01930826.2015.1085251

This research was previously published in Social Media for Communication and Instruction in Academic Libraries; pages 1-16, copyright year 2019 by Information Science Reference (an imprint of IGI Global).

Chapter 102
Social Media–Based Data Collection and Analysis in Educational Research

Liuli Huang

Louisiana State University, USA

ABSTRACT

The past decades have brought many changes to education, including the role of social media in education. Social media data offer educational researchers first-hand insights into educational processes. This is different from most traditional and often obtrusive data collection methods (e.g., interviews and surveys). Many researchers have explored the role of social media in education, such as the value of social media in the classroom, the relationship between academic achievement and social media. However, the role of social media in educational research, including data collection and analysis from social media, has been examined to a far lesser degree. This study seeks to discuss the potential of social media for educational research. The purpose of this chapter is to illustrate the process of collecting and analyzing social media data through a pilot study of current math educational conditions.

INTRODUCTION

Due to rapidly increasing advances in technology, many of today's activities are carried out online. These include mundane tasks, such as shopping and business communications. Internet connectivity and smart devices in schools, homes, neighborhoods, and communities have become increasingly pervasive, enabling expanded opportunities for formal and informal learning. Moreover, technological advancements have contributed significantly to people's adoption of social media platforms, with approximately 90% adults using the Internet regularly - 100% of people aged 18-29, 97% of people aged 30-49, and 88% of people aged 50-64 (Pew Research Center, 2019). It is also reported that 95% of teens have access to a smartphone, and 45% say they are online almost constantly (Anderson & Jiang, 2018). The combination of computers, Internet access, smart digital technologies, and social media platforms are

DOI: 10.4018/978-1-6684-7123-4.ch102

moving the ecology of education to a new era (Pew Research Center, 2018). Such shifts have impacted constructs for learning, instruction, and paths for future research (Greenhow & Robelia, 2009). In this chapter, the author seeks to address the reasons for the popularity of social media, the role of social media in educational activities, as well as how to conduct educational research with social media-based data collection and analysis.

BACKGROUND

What Social Media Are and What Makes Them Popular

Social media refers to Internet tools and applications that allow users to share content and communicate with other users. Nowadays, most users utilize social media through applications (apps) which are installed on mobile devices, such as mobile phones, which allow for near real-time sharing of information. These apps tend to be free or very inexpensive and allow users unfiltered access to a broad community. In this sense, they meet a basic human need of connecting with others. They permit connectivity across geographic and even language boundaries, and are utilized to share day-to-day life activities in the form of texts and images, express opinions, follow and interact with the postings of others. Social media allow users to share the details of their lives as they unfold on a daily basis. These features have driven the usage rates of social media to unprecedented levels, with virtual communities that extend across the globe.

Social media are used by organizations, often as a way to communicate with customers, employees, and competitors. They are also used for advertisement, to inform others of events and happenings in their organizations, as a means of professional development, and as a tool to build community among workers and peers locally and internationally.

In education, the connectivity that social media offer has significant potential to enhance educational processes. Students can use social media to interact with teachers outside of the classroom, or join and connect with collaborative groups of learners at a local school or in another country (Erjavec, 2013; Garcia, Elbeltagi, Dungay, & Hardaker, 2015; Susilo & Kaufman, 2014). Teachers can use social media to communicate with colleagues about particular students, share learning resources, and engage in peer mentoring and collaborations (Bett & Makewa, 2018). Administrators can use social media to communicate directly with parents, interact with students and teachers, and conduct a host of administrative functions (Mazer, Murphy, & Simonds, 2007).

Research on Social Media in Education

Social media is now becoming a recognized part of the educational environment. Social media tools, such as MySpace, Facebook, Twitter, Edooware, YouTube, WeChat, and Web 2, have been extensively used for educational purposes. Based on a review of recent literature, the author identified three major areas of research on social media in education: (a) The values of implementing social media into classrooms, as well as the relationship between faculty and students via social media; (b) The relation between academic achievement and social media; and (c) The impact of social media environment on learners' expectation in learning.

Researchers have examined the educational value of social media in the classroom (Boyd, 2007; Lin, 2018; Manca & Ranieri, 2014; Ng'ambi, Brown, Bozalek, Gachago, & Wood, 2016; Prescott, Stodart,

Becket, & Wilson, 2015), including the use of social networks for teaching and learning in education (Albayrak & Yildirim, 2015; Bosch, 2009; McMillan & Morrison, 2006; Gitonga, Muuro, & Onyango, 2016; Selwyn, 2007), and educators' attitudes towards social media (e.g., Facebook, Twitter) as an educational tool (O'Bannon & Thomas, 2014). The investigation of the relationship between students and faculty through social media shows that students' access to the social media of a teacher/professor could lead to higher levels of classroom participation and motivation in learning (Hewitt & Forte, 2006; Karl & Peluchette, 2011; Mazer, Murphy, & Simonds, 2007). Other researchers explored the relationship between academic achievement and social media (Al-Rahmi & Othman, 2013; Heiberger, & Loken, 2011; Junco, 2012; Junco; Yang, Wang, Woo, & Quek, 2011).

Moreover, social media make learning anytime, anywhere, any methods, and with anyone available. It has been found that social media affect learners' expectations about the availability of information, the ways in which learning takes place, as well as the methods they express and communicate feelings. Social media allow new access points to knowledge, real-time sharing, and just-in-time searching (Pew Research Center, 2011).

In addition, the accessibility of collaboration and interaction via social media regardless of location and time facilitates the educational process. Collaboration is considered one of the top skills for students, following math, science, and reading (Organization for Economic Cooperation and Development, 2003). The ability of collaboration/team-based learning has received much attention from researchers, scholars, and employers, as well (Junco et al., 2011). Active collaborative learning through social media should be encouraged in the learning and teaching process in higher education institutions (Al-Rahmi, Alias, Othman, Marin, Tur., 2018). The collaboration/team-based learning is also proved to improve academic performance significantly (Blanche, Jeffrey, & Virginia, 2013).

To conclude, it should be noted that the social influence, the information quality, and the facilitation from social media are the critical and direct determinants that affect users' continuous intention to use social media in learning, which provides a positive base for the continuous use of social media (Wu & Chen, 2015). Relatedly, students' satisfaction with the social media (i.e., positive user experience) also positively affects students' learning performance (Al-Rahmi et al., 2018). For example, the fun, enjoyable interaction in social media (Edooware) could improve students' perception of their learning experience (Balakrishnan, Liew, & Pourgholaminejad, 2015).

The Availability of Social Media Platform and Data in the Educational Setting

It has been widely acknowledged that social media offer researchers the opportunity to observe human behaviors in real time on a global scale. Social media are arguably the most extensive observational data source of human behavior to date (Mccormick, Lee, Cesare, Shojaie, & Spiro, 2017). Thus, social media-based data collection and analysis for social science research, including educational research, is growing.

The frequent use of social media platforms (e.g., Twitter), the availability of technology for data collection from social media, together with extensive data regarding educational topics or schooling life through social media make educational research with social media-based data collection and analysis possible.

Twitter data are abundant and relatively easy to access. Twitter users are approximately 269.6 million worldwide (Clement, 2019), with over 69 million Twitter users in the U.S., and roughly 46% of whom are on the platform daily (Omnicore, 2019). Importantly, most of the data (i.e., tweets, retweets, and likes) are unprotected, meaning that all these published contents are available for view to all Web users. This published material is considered public data.

Besides the text tweets, retweets, and likes, Twitter has an influential hashtag culture. Indeed, a word or phrase that follows a pound sign is used to identify posts on social media, which makes it easier gathering, sorting, and expanding searches focusing on a particular topic, when collecting data (Barbee, 2018). Moreover, Twitter allows researchers to examine people's responses and attitudes to a particular policy immediately, in ways researchers would not be able to do on such a large scale with a survey or other research methods.

Finally, a considerable amount of data about educational settings are available through social media. Education institutions are adapting their systems to incorporate social media (Education Technology, 2018). Institutions communicate campus news, make announcements, share supportive posts, and initiate an online discussion about education-related topics via YouTube, Twitter, and Facebook. Institutions can find out how the majority of people feel about a particular topic or how experts perceive and advance on specific issues. As a result, the tweets, retweets, mentions, and public tweets containing keywords from a Twitter profile, and posts, comments, likes, and shares from Facebook reveal what people are saying and the trend, and provide insights for educators and researchers to develop educational practice, policies, and strategies.

Methods of Social Media Data Collection

What Are the Techniques for Social Media Data Collection

There are primarily three ways to obtain large-scale data on social media platforms (Liang & Zhu, 2017). Firstly, the most direct way is to download the data from databases on Web servers. This kind of data is known as "log-file" data, which is not visible on Web pages. Thus, it is difficult to get this kind of data, unless researchers have close collaborations with social media companies.

The second method is Web scraping. This method is particularly useful for those Web sites that do not provide application programming interfaces (APIs). Web scraping involves writing computer programs to do what people do manually when they select, copy, and paste automatically. People parse the Web pages, extract the needed information, and organize the data in csv, excel, or txt format, which are common data formats that can be imported to most statistics software.

The third method is to collect data through APIs. APIs are special URLs that Web owners intentionally provide for developers to download data from their databases. The API is the most popular way to collect social media data today, which is also the method used in this study. Related queries are sent to social media with the API to collect large-scale data. Then, a file (usually a txt format file) including all the related contents is generated.

What Are the Strategies for Social Media Data Collection

Social media data are the collected information from social networks that show how users share, view or engage with user content or profiles (Banhart, 2018). Social media data are composed of quantitative and qualitative data. In the case of Twitter's data, the quantitative data usually include the number of tweets, retweets, and likes, while the qualitative data include tweets and comments.

For traditional educational research, qualitative, quantitative or mixed-methods (i.e., both quantitative and qualitative) data analysis are the most common methods to analyze educational researches; indeed, they have been used in educational research for decades (Creswell & Plano, 2007). However, these research methods are usually determined based on research designs. Some researchers suggested to use the mixed model of data analysis for research designs which integrate qualitative and quantitative data (Driscoll, Salib, & Rupert, 2007). Thus, the mixed model of data analysis, modified from the traditional mixed methods of data analysis, could be used for educational research, since the data collected from social media are composed of both qualitative and quantitative types.

Based on a combination of the traditional educational methods, as well as the availability of in-time big data from social media, the author applied an ensemble of two mixed methods of data collection in this study. Indeed, the author used both the sequential and the concurrent mixed method of data collection to validate one form of data with the other form, and to address different types of questions, as well as to provide more data about results from an earlier phase of the data collection and analysis (Creswell & Plano, 2007).

Social Media Data Analysis for Educational Research

In this study, the data analysis was composed of several phases, given the unpredictable content and comments data the author collected from social media. Firstly, the author quantified the qualitative data (data transformation) by clustering the raw unorganized text data (i.e., tweets and comments) into several main themes related to the study, based on the frequency of each theme (Onwuegbuzie & Teddlie, 2003). After the data transformation, the author could use the descriptive technique to explore the importance of each theme.

Next, after determining the main themes for this study, the author used the sequential mixed method of data collection to collect more data for each particular theme (Driscoll et al., 2007). During this phase, the author quantified the qualitative data by counting the frequency, or the percentage of people sharing the same attitudes toward a specific theme (Onwuegbuzie & Teddlie, 2003).

Furthermore, besides the traditional quantitative and qualitative data analysis, the author applied sentiment analysis to determine people's attitudes toward each of the theme, either positive, negative, or neutral. Sentiment analysis, which is otherwise known as opinion mining, is extremely useful in social media monitoring, as it allows researchers to gain an overview of the wider public opinion behind certain topics (Bannister, 2018). Social media such as Twitter and Facebook have become essential broadcasting platforms for institutions and individuals. The information on these platforms is often unstructured text (e.g., tweets and comments), but yields valuable insights into preferences, likes and dislikes. Thus, sentiment analysis is a methodology for mining unstructured text to identify and pattern subjective users' opinions. Typically, sentiment analysis is used to determine whether a user's attitude toward a particular topic is positive, negative, or neutral. For each specific tweet, a sentiment score is generated regarding the user's attitude toward a particular topic or product (i.e., positive, negative, or neutral), based on the wording in the tweets. For example, the expression "it is easy (+1) and fun (+1) to learn math" generates a sentiment score of 2, while "I don't enjoy learning (-1) math since it is complicated (-1)" creates a sentiment score of -2. The presence of the word "don't" before "enjoy" produces a negative score, rather than a positive score.

A PILOT STUDY OF PEOPLE'S ATTITUDES TOWARD CURRENT MATH EDUCATIONAL PERFORMANCE IN THE U.S.

Purpose and Research Questions

The previous literature reveals that the study of social media in education is focused on how social media are utilized in educational settings or impact educational performance (Prescott et al., 2015). People's voice or feelings regarding educational topics and schooling life expressed via social media are rarely explored. These expressions, however, are valuable first-hand data, compared to the traditional data which are collected through interviews, observations, and surveys. In this study, the author seeks to demonstrate the process of collecting and analyzing social media data for educational research with a case study regarding people's attitudes toward the current math educational performance in the U.S.. The population for this study were all respondents to the topics, since math education is almost related to everyone in the U.S., including educators, students, researchers, and parents. The research questions are as follows:

1. Are the public's attitudes toward the current math educational performance in the U.S. positive, negative, or neutral? If negative, what are the major problems under debate?
2. What are the financial and human resources inputs of the current educational system?
3. What are the current educational policies regarding math education, and what are people's opinions toward these policies?

Querying Data Using Twitter's API

Twitter's universe consists of terabytes of data, far too much data for an individual researcher to review, thus an automated process is required. In the following example, the author used the programming language Python as the primary technique to collect and analyze data from Twitter's API. Instead of interviewing educators, students, and others about their education-related experiences or opinions, in this example the author illustrates how to formulate a query of Twitter's API and analyze the resulting data from a variety of groups, including educators, student, and parents.

Step 1: Obtaining Twitter's API Keys

In order to access Twitter's Streaming API, it is necessary to obtain the following API information from Twitter: API key, API secret, access token, and access token secret. Several online sources illustrate how to obtain Twitter's API keys (Moujahid, 2014).

Step 2: Determining the Keywords of the Topics

This step narrows down the targets for the data of interest. The keywords the author selected for this illustration were "math education." This served as the first screener and as a means for obtaining a general idea about the topics and trends regarding math education. The author writes a Python program to select recent tweets containing "math" or "education," or both words. For purpose of this example, the author limited the count to 30,000 instances.

Step 3: Data Collection

The author settled on a total of 8885 tweets related to the keywords above. Raw data are unstructured in the txt format. This data set is relatively small, but serves the purpose of this example (i.e., removing irrelevant tweets). Figure 1 is a screenshot of how the data (one tweet) looked like. For example, this tweet was "created at" "Sun Mar 31 08:18:27," and the "id" was "1112267903057969158."

Figure 1. The screenshot of txt format data collected from Twitter's API programmed with Python

```
{"created_at": "Sun Mar 31 08:18:27 +0000 2019", "id": 1112267903057969158, "id_str":
"1112267903057969158", "full_text": "RT @theworldindex: Math and science education quality, 2017.
(out of 137 countries)
\n\n1.\ud83c\uddf8\ud83c\uddecSIN\n2.\ud83c\uddeb\ud83c\uddeeFIN\n3.\ud83c\udde8\ud83c\uddedSUI\n\n4

\ud83c\uddf1\ud83c\udde7LIB\n5.\ud83c\uddf3\ud83c\uddf1NED\n6.\ud83c\uddf6\ud83c\udde6QAT\n10.\ud83c
\uddfa\ud83c\uddf8\u2026", "truncated": false, "display_text_range": [0, 140], "entities":
{"hashtags": [], "symbols": [], "user_mentions": [{"screen_name": "theworldindex", "name": "World
Index", "id": 938419883745869824, "id_str": "938419883745869824", "indices": [3, 17]}], "urls": []},
"metadata": {"iso_language_code": "en", "result_type": "recent"}, "source": "<a href=\"http://
twitter.com/download/iphone\" rel=\"nofollow\">Twitter for iPhone</a>", "in_reply_to_status_id":
null, "in_reply_to_status_id_str": null, "in_reply_to_user_id": null, "in_reply_to_user_id_str":
null, "in_reply_to_screen_name": null, "user": {"id": 97042767, "id_str": "97042767", "name":
"quartetist", "screen_name": "tribeca71", "location": "Istanbul/Toronto", "description": "Serk's
Quartet : Questions , Knowledge, Truth, Faith", "url": "https://t.co/MCxIXMeR37", "entities":
{"url": {"urls": [{"url": "https://t.co/MCxIXMeR37", "expanded_url": "http://www.cafequartet.com",
"display_url": "cafequartet.com", "indices": [0, 23]}]}, "description": {"urls": []}}, "protected":
false, "followers_count": 116, "friends_count": 1166, "listed_count": 1, "created_at": "Tue Dec 15
19:20:20 +0000 2009", "favourites_count": 3773, "utc_offset": null, "time_zone": null,
"geo_enabled": true, "verified": false, "statuses_count": 410, "lang": "en", "contributors_enabled":
false, "is_translator": false, "is_translation_enabled": false, "profile_background_color":
"C0DEED", "profile_background_image_url": "http://abs.twimg.com/images/themes/theme1/bg.png",
"profile_background_image_url_https": "https://abs.twimg.com/images/themes/theme1/bg.png",
"profile_background_tile": false, "profile_image_url": "http://pbs.twimg.com/profile_images/
882605721514278916/D0qNuftX_normal.jpg", "profile_image_url_https": "https://pbs.twimg.com/
profile_images/882605721514278916/D0qNuftX_normal.jpg", "profile_banner_url": "https://
pbs.twimg.com/profile_banners/97042767/1361215174", "profile_link_color": "1DA1F2",
"profile_sidebar_border_color": "C0DEED", "profile_sidebar_fill_color": "DDEEF6",
"profile_text_color": "333333", "profile_use_background_image": true, "has_extended_profile": false,
"default_profile": true, "default_profile_image": false, "following": false, "follow_request_sent":
false, "notifications": false, "translator_type": "none"}, "geo": null, "coordinates": null,
"place": null, "contributors": null, "retweeted_status": {"created_at": "Fri Mar 29 19:09:28 +0000
2019", "id": 1111706959395332097, "id_str": "1111706959395332097", "full_text": "Math and science
education quality, 2017. (out of 137 countries)
\n\n1.\ud83c\uddf8\ud83c\uddecSIN\n2.\ud83c\uddeb\ud83c\uddeeFIN\n3.\ud83c\udde8\ud83c\uddedSUI\n\n4
```

Step 4: Data Cleaning with Python

The author used a Python program to clean and finalize the data. Due to the idiosyncratic and temporal nature of text information on Twitter, the author loosely monitored the tweets during the initial data collection process. The author removed the irrelevant tweets—which compose the minority of the total body of data collected—during the following data preprocessing steps. Then, the author organized and transformed the final data into a data frame with sample size n = 8885 and 17 columns. More than 300 columns were present, while only 17 variables (columns) were of interest to this study. The variables were as follows:

- **Created At:** UTC time when the tweet was created.
- **Entities Hashtags:** The hashtags indicate the category of the Tweet topic.
- **Favorite Count:** The number of times this Tweet has been liked.
- **Full Text:** The content of the Tweet.
- **id_str:** The unique identifier of the Tweet.

- **lang:** The machine detected the language of the Tweet text.
- **Retweet Count:** The number of times this Tweet has been retweeted approximately.
- **Retweeted Status Favorite Count:** The number of times the source Tweet has been liked.
- **Retweeted Status Full Text:** The content of the retweet.
- **User Created At:** UTC time the Twitter user was created.
- **User Description:** The description about the Twitter user.
- **User Favourite Count:** The number of times this Twitter user has been liked.
- **User Followers Count:** The number of followers this Twitter user has.
- **User Following:** The number of followings this Twitter user has followed.
- **User Friends Count:** The number of friends this Twitter user has.
- **User id_str:** The unique identifier of the Tweeter user.
- **User Name:** The name of the user.

DATA ANALYSIS

Among the 8885 tweets, a total of 3429 different tweets were generated from 6994 unique users. The tweets were created from March 21 to March 31. Since social media data are time sensitive, knowing the time of the tweets could be connected to the particular context about what was happening in the world then, which would help explain the behaviors better.

In addition, most of the tweets were generated on Wednesdays and Saturday.

Furthermore, the peak time of Twitter usage of a day was around 2:00 pm. Thus, the greatest time for the users to raise a topic discussion was on Wednesday or Saturday around 2:00 pm. The information about when people send tweets about a particular topic and comment on the tweets is important for behavior research, but almost impossible to collect with conventional surveys.

Figure 2. The distribution of the number of tweets & retweets during the time the data was collected in dates

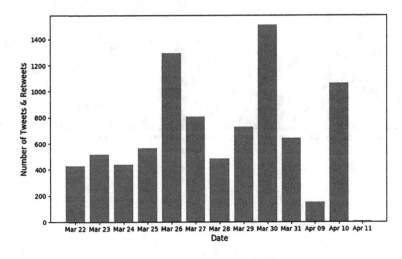

Figure 3. The distribution of the number of tweets & retweets during the time the data was collected in week time

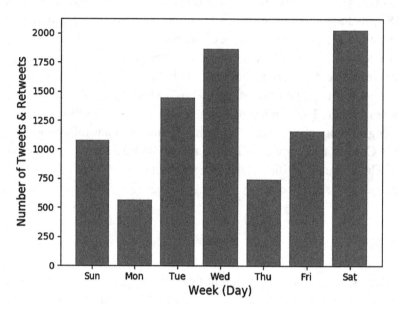

Figure 4. The distribution of the number of tweets & retweets during the time the data was collected in hours

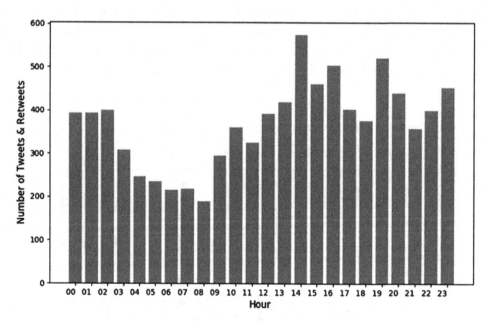

Quantitative Data Analysis for Participants in This Study (Twitter Users)

The number of followers, friends (followings), and favorites from social media platforms are good indicators of the impact of the users. For the 6994 unique users, Table 1 provides descriptive information for the number of followers, friends, and favorites, and the users have an average of 4382 followers, 1461 friends, and 14381 favorites. In conclusion, evidence shows that the participants in this study are influential users whose voice would make a significant impact on the educational system.

Table 1. Descriptive of users' followers, friends, and the total number of favorites

	Count	Mean	Std	Min	25%	50%	75%	Max
Followers	6994	4382	52,415	0	92	315	1,028	3,079,499
Friends	6994	1461	8,794	0	166	405	1,042	399,229
Favorites	6994	14381	35,948	0	597	3,139	12,173	785,427

With the significant impact of social media and emerging technology, any user could interact with particular institutions or individuals around the world via Twitter, even without knowing each other. For the 8885 tweets from 6994 unique users in this example, 729 users were mentioned or retweeted. The most frequent referred user is Norbert Elekes, a storyteller with data, minimalist, and habitual list-maker, who was mentioned 1341 times, with 52,300 followers.

Figure 5 shows the followers of Twitter users who were involved in this study. The number of followers ranged from 0 to 3,079,499. The author categorized this discrete variable into six clusters, including 0-100, 100-300, 300-500, 500-1,000, 1,000-10,000, and 10,000-40,000. The author did not assign these clusters evenly, with the purpose to focus on the extreme users. For example, some users had a comparatively large impact on the discussion of a particular topic, 11.4% of whom involving 1,000-10,000 followers, and about 5.1% of whom containing more than 10,000 followers, up to 3,079,499. Meanwhile, some of the users cared about this topic and were also important to this topic, such as parents and students, about 25.6% of whom including 0 to 100 followers.

Table 2 provides user name, number of followers, and description information for the top 25 influential users, containing more than 188,000 followers. The description provides insight about the user's background, major role in society, or purpose. These users or organizations were from a variety of areas, including education (e.g., Education.com and U.S. News Education), emerging technology (e.g., Big Data Talks), express (e.g., The Indian Express and Financial Express), agriculture (e.g., Peace Corps), women (e.g., Refinery29), and art (e.g., 947).

The quantitative data analysis focused on exploring the number of followers, favorites, and friends for each user. The results revealed that most of the participants in this study were either influential with a large number of followers, or critical to this discussion, which sets a basis for the value of the research with social media-based data collection.

Figure 5. The Twitter users are clustered into several groups based on their number of followers. The pie chart illustrates the percentage of Twitter users in each group.

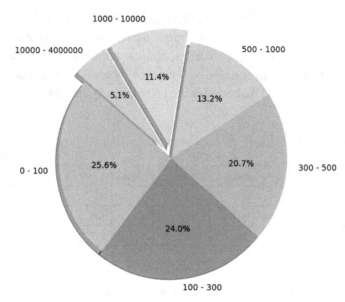

Table 2. The 25 most influential users involved in this study

N.	User Name	Followers	Description
1	The Indian Express @IndianExpress	3,079,499	The Indian Express brings to you latest news from India and the world, breaking round the clock. The "Journalism of Courage" starts here.
2	Peace Corps @PeaceCorps	1,511,918	If you are inspired by global impact that is hands-on, grassroots-driven, and lasting, get to know us.
3	Refinery29 @Refinery29	1,321,989	The catalyst for women to feel, see, and claim their power. We cover news, fashion, beauty, entertainment, wellness, and more.
4	Education.com @Education_com	1,016,699	We offer free + paid printables, lesson plans, and activities to help nurture each child's passion and curiosity (for parents + teachers!). Also @Preschoolers
5	The Spectator Index @spectatorindex	985,436	Watching the world. Focused on politics, economics, history, military affairs, sports, science, and technology.
6	CMEGroup @CMEGroup	690,430	The world's most diverse financial marketplace made up of CME, CBOT, NYMEX, COMEX, and KCBT.
7	Microsoft Azure @Azure	663,115	The official account for Microsoft Azure. Follow for news and updates from the #Azure team and community.
8	Financial Express @FinancialXpress	512,419	The #FinancialExpress - A complete up-to-date source for business news, #finance news, #stockmarket news, #economy, & #financial news online.
9	Detroit Free Press @freep	463,172	Breaking news, analysis, and chatter from Detroit and around Michigan. w/ @BrianManzullo, @lissa218, @twildt, @AEtmansHuschka and the @freep Web team. On Guard.
10	Bobby Umar | Keynote Speaker @raehanbobby	453,864	5x @TEDx | Inc Mag Top 100 Speaker, Heart-Leader, Networking, Personal Brand & Parenting. Author, @HuffPostWriter, TV Host, Comedy Actor, GMAT pro, Daddy
11	Mohandas Pai @TVMohandasPai	450,386	A global citizen and a Bangalorean at heart. Chairman at Aarin Capital | Co-founder

continues on following page

Table 2. Continued

N.	User Name	Followers	Description
12	RTtheBEST @RTtheBEST	428,446	#Videos #Photos #Music #Sports #Tech #Pets #Art & more!
13	The Wire @thewire_in	410,110	We are India's foremost independent news-site, carrying critical opinion, investigations, and reportage.
14	Amitabh Kant @amitabhk87	383,373	CEO,Niti Aayog,GOI. Author-Branding India: An Incredible Story. Driver of Make in India,Startup India,Incredible !ndia & God's Own Country campaigns.
15	947 @947	336,235	If you love Joburg, 947 loves you! #947Joburg Get your #HuaweiJoburgDayin the Park tickets now.
16	Big Data Talks @BigDataTalks	327,280	Big Data Talks estudia comunidades a través de sus conversaciones. Forma parte de @Mitofsky_group donde innovamos en investigación.
17	U.S. News Education @USNewsEducation	300,412	Education news and rankings from U.S. News & World Report.
18	Newsday @Newsday	292,266	Breaking news and daily discussion on the latest happenings on Long Island. Send news tips or questions and join the conversation.
19	Philly Inquirer @PhillyInquirer	280,990	Delivering the news since 1829. Winner of 20 Pulitzer Prizes.
20	The Quint @TheQuint	271,403	Mobile-first digital news platform. We are the signal over the noise.
21	ABC11 EyewitnessNews @ABC11_WTVD	270,634	ABC11 WTVD Eyewitness News Raleigh Durham Fayetteville.
22	Jennifer Rubin @JRubinBlogger	260,214	Conservative blogger at @WashingtonPost, MSNBC contributor, recovering lawyer and friend of @Israel.
23	Las Vegas RJ @reviewjournal	248,118	Worth talking about. Send news tips to atthescene@reviewjournal.com #RJnow
24	event di jabodetabek @EventJakartaCom	225,499	Event Media Partner In Jakarta, redaksi@eventjakarta.com, SMS/WA: 0821 3229 4600. Line ID: eventjakartacom
25	Cedar Point @cedarpoint	188,129	A Place Like No Other™. Home of Steel Vengeance - the TALLEST, FASTEST, WILDEST hyper-hybrid coaster ever!

Qualitative Data Analysis of Tweets

For the qualitative portion of the analysis, the author screened each of the 3429 tweets manually. The author removed some of the tweets which were not related to this topic, such as advertising new books about math, applying for a math activity, and school schedules including math class. The remaining tweets related to education and yielded a high frequency of discussion and retweets by diverse groups or populations. The populations included educational administrators, teachers, students, parents, etc. Views from many of these groups are difficult to collect through conventional data collection methods.

After the iterative and reflective process of reviewing tweets, the author developed five major themes relating to math education. The five major themes covered topics from the importance of math/STEM education, current educational inputs, process, and outputs to some particular hashtags under current educational reform, the efforts underway to improve education, as well as the trend of the future education. Each of the five major themes is discussed below.

Theme 1: Current Educational Output

The first theme was about current educational output, focusing on math. In general, perceptions of the current level of educational output regarding math is that it is unsatisfactory. This theme is composed of four subthemes: (1) Current educational performance; (2) The inequity/bias for underrepresented populations; (3) Students' poor math and reading abilities; (4) Some facts about charter schools. The first subtheme of current educational output lists the problems that exist in current math education, namely the high educational expenditure, but poor performance. Some of the tweets were as follows:

Spending on education has increased 180% over the past 40 years, accumulating to $1.2 trillion. The U.S. outpacing nearly every country in the world on per-student education spending; however, with very little to show for it.

The U.S. education performance dropped massively during the past two decades.

In an annual ranking of OECD countries, the United States ranked 40th in math, 24th in reading, and 25 in science.

In the latest Program for International Student Assessment (PISA) measuring math literacy in 2015, U.S. students ranked 40th in the world.

The sustainable "growth" in math education is a failure.

The second subtheme provides insights about the inequity/bias for underrepresented populations. Even though the input in education is enormous, still a considerable underrepresented population of students who do not have access to quality education.

There are approximately 57-264 MILLION kids who don't have access to an education, can't read or do basic math.

Despite the increase in access, very few children in sub-Saharan Africa reach minimum proficiency levels in reading, math or science.

The third subtheme is the description about current students' incompetence in math.

One in seven are not attaining minimum proficiency in reading and math in Europe and North America.

Today, they are hopeless thanks to the politicization of public education. Children can't read. They can't do basic math. Despite this failure, public schools ascribe to themselves a monopoly on education and money. Change, if it comes, has to come from INSIDE the system.

Teachers have the best technology in history, the least class sizes in history, and their wages are huge! Yet, math scores are abysmal! Why are we BEHIND India 2 years in math curriculum?

The last subtheme is about charter schools. Most parents want to send their children to charter schools. Nevertheless, the students' academic performance from charter schools are not as good as expected, and charter school students' academic progress is not up to those of traditional schools.

The report from the Center for Research on Education Outcomes at Stanford University shows Ohio charter school students had weaker academic progress in math than traditional students. They showed similar results in reading.

Theme 2: Current Educational Process

The second theme was about the current educational process. This theme focused on exploring users' opinions regarding the possible reasons why the current education system, especially math education fails from five aspects: (1) Qualified math teachers in low-performing schools are needed; (2) High cost for education; 3) Irrelevant or unhelpful coursework; 4) Math anxiety; and (5) The test-result driving educational system.

The first aspect was about math teacher quality, especially in low-performing schools. Some incentives are incorporated, but the impacts do not seem significant (Crowell, 2019).

Elementary math should be taught by math specialists.

The education reform of the last two decades has aimed to increase math teachers' knowledge and instructional quality. It seems that the effects were not significant.

The second reason was about the high cost for education, while the costs for math education and performance are not proportional. In addition, the high cost for campus infrastructure may not be highly correlated to math education.

Why is getting an education so freaking expensive. I don't need a luxury campus & amp… just to learn math.

Math scores are in the toilet, costs are skyrocketing, our children are less competitive.

The third reason leading to the failure of math education could be math anxiety. Math anxiety is prevalent, and math anxiety has a devastating effect on math education.

Partner with schools to eradicate math anxiety by leveraging technology.

When I decided to learn English education to avoid math, but then there's math subject at the last year.

Fear of math is in our air and water, and supported by our own system of education

Math is hard, my math anxiety…

The fourth reason could be the irrelevant or unhelpful coursework that "too much money is spent on education to value irrelevant or unhelpful coursework the way we do."

The last reason twitter users suggested could be about the test-result driving educational system. The educational policy of reinforcing standardized testing to hold schools accountable seems not to work, since math scores have been tumbling.

Research shows that an emphasis on memorization, rote procedures, and speed impairs learning and achievement,

High-stakes standardized testing teaches rote memorization and obedience. Effective education falls to the wayside as TX students are...

Competition in schools goes against the intent of education.

Effective leadership in education is not about moving everyone from 1 standardized point to the next, but moving individuals to their point A to their point B!

Standardized testing is one of the worst things created in math education. ...Nothing has been so harmful as this systemic weapon.

Theme 3: Hashtags for Educational Reform under Discussion

Theme three covered hot topics under discussion about educational reform. These topics are marked as hashtags from Twitter culture. The hashtags include #NoCutsToEducation, #IncreasingClassSize, and #DiscoveryMath. For each of the hashtags, the author conducted a second data query to gain insights into the new educational policy. Also, the author conducted sentiment analysis for each topic to determine the public's attitudes toward the particular topic. The three above-mentioned hashtags are detailed below:

- **Hashtage 1. #NoCutsToEducation:** The first hashtag under discussion was about funding, #NoCutsToEducation. People's opinions vary. Taxpayers may support the policy of funding cuts from education, while school administers, teachers, parents, and students are against the policy of funding cuts. The tweets below are examples of the attitudes participants expressed:

Spending on education has increased 180% over the past 40 years, accumulating to $1.2 trillion, but we are 24th in reading, 25th in science, and 40th in math, when compared to the rest of the world. Lack of money is not the problem, so let's STOP wasting the taxpayer's money.

$13 million cut will lead to the loss of special education teachers, educational assistants, social workers, behavioral assistant....

Cutting Federal education means students will get less funding (a short list) in the following list: 1) Intervention teachers to work with small groups of students; 2) reading & amp; math programs designed to help those behind; 3) teachers with the best training.

Taking dollars away means education will suffer.

The 9 billion cut in public education leads to the drop from 28 to 41 in reading and from 27 to 42 in math in Michigan.

No one in Ontario voted for $1.4B in cuts to education. I stand with my wife, an educator, and the students.

In the 2 weeks since your announcement, I visited 8 schools to take to over 500 teachers…, not 1 supports.

I don't think the provincial government fully appreciates just how angry parents and teachers are. And it's not just parents.

The author conducted a second data query focusing on #NoCutsToEducation. A total of 12,999 tweets were returned, while 4071 different contents were generated. The author screened the tweets manually. While most tweets were against the policy of cutting funding from education, some were in favor of funding cuts. The author carried out sentiment analysis regarding the #NoCutsToEducation. Among the 4071 tweets, 1610 tweets were positive (with a percentage of 39%), 571 tweets were neutral (with a percentage of 46%), while 1890 tweets were negative (with a percentage of 14%). Upon deeper examination, the tweets from the positive category indicated that people are taking actions to stop funding cuts to education. Examples of these tweets are as follows:

The amount of teachers and education support staff being laid off is frightening. Proud of our students for arranging a walkout tomorrow. We stand with you! Homeschooling will probably be in our near future.

Who is going to Queen's Park, on April 6 for the #NoCutsToEducation protest? Doug Ford is going to hear us roar. The students are doing their part tomorrow, now it is our turn. Our children deserve better than Doug Ford, Lisa Thompson, and their $1.4B in cuts.

Please meet with @LisaThompsonMPP and @fordnation to find ways to put students first.

Some important instructions regarding the #NoCutsToEducation Rally being held this Saturday, April 6.

Hey Peel Region! We are almost at 500 signatures online.

In addition, the tweets from the neutral category described people' intent to take action to stop the policy. The tweet of the highest frequency is "Who is going to XX Park, on XX for the #NoCutsToEducation protest? Doug Ford is going to hear us roar. The students …"

Moreover, the tweets from the negative category described the potential harm from the policy of funding cuts from education. These included loss of jobs for many teachers, larger class sizes, and mandatory online courses for high school students, which are not favored presently:

If HPEDSB has to cut the same amount of teachers,- I will be cut. If the board has to cut 60 teachers,- I will be cut. These cuts are not nameless.

This could be a terrible reality, if Ford gets his way.

Mandatory online courses for high school students "a terrible idea," expert says.

Making signs and dressing in black to protest against gov't cuts to education! Our students matter!

Changes to education will have negative impact in … [school].

In general, the discussion of hashtag #NoCutsToEducation showed most people participating in this discussion shared the same opinion. They were against the policy of cutting funding from education, since this policy would lead to job loss for teachers, larger class sizes, mandatory online courses for high school students, and inefficient use of resources. Sentiment analysis allowed to describe people' attitudes about this policy and group them into three categories: (1) The potential harm of cutting funding from education, (2) The intent to gather more people to make their voice influential, and (3) Taking actions to express their opinions to the public.

- **Hashtage 2. #ClassSizeMatters or #IncreasingClassSize:** The second hashtag was increasing the class size, #ClassSizeMatters. Almost all people were against the policy of larger class size. Some of the comments were: "Gov't is increasing class sizes to give students more challenges and an opportunity to build resilience and coping skills;" "class sizes to be increased at high school level, possible job losses for teachers; math, sex education to be overhauled;" "I know that smaller classes mean more time for connections with and between students. Connections create a positive learning environment. A great learning environment leads to a great public education. THAT is simple math."

The comments about #ClassSizeMatters were similar to those of #NoCutsToEducation, which is obvious because most people do not support this policy. A total of 111 tweets were returned with the keywords #ClassSizeMatters. Fifty-three of the tweets were positive (with a percentage of 47.7%), 44 of the tweets were neutral (with a portion of 39.6%), and 14 of the tweets were negative (with a percentage of 12.6%). Most of the tweets with the positive result described how a classroom of 40 looks like:

This is how a classroom of 40 looks; does this look like a good environment for learning?

I could only round up 25 bodies to photograph in my classroom so you'll have to imagine where I'd put 15 more.

This is what 40 bodies crammed into a biology lab looks like. This will soon be your child's reality in … schools! There is no way this is good for students. Please join us in saying no way to cuts to education.

In addition, the tweet with the most neutral attitude is "The difference between 25 and 40," suggesting how crowded a class of 40 students is.

Finally, negative tweets describe the potential harm of larger classes, which is similar to that of the policy of cutting funding from education.

Why don't you care about our kids? Cuts to education across this province will result in less opportunities for our children.

Such a sad statement on this province with the character of whom was chosen to run it. Clearly never valued a classroom.

In brief, it is clear that larger class sizes are not favored by the public and that this policy is related to the #NoCutToEducation. Cuts to education funding could lead to the larger class size.

- **Hashtage 3. #DiscoveryMath:** The third hashtag was about math learning strategy, namely #DiscoveryMath. "The NDP is failing Alberta's future generations. The UCP will focus on tried and true teaching methods, not fads like 'discovery math';" "check out our education plan that is focused on real results for students—not fads like 'discovery math';" "it's time to put away the failed teaching fads;" "our systemic embrace of discovery math has led to parents with interest and $$$ to get tutoring for kids."

The discussion showed that, when relating the policy DiscoveryMath to education, people's attitudes seemed negative. However, when digging the reason for the negative attitude toward DiscoveryMath, the author found that the negative attitude could result from the inequity of education. The author conducted a second query targeting #DiscoveryMath, resulting in a total of 30 tweets. People's attitudes were different when talking about the efficiency of DiscoveryMath. This conclusion could be supported from the following tweets: "Students are learning to construct models of prisms and pyramids using plasticine. The constructed accurate models using their 'touch' and knowledge of properties;" "exploring the parts of circle;" "exploring the relationship between perimeter, area, and our new measurement friend, volume."

In conclusion, the discussion about DiscoveryMath was disputable. When regarding implementing the policy of DiscoveryMath, people's attitudes were negative, since this policy is not accessible to most kids. However, regarding the efficiency of this policy, people's attitudes were positive. Thus, educators could try to make the best use of the positive effects, and try to improve access to DiscoveryMath.

Theme 4: Efforts Underway to Improve Education

A subset of the selected tweets addressed ways to improve math education. These included fun technologies, technology tools, and apps that could make math learning enjoyable. For example, "Ferguson HS in Miami is using xSpace for hands-on education through learning apps for science, technology, engineering, art, and math. Students can better visualize and understand abstract concepts, and collaborate in rich academic conversations." In addition, inspired by the Topobo, a robotic dog for children, educators are on a mission to bring playful tools for science and math learning to the far reaches of the world. Moreover, millions of games are available to enhance children's mathematical skills.

In addition to emerging technologies, some tweets addressed new curriculums, which are designed to increase students' academic performance. For example, "DPSCD is implementing a new curriculum that will help make students more competitive at the national level in the future."

Finally, math learning tips were also a subject of tweets in this category. The tips participants offered included the following: (1) Develop children's mathematical skills long before they enter school; (2) Early exposure to math helps kids grasp it more effectively, especially if English is their second language; (3)

Engage kids in real-world math; (4) Counting on fingers is an essential technique for early math development, as students see more success on fingers is an essential technique for early math development; and (5) Students see more success when they tackle math, science, and tech in early grades.

Theme 5: The Trend of Education

The tweets the author categorized into theme five focused on recommendations and future trends in education. For example: "The new trend in education should be STEAM (Science, Technology, Engineer, Arts, and Mathematics) instead of STEM." Typical tweets include "Time to turn STEAM into STEAM;" "a new study showed students who are exposed to the arts in school had significantly higher GPAs and math and reading scores;" "the arts are not important because they improve math scores, they are important because they speak to a child's wellbeing;" "There's evidence that arts classes can have significant benefits, especially for disadvantaged students;" "arts in education is as valuable as math, science, and reading;" "if we want students to excel in both the short and long term, both academically and behaviorally, the arts are not an expendable part of education;" "did you know that children develop pattern-recognition and math skills with the help of music education?" All these tweets support this statement. Even cooking is helpful in math, as these comments indicate: "Cooking is a health hobby plus, great help with math and reading skills;" and "arts education is not an 'extra'-it is necessary to great schooling."

RESULTS

In sum, the five themes the author discussed above provide a description of the current educational input, process, output, and future trends. Regarding the research questions, some problems exist in current math education, which raises an outcry in public. The most debating topic is the vast input, but poor output. Other topics raising outcry are funding cuts from education and increasing class size. The opinion is almost identical for most Twitter users, namely that the funding cut could lead to suffering in education, and the larger class sizes would result in inefficient learning. Among all the discussions about these topics, the root reasons for the poor output are yet to be confirmed. The tweets from users could provide some insights about the root reasons for the current educational conditions. "We fail to recognize the resources teachers require as budget worthy, and we add more stress to teachers, strain on classroom sizes, we create an injustice for kids." Thus, the gap between the input and the output could be the reason that the input is not targeting the problems which need to be solved.

DISCUSSION

As evidenced in the above discussion, social media data provides enormous potential to educational research. However, current social media-based educational research also comes with several major challenges. The first challenge is concerned with the idiosyncratic nature of the data. Unpredictable content and comments which are unrelated to a specific query may find their way into the data stream and skew results.

Table 3. Social-media-based and traditional data collection methods for educational research

	Description	Pros	Cons
Traditional			
Interviews	Structured or unstructured, one-on-one directed, or one-on-group conversations	• Low cost (small sample size) • Respondents define what is important • Rapid data collection • Possible to explore issues in depth • Opportunity to clarify responses through conversations	• Can be time-consuming to set up interviews • Can be difficult to interview influential individuals • Can be difficult to guarantee the interviewers' skills • Can be challenging to reach generalizability • Data are unstructured • Can be difficult to follow-up if more data are needed • Can be challenging to analyze and summarize results
Survey	Standardized paper-and-pencil, one-line, or phone questionnaires that ask predetermined questions	• Can be highly accurate • Can be highly reliable and valid • Allows for comparisons with other/larger populations • Data are structured and standard • Easy to conduct quantitative data analysis	• Accuracy depends on particular samples and the sample size • Relatively slow on design, implement, and analyze • May have low responses rates • Little opportunity to explore issues in depth
Social Media			
Twitter	Number of likes (positive), retweets, and unstructured comments from Twitter's API with keywords or hashtags regarding particular topics (e.g., "math education" and "NoCutsToEducation")	• Low cost (both time, money) & immediate data collection • Easy to follow up with extra new data • Allows for large samples from various populations (educators, parents, and teachers for educational researches) • Easy to link to any individuals or organizations of interest • Easily generate quantitative data analysis with the number of likes, retweets, and sentiment analysis to determine participants' attitudes • Easily generate sentiment analysis, even with unstructured text tweet data	• Some programming background is required for researchers (e.g., R and Python) • Unstructured comment data • Screen comments manually • Difficult to get demographical information

Second, analyses that use Twitter data must be careful to consider issues of representation when interpreting results. The analysis relies on voluntary information. Its findings represent only those individuals who offer information about their opinions. It does not reflect individuals who do not express their opinions. It could be true that this group of people holds the opposite opinions.

Third, the demographic factors such as gender, race, and age being common variables included in educational research are still difficult to identify. Some studies about identifying race and gender from social media data involve massive extra data for model validation, which are not commonly accepted and utilized in research, yet.

Fourth, the majority of researchers who are taking advantage of social media data for social science research are not social scientists or educators, but rather computer scientists. Even though the researchers do not need to be equipped with extensive background knowledge in programming and coding, there still exists gaps in the areas of educational research and computer science.

Apparently, both traditional and social media-based data collection methods have advantages and disadvantages. Table 3 lists the pros and cons of both methods.

CONCLUSION

This study provides guidelines on how to conduct educational research with social media-based data collection methods. With the popularity of the Internet and emerging technology, social media are becoming one of the most popular access to research data. Social media-based educational research is the trend for future research, since future children are born in the technology time, more and more educational activities will be moving online, and researchers need the skills to collect and analyze the data. Fortunately, compared to traditional data collection methods, emerging technology provides a more efficient approach to data collection.

REFERENCES

Al-Rahmi, W., & Othman, M. (2013). The impact of social media use on academic performance among university students: A pilot study. *Journal of Information Systems Research and Innovation*, *4*(12), 1–10.

Al-Rahmi, W. M., Alias, N., Othman, M. S., Marin, V. I., & Tur, G. (2018). A model of factors affecting learning performance through the use of social media in Malaysian higher education. *Computer Education*, *121*, 59–72. doi:10.1016/j.compedu.2018.02.010

Albayrak, D., & Yildirim, Z. (2015). Using social networking sites for teaching and learning. *Journal of Educational Computing Research*, *52*(2), 155–179. doi:10.1177/0735633115571299

Anderson, M., & Jiang, J. (2018, May 31). *Teens, social media & technology 2018*. Retrieved from https://www.pewinternet.org/2018/05/31/teens-social-media-technology-2018/

Balakrishnan, V., Liew, T. K., & Pourgholaminejad, S. (2015). Fun learning with Edooware – A social media enabled tool. *Computers & Education*, *80*, 39–47. doi:10.1016/j.compedu.2014.08.008

Banhart, B. (2018). *How to mine your social media data for a better ROI*. Retrieved from https://sprout-social.com/insights/social-media-data/

Bannister, K. (2018). *Understanding sentiment analysis: What it is & why it's used*. Retrieved from https://www.brandwatch.com/blog/understanding-sentiment-analysis/

Barbee, B. (2018). *Are you #stoked or #overit? The complete guide to hashtags on social media*. Retrieved from https://www.digitaltrends.com/social-media/what-is-a-hashtag/

Bett, H., & Makewa, L. (2018). Can Facebook groups enhance continuing professional development of teachers? Lessons from Kenya. *Asia-Pacific Journal of Teacher Education*, 1–15. doi:10.1080/135986 6X.2018.1542662

Bosch, T. E. (2009). Using online social networking for teaching and learning: Facebook use at the University of Cape Town. *Communication*, *35*(2), 185–200.

Boyd, D. (2007). *Viewing American class divisions through Facebook and MySpace*. Retrieved from http://www.danah.org/papers/essays/ClassDivisions.html

Clement, J. (2019). *Number of Twitter users worldwide from 2014 to 2020 (in millions)*. Retrieved from https://www.statista.com/statistics/303681/twitter-users-worldwide/

Creswell, J. W., & Plano, C. (2007). *Designing and conducting mixed methods research*. Thousand Oaks, CA: Sage.

Crowell, R. (2019). Do bonuses for teachers lead to math test score gains for kids? *Forbes*. Retrieved from https://www.forbes.com/sites/rachelcrowell/2019/03/23/do-bonuses-for-teachers-lead-to-math-test-score-gains-for-kids/

Driscoll, D. L., Salib, P., & Rupert, D. J. (2007). Merging qualitative and quantitative data in mixed methods research: How to and why not. *Ecological and Environmental Anthropology*, *3*(1), 18–28.

Erjavec, K. (2013). Informal learning through Facebook among Slovenian pupils. *Comunicar*, *21*(41), 117–126. doi:10.3916/C41-2013-11

Garcia, E., Elbeltagi, I. M., Dungay, K., & Hardaker, G. (2015). Student use of Facebook for informal learning and peer support. *International Journal of Information and Learning Technology*, *32*(5), 286–299. doi:10.1108/IJILT-09-2015-0024

Gitonga, R., Muuro, M., & Onyango, G. (2016). Technology integration in the classroom: A case of students experiences in using Edmodo to support learning in a blended classroom in a Kenyan University. In *Proceedings of the 2016 IST-Africa Week Conference*, (pp. 1-8). New York, NY: IEEE. 10.1109/ISTAFRICA.2016.7530591

Greenhow, C., & Robelia, B. (2009). Informal learning and identity formation in online social networks. *Learning, Media and Technology*, *34*(2), 119–140. doi:10.1080/17439880902923580

Hewitt, A., & Forte, A. (2006). *Crossing boundaries: Identity management and student/faculty relationships on the Facebook*. Paper presented at the CSCW Conference, Canada.

Junco, R. (2012). Too much face and not enough books: The relationship between multiple indices of Facebook use and academic performance. *Computers in Human Behavior, 28*(1), 187–198. doi:10.1016/j. chb.2011.08.026

Junco, R., Heiberger, G., & Loken, E. (2011). The effect of Twitter on college student engagement and grades. *Journal of Computer Assisted Learning, 27*(2), 119–132. doi:10.1111/j.1365-2729.2010.00387.x

Karl, K. A., & Peluchette, J. V. (2011). "Friending" professors, parents and bosses: A Facebook connection conundrum. *Journal of Education for Business, 86*(4), 214–222. doi:10.1080/08832323.2010.507638

Liang, H., & Zhu, J. J. H. (2017). Big data, collection of (social media, harvesting). The International Encyclopedia of Communication Research Methods, 7. doi:10.1002/9781118901731.iecrm0015

Lin, C. W. (2018). Gender as a moderator of the relationship between Facebook addiction and self-efficacy for learning in a college sample: The mediating effect of deliberative belief. *Quality & Quantity, 52*(6), 2435–2454. doi:10.100711135-017-0576-6

Manca, S., & Ranieri, M. (2014). Does Facebook provide educational value? *The Social Classroom,* 311-336.

Mazer, J., Murphy, R., & Simonds, C. (2007). I'll see you on "Facebook": The effects of computer-mediated teacher self-disclosure on student motivation, affective learning, and classroom climate. *Communication Education, 56*(1), 1–17. doi:10.1080/03634520601009710

McCormick, T. H., Lee, H., Cesare, N., Shojaie, A., & Spiro, E. S. (2017). Using Twitter for demographic and social science research: Tools for data collection and processing. *Sociological Methods & Research, 46*(3), 1–26. doi:10.1177/0049124115605339 PMID:29033471

McMillan, S., & Morrison, M. (2006). Coming of age with the Internet: A qualitative exploration of how the internet has become an integral part of young people's lives. *New Media & Society, 8*(1), 73–95. doi:10.1177/1461444806059871

Moujahid, A. (2014). *An introduction to text mining using Twitter streaming API and Python.* Retrieved from http://adilmoujahid.com/posts/2014/07/twitter-analytics/

Ng'ambi, D., Brown, C., Bozalek, V., Gachago, D., & Wood, D. (2016). Technology-enhanced teaching and learning in South African higher education - A rearview of a 20-year journey. *British Journal of Educational Technology, 47*(5), 843–858. doi:10.1111/bjet.12485

O'Bannon, B. W., & Thomas, K. (2014). Teacher perceptions of using mobile phones in the classroom: Age matters! *Computers & Education, 74,* 15–25. doi:10.1016/j.compedu.2014.01.006

Omnicore. (2019). *Twitter by the numbers: Stats, demographics & fun facts.* Retrieved from https://www.omnicoreagency.com/twitter-statistics/

Onwuegbuzie, A. J., & Teddlie, C. (2003). A framework for analyzing data in mixed methods research. In A. Tashakkori & C. Teddlie (Eds.), *Handbook of mixed methods in social and behavioral research* (pp. 351–383). Thousand Oaks, CA: Sage.

Organization for Economic Cooperation and Development. (2003). *The PISA 2003 Assessment Framework*. Retrieved from https://www.oecd.org/education/school/programmeforinternationalstudentassessmentpisa/33694881.pdf

Pew Research Center. (2011). *The new education ecology* [Report]. Retrieved from https://www.pewinternet.org/2011/11/09/the-new-education-ecology/

Pew Research Center. (2018). *Social media use continues to rise in developing countries* [Report]. Retrieved from https://www.pewresearch.org/global/2018/06/19/social-media-use-continues-to-rise-in-developing-countries-but-plateaus-across-developed-ones/

Pew Research Center. (2019). *Internet/broadband fact sheet, 2019*. Retrieved from https://www.pewinternet.org/fact-sheet/internet-broadband/

Prescott, J., Stodart, M., Becket, G., & Wilson, S. (2015). The experience of using Facebook as an educational tool. *Health and Social Care Education, 0*(0), 1–5.

Selwyn, N. (2007). *"Screw blackboard … do it on Facebook!": An investigation of students' educational use of Facebook*. Paper presented to the Pole 1.0 – Facebook social research symposium. University of London. Retrieved from http://www.scribd.com/doc/513958/Facebook-seminar-paper-Selwyn

Selwyn, N., & Stirling, E. (2016). Social media and education … now the dust has settled. *Learning, Media and Technology, 41*(1), 1–5. doi:10.1080/17439884.2015.1115769

Susilo, A., & Kaufman, D. (2014). Exploring Facebook (FB) as an online tutorial complement in distance education. *International Journal of Online Pedagogy and Course Design, 4*(4), 60–75. doi:10.4018/ijopcd.2014100105

TechnologyPlus. (2018). *The role of social media in education*. Retrieved from https://education.cxotv.news/2018/04/30/the-role-of-social-media-in-education/

Wu, C. H., & Chen, S. C. (2015). Understanding the relationships of critical factors to Facebook educational usage intention. *Internet Research, 25*(2), 262–278. doi:10.1108/IntR-11-2013-0232

Yang, Y., Wang, Q., Woo, H. L., & Quek, C. L. (2011). Using Facebook for teaching and learning: A review of the literature. *International Journal of Continuing Engineering Education and Lifelong Learning, 21*(1), 72–86. doi:10.1504/IJCEELL.2011.039695

KEY TERMS AND DEFINITIONS

Concurrent: A mixed method data collection strategy to validate one form of data with the other form, or to address different types of questions, while the data are collected simultaneously.

Data Transformation: The process of transforming the qualitative data into quantitative data.

Hashtag: The word or phrase that is used to identify specify posts on social media, such as Twitter Facebook.

Key Words: The words researchers determine to query from the tweets.

Sentiment Analysis: A technique used to gain an overview of people' opinion toward certain topics through text data.

Sequential Strategy: A mixed-methods strategy for data collection to provide more data based on the results from the earlier phase of the data collection.

Twitter API: The special URLs that web owners intentionally provided for developers to download data from their databases.

This research was previously published in Advancing Educational Research With Emerging Technology; pages 54-77, copyright year 2020 by Information Science Reference (an imprint of IGI Global).

Chapter 103

Use of Facebook in Primary Teacher Training:
Experimental Analysis

Inmaculada Gómez-Hurtado
University of Huelva, Spain

ABSTRACT

This chapter presents a study carried out to describe and determine the relevance of the Facebook network as a tool for development of the teaching-learning processes in the teacher-training classroom, and knowledge of the same for use in a research model. This study is based on an analysis of the latest research on the use of social networks in higher education to describe an experiment performed in a group of future primary teachers at a Spanish university in which Facebook was used as a resource to improve the teaching-learning processes. The outcomes point towards a positive evaluation of Facebook as a resource for the creation of collaborative learning communities, improving teaching-learning processes, knowledge construction and social learning, the classroom climate, tutoring among peers and with faculty, foreign-language practice, and digital competence. Among the initial conclusions, the authors highlight the need to demonstrate tools like Facebook to student teachers to ensure their appropriate professional and personal development.

INTRODUCTION

The use of social networks is an increasingly common practice in university education. Nowadays, the application of social networks in the academic field of higher education is a reality (Mendiguren, Meso & Perez, 2012). Social networks are prompting a rethink of the traditional teaching model consisting of lectures as the only strategy, with the student treated as a mere spectator in the teaching-learning process. At present, Higher Education and European Higher Education mostly rely on a didactic researcher model where the student is the main actor in the teaching-learning process and the teacher is merely a guide to the use of different resources and strategies to access the knowledge (Pasadas, 2010). Within

DOI: 10.4018/978-1-6684-7123-4.ch103

these resources nowadays, as we have seen, it is necessary to talk about the Internet and Web 2.0 as its constituents, and of social networking as a springboard to collaborative learning by students.

This fact exerts a powerful influence in the educational sphere. When talking about the incorporation of technologies in education and the didactic resource, it is a technological innovation, but only with these new integrated, alternative pedagogical models and search of pedagogical innovation (Mayorga & Madrid, 2010). With this contextual framework, in terms of use and familiarization with social networks, education is in the position of having to address a new dimension in the process of student training.

This chapter presents a study carried out to describe and determine the relevance of the Facebook network as a tool for development of the teaching-learning processes in the teacher-training classroom, and knowledge of the same for use in a research model.

After proposing a theoretical foundation for the use of Facebook in Higher Education, specifically in the training of primary teachers, we go on to describe an experiment performed with a group of 2nd year students on the primary education degree course at the University of Huelva, which was also carried out in subsequent courses. This experiment was analysed through a case study including interviews, discussion groups, observations and document analysis (Gómez & Coronel, 2014). Finally, we contrasted the results obtained in this experiment with the research works described in the theoretical grounding.

It also means the beginning of the training for teachers, who have had to learn to distinguish between the advantages and disadvantages of social networks in order to make them a suitable educational resource for the classroom.

BACKGROUND

The Importance of ICTs in Higher Education

Information and communications technologies (ICTs) have become an important and inseparable part of daily life. Among them, the Internet has brought about a revolution in our society (Buabeng-Andoh, 2012; Castells, 2002, 2006; Sharma, 2010; Murati & Ceka, 2017). Authors such as Silverstone and Hirsch (1994) considered the great influence that ICTs are having on socialisation of the individual and defend the benefits that they can develop.

Information and communication technologies are changing all areas of our life, home, work... The way we communicate, analyse and socialise is different. One might say that ICTs are transforming our way of thinking and perceiving the world (Attard, 2011).

These new information and communication technologies have largely been considered and intended for personal and recreational use. However, these "conversation technologies" and "constructivist learning tools", along with the power and reach of the Internet, have made them viable options both for educational learning and for applications focused on the construction of learning (Hsu, 2007). ICTs, with their possibilities, provide excellent opportunities to develop meaningful, collaborative and socially relevant learning. (Greenhow, Robelia & Hudges, 2009). The interest in using information and communication technologies derives not only from the educational benefits achieved, but also from the basic need to be in tune with the focus and reality experienced by students today (Hsu, 2007). This has led to the development of changes in education, where one of the main objectives is the inclusion of Information and Communication Technologies as a means to develop new types of classroom interaction and engage in the teaching-learning processes (De Haro, 2010; Infante & Aguaded, 2012; McGarry et al., 2012; Sandy & Jared, 2014; Silverstone & Hirsch, 1994; Simons, 2011).

The use of Information and Communication Technologies in education has become a need in the development of student learning, although their mere use does not necessarily entail suitable learning. Educators need suitable training for the implementation of teaching-learning processes that include ICTs. (Keane, Keane & Blicblau, 2016). Thus, the new needs of students inserted in a generation of communication and information give rise to the development of new methodologies that respond to their demands (Tapscott & Williams, 2010).

Cabero and Gisbert (2005), quoted by Túñez and Sixto (2012, p. 4) enumerated a series of transformation-causing aspects in the teaching field, such as:

- ICTs make a large volume of information available to the students.
- They facilitate the updating of information and contents.
- Making information more flexible, regardless of the space and time in which educator and student are present.
- Allowing the delocalisation of knowledge.
- Encouraging student autonomy.
- They provide just-in-time and just-for-me learning.
- Offering different synchronous and asynchronous communication tools for students and teachers.
- They favour multimedia learning.
- Facilitating group and collective training.
- Favouring interaction in different scopes.
- Fostering the use of learning materials and/or objects.
- They allow servers to keep a record of the activity carried out by students.
- Saving on costs and travel.

In view of the above, Kirkgöz (2016) posits that the university teachers of a group of future teachers see information technologies as having multiple advantages in the teaching-learning processes, although they acknowledge the scant use made of them.

In particular, social networks are one of the main aspects that have grown in popularity and led millions of young people worldwide to become increasingly internet dependent (Wodzicki, Schwämmlein, & Moskaliuk, 2012). For example, according to the ONTSI (2011), most social networking in Spain takes place on a daily basis. Young people between 18 and 34 are the most avid users of these networks. In 2017, use of the internet to access social networks is increasing, with 62.7% of the Spanish population using the internet to do so, a percentage only exceeded by instant messaging users, at 71.5% (ONTSI, 2017).

Likewise, the Centre for Children in Andalusia observed in a 2010 Report on ICT use and activities among girls and boys in Andalusia that 92% of respondents used the computer to access internet and 89.1% were using it to chat via instant messaging (social networks), while 58.8% used it for this purpose every day, or most days.

In the United States, the Association for Media Research (AIMC), in its Infographic Summary n° 19 on Net Browsers published in March 2017, explains that 87% of the population uses Facebook as the main network. In the United States, 87% of young people and adults between 18 and 29 have a Facebook account, compared to 71% of the general population aged 18-65 years. (Duggan et al., 2015). Today, 90% of young Americans use social networks, compared to the 12% who were using it in 2005 (Perrin,

2015). This exerts a powerful influence in the educational scope. Siemens and Weller (2011) argued that the Internet has brought about a change in the traditional relationships formerly found in education, as tasks such as searching for information and knowledge, previously the domain of teachers, are currently available to students. In doing so, internet and social networks in particular become a perfect vehicle to reach those people who, for various reasons, are unable to attend school regularly. The most important thing is that a good information tool should be able to end the teacher's monopoly as the main source of knowledge.

UNESCO (2017), in the Global Education Monitoring Report for 2016, recognises the importance of ICTs in education for the development of an effective learning environment, directly linking ICT in schools and learning outcomes. However, the report acknowledges that this depends directly upon the connectivity and IT infrastructures available, which means that there will be differences among the different countries worldwide in terms of options.

Social Networks as Resource in the University Scope

The use of social networks changes our lives and directly influences our way of managing knowledge and information (Kolbitsch & Maurer, 2006). Social networks are one more resource to be introduced in learning environments for the development of learning communities in communication. Nevertheless, they entail a series of risks and different challenges for the teacher to face (McCarroll & Curran, 2014).

However, the use of social networks in Higher Education and their use as a didactic resource to link the different contexts in which users take part in the teaching-learning process have not been studied in depth, leaving much to be done regarding how the use of networks affects the students (Cabero, Barroso, Llorente, & Yanes, 2016).

Several studies have brought to light various initiatives concerning the current use of social media as an educational tool which can also be considered a valuable alternative in the construction of knowledge and social learning (Dziuban et al.,2013; Meso, Perez, & Mendiguren, 2010b; Selwyn, 2007, 2012). In Higher Education, teaching using the Internet provides opportunities for students to achieve their learning development beyond what is acquired in the classroom (Betts, Kramer, & Gaines, 2011; Eynon, 2005; Gao, 2013), even though there is little experience and not many teachers are using this type of education. In addition, university learning is shifting away from the reception and storage of data and is focusing more on promoting analysis, seeking and reprocessing information found on the network and shared with peers through it, and encouraging student autonomy by always taking into account the flexibility and adaptability of space, achieving directions and a different interaction between teachers and students in order to enable, facilitate and promote collaboration beyond the physical boundaries of the university and academic spheres to which they belong (Area, 2000).

Specifically, Facebook is now one of the most popular social networks worldwide, with 1.71 million active users. In the USA, 72% of adult Americans online use Facebook (Duggan, 2015), a popular network that allows collaboration and connectivity in a massive way, while enabling users to create and share content and build relationships. Facebook is the social network most widely used by educators. Some 80% of educators have a social network account and use this network to communicate with students (Tinti-Kane et al., 2010, as cited in Chugh & Ruig, 2017).

Lohnes and Whitfield (2016), Sheldon (2008) and Wang (2012) analysed research into the use of Facebook in Higher Education in three categories: communication and relationship practices, privacy concerns and its use in the academic context. The research focused on responding to how Facebook is integrated in student routines, how students negotiate the use of Facebook, and why some of them prefer not to use it. Notable among their conclusions was that university students are not always users of Facebook, which is not always well received by students, but rather decide when they want to use the network or not depending on their own criteria and the issue to be approached.

The rise of social media has also been a challenge for teaching in higher education, representing an advantage for students by encouraging dialogue between peers and promoting resources that foster collaboration and develop communication skills (Siemens & Weller, 2011, p. 157).

Specifically, Facebook has given rise to a new dimension in learning and knowledge processes (Rouis et al., 2011; Wodziki, Scfhwämmlein, & Moskaliuk, 2012). According to different studies (Boyd & Ellison, 2007; Álvarez & López, 2013; Climent Sanchís, 2013; Gray & Carter, 2012; Liccardi et al., 2007; Mendiguren et al., 2012; Reina Estévez et al., 2012; Tuñez & García, 2012), this has led to the development of a series of aspects to take into account when using this network in the classroom, such as the methodological opening whereby the teacher increases the activity and involvement of the students in the classroom, creating a family space rated positively among the students, while acknowledging the pros and cons of using the network. It constitutes an alternative in the construction of knowledge and social learning among the students, which gives rise to learning communities and becomes an important complement to face-to-face and virtual teaching, requiring suitable strategies for proper use. This social network thus becomes a fundamental resource as part of the innovative elements being introduced in Higher Education (Castro & González-Palta, 2016; Igartua & Rodríguez de Dios, 2016).

Authors such as Watulak and Whitfield (2017, p. 180) classified the uses for which Facebook is deployed in higher education teaching processes, according to students, on three issues: communication and relationship practices, privacy concerns and use of the academic context. Chugh and Ruhi (2017, p. 9) noted that the main reasons for using Facebook are to improve learning, increase participation and commitment, dissemination of content, and to improve pedagogy and the exchange of information.

Facebook thus becomes an important tool for teaching-learning processes in Higher Education, as it has several benefits for students and teachers, although it also presents some drawbacks (see Figure 1).

Social Networks in Primary Teacher Training

Teacher training faces a new challenge, due to the need to improve the capacity of new teachers to implement new pedagogical approaches and take advantage of ICTs for teaching and learning. This training persists in the struggle to disconnect theory and practice. However, collaborative learning defended by theories (Kugelmas, 2001) is needed so that students can bring knowledge and ideas together in collaborative situations, problem solving and the creation of new knowledge information. To this end, experiences in Higher Education that promote these aspects are needed (Häkkinen et al., 2017).

ICTs can become a good mediation tool for teacher training and teacher development. These technologies can be used for self-reflection by the future teachers on their practices, creating collaborative peer networks among colleagues (Altinay-Gazi & Altinay-Aksal, 2017). However, any tool that can foster collaboration and development among professionals embarking on a career in education, or those already teaching, is a positive aspect. ICTs can create learning communities where different educational stakeholders communicate and exchange ideas, enriching their training and, in turn their practice (Lieberman & Pointer, 2010). This implies that in the training of future teachers, all possible tools should be provided to achieve suitable training of education professionals, not only initially but also in continuous training.

Figure 1. Benefits of using Facebook in the university classroom

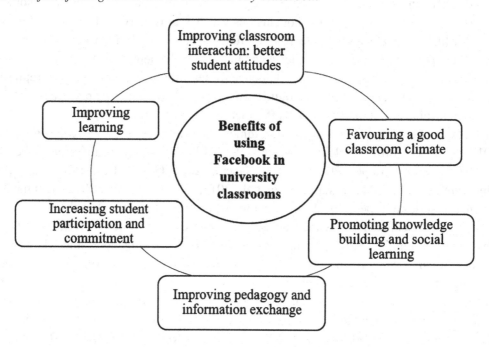

To this end, the training of primary teachers calls for a new dialectic model which involves the students developing understanding of content through a variety of pedagogical approaches. The teacher should consider the characteristics of student and context and reflect on the teaching process. One essential point is that the students themselves should create the connections through an open and flexible curriculum, rather than the teacher transmitting the truths and methodologies of a subject (Domínguez & Llorente, 2009).

The teachers studied by Starkey (2010) showed that their practices are based on learning theories prior to the digital age, which implies a limitation in the development of innovative practices. This is why primary teachers in training must be aware of the utility of different tools that improve the teaching-learning process (Kelly, Thompson, Green & Vice, 2017). To this end, the university teacher's role is fundamental in the development and improvement of the teaching-learning processes. Facebook becomes a tool that can influence group interaction. Student perceptions of the class group are different among students who use Facebook and those who do not, being more positive in the former, as they feel closer to the teacher and display greater interest in the course (Akcaoglu & Bowman, 2016). In turn, there is a positive correlation between the students using Facebook and their knowledge development. (Lambic, 2016).

However, the use of social networks remains limited and restricted by teachers. Teachers are not willing to integrate these resources into their practices, for reasons such as cultural resistance, pedagogical issues or institutional constraints. However, there are differences of opinion and attitudes among university faculty members regarding the use of social networks, namely Facebook, for the development of teaching-learning processes. (Manca & Ranieri, 2016).

Some of the reasons why social networks are less used may be embedded in the limitations considered by Chugh and Ruhi (2017) on the basis of other research, namely teacher dominance, passive behaviour, lack of use of academic language, technological issues, privacy and discrimination. Based on the above, we summarise these limitations in Figure 2.

Figure 2. Teacher limitations on the use of Facebook in class, according to the research works studied

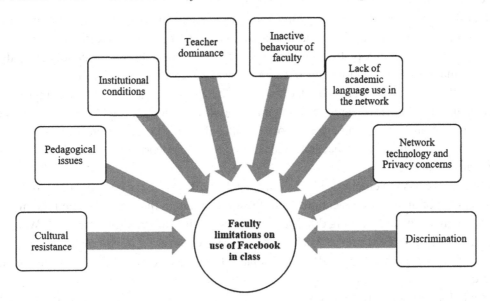

Moreover, today's students are experiencing a new form of interpersonal communication that encourages collaboration among peers and the emergence of stronger work and friendship-related relationships between them (Guiza, Salinas, & Flores, 2011; Meso, Perez, & Mendiguren, 2010a; Sotomayor, 2010). Thus, our students are learning a new way of forming and nurturing relationships through a digital channel rather than the old approaches, which were based on face-to-face interaction (Moorman & Bowker, 2011). This new experience in forging and maintaining interpersonal relationships can be applied in the field of higher education, using social networks as a teaching resource to enhance learning and the acquisition of our students' basic skills (Cho & Kim, 2013; Davis III et al.,2012; Wodzicki, Schwämmlein, & Moskaliuk, 2012).

This way, social networks as communication and information-exchanging systems can be provided to groups of students and/or teachers that constitute virtual collaborative communities with certain academic and social skills. This allows teachers to work cooperatively with other universities and conduct collaborative educational experiences among their students, who opt for inclusive higher education that supports the idea of collaborative networks within and between schools (Ainscow, 2012).

Moreover, social networks support virtual teaching of the subject and call for different teaching strategies and methods that contribute to the development of student learning (Reid, 2012). Thus, some studies consider that the use of these technologies (Brill & Park, 2008; Duart, 2009; Stollak et al.,2011) and, in our case, social networks, encourages the development of learning communities among students by promoting their inclusion in the development of knowledge of the subject matter (Lampe et al., 2007; Gray & Carter, 2012).

University students decide to use Facebook mainly to exchange materials and resources, although other factors can influence their decision to use social networks or not, such as the perceived usefulness of the network for material development and the enjoyment or motivation through it, as well as collaboration and social influences. In addition, collaboration is the most important predictor for adopting Facebook for academic purposes. (Sharma, Joshi, & Sharma, 2016).

The research into the use of Facebook in Higher Education analysed by Chugh and Ruhi (2017) showed that the use of Facebook for teaching and learning activities can be seen as a strategic change designed to improve student academic achievement and participation. In addition, educators may see Facebook as a complementary platform for teaching and interaction. Facebook should not only be seen as a platform that improves relationships but as a gateway to learning and teaching. Despite the limitations, these authors consider that Facebook offers many benefits that should be used to improve students' educational outcomes. Their research shows that Facebook was good for improving learning, increasing participation and commitment, and diffusion of content, enhancing pedagogy and information exchange. The popularity and familiarity of Facebook make this social network a suitable choice for use in the teaching-learning processes.

In particular, we wish to emphasise two elements when discussing social networks and their application in the sphere of university education. First, the atmosphere in the classroom and its importance in classroom management and learning development in university students (Fraser, 2012; Wang, Haertel, & Walberg, 1997). Lecture theatres and other scholarly spaces are areas of communication and learning, where interaction, communication and interpersonal relations as well as with objects are key elements to ensure quality education. Improving classroom climate thus becomes a fundamental aspect in the development of learning in our student body. It is therefore assumed that improving the atmosphere and resolving conflicts in the classroom leads to improvement and appropriate learning development (Lazaros & Jeffery, 2013; Lei, 2010; Myers & Claus, 2012). Secondly, the configuration of collaborative learning communities and their close relation with improvement in online learning (Bonk & Wisher, 2000; Lieberman & Pointer, 2010; Mendiguren, Meso, & Pérez, 2012; Rovai, 2002). Collaborative learning communities are instructed with a dual purpose: a) that students should make a connection between all the subjects they study, and b) to foment social relations among them and with the teaching body, developing a real vision of the world through academic and social experiences (Mei-Zhao & Kuh, 2004). In this sense, these communities encourage improved social interaction, acknowledged as one of the most important factors in knowledge construction (Brook & Oliver, 2003). There are multiple benefits to be found in the formation of online learning communities, among them promotion of the development of a classroom climate suitable for the development of a better teaching-learning process (Baghdadi, 2011). Studies similar to the experiment presented here consider social networks not only as a teaching-learning resource, but also as a strategy for the creation of collaborative learning communities that will enhance social interaction in the classroom, leading to an improvement in academic performance (Moorman & Bowker, 2011).

Briefly, and supported by similar studies (Getzlaf et al., 2012; Gray & Carter, 2012), the aim of our research is to analyse the use of social networks in the context of the teaching and learning process and explore the influence of this emerging technology on the construction of knowledge and the forging of closer bonds between students and students and teachers.

Specifically, in research carried out in Higher Education students in training to become teachers, the results indicated that students who normally used Facebook to seek formal and informal academic support considered that the network generated a sense of community and helped complete their academic tasks (Amador & Amador, 2017) (see Figure 3).

Figure 3. Summary of the most important aspects of use of ICTs in higher education

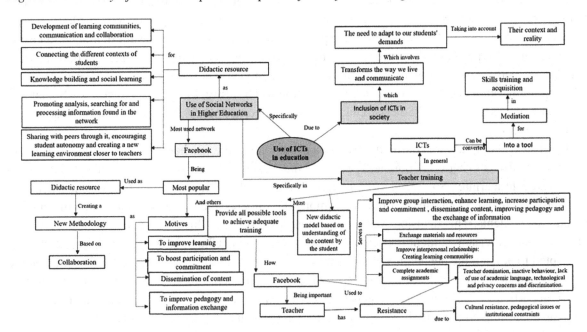

MAIN FOCUS OF THE CHAPTER

What Did We Learn From Our Experience With the Use of Facebook in Primary Teacher Training?

Our First Steps

The experiment began in academic year 2010-2011, with the participation of teaching staff from the Department of Education and the Department of Integrated Didactics, and is still underway today. Pre-service teachers in Early Childhood and Primary Education Degrees took part. A total of 260 students were involved in each course, split into four groups of 65 pupils each. However, the researchers focused the experiment on a class where the teacher opted to use Facebook as a resource to enhance the classroom climate and teaching-learning process.

This experience provided a case study on how a multilingual group of students and a teacher from a small university attempt to improve relationships in the classroom and enhance the teaching-learning process by using Facebook (Gómez & Coronel, 2014). This option was applied with the aim of improving the classroom climate and furthering teaching and learning of the subject. So, when choosing the social network, we asked students what network they most commonly used, and 90% of them used Facebook. For this reason, we decided to create a website and Facebook profile for the subject. In the study conducted by Moorman and Bowker (2011) they managed to determine a definition and appropriate assessment method for social networks in teaching regarding the relationships among students and between students and teacher.

During 2010/2011, a female teacher from the University of Huelva Education Department decided to use Facebook as a classroom teaching resource in the course on Teaching, Curriculum Development and School Organisation. This was a unique experience, as the use of networks was not limited to virtual learning. In subsequent courses, the teacher, along with other faculty members, carried out the same experiment with other groups, reaching more than 260 students per academic year. The experiment was applied in other course subjects such as Attention to Diversity, Integrated Projects for Social and Cultural Knowledge or Social Science Didactics. The outcomes obtained were similar to those shown in this experiment.

Use of Facebook in the classroom arises as a need. One of the teachers involved in the experiment observed conflicts in her classroom and perceived them as giving rise to a climate that was not conducive to student learning. So, this teacher decided to use Facebook as a resource to foster interpersonal student-student and student-teacher relations among the students and as a way of mediation in conflicts among the students. This decision was based on previous studies which found Facebook to be a suitable tool for increasing student participation and commitment (Chugh & Ruhi, 2017). Similarly, she attempted to add a more academic component to the use of this tool as a means to hold forums on the issues raised in lectures and virtual tutorials, while improving learning in general and the second language in particular. This way, the social network brings about a change in the learning environment by creating a learning community based on collaboration (McCarroll & Curran, 2014). The students were required to use the Facebook network address to access a private network for the exchange of e-learning. (Panckhurst & Marsh, 2011).

The purpose of this experiment, which was developed over two years and is still ongoing today in other subjects, was to place students at the centre of the learning process, allowing them to experience and reflect upon collaborative learning in networks. In addition, it was important that they should acquire and develop knowledge of teaching strategies such as peer tutoring and learning by doing, while building their knowledge and acquiring the subject content, as one of the most important limitations that teachers find for the use of Facebook consists of their own concerns, arising from their ignorance of these technologies (Chugh & Ruhi, 2017).

However, the main aim of this experiment is to analyse the use of Facebook as a teaching resource network for teaching practice that improves student-teacher relations, assuming that classroom climate is a key element to development of the teaching-learning process, a similar aim to those of other research works carried out in higher education with Facebook (Lohnes & Whitfield, 2016).

The teacher invited her students to take part in the Facebook network. First of all, she set up a Facebook page with a Facebook profile to act as developer of the initiative. Thus, different activities were carried out through the network: using a common forum to discuss links to a photo on issues related to network learning, the teacher encouraged discussion of the contents presented in different subjects through her Facebook status and asked open questions from which students had to build the contents of the subjects. Tutorials were held with students at the times previously scheduled by the teacher, setting out guidelines for individual and group work linked to the subjects, discussing personal issues involved in the teaching-learning process and inviting students to practice the foreign language.

Throughout the course, teachers made use of Facebook as a promoter at all times, using the network as a teaching resource linked to the classroom subject. The use of Facebook among students was 90%, notably for mentoring sessions and tutorials. It is very difficult to estimate the number of postings due to the high degree of involvement of faculty and students, to the point that interaction activity overflowed initially the working hours assigned for that purpose. Even some students, who initially did not have Facebook, quickly changed their situation to actively participate in the experience.

For information gathering, we found 20 candidates who showed interest in taking part in the study, with whom an interview was held. Likewise, another teacher involved in the experience held an in-depth interview with the teacher to find out her perspective and reflections on the subject of study and her own assessment of the experiment.

In addition to the interviews, the researchers analysed the classroom materials used, the teachers' planning and several conversations from the students' and teachers' Facebook pages. Finally, the researchers held a discussion group with the teacher and six randomly chosen students taking part.

To triangulate the data, an inductive analysis was performed (Strauss & Corbin, 2002) on all the information gathered. After analysing the material compiled, the researchers drew up a system of categories. Transcripts of the interviews, focus group and dialogues in Facebook were analysed inductively to identify key themes affected by the experience, as outlined below: a) classroom climate; b) teaching and learning of course contents; c) virtual tutoring; d) second language practice, and e) acquisition of digital competence.

Our Experimental Details/Data

The researchers present the outcomes of the experience from the standpoint of the teacher involved and from the point of view of the students themselves.

Classroom Climate

Consistent with the findings of Akcaoglu and Bowman (2016) and Gao (2013) on the influence of social networks on collaboration between students and teachers, the results stress that the teacher-student relationship was also affected by the use of the social network.

The classroom atmosphere improved through use of the Facebook network. The teacher introduced Facebook as a strategy that helped her mediate conflicts between students, so that many students began to use the network to tell the teacher the problems present in the small groups that affected the larger group, giving the teacher the opportunity to propose different solutions to these issues, consequently giving rise to improved function of the small groups and the larger group, as well as a closer relationship with the teacher.

As in the study by Túñez and Sixto (2012), teacher-student and student-student relations improved, generating networks of collaboration and support that went beyond professional issues and reached more personal questions, which led to the development of great friendships between students and a closer relationship with the teacher (Moorman & Bowker, 2011), creating a familiar environment (Álvarez & López, 2013). Throughout this experience, the students developed skills such as cooperative working, responsibility, effort, collaboration and empathy, which improved the group cohesion, in agreement with the literature, which shows that a substantial benefit of Facebook in the university classroom is the construction and development of social learning (Gray & Carter, 2012). This constituted a great step forward in class development, as students began to fully trust in the teacher and their motivation increased considerably towards the subject matter, which, moreover, subsequently led to them achieving higher marks as a result of this motivation.

For the teacher, the experiment was an excellent opportunity to discover common elements among the development of course content, classroom management and relationships among students. The classroom shared the space given over to learning and teaching, contact and interaction with the students with the network and, in some cases, Facebook represented an opportunity for the emergence and cultivation of personal relationships between students and teacher which were subsequently reflected positively in the classroom dynamics and activities. The classroom climate thus underwent an improvement, with positive consequences on how the teacher's work was carried out. Researchers should note that the role of the teacher in this experiment was management and coordination of the activities, with her as the guide to learning about the subject on the network, while giving students an important role in its development and management. The teacher makes decisions about what to do through virtual forums and tutorials, planning the process of learning through Facebook, proposing the subject for debate through her Facebook status, guiding the work and activities through virtual tutoring via network chat, and most importantly, mediating between the students. Students are responsible for constructing their own knowledge, with the teacher using an open and flexible curriculum that enables her to attend to the needs of all the students (Domínguez & Llorente, 2009).

For the students, this experience constitutes a breakthrough both in their professional and personal development. In the professional sense, they have learnt to handle Facebook as a resource in the classroom and been able to share knowledge with their peers and the teacher, gradually constructing their own knowledge on the subject matter. And in the personal scope, it enabled them to develop attitudes of collaboration, mutual respect and honesty, etc., and share personal experiences with their classmates, managing to form strong friendships and finding out that a collaborative learning community achieves more and better learning than studying alone at home without the help of others.

The perceptions of the students who were not using Facebook previously varied, considered that this tool enabled them to feel closer to the teacher and to their peers (Akcaoglu & Bowman, 2016).

The network becomes a substantial tool for innovation in the university classroom (Castro & González-Palta, 2016; Igartua & Rodríguez de Dios, 2016).

Teaching-Learning Process of Course Contents

Training of future teachers must be adapted to the demands of today's information society. ICTs can be a good tool for teacher training and development, as using them can encourage self-reflection and group reflection on their practices (Altinay-Gazi & Altinay-Aksal, 2017).

The teaching-learning process was improved significantly with the use of Facebook as a tool. One of the main tasks of the teacher in the use of Facebook concerned monitoring to ensure that the tasks carried out by the students and checked through Facebook were focused on achieving the course objectives. So, we see how this tool allowed the creation of a learning community formed by the students and the teacher, where the teacher is participant and observer of the students' whole learning process and the students are researchers in their own teaching-learning process, which enabled them to learn not only the knowledge, but even more importantly, how and where to acquire it, as Facebook improved or encouraged the skill of learning to learn. The teacher allowed the students to work on their own, with her guidance through the network, building connections in their own knowledge, the students themselves being responsible for the construction of their own knowledge (Domínguez & Llorente, 2009).

Facebook was therefore a didactic resource which enabled the development of knowledge, reinforcing in some cases and facilitating in others. Facebook has thus become an important tool in the processes of learning and knowledge development (Wodziki, Scfhwämmlein, & Moskaliuk, 2012). Students and teachers therefore need to know the features and uses of different tools suitable for the characteristics of today's students and which can improve the teaching-learning processes (Kelly, Thompson, Green, & Vice, 2017).

The subject content was debated on Facebook by the students, guided by the teacher, who was also able to introduce key questions from the subject so that the students could develop their own learning through an investigative approach. The students think that their role as a researcher in the teaching-learning process enabled them to learn not only knowledge but something even more important, i.e. how and where to learn them, in such a way that Facebook has improved or encouraged their learning-to-learn skill. In agreement with Lambic (2016), there is a positive correlation between Facebook users and their knowledge development. Both teacher and students highlighted the considerable improvement in the knowledge and outcomes of the student body as use of Facebook increase. Using Facebook allowed the teacher to guide the learning and explain some contents via the network, supplementing the classroom learning and dedicating more time to helping students understand the contents.

The tool allowed students the chance to have more contact hours with the teacher, in such a way that her working time, while acknowledging that it became more intensified, enabled her to explain the course contents more fully, fostering discussion and debate, the exchange of views and knowledge construction.

Virtual Tutoring

The teachers engaged in this experiment believe that virtual mentoring is one the main tasks they carry out through Facebook and is, in turn, the task most rated by the students. The teachers of the different courses and the teacher of the specific experiment in question consider that it is the most important task, as it is the one that promotes a better climate, builds the collaborative learning community and contributes to the acquisition of knowledge. Facebook is the promoter of the creation of learning communities in which the different educational agents exchange and communicate viewpoints (Lieberman & Pointer, 2010). The students start to use the network to consult the teacher about their course contents.

Facebook is a vital medium, giving them the chance to have personalised and individualised contact with the teacher at all times, facilitating the construction of knowledge of both teachers and students. In other words, tutoring hours increased and the teacher attended each student personally, taking their personal features into account and providing a response to the diversity present in the classroom. Facebook was not only very supportive in tutoring with the teacher. Students explained that it was an essential tool that encouraged peer-to-peer tutoring, i.e. among classmates. In this sense, they consider that it promoted mutual aid, concern for others, respect and the need to improve as groups, etc.

The collaboration was positively valued by both students and faculty. Collaboration theories (Kugelmas, 2001) were promoted in this experiment using the Facebook network.

Second Language Practice

Practising a second language only occurred in one specific case; in subsequent courses there were no multilingual groups. Although language improvement was not a priority objective to be achieved through Facebook, both teacher and students claim that this network allowed them to acquire vocabulary and practice their grammar and comprehension, thus improving their second language writing skills. This constituted improved communication and language development through the network (Sotomayor, 2010).

This didactic resource encouraged the use of English on the network, as both teacher and students had to make an effort to express what they wanted to say and use the language correctly

Acquisition of Digital Competence

The digital skills of faculty were considerably improved. Overcoming one of the limitations of teachers in use of Facebook, namely technological knowledge (Chugh & Ruhi, 2017), Facebook gave faculty the chance to raise concerns about training in issues related to the use of online tools, increasing their digital competence every day and transmitting this to their students. The students positively rated the teachers' efforts to use different resources to improve the teaching-learning process.

All agreed that using Facebook was initially a challenge, as none of them were using social networks in their personal life, but they all consider that using this tool has enabled them to discover other educational resources on the net that allow them to engage in better pedagogy online, such as: wikis, web quests, treasure hunts, etc.

Facebook also provided an opportunity for teachers to share and discuss their practices among themselves, encouraging self-reflection regarding improvement of the same in the classroom (Altinay-Gazi & Altinay-Aksal, 2017).

However, the students' digital skills were not developed to any great extent, as the use of Facebook in the personal sphere was already a reality. They consider that they learnt more about other tools along with the teacher, such as wikis and web quests, etc.

So, the researchers may conclude that Facebook has given teachers the chance to raise concerns about training in issues related with the use of online tools, gradually increasing their digital competence and transmitting this to their students.

Finally, we can say that this experiment in the use of Facebook successfully led to better student learning development, while taking advantage of social networking as a facilitator of cooperative work which promotes the student's overall development. Moreover, the results were very favourable, with over 90% of the students successfully completing the academic subject and in turn creating a teacher-student relationship that still remains today.

Social networks, in this case Facebook, allowed the development of collaborative communities (McCarroll & Curran, 2014), based on cooperative work contributing to improvement of the classroom climate and the results of the students themselves.

SOLUTIONS AND RECOMMENDATIONS

This research shows that there is an eminent need to update primary teacher training. It is essential to adapt training to the new reality of society by furnishing future teachers with tools that can contribute to the improvement of teaching-learning processes. We have seen that among them are ICTs and, within them, social networks.

This research has further shown that incorporating a digital dimension or competence into the curriculum led to significant learning and change in the participants, both in personal and professional terms. The contact and interaction with other students through Facebook gave rise to positive effects on behaviour as well as on the development of attitudes and knowledge about the subject, while fostering a special sensitivity to building learning through cooperative work and improving student-student and student-teacher relations. The effects of the experience are projected into the reality of participants' lives, reflected in their actions and subsequent commitment and in changes in how they deal with professional and personal situations.

FUTURE RESEARCH DIRECTIONS

This study leads us to envisage possible future lines of work and research related to social networks as a teaching resource to improve student learning, such as Facebook as a classroom strategy for resolving conflicts, use of internet in the classroom to mediate students' interpersonal relationships and several other topics that might be interesting subjects for more in-depth study in this area with a view to enhancing our teaching practice. Specifically, from this experiment, the researchers can point out three issues to develop a research agenda. Thus, it would be interesting to delve deeper into the use of Facebook: a) as a tool for improving the teacher-student relationship; b) to analyse the impact of Facebook use on the teacher's work; or c) to improve second language learning.

CONCLUSION

This experiment has been an opportunity for students and teachers to verify that learning through building learning communities based on collaboration and teamwork entails an improvement in relations and interaction in the classroom and thus improves the teaching-learning process leading to the students' overall development. The main aim of the experiment - to improve interaction in the classroom and teaching and learning processes - was achieved through the Facebook social network, complementing the attention to the individual characteristics of students and their diversity along with the development of the class as a group and as a working group, making this process a true reflection of the society we live in.

Nevertheless, some limitations were encountered throughout the experience. The first, and most important, was the amount of time invested in virtual tutoring virtual, forums and chats, i.e. attention to students, which intensified the teachers' already heavy workloads. It seems appropriate to limit the time devoted to this end within a set timetable. Secondly, the breach of trust by some students during network interaction, obliging the teacher to exert her authority and lay down the boundaries between them. Finally, the occasional excessive use by students of virtual tutoring as compared to traditional one-on-one mentoring, thereby losing the expression and knowledge the researchers gain from non-verbal language and face-to-face contact.

Overall, use of the Facebook network has worked as a knowledge-building teaching resource for students and teachers as well as a way to build citizens with teamwork, cooperation, collaboration and interdisciplinary work-related skills, in preparation for a digital society as committed professionals who not only know their subject matter but have also acquired the necessary skills to work on it with the group.

Summing up, we believe this new tool may result in subsequent related multiple research works which will help improve traditional as well as virtual teaching-learning processes. Digital competence is one of the basic skills that school children should acquire. Pre-service teachers must therefore also be competent in this area. Social networks, especially Facebook, can be a tool to achieve this and open up a world to teaching and learning where closer interaction between people (Lampe, Ellison, & Steinfield, 2007) brings us closer to the globalisation of knowledge.

ACKNOWLEDGMENT

This research received no specific grant from any funding agency in the public, commercial, or not-for-profit sectors.

REFERENCES

AIMC. (2017). *Infografía de la 19ª Encuesta AIMC a usuarios de Internet - Navegantes en la Red*. Retrieved August, 2017, from http://download.aimc.es/aimc/REP2a3z/Infografia_naveg_19.pdf

Ainscow, M. (2012). Moving knowledge around: Strategies for fostering equity within education systems. *Journal of Educational Change*, *13*(3), 289–310. doi:10.100710833-012-9182-5

Akcaoglu, M., & Bowman, N. D. (2016). Using instructor-led Facebook groups to enhance students' perceptions of course content. *Computers in Human Behavior*, *65*, 582–590. doi:10.1016/j.chb.2016.05.029

Altinay-Gazi, Z., & Altinay-Aksal, F. (2017). Technology as Mediation Tool for Improving Teaching Profession in Higher Education Practices. *EURASIA Journal of Mathematics*, *Science & Technology Education*, *13*(3), 803–813.

Álvarez, G., & López, M. (2013). Análisis del uso de Facebook en el ámbito universitario desde la perspectiva del aprendizaje colaborativo a través de la computadora. *Edutec, 43*, 1-15. Retrieved August, 2017, from http://edutec.rediris.es/Revelec2/Revelec43/pdf/Edutec-e_n43-Alvarez_Lopez.pdf

Amador, P.; & Amador, J. (2017). Academic Help Seeking: a Framework for Conceptualizing Facebook Use for Higher Education Support. *TechTrends: Linking Research & Practice to Improve Learning, 61*(2), 195-202. Doi:10.1007/s11528-016-0135-3

Area, M. (2000). ¿Qué aporta internet al cambio pedagógico en la Educación Superior? In R. Pérez (Coord.). *Redes multimedia y diseños virtuales* (pp. 128-135). Actas del III Congreso Internacional de Comunicación, Tecnología y Educación. Oviedo: Universidad de Oviedo.

Attard, C. (2011). Teaching with Technology. *Australian Primary Mathematics Classroom*, *16*(2), 30–32.

Baghdadi, Z. D. (2011). Learning community in Online Education. *Online Journal of Distance Education, 12*(4), 1-2. Retrieved August, 24, 2012, from http://tojde.anadolu.edu.tr/tojde45/notes_for_editor/notes_for_editor_2.htm

Betts, K., Kramer, R., & Gaines, L. (2011). Online Faculty and Adjuncts: Strategies for Meeting Current and Future Demands of Online Education through Online Human Touch Training and Support. *International Journal of Online Pedagogy and Course Design*, *1*(4), 20–38. doi:10.4018/ijopcd.2011100102

Bonk, C. J., & Wisher, R. A. (2000). *Applying Collaborative and e-learning Tools to Military Distance Learning: A Research Framework*. United States Army Research Institute for the Behavioral and Social Sciences. Retrieved February, 13, 2013, from http://www.publicationshare.com/docs/Dist.Learn(Wisher).pdf

Boyd, D. M., & Ellison, N. B. (2007). Social Network Sites: Definition, history and scholarship. *Journal of Computer-Mediated Communication, 13*(1), 201–230. doi:10.1111/j.1083-6101.2007.00393.x

Brill, J. M., & Park, Y. (2008). Facilitating Engaged Learning in the Interaction Age: Taking a Pedagogically Informed Approach to Innovation with Emergent Technologies. *International Journal on Teaching and Learning in Higher Education, 20*(1), 70–78.

Brook, C., & Oliver, R. (2003). Online Learning communities: Investigating a design framework. *Australian Journal of Educational Technology, 19*(2), 139–160.

Buabeng-Andoh, C. (2012). Factors influencing teachers' adoption and integration of information and communication technology into teaching: A review of the literatura. *International Journal of Education and Development Using Information and Communication Technology, 8*(1), 136–155.

Cabero, J., Barroso, J., Llorente, M. C., & Yanes, C. (2016). Redes sociales y Tecnologías de la Información y la Comunicación en Educación: Aprendizaje colaborativo, diferencias de género, edad y preferencias. *Revista de Educación a Distancia, 51*. doi:10.6018/red/51/1

Castells, M. (2002). *The Information Age: Economy, Society and Culture: The Rise of the Network Society* (2nd ed.; Vol. 1). Oxford, UK: Blackwell Publishing.

Castells, M. (2006). *La Sociedad Red*. Madrid: Alianza Editorial.

Castro, P. J., & González-Palta, I. N. (2016). Percepción de estudiantes de psicología sobre el uso de Facebook para desarrollar pensamiento crítico. *Formación Universitaria, 9*(1), 45–56. doi:10.4067/S0718-50062016000100006

Cho, M. H., & Kim, B. J. (2013). Students' self-regulation for interaction with others in online learning environments. *Internet and Higher Education, 17*, 69–75. doi:10.1016/j.iheduc.2012.11.001

Chugh, R., & Ruhi, U. (2017). Social media in higher education: A literatura review of Facebook. *Education and Information Technologies*. doi:10.100710639-017-9621-2

Climent Sanchís, S. (2013). La comunicación y las redes sociales. *Revista 3C TIC, 2*(1). Doi:10.17993/3ctic.2013.21.+

Davis, C. III, Deil-Amen, R., Rios-Aguilar, C., & Gonzalez Canche, M. (2012). *Social Media in Higher Education. A literature review and research directions*. Center for the Study of Higher Education. University of Arizona, Claremont Graduate University.

De Haro, J. J. (2010). *Redes sociales para la educación*. Madrid: Anaya.

Dominguez, G., & Llorente, M. C. (2009). La educación social y la web 2.0: Nuevos espacios de innovación e interacción social en el espacio europeo de educación superior. *Pixel-Bit. Revista de Medios y Educación, 35*, 105–114.

Duart, J. M. (2009). Internet, redes sociales y educación. *Revista Universidad y Sociedad del Conocimiento, 6*(1), 1–2.

Duggan, M., Ellison, N. B., Lampe, C., Lenhart, A., & Madden, M. (2015). *Social Media Update 2014*. Pew Research Center, January 2015. Retrieved August, 2017, from http://www.pewinternet.org/2015/01/09/social-media-update-2014/

Dziuban, C., Moskal, P., Kramer, L., & Thompson, J. (2013). Student satisfaction with online learning in the presence of ambivalence: Looking for the will-o'-the-wisp. *Internet and Higher Education*, *17*, 1–8. doi:10.1016/j.iheduc.2012.08.001

Ellison, N. B., Steinfield, C., & Lampe, C. (2007). The Benefits of Facebook Friends: Social Capital and College Students Use of Online Social Network Sites. *Journal of Computer-Mediated Communication*, *12*(4), 1143–1168. doi:10.1111/j.1083-6101.2007.00367.x

Eynon, R. (2005). The use of the internet in higher education: Academics' experiences of using ICTs for teaching and learning. *Aslib Proceedings*, *57*(2), 168–180. doi:10.1108/00012530510589137

Fraser, B. J. (2012). Classroom Learning Environments: Retrospect, Context and Prospect. In B. Fraser, K. Tobin, & C. McRobbie (Eds.), *Second International Handbook of Science Education* (pp. 1191–1239). Dordrecht, The Netherlands: Springer. doi:10.1007/978-1-4020-9041-7_79

Gao, F. (2013). A case study of using a social annotation tool to support collaboratively learning. *Internet and Higher Education*, *17*, 76–83. doi:10.1016/j.iheduc.2012.11.002

Getzlaf, B., Melrose, S., Moore, S., Ewing, H., Fedorchuk, J., & Troute-Wood, T. (2012). Online Interest Groups: Virtual Gathering Spaces to Promote Graduate Student Interaction. *International Journal of Online Pedagogy and Course Design*, *2*(4), 63–76. doi:10.4018/ijopcd.2012100105

Gray, K., & Carter, M. (2012). "If Many Were Involved": University Student Self-Interest and Engagement in a Social Bookmarking Activity. *International Journal of Online Pedagogy and Course Design*, *2*(4), 20–31. doi:10.4018/ijopcd.2012100102

Greenhow, C., Robelia, B., & Hudges, J. E. (2009). Learning, teaching, and scholarship in a digital age: Web 2.0 and classroom research — What path should we take "now"? *Educational Researcher*, *38*(4), 246–259. doi:10.3102/0013189X09336671

Guiza, M., Salinas, J., & Flores, E. (2011). Desarrollo e implementación de un entorno virtual para trabajo colaborativo. In *XIV Congreso Internacional EDUCTEC*. Pachuca de Soto.

Häkkinen, P., Järvelä, S., Mäkitalo-Siegl, K., Ahonen, A., Näykki, P., & Valtonen, T. (2017). Preparing teacher-students for twenty-first-century learning practices (PREP 21): A framework for enhancing collaborative problem-solving and strategic learning skills. *Teachers and Teaching*, *23*(1), 25–41. doi:10.1080/13540602.2016.1203772

Hsu, J. (2007). Innovative Technologies for education and Learning: Education and Knowledge-oriented applications of blogs, Wikis, podcasts, and more. *International Journal of Information and Communication Technology Education*, *3*(3), 70–89. doi:10.4018/jicte.2007070107

Hurtado, I. G., & Llamas, J. M. C. (2014). Social Networks in University Classrooms: An experience of teaching and learning with pre-service teachers through Facebook. *International Journal of Online Pedagogy and Course Design*, *4*(3), 34–48. doi:10.4018/ijopcd.2014070103

Igartua, J. J., & Rodríguez-de-Dios, I. (2016). Correlatos motivacionales del uso y la satisfacción con Facebook en jóvenes españoles. *Cuadernos.Info, 38*(38), 107–119. doi:10.7764/cdi.38.848

Infante, A., & Aguaded, J. I. (2012). Las redes sociales como herramientas educativas. In Y. Sandoval, A. Arenas, E. López, J. Cabero y J.I. Aguaded (Coords.), Las tecnologías de la información en contextos educativos: nuevos escenarios de aprendizaje (pp. 163-176). Santiago de Cali: Universidad Santiago de Cali.

Keane, T., Keane, W., & Blicblau, A. (2016). Beyond Traditional Literacy: Learning and Transformative Practices Using ICT. *Education and Information Technologies, 21*(4), 769–781. doi:10.100710639-014-9353-5

Kelly, T., Thompson, S., Green, B., & Vice, J. (2017). Facebook Faculty and Tweeting Teachers: Social Media as a Learning, Development, and Support Mechanism for Pre-Service, In-Service, and Post-Service Educators. In P. Resta & S. Smith (Eds.), *Proceedings of Society for Information Technology & Teacher Education International Conference* (pp. 1655-1659). Austin, TX: Association for the Advancement of Computing in Education (AACE).

Kirkgöz, Y. (2016). The Use and Uptake of Information and Communication Technology: A Turkish Case of an Initial Teacher Education Department. In M. Khosrow-Pou (Ed.), *Mobile Computing and Wireless Networks: Concepts, Methodologies, Tools, and Applications* (pp. 773–796). IGI Global. doi:10.4018/978-1-4666-8751-6.ch034

Kolbitsch, J., & Maurer, H. (2006). The transformation of the Web: How emerging communities shape the information we consume. *Journal of Universal Computer Science, 12*(2), 187–213.

Kugelmass, J. W. (2001). Collaboration and Compromise in Creating and Sustaining an Inclusive School. *International Journal of Inclusive Education, 5*(1), 47–65. doi:10.1080/13603110121498

Lambic, D. (2016). Correlation between Facebook use for educational purposes and academic performance of students. *Computers in Human Behavior, 61*, 313–320. doi:10.1016/j.chb.2016.03.052

Lampe, C., Ellison, N., & Steinfield, C. (2007). A Familiar Face(book): Profile Elements as Signals in an Online Social Network. In *Proceedings of Conference on Human Factors in Computing Systems.* New York: ACM Press. 10.1145/1240624.1240695

Lazaros, E. J., & Jeffery, C. (2013). Promoting a positive classroom climate in higher education in the United States. *Continental Journal of Arts and Humanities, 5*(1), 8–12.

Lei, S. A. (2010). Classroom physical design influencing student learning and evaluations of college instructors: A review of literature. *Education, 131*(1), 128–134.

Liccardi, I., Ounnas, A., Pau, R., Massey, E., Kinnunen, P., Lewthwaite, S., ... Sarkar, Ch. (2007). The Role of Social Networks in Students' Learning Experiences. *ACM Sigcse Bulletin, 39*(4), 224–237. doi:10.1145/1345375.1345442

Lieberman, A., & Pointer, D. (2010). Making Practice Public: Teacher Learning in the 21st Century. *Journal of Teacher Education, 61*(1-2), 77–88. doi:10.1177/0022487109347319

Lohnes, S., & Whitfield, D. (2016). Examining college students' uptake of Facebook through the lens of domestication theory. *E-Learning and Digital Media*, *13*(5–6), 179–195.

Manca, E., & Ranieri, M. (2016). Facebook and the others. Potentials and obstacles of Social Media for teaching in higher education. *Computers & Education*, *95*, 216–230. doi:10.1016/j.compedu.2016.01.012

Mayorga M.J. & Madrid, D. (2010). Modelos didácticos y Estrategias de enseñanza en el Espacio Europeo de Educación Superior. *Tendencias pedagógicas, 15*, 91-111.

McCarrol, N., & Curran, K. (2014). Social Networking in Education. In M. Khosrow-Pou (Ed.), *Digital Arts and Entertainment: Concepts, Methodologies, Tools, and Applications* (pp. 731–745). IGI Global. doi:10.4018/978-1-4666-6114-1.ch034

McGarry Wolf, M., Wolf, M., Brady, L., Peszynski, H., & Higgins, L. (2012). Using Social Media for Collaboration about Industry News in Higher Education. *Proceedings of American Association Wine Economists Sixth Annual Conference.*

Mei-Zhao, C., & Kuh, G. (2004). Adding Value: Learning Communities and Student Engagement. *Research in Higher Education*, *45*(2), 115–138. doi:10.1023/B:RIHE.0000015692.88534.de

Mendiguren, T., Meso, K., & Pérez, J. (2012). El uso de las redes sociales como guía de autoaprendizaje en la Facultad de Comunicación de la UPV/EHU. *Didáctica de la Lengua y la Literatura*, *6*, 107–122.

Meso, K., Pérez, J., & Mendiguren, T. (2010a). Estrategias de enseñanza formal e informal. In *J. Sierra y J. Sotelo (Coords.), La incorporación de las redes sociales como herramienta en las aulas. Métodos de innovación docente aplicados a los estudios de Ciencias de la Comunicación.* Madrid: Fragua.

Meso, K., Pérez, J., & Mendiguren, T. (2010b). *Las redes sociales como herramientas para el aprendizaje colaborativo. Presentación de un caso desde la UPV/EHU. Congreso Internacional Europa/ América Latina ATEI. Alfabetización mediática y cultural digitales.* Sevilla: Gabinete de Comunicación y Educación.

Moorman, J., & Bowker, A. (2011). The University Facebook Experience: The Role of Social Networking on the Quality of Interpersonal Relationships. *American Association of Behavioral and Social Sciences Journal*, *15*, 1–23.

Murati, R., & Ceka, A. (2017). The Use of Technology in Educational Teaching. *Journal of Education and Practice*, *8*(6), 197–199.

Myers, S. A., & Claus, C. J. (2012). The relationship between students' motives to communicate with their instructors and classroom environment. *Communication Quarterly*, *60*(3), 386–402. doi:10.1080 /01463373.2012.688672

ONTSI. (2017). *Las Tics en los hogares españoles. Estudio de demanda y uso de Servicios de Telecomunicaciones y Sociedad de la Información.* Retrieved August, 2017, from http://www.ontsi.red.es/ontsi/ sites/ontsi/files/LIV%20Oleada%20del%20Panel%20Hogares.pdf

Panckhurst, R., & Marsh, D. (2011). Utilización de redes sociales para la práctica pedagógica en la enseñanza superior impartida en Francia: Perspectivas del educador y del estudiante. *Revista de Universidad y Sociedad del Conocimiento*, *8*(1), 233–252.

Pasadas, C. (2010). Multialfabetización y redes sociales en la universidad. *Revista de Universidad y Sociedad del Conocimiento, 7*(2), 17–27.

Perrin, A. (2015). *Social Networking Usage: 2005-2015*. Pew Research Center. Retrieved August, 2017, from http://www.pewinternet.org/2015/10/08/2015/Social-Networking-Usage-2005-2015/

Reid, S. (2012). The Changed Role of Professor in Online Courses. *International Journal of Online Pedagogy and Course Design, 2*(1), 21–36. doi:10.4018/ijopcd.2012010102

Reina Estévez, J., Fernández Castillo, I., & Noguer Jiménez, A. (2012). El uso de las Redes sociales en las Universidades andaluzas: El caso de Facebook y Twitter. *Revista Internacional de Relaciones Públicas, 4*(2), 123–144.

Rouis, S., Limayen, M., & Salehi-Sangari, E. (2011). Impact of Facebook Usage on Student's Academic Achievement: Roles of Self-Regulation and Trust. *Electronic Journal of Research in Educational Psychology, 9*(3), 961–994.

Rovai, A. (2002). Development o fan Instrument to Measure Classroom Community. *The Internet and Higher Education, 5*(3), 197–211. doi:10.1016/S1096-7516(02)00102-1

Sandy, M., & Jared, K. (2014). Information Communication Technology Planning in Developing Countries. *Education and Information Technologies, 19*(4), 691–701. doi:10.100710639-013-9248-x

Selwyn, N. (2007). '*Screw Blackboard... do it on Facebook!': An investigation of students' educational use of Facebook*. Paper presented to the 'Poke 1.0 - Facebook social research symposium', London, UK.

Selwyn, N. (2012). *Social Media in Higher Education. The Europa World of Learning.* London: Routledge.

Sharma, R. C. (2010). Emerging Trends of Student Support Services in Indian Distance Education. In D. Gearhart (Ed.), *Cases on Distance Delivery and Learning Outcomes: Emerging Trends and Programs* (pp. 245–258). Hershey, PA: IGI Global; doi:10.4018/978-1-60566-870-3.ch015

Sharma, S. K., Joshi, A., & Sharma, H. (2016). A multi-analytical approach to predict the Facebook usage in higher education. *Computers in Human Behavior, 55*, 340–353. doi:10.1016/j.chb.2015.09.020

Sheldon, P. (2008). The Relationship between Unwillingness-to-communicate and Students' Facebook Use. *Journal of Media Psychology, 20*(2), 67–75. doi:10.1027/1864-1105.20.2.67

Siemens, G., & Weller, M. (2011). El impacto de las redes sociales en la enseñanza y el aprendizaje. *Revista de Universidad y Sociedad del Conocimiento, 8*(1), 157–163.

Silverstone, R., & Hirsch, E. (Eds.). (1994). Consuming Tecnologies. Media and Information in Domestic Spaces.

Simons, H. (2011). *El estudio de caso: Teoría y práctica*. Madrid: Morata.

Sotomayor, G. (2010). Las redes sociales como entornos de aprendizaje colaborativo mediado para segundas lenguas. *Revista Electrónica de Tecnología Educativa, 34*, 1–16.

Starkey, L. (2010). Teachers' pedagogical reasoning and action in the digital age. *Teachers and Teaching, 16*(2), 233–244. doi:10.1080/13540600903478433

Stollak, M. J., Vandenberg, A., Burklund, A., & Weiss, S. (2011). Getting social: the impact of social networking usage on grades among college students. *Proceedings of ASBBS. ASBBS Annual Conference.*

Strauss, A., & Corbin, J. (2002). *Bases de la investigación cualitativa. Técnicas y procedimientos para desarrollar la teoría fundamentada.* Medellín, Colombia: Universidad de Antioquia.

Tapscott, D., & Williams, A. D. (2010). *Wikinomics. How Mass Collaboration Changes Everythings, Portfolio.* Penguin Group.

Túñez, M., & Sixto, J. (2012). Las redes sociales como entorno docente: análisis del uso de Facebook en la docencia universitaria. *Pixel Bit, 41,* 77-92. Retrieved August, 2017, from, de http://acdc.sav.us.es/pixelbit/images/stories/p41/06.pdf

UNESCO. (2017). *Informe de Seguimiento de la Educación en el Mundo 2016.* La educación al servicio de los pueblos y los planetas. Creación de futuros sostenibles para todos. Retrieved August, 2017, from http://unesdoc.unesco.org/images/0024/002485/248526S.pdf

Wang, C. M. (2012). Using Facebook for Cross-cultural Collaboration: The Experience of Students from Taiwan. *Educational Media International, 49*(1), 63–76. doi:10.1080/09523987.2012.662625

Wang, M., Haertel, G., & Walberg. (1997). Learning Influences. In H. Walberg & G. Haertel (Eds.), *Psychology and Educational Practice.* Berkeley, CA: McCuthan.

Watulak, S. L., & Whitfield, D. (2017). Examining college students' uptake of Facebook through the lens of domestication theory. *E-Learning and Digital Media, 13*(5-6), 179–195. doi:10.1177/2042753016689633

Wodzicki, K., Schwämmlein, E., & Moskaliuk, J. (2012). "Actually, I Wanted to Learn": Study-related knowledge exchange on social networking sites. *Internet and Higher Education, 15*(1), 9–14. doi:10.1016/j.iheduc.2011.05.008

KEY TERMS AND DEFINITIONS

Classroom Climate: The intellectual, social, emotional, and physical environments in which our students and teachers learn and teach.

Collaborative Peer Networks: Collaborative relationships between students and teachers to build on the teaching-learning process.

Facebook: It is the most used social network.

Flexible Curriculum: It is a curriculum for students that is open to change.

Learning Communities: Groups of teachers and students who establish relationships of mutual support to learn and have the same goals and attitudes in the teaching-learning process.

Social Networks: They are websites or applications that allow people to communicate and share information on the computer or mobile phone.

Teacher Dominance: The teacher's freedom and authority in class.

This research was previously published in Innovative Applications of Online Pedagogy and Course Design; pages 258-279, copyright year 2018 by Information Science Reference (an imprint of IGI Global).

Chapter 104
Social Media Use in Career Guidance Delivery in Higher Education in the United Arab Emirates:
A Literature Review

Sophia Alim

https://orcid.org/0000-0002-0413-3893

Independent Researcher, UK

ABSTRACT

This literature review examines the use of social media in higher education career guidance delivery in the UAE (United Arab Emirates). Previous research has revealed UAE youth feel unprepared for work, highlighting a need to improve the quality of career guidance. With social media becoming popular, social media integrated with career guidance can expand opportunities for students. The current use of social media in career guidance, highlighted that the UAE is utilizing social media as an information source rather than an interactive workspace. UAE universities use online career planning systems mainly. One of the main reasons being that social media delivery in career guidance leads to pressure for career guidance practitioners, in terms of moderating content. Coupled with the strict privacy laws governing the use of social media in the UAE, this can present challenges. For social media to become successfully integrated into career guidance delivery, universities in the UAE need to understand what their students want in terms of career guidance delivery.

1. INTRODUCTION

The United Arab Emirates (UAE) is a federation of seven states located in the Middle East. With 13.53% of the population in the UAE in 2017 between 15-24 years old, the youth represent the third largest age group in the UAE. Youth unemployment figures in 2017 across the Gulf States and North Africa

DOI: 10.4018/978-1-6684-7123-4.ch104

including the UAE indicated the highest collective percentage of youth unemployment in the world (Central Intelligence Agency, 2018; Oxford Business Group, 2018. In 2017, youth unemployment among 15-24-year-olds in the UAE was 11.7% (Statistica, 2018).

A lack of good quality career guidance was one of the reasons cited behind youth unemployment in the UAE. Career guidance is defined as "advice and information about careers that helps individuals, especially young people, decide on a career and also teaches them how to pursue their chosen career" (Collins, 2018). Other reasons behind youth unemployment included slow economic growth, low-quality education, rising social unrest and a tough private sector environment (ASDA'A Burson-Marsteller, 2017; Dilshad, 2017; The International Council of Security and Development, 2010; The World Bank, 2017; Wilkins, Balakrishnan, & Huisman, 2012). The reasons were reflected in findings of the Arab Youth Survey in 2018 (ASDA'A Burson-Marsteller, 2018). The Arab Youth Survey carried out annually, aims to provide evidence-based insights into the attitude of Arab youth. This information is beneficial to the public and private sector in the creation of policies and decision making.

The 2018 Arab youth survey conducted 3,500 face-to-face interviews with 18-24-year-old Arab men and women across 16 Arab states which included the UAE. The survey highlighted that 23% of Arab youth associate the UAE with having a high-quality education system and 29% associate the UAE with offering a wide range of work opportunities. The UAE was also stated as the top country to live in by 35% of the youths questioned due to being associated with high paid jobs and strong career opportunities (ASDA'A Burson-Marsteller, 2018).

One method of making career guidance more accessible is incorporating it with social media. Social media platforms especially Facebook are very popular amongst UAE youth and the population in general. Types of social media platforms include social networking sites (Facebook, Google+); microblogging (Twitter); blogs; virtual worlds (Second Life), social bookmarking sites (Delicious, Digg); photo or video-sharing sites (Flickr, YouTube); forums and discussion groups.

UAE, with a population of 9.5 million people, 9.4 million are Internet users with a 99% Internet penetration rate. In terms of Facebook users in the UAE, there are 9.38 million Facebook users with 99% of them having active accounts at the beginning of 2018 (ASDA'A Burson-Marsteller, 2018). Other popular social media platforms used in the UAE include YouTube 7.47 million users, 79% active users; Instagram 5.01 million users, 53% active users; Twitter 3.87 million, 41% active users; LinkedIn 3.78 million, 40% active users (Dubai Digital Interactive Agency, 2018).

Focusing on the UAE youth, in 2016, the social media survey of Arab countries highlighted that from the 5,530 users who answered the online survey, the UAE had high penetration rates in terms of the population in 2016: for Facebook (81.1%). Whereas the social media platforms with the lowest penetration rate were Instagram (12.9%) and LinkedIn (32.5%) (Salem, 2017).

Overall usage indicated that the most popular social media platforms used in the UAE were Facebook, WhatsApp, and YouTube. The least popular were Snapchat and LinkedIn. Age breakdown for Facebook users highlighted that there was a balance between the percentage of young users of Facebook in the UAE aged 15-29 years (49.2%) and older users aged 30+ (50.8%) (Salem, 2017). As far as the author is aware, there are no up to date statistics for UAE youth usage of social media.

With the issue of social media use in career guidance in mind, the aim of this study is to present a literature review which explores the role of social media in UAE university career departments and whether the integration of social media platforms into career guidance has taken place in the UAE and if so how. The literature review aims to answer the following research questions:

RQ1: What roles can social media play in university career departments in the UAE?

RQ2: What is the current state of career guidance delivery in terms of social media integration in UAE universities?

RQ3: What recommendations can be made for the future in terms of successful social media integration in UAE universities career departments?

The literature review will cover areas such as: youth unemployment in the UAE, the role social media can play in careers department; the impact social media can have on staff who deliver career guidance; the state of career guidance in UAE universities; how social media has been integrated and the impact it is having. If social media is utilised by students for career guidance purposes, how do they use it? Does the culture in the UAE impact on social media use in the careers guidance sector? There is currently a gap in research for literature surveys which look at social media use in higher education career guidance, in the UAE.

Previous research studies by (Kettunen, Vuorinen, & Sampson, 2013; Osborn & LoFrisco, 2012; Vuorinen & Kettunen, 2012) have highlighted how successful the integration of social media platforms into career guidance has been for students in Finland and Denmark.

The structure of the literature review will be as follows: Section 2 explores in more detail the background behind youth unemployment in the UAE and examine why there is a need for good quality career guidance. Section 3 looks at the role social media can play in career services as well as the advantages and disadvantage of using social media. Section 4 presents the current state of the career guidance sector in UAE universities. Section 5 explores current social media use in career departments at UAE universities. Section 6 presents a discussion of the literature review and Section 7 concludes the article.

2. FACTORS AFFECTING YOUTH UNEMPLOYMENT IN THE UAE

Factors such as low-quality education, slow economic growth, rising social unrest and a tough private sector environment have all contributed to UAE youth unemployment. The price and quality of higher education have long been debated in the UAE. The focus is on the business side of education rather than the quality of the graduates they produce as stated by a student, Kareem, a graduate of the Canadian University of Dubai (Fanack, 2017). This has an impact when searching for jobs and fighting with other graduates for job vacancies. More education choices are needed as well as modernising teaching theory through the use of technology in comparison to the use of traditional teaching methods (United Arab Emirates Government, 2018; Westley, 2017). The quality of higher education also affects the delivery of career guidance provisions.

In 2017, with the realisation that standards in education need to improve, Vision 2021 was established by the prime minister of the UAE Sheikh Mohammed bin Rashid al-Maktoum. The vision was to develop eight education pillars by 2021. They included increasing the average PISA score to be in the top 20 countries. Currently, the UAE is 48th and as a whole is achieving well below the Organisation for Economic Co-operation and Development (OECD) average for children. PISA tests the reading, writing and science skills of 15-year-olds. Another education pillar of interest to career guidance practitioners included increasing the percentage of 18-year-old national students who graduate from secondary education (United Arab Emirates Government, 2018b).

The history of the UAE has led to economic issues and consequently impacting youth unemployment. Sixty years ago, the discovery of oil allowed the UAE to transform from a cluster of small principalities into a modern state with a high standard of living. However, the UAE's dependence on oil has presented challenges, e.g., having to cut expenditure on social programmes due to low oil prices. For the next few years, the strategic plan for the UAE is to promote tourism and trade, develop industry and create more jobs for nationals through the improvement of education and increasing opportunities in the private sector (The World Bank, 2017).

Large-scale youth unemployment is one of the drivers of rising social unrest. Social unrest was illustrated in the Arab spring which occurred in 2011. The Arab spring involved high profile protests in Tunisia, Libya, Egypt, Bahrain, and Syria. The Arab spring was described as a youth rebellion against governments because it was time to reform and modernise their respective countries for the future (Hoffman & Jamal, 2012). Untapped potential can cause frustration amongst the young, trapped in their surroundings with family to support and little chance to earn an income and move elsewhere.

Various studies (Benchiba-Savenius, Mogielnicki, Owens, & Scott-Jackson, 2016; Daleure, 2017; The International Council of Security and Development, 2010; Zeffane & Bani Melhem, 2017) have explored the state of the public and private sectors in the UAE as well as the tough conditions of the private sector.

Benchiba-Savenius et al. (2016) used telephone interviews to gather data from 300 working Emirati nationals about their views on employment. Respondents were aged between 18-69 years old, with 19.6% of the participants being aged 19-25 years old. 87% of respondents worked in government and semi-government and 13% worked in either family businesses or the private sector. The results found that 60% of participants aged over 30 were more likely to work in the public sector in contrast to 49% of those under 30. This is in comparison to The International Council of Security and Development's (2010) survey of 310 Emirati youths aged between 16-26 years old. The results of this survey highlighted that 47% of participants would consider working in the private sector and 74% felt that the private sector played an important part in the employment sector.

Characteristics of the private sector have included long working hours, low salary, high workload, low job security, unrewarding and cultural insensitivity (Alboushi, 2017). Zeffane and Bani Melhem (2017) studied private and public sectors utilising a sample of 311 employees (129 public and 182 private sector) from the services sector in the UAE. The study found that public centre employees were more trusting, more satisfied and have less intention to leave their job.

The private sector can become more appealing by providing a better salary, better working conditions, increasing the awareness of the private sector amongst the youth, increasing the employment of Emirati citizens over non-Emirati citizens (Emiratization), flexible working schedules, and introducing more personal and workspaces in mixed gender environments (Daleure, 2017; International Council of Security and Development, 2010). Youth unemployment and its contributing factors are drivers for a need in better quality career guidance to be delivered to UAE youth to prepare them for the working world. Holman's (2014) benchmarks for good career guidance include:

- Learning from career and labour market information;
- Addressing the needs of the students;
- Encounters with employees/employers through workplace visits;
- Linking curriculum learning to careers;
- Experience of workplaces;
- Personal guidance;

- A stable careers programme.

Every student should be given enough information and support in order to navigate themselves through the world of work and make informed career choices in an ever-changing work environment despite the obstacles. Good quality career guidance is measured mainly by the destination of graduates. What sectors do graduates ultimately work in? What salaries do they start on? In the case of the UAE, there are various obstacle which young people face when searching for work. The use of social media is beneficial in career guidance in terms of opening doors in the job market. Also, social media use can help universities achieve the career guidance benchmarks highlighted by Holman's (2014). This is discussed in more detail in Section 3.

3. THE ROLE OF SOCIAL MEDIA IN CAREER DEPARTMENTS

The use of social media in a career department can affect not only the students but also career guidance practitioners who deliver career guidance to the students. Section 3 firstly explores the role of social media in the careers department for both the career guidance practitioners and the students. Secondly, Section 3 delves into the impact social media integration has for the guidance practitioner. Finally, there is an exploration of advantages and disadvantages of utilising social media for career guidance.

Social media can be used for a variety of functions for the guidance practitioner ranging from delivering access to career information, creating an interactive working space, providing a medium for one-to-one education and being a catalyst for policy change and reform (Kettunen, Sampson, & Vuorinen, 2015). Listed below are the main roles of social media in relation to career guidance from a students' perspective.

3.1. Creating Connections

At present, social media plays a big part in networking and creating connections with other people, e.g., potential employers. This is important when searching for a job. Previous research by Granovetter (1974) on how people found jobs, studied 282 men in the United States and explored how they found their jobs. Granovetter (1974, p. 20) discovered that job searching is "not what you know but who you know." The use of social media opens up your profile to a large audience and enables you to create connections and acquire more knowledge outside your own social circle.

3.2. Different Social Media Platforms Produce Different Guidance Options

Different social media platforms can provide different opportunities for students. Twitter, is a very public platform, can be used to network with potential employers and research job occupations and vacancies. Content posts on Twitter must be succinct and to the point due to the 280-character limit. In comparison, LinkedIn, which is a less open platform, allows a student to create an online CV and network with colleagues, alumni, and organisations. Students also can research job opportunities and discover what previous students have gone on to do career-wise. Facebook profiles can be created by students and used to receive updates from companies, join groups associated with job searches and interact with fellow job seekers. Other social media platforms of use include Pinterest, a visual pinboard to showcase research, resources, and work. Students can demonstrate their work and skills via blogging tools, e.g.,

WordPress. Blogging can be used to establish an online identity and highlight to potential employers what a candidates' skills are.

3.3. Standing Out From the Crowd

Social media platforms allow students to find out about key influencers in their chosen job sectors and hopefully get noticed by standing out from the crowd (Sheffield Hallam University, 2017; University of Edinburgh, 2016). The use of social media fits into the communication function as highlighted by Barnes, La Gro, and Watts' (2010) four functions of Information Communication Technology (ICT) in delivery of career guidance. The other functions include: informing by allowing access to career information; experiencing through learning from virtual online simulations and constructing through understanding their situation using online assessments.

3.4. Integration of Other Digital Technologies

Social media is not the only digital technology associated with career guidance delivery.

Other digital technologies which can be utilised for career guidance (Barnes, 2015) which can be beneficial to students, includes online peer mentoring; Web chats with career practitioners; E-portfolios; Career guidance platforms, e.g., CareerGuide.com. The platform solves career queries in three ways. The platform has an online forum with questions answered by over 1100 career guidance practioners; Applications for phone, e.g., Smart Career UK, Career Planner and Interest and Career Advice; Games, e.g., The Skills Game; Quizzes; E-learning, e.g., Massive Open online Courses (MOOCs) and Open badges are based on a digital standard created by the Mozilla Foundation to recognise learning, know-how, achievements, skills, and attitudes.

The integration of digital technologies into career guidance was highlighted by Hooley, Matheson, and Watts (2014) exploring what makes career guidance in schools effective. One of the recommendations centred on how online technology was important and how the government should develop a strategy to stimulate the development of tools to meet the needs of schools. This finding highlights one of. Holman's (2014) benchmarks for good career guidance which is for career guidance to address the needs of the students.

3.5. The Effect of Social Media use on Career Guidance Practitioners

The increased use of social media and digital technology has brought about extra challenges for career guidance practitioners. Kettunun et al. (2013) and Kettunen et al. (2015) explored practitioners' views on social media and technology. Kettunen et al. (2015) analysed the competency of 16 Finnish and Danish career guidance practitioners with experience in social media and found that there were various dimensions to the role. The role of the practitioners includes using social media to deliver information, delivering career services, establishing a collaborative approach for exploring careers and utilising social media for co-careering.

The various aspects of the role mean the practitioners have to have good online skills, knowledge of ethics as well as being innovative, patient, confident and motivated. The expert role of the career guidance practitioner, which is highlighted in Kettunun et al. (2013), emphasises the importance of delivering up-to-date information and coming up with innovative ways to engage students. This finding was validated by Bright, Pryor, Wilkenfeld, and Earl (2005) who studied 651 university students' experiences of career decision making. The study found that web-based information and media were significant in making career decisions.

The importance of innovation and using new technology in career guidance ties in with the 7C's of digital career literacy (Hooley, 2012) (see Table 1). The 7C's demonstrates how a career guidance practitioner can get the best out of the digital environment. This is so they can provide an up to date tailored guidance service to their students.

Table 1. The 7Cs of digital literacy adapted from (Hooley, 2012)

Name of 'C'	Description
Creating	Using social media and other digital technologies to create online CVs, portfolios and career blogs.
Communicating	The type of media you are communicating with, the audience you are communicating with and can you improve your communicating skills.
Connecting	Building networks.
Critiquing	Analysing the quality of the information such as who is telling me this, what message are they telling me, the purpose of the site, is someone paying for the site and why.
Collecting	Retrieving and storing information.
Changing	Keeping with the latest technical skills.
Curating	Managing your presence in the online world, i.e., how you are seen in the world, how you interact with the world and how this links in with your career.

The 7C's can put pressure on practitioners to be technically able and up-to-date on the latest technical trends. Trying to balance the use of social media and face-to-face interactions with students can be challenging for practitioners due to deciding the best method of information delievery the student. Another challenge is deciding how much of the career guidance is done online versus face to face interaction. Different models of learning can produce a variety of experiences for the students as well as impact the workload of the practitioners as illustrated by Staker and Horn's (2012) blended learning model in Table 2. Table 2 illustrates how carear guidance can be delivered and who takes the lead.

Table 2. Models of blended career development learning adapted from Staker and Horn's (2012)

Professional or Client Led Career Guidance Delivery	Primarily Face to Face Career Guidance Delivery	Primarily Online Career Guidance Delivery
Professional Led	Rotational Model	Enriched Virtual Model
Client Led	Self-blend model	Flex Model

There are four varieties of model which stipulate whether the student or practioner lead in the career guidance sessions. The models include:

- **Rotational Model:** Students rotate on a fixed schedule between learning modalities. One of the modalities is online learning. An example is students researching a topic online before coming together for a discussion with their career guidance practitioner on the topic;
- **Enriched Virtual Model:** A whole school experience where students' time is divided between learning online remotely and attending a brick and mortar campus. The model differs from the rotation model because it focuses on the whole school experience and not just a module by module model;
- **Self-blend Model:** Students take online courses to supplement their traditional courses. Online courses can be taken off site or on a brick and mortar campus. Self-blend differs from the Enriched Virtual Model because it is not a whole school experience;
- **Flex Model:** The content and instruction of the programme are mainly delivered online. Students can request time with the teacher in a flexible way, i.e., a face-to-face meeting to discuss topics they are finding difficult.

Table 2 demonstrates how the students are in control of their learning and what they get out their learning when using a client-led model. This makes them more self-sufficient when searching for a career. In turn, the career guidance practitioners provide a more supporting role rather than a facilitator. For both the student and practitioner, there can be advantages and disadvantages to using social media for career guidance activities.

3.6. Advantages and Disadvantages of Social Media Use for Career Guidance

Some of the advantages (Cochrane & Bateman, 2010; McNeill, Rice, & Wright, 2016; Osbourne, 2012) include:

- **Creation of a community:** The use of social media and its accessibility allows for the creation of networks of larger size created communities by its users. Social media platforms are well-known, and they can be useful for students to exchange knowledge, collaborate or encourage them to open up about their career choices or issues. Social media facilitates a wide range of communication and generates a vast amount of collective knowledge through the use of user-generated content and opinion as a result of answering questions and discussing experiences and problems (Cochrane & Bateman, 2010).

The use of social media builds up research and analytical skills in terms of the student deciding what information is useful and whether it can be trusted. For both practitioners and students, this is an important skill career-wise. Social media takes place in real time so depending on how active the community is, the information posted can be up-to-date. This is important because of the dynamic world of careers. New jobs are posted all the time. The use of social media allows barriers such as time, social stigma and distance to be overcome when seeking out assistance (Morris & Aguilera, 2012; Shallcross, 2011).

- **Individualised Experiences:** Different tools and technologies are available for students to use for career development and interaction with career practitioners. Students take in knowledge and apply it in different ways as illustrated by Staker and Horn's (2012) models of blended learning.

Students can tailor the relationships they have with online content and search out content which fits with their aims;

- **Time and Place:** The use of social media and digital technology means the online world is open 24 hours a day, 7 days a week. This fits in with the working world around the world. Technology has the beauty of storing the time and place of the content generated. This enables us to track trends, perspectives from different countries and this is important when researching careers (Osbourne, 2012);

- **Free Resources:** Apart from paying for Internet access, the cost of generating social media content and content for digital applications can be free. The cost of publication and development has decreased over time and this has allowed a greater amount of resources to be available for students. Resources include video-based commentary, debates, and news reports. The search functions on social media platforms allow for historical research to take place (Osbourne, 2012);

- **Diverse range and integration of technologies:** The use of the Internet and telephony offers a wide range of social media platforms and applications. This opens up opportunities for career learning and communication with practitioners, employers, and fellow colleagues;

- **Interactive Fun:** With the increased popularity of gaming across society, incorporating online games into career education can make it fun, engaging and memorable for the student. Technology use can be useful in the initial stages of career planning. Applications such as psychometric and personality tests are used to explore the personality and competencies of the student. Games and simulations explore the world of work and learning. The use of technology encourages students to take control of their learning and become self-sufficient (McNeill, Rice, & Wright, 2016);

- **Increased Collaborative modes of enquiry:** Social media platforms encourage collaborative modes of enquiry to acquire knowledge and results when learning. Hemmi, Bayne, and Land (2009) explored the use of social media in three courses across two semesters. Two courses were on campus undergraduate courses and one online postgraduate course. One undergraduate course used wikis which are visually rich to support teaching and learning. The other undergraduate course used blogs. The online postgraduate course used a range of social media platforms, e.g., Facebook, Second Life, blogs, and Wikis to support learning activities. The study found the use of social media and Wikis provided significant potential for formal learning;

- **Responsibility:** The introduction of social media platforms forces the student to understand the role of social media in society today and the issue of privacy. Everything they write on social media has an impact and this prepares them for life in the digital age where boundaries are only there if you define them.

Alongside advantages, there are also disadvantages to using social media and digital technologies for career learning which include:

- **Lack of Access:** Not every student will have access to the Internet or computers outside the university. This can cause issues especially if the support is fully online with minimal face-to-face contact. Even with students able to access the Internet, for disabled students, assistive technology has to be compatible with social media platforms and resources. An example for a blind student is the screen reader able to decipher the material and convey to the student exactly what is on the webpage (McNeill, Rice, & Wright, 2016).

Computer users have a wide variety of digital literacy skills. With the fast speed of social media development, digital skills have to be developed constantly. This can cause issues for students and practitioners alike if they struggle with technology. In order to attract users to social media platforms, the interface has to be usable for both students and practitioners.

- **Motivation:** The use of social media platforms and digital technology means that there is a lack of face-to-face with career guidance practitioners. If there is too much technology in use, the students can feel alone due to the lack of social interaction with the practitioner (Osbourne, 2012). This, in turn, can decrease motivation in using the technology;
- **Time Wasting:** Studies (e.g., Alwagait, Shahzad, & Alim, 2015; Livingstone, 2008; Malita, 2011) have indicated that the use of social media can lead to wasting time which can have an impact on the progress of career learning. Productivity decreases places pressure on the practitioner in terms of what advice to give out. Understanding students and what motivated them can help them with face-to-face interaction to get the best performance out of the students;
- **Privacy and Ethical Issues:** One of the major disadvantages of putting personal and job details on online profiles is privacy and ethics, i.e., where the boundary lies between personal and professional. Security has an impact on the privacy and confidentiality of student records. Phishing scams, viruses, and malware infections can retrieve personal data and passwords. This can compromise private sensitive data of students. The National Career Development Association's (NCDA; 2015) examination of ethical challenges (see Table 3) highlight that the field of ethics spans various areas from consent through to access of data.

The challenges are mainly associated with the issues of privacy, security, and confidentiality. The changing nature of the relationship between the practitioner and the student may distort the boundaries between personal and professional. This is due to social media being so accessible. Many companies do background checks on social media posts of potential candidates. There have been instances where personal lives have mixed in with professional lives with a negative impact. An example is a member of parliament (MP) turning down a student for work experience at his office due to tweets containing many swear words (Sherriff, 2014). Facebook has the option for job seekers to create separate professional and personal profiles. This is due to personal profiles being public by default.

Table 3. Ethical challenges for core ethical commitments adapted from National Career Development Association (NCDA), 2015). The symbol 'X' signifies the challenge met by the corresponding core ethical commitment.

Challenges	Core Ethical Commitments					
	Confidentiality	Privacy	Consent	Data Security	Tested Tools	Fair Treatment
Protection of client information	x	x		x		
Managing Interactions	x	x	x	x		
Digital Exclusions						x
Changing Nature of relationships	x	x	x	x		
The rapid development of technology					x	

The rapid development of technology can impact in the area of professional competence. Practitioners' competence in technical skills impacts the services delivered to the students. Practitioners have to understand how the technology works, the terms of service of the technology they are using, how to troubleshoot issues with technology, the end user agreement regarding technology use and what the capabilities and disadvantages of the technology (Vuorinen,Sampson, & Kettunen, 2011).

3.7. Quality of Assessments and Information

Having career based assessments on the Internet can produce validity issues such as: selecting career assessments which measure what they claim to measure; lack of a valid process when developing an assessment for the online world and trying to decipher results from an online assessment which has been done using pen and paper previously (Sampson & Makela, 2014). Computerised assessments can dehumanise the process of recruiting staff. Computers are put in charge of generating results as a result of inputs by a human. The computer will follow a set of rules and not necessarily see the whole picture. A computer is only as good as the knowledge programmed into it. The issues with online assessments also affect the career-based information accessed by students.

There are several factors which can compromise the validity of information. Information can be developed to promote a particular point of view rather than present the whole picture. This can have an impact on students' decisions in terms of what occupations and companies to work at. Indeed (https://www.indeed.co.uk/), a recruitment site, contains employee reviews of workplaces where they have worked. The review section contains a pros and cons column to depict an accurate picture of the company. Due to the ability to store information on the Internet, users do not always remove out-of-date information. This can make it difficult for students to search out the relevant information that they need for decision making in terms of education, training, and employment (Sampson & Makela, 2014).

4. CAREER GUIDANCE IN UAE UNIVERSITIES

The current state of career guidance in the UAE forms the foundation for the integration of social media. Despite the feelings amongst some young Emiratis that the quality of career development needs to be improved, the issue of career guidance is one of the areas being considered at universities. This is illustrated in Wilkins et al.'s (2012) study into students' perceptions of study at international branch campuses in the UAE. The study looked at areas such as student learning, programme effectiveness, quality of teaching, learning resources, use of technology and facilities which included career guidance and library services. The sample of 247 students were asked to rate statements based on the corresponding areas. The rating scale was a 7-point rating scale, where 1= disagree strongly, 4= neutral and 7 = agree strongly. The mean score for the statement 'My university has a good careers advice and internships service' was 4.84 indicating slight agreement but room for improvement.

Section 4 will now explore firstly the main themes surrounding career guidance delivery in UAE universities such as the focus on internships; increased relationship with employers and the increased desire for young Emiratis to become entrepreneurs. Secondly, Section 4 will also investigate what social media tools are currently being utilised in career guidance delivery in the UAE.

4.1. Internships

In the UAE career guidance curriculum, there is a focus on internship services due to the introduction in 2002 of internships to the academic curriculum for various subjects (Downey & Raja, 2017).

An internship is when a student undertakes a period of work experience offered by a company for a fixed period of time. An internship offers students exposure to the working world and builds upon course material learned in university lectures. The use of the internship is to make students more work ready.

Studies such as (Bhattacharya & Neelam, 2018; Silva et al., 2016) highlighted the value of graduates doing an internship during their studies. The study by Silva et al., 2016 explored the effect of internships in graduate unemployment levels in Portugal before and after the introduction of internships. The study methodology involved examining empirical data from a database which contained data from 138 Portuguese first cycle degrees (FCDs) with study programme. The data included internship data and graduate unemployment data. The results indicated that the inclusion of internships in the degree programs led to a reduction in the graduate unemployment rate. It was also found that internships can help students enhance their chances of getting a job.

In terms of UAE universities and internships, Zayed University incorporated a for-credit internship model where students had to undertake internships in order to get credit. In contrast, New York University Abu Dhabi created an online portal advertising internship vacancies, but internships are not compulsory.

4.2. Relationships With Employers

Ties with employers are highly valued and recognised in UAE universities, e.g., New York University Abu Dhabi builds up relationships with employers by inviting them to sessions and events. Adu Dhabi University has a career fair every year, which attracts regional and multinational companies. Other activities which are carried out in university career guidance departments, include: CV writing; interview preparation; internship preparation; skills analysis to enable individually tailored career guidance; learning how to market themselves as potential employees; learning about different industries and sectors; tips on how to search for jobs and networking and employment engagement activities such as site visits, interviews on campus, employer days, student/graduate recruitment (Downey & Raja,2017; Zayed University, 2017).

Career decision making forms a big part of university students' life. This is highlighted in Daniels and Ratliff's (2017) study which looked at career decisions making amongst 233 female Emirati undergraduate students. The study found that friends and family were the biggest influence on the career decision-making process. However, the study also found the family can serve as an obstacle in this process of job hunting due to their opinions on certain courses and jobs.

Universities in the UAE use a variety of career planning online systems, e.g., (Kuder Atlas, 2018; Kudos, 2018) to distribute career guidance and aid the career guidance practioner as well as the students. Career guidance information which is distributed by the Kudos system includes what employers are looking for, information on labour markets, what salary students can earn and what qualifications they will need. It gives students the ability to explore the future and make decisions about their future. Kuder Atlas offers tools and resources for planning careers for various service users. Some features include assessments designed to helps students discover their career paths, search for information about occupations of interest and what meets the students' interests. Kuder assessments also measure work values and skills confidence. As of present, there are no academic studies present which have looked into the validity or assessment reliability of Kuder (Kuder Atlas, 2018; Kudos, 2018).

In terms of the quality of career guidance given, the UAE government is taking the quality of education services including career guidance very seriously through its 2016 reforms as described by Warner and Burton (2017) which include:

1.   Improved student experience and attainment at all levels of education;
2.   Improved quality and professionalism among education practitioners;
3.   Higher standards on an international scale. This means scoring higher on educational tests e.g. PISA;
4.   Greater accountability among leaders in the education sector.

With these reforms in mind as well as, the Abu Dhabi Education Council (ADEC) has trained 37 staff from various schools, colleges, and universities with the internationally recognised career advisor training. This means that all higher education establishments now have an internally certified career guidance practioner who can advise students on their careers (Teach Middle East, 2016). One of the most popular career paths with young people in the UAE is entrepreneurship.

4.3. Entrepreneurship

Some studies (El-Gohary, Selim & Eid, 2016; Jabeen, Faisal & Katsioloudes, 2017; Rixon. Maritz & Fisher, 2017) have touched on the popularity of entrepreneurship as a career choice for young Emiratis. Jabeen et al. (2017) looked at drivers which influence a young Emirati to follow a career path in entrepreneurship. The findings of the study surprisingly illustrated that despite young people ranking entrepreneurship as the top choice of employment, they had never attended any course on entrepreneurship. This illustrates that like Daniels and Ratliff's (2017) finding, friends and family have a big influence on career choice. El-Gohary et al. (2016) researched the factors which influenced entrepreneurship education and UAE students' decision to start a business including: module content, module delivery, teaching environment, age, motivation, risk aversion and entrepreneurial ability. In contrast, Al-Harrasi and Al-Salti (2014) studied Omani university students and their relationship with entrepreneurial education, finding that work flexibility, money, and independence had a positive impact on entrepreneurial intention.

The benefits of young people becoming entrepreneurs for the economy is that they are innovative and create new sectors of work. They have a greater satisfaction with life and are more likely to hire fellow youths. Disadvantaged as well as advantaged youth can become entrepreneurs and young entrepreneurs are more adaptable to economic trends. They can spot opportunities due to being digitally native. Their ability to network in high growth sectors reaffirms UAE's position in markets. Entrepreneurship also enriches the private sector which is unpopular work in the UAE (Rixon et al., 2017).

4.4. UAE Career Guidance and Social Media

In addition to career development systems, some universities have incorporated the use of social media into career guidance. An example is NYU Abu Dhabi, which allows current students to utilise LinkedIn to explore the profiles of the NYU Abu Dhabi alumni. This allows students to see what previous students with an internship have achieved (Ismail & Koshy, 2017; NYU Abu Dhabi, 2018). Research into the use of Linkedin in the UAE carried out by (Ismail & Koshy, 2017) involved conducting in-depth interviews with five organisations and five recruitment companies. The study found that LinkedIn was a cost-effective tool for recruitment.

Furthermore, the use of video clips is becoming increasingly popular method in career guidance. In 2017, the Canadian University in Dubai presented a career workshop where a representative from InternsME (a company which helps students find internships in the UAE) introduced students to video CVs. These types of CVs can make the student stand out and give employers an indication of the candidate's personality and presence. The workshop also taught students how to make a professional video CV (Canada University Dubai, 2017).

Equally important is that career development departments in universities are starting to have their own individual social media presence rather than feed information into the Universities' main social media channels. An example is Abu Dhabi University's career department, who have their own Facebook page. Their Facebook page advertises opportunities, details of training and career-related events, e.g., career fairs at Abu Dhabi University. NYUAD Career Development Center Facebook page presents stories about current students who are doing internships as well as advertising what the career department offers students in terms of guidance and support. The NYUAD Career Development Center Instagram platform presents videos of alumni of NYUAD.

5. DISCUSSION

RQ1: What roles can social media play in university career departments in the UAE?

Social media integration in career guidance plays a variety of roles for both the career guidance practitioner and the student. The roles from the career guidance practitioner centre on creating an interactive working space so the guidance practitioner student working relationship can be a partnership in comparison to solely an advisory role by the career guidance practitioner.

However, as highlighted in this paper, the social media platforms in UAE universities are mainly used as an information distributor rather than a combination of student interaction and information distribution. This is highlighted in Kettunen et al.'s (2013, p313) analysis of career practitioners' thoughts on social media, finding that "shifts in guidance locus were the transitions from a supplier-driven service, formally bounded in time and space, to a citizen/ user-centered service that is ubiquitous…" The use of social media for guidance, allows students themselves to generate content through the interactions they have on social media undertaking career based activities. The interactions in conjunction with support from the career guidance practitioners enables a more tailored career guidance to be delivered to the student. The roles of social media use for students identified from the literature review in this paper (creating connections; access different guidance options; standing out from the crowd and integration of other digital technologies) highlights that a tailored approach to career guidance allows the student to be in more control of the task of preparing themselves for the world of work.

RQ2: What is the current state of career guidance delivery in terms of social media integration in UAE universities?

An analysis of literature on the use of social media in career guidance in UAE higher education has shown that some universities are utilising social media for career guidance purposes. Applying Kettunen et al.'s (2015) evolution of the use of social media in career guidance, the UAE is in-between the first and second stage: delivering information and using social media platforms for one-to-one communication via real-time texts, visual or audio. The subsequent stages are creating an interactive workspace which is integrated into the career department and finally co-careering. This involves sharing expertise and collaborating over career issues amongst members who belong to a community, e.g., career guidance practitioners. The UAE uses a combination of career planning online systems and social media platforms rather than social media platforms solely.

Countries such as Denmark and Finland have illustrated that social media use integrated into career guidance can be achieved. Denmark's eGuidance system offers guidance about education choices through the use of mail, phone, webinars, and chat. The service is available 68 hours a week and all counselling is done anonymously. The eGuidance Facebook page allows students to discuss, share and reflect on their experiences regarding education choices (Kettunen et al., 2015; The Education Guide, 2018).

In Finland, every student completing basic education is introduced to the online national career services. The use of ICT is a compulsory module of career education which is taught to all students aged 7-16 years old who go through basic education. This will set the students up from an early age to think about their career options. The ethos of instilling guidance and counselling services for students early on in their education means staff can understand the student and tailor career services to their needs. In Finnish higher education, specialist practitioners and teachers provide guidance and counselling to students. The methods of integration include web-based, distance learning guidance, integrated into teaching, via the careers and recruitment service, individual guidance and guidance into study affairs (Finnish National Agency for Education, 2011).

A report by the European Commission in 2017 highlighted the success of social media integrated career guidance with the 2016 graduate employment rate for Finland being 77.4% and 83.9% for Denmark (European Commission, 2016a; European Commission, 2016b).

A concept which is not covered in-depth in the literature reviewed in this paper is personal branding (Ambrose, 2015). Personal branding will allow a student to create an online profile viewable to employers. With employers in the UAE using LinkedIn to search and analyse candidates for senior manager level positions who have technical skills that are hard to find, personal branding is more important than ever to get noticed by recruiters. Recruiters have stated that LinkedIn is a trustworthy platform for sourcing candidates (Ismail & Koshy, 2017). However, profile information on candidates is only as true as the candidate posting it.

One of the strategies for sourcing the best candidates in areas such as IT security and Geographical Information Systems in the UAE is using LinkedIn to get in touch with candidates who have eight years or more experience and who are satisfied in their current job role (Ismail & Koshy, 2017). Personal branding is important in the UAE working environment where local citizens make up a small percentage of the population in comparison to expatriates.

Waxin, Lindsay, Belkhodja and Zhao (2018) studied recruitment and interviewed five private organisations and six public organisations from a variety of industries in the UAE. The results of the study highlighted that the common recruitment issues related to local candidates, included their high salary expectations, the lack of relevant skills, education, and experience as well as lack of career, business and industry awareness.

One reason for the lack of uptake of social media use amongst university career departments is the utilisation of social media data and the control of the data in which social media generates. In one example from 2017, 102 UAE youths were blackmailed over indecent pictures on social media platforms

Facebook, Instagram, and Snapchat. The victims were aged 20-25 years old. The victims were befriended by the blackmailers and encouraged to share personal details including indecent images. The blackmailers then used the indecent images to exploit the victims financially (Al Quwain, 2017). Some studies (Khan, Rakhman, & Bangera 2017; Rajan, Ravikumar, & Al Shaer, 2017) have highlighted how the UAE has become a target for cybercrime.

The UAE has a very strong attitude towards privacy and the protection of an individual's privacy. An example is posting photographs of others online and via social media which is a breach of Article 21, Cybercrime Law. The law makes it an offense to breach a person's privacy by taking, displaying or publishing pictures of others. The sanction is at least six months in prison and/or a fine of £29,234 pounds. Other rules which carry punishments include: disclosing details of a person's private life without consent, an employee disclosing confidential information, making defamatory statements and using social media to spread public hatred (Dowle & Judson, 2016; Khaleej Times, 2017).

These issues along with inappropriate actions on social media, maintaining technical skills, moderating content generated by the students and applying sanctions for misbehaviour creates extra work for the career guidance practitioners. Despite the negatives, the positives are that with the integration of social media into career guidance, social media can open doors for UAE students, allow them to network with employers and give them tools to explore careers and themselves as people.

RQ3: What recommendations can be made for the future in terms of successful social media integration in UAE universities career departments?

Despite the UAE government advertising how social media is widely used in the UAE (United Arab Emirates Government, 2018a), one of the reasons for lack of uptake on social media use in career guidance are the privacy laws and laws regarding disclosure of protection of an individual's privacy. The privacy and data laws need to be highlighted to students especially when the UAE universities start introducing more interactive workspaces into their digital strategy for career guidance.

There is a worry that moderation of social media platform content would be extra work for career guidance practioners. Unfortunately, this is the case with online systems. However, educating responsible use of social media amongst students, having clear terms of use for social media platforms and selling the advantages of social media integration such as tailored career guidance services and the ability to use various technologies should give a purpose to the careers department and its students. The success of interactive career guidance tools which includes social media, in both Finland and Denmark has shown there is a market for it and that it works.

Universities in the UAE need to understand what their students/career guidance practitioners want in terms of social media integrated career guidance delivery before implementing a digital strategy which all UAE universities can follow. This will allow students to have a voice in terms of suggesting what types of social media delivery are most effective in career guidance. Career guidance practitioners also need to have an input into the digital strategy so they can identify training needs and what platforms will work.

Various social media platforms offer different opportunities regarding the integration of social media into career services. Utilising a variety of media will give students the options to utilise their creative skills. Some of these platforms e.g. LinkedIn are already utilised in the UAE. Other platforms include:

- Filming a video CVs and posting it on Instagram;

- Use LinkedIn to create and build a brand for as well as build a network of people who have similar career interests;
- Create a professional Facebook profile to join a career-related group to share and exchange experiences of job hunting and career-related thoughts with fellow students;
- Share career achievements via video on YouTube;
- Use Google+ to present and share information such as a CV;
- Flickr and Pinterest to share photos and get inspiration for creative jobs or just to show off other talents (Ambrose, 2015).

6. CONCLUSION

With the quality of education and career guidance being criticised by the youth of the UAE, more needs to be done to improve career guidance delivery in order to prepare and support students for the world of work. The use of social media is becoming ever popular amongst UAE youngsters. This literature review explored the background behind why social media in career guidance is needed, the role of social media in career guidance, the current state of career guidance in the UAE and recommendations for future. The review highlighted instances of where social media is used in career guidance in the UAE.

However, social media is currently used as an information source rather than an interactive workspace where students can generate the content. One of the main barriers to lack of social media adoption in career guidance delivery is the strict privacy and data laws. Recommendations such as educating responsible use of social media amongst students, having clear terms of use for social media platforms and selling the advantages of social media integration such as tailored career guidance services and the ability to use various technologies will focus the digital strategies of university career services. A further motivation for social media use in career guidance is that employers in the UAE use LinkedIn as a recruiting tool. LinkedIn is used in the UAE by its youth but not as frequently as other social media platforms. This is an area for further research. This review sets the foundation for more research into what students think about career guidance and what career guidance practitioners think about the use of social media on a wider level.

REFERENCES

Abu Dhabi, N. Y. U. (2018). Career Development. Retrieved from https://nyuad.nyu.edu/en/academics/undergraduate/career-development.html

Al-Harrasi, A. S., & Al-Salti, Z. S. (2014). Entrepreneurial intention among information systems (IS) students at Sultan Qaboos University: An exploratory study. *Global Journal of Management and Business Research*, *14*(9). Retrieved from https://journalofbusiness.org/index.php/GJMBR/article/download/1474/1381

Al Quwain, U. (2017). 102 UAE youth blackmailed over indecent photos on social media. *Khaleej Times*. Retrieved from https://www.khaleejtimes.com/nation/umm-al-quwain/102-uae-youth-blackmailed-over-indecent-photos-on-social-media

Albloushi, I. (2015). Exploration of the challenges of Emiratisation in UAE in the 21st century [Doctoral dissertation]. University of Salford.

Alwagait, E., Shahzad, B., & Alim, S. (2015). Impact of social media usage on students' academic performance in Saudi Arabia. *Computers in Human Behavior*, *51*, 1092–1097. doi:10.1016/j.chb.2014.09.028

Ambrose, J. (2015). Embedding Social Media Within Career Education. Retrieved from http://www. thecdi.net/write/Events/Presentations/AC%20for%20Schools/Embedding_Social_Media_within_Career_Education_-_John_Ambrose,_Lincolnshire_CC.pdf

ASDA'A Burson-Marsteller. (2017). Arab Youth Survey 2017. Retrieved from http://arabyouthsurvey. com/findings.html

ASDA'A Burson-Marsteller. (2018). Arab Youth Survey 2018. Retrieved from http://www.arabyouthsurvey.com/about_the_survey.htm

Barnes, A. (2015). Delivering career development with digital tools. Retrieved from http://player.slideplayer.com/26/8873939/#

Barnes, A., La Gro, N., & Watts, A. G. (2010). Developing e-guidance competencies: The outcomes of a two-year European project to transform the professional development of career guidance practitioners. *Career Research and Development*, *25*, 12–25.

Benchiba-Savenius, N., Mogielnicki, R., Owens, S., & Scott-Jackson, W. (2016). UAE Employment Report Insights for 2016. Oxford Strategic Consulting. Retrieved from http://www.oxfordstrategicconsulting.com/wp-content/uploads/2017/09/OxfordStrategicConsulting_EmiratiEmployment_Aug2016.pdf

Bhattacharya, S., & Neelam, N. (2018). Perceived value of internship experience: a try before you leap. Higher Education, Skills And Work-Based Learning. doi:10.1108/heswbl-07-2017-0044

Bright, J. E., Pryor, R. G., Wilkenfeld, S., & Earl, J. (2005). The role of social context and serendipitous events in career decision making. *International Journal for Educational and Vocational Guidance*, *5*(1), 19–36. doi:10.100710775-005-2123-6

Canadian University Dubai. (2017). CUD Career Services Prepare Students for Professional Success. Retrieved from http://www.cud.ac.ae/news/cud-career-services-prepare-students-professional-success

Cannon. (2015). How are universities using social media? Retrieved from https://www.redbrickresearch. com/2015/07/27/how-are-universities-using-social-media/

Central Intelligence Agency. (2018). The World Factbook- United Arab Emirates. Retrieved from https:// www.cia.gov/library/publications/the-world-factbook/geos/ae.html

Cochrane, T., & Bateman, R. (2010). Smartphones give you wings: Pedagogical affordances of mobile Web 2.0. *Australasian Journal of Educational Technology*, *26*(1), 1–14. doi:10.14742/ajet.1098

Collins. (2018). Definition of 'careers guidance.' Retrieved from https://www.collinsdictionary.com/ dictionary/english/careers-guidance

Daleure, G. (2017). Social Transitions Contributing to Emirati Unemployment. In *Emiratization in the UAE Labor Market* (pp. 85–94). Singapore: Springer. doi:10.1007/978-981-10-2765-9_8

Daniels, L., & Ratliff, J. R. (2017). Career Decision-Making: Empowering Emirati Females for Future Success. Retrieved from https://www.zu.ac.ae/main/en/research/publications/_documents/Career%20Decision%20Making%20Empowering%20Emirati%20Females%20for%20Future%20Success.pdf

Dilshad, T. (2017). The Youth Unemployment Problem: Why it Matters & What You Can Do. Retrieved from https://www.internsme.com/employers/blog/youth-unemployment

Dowle, C., & Judson, C. (2016). Privacy in the United Arab Emirates: overview. Retrieved from https://uk.practicallaw.thomsonreuters.com/8-570-7305?transitionType=Default&contextData=(sc. Default)&firstPage=true&bhcp=1

Downey, D., & Raja, H. (2017). Career Counselling in the United Arab Emirates. Retrieved from https://www.ncda.org/aws/NCDA/asset_manager/get_file/156399?ver=1243

Dubai Digital Interactive Agency. (2018). UAE Social Media Usage Statistics 2018. Retrieved from https://www.globalmediainsight.com/blog/uae-social-media-statistics/

Dunn, L. (2013). Teaching in Higher Education: Can Social Media Enhance the Learning Experience. Retrieved from https://www.gla.ac.uk/media/media_276225_en.pdf

El-Gohary, H., Selim, H. M., & Eid, R. (2016). Entrepreneurship education and employability of Arab HE business students: An attempt for a primary investigation. *International Journal of Business and Social Science*, 7(4), 52–72.

European Commission. (2016a). Education and Training Monitor 2017 Finland. Retrieved from https://ec.europa.eu/education/sites/education/files/monitor2017-fi_en.pdf

European Commission. (2016b). Education and Training Monitor 2017 Denmark. Retrieved from https://ec.europa.eu/education/sites/education/files/monitor2017-dk_en.pdf

Fanack. (2017). The UAE Reforms Education System as Part of Vision 2021. Retrieved from https://fanack.com/united-arab-emirates/society-media-culture/society/education/uae-reforms-education-system/

Finnish National Agency for Education. (2011). Lifelong Guidance in Finland. Retrieved from http://www.cimo.fi/instancedata/prime_product_julkaisu/cimo/embeds/cimowwwstructure/25493_Lifelong_guidance_in_Finland.pdf

Granovetter, M. (1974). *Finding a job: A study on contacts and careers*. Cambridge, MA: Harvard University Press.

Hemmi, A., Bayne, S., & Land, R. (2009). The appropriation and repurposing of social technologies in higher education. *Journal of Computer Assisted Learning*, 25(1), 19–30. doi:10.1111/j.1365-2729.2008.00306.x

Hoffman, M., & Jamal, A. (2012). The youth and the Arab spring: Cohort differences and similarities. *Middle East Law and Governance*, 4(1), 168–188. doi:10.1163/187633712X632399

Holman, J. (2014). Good career guidance. Retrieved from http://treviglas.net/wp-content/uploads/2008/12/Gatsby-Good-Career-Guidance-Summary.pdf

Hooley, T. (2012). How the internet changed career: Framing the relationship between career development and online technologies. *Journal of the National Institute for Career Education and Counselling*, *29*(1), 3–12.

Hooley, T., Matheson, J., & Watts, A. G. (2014). Advancing ambitions: The role of career guidance in supporting social mobility. https://www.suttontrust.com/wp-content/uploads/2014/10/Advancing-Ambitions-16.10.pdf

Ismail, I., & Koshy, S. (2017). The Use of Linkedin as a Recruitment Tool in the UAE: An Evaluation. *Paper presented at the International Conference on Education, Humanities and Management (ICEHM-17)* (pp. 113-119). doi:10.15242/HEAIG/IAH0317535

Jabeen, F., Faisal, M., Nishat, I., & Katsioloudes, M. (2017). Entrepreneurial mindset and the role of universities as strategic drivers of entrepreneurship: Evidence from the United Arab Emirates. *Journal of Small Business and Enterprise Development*, *24*(1), 136–157. doi:10.1108/JSBED-07-2016-0117

Kettunen, J., Sampson, J. P. Jr, & Vuorinen, R. (2015). Career practitioners' conceptions of competency for social media in career services. *British Journal of Guidance & Counselling*, *43*(1), 43–56. doi:10.1080/03069885.2014.939945

Kettunen, J., Vuorinen, R., & Sampson, J. P. Jr. (2013). Career practitioners' conceptions of social media in career services. *British Journal of Guidance & Counselling*, *41*(3), 302–317. doi:10.1080/03069885.2013.781572 PMID:24009407

Khaleej Times. (2017). 6 legal risks social media users in UAE should know. Retrieved from https://www.khaleejtimes.com/legalview/legal-risks-for-social-media-users-in-uae

Khan, Z. R., Rakhman, S., & Bangera, A. (2017). Who Stole Me? Identity Theft on Social Media in the UAE. *Journal of Management and Marketing Review.*, *2*(1), 79–86.

Kuder Atlas. (2018). Abu Dhabi Education Council Career Planning System. Retrieved from http://adeccps.kuder.com/

Kudos. (2018). Kudos is the leading career development service helping you to explore, develop and maximise your potential. Retrieved from https://kudos.cascaid.co.uk/#/

Livingstone, S. (2008). Taking risky opportunities in youthful content creation: Teenagers' use of social networking sites for intimacy, privacy, and self-expression. *New Media & Society*, *10*(3), 393–411. doi:10.1177/1461444808089415

Malita, L. (2011). Social media time management tools and tips. *Procedia Computer Science*, *3*, 747–753. doi:10.1016/j.procs.2010.12.123

McNeill, L., Rice, M. L., & Wright, V. H. (2016, June). Advantages and barriers to using social media in online education. *Presented at Distance Learning Administration Conference 2016 (DLA2016)*. Georgia, USA: University of West Georgia.

Morris, M. E., & Aguilera, A. (2012). Mobile, social, and wearable computing and the evolution of psychological practice. *Professional Psychology, Research and Practice*, *43*(6), 622–626. doi:10.1037/a0029041 PMID:25587207

National Career Development Association. (2015). Ethical use of social networking technologies in career services. Retrieved from https://www.ncda.org/aws/NCDA/asset_manager/get_file/110167

Osborn, D. S., & LoFrisco, B. M. (2012). How do career centers use social networking sites? *The Career Development Quarterly*, *60*(3), 263–272. doi:10.1002/j.2161-0045.2012.00022.x

Osbourne, C. (2012). The pros and cons of social media classrooms. Retrieved from http://www.zdnet.com/article/the-pros-and-cons-of-social-media-classrooms/

Oxford Business Group. (2018). Bahrain's young population has potential to boost economy. Retrieved from https://oxfordbusinessgroup.com/overview/managing-growth-youthful-population-has-potential-boost-gulf-economies

Rajan, A. V., Ravikumar, R., & Al Shaer, M. (2017, June). UAE cybercrime law and cybercrimes—An analysis. In *2017 International Conference on Cyber Security And Protection Of Digital Services (Cyber Security)* (pp. 1-6). IEEE.

Rixon, A., Maritz, A., & Fisher, R. (2017). Youth Entrepreneurship in an Islamic Context. In V. Ramadani, L. P. Dana, S. Gërguri-Rashiti, & V. Ratten (Eds.), *Entrepreneurship and Management in an Islamic Context*. Cham: Springer. doi:10.1007/978-3-319-39679-8_11

Russell, J. (2017). Social Media in Higher Education: Strategies, Benefits, and Challenges. Retrieved from https://blog.hootsuite.com/social-media-in-higher-education/

Salem, F. (2017). The Arab Social Media Report 2017. Arab Social Media Report Series (Vol. 7). Dubai: Governance and Innovation Program, MBR School of Government. Retrieved from www.mbrsg.ae/getattachment/1383b88a-6eb9-476a-bae4-61903688099b/Arab-Social-Media-Report-2017

Sampson, J. P., & Makela, J. P. (2014). Ethical issues associated with information and communication technology in counselling and guidance. *International Journal for Educational and Vocational Guidance*, *14*(1), 135–148. doi:10.100710775-013-9258-7

Shallcross, L. (2011). Do the right thing. Retrieved from http://ct.counselling.org/2011/04/do-the-right-thing/

Sheffield Hallam University. (2017). Using social media to enhance your employability. Retrieved from https://students.shu.ac.uk/lits/it/documents/pdf/SocialMediaEmployability.pdf

Sherriff, L. (2014). Effects Of Social Media On Job Prospects. *Huffington Post*. Retrieved from http://www.huffingtonpost.co.uk/2013/01/25/social-media-job-prospects-impact-should-we-be-scared_n_2550921.html

Silva, P., Lopes, B., Costa, M., Melo, A., Dias, G., Brito, E., & Seabra, D. (2016). The million-dollar question: Can internships boost employment? *Studies in Higher Education*, *43*(1), 2–21. doi:10.1080/03075079.2016.1144181

Staker, H., & Horn, M. B. (2012). Classifying K-12 blended learning. Innosight Institute. Retrieved from https://files.eric.ed.gov/fulltext/ED535180.pdf

Statistica. (2018). United Arab Emirates: Youth unemployment rate from 2007 to 2017. Retrieved from https://www.statista.com/statistics/813136/youth-unemployment-rate-in-the-united-arab-emirates/

Teach Middle East. (2016). ADEC: Higher Education Institutes now have an internationally certified Career Guidance Advisor. Retrieved from http://teachmiddleeastmag.com/3949-2/

The Education Guide. (2018). Education Guide. Retrieved from https://www.ug.dk/evejledning

The International Council on Security and Development. (2010). *Unemployed Youth in the UAE: Personal Perceptions and Recommendations. Collingdale.* Pennsylvania: Diane Publishing Co.

The World Bank. (2017). United Arab Emirates' *Economic Outlook*. Retrieved from http://www.world-bank.org/en/country/gcc/publication/united-arab-emirates-economic-outlook-october-2017

United Arab Emirates Government. (2018a). Media in the UAE. Retrieved from https://government.ae/en/media/media

United Arab Emirates Government. (2018b). Retrieved from https://www.vision2021.ae/en/national-priority-areas/national-key-performance-indicators

University of Edinburgh. (2016). Using social media in your job search. Retrieved from https://www.ed.ac.uk/careers/looking-for-work/social-media

Vuorinen, R., & Kettunen, J. (2012). The Perceived Role of Technology and Social Media in Career Guidance among practitioners who are experienced Internet users – Chances and Challenges. Retrieved from https://warwick.ac.uk/fac/soc/ier/research/.../finalglasgow_vuorinenkettunen1.ppt

Vuorinen, R., Sampson, J. P., & Kettunen, J. (2011). The perceived role of technology in career guidance among practitioners who are experienced internet users. *Australian Journal of Career Development, 20*(3), 39–46. doi:10.1177/103841621102000307

Warner, R. S., & Burton, G. (2017). A fertile oasis: The current state of education in the UAE. MBRSG. Retrieved from http://www.mbrsg.ae/getattachment/658fdafb-673d-4864-9ce1-881aaccd08e2/A-Fertile-OASIS-The-current-state-of-Education-in

Waxin, M. F., Lindsay, V., Belkhodja, O., & Zhao, F. (2018). Workforce localization in the UAE: Recruitment and selection challenges and practices in private and public organizations. *Journal of Developing Areas, 52*(4), 99–113. doi:10.1353/jda.2018.0054

Westley, J. (2017). Using PISA to Benchmark UAE Schools – Why, & Why Not. Retrieved from https://schoolscompared.com/guides/using-pisa-benchmark-uae-schools-not/

Wilkins, S., Balakrishnan, M. S., & Huisman, J. (2012). Student choice in higher education: Motivations for choosing to study at an international branch campus. *Journal of Studies in International Education, 16*(5), 413–433. doi:10.1177/1028315311429002

Zayed University. (2017). Career Fairs and Employer Engagement Activities. Retrieved from https://www.zu.ac.ae/main/en/student_affairs/student_careers/career_fairs_engagement.aspx

Zeffane, R., & Bani Melhem, S. J. (2017). Trust, job satisfaction, perceived organizational performance and turnover intention: A public-private sector comparison in the United Arab Emirates. *Employee Relations*, *39*(7), 1148–1167. doi:10.1108/ER-06-2017-0135

This research was previously published in the International Journal of E-Adoption (IJEA), 11(1); pages 25-44, copyright year 2019 by IGI Publishing (an imprint of IGI Global).

Chapter 105
Social Media Usage for Informal Learning in Malaysia:
Academic Researcher Perspective

Mohmed Y. Mohmed Al-Sabaawi

Department of Management Information Systems, College of Administration and Economics, University of Mosul, Iraq

Halina Mohamed Dahlan

Information Systems Department, Azman Hashim International Business School, Universiti Teknologi Malaysia, Malaysia

Hafiz Muhammad Faisal Shehzad

Department of Computer Science and IT, University of Sargodha, Pakistan

ABSTRACT

Social media (SM) has gained a huge acceptance from all and sundry. A huge potential exists for academic researchers in the use of SM for intellectual exercise. Informal learning (IL) has redefined the entire learning process, creating a new dawn from the formal learning rigid structures. However, there is lack of research on why some researchers fail to accept SM for IL. Therefore, the aim of this paper is to explore the use of SM for IL, barriers, benefits, and effect of individual factors. For this reason, a thorough literature review was conducted, and items were extracted from prior studies. Using a survey, a total of 170 responses were received from academic researchers using paper-based questionnaire. The authors discovered from the survey that lack of encouragement, lack of quality information, threat to research material are the barriers affecting SM use. Furthermore, they found that the benefits of using SM by academic researchers are to communicate with peers, share knowledge, and enhance collaboration. Thus, these findings will help stakeholders in encouraging the use of SM for IL.

DOI: 10.4018/978-1-6684-7123-4.ch105

1. INTRODUCTION

The emergence of SM such as YouTube and Facebook has made academic researchers consider its usage in several academic activities. Facebook has created an avenue for academic researchers to connect, engage, and share ideas. YouTube also provides a chance for academic researchers to disseminate novel finding using multimedia, and also improve their understanding of areas of expertise. The widespread popularity of SM has led to its acceptance and usage in the academic environment (Jaffar, 2012; Kirschner & Karpinski, 2010; Krauskopf, Zahn, & Hesse, 2012; Manasijević, Živković, Arsić, & Milošević, 2016; Moran, Seaman, & Tinti-Kane, 2011). Facebook was founded in 2004 with one million users which has now increased to two billion users (Facebook, 2018). Furthermore, YouTube came into existence in 2005 with eight million users. YouTube now commands followership of 1.32 billion subscribers (Statistic Brain Research Institute, 2018). However, the low rate of SM acceptance for IL calls for investigation (Bullinger et al., 2011; Church & Salam, 2010).

This paper empirically examines the barriers and benefits of using SM for IL in Universiti Teknologi Malaysia (UTM) being one of the foremost research universities in Malaysia. Altbach (2009) is of the view that research universities are of paramount importance to developing nations for them to effectively compete in the knowledge economy (Madhusudhan, 2012). He et al. (2009) stated innovations that make it easy to transfer knowledge and maximize collaboration among researchers play a major role in research growth and productivity. Researchers have shown that productivity in research output will eventually lead to favorable rankings in the global university rankings (Da Silva & Davis, 2011; Liu & Cheng, 200). Therefore, sufficient productivity among researchers is usually determined by the level of collaboration and interaction. Hence, the ability of researchers to produce quality research output is highly influenced by the creation of a collaborative environment (Abramo et al., 2013). Conversely, the use of SM as a means of communication, interaction, and collaboration will effectively improve research output, thereby resulting in favorable ranking among other universities. The paper aims to bring forth the barriers and benefits of using SM for IL among academic researchers in Malaysia. The main objectives of the study are:

1. To discover the level of usage of SM in IL by academic researchers.
2. To explore the role of gender, age, position, academic discipline, and experience on SM for IL use by academic researchers.
3. To identify specialized SM tools for IL among researchers.
4. To identify the benefits of using SM for IL by academic researchers.
5. To identify the barriers affecting the use of SM for IL by academic researchers.

This paper is organized as follows: prior studies were reviewed in section 2, followed by the research methodology in Section 3. The data analysis is carried out in section 4. Section 5 provides a discussion of results and the Conclusion and limitations are discussed in Section 6.

2. LITERATURE REVIEW

There is a lack of research on the use of SM for IL (Manca, & Ranieri, 2017). Subsequently, previous reviews on SM for IL and their limitations were presented in this section. Social Networking Sites

(SNSs) such as Facebook, has revolutionized the Internet to be a social platform which supports IL and information dissemination effectively (Rashid & Rahman, 2014). The usage of SNSs in academia has been there for quite some time now. An additional number of researches in past years has explored the pedagogical potential of SNSs and its effectiveness as a learning tool. The outcome showed that a greater number of the participants use YouTube and Facebook for communication and collaboration not necessarily for IL (Nentwick & König, 2014). The theoretical background of this study is based on the Constructionist Theory and Technology Acceptance Model (TAM). TAM is the Information Systems theory to explain and measure the acceptance of new technology such as social media. The experience-based knowledge building is referred to as the constructionist theory. The learning through conditions and culture is social constructivism. Knowledge building through interaction and collaboration is cognitive constructivism. The research community believes that social media technologies affirm constructivism (Catherine McLoughlin, 2008; Schroeder, Minocha, & Schneider, 2010).

The concept of IL plays a growing role in how individuals think of everyday learning. If there is a need to know or learn something, individuals may look it up in a book, look it up online, or contact someone for support. IL transpires outside the normal school settings or other educational programs (Clough, 2010; Smaller, 2005). This implies that IL means a form of learning without stringent structures of time and space (Schöndienst, V., Krasnova, H., Günther, O., Riehle, D., & Schwabe, G, 2011). It was observed that IL is defined by the activities of peoples, and not defined by institutional settings or any standard curricula. In that direction, IL is not directed by any planned or structured objectives, time, or learning support (Behringer & Coles, 2003). A survey was conducted by Lupton (2014) on 711 researchers to examine how they integrate SM in their research activities. The majority of the respondents in the research assert that they use SM for their daily research work. Another study was also conducted by Nature Publishing Group (2014) that explores the SM tool used by researchers. It was discovered that 55% of the respondents claimed that they mostly use Facebook to carry out their research. Furthermore, Thelwall & Kousha (2014) explores the usage of Facebook among different age groups. They found that females and younger populations are frequent users. This finding was supported by Poellhuber (2013) who discover gender and age differences in SM usage. Research conducted by Jordan (2014) highlights the structural difference of SM across disciplines. The investigation found that disciplines played a major role in SM usage. Bullinger et al. (2011) noted that a good number of SM features are adopted based on disciplines. As endorsed by Jamali, Russell, Nicholas, & Watkinson (2014), differences exist among SM membership rates based on disciplines. Given the thorough review carried out by the researchers, it can be deduced that researchers mainly focused on the influence of SM rather than the benefits and barriers of these tools as they relate to academic researchers. Thus, the major aim of this research is to identify the barriers and benefits of SM usage among academic researchers in Malaysia.

3. METHODOLOGY

This study adopts the causal approach to investigate the cause and effects of the benefits and barriers (Alsabawy et al., 2013). A survey method was employed in this study to collect data. The questionnaire administered consists of twelve (12) questions are adapted from (Jamali, Russell, Nicholas, & Watkinson, 2014; Madhusudhan, 2012; Rowlands, Nicholas, Russell, Canty, & Watkinson, 2011; Schöndienst, Krasnova, Günther, & Riehle, 2011) and questioner items are already validated in mentioned studies. The convenience sample was used to examine the barriers and benefits of using SM for IL in Malaysia.

The study sample explored different samples; ranging from Postgraduate Students, Research Fellow, Academic Staff in UTM. A total of 170 responses were collected using the paper-based and online-based questionnaire. The data collection process began in February 2018 and lasted for one month. Statistical Package for Social Science for Windows (SPSS for Windows Version 25.0) was used in analyzing the data. The level of significance at a probability level of 5% was employed.

4. RESEARCH FINDINGS

The study indicates that the majority of the respondents were male (63.5%) and also 36.5% were female, respectively. Showing a justifiable representation of members of both sexes in academia (see Table 1). A greater percentage of the respondents are young below the age of 25 to 30 years (34.7%). In terms of position, 106 (62.4%) of the respondents were Postgraduate students (Ph.D. and Master). Table 1 indicates that a large percentage of the respondents were found not to use SM (62%, n=106). Whilst, a lesser number of the respondents (38%, n=64) have experience in using SM for IL.

Table 1. Characteristics of respondents

	Users		Non-Users		Total	
	n	%	n	%	n	%
Gender						
Male	45	26.4%	63	37.1%	108	63.5%
Female	19	11.2%	43	25.3%	62	36.5%
Age						
Less than 25-30 years	19	11.2%	40	23.5%	59	34.7
31-35	14	8.2%	16	9.4%	30	17.6
36-40	13	8.8%	18	9.4%	31	18.2
41-45	11	6.5%	11	6.5%	22	12.9
More than 45	7	4.1%	21	12.4%	28	16.5
Position						
Academic Staff (Lecturer, Senior Lecturer, Associate Professor, Professor)	19	11.2%	33	19.4%	52	30.6%
Research Fellow	5	3%	7	4%	12	7%
Postgraduate Student	40	23.5%	66	38.9%	106	62.4%
Experience as a researcher						
less than 1 year	6	3.5%	14	8.2%	20	11.8
1-3 years	18	10.6%	35	20.6%	53	31.2
3-5 years	15	8.8%	25	14.7	40	23.5
5-10 years	13	7.6%	14	8.2	27	15.9
More than 10 years	12	7.1%	18	10.6	30	17.6

4.1 Gender and Social Media Usage for Informal Learning

The effect of gender in SM acceptance is investigated in the present study. An independent sample T-test was adopted to examine the difference in gender and use of SM for IL (see Table 2). The results show that the F-statistics is 9.016 and the related p-value is 0.115. Given that the p-value is greater than 0.05, the researcher's gender exhibits no effect on the use of SM. All genders exhibit the same attraction to technology use. This contradicts previous studies that indicate a strong impact of gender on the use of SM for IL (Thelwall & Kousha, 2014). This finding could be attributed to the nature of the academic environment were both male and female academics exhibit similar features in the use of technology. The finding is consistent with (Manca & Ranieri, 2017; Ja-mali et al., 2014).

4.2 Age and Use of Social Media for Informal Learning

In investigating the effect of the age difference and SM use for IL, a one-way ANOVA was employed. The Tukey's HSD Post-hoc test was carried out to identify if there exists any difference between age groups in terms of SM for IL use. Table 3 present the result of the ANOVA analysis. The findings showed that there is no effect of age difference on SM for IL use (p=0. 256).

4.3 Position and Use of Social Media for Informal Learning

Academic positions are believed to influence the acceptance of SM for IL. On investigating the effect of academic positions and SM use (see Table 4), it shows a strong effect (p=0. 947). Tukey HSD test is carried out to ascertain the group that creates the difference. This result showed that there exists a strong effect between users and non-users of SM (p=0.024). This indicates a strong difference between student and re-searchers (p=0.045). The findings in this study showed that position has a strong impact on SM use for IL. This result is expected as most of the respondents are postgraduate students. The findings are consistent with that of (Manca &Ranieri, 2017).

Table 2. T-test for the association between gender and Use of SM for IL

	Levene-Test of Equal Variance T-test for Equal Means				Sig(2-sided)
	F	Significance	T	df	
Variances are equal	9.016	0.003	-1.428	168	0.155
Variances are not equal			-1.452	140.182	0.149

Table 3. Simplified ANOVA for age and use of SM for IL

	Sum of Square	df	Square Means	F	Significance
Between the groups	1.2594	4	0.315	1.344	0.256
Within the groups	38.646	165	0.234		
Total	39.906	169			

Table 4. ANOVA for position and Use of SM for IL

	Sum of Square	df	Square Means	F	Significance
Between the groups	0.026	2	0.013	0.054	0.947
Within the groups	39.880	167	0.239		
Total	39.906	169			
Tukey HSD Post-hoc test					
Position(I)	Position(J)	Mean difference(I-J)	Std. Error	Significance	
Academic Staff	Research Fellow	0.051*	0.157	0.943	
Research Fellow	Academic Staff	-0.051*	0.157	0.943	
Postgraduate Student	Academic Staff	-0.012*	0.083	0.989	

*The mean difference is significant at the 0.05 level.

4.4 Discipline and Use of Social Media for Informal Learning

A key question as regards SM use for IL is the effect of academic discipline, which was assessed with the help of ANOVA. Table 5 present the users and non-users of SM for IL according to disciplines.

ANOVA was employed to assess the relationship between discipline and SM for IL use (see Table 6). There exist no effect of discipline on SM use for IL (p= 0.499). This contradicts previous studies that indicate a strong impact of discipline on SM use for IL (Jordan, 2014; Jamali, Russell, Nicholas, & Watkinson, 2014; Sugimoto, 2017).

Table 5. Use and non-use of SM for IL in research by narrow subject discipline

Use Social Media for Informal Learning in Research Faculty	Yes	No
Faculty of Civil Engineering	62.50%	37.50%
Faculty of Bioscience and Medical Engineering	37.50%	62.50%
Faculty of Computing	37.50%	62.50%
Faculty of Electrical Engineering	38.90%	61.10%
Faculty of Chemical Engineering	27.30%	72.70%
Faculty of Mechanical Engineering	28.60%	71.70%
Faculty of Geoformation and Real Estate	55.60%	44.40%
Faculty of Education	38.90%	61.10%
Faculty of Management	40.00%	60.00%
Faculty of Science	23.50%	76.50%
Faculty of Islamic Civilization	50.00%	50.00%
All disciplines	**37.60%**	**62.40%**

Table 6. Simplified ANOVA for discipline and Use of SM for IL

	Sum of Square	df	Square Means	F	Significance
Between the groups	2.245	10	.225	.948	.499
Within the groups	37.661	159	.237		
Total	39.906	169			

4.5 Experience and Use of Social Media for Informal Learning

Figure 1 presents the duration of SM use for IL by researchers. Considering the usage duration, a large part of the respondents (73.4%, n=47) indicate a usage duration of more than 2 years, this is followed by 21.9% that are using SM for about 1-2 years, 1.6% indicate from 7 months to a year, and 3.1% for less than 6 months. Prior studies have shown the effect of experience on technology use. However, the ANOVA result in this study (see Table 7) indicate a lack of effect of experience on SM use for IL (p=0.379). According to Nysveen & Pedersen (2016), this finding could be attributed to the emergence of technology and the user's lack of experience.

Figure 1. SM for IL Usage (N=64)

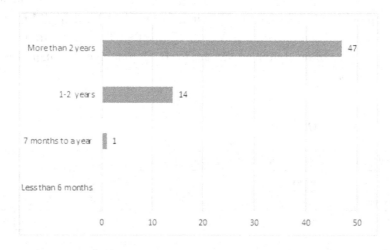

Table 7. ANOVA for experience and Use of SM for IL

	Sum of Square	df	Square means	F	Significance
Between the groups	1.009	4	.252	1.056	0.379
Within the groups	48.972	205	.239		
Total	49.981	209			

4.6 Use of Specialized Social Media for Informal Learning

Academic researchers are the major components of academia. The importance of SM for IL is to help researchers discover their potential and have a global reach. As presented in Figure 2, respondents with more than one SM membership were required to indicate the most frequently used SM tool. A large part of the respondent (30.20%) indicates Facebook as the most utilized SM, followed by YouTube (26.56%), Wikipedia (17.16%), LinkedIn (12.50%), other (5.76%), Blogs (4.18%) and Twitter (3.64%). The finding in this study is consistent with prior studies (Al-Aufi et al., 2015). They found that a larger percentage of respondents used Facebook and YouTube. It should be known that certain respondents are using LinkedIn for IL. However, the present study does not consider LinkedIn because it serves as a professional social network (business-oriented).

Figure 2. Use of specialized SM for IL (multiple answers are permitted (N=64))

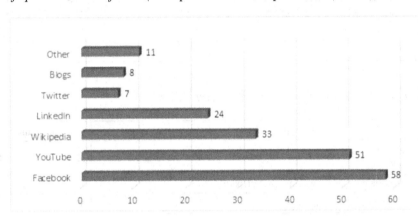

4.7 Barriers to Using Social Media for Informal Learning

Barriers that impede academic researchers from using SM for IL were discovered from the survey carried out by the researcher (see Table 8). The greatest barrier as indicated by the respondents was a lack of encouragement from colleagues on the need to use SM for IL (66.04%, n=70). This barrier is closely accompanied by lack of quality of information (59.43%, n=63), threat to research materials and data (57.55%, n=61), lack of necessity to use SM for IL (57.55%, n=61) and finally time constraints (52.83%, n=56).

4.8 Benefits of Using Social Media for Informal Learning by Academic Researchers

The emergence of SM has paved the way for a new forum for collaboration among researchers that enable them to share ideas and resources. The benefits of SM for IL as indicated by the respondents are presented in Table 9. The findings showed that researchers need to keep up to date is the most common of SM (81.25%), communicating my research with other colleagues (81.25%), facilitating interaction with my research partners (81.25%), creating a global network for sharing my research with other colleagues

(79.68%), sharing my findings with another researcher faster(78.12%), knowledge sharing with other researchers (75.00%), communicate with more experienced researchers in my field (67.18%), encourage collaboration with my co-researchers (64.06%), get input about my research from other researchers (60.93%), communicate my research method with other researchers (57.81%), share my research findings with other researchers (56.25%), encourage collaboration with my research respondents to collect the required data (53.12%), communicate with other researchers to my literature review better (51.56%), and seek for collaborators for my research projects (50.00%).

Table 8. Barriers associated with use of SM for IL by academic researchers

Barriers	Respondents	Percentage
There is a lack of encouragement from colleagues on the need to use SM for IL.	70	66.04%
I don't use SM for IL because most information obtained is a lack of quality.	63	59.43%
I don't use SM for IL because it is a threat to my research materials and data.	61	57.55%
I don't feel any necessity to use SM for IL.	61	57.55%
I don't have time to use SM for IL.	56	52.83%

Table 9. Benefits of using SM for IL by academic researchers

Benefits	Respondents	Percentage
I use SM to communicate with other researchers to keep up to date with the new information related to my research field.	52	81.25%
I use SM to communicate about my research with my research partners.	52	81.25%
I use SM to facilitate interaction with my research partners.	52	81.25%
I use SM to communicate about my research with researchers globally.	51	79.68%
I use SM to exchange knowledge more quickly with other researchers.	50	78.12%
I use SM to share knowledge with other researchers.	48	75.00%
I use SM to communicate with renowned experts in my research field.	43	67.18%
I use SM to facilitate collaboration with my researcher partner.	41	64.06%
I use SM to get feedback about my research from other researchers.	39	60.93%
I use SM to discuss my research method with other researchers.	37	57.81%
I use SM to discuss my research finding with other researchers.	36	56.25%
I use SM to facilitate collaboration with my research respondents to collect the required data.	34	53.12%
I use SM to discuss with other research in conducting a literature review.	33	51.56%
I use SM to find collaborators for my research projects.	32	50.00%

Note: multiple answers are permitted (No. of user=64).

5. DISCUSSION

The first objective of the study was to find the usage of SM in IL in the academic community. From the overall findings of this research, it has shown that the majority of the respondents do not use SM for IL.

(Al-Sabaawi and Dahlan, 2018). From the problem confirmation survey, it was found that 62.40% of the 170 respondents do not use social media use for informal learning as against 37.60% as shown in Figure 1. Thus, validating the claim that few academic researchers use social media use for informal learning. The second objective was to test the moderating effects of gender, position, and experience. All the effect factors such as gender, age, position, discipline, and experience exhibit no significant impact on the use of SM for IL by academic researchers. This implies that these factors do not influence the academic researcher's behavior as regards the use of SM for IL as demonstrated in section 4.1-4.5. Thirdly, the objective was to find the SM tools for learning in researchers. Figure 2 demonstrates that the most popular SM in a research setting is Facebook and YouTube. On the other hand, Wikipedia, LinkedIn, and Tweeter is utilized more for social activities as compared to informal learning. Perhaps the social media advertisements and digital marking attract more to use Facebook and YouTube as compared to other SM.

The fourth objective was to identify the benefits of SM for IL. Table 9 represents the benefits the research community perceived from SM. Some of the respondents who have experienced the use of SM believe that the most common benefit derived is as follows: keeping up to date, encourage interaction with research partners, share my research with researchers globally, sharing my research activities with other researchers, exchange and share knowledge better and faster with other researchers. The greatest benefit of SM is to learn from specialized persons and make a network of collaborators. The younger respondents are happier than older and rate SM a highly important learning tool. Finally, the major barrier as represented in Table 8 to the use of SM for IL by academic researchers is as follows: the absence of support from colleagues, most information lack substance, and lack of security of information leading to serious threats to research work, lack of any need to use SM for IL and time constraints. To this extent, the overall findings in this research paper will help policymakers to tackle these identified barriers and maximize the highlighted benefits of using SM for IL to the research community.

6. CONCLUSION AND LIMITATIONS

The use of SM as a means of communication, interaction, and collaboration effectively improves informal learning and research output, thereby resulting in favorable ranking among other universities. Existing research did not reveal that the learning potential of SM and inhibitors of SM in informal learning. The paper aims to bring forth the barriers and benefits of using SM for IL among academic researchers in Malaysia. Social media are one of the choices that researchers consider to examine domain or adjacent research areas. SM plays a vital role in lower-order informal learning and enhances knowledge outcomes. However, the general perception of researchers is not in favor of social media to be a serious learning platform. Therefore, to achieve the actual learning benefits of SM the perception of the scholars plays a vital role. Similarly, some researchers believe that information overload on SM has a negative influence on informal learning.

In conclusion, decision-makers and policymakers should encourage the use of SM for IL to overcome the identified barriers in this study, and to maximize the benefit associated with SM use for IL by academic researchers. This will greatly help to curtail the immense burden on the limited resources in our institutions. Additionally, encouraging academic researchers to use SM for IL will greatly influence their productivity in the research arena. This will also facilitate interaction and collaboration with a wide range of other researchers globally eventually leading to a higher ranking for the university in particular and national development for the country in general. Even though the findings of this study have a lasting impact, they are not without inadequacies. Firstly, one university provided the sample for this study (UTM), generalizing its findings to the whole population must be done with caution. The research used a quantitative method; other research in the future should try to use alternative methods as this might provide interesting results. The data used was obtained from one Research University. Future studies should consider other research universities in Malaysia to extend the finding of this study.

ACKNOWLEDGMENT

The authors are very grateful to the University of Mosul/ College of Administration & Economics for their provided facilities, which help to improve the quality of this work.

REFERENCES

Abramo, G., D'Angelo, C. A., & Murgia, G. (2013). Gender differences in research collaboration. *Journal of Informetrics*, *7*(4), 811–822. doi:10.1016/j.joi.2013.07.002

Al-Aufi, A., & Fulton, C. (2015). Impact of social networking tools on scholarly communication: A cross-institutional study. *The Electronic Library*, *33*(2), 224–241. doi:10.1108/EL-05-2013-0093

Altbach, P. G. (2009). Peripheries and centers: Research universities in developing countries. *Asia Pacific Education Review*, *10*(1), 15–27. doi:10.100712564-009-9000-9

Al-Sabaawi, M. Y. M., & Dahlan, H. M. (2018, June). Social Media for Informal Learning Usage in Malaysia. In *Barriers and Benefits. In International Conference of Reliable Information and Communication Technology* (pp. 995-1001). Springer.

Alsabawy, A. Y., Cater-Steel, A., & Soar, J. (2013). IT infrastructure services as a requirement for e-learning system success. *Computers & Education*, *69*, 431–451. doi:10.1016/j.compedu.2013.07.035

Behringer, F., & Coles, M. (2003). *The role of national qualifications systems in promoting lifelong learning*. OECD Education Working Papers, No. 3, OECD Publishing.

Bullinger, A., Renken, U., & Moeslein, K. (2011). *Understanding online collaboration technology adoption by researchers–a model and empirical study*. Academic Press.

Church, M., & Salam, A. F. (2010). Facebook, the spice of life? In ICIS (p. 212). Academic Press.

Clough, G. (2010). Geolearners: Location-based informal learning with mobile and social technologies. *IEEE Transactions on Learning Technologies*, *3*(1), 33–44. doi:10.1109/TLT.2009.39

Da Silva, N., & Davis, A. R. (2011). Absorptive capacity at the individual level: Linking creativity to innovation in academia. *The review of higher education*, *34*(3), 355–379. doi:10.1353/rhe.2011.0007

Catherine McLoughlin, M. J. W. L. (2008). The Three P's of Pedagogy for the Networked Society: Personalization, Participation, and Productivity Catherine. *International Journal on Teaching and Learning in Higher Education*, *20*(4), 10–27. doi:10.10171537592709991423

Jamali, H. R., Russell, B., Nicholas, D., & Watkinson, A. (2014). Do online communities support research collaboration? *Aslib Journal of Information Management, 66*(6), 603–622. doi:10.1108/AJIM-08-2013-0072

Madhusudhan, M. (2012). Use of social networking sites by research scholars of the University of Delhi: A study. *The International Information & Library Review, 44*(2), 100–113. doi:10.1080/10572317.20 12.10762919

Rowlands, I., Nicholas, D., Russell, B., Canty, N., & Watkinson, A. (2011). Social media use in the research workflow. *Learned Publishing, 24*(3), 183–195. doi:10.1087/20110306

Schöndienst, V., Krasnova, H., Günther, O., & Riehle, D. (2011). Micro-Blogging Adoption in the Enterprise: An Empirical Analysis. Wi, (2011), 931–940.

Schroeder, A., Minocha, S., & Schneider, C. (2010). The strengths, weaknesses, opportunities and threats of using social software in higher and further education teaching and learning. *Journal of Computer Assisted Learning, 26*(3), 159–174. doi:10.1111/j.1365-2729.2010.00347.x

He, Z. L., Geng, X. S., & Campbell-Hunt, C. (2009). Research collaboration and research output: A longitudinal study of 65 biomedical scientists in a New Zealand university. *Research Policy, 38*(2), 306–317. doi:10.1016/j.respol.2008.11.011

Jamali, R., Russell, H., Nicholas, B. D., & Watkinson, A. (2014). Do online communities support research collaboration? *Aslib Journal of Information Management, 66*(6), 603–622. doi:10.1108/AJIM-08-2013-0072

Jordan, K. (2014). Academics and their online networks: Exploring the role of academic social networking sites. *First Monday, 19*(11). Advance online publication. doi:10.5210/fm.v19i11.4937

Jaffar, A. A. (2012). YouTube: An emerging tool in anatomy education. *Anatomical Sciences Education, 5*(3), 158–164. doi:10.1002/ase.1268 PMID:22383096

Kirschner, P. A., & Karpinski, A. C. (2010). Facebook® and academic performance. *Computers in Human Behavior, 26*(6), 1237–1245. doi:10.1016/j.chb.2010.03.024

Krauskopf, K., Zahn, C., & Hesse, F. W. (2012). Leveraging the affordances of Youtube: The role of pedagogical knowledge and mental models of technology functions for lesson planning with technology. *Computers & Education, 58*(4), 1194–1206. doi:10.1016/j.compedu.2011.12.010

Liu, N. C., & Cheng, Y. (2005). The academic ranking of world universities. *Higher Education in Europe, 30*(2), 127–136. doi:10.1080/03797720500260116

Lupton, D. (2014). *'Feeling better connected': Academics' use of social media*. News & Media Research Centre, University of Canberra.

Madhusudhan, M. (2012). Use of social networking sites by research scholars of the University of Delhi: A study. *The International Information & Library Review, 44*(2), 100–113. doi:10.1080/10572317.20 12.10762919

Manca, S., & Ranieri, M. (2017). Networked scholarship and motivations for social media use in scholarly communication. *The International Review of Research in Open and Distributed Learning, 18*(2). Advance online publication. doi:10.19173/irrodl.v18i2.2859

Manasijević, D., Živković, D., Arsić, S., & Milošević, I. (2016). Exploring students' purposes of usage and educational usage of Facebook. *Computers in Human Behavior, 60*, 441–450. doi:10.1016/j.chb.2016.02.087

Moran, M., Seaman, J., & Tinti-Kane, H. (2011). *Teaching, Learning, and Sharing: How Today's Higher Education Faculty Use Social Media*. Babson Survey Research Group.

Nentwich, M., & König, R. (2014). Academia goes Facebook? The potential of social network sites in the scholarly realm. In *Opening science* (pp. 107–124). Springer. doi:10.1007/978-3-319-00026-8_7

Nature Publishing Group. (2014). *NPG 2014 social networks survey*. Figshare.

Nysveen, H., & Pedersen, P. E. (2016). Consumer adoption of RFID-enabled services. Applying an extended UTAUT model. *Information Systems Frontiers, 18*(2), 293–314. doi:10.100710796-014-9531-4

Poellhuber, B., Anderson, T., Racette, N., & Upton, L. (2013). Distance students' readiness for and interest in collaboration and social media. *Interactive Technology and Smart Education, 10*(1), 63–78. doi:10.1108/17415651311326455

Rowlands, I., Nicholas, D., Russell, B., Canty, N., & Watkinson, A. (2011). Social media use in the research workflow. *Learned Publishing, 24*(3), 183–195. doi:10.1087/20110306

Rashid, R. A., & Rahman, M. F. A. (2014). Social networking sites for online mentoring and creativity enhancement. *International Journal of Technology Enhanced Learning, 6*(1), 34–45. doi:10.1504/IJTEL.2014.060024

Smaller, H. (2005). Teacher informal learning and teacher knowledge: Theory, practice and policy. In *International handbook of educational policy* (pp. 543–568). Springer. doi:10.1007/1-4020-3201-3_27

Sugimoto, C. R., Work, S., Larivière, V., & Haustein, S. (2017). Scholarly use of social media and altmetrics: A review of the literature. *Journal of the Association for Information Science and Technology, 68*(9), 2037–2062. doi:10.1002/asi.23833

Schöndienst, V., Krasnova, H., Günther, O., Riehle, D., & Schwabe, G. (2011). *Micro-blogging adoption in the enterprise: An empirical analysis*. Academic Press.

Thelwall, M., & Kousha, K. (2014). Academia.edu: Social network or Academic Network? *Journal of the Association for Information Science and Technology, 65*(4), 721–731. doi:10.1002/asi.23038

This research was previously published in the International Journal of Information and Communication Technology Education (IJICTE), 17(2); pages 103-117, copyright year 2021 by IGI Publishing (an imprint of IGI Global).

APPENDIX: PROBLEM CONFIRMATION SURVEY

Welcome to the Acceptance of Social Media for Informal Learning Survey!

Social Media: Refers to online technologies that enable multiple users to interact, generate content, and collaborate in real time or through postings such as images, text, audio, or video, viewed later. Some examples of social media are Facebook and Twitter.

Informal Learning: Refers to a form of learning that is not professionally organized or highly structured and occurs outside of the formal learning framework for the purpose of acquiring required knowledge or skills.

Informal Learning Using Social Media: Can be considered as the use of social media for communication, interaction and collaboration in supporting a form of learning that is not organized or highly structured. This process leads to knowledge and skills acquisition.

This questionnaire is to find out about the acceptance of social media for informal learning among the academic researcher.

Informal Learning Using Social Media Based on Academic Researcher: Can be considered as the use of social media for communication, interaction and collaboration in supporting a form of learning that is not organized or highly structured related in conducting the academic research. This process leads to enhancement of knowledge and skills about the research.

Please complete all following questions by inserting tick (√) the boxes or by writing in the spaces provided.

Table 10. General questions

1. Gender	Male ☐ Female ☐
2. Age	Less than 24 – 30 years ☐ 31 – 35 years ☐ 36 – 40 years ☐ 41 – 50 years ☐ More than 45 years ☐
3. Level of education	Postdoctoral ☐ PhD ☐ Master ☐
4. Level of education	Professor ☐ Associate Professor ☐ Senior Lecturer ☐ Lecturer ☐ Research Fellow ☐ Research Assistant ☐ Postdoctoral ☐ Student ☐ Other (please specify) ☐
5. Which faculty do you belong to?	

6. How long have you been working as a researcher?	Less than 1 year ☐ 1-3 years ☐ 3-5 years ☐ 5-10 years ☐ More than 10 years ☐
7. Do you use social media for informal learning?	Yes ☐ No ☐
8. How long have you been using social media for informal learning?	Less than 6 months ☐ 7 months to a year ☐ 1-2 years ☐ More than 2 years ☐
9. Which of the following social media do you use frequently for informal learning? (Multiple answer are permitted).	Facebook ☐ Twitter ☐ YouTube ☐ Wikipedia ☐ LinkedIn ☐ Blogs ☐ Myspace ☐ Other (please specify) ☐

Instruction: Please Circle the number that best matches your view of the statement (which fall between 1= Strongly Disagree to 5= Strongly Agree).

Table 11. Benefits of using SM for IL by academic researchers

	10- How do you use social media for informal learning?	1	2	3	4	5
a.	I use social media to communicate about my research with researchers globally.					
b.	I use social media to communicate about my research with my research partners.					
c.	I use social media to communicate with the renowned experts in my research field.					
d.	I use social media to communicate with others researcher to keep up to date with the new information related to my research field.					
e.	I use social media to facilitate interaction with my research partners.					
f.	I use social media to exchange knowledge more quickly with other researcher.					
g.	I use social media to share knowledge with other researcher.					
h.	I use social media to get feedback about my research from other researchers.					
i.	I use social media to discuss with other research in conducting literature review.					
j.	I use social media to discuss my research method with other researchers.					
k.	I use social media to discuss my research finding with other researchers.					
l.	I use social media to find collaborators for my research projects.					
m.	I use social media to facilitate collaboration with my researcher partner.					
n.	I use social media to facilitate collaboration with my research respondents to collect the required data.					

Table 12. Barriers associated with Use of SM for IL by academic researchers

11- Why you don't use social media for informal learning?		1	2	3	4	5
a.	There is a lack of encouragement from colleagues on the need to use SM for IL.					
b.	I don't use SM for IL because most information obtained is a lack of quality.					
c.	I don't use SM for IL because it is a threat to my research materials and data.					
d.	I don't feel any necessity to use SM for IL.					
e.	I don't have time to use SM for IL.					
12- Do you think social media can be used for informal learning?		1	2	3	4	5

Thank you very much for your cooperation and participation.

Index

Ensure Quality Research is Introduced to the Academic Community

Become an Evaluator for IGI Global Authored Book Projects

Premier Reference Source

Stabilizing Currency and Preserving Economic Sovereignty Using the Grondona System

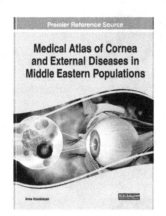

Premier Reference Source

Medical Atlas of Cornea and External Diseases in Middle Eastern Populations

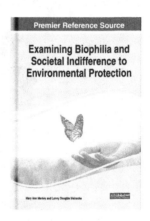

Premier Reference Source

Examining Biophilia and Societal Indifference to Environmental Protection

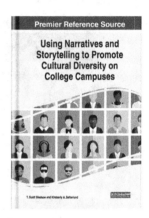

Premier Reference Source

Using Narratives and Storytelling to Promote Cultural Diversity on College Campuses

The overall success of an authored book project is dependent on quality and timely manuscript evaluations.

Applications and Inquiries may be sent to:
development@igi-global.com

Applicants must have a doctorate (or equivalent degree) as well as publishing, research, and reviewing experience. Authored Book Evaluators are appointed for one-year terms and are expected to complete at least three evaluations per term. Upon successful completion of this term, evaluators can be considered for an additional term.

If you have a colleague that may be interested in this opportunity, we encourage you to share this information with them.

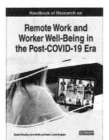

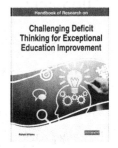

Printed in the United States
by Baker & Taylor Publisher Services